The New Mediterranean Diet Cookbook

The New Mediterranean Diet Cookbook

A Delicious Alternative for Lifelong Health

Nancy Harmon Jenkins

With a Foreword by Marion Nestle

BANTAM BOOKS

THE NEW MEDITERRANEAN DIET COOKBOOK
A Bantam Book

PUBLISHING HISTORY
The Mediterranean Diet Cookbook hardcover edition published June 1994
The New Mediterranean Diet Cookbook / January 2009

Published by
Bantam Dell
A Division of Random House, Inc.
New York, New York

Book design by Ralph Fowler

Library of Congress Cataloging-in-Publication Data
Jenkins, Nancy Harmon
The new Mediterranean diet cookbook : a delicious alternative for
lifelong health / Nancy Harmon Jenkins ; with a foreword by Marion Nestle.
p. cm.
Includes bibliographical references and index.
ISBN: 978-0-553-38509-0 (hardcover)
1. Cookery, Mediterranean. 2. Diet—Mediterranean Region.
3. Low-fat diet—Recipes. I. Title.

TX725.M35 J46 2009   2008040982
641.59182/2 22

Printed in the United States of America
Published simultaneously in Canada

www.bantamdell.com

10 9 8
RRDW

The United States poet laureate Charles Simic

was asked by a *New York Times* reporter early in 2008

what he might advise people who are

"looking to be happy."

"For starters," the poet laureate said,

"learn how to cook."

Good advice!

For Nadir—
and the future

CONTENTS

ACKNOWLEDGMENTS

My deepest thanks go to Christopher Speed, who agreed to be my chief nutrition consultant for this book, and who has doggedly and determinedly helped me thread my way through the mysteries of antioxidants, phytochemicals, fatty acids, glycemic loads, and other arcane aspects of nutrition, diet, and health. My hat goes off to anyone who can keep all those n-numbers straight, and that also includes Antonia Trichopoulou of the University of Athens (Greece) Medical School and her husband Dimitri Trichopoulos of the Harvard School of Public Health, who jointly provided the meticulous outline of the Mediterranean diet on pages 467–475; Marion Nestle of the Department of Nutrition, Food Studies, and Public Health at New York University, who has done so much to push Americans in the right direction as far as their eating habits are concerned, and who graciously provided the Foreword for this edition; and Frank Sachs, Eric Rimm, Walter Willett, and their many colleagues at the Harvard School of Public Health who, largely through a remarkable series of encounters at the Culinary Institute of America in California, introduced me to new ideas and theories and elaborated on old ones.

And speaking of the CIA (the food one, that is), I also want to acknowledge Greg Drescher, Executive Director of Strategic Initiatives at that organization, and his role in channeling Oldways Preservation & Exchange Trust, of which he was then a director, toward the initial Mediterranean diet work. Together with Dun Gifford, Greg labored mightily to gain recognition for the importance of diet in general, and the Mediterranean diet in particular. Under their leadership, Oldways was instrumental in bringing together scientists, journalists, chefs, and concerned members of the public to discuss these issues. At the CIA, Greg continues to work closely with institutions like the Harvard School of Public Health to promote greater understanding of the importance of a healthy diet. The CIA/HSPH annual conference, World of Healthy Flavors, is a landmark occasion for that.

My agent, David Black, was admirable in his pursuit of my dream of updating this book, fifteen years after the first edition, for which I thank him mightily, and I thank him too for finding me exactly the right editor at Bantam, Beth Rashbaum, who had never before taken on a food book and turned out to be every writer's fantasy editor—attentive, intelligent, quick to respond, quick to act, full of good ideas, lots of fun to work with, and, like my agent, with a fine palate to boot.

Finally, the book would simply not have happened without the constant attention of two essential people—faithful recipe tester Pam Elliott, who appeared on my front porch at the oddest times of the day with the oddest kind of something for me to taste yet another time until we got it right; and my equally faithful assistant Martha Lohnes, who searched, filed, photocopied, faxed, paid bills, traced recalcitrant contractors, boxed, hauled, mailed, took out the garbage, and looked after the dog while I roamed the Mediterranean having fun.

As is usual with a book of this nature, many, many other people had a hand in what success it may claim—anonymous chefs, growers, and food producers, in Europe and the U.S., who showed me new ways with recipes or ingredients, as well as old friends and family members who accompanied me on my travels all around the Mediterranean and waited patiently while I negotiated yet another detail. To all of you, everywhere, my deepest thanks.

—Nancy Harmon Jenkins
Teverina di Cortona
May 2008

FOREWORD

BY MARION NESTLE

When Nancy Jenkins's *Mediterranean Cookbook* first appeared in 1994, it was distinguished not only by the gorgeous writing but also by its then revolutionary approach to eating healthfully. Eat, she told us, as the Greeks and Southern Italians have done since ancient times, and you might live as healthfully and long as they do. By this, she meant a largely plant-based diet—one with lots of fruits and vegetables, small amounts of meat, fish, and dairy products, with olive oil as the principal fat, and accompanied by a glass of wine. This diet, based on foods grown in the region surrounding the Mediterranean Sea, has been consumed since ancient times.

Its discovery as a health-promoting diet pattern, however, began only after World War II when investigators from Rockefeller University went to the island of Crete to try to figure out why its people, although existing under conditions of extreme poverty, were unusually healthy and long-lived. If they survived early childhood, their longevity was the highest in the world, rivaled only by the Japanese. Subsequent researchers concluded that one could hardly eat a healthier diet than that consumed by the people of Crete and Naples in the early 1950s.

Americans, however, did not really discover the Mediterranean diet until 40 years later when two groups with vested interests in promoting consumption of its distinct components—particularly olive oil—realized that its health benefits could be used as a basis for marketing. Oldways Preservation & Exchange Trust and the International Olive Oil Council (IOOC), a trade association formed under the auspices of the United Nations, began sponsoring conferences on traditional dietary patterns in the early 1990s. These meetings, often held in olive-growing countries, brought together food writers, chefs, restaurateurs, and academics to learn about Mediterranean foods and ingredients, and their separate and collective health benefits. I met

Nancy Jenkins at one of these meetings in 1990, co-chaired (with Walter Willett of the Harvard School of Public Health) the first international conference on diets of the Mediterranean in 1993, and edited a collection of papers presented at that conference for a special supplement to the *American Journal of Clinical Nutrition* in 1995.

The Olive Oil Council's purpose in sponsoring meetings and publications was to promote sales of olive oil in the United States and elsewhere. Oldways organized conferences to bring people together to explain the health benefits of olive oil and other Mediterranean foods to people who would write about them. Although olive oil is a fat that like other fats has about 130 calories per tablespoon, it is a "good" fat. Plenty of independently funded research then and since demonstrates that substituting olive oil for more saturated fats lowers the "bad" form of cholesterol in blood and raises the "good" kind. But olive oil has one other benefit. It tastes good. It tastes good itself and makes other foods taste good. As Antonia Trichopoulou and Dimitrios Trichopoulos have always maintained, olive oil makes vegetables palatable so people will eat and enjoy them (see Appendix I).

The Oldways-IOOC meetings worked splendidly to increase sales of olive oil. In 1993, you were lucky if you could find a decent bottle of extra-virgin olive oil in your local supermarket and if you did find one, it cost a fortune. Today, you can get oils of the highest quality at your local grocery, and specialty stores offer dozens of options. Except for the blessedly brief, unhappy period of the Atkins diet craze when Americans stopped eating bread or pasta, the Mediterranean diet is now mainstream. It represents a model of the ideal dietary pattern recommended by health agencies in the United States and worldwide.

Let's give the IOOC and Oldways credit for the mainstreaming of the Mediterranean diet. Their conferences did much more than increase sales of olive oil. The conferences stimulated participants to conduct further research, to initiate clinical trials, to compare Mediterranean diet patterns to those recommended by health authorities, and to write superb cookbooks using Mediterranean ingredients and recipes—this book is one such example.

The research has been especially valuable. Virtually all studies on the separate components of Mediterranean diets or on overall Mediterranean dietary patterns have been funded independently by government research agencies. As might be expected because they remove foods from their dietary context, studies of individual components—olive oil, fruits and vegetables, fish, and grains—do not always produce results as consistent or compelling as one would like.

But the results of studies of Mediterranean dietary patterns are much less ambiguous. Then and now, they indicate how people who follow traditional

Mediterranean diets display much lower rates of heart disease, for example, than those who follow "Western" dietary patterns. The most recent of these studies (*American Journal of Clinical Nutrition*, August 2007) examined the diet and health patterns of nearly 41,000 Australians. Those who typically followed a traditional Mediterranean pattern with more plant foods and fish, fewer animal products, and an occasional glass of wine displayed rates of heart disease 30 percent lower than their peers who ate like the typical Australian.

The best reason for following a Mediterranean diet is how good it tastes. Mediterranean dietary patterns unite taste and health. The recipes in this book are wonderful—a pleasure to read, to follow, and to eat. Pasta, vegetables, fish, and good bread, accompanied by a glass of wine? That's my idea of how to eat well and healthfully. Read this book and enjoy!

Marion Nestle is the Paulette Goddard Professor of Nutrition, Food Studies, and Public Health, and Professor of Sociology, at New York University, and the author of Safe Food *(2002),* What to Eat *(2006), and* Food Politics *(revised ed., 2007).*

The New Mediterranean Diet Cookbook

INTRODUCTION

This book began life in a rugged stone farmhouse that stands high on a rocky outcropping in the middle of a long Tuscan valley. The valley flows eastward as it descends, gradually opening into Umbria and the upper reaches of the Tiber, one of the river-roads that has always led to Rome. From the house on its hilltop, the view encompasses woods and forests of chestnut and oak, cleared fields and terraces planted to wheat, corn, and sunflowers, and the ordered regiments of vineyards and groves punctuated with olive trees, their leaves, even at a distance, a distinctive silvery green. Here and there across the landscape are scattered our neighbors' farms, appealing if architecturally undistinguished clusters of stone buildings that have evolved over the centuries, and sometimes occupied over those same centuries by the ancestors of the people who live and work there today. If you blur your vision a little to erase the telephone poles and electric lines, you might almost be looking at a scene that has persisted for centuries as well.

Some decades ago I brought my small family to live on this hilltop farm, after years spent roaming the Mediterranean, from Spain to France to Spain again, then to Lebanon and Cyprus, and finally, after a brief stint in East Asia, to Rome. (The children's father was a foreign correspondent for an American newsmagazine; we followed wherever his work led him.) The farmhouse, with its fields and olive orchards, and the little community that embraced it, became our home and focus in the world, a place where we gathered for celebrations—the olive harvest, Thanksgiving, Easter, the launch of a book or a career change—and equally a place of solace and recovery when times seemed out of joint.

On an adjacent farm, just a short walk over the fields, lives the Antolini family—Arnaldo and Maura and their two young daughters, and Arnaldo's mother, Mita, now enjoying a somewhat sedentary old age after long years of working the fields and vegetable gardens, tending pigs and chickens, while her husband, Bruno, just recently passed away, logged the forest and made charcoal, threshed wheat and pressed grapes and olives to make wine and oil, all the staples of the family table. The Antolinis have been good neighbors, good friends, and partners in happy times and a few sorrowful ones, constants in the changing face of the valley community as babies are born, children grow to adulthood, new people arrive with new ideas, and old people pass on. Over the years that we have known them, we have witnessed together how the subsistence agriculture of this mountain valley has changed from wheat, vines, and olives that met the needs of the people who live here, to commodity crops like sunflowers and tobacco, subsidized by the government and grown for distant markets. Now more momentous changes are in the offing as many farms, no longer able to sustain a family, are abandoned and sold to foreigners who install central heating and swimming pools and proceed to rent out the reconstructed farmhouse for exorbitant sums to visitors who come in the summer for a week or two and then move on.

When we first came to live in the valley, the Antolinis, like most of their neighbors, had no electricity, no plumbing, no telephone, and no tractor or other mechanized means of transportation. A profound and appealing stillness pervaded the valley, broken only by human voices and the rooster's crow. Terraces of wheat, studded with gnarled olive trees and edged with grapevines, marked the contours of the steep hillsides, and around them climbed forests of oak, chestnut, and Aleppo pine.

Today the forests are still there, but the terraces have long since been plowed into dikes and broad fields for easier cultivation with tractors, and the Antolinis have passed, with stunning rapidity, from a mid-19th-century way of life to an early-21st-century one without, it seems, so much as the blink of an eye. Electricity hums in their comfortable farmhouse, running everything from a *frullatora* for beating eggs to a washing machine to that icon of modern times, the television set. The telephone rings with news of family and friends. The bathroom sparkles with toilet, washbasin, and shower, and outside the little Fiat car and the big Lamborghini tractor gurgle periodically to life, ready to plow fields or carry goods and people to market.

Yet, despite all these changes, the food that is prepared and set before the family twice a day has remained the same, much of it still grown and harvested on the farm—pasta with fresh vegetables from the gardens, chickens and rabbits from the farmyard, and pork from the pig that is slaughtered each year at Christmastime; mushrooms and chestnuts from the forest; and above all olive oil and wine that the Antolinis still proudly make themselves. They eat, in fact, an almost perfect Mediterranean diet, although they'd be perplexed to hear that—very low in saturated fats, very high in complex carbohydrates, lots of fresh vegetables, especially those cancer-blocking brassicas or cruciferous vegetables—cabbages, kale, turnip greens, broccoli, and so on.

This is not a book about the Antolinis or the community of Teverina, but I mention them with prominence because for me this place in the world, almost dead center in the Italian peninsula, which puts it almost dead center in the whole northern Mediterranean region, has been a place to think about food and its importance to communities and individuals, about what we grow and how we process it, how we prepare it and preserve it and share it among ourselves. Teverina, for all the changes that have taken place here, has been an example for me of what the Mediterranean diet means, in real terms and to real people.

So what is this Mediterranean diet and why should Americans, descendants of people from many different parts of the world, care?

Here's a good definition of the diet from Dr. Antonia Trichopoulou, Professor of Nutrition at the University of Athens (Greece) Medical School and a longtime researcher into the relationship between diet and health:★

- a high intake of vegetables, legumes, fruits and nuts, and cereals (in the past largely unrefined)

- a high intake of olive oil but a low intake of saturated lipids

- a moderately high intake of fish (depending on the proximity of the sea)

- a low-to-moderate intake of dairy products (mostly in the form of cheese or yogurt)

- a low intake of meat and poultry

- a regular but moderate intake of ethanol, primarily in the form of wine and generally during meals

Rich in antioxidants and omega-3 fatty acids from fish and greens, low in saturated fats but with a high quotient of monounsaturated olive oil, the Mediterranean diet has been shown, over and over again, to be protective against heart attack and stroke, to inhibit atherosclerosis and help control blood pressure and cholesterol, and to protect against many kinds of cancer, as well as against the effects of aging, especially macular degeneration and cataracts. And the list of benefits goes on and on. Recent research indicates that eating in a Mediterranean pattern may also reduce mortality among the elderly and help ward off Alzheimer's, and it may be of great help in managing diabetes and metabolic syndrome.

★See also Appendix I to this volume (pages 467–475), "The Mediterranean Diet and Health," written for the first edition of this book, *The Mediterranean Diet Cookbook,* by Dr. Trichopoulou with her husband Dr. Dimitrios Trichopoulos, Professor of Cancer Prevention and Epidemiology at the Harvard School of Public Health.

Apart from nutritional research, however, a quick look at Mediterranean populations who follow this way of eating shows an unmistakable correlation with good health profiles. Going back as far as the early 1960s, when the famous Seven Countries Study, under the direction of Dr. Ancel Keys, first began to examine the nature of the relationship between diet and health in a number of locations around the world including the island of Crete and a community in Puglia in southern Italy, it was clear that the traditional diet of people in the Mediterranean is a major factor in their *generally* good health profiles, their *generally* long lives, and their *general* lack of chronic and debilitating diseases. An international conference on health aspects of Mediterranean diets was convened back in 1983, when the first edition of this book was contemplated, by the Harvard School of Public Health and Oldways Preservation & Exchange Trust, a nonprofit organization to promote healthful diets. The conference, "Traditional Diets of the Mediterranean," reached a consensus that there are indeed clear health benefits to be derived from the traditional Mediterranean diet. That consensus has continued to develop and strengthen as the evidence, both scientific and anecdotal, has accumulated over the years.

Of course, as Dr. Trichopoulou would be the first to admit, the diet as she describes it is an idealized diet and doesn't necessarily reflect the way many people in Mediterranean countries eat today. Recent decades have seen an increase across the board in meat consumption, as well as a huge impact on traditional diets from highly processed foods. (One of the most insidious invasions of the latter has been in the form of individual snacks for kids, heavily sweetened and salted and replete with the most unhealthful kinds of fat—all conveniently packaged for Mediterranean moms to pick up at the local supermarket, a snack a day for each child in the family, to be tucked into each little book bag as they set off for school in the morning.) Even more dangerous, from the perspective of health and flavor alike, has been an increase in the use of cheap refined vegetable oils in place of traditional olive oil. Still, if you think of diet as a pattern, rather than as a collection of individual foods or meals, much of the traditional diet remains intact, and health profiles continue to be positive, with low incidences of chronic disease, especially heart disease, cancer, and diabetes, as a result.* Mediterranean countries continue to consume far higher quantities of fresh fruits and vegetables and far greater amounts of seafood than do North Ameri-

---

*A recent trend among Italian public health specialists has been to decry what they call an alarming increase in childhood obesity. But I have to say that, after searching available crowds of children, adolescents, and teenagers in central and southern Italy, along with some colleagues from New York University's department of nutrition and food studies, we concluded that obesity appears, at least to our eyes, to be more conspicuous by its absence. Certainly it doesn't exist on anything like the levels it has assumed in the United States.

cans. And the overriding factor is the use of extra-virgin olive oil as a major source of fat—olive oil, in fact, has had something of a resurgence most recently as publicity about its health benefits reaches down even to the lowest socioeconomic groups through the power of television.

Factors other than diet, of course, also influence good health—among them heredity, exercise or the lack of it, tobacco and alcohol abuse, and environmental pollutants in the air we breathe, the water we drink, the soil in which our vegetables and fruits grow, and the chemicals we add to our foods during growth and processing. It would be disingenuous to suggest that diet alone is a factor.

And it would be disingenuous to suggest that diet is nothing more than a quantifiable sum of nutrients. The Mediterranean diet, or the Mediterranean way of eating if you will, is the result of Mediterranean history and an integral part of Mediterranean culture. I like to describe it as a way of *thinking* about food. Tunisians or Turks, Cypriotes or Spaniards, rich people or poor, country folk or city dwellers, Mediterranean people are on the whole *conscious* of food in a way that most people, certainly most Americans, are not. I think it's because of this that what they eat is, on the whole, delicious—nourishing to the body because it's wholesome and to the soul because it tastes so very good.

I don't mean to suggest an obsession with food. Rather, it seems to me that in the countries of the Mediterranean there exists a deep-seated and largely unspoken consensus that eating is one of the most important things we humans do in our lives. As a great anthropologist once told me, it is our single most intimate act, far more intimate than sex because through food we literally re-create ourselves each and every day of our lives. And beyond individual needs, in Mediterranean countries there's a real sense of eating as a social act, a way of communicating, of expressing solidarity and relationship. Gathering around the table, literally breaking bread together, is both a symbol of communion and an act of communion in and of itself. And so from a very early age—probably, if it could be measured, from infancy—children absorb the cultural message that it's important to *pay attention,* to *be aware,* in an almost Zen way, of what food is, where it comes from, and how it gets to be the way it is when it comes into our lives.

Here in North America, on the other hand, on magazine racks and newspaper stands, from TV screens and billboards, headlines wail an uncomfortable but unavoidable truth: the industrialized diet that most Americans consume is a mess—high in heavily processed food, in saturated fat and red meat from animals that themselves have been raised and processed in an unhealthy manner, in refined sugars from high-fructose corn syrup, and way too low in fresh, unprocessed fruits and vegetables and healthy carbohydrates from whole grains. The health pattern that results is one of chronic and debilitating diseases—heart disease, cancer, diabetes, and others—that affect individuals and their families while taking a tremendous toll, economically and psychologically, on the nation as a whole. Fifteen years ago, when the first edition of this book was published, diabetes came third in the list of diet-related chronic diseases, preceded by coronary heart disease and cancer. Now it comes first. And it comes earlier as more and more children, grown obese on an industrialized diet, become victims, ironically, of what was until recently called "adult onset diabetes."

As a nation, it seems, we are on the road to perdition in the form of catastrophic illnesses caused or exacerbated, all or in part, by what and how much we eat. Diet alone will not cure our problems but diet is one factor that ought to be easy to control and easy to change.

Ought to be, but it's not. The plaint is echoed by doctors, nutritionists, and other health care professionals who gather annually at the Culinary Institute of America in California for a conference jointly sponsored with the Nutrition Department of the Harvard School of Public Health. The Harvard docs are exceptionally alarmed by increasing rates of childhood obesity. Universally and to a person, they point out enormous economic and social consequences from our poor diets: "We will not remain a superpower if we have to cope with the fallout from all this," one doctor said during the 2007 meeting.

But what's to be done? Not a month goes by without new stories proclaiming the demise of one dietary strategy, the elevation of another. Fat's in, fat's out, carbs are no-nos, trans fats and processed sugar are pure evil, brown rice and tofu are the sources of eternal youth—unless, perhaps, it's grapefruit and yogurt—tomatoes prevent cancer, oatmeal lowers cholesterol, on and on and on.

Yet, throughout the last half century of conflicting and often hostile debate, the Mediterranean way of eating has consistently earned plaudits for its sensible, holistic approach, its simplicity and easy familiarity, and the strength of the proof it offers of the connection between good eating and good health, a proof that is based on decades of both anecdotal evidence and scientifically unassailable verification.

But for enormous numbers of Americans, of all ages and economic classes, the Mediterranean way of eating remains a poorly understood mystery—indeed, a mystifying experience of its own in the kitchen. This book is written for all of them:

- for parents with growing families

- for young people starting out with their first apartment or home

- for the aging and elderly whose changing dietary needs mean less food overall, hence a real need for nutritionally dense Mediterranean foods

- for single somethings

- and for the vast majority of ordinary people who know instinctively that there's a strong connection between what we eat and how we feel, yet who've lost the ability to express that connection in their daily lives

A full 85 percent of Americans say the question of diet and nutrition is personally important, according to the American Dietetic Association. And yet, changing the kind of diet followed by so many Americans—high in unhealthy fats, high in sugar and artificial sweeteners, processed food, fast food, junk food—isn't happening. Why? Because eating well takes too much time, the ADA pollsters reported, and besides, people said, "we don't want to give up the foods we like."

With *The New Mediterranean Diet Cookbook,* there's no need to give up the foods you like. This is not a diet, on the one hand, of bean sprouts and tofu-and-lentil burgers or, on the other, of artificial fats and sugars, what a friend of mine aptly calls "fake foods," created in laboratories to substitute for things we like and know we shouldn't eat. (Trans-fat margarine, anyone?) It's a diet based on real food for real people, people like you and me. It's my hope that if you use this book, you'll never again crave a gristly, greasy Macburger or the like, piled high with sugary condiments and accompanied by a pile of limp fried potatoes.

This is good food, food you'll want to eat because it tastes so darned good, and food that, for the most part, doesn't take hours of time and all your energies to prepare. (Yes, there are some recipes for those like me who love to spend time in the kitchen, but there are many others for those with little time or skill to spare.) Almost everything used in the book can easily be found in local supermarkets, health food stores, and farmers' markets. There are occasional ingredients—the best olives and olive oils, for instance—that may call for a special trip to a Greek, Italian, or Middle Eastern neighborhood or to a specialty foods store, and there are occasional products that may require a little effort to uncover. But in this Internet Age, that sort of project has become ever so much easier, if not quite so exciting.

Because Mediterranean cooking is, by and large, home cooking and not restaurant cuisine, it is improvisational and very forgiving. You have only two cloves of garlic instead of the called-for six? Use two and don't worry. You can't find celery root, but there are loads of parsnips in the produce section? Substitute the parsnips. The chard looks good while the spinach is yellow and wilted? Use chard instead of spinach. The dish may end up a little less predominantly flavored with this or that, but somewhere in the Mediterranean, you can be certain, someone has made it like that before. Only with cakes should you be as precise as you can—and even then, only the first time out. Once you're familiar with a recipe, you can fiddle with it at will.

The most important lesson from the Mediterranean, however, is not to be found in recipes but rather in that attitude I mentioned earlier, that consciousness about food that stems from the realization that good food begins with good ingredients—truly ripe and flavorful tomatoes; fresh, crisp carrots, green beans, and peas; beets, turnips, and potatoes that are firm and full of sweet savor; naturally raised meats, chickens, and their eggs; dairy products, yogurt and cheese, without added preservatives or stabilizers; fish, even frozen fish, with a clean and pristine scent.

This will come about only when you seek out the very best of local, regional, preferably organically and naturally raised products. Only then will you have a standard by which to measure what is not regional and natural. There are times in all our kitchens when we must use other kinds of products, but only by knowing what is best can we judge what is second-best but still a possibility. When you know the flavor of a ripe local tomato at the height of its season, when you understand what makes it taste the way it does, you will also know what doesn't measure up.

Look for the best ingredients wherever you are, whether greens or fish, wine or oil, cheese or fruit. Obviously, not all of these are going to be produced locally—wine, certain types of cheese, and olive oil almost certainly not. But look for fresh or very minimally processed food, food that has been naturally raised or grown without pesticides or chemical fertilizers.

Fortunately for all of us, the Mediterranean diet is extremely palatable with great appeal to all the senses. Appetite doesn't come from knowing food is good for you—it comes from flavors and textures, from the delicious aromas that waft from a kitchen where peppers and tomatoes are simmering in olive oil with a little garlic and fresh basil, from the fragrance that rises out of a steaming soup tureen filled with chunks of seafood and leeks and a bit of orange zest, from the dazzling appearance of a bowl of crisp salad greens and ripe red tomatoes, or a platter of grilled summer vegetables, or a handsome loaf of crusty-brown country bread with a pale wedge of cheese and a sparkling glass of deep red wine to go with it. The Mediterranean diet brings to the table fragrances, colors, and textures like these along with good health and an overall sense of well-being.

Think of a meal that may be familiar to many Americans, especially those of Mediterranean ancestry: a light vegetable soup, made with chicken stock and chopped onions, carrots, celery, and garlic, flavored with fresh herbs and perhaps a spoonful of freshly grated cheese; a dish of pasta sauced with a little savory ground meat mixed with more chopped vegetables and herbs, the whole sautéed in olive oil; a green salad, crisply fresh and fragrant with garlic, more olive oil, and lemon juice; plenty of crusty country-style bread; a small piece of cheese; and fruit, either raw or poached in a very light sugar syrup.

Sound good? That's one example of the Mediterranean diet. There are more. Pizza is part of the Mediterranean diet, and so are rice dishes like pilaf, risotto, and paella. So are vegetable combinations with a very little meat or cheese added for flavor, hearty bean and lentil soups, fish and shellfish quickly grilled or broiled. And so too is a chunk of bread, a wedge of cheese, a few slices of onion and tomato, and a glass of good red wine to wash it all down.

The fact is that the people of the Mediterranean figured out a long time ago—back, if truth be told, in the mists of time—that good food, skillfully prepared, garnished with little more than fresh herbs, garlic, and olive oil, and shared in something approaching abundance around a table with friends and relations, is not only good tasting; it's good for you, too.

NOTE ON NUTRITIONAL DATA

Everything in this book tastes good and is good for you, in the Mediterranean context. That means that rich feast-day preparations and desserts should be consumed, as they are in the Mediterranean, for special occasions, perhaps a few times a year. Vegetarians and people with special health needs, for foods very low in fat or sodium for instance, will find plenty of ideas in the Mediterranean diet. The best news is that there are no hard-and-fast rules: if you want to make adjustments to account for special health problems, it's easy to do so.

Readers familiar with the first edition of this book may be surprised at the lack of nutritional data accompanying each recipe. I have long been convinced that such data, beneficial though they may appear to be on the surface, are in fact quite useless and can lead to misguided conclusions. This is in part because the information on which the data are based is at best adequate and at worst downright wrong. In any case, it is all relative and based on unquantifiable elements like portion size.

Fear of fat has dominated popular discussion of diet for such a long time that many otherwise normal, health-conscious people are still struggling to lower the fat content of their diet from the 30 percent recommended by the USDA to 20 percent or an even more drastic 10 percent. But extremely low-fat diets are terribly hard to maintain: the food seldom really tastes good, and the effort that must go into providing even minimal flavor means that most conscientious observers would rather purchase prepared, portion-controlled, industrially manufactured food. Yet there is no real evidence that, for normally active people with no obesity, there's any good reason to pursue this course.

The fact is that the extensive public health initiatives in recent years have been based largely on research indicating the need to limit *saturated* fat. One of the most appealing lessons of the Mediterranean diet is that as long as *saturated* fat remains low, and the *balance* of fat is mostly *monounsaturated,* as is the case with the recipes in this book, the amount of total fat in the diet, even above 35 percent, is probably not an issue for active people.

The health benefits of olive oil have been discussed in other parts of this book, but it is important to remember that simply *adding* olive oil to a diet already high in saturated fat is not the order of the day. *Substituting* olive oil, however, is a major key to a better health profile.

Still, for many the overriding question is: can I lose weight on the Mediterranean diet? And the answer is simple: yes, you can, but only if you reduce the amount you eat and increase the amount of exercise you get in the normal course of everyday life. For ordinary people who do not have metabolism problems (and that includes most of us), that is the only way to lose weight.

Fortunately, the traditional dishes on which Mediterranean people have nourished themselves for generations are so delicious that no one need feel deprived in the slightest when they become mainstays of our own tables. This in itself may make it easier to lose weight. By shifting meat and other animal products away from the center of the plate, by adding lots of beautiful, fresh, seasonal produce, cooked vegetables, salads, and raw fruit for dessert, by making grains and beans in the form of bread, pasta, and delightful soups the focus of the meal, you may find that the word *diet* takes on an entirely new meaning.

Making the Change

✧ ✧ ✧

C HANGING EATING HABITS may seem like a radical and difficult chore, but changing to the Mediterranean diet is easy because most of the foods and cooking techniques are already familiar to us. It's a shift of emphasis that's the key to cooking and eating in a healthy Mediterranean style.

Except for olive oil, there's no need for special foods in the larder—in fact, many of the foods featured in the Mediterranean kitchen are probably already in your pantry cupboard. Several different kinds of beans, both dried and canned, long-grain and short-grain rice, cornmeal for polenta and flour for bread, pasta in a variety of shapes, canned tomatoes, and condiments like dried mushrooms and herbs are common ingredients and take no special effort to acquire. If there's an Italian, Greek, or Middle Eastern neighborhood nearby, you'll have access to first-rate olives and cheese; otherwise, make a special trip some Saturday to a more distant market and spend time wandering around examining the offerings. If you're far from ethnic shopping areas like these, mail-order and Internet suppliers are a good, if sometimes rather expensive, resource. (See pages 465–466 for some suggestions.)

We invent all sorts of rationales for holding back on changing diets, especially where families are involved. But there are compelling reasons for making the switch, and most of the obstacles are easily overcome. Just remember that where families are concerned, change sometimes has to come slowly. Whatever you do, don't make a big deal out of it. Small, quiet, almost unnoticeable changes are more effective than noisy family food fights.

Start off by structuring mealtimes, if you don't do that already. It's hard for American families, with so many of us apart at lunch, but dinner at least should be a time for the family to come together and share whatever is on the table. Try to have meals on the table at the same hour each day and let people know they're expected to be there. It's the first step in a Mediterranean direction, building a sense of food as a fundamentally communal, shared experience.

Switch from whatever fats you now use to extra-virgin olive oil. If you find it hard to get used to the flavor of extra-virgin oil, start off by combining it 50/50 with canola oil, which has no perceptible flavor or aroma. Gradually reduce the amount of canola as you grow accustomed to the delicious flavor of olive oil. Experiment with oils by buying several different varieties in small quantities—the flavors vary enormously from country to country, region to region, and even producer to producer. Begin by throwing out all those bottles of commercial salad dressing that are crowding your refrigerator shelves. Then follow one of the recipes on pages 261–264 for tasty salad dressings using extra-virgin olive oil. Start using olive oil to sauté meat, chicken, or fish. More flavorful oils are wonderful for frying potatoes, especially with a little garlic or onion added—another way to accustom your family to the distinctive flavor. Soon you may find yourself using truly aromatic oils on steamed vegetables or baked potatoes in place of butter or sour cream. Then you'll be ready for a real summertime treat—extra-virgin olive oil lavished on fresh seasonal corn.

(For more on olive oil, see pages 30–33.)

Get out of the butter habit. A little butter from time to time is fine, but butter is *never* on the Mediterranean table, *never* assumed to be an automatic accompaniment to bread. Even at breakfast, only a little jam garnishes the bread, which is appreciated for its own good flavor. (And contrary to American restaurant custom, bowls of olive oil, even of the finest extra-virgin, are *never* put on the table, except during the autumn harvest when the flavor of new oil is appreciated.)

Use more whole grains. Even though Mediterranean cooks seldom use whole-wheat pasta or brown rice, they still get plenty of whole grains through dishes like tabbouleh, the hearty Lebanese salad, and bulgur pilafs. And breads throughout the Mediterranean are often made with unrefined wheat and barley flours. Fortunately we have much greater access to really high-quality bread than we had 15 years ago when I compiled the first edition of this book, but if you can't find the kind of bread you want nearby, try making it yourself. It really isn't time consuming once you get the hang of it, and that's quickly acquired. And presenting a homemade loaf of high-quality bread on the table is just eminently satisfying.

Begin or end each meal with a salad. Make it from crisp greens and whatever vegetables are in season—tomatoes, cucumbers, sweet peppers, scallions, shavings of carrot, sherds of fennel, celery, tender chicory, raw fava beans.

Don't use iceberg lettuce, which has almost no nutritional value, but do look for dark green leaf lettuces like oak leaf and romaine. Add some fresh green herbs for variety, but not all at once—basil at one meal, dill at another, cilantro, if you like it, at a third.

Add both more vegetables and different vegetables to the menu. Get away from the American focus on potatoes, peas, and salad greens. Nothing wrong with any of them but life is so much richer! The average American consumes just three servings of fruits and vegetables daily and many Americans don't even get that. The latest Dietary Guidelines for Americans, published by the Department of Health and Human Services, recommend up to nine servings, which is about 4½ cups, for otherwise healthy people consuming 2,000 calories a day. So let vegetables take up most of the room on your plate.

Every day try to get in at least one serving each of cruciferous (cabbage family) vegetables—broccoli, broccoli rabe, cabbage, cauliflower, turnip and mustard greens—and bright-colored vegetables and fruits that are rich in antioxidants—again broccoli and broccoli rabe, but also carrots, sweet potatoes, spinach, and yellow squash, as well as apricots and cantaloupe, just to mention a few. Experiment with different vegetables, ones that may not be familiar—artichokes, leeks, fava beans are exotic to many Americans, and vegetables like Jerusalem artichokes (sunchokes), celery root, and many greens are virtually unknown.

Vegetables don't have to be served separately—vegetable combinations, vegetables cooked in a sauce for pasta, vegetables served cut up in a soup, are all ways to increase the quantity consumed. But no single fruit or vegetable provides all the nutrients you need to be healthy. In the end, it's variety that is the key.

Cut down on the amount of meat consumed. There's no reason for normal, healthy adults to eat more than 4 ounces of lean meat a day, and much less is much better. Children, of course, need even less. (If your family is used to 8-ounce portions, start cutting the portions down gradually rather than all at once.) Eat lean red meat (beef, pork, and lamb) just once or twice a week. Other meals can feature chicken, fish, pasta, rice, beans, or vegetables.

One easy way to cut meat consumption is with stews that feature meat as an incidental to lots and lots of vegetables. You'll find recipes for such preparations throughout this book. Or make a hearty soup the main course, with plenty of bread, perhaps a little cheese, and salad to accompany it. Soup is a delicious and cheap way to get lots of vegetables on the table.

Move meat away from the center of the plate by adding complex carbohydrates like rice, beans, and pasta to fill the gap that meat once occupied. When you do serve a main course of meat or fish, get into the Mediterranean habit of offering a filling first course of pasta or soup before the meat arrives.

And if you're worried about budgetary constraints, think of this: by adding olive oil and subtracting meat, you'll probably come out even over the course of a week.

Think about portion size, especially when dining in restaurants. Americans on the whole now spend almost half their food dollars outside the home in fast-food, take-out, and family-style restaurants. It's no secret that portion sizes have increased dramatically in such food outlets—indeed, some national chains actually brag about the humongous size of burgers, fries, and soft drinks, and what a bargain they are. Some bargain! Anyone who saw the movie *Supersize Me* knows all too well the consequences of this. But when Drs. Lisa Young and Marion Nestle at New York University studied the phenomenon, they discovered that between the 1975 and 1997 editions of the *Joy of Cooking,* that venerable cookbook has decreased the number of servings it says a given recipe will yield. No wonder we're a fat nation, cradle to (often early) grave.

Now think of a deck of cards: that's about the portion size of meat or fish in a restaurant in just about any country in the Mediterranean, and the vegetables, the soups, the pasta and rice dishes are equivalent. As for dessert, most often, if it's anything at all, it's a single small portion of seasonal fruit. If there's an actual sweet involved, it will be the size of a little espresso cup, no more.

So think about portion size, whether at home, where it's much easier to control, or when eating out, where it's often quite difficult. In the right kind of restaurant, you can order from the appetizer list where portions are notably smaller. Or share a main course with a friend dining with you. Or eat half the presentation and ask to bag the rest to carry home.

Substitute wine in moderation for other alcoholic beverages. If you enjoy wine with your meals, you're already well on the way to a Mediterranean lifestyle. Except among strict Moslems, wine is part of every Mediterranean meal but breakfast. The operative words here are *part of the meal.* In the Mediterranean, wine is a companion to food and almost never taken on its own. Even a glass of wine or an aperitif as a cocktail before dinner is always accompanied by something to eat—if not a full-fledged meze, then a few olives or a handful of almonds. Wine in moderation, a couple of glasses a day served with meals, seems in fact to be protective against coronary heart disease.

If you don't care for wine, don't turn to soft drinks or fruit juices, even natural ones, as they are all potent sources of sugar and/or calories. Drink water instead—a bottle or pitcher of water is a standard feature on Mediterranean tables. It doesn't have to be expensive bottled water, either. Most of us in North America are fortunate to have access to good, clean water straight from the tap. Just don't substitute milk, which comes into the Mediterranean diet after infancy only in the form of wonderful cheeses and yogurts or a little hot milk added to morning coffee. For normal healthy adults, enough calcium should be supplied by cheese, yogurt, and vegetables.

Don't fuss with dessert. To me, dessert seems like useless and unprofitable time spent in the kitchen, and it's certainly not necessary on the table. (Far better to spend that time making soup.) Above all, don't buy packaged desserts, whether cakes, cookies, or ice cream—well, maybe ice cream as an occasional treat. Most packaged desserts are so loaded with saturated fat and sugar, not to mention stabilizers and other undesirable additives, that they are truly nutritional time bombs. All they really do is accustom the palate to sugary fats at the end of a meal. If you must have a sweet, the simplest of cookies is preferable to a rich cake; better yet is fresh or lightly poached fruit, which should be sweet enough in itself to satisfy any sugar addicts in the family. And with fruit you get valuable vitamins and fiber along with the sweet, something that cannot be said for other desserts.

Many restaurants will have a simple platter of fresh fruit or fruit with cheese on the dessert menu. Choose it instead of the sinfully chocolate drop-dead nightmare the pastry chef is so proud of. As more of us start asking for fruit, more fruit will be served.

Think about the quality of the food you buy and seek out the best. Because Mediterranean food is so simple, it's worth spending time looking for the best ingredients. How do you go about doing this? Fortunately, it gets easier with each passing season. Start with the place where you customarily shop. Many supermarkets, responding to customer demand, have established sections devoted to organically raised produce and naturally raised meats.

If supermarkets have little to offer, look for farmers' markets and health food stores that carry local, healthy ingredients. (Call the food editor of a local newspaper or your state university's college of agriculture for information. Cooperative Extension agents can also be good information sources.)

Farmers' markets are terrific sources. When you start to frequent them, you'll also start to build up contacts with local farmers. They'll not only tell you how the food is grown or produced; they may tell you how to cook it, too, and they'll start to let you know what things are coming along. The best-run health food stores and co-ops are also good outlets for local production—fruits and vegetables, whole grains and beans, free-range chickens and their eggs, all of which will be fresher and more flavorful than most supermarket offerings. Many farmers' markets and health food stores take WIC coupons and food stamps; if you're on a tightly restricted budget, keep that in mind.

In restaurants, ask questions about where food comes from and let them know that you care. The best restaurants also care and work hard to advance quality.

In the end, it's the simplicity of it all that makes the Mediterranean diet such an appealing alternative. Exotic foods, elaborate and time-consuming preparations, and special culinary techniques are not what it's all about. Good food, carefully purchased, thoughtfully if simply prepared, and lovingly served and shared: that's the secret.

Children and the Mediterranean Diet

Enjoyment is the key to supporting great nutrition, especially for young children, because if they don't enjoy their food, they simply won't eat it. But if you present food that is freshly prepared and tasty, even broccoli, children will almost always come around, especially if they see that everyone else at the table is enjoying the same thing.

All children seem to go through periods when they will eat only one thing—only white food, perhaps, or only peanut butter and jelly sandwiches (not a bad thing, as long as they're made with whole-grain bread). The best course of action, we are assured by everyone from Dr. Spock on, is not to stress out, not to wring hands, not to indicate the least shred of anxiety—and above all, not to rush to offer an alternative. But almost all children love pasta and pizza, so start your Mediterranean diet campaign with one of those, prepared to be appetizing and full of flavor, presented as a family meal to be enjoyed all together—and you may find the battle is over before it's even begun.

The Fat Picture

Few subjects of nutritional research are more confusing than the question of what fats to eat—or not to eat. Reams have been written on the subject, in prestigious peer-reviewed professional journals as well as in the popular press, and the books alone would fill a small-town library. Yet much of the advice is conflicting and each season, it seems, new evidence is presented to support the benefits or detriments of this fat or that fat or no fat at all. The more we know, it seems, the more we discover that we don't know.

So what's a thoughtful person to conclude? For the benefit of the argument, I will try to outline below what I know about fats, and what I think you should know, and you may draw your own conclusions. And if this is more than you want to know, then skip over it and join me as I come back, in the final analysis, to the typical, traditional Mediterranean diet and its emphasis on extra-virgin olive oil as the primary fat, along with the occasional use of pure lard for deep-fat frying. Why? Because, apart from the science, which has shown conclusively that olive oil, as a monounsaturated fat, works to reduce harmful LDLs, stabilize HDL cholesterol, reduce inflammation, and support healthy blood pressure as well as healthy blood flow, the anecdotal evidence is clear that people who follow a traditional Mediterranean diet, even with as much as 40 percent of their calories from fat (but most of that monounsaturated olive oil), have far better health profiles than Americans who follow diets high in saturated and polyunsaturated fats. And researchers are convinced that there is a cause-and-effect link. Where once we were told to lower our consumption of fats, state-of-the-art investigation now says the problem is not quantity so much as quality. In other words, it's not the *amount* of fat—it's the *kind* of fat that is at issue.

Basically, there are three kinds of dietary fats—saturated, polyunsaturated, and monounsaturated. All fats are a mixture of all three, with one or the other more predominant. All fats are also alike in that all are 100 percent fat and have 9 calories per gram or 120 calories per tablespoon. You will not lose weight if you substitute a tablespoon of olive oil for a tablespoon of butter. But that's not what this is about.

I won't go into the detailed chemistry of the differences among the three kinds of fat except to note that it is based on the carbon-hydrogen bonds in the molecules of each kind. Those who are interested can find discussions of fat chemistry in any number of texts (see Bibliography, pages 479–481) as well as all over the Internet. (For a particularly helpful discussion, easy for laypeople to understand, look at the Harvard School of Public Health's web site, www.hsph.harvard.edu/nutritionsource/fats.html.) Those of us who are not chemists can easily tell the difference between saturated and unsaturated fats because at room temperature, saturated fats are solid (think butter, lard, meat fats, coconut oil), while unsaturated fats, whether poly or mono, are liquid.

Saturated fat increases the risks of heart disease, primarily by raising blood cholesterol levels, and has been linked to other chronic diseases such as cancer and degenerative ailments. Many researchers believe that consumption of saturated fat should be limited, as it is in the traditional Mediterranean diet, to just a few times a month, or more often in small amounts—a good example of the latter is the use of a couple of ounces of meat or sausage in a pasta sauce to serve four to six people. Or the garnish of sautéed chopped lamb that tops Lebanese hummus bi tahini. Or the little bit of meat that adds richness of flavor to Greek or Turkish stuffed grape leaves. Saturated fat shouldn't be banned from the diet—it often accompanies other valuable nutrients—but it should be used much more moderately than it is in America, where our meat-focused diet is the cause of a lot of health problems.

But there are worse fats than saturated fats. Far worse. Trans fats are quite possibly the most dangerous fats we can put in our mouths. These are for the most part artificial fats, created through the process of hydrogenation, heating polyunsaturated liquid oils in the presence of hydrogen. Why was hydrogenation invented? Because, as any baker knows, it's hard to make a buttery cake with a liquid polyunsaturated fat such as corn oil. But hydrogenating makes the oil harder, more solid at room temperature—just like margarine, which is supposed to be just like butter, except that, as a plant-based fat, it is free of cholesterol, and we were told that cutting back on dietary cholesterol was the way to good health.* Et voilà, cakes, cookies, all manner of baked goods coming out of the oven, cholesterol free but tasting like and feeling like they had been made with butter. Along the way, it was also discovered that these hydrogenated fats have great shelf stability, meaning products made with them will last not quite forever, but darned close. Which has led the processed food industry—and we're talking an enormous industry here, one that reaches into all our lives all over the world—to rely on trans fats. Unfortunately, however, the effect of consuming trans fats is precisely the reverse of what is desirable—they increase bad LDLs, lower good HDLs, and initiate an immune system response that may lead to diabetes, heart disease, and other chronic inflammatory conditions. (Commercially prepared fried foods—french fries, fried onion rings, chicken nuggets, et cetera—are also often fried in cheap hydrogenated fats and should be avoided for that reason.)

So let's put the saturated fats high up on the pantry shelf where we won't use them often, and let's throw the trans fats out entirely. That leaves us with polyunsaturated and monounsaturated fats.

But it's still not simple. Because among the polyunsaturated fats are two that are essential to human health ("essential" meaning that if you don't consume them, you die). These are the omega-6 and omega-3 fatty acids, which help produce the material to regulate an enormous range of vital body functions like heart rate, blood pressure, and the immune system, among others. The best-known omega-3s (EPA or eicosapentaenoic acid, and DHA or docosahexaenoic acid—but you don't have to remember that) are found in fatty fish such as salmon, anchovies, tuna, mackerel, sardines—most of them, incidentally, prevalent in the Mediterranean diet. (If your mother, like mine, called fish "brain food," she was right, because they contribute to the DHA in our own brains.)

Another equally important omega-3, alpha-linolenic acid (ALA), comes from certain vegetable oils (soybean, flaxseed, and cold-pressed canola or rapeseed oils) and from walnuts; ALA is also found in certain green leafy vegetables—kale, spinach, leeks, salad greens like arugula and purslane, turnip greens, and so forth. Interestingly, it's the prevalence of ALA in many greens that accounts for its appearance in the flesh of animals and fish that

*It now appears that there is little relationship between the cholesterol we eat (dietary cholesterol) and the cholesterol in our systems (blood or serum cholesterol); instead, it's the consumption of saturated and trans fats that leads to elevated blood levels of cholesterol.

eat those greens (but not in animals or fish fed a corn-based diet, as most animals are in the United States).

Omega-6 fatty acid (linoleic acid) comes from soybean, corn, safflower, and cottonseed oils, among others—and there are far more omega-6s in most vegetable oils than there are omega-3s. In general, according to Artemis Simopoulos, one of the principal investigators of essential fatty acids, grains are high in omega-6s, while greens are high in omega-3s. In fact, one of the problems with hydrogenation is that the omega-3s are often eliminated in the process. (Since omega-3 oils are prone to oxygenation, this is a major explanation for the lengthened shelf life that hydrogenation effects.)

We should be consuming as much of these two essential fatty acids as we can. The problem, however, is that Americans, eating what nutritionists call a Westernized diet, get plenty of omega-6s—in fact, some nutritionists claim that we get too much with our corn-based meat-based diet—but nowhere near enough omega-3s. And it's the imbalance, these nutritionists say, that causes serious health problems. Our intake of omega-6 fatty acids has grown steadily over the years as we have switched to a diet that is increasingly based on processed foods. And the omega-6 fatty acids crowd out the even more valuable omega-3s. An ideal balance of omega-6s to omega-3s, scientists tell us, would be from 1:1 up to 4:1. In fact, the typical Westernized or American diet can range from 10:1 all the way up to 30:1.

So we should all eat more fatty fish, more greens, and where meat is concerned, meat from animals that have fed on grass rather than grain. This is an expensive proposition because our government's agricultural policy has been built for the best part of a half-century on promoting big commodity crops, soybeans and corn, and a great deal—I might go so far as to say an unfathomable amount—of money is invested in keeping us, and our animals, on a soy- and corn-based diet. Switching is expensive, but not switching may be more expensive still in view of the health problems we face now and in the future as we raise generations of obese children and diabetics.

That brings us to monounsaturated fats, which are actually easiest to deal with since they come primarily from olive oil and canola oil. These are the oils we should be using to dress our salads, to sauté our fish and the small amounts of meat we consume, to garnish our bean soups and steamed vegetables, even to put on our breakfast toast (try my favorite breakfast, a dribble of truly fine extra-virgin olive oil on a slice of toasted whole-grain bread—it's delicious!).

Of these two oils, my choice is always extra-virgin olive oil. One, because, unlike most canola oil and unlike olive oil that is not marked extra-virgin, extra-virgin oil is unrefined and unprocessed, the result simply of squeezing olives until the oil runs out. No chemical solvents are used to extract it, no heat is applied to transform it into something else. It is pure and natural, and moreover because of that it is also a source of important vitamins, minerals, antioxidants, polyphenols, and other phytochemicals that we are only beginning to understand. In fact it may be olive oil's polyphenolic content along with its monounsaturated fat that makes it so highly heart protective. And, as with so many other aspects of the Mediterranean diet, it may be that while olive oil on its own is good for you, olive oil in combination with vegetables, with lemon juice, with vinegar, with freshly chopped herbs, with salt and pepper and all manner of other foods to which it is suited— may be even better for you than any of those elements are in and of themselves.

EXTRA-VIRGIN OLIVE OIL

Capodacqua is a little village in the Umbrian hills south of Assisi, where during the season of the olive harvest I like to drop in on the Fancelli mill, or *frantoio* as it's called in Italy, to watch and smell and taste as the big stone presses whirl around, crushing the olives, and the fragrance rises on the air, and, finally, the thick, luscious oil flows sedately onto a crust of toasted bread, ready for the first sampling of the new oil. I like Mr. Fancelli's place in part because the oil he produces is the rich green stuff of the region that, when young and fresh from the frantoio, slides down the throat with the peppery *pizzica,* the catch at the back of the palate, that is typical of oil pressed from immature, half-green Umbrian moraiolo olives.

This is the oil connoisseurs seek out much as they do the fine red Sagrantino wines of the region. Like the wines, the oil has a unique character. It speaks of the terraced hills around Capodacqua with a voice that is subtly different from that of oils from nearby Orvieto or Cortona. And these strong-flavored, green-tasting central Italian oils are very different themselves from the rounder, more succulent oils from Puglia or Sicily. Which again are distinct from the oils of Catalonia with their hints of almond, and the richer, full-bodied oils from Greece and farther east in Lebanon, and the bland, sweet oils from North Africa.

The olive harvest begins in Capodacqua, as it does throughout the Mediterranean, in mid-autumn as farmers accompanied by family and friends work quickly to strip the trees by hand of their fruit.

The greenish violet olives, engorged with oil, are brought to the frantoio by the tractorload and tumbled through a hopper down into the crusher, two giant stone wheels that stand on edge and turn steadily, mashing the fruits to a thick, oily paste that is spread on round mats, once made of esparto grass, now made of plastic. The big mats are stacked high, one on top of the other, and carted by dolly to the presses. Gently but firmly the mats are compressed and the precious oil, glistening gold in the dim light of the frantoio, oozes out and trickles slowly down over the mats and into waiting receptacles below.

And that's it. Cloudy, greenish gold, and heady with fragrance, the new oil is ready. Most of Mr. Fancelli's clients don't bother filtering their oil because the residues precipitate, just like wine residues, with the cold winter temperature.

Mr. Fancelli's is one of the last of these traditional mills left anywhere around. Apart from the fact that electricity is the driving force, rather than mules or human labor, the system in essence is unchanged from Roman times or even earlier. Nowadays, almost everyone else has switched over to modern stainless-steel continuous-cycle machinery, which extracts the oil quickly and efficiently but without the inherent drama and romance of the Capodacqua mill. Some say you'll never get clean oil with the old-fashioned system—it's too slow, it exposes the crushed olives to oxidation—while others claim the modern method produces clean oil, yes, but without the character, the stamp of individuality, that the older mills produced.

Whether old-fashioned or newfangled, however, this is all extra-virgin olive oil. That's because the process is essentially one of simply squeezing good, sound, healthy olives to extract their oil, along with the vegetable water that is removed by precipitation or centrifuging. But no chemical solvents are used to extract or to clean the oil, and no heat is applied. This is what food writers like to call a "first cold pressing," although the term is deceptive since there is no second pressing, no hot pressing.

There are other ways of getting oil out of olives with chemical solvents, a process used only with olives that, for one reason or another, are not sufficiently high in quality to produce extra-virgin oil. The oil from poor-quality olives is stripped of its bad flavors and aromas, leaving a colorless, tasteless, aromaless oil to which a little extra-virgin is added to give some reason for calling it olive oil, plain and simple, but never extra-virgin. The only virtue of "olive oil" is that, like extra-virgin, it's primarily a monounsaturated fat, but as it's also a highly processed fat, I don't recommend using it except for deep-fat frying.

It is chilly in the *frantoio,* but that doesn't stop it from being a sort of community center during the brief weeks that it's operating. Besides the workers, there are farmers and farm wives dropping in to check the progress of their oil, buyers and curious onlookers, and always a group of old men of the village who do nothing much but make comments on the action, comments that are sometimes received as wisdom, sometimes as the foolishness of age.

In the back room a fire burns brightly on an old hearth that just escapes being an antique. The men gather around the hearth, toasting thick slices of bread on long forks until they're blackened and crusty. Then they rub the slices with a cut clove of garlic and drizzle them thickly with the newly decanted oil. A sprinkle of salt from a nearby jelly jar and the bruschetta is ready, its crust softened with oil to the point that weak old teeth can masticate it with evident satisfaction. It is a scene that has been repeated every year at this time for as long as the old men can remember, for as long as they've heard tell.

Is it strange that a product as ancient as olive oil has been given new life and validity by the discoveries of modern science? Not really. Not when you understand that for thousands of years olive oil has been the foundation of the Mediterranean diet, this diet that nutritionists and medical researchers tell us approaches an ideal. Olive oil is not the only healthy factor in the Mediterranean diet by any means, but scientists suspect that it is one of the most significant.

As nutritional science evolves, so does our knowledge about olive oil, its physical characteristics and chemical composition and its impact on human metabolism. We know that all olive oil, extra-virgin and regular alike, has impressive health benefits because of its high quotient of monounsaturated fat. But extra-virgin olive oil has the further virtue that, because it is so minimally processed, it retains many of the valuable phytochemicals that are present in olives, especially antioxidant carotenoids and tocopherols (vitamin E)—and these are lost during the processing that results in plain olive oil.

Vitamin E is a powerful antioxidant; like beta-carotene and vitamin C, it fights against free radicals, damaging elements that seem to suppress the immune system and may contribute to heart disease, cancer, and lung disease as well as to the aging process. Free radicals are produced in the body by pollutants like tobacco smoke and fuel exhaust, but they are also a normal, constant, and inevitable by-product of human metabolism. Anything that inhibits the formation of free radicals is likely to be beneficial in disease prevention.

Olive oil is the only fat that is high in monounsaturated fatty acids, that is easy and relatively inexpensive to produce by simply expressing the juice of olives, and that contributes welcome flavors and textures to the foods to which it's added. Moreover, olive oil has a long tradition as the principal fat used by people with a well-documented history of long and healthy lives—the people of the Mediterranean basin.

With all the talk that goes on about reducing fat consumption, why should we bother with olive oil at all? Wouldn't it be better just to eliminate all fats from our diets? No, it wouldn't, for the very good reason that, beyond questions of taste (and fat, no matter what its structure, contributes powerfully to flavor in all our foods), our bodies need a certain amount of fat to function properly—grease for the gears, you might say, in the form of fat-soluble vitamins like A, D, E, and K and in the valuable, protective HDL cholesterol levels that, without some fat in the diet, might fall dangerously low, according to researchers.

At the Cambridge conference on the diets of the Mediterranean in 1993, Dr. Walter Willett, chairman of the Department of Nutrition at the Harvard School of Public Health, startled the assembly when he exclaimed, only half-jokingly, "As far as I'm concerned, you can take the whole food pyramid and just pour olive oil over it!" Yet there's a certain amount of logic in that assertion: the Seven Countries Study of men on the island of Crete in the early 1960s showed that they received a full 40 percent of their daily calories from fat, the fat they ate was primarily olive oil, and their mortality rates from coronary heart disease and stroke were among the lowest in the world.

Mediterranean Methods, Materials, and Ingredients

✧ ✧ ✧

D ON'T BE OBSESSIVE about methods and materials: that is the motto of the Mediterranean kitchen.

If you can't quite master a new technique, don't tell anyone. I can almost guarantee you they won't know the difference.

Flavor counts far more than elaborate techniques and presentations, and flavor begins with the best ingredients. Each separate ingredient should be the finest you can afford, but if you can't afford it or you've run out of it, don't worry. Mediterranean cooks are notable for making do with what's at hand. That's an attitude I try to cultivate in my own kitchen.

With the exception of pastries, which often require a fairly precise balance of ingredients, nothing in this book is written in stone. If you don't happen to have an ingredient, or if you don't have enough to satisfy the recipe requirements, don't let that stop you from preparing it. If you get halfway through a recipe only to discover that the tomatoes you thought were fine have gone soft, or someone in a midnight feeding frenzy ate up all the pine nuts, just leave out the pine nuts. Or change fish in a tomato-parsley sauce to fish in a parsley sauce and add lemon juice or wine or just plain water to make up for the missing liquid from the tomatoes.

On the other hand, a well-stocked pantry is a great comfort in life. If you have the space, there's nothing like a wall of shelves filled with the sort of things that keep well: olive oil, vinegars, dried mushrooms, beans, and grains.

Methods

The Battuto or Soffritto

You will find, as you flip through the recipes in this book, that many begin with sautéing a mixture of finely chopped vegetables in olive oil or sometimes pork fat such as pancetta. This step is called the *battuto* or *soffritto* in Italy and the *sofrito* in Spain. I mention it because it's a useful technique for all sorts of soups, sauces, and sauced preparations, whether vegetables, meat, chicken, or fish. In Italy, the ingredients for the battuto—called *odori*, aromatics—might consist of a carrot, a stalk of celery, and a little bunch of parsley or a sprig of rosemary. The stall holders in street markets give them away to favorite customers. *"Odori, signora?"* says the market lady from whom you've just bought artichokes, and she tucks a little bundle in the bag almost as an afterthought. When you get home, you chop your aromatics with maybe half an onion and half a clove of garlic, add a little finely chopped pancetta, and sauté it all in a spoonful of olive oil. It's the foundation of an aromatic pasta sauce or soup for lunch. It's also a way of adding vegetables to your daily diet without even being aware of it.

Soaking Beans

Most beans and legumes should be soaked before cooking—lentils are a notable exception. To soak them, simply place them in a bowl with twice their quantity of fresh cool water. Set aside overnight. In the morning, discard the soaking water and start the cooking process with fresh water.

If you forget to soak the beans the night before (how many times I have forgotten!), you can use the quick-soak method: set the beans in a saucepan with twice their quantity of fresh cool water. Bring the water to a boil over high heat and boil rapidly, covered, for 1 to 2 minutes. Then remove from the heat and set aside, still covered, for an hour or more. Drain the beans and use fresh water for cooking.

Peeling and Seeding Tomatoes

To peel tomatoes, bring a large pot of water to a rolling boil, drop in one or two tomatoes (more will lower the heat of the water too much), and leave them for a slow count to 15. Then extract them with a slotted spoon and proceed until all the tomatoes are done. The skins should lift off easily, without using a knife.

Sometimes a recipe requires seeding tomatoes to make a very dry preparation. Simply cut the skinned tomatoes in half and press each half gently so that the seeds ooze out. (You don't need to get every last seed.) I do this over a sheet of newspaper, then simply fold the paper up to discard it.

Roasting Peppers

The method is the same, whether the peppers are sweet or hot, red, green, or yellow. Charcoal or wood embers are best for roasting peppers because of the smoky flavor they impart. If you have a grill, set the peppers on a grid about 4 inches above the hot and glowing coals. Turn the peppers frequently so that the skins become thoroughly blackened and blistered. If you don't have live coals, the peppers can be toasted over a gas flame on top of the stove. Use a long-handled fork and turn them constantly to toast as much of the skin as possible. Or if necessary, they can be toasted under an electric broiler. The point is to soften the peppers and turn the skins very black and loose, making them easy to peel.

No matter which procedure you follow, when the peppers are done, take them off the grill and set them aside under a kitchen towel until they're cool enough to handle. Then slit them and drain the juices into a bowl. (The flavorful pepper juices can be added to the preparation.) Peel the peppers by pulling and rubbing the blackened skin away with your fingers. Use a sharp knife if necessary to scrape away remaining bits of skin. Peeling the skins under running water washes too much of the flavor away, but a bowl of water is handy for rinsing off difficult bits.

The seeds and interior white membranes of sweet peppers are usually discarded for appearance's sake. With hot peppers, you may wish to retain some seeds and membrane, because this is where a large part of the pepper's heat is located. Taste a little bit of pepper, and if it seems not quite hot enough, add some of the seeds and membrane to the preparation.

This procedure can be done well in advance and the peppers refrigerated, if necessary, until you're ready to cook.

Trimming Artichokes

Even artichokes that are to be served whole must be prepared before cooking. You'll need a bowl large enough to hold all the artichokes, filled with cool water to which the juice of a lemon has been added to keep the artichokes from darkening. To prepare the artichokes, cut the stems back to about an inch from where they join the fruit; or, if the artichokes are to be served whole, standing up on the plate, trim the artichoke stem off flush with the fruit. Break off the very tough outer leaves. For a fancier presentation, trim the tough points of the remaining leaves with kitchen shears to present a uniform appearance. As you work, rub the cut surfaces of the artichoke with a lemon half to keep the exposed flesh from darkening. Toss each finished artichoke into the bowl of lemon water. When all the artichokes are trimmed, drain and proceed with the recipe.

To prepare artichoke hearts, trim off most of the leaves until you have only a few layers left around the heart. Using a sharp knife, cut off the tops of the artichokes down to where the heart begins. Using a serrated grapefruit spoon, pull out the spiny choke that lies on top of the heart. Again, rub the cut surfaces with lemon and toss the finished artichokes into lemon water.

Some recipes call for quartered artichokes. For this, you need not go all the way down to the heart, but when you reach the tender leaves, cut the tops off, cut the artichokes into quarters, and use a serrated grapefruit spoon to scrape away the choke. Again, place in lemon water.

Materials

Kitchen Paraphernalia

The part in Mediterranean cookbooks that I love best is the introductory chapter on *batterie de cuisine,* with its evocation of a lost world of craftsmanship and caring—artisanally sculpted earthenware pots, each form carefully molded to a specific purpose; hammered copper skillets and soup kettles so heavy they must be lifted with both hands; and an intricate variety of tools, implements, and other handy gear like a French *chinois,* a conical sieve for straining sauces, or an Italian *mezzaluna,* a half-moon-shaped knife that makes chopping parsley a breeze, or a Spanish *plancha,* a flat iron griddle for *gambas a la plancha* (shrimp on the grill) and other similar treats.

These are all eminently useful objects and often very beautiful ones, too. Collecting such paraphernalia and learning how to use them is a source of great pleasure—especially when they are sought out on their home ground. Real food lovers traveling in the Mediterranean always find a trip to the local market far more enlightening than a visit to any three-star restaurant. Not only will you find food products that are perfectly legal to bring back,★ but markets are always surrounded, naturally enough, by little shops selling whatever else is needed in the kitchen.

The reality in most Mediterranean kitchens, however, is rather different. Even in the hands of truly gifted cooks, the *batterie de cuisine* often consists

---

★As a general rule of thumb for Customs, no meat products and no fresh fruits and vegetables may be brought back by travelers. But you can bring back dried beans, dried mushrooms, dried fruits, nuts, dried herbs and spices, rice and other grains, pasta, olive oil, and most cheeses.

of cheap, dented aluminum pots with lids that don't quite fit, dull stainless-steel knives that are impossible to sharpen, and various catchall, makeshift, often comical, and sometimes out-and-out dangerous arrangements for preparing and serving food. Most Mediterranean cooks make do with what's on hand. And an ordinarily well-equipped American kitchen would almost always put what's on hand to shame.

Although you don't need any specialized equipment to adopt a Mediterranean way of cooking, there are a few tools, most of them inexpensive, that I consider essential. Here's my short list (see Resources):

Good carbon-steel knives, kept sharp with a stone. You'll know a good knife when you heft it—it feels well balanced and comfortable in the hand. A repertoire of knives might include an 8-inch chef's knife, indispensable for chopping and slicing, a couple of 5-inch paring knives, a serrated bread knife, and a smaller stainless-steel serrated knife for slicing tomatoes, lemons, and other fruit. Carbon-steel knives are very expensive and should be treated like jewels—washed after use, dried to prevent rust, sharpened before being put away in a special knife drawer or stand where each blade lies separate from the others, and sharpened again just before being used.

A large, heavy cutting board or a wooden countertop. Try to have at least two boards—one for chopping garlic and onions, cutting up meat and fish, and so forth; one for making breads and pastry—so the *pasta frolla* won't taste of onions. Keep your boards or countertops scrupulously clean and scrubbed, especially after cutting up chicken. One way salmonella spreads is through raw salad greens that have been contaminated by being cut up on a board used to cut chicken. Thorough cooking kills off the salmonella in chicken, but the uncooked salad becomes a fertile breeding ground for the invisible bugs. (A plastic cutting board, contrary to what we were told recently, is actually more likely than wood to engender this type of accidental contamination.)

A mortar and pestle is not just a nostalgic symbol of Old World craftsmanship, but a useful and necessary tool. More easily than with a food processor or blender, you can see when the food you're working with reaches precisely the right texture and consistency. Garlic, especially, should almost always be pounded in the mortar rather than tossed into the food processor— I'm persuaded that mechanical processing and blending give garlic a bitter aftertaste. And for small batches of food—half a cup or so of nuts, for instance—it's actually easier to use a mortar and a whole lot quicker to clean up.

I keep two mortars—one for pounding garlic and other strong-flavored foods, one for sweet spices and nuts; this way you'll keep the cookies from tasting of garlic and anchovies.

Spice mills: Because the flavor impact of freshly ground spices like allspice, cinnamon, and clove is so important in eastern Mediterranean dishes, I buy whole spices instead of previously ground ones. I keep a separate, small pepper mill with allspice berries in it and a separate small electric coffee grinder that I use when necessary for cinnamon, cloves, and other hard spices. These appliances, if they deserve such a fancy name, are cheap, and the convenience and flavor they afford is worth every penny.

A hand-turned food mill, with three different disks, along with the mortar and pestle, is indispensable for pureeing—especially for tomatoes since, unlike the processor or blender, it holds back seeds and bits of skin that can embitter a tomato sauce. And now and then, when you want an elegantly strained, velvety pureed soup or sauce, you will find it can really be done only with a food mill. Mechanically processed or blended purees must be further strained through a fine sieve to achieve this consistency.

Tongs are not something you see in domestic kitchens in the Mediterranean, but all professional chefs, there as well as here, find them so indispensable that, slid into the apron strings in back, they become part of the professional costume. I was introduced to tongs only a few years ago, but I can't cook without them today. Both my kitchens have three or four sets of the spring-loaded variety. For turning fried or grilled foods, for moving hot pots about on top of the stove, they are without peer.

A baking stone and a wooden peel are not quite mandatory but are certainly very useful if you intend to bake bread or pizza. For my money, the heavy rectangular stones are superior to so-called pizza disks. The stone mimics, to some degree, the action of a traditional baking oven lined with fireproof brick. You can devise your own system, using unglazed ceramic tiles, available at building supply houses.

Whichever you use, the stone or tiles *must* heat up for at least 30 minutes before you put in the bread or pizza. (Be sure to put the cold stone into the cold oven to prevent cracking.) Even when the oven light goes off, indicating that the proper ambient temperature has been reached inside, the temperature of the stone may be lower.

Note too that the bread or pizza is placed *directly* on the stone, not in a pan or on a baking sheet. This is known as *casting* and imitates the action in a traditional oven where the bread or pizza is cast directly onto the floor or hearth of the oven. (Traditional American baking powder biscuits, by the way, are terrific baked on a baking stone.)

A long-handled wooden peel is also useful in baking, especially for pizza. The best peels have a beveled edge so that pizza or bread loaves slide off the peel and onto the stone with a quick jerk of the hand, an action that seems to give most people who practice it an enormous amount of pleasure and satisfaction.

Ingredients

Olives and Olive Oils

The subject of olive oil raises questions in the minds of American consumers, probably because for many of us it's a new product, a new taste, one we're not accustomed to using. Why is olive oil so expensive? Are we really getting what we pay for? If we buy cheap oils, are they bound to taste like rancid crankcase grease? What is extra-virgin oil, and why should I buy it?

The International Olive Oil Council, a United Nations–backed organization of oil-producing countries, sets world standards for different grades of olive oil. Only two concern us as consumers. The finest is extra-virgin oil, an unrefined product that is produced simply by extracting the oil from the olives through mechanical or physical (but not chemical) processes, whether an old-fashioned crush-and-press operation or a newfangled centrifugal extractor. No matter how it's produced, extra-virgin oil must have a free oleic acid content of 0.8 percent or less and "perfect" aroma, color, and flavor.

The second quality of oil is called *pure olive oil* or just plain *olive oil*—somewhat confusingly, since both extra-virgin and pure oils are pure in the sense that they are clean and contain nothing but the oil of olives. Pure oil is extracted from lesser-grade olives, those that, for a number of reasons, have undesirable characteristics of acidity, odor, and taste. This oil is refined to make a colorless, odorless, flavorless oil; then extra-virgin or virgin oil (an intermediate category that is not generally for sale) is added in small quantities to give the oil some character.

Extra-virgin olive oil is a great food product, lending taste and structure to dishes in which it is used. Each extra-virgin oil has its own particular color, flavor, and aroma—what professional tasters call *organoleptic characteristics*. I compare it to wine: in oil, as in wine, the complex of flavors and aromas in the finished product depends on a number of critical variables—the variety of the plant, whether vine or tree, the structure of the soil, the microclimate of the immediate environment, the quantities of fertilizer and irrigation used during the growing season, the time and method of harvest, and finally the care with which the raw fruit is turned into the finished product, bottled, and stored. Like wines, the finest extra-virgin oils vary from one region to another and from one season to another. But they are almost invariably made from immature olives that are handpicked and pressed quickly in cool temperatures before the oil starts to oxidize and ferment.

One caveat in comparing olive oil to wine: unlike wine, extra-virgin olive oil doesn't improve with age. Anyone who's had the privilege of tasting olive oil in the first few weeks after pressing knows that the fresher it is, the better it tastes. While a freshly pressed and unfiltered oil is not especially good for high-temperature cooking, since the unprecipitated vegetable matter may burn in the process, it is superb for consuming raw. A sauce in and of itself, it needs no embellishment beyond perhaps a few grains of salt.

Carefully stored in a sealed metal or glass container, preferably in a cool (but not refrigerated), dark cupboard, olive oil is good for up to two years, but after that the oil will have passed its prime and should be used as soon as possible. Olive oil that is exposed to heat and light for a period of time, on the other hand, can turn rancid. Keep a small quantity in a metal oil can by the work counter and store the rest in the cupboard.

I sometimes hear American chefs assert that extra-virgin olive oil is no good for cooking and should be reserved for dressing salads and garnishing plates. Nothing could be further from the truth. Chefs in the best restaurants in Spain, southern France, Italy, and Greece would be as perplexed as I am to hear that since they would not dream of using anything else. I take my cue from these experts and use extra-virgin olive oil for all cooking except deep-fat frying when, because it's cheaper, I mostly use refined plain olive oil or canola oil.

Even then, extra-virgin olive oil is fine if you can afford it. Of course you won't use first-rate, estate-bottled oil for deep-fat frying, any more than you would use a top-quality Châteauneuf-du-Pape to make a stew. But the suggestion that somehow extra-virgin olive oil has a very low flash point is mistaken. The optimum temperature for deep-fat frying is 350 to 375 degrees, and olive oil has no problems at that temperature, or even higher. Once, with my friend the olive oil maven Mort Rosenblum, I deep-fried a turkey for Thanksgiving. It came about because I discovered in the back of my pantry a stainless-steel container with a good 15 quarts of olive oil in it, fine extra-virgin oil that had been pressed from another friend's crop and hidden in the cool, dark cantina in Tuscany for at least four years. The oil had lost a lot of its flavor and aroma but it wasn't the least bit rancid. What better use could it serve than deep-frying a turkey? In the end, a whole turkey was way too big to fit in the cooking pot but we managed to fry an enormous leg quarter and the consensus around the Thanksgiving table was impressive—crisp and golden on the outside, succulent on the inside, it was the best turkey, we all agreed, we had ever eaten.

Which olive oil is best? It's a question I'm often asked and it's impossible to answer. Which cheese is best, you might well ask, or which wine? It all depends on how and when you want to use it, how much you want to spend, and various other variables. In fact, there are great oils from all over the Mediterranean and from farther afield—California, Chile, New Zealand, and South Africa, among the many places that have initiated olive oil production in recent years. Many of these great oils are produced in small quantities and aren't generally available. So if my specialty foods market in Maine, for instance, has access to a terrific little oil from the Mani peninsula of Greece, that doesn't necessarily mean you too can find it in a food shop in another part of the country.

A couple of buying tips:

- Look for the name of the place where the olive oil was produced (if it doesn't have a place name, it may well be generic oil made by combining oils from several different places—nothing wrong with that but such an oil should be kept for cooking, rather than treated as a fine oil).

- Extra-virgin olive oils from Spain, France, Italy, and Greece may be marked with a DOP or Protected Denomination of Origin, a guarantee by the European Union that the oil is produced and bottled under stringent regulations—although many oils that are not DOP may still be very high quality.

- More and more producers are adding the date when the oil was pressed (it could be simply 2007–2008 harvest), which is a better indication of freshness than the date the oil was bottled; be aware that the very finest and most expensive oil is not worth the price if it's more than two years past its harvest date.

- More important even than the brand of oil or where it comes from is how oil is treated in the markets you frequent. Beware of any vendor who puts her oils on display in the window of the shop. That's a certain road to ruin as sunlight and heat are the two enemies of fine olive oil. In fact, most shopkeepers would be a whole lot better off displaying one bottle only of each brand they carry, keeping the rest in a cool, dark back room. But just try convincing a shop owner of that! Shop owners should know something about the oils they carry and if they don't, perhaps you should take your custom elsewhere.

A good web site for olive oil information, with a selection of oils for sale from all over the world, is www.oliveoilsource.com. And the Internet resources listed in the back of this book include many outlets for fine extra-virgins.

The best thing to do is taste, taste, taste, as many different oils as you can find, preferably purchased in small bottles, until you find what you like. Let your suppliers know you're interested in oil and would appreciate an invitation to a comparative tasting if one is in the works. Taste oil on its own, not with a piece of bread or anything else that may confound the flavor. And when you travel to parts of the world where olive oil is produced, continue tasting and questioning, visit olive mills when they're in operation to deepen your understanding of how oil is produced, and bring samples home with you—it's perfectly legal to bring in olive oil, although you may have some problems with security restrictions if you try to carry liquid on board a flight.

Grains and Flours

Wheat is the very foundation of the Mediterranean diet, whether in the form of bread, of pasta and couscous, or of bulgur. The many types of wheat range from farro or emmer (*Triticum dicoccum*), an ancient wheat newly popular in Italy, to regular bread wheat, similar to our all-purpose flour, to hard durum semolina, used for pasta—in fact, legally required for commercial pasta in Italy—and for bread making alike. Durum is the quintessential Mediterranean wheat. As such it is still grown in some parts of the Mediterranean, but a lot of the semolina used today comes in fact from the western prairies of the United States and Canada. Durum yields a gritty semolina, the result of the vitreous nature of its grains, with a creamy yellow color from the carotenoids naturally present in the wheat.

For all-purpose flour, I prefer unbleached, unbromated King Arthur from Norwich, Vermont; it is widely available throughout the country and from the King Arthur web site, www.kingarthurflour.com. This is actually a great site for all kinds of flour, including semolina and barley flour, as well as French- and Italian-style flours and an excellent flour for bread making, European-style Artisan Bread Flour.

Bulgur (in Turkish, the word most commonly used in this country) or *burghul* (in Arabic) is made of whole wheat berries that are steamed, then dried and cracked. It needs no further cooking for salad preparations but should be soaked in warm water to soften it before using. (Cover it with warm water—2 cups of water to 1 cup of bulgur—and set it aside for 20 to 30 minutes. Then drain and squeeze dry in a kitchen towel.) Bulgur also makes an elegant pilaf (page 244); for cooking, it does not need to be soaked beforehand.

Bulgur is commonly available at health food stores and specialty shops, as well as in Arab and Armenian neighborhood stores. It comes in three grades, depending on the size of the cracked grain. Number three (coarse) is best for pilaf. Number two (medium) is best for tabbouleh and other salads. Number one (fine) is for making kibbe.

Couscous is not a distinct grain but rather a type of pasta, made, like commercial pasta, from hard durum semolina and water—nothing more. Once upon a time couscous was made at home, but nowadays, even in North Africa, most cooks use commercially prepared couscous.

Pasta comes in hundreds of shapes and sizes, mostly classifiable as either long and skinny noodles or short, stubby forms that capture dense sauces. Whatever shape it takes, however, commercial dried pasta must be made from semolina and water, with eggs added in the north of Italy but not generally elsewhere.

Among commercial pastas that are widely available are the Italian brands Barilla, the largest pasta-maker in the world, as well as De Cecco and Delverde. But look too for artisanal pastas made in Italy using old-fashioned bronze dies and slow, low-temperature drying methods that yield a superior product. Among the brands available are Benedetto Cavalieri, Rustichella d'Abruzzo, and Latini.

Rice is almost as complex a subject as wheat, but fortunately, in the Mediterranean it is simplified into two types—short-grain, used in risotto and paella, and long-grain, used in pilaf. (And, yes, there is a medium grain, grown in Spain and also used in paella.) Arborio is the most widely available short-grain rice, traditionally used for risotto but also an acceptable rice for paella. If you can find them, carnaroli and vialone nano are superior for risotto. The best rice for paella is *arroz bomba* or *calasparra* from Spain's eastern rice-growing regions, increasingly available in this country.

For pilaf, any long-grain rice is good. The best is basmati, a very fragrant rice originally from India but now grown in California and Texas. Other long-grain specialty rices grown in this country, like popcorn rice and pecan rice, are also good in pilaf.

Polenta is just cornmeal, either white or yellow, though yellow is more typical. In polenta recipes you can use any American cornmeal (except self-rising cornmeal, which contains chemical leavening), and it is often a better choice than run-of-the-mill imported polenta, which may be less than fresh. The best Italian polenta, like the best American cornmeal, is stone ground using the whole grain, including the germ. For polenta, a rather coarse-textured meal is preferred. An interesting variation, available from many suppliers (see Resources), is *polenta taragna,* a mixture of cornmeal and ground buckwheat. It can be substituted for plain polenta in any recipe.

Two of the best stone-ground American cornmeals come from Rhode Island—Gray's Grist Mill in Adamsville (graysgristmill.com) and Kenyon Cornmeal Company (kenyongristmill.com) in Usquepaugh. But there are small mills all over the country that are good sources for this native American product.

Dairy Products

Yogurt: Fernand Braudel quotes Busbecq the Fleming, writing in 1555: "The Turks are so frugal and think so little of the pleasures of eating that if they have bread, salt, and some garlic or an onion and a kind of sour milk which they call yoghoort, they ask nothing more. They dilute this milk with very cold water and crumble bread into it and take it when they are hot and thirsty . . . it is not only palatable and digestible, but also possesses an extraordinary power of quenching the thirst."

The Turks probably introduced yogurt into the Mediterranean, and it is still more often used in the old Ottoman Empire countries of the eastern Mediterranean than it is in the West. Yogurt, sweetened with a little honey, is sometimes served for dessert in France, but it is not otherwise used in cooking. In the East, travelers will find rich and tangy yogurts made from sheep's or goat's milk, and this style of yogurt is becoming more available in this country from small local dairies. Look for such products in specialty and health food stores.

Another useful yogurt product is labneh or yogurt "cheese" (it's not really a cheese at all), made by straining the whey from ordinary yogurt (page 278).

Look for pure unflavored yogurt with live acidophilus cultures and no added gelatin or other stabilizers.

Cheeses: Parmigiano is, to my mind, the finest cheese in the world. Only the genuine product, parmigiano reggiano, should be used. It comes in giant wheels of cheese stamped proudly all over their waxy outsides with the words *parmigiano reggiano.* Avoid Argentine parmesan or the previously grated stuff that comes in a shiny green tube (*any* freshly grated cheese is better than that). Real parmigiano has a remarkable nutty, sweet, slightly caramel flavor and a texture that is smooth and hard with pleasing bits of crunch from the embedded crystals that form as the cheese ages. It is expensive, but a little goes a long way. If you can't afford parmigiano reggiano for cooking, use a well-made local hard cheese, even a local cheddar. The flavor will be totally different, but the integrity of the dish will remain.

Parmigiano should not be cut with a knife but rather broken away from the mother wheel using a wedge-shaped cutter so that the grain and texture of the cheese are exposed. Grate it freshly to use in cooking or serve it in chunks with the salad or fruit or to finish off a bottle of fine red wine. Parmigiano can be kept in the refrigerator, wrapped in paper and then loosely in plastic wrap, for months. It may get too hard for eating but will still be an excellent grating cheese.

Mozzarella is traditionally made from the milk of water buffalo that graze in pastures in the territory around Naples. Imported mozzarella di bufala is increasingly available in this country, but, alas, it is made by machine rather than the old-fashioned way by hand. Mozzarella from cow's milk is properly called *fior di latte* but may be marketed just as mozzarella or muzzarel'. You can often find handmade *fior di latte* in cheese shops in Italian neighborhoods. It can also be ordered from Paula Lambert's Mozzarella Company (mozzco.com). What is not to be used is the rubbery skim-milk cheese called mozzarella available in supermarket dairy cases. It bears no relationship whatsoever to the real thing, and how it came to be called mozzarella is a mystery.

Mozzarella is not meant for long keeping and should be used within a few days of purchase.

Pecorino from Italy and *manchego* from Spain are sheep's milk cheeses, increasingly available in fine cheese shops in this country. The best are 100 percent sheep's milk; they are aged for varying periods of time. At three months the cheese has a lovely nutty flavor and a creamy paste, a fine eating cheese. Aged longer, it becomes hard and dense and is good for grating. *Pecorino romano* is a very hard cheese with a distinctive sour flavor that is good in strong-flavored dishes but not universally appropriate.

Feta is the most characteristic Greek cheese. In Greece it is made only from sheep's or goat's milk, while in North America it is most often made from cow's milk. For this reason only imported Bulgarian or Greek feta is recommended in the recipes in this book, but if you can find feta from a local sheep or goat dairy, by all means use it. Feta is cured in a salt brine, and it varies in quality and in saltiness—ask to taste a bit before you buy. If you don't use it right away, store feta in the brine that comes with it in the refrigerator.

Manouri or manourgi is a soft, fresh Greek cheese, made like ricotta from whey with a little cream or milk added. *Mizithra* is similarly soft and fresh, made from the whey rendered in feta production. Like ricotta, too, they are not meant for long keeping. Paula Lambert at mozzco.com makes delicious goat's milk ricotta and feta.

Cured Meats

Pancetta is unsmoked, salt-cured bacon, widely available, especially in Italian specialty food shops, but also often found at supermarket deli counters. Like bacon, pancetta, well wrapped in foil, may be stored in the freezer for months.

Prosciutto and *jamón serrano* are raw dry-cured hams, prosciutto from Italy and jamón serrano from Spain. The finest kind is thinly sliced from a ham with the bone left in, but that is almost never available in this country where convenience rules over all and the bones are removed before the ham ever arrives here. These are very fine products, and expensive, so they should be treated with respect. Sliced thin (but not paper thin), they are usually served as part of a tapa or antipasto course, often with melon slices, fresh figs, or other fruits to accompany the salty ham. But prosciutto, like pancetta, is also used in very small quantities (a tablespoon or so of very finely chopped meat) in the battuto that forms the basis of many Italian sauces.

Tomatoes

The best tomatoes are of course the ones you grow in your own garden and harvest at the peak of ripeness about 30 seconds before you slice and eat them. Failing that, a farmers' market is a close second.

Like most Mediterranean cooks, I use canned tomatoes when fresh ones are not suitable. For those who live in New England and are fortunate enough to have gardens, the season usually lasts about two and a half days before the first frost, so when I'm in Maine I use a lot of canned tomatoes. The best canned tomatoes are San Marzanos from the area around Naples. Look for San Marzano DOP, indicating a protected denomination of origin. Academia Barilla's Pomodorini Pelati are peeled cherry tomatoes, also very good. Among American brands, I like Muir Glen organic whole tomatoes for their firm texture, their thick juice, and their flavor, which is thoroughly tomato, with nothing added. Whatever brand you use, make sure it contains nothing but whole tomatoes—often processors add other ingredients to boost the flavor.

Estratto di pomodoro is a pure tomato extract, about the same texture as tomato paste (the stuff that comes in a tube or a squat little can) but worlds apart in flavor. The best is made from tomato puree dried in the Sicilian sun. Both manicaretti.com and gustiamo.com have estratto from Sicily. It is very expensive but a little goes a long way to enliven soups and sauces.

Herbs, Spices, and Condiments

I mention here only those herbs and spices that seem to need comment.

Use *flat-leaf parsley* if at all possible, and if your supermarket can't or won't stock it, grow your own—it's very easy, in a pot on the window ledge if nowhere else, although you'll probably need several pots to supply a Mediterranean kitchen. (Cilantro will also grow well in a pot.)

Thyme is used both fresh and dried, both garden cultivated and wild, throughout the Mediterranean. It's a typical plant of the macchia or maquis, the low scrub forest that covers barren lands of the region. The flavor varies in intensity, depending on where the plant grows, but wild thyme generally contains more of a powerfully fragrant essential oil called *thymol,* a disinfectant, which is probably why I was given an infusion of wild thyme in Morocco to cure an unhappy stomach. Wild thyme, called *za'atar* in Arabic, is an ingredient in a fragrant mixture of thyme, sesame seeds, and sumac that is mixed with olive oil and sprinkled over freshly baked bread in the morning. (Confusingly, the mixture itself is also called *za'atar.* You can find both the mixture and the thyme in shops in Middle Eastern neighborhoods, so be sure you know what you're getting.)

Oregano is, like thyme (basil, too, for that matter), a pungent member of the mint family (*Labiatae*) that is used in both cultivated and wild versions. It is a quintessential ingredient in true Neapolitan pizza. Oregano, called *rí-gani,* is also important in the Greek kitchen, and the wild version is used in Greece to make tea. Dried wild oregano, which has a delightfully astringent aroma, can be found in shops in Greek neighborhoods, often tied up in pretty bundles. (Mexican oregano is a different plant, botanically, but with a similar pungency. Marjoram is a variety of oregano, with a sweeter and more delicate flavor.)

Bay leaves, or laurel, are not hard to find, but do use Turkish bay leaves if possible rather than the stronger, more medicinal-tasting bay leaves from California. McCormick's packages the Turkish ones, as do other commercial spice companies, and they are worth seeking out for the subtler flavor.

Sumac, the pleasantly astringent red berries of a Mediterranean shrub related to the sumac that grows in this country, is used in the eastern Mediterranean to impart an agreeably acid flavor to everything from salads to meat and chicken stews. It is part of the breakfast spread called zaʿatar in Lebanon and always used in the Lebanese salad *fattoush* (page 87). In Turkey, sumac is sprinkled on kebabs and other grilled meats. You'll find both whole berries and ground powdered sumac in shops in Middle Eastern neighborhoods.

Saffron came with the Arabs to Spain—the word comes from the Arabic *zafaran,* meaning "yellow." Some of the world's best saffron comes from southern Morocco. It's said to be the most expensive aromatic in the world since it takes the hand-collected stigmata of about 75,000 wild autumn-flowering crocuses to make a pound of saffron. Don't buy powdered saffron, which is often just cheap coloring with none of the musky, earthy flavor of true saffron. Saffron threads can be crumbled directly into a dish or steeped in water or broth first, then the saffron with its steeping liquid tipped into the sauce. Be discreet with saffron—too much can be overpowering.

Wild fennel pollen, sometimes called fennel flowers or finocchietto (the Italian name for wild fennel), is creating a small sensation among North American chefs who are apt to describe it as rare, mysterious, hard to find. In fact, it is sold in season (late summer to early autumn) in every country market in Tuscany and Umbria and while it is expensive, because it's hard to collect the dusty little mustard-colored flowers of wild fennel, it's worth every penny for its deep, almost musty but floral aroma—more like a fine garam masala than anything Mediterranean. But it's traditional in central Italian cooking for pork and rabbit especially, and is also good with fatty fish like salmon and mackerel. Imported Tuscan fennel pollen is available through many of the importers listed in Resources, pages 465–466; it grows along roadsides in California—try fennelpollen.com for wild California fennel pollen.

The best *salt* I have ever tasted comes from the island of Gozo in the Maltese archipelago. It has a crisp, penetrating, but never acrid flavor that is more appreciated as a garnish added at table than as an ingredient in a stew or sauce. It may seem strange to attach so much importance to salt, but if you don't believe it's important, try a taste test: buy several different varieties of salt, including sea salt, kosher salt, and ordinary shaker salt. Taste them on their own, completely nude. I think you'll be amazed at the difference.

In the Mediterranean, a squeeze of lemon juice or a splash of vinegar, what the French call *un filet de vinaigre,* often serves the same function as salt in bringing out the flavors of a dish. In places like Turkey and Tuscany, where meat is important in the cuisine, grilled meat always comes with a garnish of lemon wedges so that each diner can add a refreshing fillip of lemon juice to his or her plate. For people who must watch the amount of sodium in their diets this is an especially good practice.

Vinegar is almost as important for discriminating cooks as olive oil. Use red wine or white wine vinegar, depending on the color of the sauce. Many wine vinegars strike my palate as too acerbic and acid; I prefer imported aged sherry vinegar for its mellow yet robust flavor.

Balsamic vinegar *(aceto balsamico)* became hugely popular a few years back, and for a while chefs were throwing it indiscriminately on all kinds of preparations. It's a unique product; the best artisanally made balsamic vinegar, called *aceto balsamico tradizionale di Modena* or *di Reggio,* is produced under stringent regulations in and around Modena and Reggio Emilia and aged in fragrant wooden casks for 10 years or more. It's a rare treat, with a price to match, and should be reserved for very special occasions.

Once at Badia a Coltibuono, a fine Tuscan wine estate (also makers of excellent olive oil), I sampled 100-year-old *aceto balsamico,* served around the table, from small silver spoons, like some strange gourmet rite of communion. It was dark colored, almost black, with flashes of red lights, rather syrupy, and with an extraordinary flavor, penetrating and lush, mellow and palate filling, all at the same time. Another time, in Florence, a particularly fine parmigiano from Lodi, north of Parma, was served with drops of *aceto balsamico* poured lovingly on each shard of cheese. This is the best way to serve *aceto balsamico tradizionale*—with love, awe, and respect.

A more commonly available, but still rather expensive, balsamic vinegar is produced commercially of wine vinegar to which caramel and herbal essences have been added, producing a rather similar, but by no means comparable, product. Even this should not be used with a lavish hand, however. A few drops in a salad dressing are all that is necessary. Among balsamic vinegars generally available in this country, the best is available from Academia Barilla.

Tahini is a paste, the consistency of peanut butter, made from ground sesame seeds. I have tried health-food-store tahinis and mostly find them wanting, insipid in flavor and sticky in texture. The best I've found is Joyva, made in Brooklyn but widely available. Tahini may separate in the can—just stir it back together with a fork. Once you've opened a can of tahini, store it in the refrigerator.

Peppers used in Mediterranean recipes are usually sweet (not hot) peppers, either round bell peppers or long skinny ones such as are marketed in this country as Italian or cubanelle long peppers. Fiery peppers, like the chilies we're used to from Mexican cuisine, are appreciated only in parts of North Africa. The small hot red pepper used in Italy is called *peperoncino rosso,* but it is used in *very* small quantities. For the rest, though Spaniards and Turks may *tell* you their dishes are hot, you probably won't find them so. A single hot dried chili or a teaspoon of hot red pepper flakes will flavor a sauce to serve six people.

Paprika or *pimentón* or *piment* is made of crushed or ground dried red chili peppers, nothing more (it should not be confused with Southwestern chili powder, which is usually a mixture of chilies, cumin, and other spices). Like chilies themselves, the ground stuff comes in a broad range of heats, but most of the Mediterranean is seduced more by chilies on the mild side than really hot ones. Those of us who like fiery Mexican or Thai chilies will find Mediterranean red peppers decidedly un-hot. The best, however, have a distinctive flavor that adds tremendously to dishes in which they are used. My favorites are Aleppo red pepper from Syria, mostly available as crushed pepper flakes, and *piment d'Espelette,* from the Basque region of southern France, which is mostly ground pepper. The Spanish are particularly attuned to the different flavors of their pimentones, with *ñoras* as the all-time favorite. *Pimentón de la Vera* should also be mentioned—it's a chili grown in the Vera valley of western Spain where the climate is so moist that the peppers must be dried over oak fires, giving the pimentón a distinctive smoky aroma.

Anchovies are at their best when packed in salt. In Greek, Middle Eastern, and Italian neighborhood shops you will find them in big round cans to be purchased by the piece or by the pound. Buy them in quantity if you find them: wrap carefully in foil and place in a sealable plastic bag to avoid contaminating other food with their strong aroma. They will keep for several months in the refrigerator. Before using, rinse each anchovy well under a running tap to rid it of salt. Then pull the two fillets away from the spine and discard the backbone and tail. Don't worry about the tiny side bones—they will be unnoticeable in a sauce or pizza topping.

The flavor of anchovies is unique and not to everyone's taste, but you might be surprised, if you say you detest anchovies, at the number of times you have eaten them thoroughly disguised in a sauce. The best chefs know that anchovies give a deep and complex flavor to dishes in which they're used.

In the absence of salt-packed anchovies, canned oil-packed anchovy fillets can be used instead. Because the fillets are so small, I substitute on a roughly two-to-one ratio—two oil-packed fillets to one salt-packed fillet.

Like anchovies, salt-packed *capers* are best. What are capers exactly? The unopened bud of a flowering plant that grows in crannied walls all over the Mediterranean. They are gathered in the late spring and preserved by packing in salt or pickling in brine. Brine-cured capers are widely available, but if you can find salt-cured ones in Greek or Italian neighborhood stores, they are superior. Rinse them under running water to rid them of salt before using.

The Small Dishes
of the Mediterranean

*Meze, Antipasti, Tapas, Street Food, Bar Snacks,
and Other Introductions to the Meal*

$$\diamondsuit \quad \diamondsuit \quad \diamondsuit$$

THE GREEK CYPRIOTES who used to live in the village of Bellapais
had a reputation as the laziest folk on the island. And with good
reason, since the infamous Tree of Idleness cast its shadow over the
village square and the dusty quadrant in front of Dmitri's café. Beneath its
branches mustachioed old men, clad in the black baggy trousers that were
once the uniform all over the eastern Mediterranean, passed long and tranquil hours sipping thick, heavily sweetened coffee or anise-flavored ouzo,
nibbling on olives or bits of the local goat's milk cheese, playing endless
games of backgammon, or trictrac as they called it, and keeping an eye on
village comings and goings. Unlike the women of the village, who kept up
a constant chatter as they went about their work (no idleness for them), the
old men were often silent, contemplative, deep into what Lawrence Durrell
supposed to be a Moslem quality called *kayf,* in his words, "a fathomless re-
pose of the will."

Bellapais was the village Durrell wrote about in *Bitter Lemons.* We lived
there in the early 1970s, long after Durrell had left, in a happy lull between
two periods of political struggle on the island. What kind of tree it was that

cast its invidious shade over the old men I no longer even remember—walnut perhaps, since walnuts encourage indolence, or so they say. In tribute to the tree's powers, the new and sparkling café-restaurant that opened opposite Dmitri's shortly after we arrived in the village was also called the Tree of Idleness, and that was appropriate, too, since it was on the terrace of the Tree of Idleness Café that we were introduced to an even more seductive form of indolence, the meze table.

The café quickly became famous island-wide for the extent and variety of its meze, or mezedakia as the Greeks say, and we became frequent and enthusiastic customers. Entire Sunday afternoons were idled away over the meze table while houseguests came and went from Kyrenia, Beirut, and farther afield and the children wandered in for a bite of this or a nibble of that between the games they played—Saracens and Crusaders instead of cowboys and Indians.

The food came on white china saucers and oval platters, and the dishes piled up in the center of the table as the afternoon wore on. There would always be hummus, pureed chickpeas or garbanzos mixed with sesame paste, and baba ghanouj or *melitzanosalata,* charcoal-roasted eggplant pureed with garlic and olive oil, along with wedges of flat pita bread for dipping. There were always olives, both shiny plump black ones and little bitter green ones flavored with coriander, and chunks of that tangy, salty sheep's milk feta cheese that seems to have been created solely because it goes so well with black olives. These were the sine qua nons of the meze table. And then, depending on the season, there would be grape leaves, stuffed with meat and served hot or stuffed with rice and currants and served cold. And since we were only 15 minutes from the sea, there would almost always be something fishy, if only salted anchovies or canned sardines or rosy-colored taramosalata, made with salted cod's roe. But if the fishing had been good lately, there might also be a little plate of fried whitebait or a pile of sweet red mullet no more than five or six inches long or chunks of octopus braised in red wine with bay leaves and cinnamon—as well as lamb sausages flavored with grains of coriander, deep-fried and melting haloumi cheese, fresh radishes and scallions and creamy, garlic-scented yogurt to dip them in, fat fasoulia beans dressed with rich, dark green Cypriote olive oil and juice from lemons grown in the orchards below the village. And so on till the afternoon had magically melted away, till twilight began to creep along the craggy peaks above the village, till the last honey touch of sun mellowed the old Crusader-built walls around the abbey church. Then *kayf,* whether Moslem or not, really did set in, the contemplation, Durrell says, that comes of silence and ease.

What exactly is a meze? Like so many ideas about food, a meze is vastly different depending on where you are and whom you're with and what you're planning to do with the day. In its simplest form it might be like what the old men had at Dmitri's, a few black and green home-cured olives on a plate with a chunk of sheep's milk cheese and a little olive oil sprinkled over it. Add slices of cucumber and quarters of dark red sweet tomatoes, dressed with a few grains of sea salt, perhaps some pickled green peppers or beet-dyed red turnips, and you start to have something worth talking about. Add more dishes, especially freshly cooked dishes, and you begin to approach a spread like that at the Tree of Idleness with which to while away a Sunday afternoon.

The elements of the meze table are part of a category I've called "the small dishes of the Mediterranean," a panoply of little dishes that are eaten informally and without a great deal of ceremony, whether meze in the eastern Mediterranean, tapas in Spain, antipasti in Italy, or the variety of *merendas* and *casse-croûtes* and snacks that are taken between meals all over the region.

Meze may have evolved, as Turks like to claim, to accompany their favorite alcoholic drink, *raki,* an anise-flavored distilled spirit that, like Greek ouzo, Arab arak, and Provençal pastis, all of which it resembles, turns cloudy when mixed with ice or water. If the Turks are right, then meze's closest cousin around the Mediterranean is surely Spanish tapas, which seem devised specifically to encourage drinkers and revive flagging spirits or at least to keep them going till a proper meal can be served.

Tapas, strictly speaking, are served only in a bar, never in a restaurant, and even more properly eaten only while actually standing up at the bar, one foot resting on the brass rail. But that custom is changing, and even in deeply traditional Andalusia, where some suspect the custom began, you'll find tapas served at restaurant tables these days. The nature of the fare is changing, too. No longer will you find the things that were served free or for a couple of pesetas with a well-chilled fino or a late-night *coñac* in the *tasca* bars where the bullfighters used to hang out around the Plaza Santa Ana in Madrid, things like little cubes of coagulated lamb's blood speared with toothpicks, or *percebes,* a strange kind of goose barnacle that looks like miniature elephants' toes—tastes like them, too, some would say. But there are still chunks of well-aged *queso manchego* or sheep's milk cheese, wedges of tortilla, the Spanish potato and onion omelet, and slices of jamón serrano, hand-cut from hams that hang over the bar with a little plastic cup beneath them to catch the dripping juices. In season you might get *gambas al ajillo,* tiny shrimps roasted in olive oil with garlic and chilies and presented in the terra-cotta dishes in which they were cooked, or in the springtime *chanquetes,* horrifyingly expensive baby eels, no more than an inch or two long and given a similar treatment. And there are always crackling fresh salted almonds, whose flavor is so complementary to the nutty taste of chilled fino sherry, and as with meze there are always olives, big fat green ones called *gordales* often stuffed with an almond or a bit of salted anchovy.

In Italy the "small dishes" are almost always served at the table, as antipasti to begin a meal. An antipasto course (the name means "before the meal," not before the pasta) is by no means invariably included in a meal; rather it indicates that the courses that follow will border on elegance or at least on showy presentation. Unlike tapas and meze, antipasti are not particularly connected with bars and drinking, although of course, like every part of an Italian meal, they are served with the appropriate wine. This is really restaurant food and rarely part of family dining except on special feast days or to impress an honored guest. In that way antipasti are more like what the French call an *amuse-gueule* or an hors d'oeuvre (literally, "outside the work"), a little something to stimulate the appetite for the real food that will follow. In an Italian country restaurant the antipasto might be a platter of local *salumi*, all sorts of cured hams and sausages flavored with garlic or the seeds of wild fennel; there might also be a few crostini, little bread crusts topped with a mash of chicken livers and capers or with fresh ripe tomatoes minced and sprinkled with basil and salt.

Sometimes vegetables, especially fresh ones just coming into season, will star in an antipasto. They might be served raw, as in a salad like puntarelle, chicory shoots dressed with an anchovy-garlic sauce that are treasured in Rome in late winter and early spring, or they might be cooked—the first wild mushrooms of the season are often simply grilled and presented as an antipasto. Raw or cooked, a singular presentation like this carries a clear message: "This is so special it is to be savored and cherished on its own, undistracted by anything else." An admirable attitude and one we would do well to adopt.

Provençal hors d'oeuvres and crudités are similar to Italian antipasti—a platter napped with slices of rosy pink and dark red sausages, for instance, alternating with some of the spectacular early vegetables cooks in the region dote on—tiny artichokes, fennel, and broad beans to be eaten raw, or barely steamed haricots verts, the most delicious of all green beans. Or the feature might be the startling goodness of those big, deeply ridged Provençal tomatoes, thickly sliced and eaten with wedges of crusty bread and salty local jambon or with aïoli, that garlic lovers' died-and-gone-to-heaven sauce of mounted egg yolks and olive oil and cloves and cloves and cloves of garlic.

Of all these presentations, the most spectacular is surely the Italian *pinzimonio,* a cornucopia of the earliest spring vegetables, either raw or barely blanched: baby onions, tender little carrots, tiny violet artichokes, pencil-thin wild asparagus, young lettuces, cucumbers, fennel. These are served with a simple glass cruet of the finest olive oil of that year, perhaps still with the slight throat-catching edge of bitterness that denotes oil of the highest quality, along with salt and pepper—nothing more. Each diner pours a puddle of golden-green oil in the center of the plate, adds judicious amounts of salt and pepper, scrambles them with a fork to mix, and then happily dips the vegetables, one by one, and consumes them out of hand.

Outside of restaurant kitchens, few cooks these days are both willing and able to produce a full-blown meze like the one at the Tree of Idleness or a succession of tapas like those still served in bars and cafés throughout Spain. But the idea behind these small dishes—to produce something quick and tasty out of a lively and informal attitude toward eating—is a good one, and for that reason I have also included in this chapter recipes for salads and egg dishes that seem to fit the job description well.

Many of the recipes here can be served singly or in a small group of two or at most three to keep guests happy with a bottle of wine while the cook gets on with the rest of the meal. Others can form the basis of a meal, either as a main course or as a garnish for something more substantial. Most of these small dishes are based on vegetables, beans, or grains; where meat is used, it is as a flavor adjunct. In the midst of the bustle of modern life, this is one way to get in those multiple servings of fresh vegetables that we are told should be our goal. A couple of small vegetable dishes to start, a substantial green salad in the middle, and a finish of fresh fruit should keep even the most confirmed carnivore happy and healthy and perhaps even wise. And whether the small dishes come at the start or in the middle of the meal, be sure there's always plenty of good, crusty bread served with them.

Keep in mind too that various savory pies (pages 171–190)—whether pizza, Catalan *cocas,* or the spinach-and-cheese-stuffed tarts of the eastern Mediterranean—can make appealing small dishes or first courses, as do many of the poultry or meat dishes (pages 403–443) served in small portions. Where it's appropriate, I have made suggestions about when and how to serve. Anyone who wants to attempt a full-scale mezedakia should keep in mind that many dishes can be prepared ahead of time and indeed benefit from it.

Marinated Olives

Makes 1 pound; 16 servings

Anywhere you go in the Mediterranean, at any time of day or night, you will most likely be offered olives in some form or another—large or small; green, black, or purply brown; brine-, salt-, or oil-cured; wrinkled and shriveled or plump and full of rich oil. In the eastern Mediterranean olives are eaten even for breakfast—and an excellent breakfast they make, served with the thickened yogurt called *labneh* and some fresh rounds of Arab bread. Elsewhere, olives are quintessential as tapas and on hors d'oeuvre and antipasto platters. One of the region's most ancient foods (wild olives were part of the diet of Mesolithic cave dwellers in the Grotto dell'Uzzo on Sicily some 10,000 years ago), olives, like their precious oil, define the region and its cuisine. Durrell's sonorous and much quoted line about their savor—"Older than meat, older than wine, as old as cold, clear water"—has its own antique flavor, memorable because it rings true.

Selecting olives is important. It's worth a special trip to a big-city delicatessen or an Italian, Greek, or Middle Eastern neighborhood shop for a look at what's available. We actually have a much wider variety of olives in this country than in any single market in the Mediterranean. In Italy, for instance, you can find only Italian olives, but at one of my favorite Italian food suppliers, Al Capone in Somerville, Massachusetts, I can find Greek, Italian, French, and often North African olives, and just a few doors away is a shop selling the rather bitter green olives from the Middle East.

Most supermarket deli departments have the lusciously oily Greek black olives called Kalamata, from the region of the Peloponnisos where they originated. Even when not the best quality, they're far superior to anything that comes in a can—the texture, combined with the extraordinary burst of flavor in your mouth, makes you realize that olives really are a food and not just a garnish for cocktail canapés. Canned California olives, whether black or green, are not to be used in any of the recipes in this book.

Although many different varieties of olives are grown, many of them specifically for eating, the most significant difference for the cook is in the curing. As you know if you've ever tasted an olive right off the tree, table olives must go through a curing process to eliminate their acrid flavors. The curing, during which the olives undergo lactic fermentation just like yogurt and other fermented products, is accomplished through different mediums—a salt brine, for instance, or, when olives are very mature and black, a dry marinade directly in salt. Such home-style curing methods are almost unchanged since Columella, the great Spanish Latin writer on things agricultural, described them back in the first century AD. In winter months, in farmhouse cantinas and attics throughout the Mediterranean basin, olives ferment in woven willow baskets and massive earthenware amphorae, just like the 3,000-year-old ones Sir Arthur Evans found in the ruined palace storerooms of Knossos on Crete.

Once olives have been cured, they may be marinated in aromatics to add other complementary flavors such as garlic, bay leaves, fresh thyme, citrus peel, lightly cracked coriander seeds, or a little hot chili pepper. Here are my personal favorites, but use your own taste to guide you in creating olives for your table.

1 pound small black Niçoise olives, drained

2 lemons

a pinch of ground or crushed red chili pepper, preferably piment d'Espelette or Aleppo pepper

½ teaspoon sweet paprika

¼ teaspoon ground cumin

1 tablespoon extra-virgin olive oil, or more if necessary

Place the olives in a bowl. Carefully pare away the zest of the lemons and slice into fine julienne (or use a zester). Peel the white rind away from the lemons and discard it. Cut the juicy yellow flesh into thin sections, discarding the seeds. Toss the zest and lemon flesh with the olives, adding the spices. Add the tablespoon of olive oil and toss again. Set aside to let the flavors blend for a couple of hours or several days before serving. To keep them longer than a few days, pack the olives in a jar; add a tablespoon of salt and enough oil to cover. The olives may be kept refrigerated for 2 to 3 weeks but should be brought to room temperature before serving.

Variation

1 pound large black Greek olives, drained

zest of 1 orange, grated or sliced into julienne

2 bay leaves, chopped

1 garlic clove, cut into thin shavings

1 teaspoon hot red pepper flakes, or to taste

1 tablespoon extra-virgin olive oil

Combine all the ingredients and mix well. Set aside to marinate for a couple of hours before serving. Or pack in a jar, as in the preceding version, to keep for 2 to 3 weeks.

TREATING FRESH GREEN OLIVES

In some Italian and Greek neighborhoods, freshly harvested olives are available seasonally. If you can find them, follow the example of Niko Stavroulakis, a friend who lives in the old city of Hania on the Greek island of Crete. Niko cracks freshly harvested green olives with a hammer and leaves them for three weeks in fresh (not salted) water, changing the water each day. Then he drains them and packs them in jars, layered with lemon slices, each layer sprinkled liberally with salt. He fills the jar with olive oil, covers it, then leaves it in a cold pantry. The olives are ready to eat in another three weeks. Cracked coriander seeds are a nice addition with the lemon layers.

Spiced Green Olives

Makes 1 pound; 16 servings

FOR THIS NORTH AFRICAN TREATMENT, you'll want to use large green olives, plainly cured in a salt brine, such as Bella di Cerignola from Puglia in the heel of Italy's boot, or Manzanillas or Sevillanas (sometimes called *gorditas,* fat ones) from southern Spain. Rinse the olives of their brine in cool running water before you start to treat them.

Cardamom seeds should have the outside husks opened and the little inside seeds spilled out. If you don't have a salt-cured lemon, add the juice and grated zest of half an organically raised lemon.

1 pound plain large green olives

1 teaspoon whole fennel seeds

1 teaspoon whole coriander seeds

½ teaspoon cardamom seeds

1 teaspoon (or more to taste) good-quality red chili pepper, such as piment d'Espelette or Aleppo pepper

3 tablespoons extra-virgin olive oil

1 tablespoon freshly squeezed orange juice

1 tablespoon freshly squeezed lemon juice

3 plump garlic cloves, crushed with the flat blade of a knife

½ salt-cured lemon (page 281; optional)

Rinse the olives in a colander to get rid of excess brine and shake dry, then toss in a kitchen towel to dry thoroughly.

Combine the fennel, coriander, and cardamom in a small skillet and toast the seeds over medium heat until the fragrance starts to come out, but be careful not to let the seeds burn. Transfer the toasted seeds to a clean coffee mill or spice grinder and add the chili pepper. Grind briefly—not to a fine powder but rather a coarse texture.

Combine the spices in a bowl with the oil and citrus juices. Mince the garlic along with the lemon, if using, and add to the bowl. Add the olives, stirring to mix well and coat the olives with the spicy mixture.

Cover the bowl with plastic wrap and set aside to marinate at room temperature for at least 6 hours before serving. The olives may also be stored in a jar, refrigerated, for 2 to 3 weeks but they should always be brought to room temperature before serving.

Roasted Almonds

Makes 2 cups; 8 servings

ONCE UPON A TIME the Fuente del Berro district was a suburb on the eastern outskirts of Madrid, but the city has long since grown up around it. Fuente del Berro means "watercress fountain," after a spring-fed fountain on the edge of the nearby park where peacocks wandered. Entering the little barrio of single-family homes with front gardens facing cobblestoned streets, you leave the clangor of the city behind and walk into a very different, much older, and more tranquil Spanish town. When we first went to live in the barrio, there were still gaslights at every street corner and a lamplighter who came around at dusk with his ladder to light the flares.

The little house in Fuente del Berro was within walking distance of Ventas, Madrid's plaza de toros, where the greatest bullfighters in the world came for the San Isidro corridas in May, and so the garden became a gathering spot before the corrida for a ritualistic glass or two of well-chilled fino sherry and a handful of these almonds. I used to fry them, but oven roasting uses much less oil. The flavor of roasted almonds goes especially well with the nutty flavor of fino or palo cortado sherry—but these almonds are so delicious they can accompany any other wine just as well.

Almonds and almond oil, like olives and olive oil, are a good source of monounsaturated fat. In North America the best almonds come from natural foods stores, where a steady turnover ensures freshness. Don't buy blanched almonds, because the skin helps keep the nuts fresh. Above all, avoid nuts with any hint of rancidity. Note too that the taste of the almonds is actually better a couple of hours *after* roasting.

2 cups unblanched shelled almonds

2 teaspoons almond oil or very light-flavored extra-virgin olive oil

½ teaspoon sea salt, or more to taste

Preheat the oven to 300 degrees. Bring a large pot of water to a boil, plunge the almonds in, and boil rapidly for 1 minute. Turn the almonds into a colander, and as soon as you can handle them but before they are really cool, slip the skins off. If any skins don't come off easily, return the offending nuts briefly to the boiling water.

Spread the skinned nuts in a baking dish large enough to hold them in a single layer. Bake for 5 minutes to dry them out. Remove from the oven and stir in the oil and salt. Return to the oven for another 10 minutes, stirring occasionally with a wooden spoon, until the almonds are a pale golden brown. During the last few minutes, check frequently to make sure they're not getting too brown. Set aside for a few hours before serving.

Tapénade

Black Olive Paste

❧ Makes 1½ to 2 cups; 6 to 8 servings (more if part of a meze)

THE ANCIENT ROMANS made a sauce called *epityrum,* pounding black or green olives in a mortar with oil, vinegar, a little cumin, and green herbs like fennel tops, rue, mint, and cilantro. Tapénade, which is similar, comes from the south of France—the word derives from the Provençal *tapéno,* meaning capers, although the principal ingredient in the sauce is black olives. The late Elizabeth David, who wrote so movingly about Mediterranean food, always added a few ounces of tuna and a little cognac to her tapénade. Mrs. David served the sauce as an hors d'oeuvre, topped with hard-boiled eggs sliced in half lengthwise. In my family it goes on the meze table with toasted flatbread and sometimes strips of raw vegetables—fennel, carrots, celery—to dip in it; it's also a first-rate topping for *crostini neri.*

This calls for the very best-quality brine-cured black olives you can find. Niçoise or Gaeta olives are an excellent choice. Do not use canned Spanish or California black olives; they are simply green olives processed to turn black and peculiarly lacking in either flavor or texture.

1 pound black olives, pitted

½ cup drained capers

1 small garlic clove, coarsely chopped

½ 6-ounce can tuna packed in olive oil, drained

Combine the ingredients in a food processor and process very briefly. Tapénade should be a coarse-textured paste (the original method of pounding in a mortar, while tedious, still produces the best quality). This may be prepared up to a week ahead and stored in the refrigerator with a thin layer of

2 tablespoons brandy

½ cup olive oil

a few drops of fresh lemon
juice

olive oil poured over it, but be sure to bring it to room temperature before serving since olive oil solidifies when chilled. Stir the excess olive oil into the paste before serving. Taste and add a few drops of lemon juice if desired.

Provençal Anchovy Dip

Anchoïade

⚜ Makes about 1¼ cups; 8 to 10 servings

A PROVENÇAL FAVORITE that mixes olive oil with anchovies and garlic, this is traditionally served as a thick smear over toasted French bread but it is also a great dip for fresh raw vegetables—celery, cucumbers, carrot sticks, scallions, and so on. Don't worry if you don't get all the bones out of the anchovies—they're soft enough to go down easily and in any case provide extra calcium.

If you can only get oil-packed fillets, by all means use them, but salt-packed anchovies, available in Greek and Italian markets, are usually better, as they have more flavor and a better texture than oil-packed ones. Salt-packed anchovies should be rinsed under running water to rid them of any chunks of salt, then split apart in your hands and the center spine lifted out, along with any fins or tail pieces. In Catalonia those center spines are deep-fried in olive oil to make a crispy snack. Try it—you'll be surprised at how delicious it is.

10 whole salt-packed anchovies, rinsed, filleted, and coarsely chopped

4 garlic cloves, coarsely chopped

2 tablespoons unsalted butter, at room temperature

½ cup extra-virgin olive oil

1½ teaspoons aged red wine vinegar

[cont. next page]

Combine the anchovies with the garlic in a food processor and pulse till they are pureed. Add the butter and blend it in. With the blade spinning, add the olive oil, a tablespoon at a time. Lastly, add the vinegar. Transfer the *anchoïade* to a serving bowl and stir in lots of black pepper.

Cut a baguette in two the long way, then cut each half into chunks about 4 inches long. Lightly toast the cut side of each chunk on a grill or under the broiler. Spoon lots of anchoïade on each toast,

freshly ground black pepper

grilled or toasted bread or
raw vegetables for serving

letting it sink in. Or, if you prefer, assemble a tray of raw vegetables, as described above, and serve the anchoïade as a dipping sauce in the middle.

Chickpea Salad or Dip with a Lamb Garnish

Hummus bi Tahini

*H*UMMUS BI TAHINI, mashed chickpeas with sesame paste, is quintessential to an eastern Mediterranean meze table. Served on its own, the hummus goes well with crackers, or toasted triangles of Arab pita bread, but it's also good as a dip for raw vegetables—scallions, carrot and celery sticks, strips of cucumber, or of sweet red peppers. This is good finger food with a glass of wine (or arak or ouzo) before dinner, but it could also be a substantial side dish to accompany a main-course soup or salad, especially if you add the variation with a lamb-and-onion topping at the end.

Tahini, or sesame paste, is widely available in supermarkets and specialty food stores, as is sesame oil. Be sure to use dark roasted sesame oil rather than the lighter quality that is sold in many health food stores and lacks the flavor boost of the darker kind.

1 cup dried chickpeas, soaked overnight and drained

½ cup tahini (sesame paste)

1 tablespoon roasted (dark) sesame oil

sea salt

½ teaspoon ground cumin

juice of 2 lemons, or more to taste

¼ garlic clove, finely minced

Add the chickpeas to a saucepan with water to cover to a depth of 1 inch. Bring to a boil, cover, and simmer gently until the chickpeas are very tender but not falling apart. Cooking time will depend on the age and size of the chickpeas, but count on at least 30 to 40 minutes. Remove from the heat and drain, reserving about ½ cup of the cooking water to be used to thin the sauce if necessary. Set aside half a dozen chickpeas to use as a garnish.

Transfer the chickpeas with about ¼ cup of the cooking liquid to a food processor and process in

1 tablespoon extra-virgin
olive oil

a pinch of ground hot red
chili pepper

a little finely minced flat-leaf
parsley

brief bursts until the chickpeas are a coarse and
grainy puree, adding more of the cooking liquid if
necessary.

Combine the puree in a bowl with the tahini,
sesame oil, salt, and cumin. Add the lemon juice
and stir to mix well, then stir in the minced garlic.
Spread the puree on a deep platter, swirling the top
with a spoon or fork. If you are not using the
lamb-and-onion garnish below, combine the olive
oil with the ground chili and dribble it over the
swirls. Sprinkle the top with the parsley and
reserved chickpeas.

Hummus is usually served at room temperature. If
you must refrigerate it, bring it back to room
temperature before adding the garnish and serving.

Variation

Makes 6 to 8 servings, more if part of a meze

To make a more substantial dish, one appropriate as a main course or as a side
with a robust winter soup, garnish the hummus with this savory lamb and
caramelized onion topping, which should be prepared ahead, ready to top the
chickpea puree when it's about to be served. It is best if served hot or somewhat
warmer than room temperature.

2 tablespoons pine nuts

1 medium yellow onion,
chopped

2 to 3 tablespoons extra-
virgin olive oil

½ teaspoon ground
cinnamon, or more to taste

½ pound ground lean lamb

sea salt and freshly ground
black pepper

Toast the pine nuts in a dry skillet over medium
heat until they are golden, being careful not to
burn them. When done, set aside.

To the same skillet add the chopped onion and 2
tablespoons of olive oil. Cook over medium-low
heat, stirring frequently, until the onions are
thoroughly cooked and golden. This may take as
much as 20 to 30 minutes and you must be very
careful not to let the onions brown, as they will
give an acrid flavor to the topping.

When the onions are done, add the cinnamon and
the lamb, along with another tablespoon of oil if it

seems necessary, and raise the heat slightly. Cook, breaking up the lamb with the side of a spoon or cooking fork and mixing it thoroughly with the onion. Add salt and pepper to taste—the mixture should be very well seasoned. Finally, stir in the pine nuts and distribute over the top of the hummus. At this point, add the minced parsley and chili pepper in the basic recipe ingredient list—but you will not need the additional tablespoon of olive oil.

Tart and Spicy Roasted Eggplant Salad

Melitzanasalata

✤ Makes about 2 cups; 8 servings as part of a meze

THIS IS SIMILAR to the well-known Lebanese eggplant puree called baba ghanouj but the addition of yogurt and green chilies gives it a pleasantly tangy spice. If you have a fireplace or an outdoor grill, roast the eggplant over live coals for a delectably smoky aroma.

Select eggplants with smooth, shiny skins that are hefty for their size. Eggplant doesn't store well so be sure to use any you buy within a day or two; keep cool, but don't refrigerate—that only hastens deterioration.

Fresh green poblano peppers are best in this recipe, but if you cannot find them, use jalapeños or serranos—as long as they are agreeably spicy but not fiery hot.

1 pound eggplant (1 medium eggplant)

2 spicy but not fiery green chilies, such as poblanos

½ cup plain yogurt (nonfat or low-fat is fine)

2 tablespoons extra-virgin olive oil

If you have a charcoal or other type of grill, or a fireplace, light a fire in plenty of time to have hot coals by the time you're ready to roast the eggplants. Otherwise, preheat your oven to 375 degrees.

Using a fork, prick the eggplant at least an inch deep in a dozen places. (This is important. I once

juice of ½ lemon, or more to taste (about 1 tablespoon)

1 large garlic clove, chopped

1 teaspoon sea salt

had a large unpricked eggplant explode in my oven; the cleanup took days.)

Set the eggplant on a grill about 8 inches above the coals, or place on a rack in the preheated oven. Roast the eggplant on the grill for about 20 minutes, turning frequently, until the outside is black and charred and the inside is tender all the way through. In the oven, it will take 40 minutes and should also be turned frequently.

At the same time, roast and peel the chilies, following the directions on page 26. Trim them of seeds and white membranes. Any juices from the chilies should be kept to add to the eggplant puree. Slice one of the chilies into narrow strips and set aside. Chop the other one roughly.

When the eggplant is cool enough to handle, strip away and discard the dark skin and mash the flesh with a potato masher or an immersion blender, gradually mixing in the yogurt, olive oil, lemon juice, and any juices from the chilies.

Combine the garlic and salt in a mortar and pound to a paste. Add the chopped chilies to the mortar and crush with the paste. (You may use a blender or food processor for this step if you wish, but don't put the eggplant into the blender; the texture is much better when it's done by hand.) Fold the chili-garlic mixture into the eggplant. Transfer to a serving bowl and garnish with the chili strips, like the spokes of a wheel.

Melitzanasalata could also be served as a side dish with meat, especially lamb, in which case it will make 4 to 6 servings.

Mhammara

Red Pepper and Walnut Sauce

MHAMMARA (PRONOUNCED MUH-HAHM-ahrah) comes from the eastern Mediterranean and the Arabo-Turkish region of northern Lebanon and Syria and southeastern Turkey, around the old trading cities of Aleppo and Gaziantep. Red peppers from Aleppo are renowned for their flavor and quality. They are spicy, decidedly in the chili branch of the pepper family, but not searingly hot. Ground red Aleppo pepper is available in Middle Eastern specialty stores but you could also substitute crushed dried New Mexico or ancho chilies, or a Spanish pimentón (paprika), as long as it's not the smoky kind from La Vera.

Pomegranate syrup, widely available in Middle Eastern markets, is simply the reduced juice of pomegranates. It has a pleasant, sweet-tart tang, but if you cannot find it, add more lemon juice to taste.

Mhammara is served as part of the meze table, with toasted triangles of Arab pita bread or raw vegetables to dip in it. I've found that it also makes a splendid garnish for grilled or braised lamb.

This is best made with a mortar and pestle but if you must use a food processor, be careful not to overprocess. The sauce should have considerable texture from the nuts.

To toast fresh bread crumbs, simply stir them in a skillet over medium heat until they turn golden and crisp.

4 sweet red peppers

1 garlic clove, crushed with the flat blade of a knife

sea salt

1½ cups walnut halves, very finely chopped

½ cup toasted bread crumbs

Roast the peppers until they are black and blistered, then set them in a paper bag to steam in their own heat for 20 minutes or so before peeling them, discarding the stems, seeds, and internal white membranes (see page 26 for instructions). Coarsely chop the peeled peppers. You should have 3 to 4 cups of chopped peppers.

In a mortar, pound the crushed garlic to a paste with a pinch of salt, then pound in the walnuts and toasted bread crumbs. Add the chopped peppers

1 teaspoon ground or crushed red Middle Eastern chili pepper, preferably Aleppo or Turkish pepper

¼ teaspoon ground cumin (optional)

1 tablespoon + 1 teaspoon pomegranate syrup

2 teaspoons fresh lemon juice

extra-virgin olive oil

toasted pine nuts for garnish

and continue pounding to a paste. Then stir in the ground red pepper, cumin, if using, pomegranate syrup, lemon juice, and a tablespoon of olive oil. Taste and adjust the seasoning, adding another tablespoon of oil if you wish.

If you use a food processor, after chopping the peppers, transfer them to the processor with the garlic and salt and puree until smooth. Add the walnuts, bread crumbs, and ground red pepper and pulse to a granular mixture. Scrape the contents of the processor into a bowl and stir in the cumin, if using, pomegranate syrup, and lemon juice. Finally stir in a tablespoon of oil and taste, adding more oil and/or salt if you wish.

Heap the finished sauce in a bowl and garnish with toasted pine nuts.

Cacık/Tzatziki

Yogurt and Cucumber Sauce, Salad, or Dip

Makes about 2 cups; 6 to 8 servings (if thinned with 1 cup of ice water, makes 4 to 6 servings of chilled yogurt soup)

IT's CALLED *CACIK* (pronounced DJAH-djuk) in Turkish, *tzatziki* in Greek, but wherever you find it, this is a healthful addition to the meze table. You can use this as a sauce or as a salad, or you might serve it as a dip with crackers or raw vegetable crudités—or thin it with ice water for a refreshing, summertime cucumber-yogurt soup.

Look for fresh, firm cucumbers that are slender for their length and free of any soft spots or wilted ends. I like the shrink-wrapped cukes sometimes called English cucumbers. Cucumbers with greasy waxed skins are to be avoided. That wax adds nothing to your diet and is probably a good indication that the cuke was harvested days, if not weeks ago. Good-quality unwaxed Kirby or pickling cucumbers, although small, are an acceptable alternative.

Dried mint has a sweeter, less wild taste than fresh mint and is preferred for this dish, although fresh mint is an appropriate garnish.

1½ cups plain yogurt (low-fat or nonfat is acceptable)

1 long English cucumber or 2 slender unwaxed regular cucumbers

sea salt

2 garlic cloves, chopped

1 tablespoon white wine vinegar

2 tablespoons extra-virgin olive oil

1 tablespoon dried mint

a pinch of dried red chili pepper such as piment d'Espelette or Aleppo pepper

2 tablespoons slivered fresh mint leaves for garnish

Strain the yogurt for about 30 minutes to thicken it slightly (see page 278 for instructions).

Peel the cucumber. Cut in half and if it's very seedy, cut out and discard the seeds (seeds are not usually a problem with English cucumbers). Grate the cucumber on the large holes of a grater into a colander. Add a pinch of salt and toss to mix well. Set the colander in the sink to draw some of the liquid out of the cucumbers.

In a bowl in which you will serve the cacık, use the back of a spoon to mash the garlic to a paste with a half-teaspoon of salt. Stir the vinegar into the paste and then stir in the oil. Add the strained yogurt, dried mint, and chili and mix well.

Rinse the salt from the grated cucumber and toss to drain of excess water. Pat dry with paper towels and fold into the yogurt mixture. Garnish the dish with the slivered fresh mint.

Serve this as a sauce (it's wonderful with poached or grilled salmon, or poured atop plain eggplants, halved and baked in olive oil), or as a dip with wedges of toasted pita bread or crackers, or fresh vegetables such as carrots or celery sticks.

Variation: In Greece, fresh dill is often substituted for dried mint, and snipped dill is used to garnish the tzatziki.

Feta Salad with Vegetables

LEBANESE COOKS use a white cheese called *jibneh baidha* (which means simply "white cheese") for this. Barrel-aged Greek feta is close enough to substitute and makes a fine, substantial salad. It's also a great sandwich mix, stuffed into crisp rolls or Arab pita bread.

Lebanese za'atar is a savory combination of wild thyme, sumac, and sesame seeds, mixed together and coarsely ground. You will find it in Middle Eastern specialty shops.

1 sweet red pepper

1 medium red onion

2 very ripe medium tomatoes

1 small cucumber

½ pound barrel-fermented Greek feta cheese

3 or 4 tablespoons extra-virgin olive oil

2 tablespoons finely chopped flat-leaf parsley

Lebanese za'atar (mixed spices) if available, or sprigs of thyme

ground or crushed red pepper, preferably piment d'Espelette or Aleppo pepper

sea salt

Discard the seeds and white membranes from the pepper and chop it coarsely. Chop the red onion and combine with the pepper. Halve the tomatoes and squeeze out some of the seeds and watery pulp. Chop the tomatoes and add to the other vegetables. Peel the cucumber and remove the seeds. Chop the cucumber and add to the other vegetables.

Dice or crumble the cheese and add to the vegetables. Gently stir in the olive oil and parsley, then add a pinch of za'atar or the leaves stripped from the thyme sprigs. Add a pinch of red pepper, then taste the salad, adding salt if it seems necessary. (Some feta is quite salty, so you may not need to add more.) May be served immediately or kept for a few hours to develop the flavors—but do not refrigerate.

Variation: This is the way the salad is usually made for a Lebanese meze but you could of course add other raw vegetables—fennel, I think, would be very nice, as would carrots or slightly underripe, firm tomatoes, or bright red Spanish *pimientos de piquillo* (the kind that come already peeled in jars), sliced into narrow strips. Instead of za'atar, try the salad with slivered fresh basil or a handful of snipped chives.

Little Deep-Fried Ricotta Balls

Polpettine di Ricotta from Puglia

Makes 24 to 30 ricotta balls; 6 to 8 servings

ONE OF MY FAVORITE RESTAURANTS in southern Italy is Al Fornello da Ricci, just outside the Pugliese town of Ceglie Messapico. Angelo and Dora Ricci established the restaurant many years ago, but today their daughter Antonella and her husband Vinod Sookar are in charge of the kitchen. Still, Dora's Deep-Fried Ricotta Balls are always a feature on the extensive antipasto menu.

Fresh goat's or sheep's milk ricotta is best for this and you can often find one or the other in farmers' markets; a good mail order source is Paula Lambert's Mozzarella Company in Dallas (page 466). Otherwise, use regular ricotta, available in supermarkets, but you will have to boost the flavor considerably by increasing the amounts of grated cheese and the aromatics. Be sure to drain the ricotta for at least 30 minutes, longer if it's very moist, before mixing it with other ingredients.

1⅓ cups fresh goat's or sheep's milk ricotta, well drained

½ to ¾ cup freshly grated aged pecorino or parmigiano reggiano

2 to 3 tablespoons finely minced flat-leaf parsley

1 garlic clove, finely minced

a pinch of freshly grated nutmeg

2 eggs

sea salt and freshly ground black pepper

1 or 2 cups extra-virgin olive oil for frying

⅔ cup freshly grated bread crumbs

Put the ricotta through a food mill or beat it briefly with an electric beater to lighten the texture. Then mix it with the grated cheese, parsley, garlic, nutmeg, and the yolk of only one of the eggs, reserving the white to use later. Mix with a wooden spoon to combine all these ingredients thoroughly, then taste and add salt and pepper. (If you're using ordinary cow's milk ricotta, you may also want to increase the quantities of parsley, garlic, and grated cheese.)

Roll the ricotta mixture into balls about the size of small walnuts and set on a rack to dry slightly for about 15 minutes.

When you're ready to fry the ricotta balls, heat the oil over medium heat to about 360 degrees. (The amount of oil depends on the size of the pan, but the oil should be at least 2 inches deep.)

In a shallow bowl, mix the reserved egg white with the remaining egg, beating with a wire whisk. Place the bread crumbs in another shallow bowl.

Dip each ricotta ball in the egg to coat it lightly, then roll it quickly in the bread crumbs. Drop the balls, a few at a time, in the hot oil and fry until golden brown. Remove with a slotted spoon and drain briefly on a rack, then serve immediately, crisp and hot.

Mechouia

Tunisian Grilled Vegetable Salsa

Makes 6 to 8 servings

IN SEASON *MECHOUIA* (MESH-WEE-YAH) appears on Tunisian tables at almost every meal, as a first course on its own, as a garnish or salad to accompany a main course, or as one of several small dishes to nibble at while waiting for more substantial food. If you add the optional garnishes of pitted black olives, hard-boiled eggs, and tuna (use the best-quality oil-packed tuna available) or anchovies, the dish is substantial enough to stand on its own accompanied by a good crusty bread and with fruit and cheese to follow.

For the finest sweet and smoky flavor, Tunisian cooks roast the vegetables over charcoal or wood embers, but in her tiny kitchen in Sidi bou Said, on a hilltop above the sea outside Tunis, Fatouma Mbrahim grills the peppers under a gas broiler and roasts the tomatoes and onion in a very hot oven. Either way, *mechouia* is best made at least an hour ahead of time and set aside for the flavors to meld somewhat before serving.

The ratio between sweet and hot peppers is meant only as a guide. If you want more or less heat, change the balance—but be sure to use a total of about 1½ pounds.

1 pound green and sweet red peppers, about 3 medium

3 or 4 fresh chilies, to taste

a little olive oil for baking

1 pound ripe but firm tomatoes, about 3 medium

2 medium onions, unpeeled

sea salt

4 garlic cloves

1 tablespoon crushed caraway or 1 tablespoon ground or crushed coriander seeds

½ cup extra-virgin olive oil

juice of 2 lemons

freshly ground black pepper (optional)

GARNISHES (OPTIONAL)

hard-boiled eggs, coarsely chopped; pitted olives; chunks of well-drained tuna; or salted anchovies, boned and refreshed in running water

Roast and peel the peppers and chilies, following the directions on page 26. Cut the peppers and chilies into small dice, add to the bowl with their juices, and set aside.

Preheat the oven to 450 degrees. Brush a little olive oil over the bottom of a small roasting pan, then pour a little oil into your palms and rub it over the tomatoes and onions. Place the vegetables in the roasting pan and roast for about 10 minutes, turning occasionally. When the tomato skins are cracking and easy to peel, remove the tomatoes from the pan but let the onions continue roasting for another 15 to 20 minutes.

Lift the skins off the tomatoes and slice them in half, letting the juices run out. Dice the tomatoes and toss in the bowl with the peppers. Remove the onions, discard the skins, dice the onions, and add to the other vegetables.

Pound the garlic with a little salt in a mortar or use the back of a spoon to crush the chopped garlic in a bowl with salt to a paste. Add the crushed caraway and mix the garlic paste into the vegetables. Set aside for at least an hour or until you're ready to serve.

Just before serving, mix the olive oil with the lemon juice to taste and stir into the vegetables, adding pepper if you wish. Garnish if desired and serve immediately.

Note: Fresh herbs or greens, such as basil or purslane, can be slivered and stirred into the salad at the last minute before serving.

Escalivada

Catalan Roasted Peppers, Eggplants, and Tomatoes

Makes 6 servings

MEDITERRANEAN KITCHENS are full of variations on this combination of summer vegetables. In this version from Catalonia in northeast Spain, cooks insist that the finest flavor comes from eggplant and peppers roasted on a charcoal grill or over the embers of a wood fire. The word *escalivada,* they say, means exactly that—cooked in the *caliu,* the embracing warmth of the fire. If you have access to a charcoal grill or a fireplace, this makes perfect picnic food and you will appreciate the delicious smoky flavors the method will give; but if you don't have that luxury, you can have almost as fine a dish roasting the vegetables in the oven.

2 sweet red peppers

1 medium eggplant

3 medium ripe tomatoes, cut in half

6 small spring onions or fat scallions, cut in half

2 tablespoons extra-virgin olive oil

1 tablespoon aged red wine vinegar

2 garlic cloves, finely chopped

2 tablespoons or more finely chopped flat-leaf parsley

coarse sea salt

Build up a charcoal or hardwood fire and let it die down to roasting coals. Set a grill over the embers and roast the whole peppers and whole eggplants directly on the grill, turning them over and over to blacken them thoroughly and tenderize them all the way through. When done, remove and wrap tightly in paper bags.

While the eggplant and peppers are resting, set the tomato and onion halves on the grill and roast for about 5 minutes on each side.

As soon as the eggplant and peppers are cool enough to handle, remove them from the paper bags and pull away the charred and blackened skin. Tear the eggplant flesh into long strips. Discard the seeds and white membranes of the peppers and slice into fleshy strips. Cut each tomato half into three or four pieces. Arrange all these vegetables on a platter. Just before serving, dribble over the olive oil and vinegar. Scatter garlic, parsley, and salt over the top.

Serve immediately or set aside to serve later at room temperature as a cooked salad. If you set the vegetables aside, you may find that they give off a great deal of liquid. Strain this off before dressing with the oil and vinegar. (Ideally, you would save that savory liquid to add to a broth or soup.) Guests may help themselves, mixing the vegetables together or taking each one separately.

If you don't have a charcoal grill or a fireplace, you can still make escalivada. Preheat your oven to 375 degrees. Rub the peppers and eggplant with a little of the olive oil and set in a roasting pan in the oven to roast for 40 to 50 minutes. They will not blacken as they will when set over live embers, but their skins will loosen enough so that they can be stripped. The tomato and onion halves should be roasted for about 30 to 40 minutes. The point is to have all the vegetables thoroughly roasted all the way through and slightly caramelized on the surface. Once they are roasted, proceed as described above.

This also makes a delightful topping for an open-face sandwich, piled on top of toasted slices of a rustic, grainy bread.

Ratatouille, Pisto Manchego, and Caponata

Makes 8 to 10 servings

I FIRST ENCOUNTERED RATATOUILLE, the brilliant Provençal mixture of summer vegetables stewed in olive oil, in the pages of Elizabeth David's *French Provincial Cooking*. That book, with its precise evocation of the good fresh flavors, the balance, and the attention to detail that still characterized French cooking in the early 1960s when it was published, changed my life in the kitchen as it did that of so many others. This recipe is basically Mrs. David's, with a few refinements added over the years. Make it at the height of summer, when tomatoes are at their peak.

Despite all precautions, the eggplant absorbs a lot of olive oil, making this a dish that's relatively high in fat. Use it, then, sensibly—it is a rich and delicious preparation, to be consumed in small quantities as a first course or as an accompaniment to a plain main course, perhaps an oven-roasted chicken or some exceptionally tasty grilled swordfish steaks. In Provence ratatouille often accompanies a roast leg of lamb, and it's especially good with a humble plate of meltingly soft white beans dressed with a little olive oil.

3 medium eggplants, about 1½ pounds

3 tablespoons sea salt, or more to taste

1½ pounds red peppers, both sweet and hot, to taste

¾ cup extra-virgin olive oil

3 medium onions, chopped

2 garlic cloves, chopped

3 medium zucchini, about 1½ pounds

4 large tomatoes, about 1½ pounds, peeled (page 25) and chopped

½ teaspoon sugar

1 teaspoon coriander seeds, lightly crushed with a rolling pin or coarsely ground in an electric grinder

1 tablespoon drained capers, coarsely chopped

freshly ground black pepper

a handful of chopped fresh basil for garnish

a handful of pitted black olives for garnish (optional)

Rinse the eggplant and cut into 1½-inch cubes. Place the cubes in a bowl and add the salt and water to cover. Set a plate inside the bowl with a weight on it (a can of tomatoes is ideal) to hold the cubes under the brine. Set aside for 1 to 2 hours.

Roast and peel the peppers, following the directions on page 26 and saving any juices from the peppers in a bowl. Cut the peppers into long strips and add to the juices in the bowl.

Heat about ¼ cup of the olive oil in a sauté pan over medium-low heat and add the onions and garlic. Cook, stirring occasionally, until the onions are very soft and melting, about 15 minutes. Do not let the onions brown. Remove the onions from the pan with a slotted spoon and add to the peppers.

Drain the eggplant cubes and pat dry with paper towels. Add another ¼ cup oil to the sauté pan and raise the heat to medium. Toss the eggplant cubes in the hot oil and fry them until they are light brown or golden on all sides, about 10 to 15 minutes. When thoroughly browned, remove with a slotted spoon and add to the other vegetables. While the eggplant is cooking, cut the zucchini into ½-inch cubes. When the eggplant is done, brown the zucchini, adding the last ¼ cup oil as needed. (Try to add oil between frying batches, so that you're not adding cold oil to the hot vegetables in the pan.)

When the zucchini is done, add the tomatoes to the oil in the pan. Lower the heat slightly, stir in the sugar and coriander, and simmer, stirring frequently, until the tomatoes have reduced to a thick jam, about 20 minutes. Stir in the capers.

Now combine all the vegetables with the tomato sauce, stirring carefully with a wooden spoon to avoid breaking up the vegetables. Add some salt if necessary and several grinds of freshly ground black pepper. Just before serving, stir in the basil and the black olives if desired.

Ratatouille can be refrigerated for several days, but it is best served at room temperature or even a little warmer.

Variations: *Pisto manchego,* from the high central plateau of Spain, is made in much the same manner except that the coriander and capers are omitted and only green peppers are used. After cooking, the whole pisto can be put into a terra-cotta baking dish and one fresh egg per serving broken over the top with a little salt and pepper and perhaps a few drops of olive oil on each egg. Placed in a hot oven, the pisto bakes until the eggs have set.

Caponata, from Sicily, is another similar preparation, but ½-inch chunks of celery are fried with the eggplant and zucchini cubes. (The celery lends a little crunch to the finished product.) Add 2 teaspoons sugar and ¼ cup red wine vinegar to the tomatoes as they cook down to give it the proper sweet-sour *(agrodolce* in Italian) flavor. Green olives, rather than black ones, will garnish caponata, which is most often served as an antipasto, although it's also very good as a side dish with meat, beans, or eggs as for pisto manchego.

CROSTINI AND BRUSCHETTA

Pieces of bread with something delicious piled on top are favorites on antipasto platters in country homes and restaurants throughout central Italy. Basically, the preparation is simply a way of using up bread that is no longer fresh. (Although we think of Italians as predominantly pasta eaters, bread has always been important in the diet throughout Italy.)

Strictly speaking, the term *bruschetta* (and please pronounce it correctly: broos-KETT-ah, never brooshedda which grates on Italian ears) refers to a slice of bread, preferably toasted over the embers of a wood fire; *crostini*, on the other hand, are thick little untoasted crusts that are dipped briefly in wine or broth or salted water to refresh them. The two terms are used quite interchangeably these days, however. Travelers in Italy, especially around Florence, during the autumn olive harvest may also encounter another variation called *fett'unta* ("anointed slice"), a slice of toasted bread that is rubbed gently with a cut clove of garlic then lavishly anointed with freshly pressed olive oil. This is a great favorite in the *frantoi,* the olive mills, when the new oil first emerges from the press. It is an addictive confection.

Years ago in Rome, Italian food writer Ada Boni says, crostini dipped in wine and topped with sugar were a favorite snack or merenda for young and old alike. Or you might dip them in water or broth, one side only, dribble olive oil over the top, then lay on slices of good provola cheese and a couple of anchovy fillets set crisscross, put them in a very hot oven, and leave for just a few minutes until the cheese is melting and the bread is crisp. You can see how pizza might evolve from a production like that, which must be very old indeed.

I must confess that I don't really like bread dipped in liquid—it's too mushy for my taste. Instead I like to grill the slices on one or both sides before piling on the topping. I suspect most people on this side of the Atlantic would agree.

Whether it's bruschetta or crostini, these are basically open-faced sandwiches. It's fun to experiment beyond the usual chopped tomato topping found in so many North American restaurants. Take some leftover creamy white beans, for instance, mix with olive oil, lemon juice, and chopped garlic, and pile on crostini or bruschetta for Tuscan baked-bean sandwiches. Or chop steamed bitter greens (arugula, broccoli rabe, collards, or turnip greens) and toss with oil, salt, and garlic; pile them on top of the bread and top with a few drops of balsamic vinegar.

Another variation on the theme is a Catalan breakfast favorite called *pa amb tomaquet,* bread with tomatoes, in which small rolls are split open, the insides briefly toasted and rubbed with a cut clove of garlic, then small, very ripe tomatoes, cut in halves, are rubbed over the surface, smooshing the tomato flesh down into the bread until nothing but the skins are left. The skins are discarded and the whole is lavishly dressed with good Catalan olive oil, made from local small, sweet arbequina olives.

The success of these preparations overall depends on the quality of the bread used. It should be a dense and grainy country-style loaf, preferably made at least in part with whole-grain flour, either a long narrow baguette or a round boule, like the bread from the recipe on page 158, or, for *pa amb tomaquet,* individual rolls made from the same kind of bread dough.

Crostini di Fegatini

Makes 6 servings

MADE WITH CHICKEN LIVERS, these are among the most substantial of all crostini. My Tuscan neighbor Mita Antolini always served them as little appetite seducers before important meals like the annual tobacco harvest dinner. In addition to a first course or antipasto, crostini are appropriate for extending a main-course salad or soup—a creamy puree of butternut squash or pumpkin goes beautifully with crostini di fegatini.

½ pound fresh chicken livers

2 tablespoons extra-virgin olive oil

½ cup minced onion

½ small garlic clove, minced

2 tablespoons minced flat-leaf parsley

2 anchovy fillets (optional)

Pick over the chicken livers, cutting away any green spots and removing any tough bits of fiber. Rinse briefly in a colander and set aside.

In a skillet over medium-low heat, heat the oil and gently sauté the onion, garlic, and half the parsley until the onion is very soft and pale yellow, about 10 minutes. Add the anchovy fillets if desired and mash into the oil in the pan.

⅓ cup vin santo or dry amontillado or oloroso sherry

2 tablespoons chicken broth (page 108) or water

1 tablespoon coarsely chopped drained capers

juice of ½ lemon

sea salt and freshly ground black pepper

good-quality bread, slightly stale, about 12 half-inch slices of baguette or 6 half-inch slices of boule cut in half, grilled on one or both sides

Pat the chicken livers dry. Raise the heat under the pan to medium, push the vegetables to the sides of the pan, and add the livers to the middle. Toss to brown them quickly. As the livers cook, chop them coarsely with a wooden spoon. After a few minutes, when their rosy color has disappeared, add the wine and broth, lower the heat to medium-low, and cook the livers for another 15 minutes or until they have changed color all the way through and most of the broth has been absorbed or has evaporated. As they cook, continue crushing them with the wooden spoon or a fork to make a coarse paste.

If you prefer a smoother mixture, remove the livers from the pan and process briefly in a food processor. (Traditionally they are served as a coarse paste.) Stir in the capers and remaining parsley along with the lemon juice and mix very well. Taste and add salt (the capers may provide enough), lots of pepper, and more lemon juice if desired.

The chicken liver paste is best served warm or at room temperature. Serve it in a bowl, accompanied by the grilled bread. Or pile it on the bread, topping each slice with a caper or a bit of lemon zest, and arrange on a platter.

Sicilian Tomato Bruschette

Makes 4 servings

INSTEAD OF THE USUAL BRUSCHETTE or crostini topped with chopped raw tomato, try this roasted tomato version. This is especially good if you roast the tomatoes on a charcoal grill or over the coals of a wood fire, although you can also do them in a very hot oven.

2 pounds small very ripe tomatoes

2 tablespoons extra-virgin olive oil, if necessary

2 garlic cloves, chopped

2 tablespoons minced fresh basil

sea salt

1 teaspoon crumbled dried oregano

½ teaspoon dried red chili pepper (not too hot) such as piment d'Espelette, Aleppo pepper, or crumbled dried ancho chilies

¼ cup extra-virgin olive oil

slices of country-style bread, toasted if you prefer

Have ready a charcoal fire or glowing wood embers in a fireplace. Set up a grill. Rinse and dry the tomatoes and set them on the grill about 3 inches above the coals. Grill or roast until they have softened and the skins are starting to split open. Remove the tomatoes, using tongs, before they go totally soft and slip between the grill spaces. Transfer the tomatoes to a serving dish and squash them lightly with a fork, so that the juices run out a little.

(If you don't have a grill or a fireplace, turn the oven on as high as it will go—450 to 500 degrees. Set the tomatoes in a single layer in a roasting dish—a gratin dish is perfect for this. Add 2 tablespoons of olive oil and stir the tomatoes to coat them all over with the oil. Set in the preheated oven and let them roast until they have softened and the skins are splitting open.)

While the tomatoes are roasting, pound the garlic and basil together with the salt in a mortar until you have a coarse paste. Mix in the oregano and dried red pepper, then stir in the olive oil. Taste and adjust the seasoning, adding salt if necessary.

As soon as the tomatoes are done and squashed on the platter, pour the dressing over them and mix vigorously to break up the tomatoes even further. Pile onto slices of bread, first toasting them if you wish. (The tomato juices will soak into untoasted bread so that it really must be eaten with a knife and fork. Toasted bread can be eaten in the hands though it too can be a little messy—but delicious!)

Variation: Sicilian Roasted Tomatoes also make a dandy topping for pasta—I like to serve them with a short stubby pasta such as fusilli or penne.

Tabbouleh

T HE EARTHINESS OF BULGUR, or *burghul* (cracked steamed wheat), combines beautifully with the sharp sweetness of mint and parsley and the tang of lemon in what may be the best known of all dishes from the eastern Mediterranean. Tabbouleh became a hit back in what my children call the hippy-dippy days, when the counterculture was first exploring alternatives to the conventional American diet. In one form or another (some of them pretty strange), it has remained a favorite in the deli sections of health food stores ever since. This version, more green than grain, is the way it appears on meze tables all over Lebanon.

Please note that bulgur is not the same thing as cracked wheat and cracked wheat will not work in this recipe. Bulgur is wheat that has been first steamed, then dried and cracked. It's a time-honored way of preserving wheat through the winter that goes back over centuries, maybe even over millennia, in Lebanon and Syria. You can find bulgur on the shelves of well-stocked supermarkets as well as in most health food stores, and of course in Middle Eastern specialty stores. It comes in three grades—fine, medium, and coarsely ground. If you have a choice, buy medium ground for tabbouleh.

¾ cup medium-grain bulgur

3 large bunches of flat-leaf parsley, finely chopped, 2 cups

1 bunch of fresh mint, leaves only, finely chopped, ½ cup

1 bunch of scallions, thinly sliced

2 or 3 tomatoes, diced

1 lemon

½ cup extra-virgin olive oil

sea salt and freshly ground black pepper

large crisp romaine lettuce leaves for serving

Cover the bulgur in a bowl with fresh cold water to a depth of about 1 inch. Set aside to soak for 20 to 30 minutes while you chop and dice the vegetables. When the bulgur grains are nicely plump, drain them, squeezing out as much water as you can. Turn the grains into a clean kitchen towel and squeeze out the remaining water. Each grain of bulgur should be moist and plump but without a trace of liquid.

Pour the bulgur into a dry bowl, add all the chopped and diced vegetables, and mix well with your hands, squeezing slightly to release the flavors. When the bulgur is well mixed, squeeze the lemon over it. Then add the oil and toss to blend all together well.

A common mistake is to use too much bulgur in proportion to the greens. You should have a very green-looking salad in which the bulgur garnishes the parsley rather than vice versa. Taste the salad and add salt and pepper, lemon juice, and oil as desired.

To serve, arrange overlapping leaves of romaine lettuce all around an oval platter and heap the tabbouleh in the middle. Use the romaine leaves as scoops for the tabbouleh.

Variation: A substantial dish for wintertime menus is another Lebanese favorite, Chickpea and Bulgur Salad. Simply soak a cup of dried chickpeas overnight, then drain and cover with fresh water. Boil until the chickpeas are tender but not falling apart—30 to 45 minutes. Drain and add to the tabbouleh mixture, omitting the tomatoes but adding, if you wish, about ¼ teaspoon of freshly ground cinnamon.

Falafel (Crisp Bean Fritters) with Tahini Sauce

Makes about 2 dozen falafel balls; 8 to 10 servings

THESE SAVORY LITTLE BALLS of crispness are the street food par excellence throughout the Middle East, but especially in Lebanon and Egypt. (In Egypt they're called *ta'amiya,* tasty bits, from the Arabic word *ta'am,* or taste.) They were made popular in the United States at Israeli fast-food emporia, but unfortunately, made in advance and left to chill in a deli case, their charm is quite imperceptible. Hot from a Beirut or Alexandria fry shop, however, falafel are an entirely different thing—and utterly irresistible.

Falafel are a little fiddly to prepare but once the batter is mixed it can be left, refrigerated if necessary, for several hours or even overnight. Then it's just a question of heating some good oil in the frying pan and popping the little nuggets in to sizzle and crisp. Make them small to serve as hors d'oeuvres with a glass of wine, or larger to offer as part of a meze. They can also be stuffed into an Arab pita bread sandwich, along with some shredded lettuce and plenty of the tahini sauce that goes with them.

You can find dried peeled fava beans in many specialty food shops or health food stores, especially in Italian and Middle Eastern neighborhoods. If peeled beans are unavailable, buy dried whole fava beans (i.e., with the skins still on), soak them for several hours or overnight, then pull off and discard the tough outside skins. (Just cut or tear a small slit at the end of each bean and the inside will pop right out.)

1 cup dried peeled fava beans, soaked several hours or overnight

½ cup dried chickpeas, soaked several hours or overnight

1 small yellow onion, minced (⅓ to ½ cup)

½ cup minced flat-leaf parsley

2 tablespoons minced cilantro

1 garlic clove, crushed

1 teaspoon baking powder

sea salt and freshly ground black pepper

¾ teaspoon ground cumin

1 teaspoon ground coriander

a pinch of ground red chili pepper (optional)

olive oil or a mixture of olive oil and canola oil for deep-fat frying

tahini sauce (recipe follows)

Combine the drained fava beans and chickpeas, uncooked, in a food processor. Pulse briefly, just to break up the legumes which, having been soaked a sufficient amount of time, should be soft enough to crumble easily.

Add all the other ingredients except the frying oil and the tahini sauce and pulse, scraping down the sides of the bowl as you do so. When you have a coarse paste, continue pulsing, adding a few tablespoons of cool water through the feed tube of the processor.

Stop the processor and extract a little of the mixture. It should be quite gritty in texture but hold together in a little ball when gently squeezed. If necessary, add a little more water. When the mixture seems right, scrape it out into a bowl and set it aside to rest for 15 minutes or so, to make the batter easier to shape.

If you wish, you can make the batter ahead of time, but cover the bowl with plastic wrap and refrigerate in hot weather.

When ready to cook, heat about 2 inches of oil in the bottom of a deep frying pan to 360 degrees (a small cube of bread, dropped in the hot oil, will toast golden brown in less than a minute). Scoop out rounded patties of the falafel mix, 2 or 3 tablespoons in each, and shape gently into round balls or flatter patties, 1½ to 2 inches in diameter, and drop into the hot oil. Fry in batches until crisp and brown, turning once to brown both sides. Drain on paper towels set on a rack. Serve immediately, piping hot, with tahini sauce.

Tahini Sauce

Makes about 1¼ cups

This sauce, made from the sesame paste called tahini (which is available in jars in most well-stocked supermarkets), also goes very well with other dishes, especially with fish, whether fried, grilled, or roasted.

½ teaspoon very finely minced garlic

1 cup tahini

freshly squeezed juice of 1 lemon

sea salt

Stir the garlic and tahini together in a bowl. Add water, a teaspoon at a time, stirring well, until the sauce has the consistency of heavy cream. Oddly, the more water you add to the tahini, the thicker the cream will be, so don't worry, if the sauce seems watery, just stir in some more water. Then stir in the lemon juice and salt to taste.

Farro Salad

Makes 6 to 8 servings

*F*ARRO IS THE ITALIAN NAME for an ancient subspecies of hard durum wheat, *Triticum dicoccum*. It was one of the earliest wheats to be domesticated back in the earliest years of Mediterranean farming, and it still exists to this day principally in Italy but also in Spain and possibly in other parts of the Mediterranean as well. Archeologists, who often find it in Neolithic sites, call it *emmer* but chefs and food writers use the Italian name, farro. (The name is sometimes translated as spelt but spelt is an entirely different species, *Triticum speltum,* and apparently came along considerably later.)

I often see the statement made in health food stores that farro is lower in gluten than ordinary wheat and therefore safe for people with gluten allergies, such as celiac disease. I think that's a very dangerous claim to make and would never recommend that a celiac consume anything made with any variety of wheat whatsoever.

If you can't find farro, substitute barley or kamut, another wheat variety often available in health food stores.

Soaking and cooking times for all these grains vary enormously. It's a good idea to test a small amount before you set out with the recipe.

1½ cups farro (or see headnote for alternatives)

3 cups vegetable broth (page 107) or chicken stock (page 108)

3 tablespoons extra-virgin olive oil, or more to taste

2 tablespoons fresh lemon juice, or more to taste

1 medium cucumber, peeled and diced

6 scallions, sliced on the diagonal, including green parts

6 radishes, trimmed and sliced

2 tablespoons finely chopped red onion

2 tablespoons finely chopped celery

1 tablespoon minced basil, flat-leaf parsley, or mint

sea salt and freshly ground black (or white) pepper

a pinch of red chili pepper, preferably piment d'Espelette or Aleppo pepper

Set the farro in a bowl and cover with cool water to a depth of about 1 inch. Set aside to soak for an hour or so. Drain the soaked farro and transfer to a saucepan along with the vegetable broth or chicken stock. Set over medium-low heat, bring to a simmer, and cook, covered, until the farro grains are tender but not falling apart. This may take as little as 15 or as much as 40 minutes—it all depends on how old and dry the farro is and how well it absorbed the soaking water.

Drain the cooked grains, transfer to a salad bowl, and immediately, while the wheat is still hot, dress with the oil and lemon juice. Add all the remaining ingredients, then taste and adjust the seasoning.

Set aside for 30 minutes or longer to let the wheat absorb all the flavors, then taste again just before serving and add salt, pepper, oil, or lemon juice if it seems to need it.

Fresh Bean and Tuna Salad

Fagioli con Tonno

IN TUSCANY, where this hearty salad is a summer favorite, the beans used are fresh borlotti, creamy white beans beautifully speckled with red that come in pods equally streaked with ivory and maroon. Borlotti and similar beans are dried on the pods, then threshed and stored for winter, but in August, before the tender beans have dried, they are shucked and cooked up quickly. The colors disappear when the beans are cooked, alas, but the flavor more than makes up for the loss.

But you don't need to wait for fresh shell beans—dried beans will do just as well, as long as they're thoroughly soaked and cooked at a very slow temperature so they don't burst in cooking.

Serve this salad Tuscan style, as part of an antipasto, or as a first course for an important meal, or, perhaps accompanied by a fresh tomato or green salad, as a light main course for lunch or supper.

Tuna is the traditional garnish nowadays but salted anchovies or sardines were once used, and Florentines, in an extravagant gesture that recalls their Medicean past, sometimes serve this humble country salad with a healthy dollop of beluga caviar to replace the tuna.

Depending on the size of the beans, you will need 2 to 3 pounds of beans in the pod to get 2 cups of shucked beans.

2 cups shelled (shucked) fresh beans

2 bay leaves or 1 sage sprig

3 tablespoons extra-virgin olive oil

1 tablespoon red wine vinegar

sea salt and freshly ground black pepper

1 6-ounce can best-quality tuna, preferably packed in olive oil

Bring a pot of lightly salted water to a rolling boil, add the beans to the pot with the bay leaves or sage, and cook until the beans are tender but still firm and not falling apart—about 15 to 20 minutes, depending on the size and age of the beans. Drain thoroughly, discarding the aromatics, and transfer to a bowl.

Immediately dress the warm beans with the oil and vinegar. Add salt to taste and plenty of black pepper. Mix well, adjusting the seasoning.

1 tablespoon salted capers, soaked and dried

2 tablespoons finely minced flat-leaf parsley

1 medium red onion, very finely sliced

Drain the tuna of its oil and flake the tuna flesh into the bean salad. Add the capers and parsley. Toss to mix well and strew the red onion slices over the top. Arrange on a platter and serve immediately, while the beans are still warm, or let cool to room temperature. Do not refrigerate.

Variation using dried beans: The trick with dried beans is not to overcook them. Soak 1 cup of dried beans (borlotti, white cannellini, or Maine beans such as Jacob's cattle or soldier beans) overnight. It will expand to make 2 cups. Drain the beans and put them in a pot with fresh cool unsalted water to cover to a depth of 1 inch. Bring to a boil over medium heat, then lower the heat so the beans just barely simmer until done—about 45 minutes to 1 hour, but time depends on the size and age of the beans. When the beans are tender but not falling apart, drain them thoroughly and transfer to a bowl. Dress and season as above while the beans are still warm.

Lentil and Green Olive Salad

꧁ Makes 6 servings

LENTILS MAKE A DELIGHTFUL SALAD, especially in late winter or early spring, when the first bitter greens and young onions are sprouting. Dressed with the finest dark green olive oil and a spritz of lemon juice, lentils have an earthy sweetness that offsets the assertive flavors of early greens and turns them into a protein-rich first course or a main course when accompanied by good crusty bread and a wedge of cheese.

½ pound brown or green lentils

1 small onion, peeled

1 garlic clove, peeled

1 bay leaf

[cont. next page]

Pick the lentils over carefully to get rid of any small stones or pieces of grit. Rinse them under running water. Place in a saucepan over medium heat with about 3 cups of water. Add one of the onions, a garlic clove, the bay leaf, and salt and pepper and bring to a boil. When the water is

sea salt and freshly ground
black pepper

1 cup pitted imported green
olives, coarsely chopped

1 sweet red pepper, cut into
long thin strips

⅓ cup extra-virgin olive oil

3 tablespoons fresh lemon
juice

bitter greens such as arugula,
chicory, frisée, radicchio, or
tender dandelions

zest of ½ lemon, cut into fine
julienne strips

1 tablespoon minced flat-leaf
parsley

boiling, turn it down, cover the lentils, and simmer for about 30 minutes—or until the lentils are thoroughly cooked and tender. (Time varies even more than with other legumes, depending on the age of the lentils.)

When the lentils are done, drain them, discarding the cooking vegetables, and mix while still warm with the olives, red peppers, olive oil, and lemon juice. Taste and adjust the seasoning if necessary. Serve piled on a bed of bitter greens. Garnish with the julienne strips of lemon and minced parsley.

Lentil and Walnut Salad

Makes about 4 cups; 4 to 6 servings

U NLIKE OTHER BEANS and pulses, lentils need not be soaked before cooking. The lentils commonly used in Mediterranean kitchens are quite small and dark slate-brown or grayish green in color. Do not use Indian dal-type lentils for these dishes, because those are meant to disintegrate into a porridge when cooked.

1 cup green or brown lentils,
picked over and washed

2 cups water

¾ cup chopped scallion

1 sweet red pepper, diced

½ cup finely chopped flat-leaf
parsley

½ cup coarsely chopped
walnuts

½ teaspoon dry mustard or 1
heaped teaspoon Dijon
mustard

Combine the lentils with the water and bring to a boil. Turn the heat down to medium-low, cover the pan tightly, and simmer for about 20 minutes or until the lentils are cooked through but still firm enough to hold their shape.

When the lentils are done, remove from the heat, drain, and place in a bowl along with the scallions, red pepper, parsley, and walnuts.

In a separate small bowl, combine the mustard with the vinegar, beating in a little at a time until the mixture is thoroughly blended. Gradually beat in

2 to 3 tablespoons red wine vinegar, to taste

⅓ cup extra-virgin olive oil

sea salt and freshly ground black pepper

the olive oil. Pour the dressing over the lentils and toss to mix thoroughly. Add salt and black pepper and serve simply as is or on a bed of bitter greens such as arugula, chicory, or dandelion greens.

Tunisian Beet Salad with Harissa

Makes 6 to 8 servings

B IG ROUND BEETS are roasted in Tunisian ovens until tender, then peeled, diced, and mixed with scallions, parsley, and garlic and dressed with oil and vinegar laced with a little peppery harissa. Oven roasting produces an altogether different texture from boiling and brings out the delicate sweetness of the vegetable. In Greece, beets roasted like this are often served with a thick garlicky sauce called *skordalia* (page 273).

a little extra-virgin olive oil

6 large beets, about 4 or 5 inches in diameter

½ cup chopped scallion

¼ cup finely minced flat-leaf parsley

1 garlic clove, minced

1 teaspoon harissa (page 279) or ½ teaspoon hot red pepper flakes or to taste

1 teaspoon red wine vinegar

2 tablespoons extra-virgin olive oil

sea salt

Preheat the oven to 325 degrees. Oil the bottom of a roasting pan and use a little oil to rub over the carefully rinsed and dried beets. Place the beets in the pan and roast in the oven for 2½ to 3 hours or until very tender. Remove and, when they are cool enough to handle, slip the skins off and cut the beets into cubes.

Toss the beets in a bowl with the scallion, parsley, and garlic. Dissolve the harissa in the vinegar, then beat in the olive oil. Pour the dressing over the beets. Taste for seasoning and add a little salt if necessary.

Turkish Grated Carrot Salad with Yogurt

Makes 6 appetizer servings

5 to 6 medium carrots, peeled

2 garlic cloves, crushed and chopped

1 teaspoon sea salt

¼ cup plain yogurt (nonfat is fine)

4 teaspoons extra-virgin olive oil

4 teaspoons fresh lemon juice

Bring a pot of water to a rapid boil and plunge the carrots in. Cook for about 5 minutes, long enough to start softening them but without really tenderizing. Remove from the heat and immediately plunge the carrots into cold water to halt the cooking and cool the carrots. When they're cool enough to handle, grate them on the large holes of the grater.

In a small bowl, crush the garlic and salt together with the back of a spoon. Mix in the yogurt, oil, and lemon juice, beating with a fork. Pour the dressing over the carrots and toss to mix thoroughly. Taste and add a little more salt if necessary. Serve piled on a lettuce leaf as a first course or in a bowl as part of a meze or as an accompaniment to a main dish.

Variation: Although Turkish cooks would consider it decidedly unorthodox, I have had great success using grated *raw* carrots in this recipe.

Tunisian Carrot Salad with Harissa and Feta Cheese

Makes 6 servings

6 medium carrots, peeled and cut into thick rounds

1 garlic clove, chopped

1 teaspoon ground caraway or cumin seeds

sea salt

Bring a pot of water to a boil, add the carrots, and cook for 5 minutes, just until they are starting to become tender. Drain, running cold water over the carrots to halt the cooking. Chop the carrot rounds very coarsely.

In a mortar, pound the garlic to a paste with the caraway and salt. Dilute the harissa with the water.

1 tablespoon harissa (page 279)

¼ cup cool water

¼ cup brine-cured black olives, pitted

¼ pound feta cheese, crumbled

¼ cup extra-virgin olive oil

2 tablespoons red or white wine vinegar

If the olives are very large, chop them coarsely. Set aside a bit of feta and a few olives for garnish.

In a bowl, combine the carrots, garlic paste, and diluted harissa. Mix together well. Add the oil and vinegar and toss once more to mix well. Sprinkle the crumbled cheese and olives over the top.

Set aside at room temperature for at least 30 minutes to develop the flavors. Garnish with the reserved olives and cheese and serve.

Moroccan Carrot Salad with Orange and Lemon Juice

⚜ Makes 6 to 8 servings

ALTHOUGH CALLED A SALAD in Morocco, this delightful mixture is in fact more like a soup and is served as part of the first course in small bowls with spoons. Freshly squeezed orange juice is essential here.

1½ pounds carrots, about 10 medium

1½ cups fresh orange juice

juice of 1 lemon

1 teaspoon sugar, or more to taste

½ cup walnut halves

Peel the carrots and grate them on the finest holes of the grater. Mix in the orange and lemon juices and add sugar to taste—the sugar should simply accentuate the flavor of the carrots rather than give them a decidedly sweet taste. Set the carrots aside to marinate while you prepare the walnuts.

Preheat the oven to 350 degrees. Spread the walnuts on a cookie sheet and bake for 10 to 15 minutes or until they become aromatic and the papery peel can be rubbed away. Remove from the oven and rub each walnut half to rid it of as much of the skin as possible. (The skin is what gives walnuts an astringent tannin flavor.)

When you're ready to serve, spoon the carrots into small bowls and garnish each with a few toasted walnut halves.

Neapolitan Cauliflower Salad

Insalata di Rinforzo

INSALATA DI RINFORZO is a Neapolitan Christmas tradition. Its curious name, "reinforced salad," comes from the fact that the salad sits on the dining room sideboard to be offered as a little taste to drop-in guests throughout the holiday season. Thus, it must be periodically reinforced, by adding more vegetables, as it diminishes in size. What a concept! I prefer to make up the salad and let it sit for a bit while the flavors mingle, then consume the whole thing (or almost the whole thing) at one sitting.

The dressing for insalata di rinforzo is quite tart. If you prefer, add 2 more tablespoons of olive oil to the mix.

1 medium cauliflower (about 1 pound)

sea salt

2 medium carrots, peeled and cut in julienne strips

1 celery stalk, preferably dark green from outer layer, cut in julienne strips

1 sweet red pepper, roasted, peeled, cut into thin slivers

a pinch of ground or crushed red chili pepper

12 large black olives, pitted and coarsely chopped

6 large green olives, pitted and coarsely chopped

2 tablespoons salt-packed capers, rinsed, drained, chopped

6 anchovy fillets, coarsely chopped

¼ cup finely chopped flat-leaf parsley

2 tablespoons wine vinegar

¼ cup extra-virgin olive oil

freshly ground black pepper

Break the cauliflower into small florets. Bring a saucepan full of lightly salted water to a rolling boil, add the cauliflower, and cook until it is just barely tender, 7 to 10 minutes, then drain thoroughly.

Combine the warm cauliflower in a serving bowl with all the other ingredients through the parsley and toss to mix well.

In a small bowl, beat together the vinegar and olive oil to mix thoroughly, then pour over the salad. Toss again and taste a bit of cauliflower. Add salt if it seems necessary—you may not need more since the capers and anchovies will add salt to the dish— and plenty of freshly ground pepper.

Set aside, lightly covered with plastic wrap, for several hours before serving. Just before serving, taste again and adjust the seasoning.

Chakchouka

Moroccan Salad of Cooked Tomatoes and Green Peppers

Makes 6 to 8 servings

A NOTHER MOROCCAN STARTER that doesn't really seem to merit the name of salad, though that is precisely what it's called. *Chakchouka,* I was told in Morocco, is a Jewish name for this dish, indicating that the preparation comes out of the rich culinary traditions of the Moroccan Jews. This is usually served, with other small dishes, at the beginning of a meal.

8 large tomatoes, peeled, seeded (page 25), and cut into chunks

1 garlic clove, slivered

¼ cup extra-virgin olive oil

4 sweet peppers

1 small fresh green chili (optional)

1 tablespoon sweet paprika

1 tablespoon minced flat-leaf parsley

1 preserved lemon (optional; page 281)

In a skillet over medium heat, cook the tomatoes with the garlic in the olive oil, adding no water but stirring frequently, until the tomatoes have thoroughly cooked down to a thick jammy sauce—about 15 to 20 minutes. They should yield up all of their liquid, and the oil should then separate slightly away from the mass of tomatoes.

While the tomatoes are cooking, roast and peel the peppers and chili, following the directions on page 26. Cut the peppers and chili into large dice. As soon as the tomatoes are thick and dense, stir in the peppers and chili and the paprika. Sprinkle with the parsley. If you have a preserved lemon, cut the skin into small cubes or julienne strips and stir in with the peppers.

Chakchouka is usually served at room temperature with pieces of bread for scooping it up.

Panzanella

Italian Bread Salad

ﾫ﹄ Makes 6 to 8 servings

H AVE YOU EVER sat around the table after the salad was finished and
dipped chunks of bread in the salad dressing left in the bottom of the
bowl? Then this Tuscan bread salad is for you, combining the full summer flavors
of red ripe tomatoes and basil with the nutty aroma of bread.

Altopascio, a town on the heights looking over the Arno Valley west of Florence as the river courses toward Pisa, is where Tuscans say the best bread in Italy
is made. "Why?" I asked the woman in the local bakery. "Because it is," she said.

Panzanella should be made with an Altopascio-style *pane integrale,* a rustic
whole-grain loaf, coarse-textured and deeply flavored, preferably baked in a
wood-fired oven. If you don't have access to a good hearty Tuscan loaf, make
your own, using the recipe on page 158, but don't try to do this with ordinary
store bread—it will make a gluey mess.

1 pound rather stale (firm
but not dried out) Tuscan
country-style bread—
4 1-inch-thick slices

4 large dead-ripe tomatoes,
full of flavor and fragrance

1 large red onion, about ½
pound, finely sliced

1 or 2 cucumbers, about ½
pound, peeled, quartered
lengthwise, and finely sliced

a handful of green basil
leaves, 1 cup firmly packed,
very coarsely chopped or
torn

½ cup extra-virgin olive oil

¼ cup red wine vinegar

1 tablespoon balsamic vinegar

sea salt and freshly ground
black pepper

Soften the bread slices in a bowl of cool water,
then squeeze each slice gently to get rid of the
excess liquid. Tear the bread into chunks, discarding
the thick crusts, and drop the chunks in the
bottom of a salad bowl. Cut the tomatoes in half
and slice thickly, about ½ inch, or cut into chunks.
Add to the bread, along with the onion, cucumber,
and basil leaves.

In a separate bowl, mix the oil and vinegars, adding
salt and pepper. Beat with a fork to emulsify and
pour over the salad. Mix well, using your hands to
turn the salad, and set aside in a cool spot (do not
refrigerate) for at least 30 minutes before serving to
allow the flavors to develop.

Fattoush

Lebanese Toasted Bread Salad

Makes 6 servings

T HE KEY INGREDIENT in *fattoush* is sumac, a dark red, lemony astringent flavoring much used in the Middle East. It is available in this country in shops in Middle Eastern neighborhoods or by mail order from specialty food stores and spice shops. If you buy whole sumac berries, grind them coarsely or pound in a mortar.

2 small Arab flatbreads (pita)

1 small head of romaine lettuce

8 radishes, sliced or cut in half

8 scallions, both white and green parts, sliced

1 or 2 cucumbers, preferably pale-skinned Middle Eastern or Armenian cucumbers, peeled and sliced

1 or 2 plain brine-pickled cucumbers, not sweetened or heavily flavored with garlic or dill, sliced

3 medium tomatoes, cut into thick chunks

⅓ cup finely chopped flat-leaf parsley

⅓ cup finely chopped fresh mint or 2 teaspoons dried, crumbled

1 or 2 garlic cloves, to taste

1 teaspoon sea salt

¼ cup fresh lemon juice

¼ cup extra-virgin olive oil

freshly ground black pepper

2 tablespoons coarsely ground sumac

Split each of the breads in half horizontally so that you have 4 thin rounds of bread. Toast the breads lightly under the broiler, just enough to turn them pale golden and crisp. Break up the crisp toast into small pieces and put in the bottom of a large salad bowl. Pile the salad vegetables on top, in the order listed, sprinkling the parsley and mint over the top.

Crush the garlic with the flat blade of a knife and chop it coarsely. In a separate small bowl, mash the garlic with the salt, using the back of a spoon. Stir in the lemon juice and oil, beating with a fork to mix well, and pour the dressing over the salad. Grind the black pepper over the top and sprinkle the sumac on last. Take the salad bowl to the table and toss the ingredients together just before serving to keep the bread from getting soggy before it is served.

Greek Salad

The Classic Horiatiki Recipe

WHEN ANTONIA TRICHOPOULOU talks about the Mediterranean diet, which she does often in her role as Director of the World Health Organization Collaborating Center for Nutrition Education in Athens, one example of good, healthy Mediterranean food that she often cites is Greek salad. This has evoked hoots of derision from Americans used to the kind of Greek salad we get all too often in mom-and-pop corner restaurants, the one that's made with wet iceberg lettuce, hard tomatoes, and canned California black olives, dressed with Wish-Bone Italian Low-Cal Dressing. The salad Antonia makes when she entertains friends and colleagues at her summer house along the sea outside Athens is altogether different. In Greece the salad is called *horiatiki,* meaning "country style." If you don't care for anchovies, try flaking a little drained white-meat tuna over the top of the salad.

This salad is robust enough to serve as a main course if accompanied by chunks of sturdy country-style bread.

1 medium head of romaine lettuce, rinsed and torn into chunks

1 long English cucumber or 2 medium slender regular cucumbers, thinly sliced

4 medium tomatoes, cut into eighths

1 medium red onion, halved and thinly sliced

1 pound imported Greek or Bulgarian feta cheese, preferably sheep's milk feta

2 sweet peppers, preferably red and green, thinly sliced

¼ cup minced flat-leaf parsley

6 or 8 anchovy fillets (optional)

Arrange the lettuce on a deep platter. Combine the cucumbers, tomatoes, and half the onion slices in a bowl. Crumble the feta and add half of it to the vegetables in the bowl, stirring to mix well. Layer this mixture over the lettuce. Arrange the peppers over the top and sprinkle with the parsley and remaining feta. Arrange the anchovy fillets, or tuna if you'd rather, on top and scatter the pitted olives over all.

In a small bowl, combine the oil, lemon juice, oregano, and salt and pepper. Beat with a fork to mix well and pour over the salad. Toss at the table just before serving.

about 18 Kalamata olives,
pitted

⅓ cup fruity extra-virgin
olive oil

juice of ½ lemon

½ teaspoon dried, crumbled
oregano

sea salt and freshly ground
black pepper

GRAPE LEAVES

If you are lucky enough to have a backyard grapevine, select tender young
leaves from the top, but be sure they're large enough to handle comfortably.
Rinse them in cold running water and place in a colander in the sink. Bring
a teakettle of water to a boil and pour the whole kettle over the grape leaves.
This should soften them enough to make them easy to handle and roll. If
they're not soft enough, repeat the procedure with more boiling water.

Canned grape leaves are of varying quality and always lack the lemony astringency of fresh ones. Most of us, however, will have to make do with them.
Canned grape leaves should be rinsed in cold running water to get rid of the
brine in which they're packed.

To stuff grape leaves, open a leaf carefully and spread it on the kitchen
counter with the smooth topside of the leaf down, the rougher veined under-
side up. If the stem is attached, cut it away. Place a spoonful of stuffing at the
base of the leaf, where the stem was attached, about ½ inch from the edge.
Fold the bottom edge up around the stuffing, then fold in each side, right and
left. Carefully roll the leaf, making a compact bundle, toward the point. Place
the stuffed grape leaves in the bottom of a heavy kettle or saucepan. They
should fit comfortably in the bottom of the pan without being wedged in
tightly, so they can expand a little as the rice in the stuffing cooks. You should
make several layers of stuffed leaves, but arrange each layer perpendicularly to
the one below; that is, if the bottom layer is in a north-south direction, the
next layer should point east-west. When all the little bundles are layered in
place, add liquid (salted water or broth, plus lemon juice) just to cover the top
layer. Set a plate a little smaller than the diameter of the pan on top of the
leaves to hold them in place while cooking. Cover the kettle and follow the
directions for steaming the leaves.

Grape Leaves Stuffed with Rice

> ❧ Makes 25 grape leaves; serves 4 as a first course,
> 6 to 8 as part of a meze

AN ANCIENT DISH from the eastern Mediterranean, these plump little bites of flavor are invariably part of a proper meze. Most of us in North America, alas, know them only from deli counters where they tend to be over-cooked, mushy, and mostly quite unappealing. Although a little fiddly to make, once you've mastered the technique of rolling them tightly—but not *too* tightly—you'll find they're perhaps not exactly a breeze but certainly well worth the effort.

1 tablespoon dried black currants

¼ cup extra-virgin olive oil

1 medium onion, minced (½ cup)

3 or 4 scallions, both white and green parts, minced

2 tablespoons pine nuts

½ cup long-grain rice

2 medium tomatoes, peeled, seeded (page 25), and chopped or 2 canned tomatoes, drained and chopped

sea salt and freshly ground pepper

¼ cup hot water

¼ teaspoon ground allspice, or more to taste

¼ cup fresh lemon juice

about 25 grape leaves, softened if fresh (page 89) or rinsed if canned

Put the currants in a small bowl and cover with hot water to soften while you prepare the rest of the stuffing.

Warm the olive oil in a saucepan over medium-low heat and gently sauté the onion and scallions for 15 to 20 minutes or until they are thoroughly softened but not browned. Add the pine nuts and continue cooking a few minutes longer, until golden. Add the rice and stir to coat thoroughly with the oil. Add the tomatoes, salt, and pepper and pour in the hot water. Mix well, cover, and cook over gentle heat until all the liquid has been absorbed, about 10 minutes. The rice will start to soften but will not be cooked. Remove from the heat, stir in the allspice and drained currants, and set aside, covered, for 10 minutes.

Stuff the grape leaves as described on page 89 and arrange in a heavy kettle or wide, shallow saucepan. Add lemon juice and water just to cover the grape leaves. Set a plate on top of the grape leaves, cover the kettle, and simmer gently for about 30 minutes or until the rice and grape leaves are thoroughly cooked.

Pile the cooked grape leaves on a platter. Serve garnished with lemon wedges and a drizzle of olive oil or with a sauce made from a cup of yogurt mixed with 2 chopped garlic cloves and salt to taste.

Variation: Sometimes a little lean ground lamb is added to make a somewhat more substantial stuffing. In that case the currants and pine nuts are omitted and the stuffing is flavored with a combination of minced fresh dill, mint, and parsley.

Spanish Tortilla with Potatoes and Onion

❧ Makes 6 to 8 servings as finger food; 2 or 3 servings as a main course for lunch

I LIVED IN SPAIN during the Franco years, when the country was very poor and cut off from the rest of Europe. Meat was expensive, but eggs, potatoes, and onions were always cheap and always available. For many Spaniards a tortilla española was the gastronomic highlight of the week.

Humble and poor it may well be, but there is an innate sense of balance and honesty about this omelet that has tremendous appeal. Frankly, I'd take it over a paella any day.

¼ cup extra-virgin olive oil

1 medium onion, finely chopped

2 medium potatoes, peeled and diced

sea salt and freshly ground black pepper

6 large eggs

Use a straight-sided iron skillet for this recipe. Warm the oil in the skillet over medium-low heat and cook the onion gently for about 5 minutes or until it starts to soften. Do not let the onion brown. Add the potatoes to the middle of the pan, pushing the onion to the sides. Continue cooking for 7 to 10 minutes, stirring and turning with a spatula, until the potatoes are also softened and thoroughly cooked. The potatoes are done when you can easily push the spatula through a little cube. Using a slotted spoon, remove the potatoes and onion from the pan, leaving the oil behind, and set aside in a bowl to cool. Add salt and pepper to taste.

In another bowl, beat the eggs with a fork until thoroughly blended. When the potato mixture has cooled enough so that it will not cook the eggs, pour the eggs over the potatoes and mix gently with a fork to make sure that all the vegetable pieces are well covered.

Turn the heat back to medium-low. When the oil in the skillet starts to sizzle, pour the egg mixture into the pan and cook, shaking the pan gently to keep the eggs from sticking to the bottom. As soon as the eggs begin to solidify around the edges, start to run a palette knife, narrow spatula, or cake icer around the edges. The tortilla will firm up gradually, beginning around the edges and across the bottom, wherever the egg mixture is in contact with the heat. The trick is to keep it from sticking to the pan, so you must keep it moving gently, both by shaking the pan and by sliding the knife around, throughout the cooking time. From time to time, lift some of the cooked egg off the bottom to let the uncooked egg run underneath. When the top is still rather liquid, invert a plate over the top of the skillet and, being careful of spilled oil, turn the plate and the skillet over. Then slide the tortilla from the plate back into the skillet to finish cooking the other side. If this seems like too much for you, you can cheat, as Spanish cooks often do. Instead of turning the tortilla over, simply run it under a preheated broiler to solidify and brown the top.

Spanish cooks consider the tortilla to be done when it is still quite moist and even a little runny in the middle. When it's done to your taste, slide it out of the pan and set aside on a plate to cool to room temperature before serving.

Note: Do not attempt to increase the recipe by adding more eggs. Because this is always served at room temperature, you can make several tortillas ahead of time if you have a number of people to serve.

Variations: Many other vegetables can be substituted for potatoes in this tortilla. Zucchini or asparagus are obvious choices, or a combination of red peppers (hot and sweet together) and tomatoes, as in the recipe for frittata that follows. Another variant is to combine about ½ pound grated raw beets with a cup of finely chopped leeks and a handful of chopped parsley or dill; stew in olive oil until the beets are soft, then mix with eggs and grated cheese and cook like the tortilla.

Italian Frittata with Tomatoes and Peppers

➵ Makes 4 servings as a main course; 8 to 10 servings as a first course

A N OMELET LIKE THIS is easy to prepare, a wonderful way to put something on the table quickly and easily. Serve this in small portions as a meze or tapas course, or divide the frittata into four servings for a light lunch or supper main course.

1 large yellow onion, chopped

2 garlic cloves, minced

3 tablespoons extra-virgin olive oil

1 medium zucchini, diced

1 medium ripe red tomato, seeded (page 25) and chopped

1 medium sweet red pepper, chopped

a handful of coarsely chopped basil, parsley, or a mix

sea salt and freshly ground black pepper

6 to 8 large eggs

[cont. next page]

Gently sauté the onion and garlic in 2 tablespoons of the oil in a skillet over medium-low heat. Cook, stirring frequently, until the vegetables are soft— about 20 minutes. Push the onion and garlic out to the edges of the pan and add the zucchini, tomato, and pepper. Cook, stirring frequently, until the vegetables are thoroughly softened—about 20 minutes. Remove from the heat and stir in the basil. Add salt and pepper and set aside.

Preheat the broiler and adjust a rack so that the upper surface of the omelet will be about 6 inches from the source of the heat.

In a medium bowl, beat the eggs with a fork. When the vegetables are cool enough not to cook the eggs, turn the vegetables into the egg mixture, scraping the pan well, and mix, adding a little pepper.

½ cup freshly grated
parmigiano reggiano cheese

Return the pan to medium-high heat. Add the
remaining oil and turn the pan to swirl the oil all
over the bottom and up the sides. Then turn the
egg mixture into the pan. Cook over medium-
high heat, continually running a palette knife or a
narrow spatula around the edge of the pan to keep
it loose. From time to time, lift some of the cooked
egg off the bottom of the pan to let uncooked egg
run underneath. When the bottom of the frittata is
set, remove from the heat, scatter the parmigiano
over the top, and run the frittata under the broiler
for 3 to 4 minutes, just to melt the cheese and
glaze the top.

Serve immediately or set aside and serve at room
temperature.

Tunisian Aijjah with Spicy Potatoes

+ Makes 4 servings

THE NORTH AFRICAN VERSION of frittata is called *aijjah* or *eggah,* and is
more like scrambled eggs than either frittata or tortilla, so much so that I
can well imagine this as the star of a wonderful summer brunch on the lawn.
Tunisians almost always add a healthy dollop of harissa.

1 pound small new potatoes,
peeled and diced

3 tablespoons extra-virgin
olive oil

½ teaspoon sea salt, or more
to taste

½ teaspoon ground caraway
seeds

2 garlic cloves, crushed with
the flat blade of a knife

2 tablespoons tomato puree

½ cup warm water

In a large skillet over medium heat, gently sauté
the potatoes in 2 tablespoons of the oil until the
potatoes are softened and starting to brown—about
15 minutes.

While the potatoes are cooking, pound the salt and
caraway to a powder in a mortar; then add the
garlic and pound to a paste. Dilute the tomato
puree with the warm water and stir in the harissa.
Combine with the garlic paste.

When the potatoes are done, add the harissa-garlic
mixture and cook briefly, stirring, for 5 to 10

1 tablespoon harissa (page 279)

freshly ground black pepper

8 large eggs

minutes, until the liquid is reduced to a thick sauce that naps the potatoes. Remove from the heat and adjust the seasoning, adding pepper and more salt if necessary. Set aside to cool slightly.

Beat the eggs with a fork in a large bowl. Then turn the potatoes into the eggs and stir to mix very well.

Rinse and dry the skillet if necessary. Set it over medium-high heat and add the remaining oil, swirling the pan to coat the bottom and sides thoroughly. Turn the egg mixture into the pan and cook, continually lifting the cooked egg mixture from the bottom and letting the liquid eggs run underneath, in order to scramble the eggs.

When the eggs have reached the desired consistency, remove from the heat and serve immediately.

Baked Zucchini and Spinach Pie

Sfougato

Makes 8 servings as an appetizer; 4 as a main course

YOU COULD CALL *sfougato* a vegetable custard and you wouldn't be far wrong, but sfougato sounds much more enticingly exotic. You could also call it a Greek frittata, baked in the oven instead of cooked on top of the stove. But whatever you call it, this simple dish from the Greek islands has all the traditional virtues of Mediterranean cooking—it's easy, it's cheap, it's good for you, and it's delicious. Moreover, you can vary it any way you want—I've seen sfougato made with nothing but onion and potato, for instance, and I've seen it with ground meat added. But zucchini is just right, and, as gardeners know, we can never have too many recipes for zucchini.

Graviera is a mild sheep's milk cheese from the island of Crete, but I sometimes make sfougato with crumbled feta when there's no graviera available. If you can't find the right Greek cheese for this, substitute parmigiano reggiano or grana from Italy.

½ cup extra-virgin olive oil

1 cup chopped scallions or spring onions

3 medium zucchini, grated on the large holes of a grater or finely sliced

½ pound potatoes, peeled and grated on the large holes of a grater

2 to 2½ cups coarsely chopped spinach or chard

½ cup finely chopped herbs, preferably dill or mint leaves, or a mix of the two

6 eggs

6 tablespoons whole milk

½ cup (about 3 ounces) grated Cretan graviera or kefalotiri, or crumbled feta, as you prefer

sea salt and freshly ground black pepper

Use a little oil to grease the insides of an 8 x 10-inch oven dish or casserole. Set the oven at 375 degrees.

Add the remaining oil to a heavy skillet and set over medium-low heat. When it is hot, toss in the scallions and cook, stirring, until they have softened considerably. Stir in the sliced or grated zucchini and the potatoes and cook till the zucchini have lost any stiffness and given up some of their liquid. Now add the spinach or chard and stir it in. Cover the pan and let the vegetables cook for about 5 minutes, or until they have softened completely. (Total cooking time for all these vegetables should be 15 to 20 minutes.) If there's a lot of liquid remaining in the pan, raise the heat and cook it off quickly. Then stir in the fresh herbs. Remove the skillet from the heat and set aside to cool.

Beat the eggs and milk together in a large bowl. Stir in the grated cheese, then add the vegetables—they don't have to be cold, but they should be cool enough so that they don't cook the eggs with their heat.

Taste the mixture before adding salt—the cheese may be very salty. Grind in plenty of pepper and tip the mixture into the oven dish. Transfer to the preheated oven and bake for 30 to 40 minutes or until the custard is golden brown and blistered on top.

Serve hot or at room temperature, with a bowl of strained yogurt to spoon over it.

Crispy Shrimp Fritters from Cádiz

Tortillitas de Camarones

✳ Makes 32 small "cocktail-size" fritters; or 16 larger ones

THESE DELECTABLE LITTLE MOUTHFULS are from the west coast of Spain, where the great Guadalquivir River empties into the Atlantic (hence, not technically part of the Mediterranean but I'm not telling!). The shrimp are tiny ones, not more than an inch long, harvested in brackish local waters. This is the way they make tortillitas at the wonderful El Faro restaurant in Cádiz.

If you can find the sweet litttle Maine shrimp that are available on the East Coast in winter, use them; otherwise use the smallest fresh shrimp you can find, peel them, and chop them coarsely. Frozen shrimp are a poor alternative, as they have so little flavor they're not worth bothering with, but any fishmonger should be able to source fresh shrimp for you. Chickpea flour (garbanzo flour) is often available in health food shops and in Indian markets, where it's sometimes called gram flour or chana flour.

2 eggs

1 teaspoon sea salt

½ cup chickpea flour

½ cup durum semolina

1 pound small shrimp, peeled and coarsely chopped

1 medium yellow onion, coarsely grated or chopped

2 tablespoons chopped flat-leaf parsley

¼ cup chopped cilantro

⅓ cup extra-virgin olive oil

a pinch of Spanish paprika (pimentón), sweet or hot, to taste

about ½ cup extra-virgin olive oil for frying

Have all the ingredients ready to mix. Add the frying oil to a skillet or wok, set over medium heat, and let the oil warm up while you mix the ingredients.

Using a wire whisk, beat the eggs in a bowl with the salt, then beat in about 1 cup water. Beat in the flours, adding a little more water if necessary to make a creamy batter. Now fold in all the remaining ingredients except the frying oil and mix well to distribute the shrimp pieces throughout the batter.

When the oil is hot enough to fry (at a temperature of about 360 degrees, or when a small cube of bread browns in 1 minute), drop in a little mound of shrimp batter and fry, turning once, until golden on both sides. Taste the fritter to see if it needs more salt or pimentón and adjust the seasoning accordingly. You may make small fritters to serve with drinks: use two soup spoons to drop in the little mounds of batter, a few at a time; or you may make larger fritters to serve at the table, perhaps on a tangle of sweet and bitter salad greens. In either case, fry the fritters until golden brown on both sides, turning once and flattening them slightly with a spatula. As the fritters finish cooking, remove and set them aside on a rack covered with paper towels while you proceed with the rest of the shrimp batter.

When all the fritters are done, serve them immediately. If necessary, they can be kept for 15 to 20 minutes in a pre-warmed oven, but they are really best hot from the pan.

Roasted Breaded Mussels

Cozze Arraganate

Makes 6 to 8 servings

PUGLIA, THE LONG, THIN HEEL of Italy's boot, is a land of passionate mussel eaters, not surprising since the bivalves have been cultivated in the brackish lagoon of Taranto, on Puglia's Ionian coast, since Roman times. These are Mediterranean black mussels, *Mytilus galloprovincialis,* which are a little different from our more common Atlantic blue mussels, *M. edulis.* The Mediterranean critters have a softer, more delicate flavor and a creamier texture. Nonetheless, Atlantic mussels, widely available from fishmongers and at good supermarket seafood counters, are fine for this recipe.

For more about mussels, see page 117.

Female mussels have a rich, reddish-orange flesh, while males are paler and cream colored.

2 pounds medium mussels
(24 to 36), scrubbed and
beards removed

about ¼ cup dry white wine

3 plump garlic cloves, finely
minced

¼ cup minced flat-leaf parsley

1 teaspoon crumbled dried
oregano

¼ cup freshly grated aged
pecorino or parmigiano
reggiano

¼ cup fresh bread crumbs

¼ cup extra-virgin olive oil

Turn the oven on to 425 degrees.

Rinse the mussels briefly under running water and pull off the beards. Discard any mussels with broken shells or shells that are gaping. If a mussel shell doesn't close up tight when rapped on the edge of the sink, it too should be discarded; also discard any that are suspiciously heavy compared to the others as they are probably packed with mud and sand.

Put the mussels in a pan with 2 or 3 tablespoons of wine and set over medium-high heat. Cook, tossing frequently, just until the shells start to open. (They will continue cooking later.) Using a slotted spoon, remove the mussels as they open and transfer to a bowl.

Strain the liquid left in the pan through a fine sieve or several layers of cheesecloth to get rid of grit. Measure the strained liquid, and add more wine if necessary to make ¼ cup.

Remove the mussels from their shells, reserving a half shell for each mussel. Set the half shells on a baking sheet and put a mussel in each one.

In a small bowl, combine the garlic, parsley, oregano, grated cheese, and bread crumbs, then sprinkle the mixture in a thin layer over each mussel. Dribble olive oil and the strained mussel liquid over the top.

Transfer to the oven and bake for about 10 minutes or until the tops are brown and crisp. Serve the mussels in their shells, piping hot, straight from the oven.

Lamb Meatballs with Pine Nuts in a Lemony Tomato Sauce

T HIS IS A MUCH-LOVED meze dish in Syria and Lebanon, where it's sometimes called *Daoud Pasha* ("Sir David" but who knows why?) and is made
in a more elaborate fashion. I've simplified it to serve as part of a meze or on its
own with a before-dinner glass of wine. Of course, as a meat dish it would function just as well as a main course, but the rich spiciness of the meatballs studded
with pine nuts, combined with the tart sweet flavors of the tomato and lemon
sauce, mark it, at least to my taste, as a perfect centerpiece on a meze table.

¼ cup extra-virgin olive oil

¼ cup pine nuts

1 pound lean lamb, ground
twice

1 medium yellow onion,
grated or minced

¼ cup finely chopped flat-leaf
parsley

1 teaspoon freshly ground
allspice

¼ teaspoon ground cumin

¼ teaspoon ground coriander

sea salt and freshly ground
black pepper

1 cup drained canned plum
tomatoes, broken up

1 tablespoon tomato
concentrate, preferably
Sicilian extract of tomatoes
(estratto di pomodoro)

grated zest and freshly
squeezed juice of 1 lemon,
preferably organic, or more
or less to taste

sugar if necessary

Combine the oil and pine nuts in a skillet and set
over medium heat. Cook, stirring, until the nuts
are golden. Using a slotted spoon, remove them
from the pan and set aside.

Combine the lamb, onion, parsley, spices, salt, and
pepper in a bowl, kneading the meat well to make
it as smooth as possible. Add the pine nuts to the
mixture and continue kneading until the nuts are
well distributed. Shape the mixture into balls the
size of a small walnut and set aside on a rack to dry
for about 30 minutes. (For cocktail presentations,
i.e., to be eaten standing up, make the meatballs
smaller, the size of hazelnuts.)

When ready to cook, reheat the oil in the skillet
over medium heat and add the meatballs in one
layer (depending on the size of the skillet, you may
have to do this in batches). Brown the meatballs
rapidly, shaking and rolling the skillet to brown
them all over. Remove the browned meatballs and
set aside.

Remove and discard all but a tablespoon of the oil
in the skillet. Add the tomatoes and cook rapidly
over medium heat, breaking the tomatoes up with
the side of a spoon. Stir in the concentrate or

extract, along with ¼ to ½ cup of water. Cook down to a thick sauce, then stir in the lemon zest and juice and continue cooking for 5 minutes. Taste and add a little sugar or more lemon juice if it seems necessary. The sauce should have a distinctive sweet-tart flavor. Add the meatballs back to the skillet, lower the heat, and continue cooking, just at a simmer, for about 20 minutes, or until the sauce is thick and jammy and the meatballs are thoroughly cooked.

May be served immediately or set aside to serve at room temperature.

Andalucian Spiced Mini-Kebabs

Pinchos Morunos

>#{ Makes 10 to 12 servings

THESE ARE AMONG my all-time favorite tapas, little kebab-skewers of bite-size pieces of pork, lamb, or veal, macerated in an East-West blend of spices with garlic and pimentón or paprika. They're especially popular in Andalucia, where tapas first evolved, and they're a nifty accompaniment to a chilled glass of fino sherry or manzanilla. In Andalucian markets you can buy an already pre-pared mixture of spices but your own mixture, made up for the occasion, will be fresher and more interesting. Try the aromatic proportions suggested below, then, if you wish, adjust them to your own taste.

In Andalucia these are strung on little bamboo skewers that have been soaked in water so they don't burn. They're grilled over a charcoal brazier but you can also cook them under an oven broiler.

In my experience, pork is the best meat to use for pinchos, especially a cut such as country-style boneless ribs, with fat mixed with lean so the bits of meat don't dry out too much.

Serve these with drinks as part of a tapas tray, along with bowls of roasted salted almonds and spicy olives.

2 garlic cloves, minced

1 teaspoon sea salt

1 teaspoon coriander seeds

1 teaspoon cumin seeds

¼ teaspoon turmeric

2 teaspoons mildly hot
Spanish paprika (pimentón)

freshly ground black pepper

3 tablespoons extra-virgin
olive oil

1 tablespoon fresh lemon
juice

1¼ pounds pork, cut into
small pieces (about ½ inch to
a side)

Crush the garlic with the salt in a mortar until you
have a paste.

Combine the coriander and cumin seeds in a dry
skillet. Set over medium-low heat and toast for
several minutes, until the spicy aromas start to rise.
Transfer the spices to the mortar and pound gently
into the garlic paste. Mix in the turmeric, paprika,
lots of black pepper, the olive oil, and the lemon
juice. Transfer the mixture to a bowl.

Add the pork pieces and stir to mix well. Set aside,
covered, for at least an hour or so, or overnight.

Half an hour before you're ready to cook, if you're
using bamboo skewers, soak them in water for at
least 30 minutes. (You will need 10 to 12 short
skewers.) Get the grill or broiler ready to cook.

Thread the meat pieces on the skewers, 4 to 5
pieces to a skewer. Each piece should touch the
others but not be jammed tightly together.

When the grill or broiler is ready, cook the
skewers, turning them once, for a total cooking
time of 5 to 6 minutes. Remove from the heat and
serve immediately with a dry fino sherry or
Manzanilla from southern Spain.

Yogurt Marinated Chicken Kebabs

★ Makes 8 servings

USE SHORT BAMBOO SKEWERS for these mini-kebabs, first soaking the
skewers in water for 30 minutes or so. If you like them extra spicy, bump
up the chili pepper and cumin to a tablespoon, more or less, according to your
own taste.

1 pound boneless chicken, breast or thighs (or both)

3 plump garlic cloves, crushed with the flat blade of a knife

sea salt and freshly ground black pepper

1 teaspoon Middle Eastern red chili pepper

1 teaspoon ground cumin

1 small yellow onion, grated

1 tablespoon extra-virgin olive oil

½ cup plain yogurt (low-fat or nonfat is fine)

Cut the chicken meat into bite-size pieces. In a bowl combine the garlic with a teaspoon of salt. Using the back of a spoon, crush the garlic and salt to a paste. Stir in plenty of black pepper, the red pepper, cumin, grated onion, olive oil, and yogurt. Add the chicken, stir to mix, cover the bowl, and set aside to marinate for a couple of hours or overnight, refrigerating if necessary.

When ready to cook, prepare a charcoal grill or heat the oven broiler. Thread the pieces of chicken onto the skewers and grill or broil, turning frequently, until the chicken is done, about 8 to 10 minutes in all.

Serve immediately.

Variation: It doesn't take a lot of imagination to see that this little marinade would be fine with chicken wings, too, creating a variation on the ever-popular Buffalo wings.

Soups

✧ ✧ ✧

René Jouveau, in *Cuisine Provençale de Tradition Populaire*, a delightful collection of recipes, folklore, and foodways, quotes the old Provençal saying about the region's best-known soup: "L'aïgo boulido sauvo la vido," to which one responds with proper irony, "Au bout d'un tèms, tuio li gent." Aïgo boulido, Jouveau says, is nothing more or less than boiled water,* flavored with sage and garlic and poured over a crust of toasted bread that has been drizzled with olive oil. Boiled water saves lives, the saying goes; and the response: And after a time, it kills people off.

Savory it may be, but aïgo boulido is not very substantial, especially on a daily basis. Yet in its very meagerness it is typical of the make-do diets of poor country folk all around the Mediterranean. (Poor on a seasonal schedule, that is, for the same country folk may well become veritable gluttons at times of the year like Christmas and Easter, when more substantial fare is available.) Italian acquacotta (cooked water) is a similar preparation, and in Spain sopa de pan, by stressing the bread (pan), only emphasizes the soup's niggardly, penurious, parsimonious nature. The ingredients change from one place to another, but the principle remains the same: making do.

We made do one year in Seville. We were there for the Feria, the great post-Easter fair, and to see the great matador Ordóñez, who had come out of retirement once more, as he did periodically, to prove that he was still the star, if the aging star, of the corrida. The Feria is usually the second week after Easter, a time of nearly explosive joy like a richly earned reward

---

*I had always assumed, as many people do, that *aïgo* means "garlic." It doesn't. It means "water."

for the penance of Semana Santa, Holy Week, which the Sevillanos take very, very seriously. Decked in fragrant orange blossoms, the city is at its loveliest, and the ladies respond, young and old alike, dressing up in the flounce-tiered costumes of flamenco dancers with flowers tucked in their hair. Riding arrogantly behind their menfolk, they parade on handsomely groomed horses, and at night they dance the sevillana to the music of guitars.

It was romantic and prodigal, but places to stay were hard to come by. We ended up in an illegal bunk on the roof of a boardinghouse kept by a slovenly woman whose breath smelled of the candied violets she sucked between her teeth all day. We reeled about the city, drunk with the scent of orange blossoms, going from casita to casita visiting these terribly proper but warm and welcoming Sevillanos in the hospitality tents they had set up. We drank chilled fino sherry and nibbled freshly fried almonds and little pinchitos, miniature savory kebabs of pork or veal. At precisely five in the afternoon *("a las cinco en punto de la tarde,"* we said, quoting Lorca) we went to the bullfights and then, much later, home to the woman who smelled of violets and who gave us, as part of the demi-pension for which we had paid royally, sopa de pan, crusts of bread over which garlic-flavored water was poured and to which was added, at table, by the señora herself to prevent excess, a thin drizzle of a peculiarly rancid olive oil that we suspected had been used to fry the fish at lunch.

I will spare you the recipe for this meager soup, which exists, in one form or another, all over the Mediterranean. But good cooks should keep in mind the kinds of simple enrichments that are often added to such skimpy fare to dress it up a bit and make it more appealing. Garnishes and additions such as these can make something very special out of anything from a humble minestrone or bean soup to a clear chicken or veal stock, perhaps with a handful of rice or a few sherds of pasta floating in it. Such garnishes could include some, but never all, of the following:

- A thick slice of country-style bread, toasted, rubbed with a freshly cut clove of garlic, dribbled with flavorful extra-virgin olive oil, and set in the bottom of each soup plate (especially good with beans and thick vegetable soups);

- A handful of grated cheese—parmigiano reggiano, an aged sheep's milk cheese, or even a well-aged non-Mediterranean cheddar— sprinkled over the top of the soup at the moment of serving (this is very effective with clear chicken or veal broths);

- A big dollop of plain yogurt, nonfat or low-fat if you prefer (a nice fillip for almost any meat- or chicken-based soup);

- A swirl of your best extra-virgin olive oil spooned over the top of the soup, again at the moment of serving (de rigueur with almost anything);

- A couple of handfuls of the dried yogurt and grain mixture called *kishk* in Lebanon and *tarhana* or *trahana* in Greece and Turkey—available in shops in Greek and Middle Eastern neighborhoods (cooked in stock for 10 to 15 minutes, it turns any clear broth into a hearty potion);

- An egg—one per serving—either poached in the soup itself or beaten in a separate bowl, some of the hot liquid slowly beaten into the eggs, and then the eggs returned to the soup—which must not, from this point, come to a boil lest the eggs scramble, but which can be stirred gently over very low heat until the eggs thicken the broth slightly.

Not every one of these is appropriate for every kind of soup—you will have to use your own good judgment for that. But any one of them can help turn a humble country soup into an occasion.

Do keep in mind that soup can be an important building block in a healthy diet, an easy way to get more of those all-important vegetables and legumes onto your plate. Simple broths or vegetable purees, enriched with one or two of the garnishes I mentioned, are great starters for a meal, while a robust bean or seafood stew can make a meal on its own.

The recipes in this chapter are for what I think of as basic Mediterranean soups, made of seafood or vegetables or beans (sometimes with a little meat added), and they're found, in one form or another, throughout the region. The ingredients may change from north to south, east to west, but the principle remains the same. Think of the recipes as theme and variation.

I've also given directions for three basic stocks that are useful to have on hand and far superior to canned stocks or broths. All too often the commercial offerings, even when touted as "natural," "organic," and so forth, have unpleasantly sweet/salty flavors that detract considerably from the fresh taste of a well-made soup. I do keep a little supply of commercial stocks on hand for emergencies but homemade stock or broth, prepared with a fresh, local, free-range chicken and a tasty handful of aromatic vegetables—leeks, carrots, parsley, and so forth—adds so much to anything in which it's used that it's worth putting a little time and effort into the making of it. And fortunately, that's not at all difficult. Stocks freeze well, and there's added pleasure in knowing you have a freezer full of flavorful bases for all manner of soups, stews, and sauces. I like to freeze stocks in half-cup, cup, and pint containers, so I have convenient supplies for many different uses. But if you must thaw, say, a pint in order to use only half a cup, simply bring any remaining stock to a rapid boil for a minute or two and then refreeze.

Vegetable Broth

Makes about 2 quarts; 8 cups

V EGETABLE BROTHS as such are rarely used in Mediterranean cooking—this one is for the benefit of strict vegetarians.

2 medium yellow onions, quartered

3 carrots, peeled and cut into chunks

3 dark green outer celery stalks, cut into chunks

3 garlic cloves, lightly crushed with the flat blade of a knife

2 tablespoons extra-virgin olive oil

6 plump brown mushrooms, cleaned and quartered (cremini or shiitake are more flavorful than ordinary supermarket mushrooms; wild mushrooms, if you can find them, are best of all)

1 cup dry white wine

9 cups hot water

1 fat leek, rinsed carefully

1 fennel bulb, including the leafy green tops, chopped

1 tablespoon chopped fresh thyme or 1 teaspoon dried, crumbled

1 3-inch cinnamon stick (optional)

6 whole cloves (optional)

6 slices of dried porcini mushrooms

sea salt and freshly ground black pepper

Preheat the oven to 425 degrees. In a flameproof glass or metal baking dish, turn the onions, carrots, celery, and garlic in the olive oil to coat them well. Roast for 15 minutes; then add the mushrooms and stir to mix well. Return to the oven for another 15 minutes, after which the vegetables should be brown and crispy on the edges and should give off a delicious aroma. Remove the dish from the oven and scrape the vegetables into a heavy stockpot or soup kettle. Add the wine to the oven dish and set over medium heat. Cook the wine, scraping up the brown bits in the pan, until it is slightly reduced, about 10 minutes, then add to the stockpot with the hot water. Add the leek, fennel, thyme, cinnamon, and cloves. Bring the stock to a simmer over medium-low heat, cover, and cook for at least 1 hour.

Meanwhile, put the dried mushrooms in a 1-cup measure and fill with boiling water. Let soak for 15 minutes. Remove the mushrooms (do not discard the soaking liquid) and rinse under running water to get rid of grit. Chop them coarsely and add to the stockpot along with the soaking liquid, strained through a fine-mesh sieve.

When the stock has finished cooking, strain it through a double layer of cheesecloth or a fine-mesh sieve. Discard the vegetables and aromatics. Taste the broth for seasoning, adding salt and pepper if necessary—be mindful of the salt, however, because reducing the broth later may concentrate the salt too much.

Chicken Stock

Makes 2½ to 3 quarts; 10 to 12 cups

THE CHICKENS I BUY in Italy are plump old ladies with their heads and feet, the source of much flavor, still attached. In this country I don't even bother making chicken stock with the widely available commercial birds—you can cook them forever and still get a bland and flavorless stock because the things don't have any flavor to yield anyway. Try farmers' markets and natural foods stores for chickens raised in a certain amount of freedom and fed on nonmedicated grains (so-called free-range or naturally raised chickens). This is the only way to get the flavorful chickens you need for good stock, or for any other chicken dish for that matter. If you can't find a boiling fowl, use a roaster. Or use a combination of chicken necks, backs, wings, and innards.

1 4- to 5-pound chicken or 4 to 5 pounds chicken parts, including wings and backs

2 onions, quartered

2 garlic cloves, crushed with the flat blade of a knife

1 medium to large carrot, peeled and quartered

½ cup chopped flat-leaf parsley

1 tablespoon fresh thyme or 1 teaspoon dried, crumbled

1 3-inch cinnamon stick (optional)

about 10 cups cold water

sea salt and freshly ground black pepper

Put all the ingredients except the salt, pepper, and water in a heavy stockpot or soup kettle. Add the cold water, or more if necessary to cover the bird. Over medium-low heat, slowly bring the liquid to a simmer. For the clearest stock, carefully skim the froth as it rises to the top. When the foam has ceased rising, cover the pot and cook at a slow simmer for at least 1¼ hours or longer if necessary. (A boiling fowl, depending on age, may take 2½ hours to cook thoroughly.) The bird should be so thoroughly cooked that it's starting to fall apart.

At the end of the cooking time, strain the stock through a double layer of cheesecloth or a fine-mesh sieve. Discard the vegetables and aromatics. The chicken meat will have given up most of its flavor, but if you wish to use some of it as a garnish for a soup, dice it and set aside. Taste the strained stock and add salt and pepper if desired. Be wary of too much salt—if the stock is to be reduced later, it will concentrate. Put the strained stock in the refrigerator to let the fat rise and solidify, after which it can be removed easily with a slotted spoon.

Variation: If you wish to make a golden brown stock, combine the chicken parts, onions, garlic, and carrot with 2 tablespoons of extra-virgin olive oil in the bottom of the stockpot. Set over medium heat and cook, turning the chicken and vegetables frequently until the chicken parts are browned. Then add the remaining ingredients and cook as directed.

Fish Stock

Makes 6 to 7 cups; 6 to 7 servings

FISH STOCK, IDEALLY, is made with the heads and bones of large white-fleshed fish like cod or haddock that have been cut up for fillets. There's a good deal of flesh left on the bones and in the head, and this gives flavor to the stock. The carcasses of any white-fleshed fish can be used—monkfish, snapper, weakfish, or whatever is available at your fishmonger. Do not use oily fish such as bluefish, mackerel, or salmon, however, because the taste is too strong.

In some parts of the country it may be next to impossible to get fish trimmings for stock. In that case, use a commercially prepared fish stock or a dehydrated mix—but do add the aromatics, wine, and vegetables to give it as distinctive a taste as possible. (Bottled clam juice is usually too salty.) In the absence of anything else, use a piece of plain frozen fish fillet, add the aromatics, vegetables, and wine, and simmer for 30 minutes or so—it won't be as rich and savory as using fish heads, but it's better than plain water. (Discard the fillet and aromatics after simmering.)

head and bones of 1 4- to 6-pound fish, preferably haddock, cod, or snapper

2 bay leaves

[cont. next page]

Place the fish head and bones in a heavy soup kettle or stockpot along with the bay leaves, carrot, onion, peppercorns, and parsley. Add the wine and cold water. Bring to a boil slowly, cover, turn the heat down, and simmer for 45 minutes. Strain the broth when done and discard the solids. Taste the

1 medium carrot, peeled and cut in half lengthwise

1 medium onion, halved

12 black peppercorns

12 flat-leaf parsley sprigs

1 cup dry white wine

6 cups cold water

sea salt and freshly ground white pepper

broth and add salt and pepper if desired, keeping in mind that the salt will be concentrated if the stock is later reduced.

A Note About Seafood Soups

Seafood soups, on the whole, require more time and forethought than other kinds of soup, at least in part because, for those who don't live in or near a fishing port, it isn't always easy to assemble good-quality ingredients. The Mediterranean abounds in different kinds of seafood soups and stews (I sometimes feel that every tiny fishing village has its own authentic soup, different from all others and just as good). Because of the different kinds of fish available in the Mediterranean, however, a real, authentic bouillabaisse or *kakavia* or *zuppa di pesce* is almost impossible to re-create in North America. But we can take inspiration, ideas, and flavors from the Mediterranean and, using the abundant varieties of seafood available to us, make up great fish and seafood soups of our own.

Above all, don't feel that you must duplicate each and every ingredient in the recipes that follow. If you can only get frozen shrimp and fresh haddock fillets, you can still put together a very special dish for friends or family by following these recipes.

Seafood soups do not freeze well, so if you're on your own and can't consume these in one or two meals, it's best to save them for when you have six or eight people gathered around your table.

Mediterranean Fish Soup

The Basic Recipe

Makes 8 to 10 servings

ZARZUELA, BOUILLABAISSE, BRODETTO, Greek *kakavia,* Tuscan *cacciucco,* Turkish *baliksi çorbasi,* and so on: the flavoring of these fish and seafood soups changes from one part of the Mediterranean to another. A little chopped wild fennel and a strip of dried orange peel mark a soup as Provençal, while the bright color and slightly musty flavor of saffron may indicate Spanish or Maghrebi ancestry, and a thickening of egg yolks and lemon juice, beaten together and stirred into the hot soup so that the broth naps the pieces of seafood with a creamy velour, is a technique of Greek and Turkish cooks. But while aromas and flavors vary, the basic preparation is consistent. Aromatics—leeks, garlic, a little chopped white onion, a handful of freshly picked parsley—are gently stewed in olive oil; the fish is added, perhaps with chopped ripe tomatoes or a glass of white wine; then water or fish stock and seasonings such as salt, pepper, a branch of thyme, a bay leaf, and, on the island of Cyprus, a short length of cinnamon stick are added, and the soup is set to cook.

The procedure may look daunting at first, but it is actually very simple and logical, and the most complicated parts of the cooking can often be done well ahead and the whole thing assembled at the last minute.

These fish soups can be made with a single variety of fish, but more often they are composed of several different kinds, as well as shellfish—mussels, clams, razor clams, crabs—shrimp or rock lobster, and squid or cuttlefish or pieces of octopus. When a number of different fish are used, of course, the cook must pay careful attention to cooking times so that the result is not a mishmash of disintegrating seafood. One caution: strong-flavored, oily fish like mackerel, salmon, and bluefish are not appropriate for these soups; save them for the grill.

It is often said that a true bouillabaisse, by all accounts the apotheosis of Mediterranean fish soup, can be made only in or near the port of Marseilles and that the preparation, to be genuine and authentic, must include the little spiny scorpion fish, called *rascasse* in French, that lend so much flavor, but very little substance, to the broth. That may well be, but a very fine Mediterranean-style fish soup can be made anywhere in the world where there is access to a variety of first-rate fresh fish—try haddock as the main ingredient on the East Coast, fresh Alaska halibut in the Pacific Northwest, red snapper and drum in the Southeast, redfish along the Gulf, or whatever looks good and fresh at the fishmonger that day. Supplies are getting better and better all over the country, and cooks in the interior, who once had to rely on a meager selection of frozen fish, now have access to excellent fresh fish. And frozen fish itself has improved enormously in quality in recent years. Even in large supermarkets the fish counter seems to be one place where the customer still has rights—don't be afraid to assert them.

In the Mediterranean, fish soup is usually served as the main course, with all the fish, shellfish, clams, and so forth piled into a deep bowl along with the broth in which they were cooked. But you could also serve the broth on its own as a starter, possibly adding a handful of rice or small shapes of pasta, or with a slice of toasted, garlic-rubbed, olive-oil-bathed bread in the bottom of each bowl; then follow the starter with the seafood itself as a main course, perhaps with a green sauce (sauce verte, page 270) or a dollop of aïoli (page 274).

½ cup dry white wine

½ cup water

20 hard-shell mahogany or Manila clams, the smaller the better, well scrubbed, or 20 mussels, well scrubbed

2 cups fish stock (page 109)

¼ cup extra-virgin olive oil

2 medium yellow onions, chopped

1 fat leek, white part only, rinsed well and sliced into julienne strips

3 garlic cloves, chopped

3 very ripe tomatoes, peeled, seeded (page 25), and chopped or 3 or 4 whole canned tomatoes, drained and chopped

1 tablespoon tomato extract, tomato concentrate, or sun-dried tomato paste

First, prepare the clams or mussels; combine the wine and water in a saucepan and set over medium heat. As soon as the liquid starts to simmer, add the mollusks, cover, and steam until the shells open—5 to 7 minutes. As each one opens, remove it from the liquid and set aside, leaving the shells intact. If after 10 minutes there are mollusks that refuse to open, remove and discard them.

Strain the wine broth through a fine-mesh sieve or several layers of cheesecloth directly into the fish stock. You should have 3 cups of combined fish stock and wine broth. If it's a little scant, add water or wine to bring it to 3 cups.

Add the olive oil to a casserole, Dutch oven, or similar heavy pot that is somewhat wider than it is tall and large enough to accommodate all the ingredients. You should have about ¼ inch of olive oil in the bottom of the pot. Set the pot over medium-low heat and when the oil is hot, add the onions, leek, and garlic. Cook, stirring occasionally, until the vegetables have softened and turned golden, about 20 minutes. Do not let the

1 bay leaf

1 teaspoon minced fresh thyme or ½ teaspoon dried, crumbled

1 teaspoon sea salt, or to taste

2½ pounds firm white-fleshed fish, such as wolffish, monkfish, cod, haddock, or halibut, boned and cut into serving pieces

1½ pounds medium (36–40 count) shrimp

4 squid, cleaned and cut into rings

freshly ground black pepper

2 tablespoons chopped flat-leaf parsley

vegetables brown.

Stir in the tomatoes, tomato extract or concentrate, bay leaf, and thyme, and continue cooking for about 30 minutes, until much of the liquid has evaporated and the tomatoes have melted into the onions. Add the salt.

Add the fish stock, raise the heat to medium, and, when the stock starts to simmer, add the pieces of fish. Simmer for 2 minutes, then add the shrimp, and 2 minutes later distribute the squid rings over the surface of the stew. Cook for approximately 3 to 5 minutes longer or until the seafood is thoroughly cooked but not overcooked—about 10 minutes in all. Add the clams or mussels in their shells for the last 90 seconds—just long enough to heat them thoroughly. Remove from the heat and, just before serving, sprinkle with generous amounts of pepper and the parsley.

Variations: There are almost as many variations on the basic Mediterranean fish soup as there are port towns and fishing villages in the Mediterranean. Here are just a few:

- A Catalan version, described in Colman Andrews's *Catalan Cuisine,* calls for ½ teaspoon each of ground cinnamon and ground allspice, added with the tomatoes, plus ½ cup each of dark rum and sherry, added with the fish stock.

- In Provence, cooks add a fresh fennel bulb, thickly sliced, with the onions, leek, and garlic, and a good strip of orange zest with the tomatoes; if you have dried fennel pollen, a sprinkle of that will add essential flavor to a Provençal fish stew, as will a dollop of anise-flavored liqueur, such as ouzo or Pernod.

- For an Italian *zuppa di pesce,* add lots of slivered fresh basil, a handful of capers, and a handful of pitted black olives at the end.

- *Bourdetto* or *bourtheto,* from the Greek island of

Corfu, adds potatoes to the basic stew along with lots more finely chopped onions and, a distinguishing mark, a goodly sum of ground hot red chili pepper.

- North Africans also add chili to the soup, often in the form of their favorite sauce, harissa (page 279), as well as a big spoonful of ground cumin.

- In Aegean Greece, a couple of tablespoons of freshly squeezed lemon juice are stirred into the pot at the very end, while in the Adriatic the lemon juice is replaced by aged red wine vinegar.

Greek Seafood Stew with Vegetables

Kakaviá

*Makes 6 to 8 servings

THE GREEK VERSION of Mediterranean fish soup is called *kakaviá* (the name comes from *kakavi*, the cauldron in which the soup is prepared). Greeks claim it as the original, the ur-soup from which all others are descended. After all, they say, it was Phocaean Greeks who established Massilia (modern Marseilles) in 600 B.C. or thereabouts, and no doubt brought with them from the mother country *kakaviá*, which down through the ages evolved into bouillabaisse. Of course, the original was a little different from modern *kakaviá* and quite unlike modern bouillabaisse but it makes a good story nonetheless.

The best kind of orange to use in this, for both zest and juice, is a bitter or sour orange, sometimes called Seville orange. They aren't easy to find (most of them go into marmalade) and they are strictly seasonal (February is when you're apt to find them); if you can't locate one, use the zest of a regular sweet orange and mix the orange juice half and half with grapefruit or lemon juice. The anise-flavored liqueur used should not be a syrupy liqueur, like sambuca, but rather like an unsweetened ouzo or arak.

Note that the saffron should steep ahead of time for several hours or overnight.

a big pinch of saffron

2 medium yellow onions, peeled, halved, and thinly sliced

1 fat leek (or 2 slender ones), trimmed and thinly sliced

¼ cup extra-virgin olive oil

2 medium carrots, coarsely chopped

2 celery stalks, including leaves, coarsely chopped

1 medium fennel bulb, including leafy tops, chopped

4 fresh, ripe tomatoes, peeled (page 25) and chopped, or 6 canned plum tomatoes, chopped

2 garlic cloves, chopped

1 small dried red chili pepper

1 teaspoon fresh thyme leaves or ½ teaspoon dried, crumbled

3 bay leaves

zest of 1 orange, preferably bitter orange (see headnote)

¼ cup anise-flavored liqueur (ouzo, arak, Pernod, or Ricard)

2 pounds boneless, firm white-fleshed fish, such as halibut, haddock, wolffish, monkfish, cod, or a combination, cut into 8 serving pieces

1 pound medium shrimp, preferably fresh, peeled but tails left on

½ cup bitter orange juice or ¼ cup sweet orange juice and ¼ cup lemon or grapefruit juice

minced flat-leaf parsley for garnish

Put the saffron in a half-cup measure and fill the measure with hot water. Set aside to steep for several hours or overnight.

Combine the onions and leeks with the olive oil in a large heavy soup kettle or saucepan. Set over medium-low heat and cook, stirring occasionally, until the vegetables are very soft, about 20 minutes. Do not let the vegetables brown.

Once the onions and leeks are soft, stir in the carrots, celery, fennel, tomatoes, and garlic. Add the chili pepper, thyme, and bay leaves and stir to mix well. Let cook gently for 10 minutes, then add the orange zest, the liqueur, and 5 cups water. Bring to a simmer and let simmer gently, uncovered, for 20 minutes, then stir in the saffron and its water, and the fish. Let the fish pieces simmer for about 5 minutes, then stir in the shrimp and continue simmering until the shrimp have changed color, indicating that they are cooked through.

Remove the *kakaviá* from the stove and transfer the fish and shrimp to a deep serving platter. Add the citrus juice to the liquid in the pan and return to a simmer, then pour over the fish in the platter. Sprinkle with freshly minced parsley and serve immediately.

Variation: You could, if you wish, make this Greek chowder with only shrimp or only fish, depending on what's available in your market. If you find some nice calamari or squid that have not been treated with chemicals to bleach them (not an easy thing to find these days), add a few small squid, whole or cut in rings, to the mixture.

It's not Greek, but a dollop of Provençal aïoli (page 274) is terrific with this soup.

Mussel or Clam Soup
from the South of France

Makes 4 servings

T HIS DELICIOUSLY GOLDEN SOUP, which comes from the territory around Nice, is traditionally made with mussels but I have also made it with hard-shell clams (cherrystones, mahoganies, or Manilas), and it's every bit as tasty. This is another great soup to serve over slices of toasted bread, rubbed with garlic and dribbled liberally with olive oil. (See About Mussels, page 117, before cooking.)

a pinch of saffron threads

2 medium onions, coarsely chopped

3 garlic cloves, crushed with the flat blade of a knife

1 bay leaf

2 cups water

2 quarts hard-shell clams or mussels, rinsed, the mussels cleaned of their beards if necessary and gaping mussels or clams discarded

3 tablespoons extra-virgin olive oil

1 leek, white part only, rinsed well and sliced

1 small fennel bulb, chopped

1 teaspoon chopped fresh thyme or ½ teaspoon dried, crumbled

2 tomatoes, chopped, or canned whole tomatoes, drained and crushed with a fork

dry white wine as needed

⅓ cup vermicelli, broken into 1-inch lengths

sea salt and freshly ground black pepper

Mix the saffron in a cup with a couple of tablespoons of very hot water and set aside to steep.

Combine half the onions, 2 garlic cloves, and the bay leaf with the water and bring to a boil in a soup kettle large enough to hold all the clams or mussels. As soon as the water boils, add the shellfish and steam until they are all fully open—about 10 minutes. Discard any that have not opened after this point.

As soon as they are cool enough to handle, remove the clams or mussels from their shells and set the meat aside with a teaspoon of the olive oil drizzled over it to keep it from drying out. Strain the broth through a fine-mesh sieve to rid it of all sand. Set aside.

In another pan over medium heat, sauté the remaining onion, remaining garlic clove, and leek in the remaining olive oil until the vegetables are soft but not brown—about 10 minutes. Add the fennel, thyme, and tomatoes and cook together for a few minutes, until the tomatoes have released their juices. Add enough wine to the strained broth to make up 1 quart, then pour the liquid into the vegetables in the pan. Cook briefly to evaporate the alcohol from the wine, then add the saffron with its soaking liquid and the vermicelli and cook about 10 minutes or just until tender. Taste the soup and add salt or pepper if desired. Add the mussels or clams, and when they are just heated through, serve the soup over toasted bread slices. (Don't let the soup come to a boil, or the shellfish will toughen.)

Garnish with a dollop of olive oil, a little handful of minced flat-leaf parsley, or a very little grated parmigiano cheese.

ABOUT MUSSELS

Mussels used to be a bother to clean, so much so that many cooks felt it wasn't worth the effort. But with cultivated mussels widely available, it's a whole lot easier. You should still pick them over carefully before cooking and discard any with cracked or gaping shells. Using a sharp little paring knife, pull or cut away the beard—but only do this right before cooking them. Bring a scant inch of water (or dry white wine) to a boil in the bottom of a pot in which the mussels will fit in a crowded single layer—if you have a lot of mussels you may wish to cook them in several batches. Bring to a boil and add the mussels, cooking them just until they open—in about 5 to 7 minutes. Remove the mussels as they open and if, after 10 minutes or so, there are any that simply do not open, discard them. Then strain the mussel liquor through a fine-mesh sieve or several layers of cheesecloth to get rid of any sand or grit. The flavorful but often quite salty liquid may be added to any seafood stew or broth.

If you gather mussels from the wild, be absolutely certain that the waters from which you harvest them are clean—local departments of fish and wildlife or marine fisheries (the name varies from one state to another) can advise you about where and when to harvest.

Aegean Fish Soup with Rice

Asplendid Turkish take on the traditional Mediterranean fish soup, this was made for lunch one day by the skipper of the *Hasret,* a 72-foot *golet* or motor sailer that cruises the south Turkish coast out of the ancient port of Bodrum (once Halicarnassos, birthplace of Herodotus). Captain Bayram makes the soup from time to time when a coastal fishing vessel ties up next to *Hasret* with a particularly good catch. He prefers rather large Mediterranean groupers, called in Turkish *orfoz* or *lahoz,* but on the Atlantic shores I have made the soup successfully with firm white-fleshed fish like cod or haddock. Halibut is also a good choice.

Be sure to soak the rice overnight—it adds both comforting density and delicate flavor to the broth.

1 quart fish stock (page 109) plus 2 cups water, or 6 cups water

2 Turkish bay leaves

1 teaspoon dried oregano, crumbled

1 teaspoon freshly ground black pepper

1 dried ancho chili

1 large onion, quartered

1 large carrot, peeled and cut into chunks

2 ripe medium tomatoes, quartered, or 3 canned tomatoes, drained and quartered

1 3- to 3½-pound whole fish or about 2 pounds fish steaks or fillets: cod, haddock, halibut, sea bass, or snapper

2 tablespoons extra-virgin olive oil, to taste

1 large potato, peeled and cut into bite-size cubes

Combine the stock and water in a stockpot and add the bay leaves, oregano, pepper, chili, onion, carrot, and tomatoes. Bring to a boil and cook over medium-low heat until the vegetables are very soft, about 30 to 40 minutes. Strain the stock, pressing the vegetables firmly to extract all the juices.

Return the strained stock to the pan and add the fish. Cook the fish at a slow simmer until the flesh flakes easily. Boneless fillets will cook in 2 to 3 minutes, depending on their thickness; a whole fish may take 25 to 30 minutes. Remove the fish when done and, if you're using a whole fish or fish steaks, discard the skin and bones. Set the flesh aside in a bowl, drizzling 1 tablespoon of oil over the top to keep it from drying out.

Add the potato to the stock and cook, covered, over medium heat for 10 to 15 minutes or until the potato pieces are tender. Using a slotted spoon, remove and pile on top of the fish pieces. Drizzle another tablespoon of oil over the top of the potatoes.

⅓ cup long-grain white rice, soaked overnight in 1 cup water

2 large eggs

juice of 2 lemons

¼ teaspoon hot red pepper flakes, or more to taste

sea salt and freshly ground black pepper

finely chopped flat-leaf parsley for garnish

Add the rice to the fish stock and cook, covered, very slowly and gently for another 30 to 40 minutes. The rice should disintegrate into the stock and give it a slightly gelatinous consistency. The recipe may be made ahead of time up to this point.

When you're ready to serve, add the fish and potatoes to the stock and return it slowly to a simmer. In a bowl, beat together the eggs and lemon juice until thoroughly blended. Slowly beat a ladleful of hot stock into the egg mixture and continue adding ladlefuls, one by one, beating constantly, until the egg mixture is close to the temperature of the simmering stock. Carefully stir the hot egg mixture into the stock. Continue to cook for a few minutes, stirring constantly, until the stock has thickened slightly. Do not let the stock boil, or the eggs will scramble.

When the soup is pleasantly thickened, remove from the heat and stir in the hot pepper flakes as well as salt and black pepper. Serve immediately, garnished with a little parsley.

Mediterranean Vegetable Soup

Minestrone

THE BASIC RECIPE

Makes 6 to 8 servings

THERE ARE AS MANY VARIATIONS of Mediterranean vegetable soup, or minestrone, as there are of Mediterranean fish soup. All rely on a panoply of fresh seasonal vegetables, and for vegetarians especially they offer a rewarding study. While pancetta (unsmoked Italian bacon), bacon, or some other type of preserved pork often adds richness to the broth, the meat is just as often left out entirely, and the richness comes from a dollop of finest-quality olive oil added at the very end as the soup is served. In Italy, freshly grated parmigiano cheese is always added at the table, and leftover minestrone forms the basis for another frugal soup, the Tuscan favorite called *ribollita* (boiled again!), the next day.

As with fish soups, the technique is similar no matter where you are: aromatics (including pancetta or prosciutto or bacon, if you wish) are sautéed in olive oil, then the vegetables and broth are added. Finally, an enrichment of oil, grated cheese, or whatever is added just before serving.

I've evolved the following basic recipe over the years from the minestrone described by Pellegrino Artusi in *La Scienza in cucina e l'arte di mangiar bene,* a great cookbook first published in Florence in 1891, still in print (my copy is the 109th edition of the original) and still used regularly in northern Italian home kitchens.

Don't be constrained by the vegetables listed, Artusi counsels—almost anything fresh and seasonal is a happy addition to this spectrum. Cabbage-family vegetables (cabbage itself, Brussels sprouts, turnips, kohlrabi, and so forth) should be added at the end or cooked separately. If cooked a long time in the soup, their strong flavors will dominate.

½ cup white beans, such as cannellini or Great Northern, or borlotti (cranberry) beans, soaked overnight, or use the quick-soak method (page 25)

6 cups chicken stock (page 108), vegetable broth (page 107), or water

½ green or Savoy cabbage, slivered

3 or 4 large leaves of red or white Swiss chard, slivered

1 tablespoon finely minced pancetta or prosciutto

1 garlic clove, minced

¼ cup chopped flat-leaf parsley

¼ cup finely chopped onion

2 tablespoons extra-virgin olive oil

2 celery stalks, sliced

In a small covered saucepan, simmer the drained beans in about 2 cups of the stock until tender but not falling apart—40 minutes to 1 hour, depending on the age of the beans. When done, set aside in the cooking liquid.

Rinse the slivered cabbage and chard in running water and steam for about 15 minutes in the water clinging to the leaves, adding a few tablespoons of water if necessary to keep the vegetables from scorching. When the vegetables are tender but not falling apart, set aside.

Combine the pancetta, garlic, parsley, and onion and sauté gently in the oil in a heavy stockpot or soup kettle large enough to hold all the vegetables and the stock until just tender but not brown—about 10 to 15 minutes.

Add the remaining vegetables to the pot along with the remaining broth. Bring to a simmer, cover, and cook gently for 20 to 30 minutes, just until the vegetables are tender. Add the cabbage,

2 medium carrots, peeled and diced

1 large potato, peeled and diced

1 large or 2 small zucchini, diced

½ pound ripe tomatoes, peeled (page 25) and chopped, or about 6 canned whole tomatoes, drained and chopped

other vegetables, such as green beans or peas, greens (kale, turnip greens, broccoli), leeks, pumpkin, acorn or butternut squash, turnips, diced or slivered, as desired

sea salt and freshly ground black pepper

½ cup Arborio rice

6 to 8 tablespoons freshly grated parmigiano cheese

the chard, and the beans with their cooking liquid. Taste the soup and add salt and pepper if you wish. Stir in the rice and continue cooking for 15 to 20 minutes or until the rice is done. Remove from the heat and serve immediately, with a spoonful of grated cheese on top of each serving.

Variations: In Majorca, roasted and peeled sweet red peppers, cut into strips, are added, along with a little hot red pepper.

In Lucca, in the lower Arno Valley, a springtime minestrone called *garmugia* includes spring onions, fresh fava beans and peas, diced hearts of small artichokes, and the tips of fresh asparagus, served up with a dollop of the fine, light olive oil for which the region is famous.

In Provence the magnificent soup called *pistou* ("Pee stew!" said Nicholas, age four, when I told him what we were having for supper) is made by stirring a healthy dollop of fragrant basil sauce, similar to Italian pesto, into the basic vegetable mixture at the end. To make pistou sauce, pound in a mortar 3 crushed garlic cloves, 1 cup firmly packed fresh basil leaves, and a pinch of salt. When the mixture is a paste, stir in 3 tablespoons freshly grated parmigiano and 2 or 3 tablespoons extra-virgin olive oil. You may also substitute a handful of broken vermicelli for the rice in the original.

Tuscan *ribollita,* an old-fashioned peasant dish once scorned by the gentry and now enjoying tremendous vogue, is made with leftover minestrone, one in which rustic white or borlotti beans are dominant and bourgeois rice is absent. The leftover soup is reheated the next day with 4 or 5 slices of good country bread torn into chunks and mixed in to absorb all the soup's juices. A healthy dollop of the best-quality extra-virgin, preferably unfiltered, olive oil is poured over the top of the very thick soup before serving—robust fare!

In the eastern Mediterranean, and especially in Islamic countries, mutton or preserved mutton (*qawarma*) takes the place of prosciutto, pancetta, or other pork products. To give a vegetable soup an eastern flavor, sauté some lean cubed lamb with the onions and garlic and add a cinnamon stick and a small amount of allspice to the seasoning of the soup.

Tomato Soup with Rice and Lemon from the Eastern Mediterranean

Makes 6 to 8 servings

THIS SOUP HAS MAXIMUM IMPACT late in August and early in September, at the height of tomato season. Take the time to seek out red, ripe, juicy tomatoes from a local farmer who grows them. There's just no point in trying to make something tasty from out-of-season and flavorless ingredients.

2 medium onions, coarsely chopped

1 medium leek, trimmed and sliced

1 garlic clove, crushed

3 tablespoons extra-virgin olive oil

About 6 pounds red, ripe tomatoes, peeled, seeded (page 25), and quartered

sea salt

a pinch of sugar, or to taste

grated zest of half an organic lemon

3 fresh thyme sprigs or ½ teaspoon dried thyme, crumbled

1 bay leaf

Combine the onions, leek, and garlic with the oil in a saucepan large enough to hold all the tomatoes, set the pan over medium-low heat, and cook until the onions are soft and golden, but not brown, about 10 to 15 minutes. Toss in the tomatoes and add salt, sugar, grated lemon zest, thyme, and bay leaf. Stir to mix well and bring to a boil. The tomatoes should exude a good deal of juice but if necessary, add chicken or vegetable stock or plain water. Cook, uncovered, for about 20 minutes or until the tomatoes are thoroughly cooked and disintegrating.

Remove the bay leaf and puree the soup. You may do this with a stick blender right in the saucepan or transfer the contents to a food processor or vegetable mill. Once pureed, return the soup to the pan over medium heat and when the soup is

2 cups chicken or vegetable stock or water if necessary

½ cup long-grain rice

2 egg yolks

juice of 1 lemon

a pinch of dried red chili pepper (optional)

freshly ground black pepper

garnishes (optional): ¼ cup slivered fresh basil leaves; extra-virgin olive oil; and/or a little handful of small bread cubes or croutons gently browned in olive oil

simmering once more, add the rice. Let cook for about 20 minutes, or until the rice is very soft.

Meanwhile, beat the egg yolks to a thick foam, then slowly beat in the lemon juice, making an avgolemono. When the rice is very soft, take a ladleful of soup and slowly beat it into the avgolemono, then another and another. This tempers the egg sauce so it won't shock into stiffness when it's stirred into the soup. Now turn the heat down under the soup so that it is barely simmering, and, stirring constantly, slowly tip the egg sauce into the soup. You must not let the soup come to a boil for fear of curdling the sauce, but you do want to let it warm and thicken to a rich texture. When the soup is thick enough to coat a spoon, remove from the heat, add plenty of black pepper and one or more of the garnishes listed, and serve immediately.

Variation: Some cooks add a short piece of cinnamon stick along with the bay leaf; if you like the flavor of cinnamon, by all means do so. Also, in some parts of Greece, bulgur wheat is used in place of the rice. Soak ½ cup of bulgur for about 20 minutes in warm water, then strain in a colander before you add it to the soup.

Tuscan Onion Soup

Carabaccia

Makes 6 to 8 servings

Tuscans claim they taught the French how to cook, and they cite this very tasty onion soup as evidence. It's the ancestor, they say, of French soupe à l'oignon. It was Caterina de' Medici, they also say, who brought onion soup, along with forks, petits pois, parsley, and artichokes, to France when she was sent over the Alps to marry the future Henri II in 1533. (The French, predictably, deny that anything of the sort ever happened.)

Nonetheless, there are ancient Tuscan recipes for onion soup going back to the 14th century that sound and taste very much like the onion soups made in Tuscany, and in France, to this day. This is a first-rate example of how the simple good things of the Mediterranean countryside, the work of humble farmhouse cooks, have persisted over the centuries.

Pancetta is the Italian version of unsmoked bacon, widely used all over the Mediterranean and widely available in North America, too.

2 ounces pancetta, cut in small dice

2 medium carrots, coarsely chopped

2 celery stalks, coarsely chopped

¼ cup coarsely chopped flat-leaf parsley

2 tablespoons extra-virgin olive oil

2 pounds yellow onions, very thinly sliced

sea salt and freshly ground black pepper

4 cups chicken stock (page 108), or stock and water mixed

½ cup dry white wine

½ cup freshly grated aged pecorino or parmigiano reggiano, plus more for passing at the table

slices of toasted country-style bread

Combine the pancetta, carrots, celery, parsley, and oil in a heavy saucepan over medium-low heat and cook very gently until the fat starts to run. Add the onions, with salt and pepper, and stir to mix well. Cook very gently, covered, for 1 hour while the onions soften and give off considerable liquid. If the liquid is insufficient and the onions start to brown, add a little of the broth or plain water—but the idea of this initial cooking is that it should be so gentle that the onions never do actually brown but rather simply turn golden and deepen in color. In the end, they should be reduced to a soft, golden mass.

At the end of the cooking time, add the wine and raise the heat slightly to burn off the alcohol. When the alcohol has evaporated, add the remaining broth. Cook at a steady simmer, uncovered, for about 15 minutes. Stir in the cheese, taste, and adjust the seasoning.

Serve immediately over toasted bread slices and pass more grated cheese at the table.

Castilian Garlic Soup

Sopa de Ajo

Makes 4 servings

*S*OPA DE AJO is a classic soup from the high central plateau of Castile, where it's a welcome winter treat when chill winds sweep across the meseta. But it's even better made in summer when fresh, new garlic is in season. Farmers' markets in North America usually have fresh garlic from about the middle of July. Its sweet and delicate flavor is a revelation to those of us who only know dried stored garlic from the supermarket. Spanish cooks often float a poached egg on the surface of the hot soup to enrich it further but it's also good just with a toasted slice of country-style bread, perhaps rubbed liberally with a cut clove of garlic as soon as it comes out of the toaster.

A well-flavored homemade chicken stock is essential for this. For the dried red pepper, use a chili pepper that is on the sweet side, piquant but not too fiercely hot, such as Spanish ñoras, Aleppo pepper, or piment d'Espelette. If you like the smoky flavor, Spanish pimentón de la Vera is also a good choice.

5 or 6 whole heads of garlic, the cloves separated and peeled (about 1 cup or ½ pound of peeled garlic cloves)

¼ cup extra-virgin olive oil

1 tablespoon dried red chili pepper

6 cups chicken stock (page 108)

⅓ cup Spanish amontillado or oloroso sherry

a pinch of ground cumin

a pinch of saffron threads

sea salt

[cont. next page]

In a heavy soup kettle or a 2-quart saucepan, gently cook the garlic in the olive oil over low heat until the cloves are thoroughly softened, about 10 to 15 minutes. Do not let the cloves get brown. Remove them with a slotted spoon and set aside.

Stir the red chili pepper into the hot oil in the pan, then add the stock and sherry. Bring to a simmer while you stir in the cumin and saffron.

Use a fork to crush the tender garlic cloves to a paste and stir the paste into the soup. Taste and add salt if necessary. Cover the soup and leave to simmer very gently for about 15 minutes.

While the soup cooks, toast the bread slices. Cut the garlic clove in half and rub over the toasted slices. If you want to add an egg to each serving, poach the eggs gently in simmering acidulated water (water to which a couple of spoonfuls of white vinegar have

4 half-inch-thick slices of crusty bread

1 garlic clove

4 poached eggs (optional)

freshly grated manchego cheese (optional)

been added), remove with a slotted spoon when done to taste, and drain on paper towels.

Serve the soup as is, hot from the pot, floating a slice of garlicky toast on each serving. If you wish, add a poached egg and a sprinkle of grated cheese. When you eat the soup, break the egg and stir it and the cheese into the hot soup.

Variation: This is the classic Spanish *sopa de ajo* from Castile. North over the Pyrenees, the French in Gascony make a similar soup called *tourain d'ail*. They use duck fat instead of olive oil and omit the typical Spanish flavorings of cumin and saffron. But the biggest difference is in the delicious thing they do with the eggs: for four servings, take the yolks of three eggs and a tablespoon of white wine vinegar. Beat the yolks and vinegar to a light froth, then whisk a few tablespoons of simmering soup into the egg mixture to warm it. When the eggs are warm, slowly stir the mixture into the simmering soup, whisking together over medium-low heat just until the soup begins to look creamy. Do not bring the soup to a boil or the eggs will curdle. Taste and add a little more vinegar if you wish and plenty of black pepper. Serve immediately, pouring the hot soup over toasted slices of crusty bread.

Pumpkin or Squash Soup
North African Style

Makes 4 to 6 servings

THE SPICY FRAGRANCE of this soup makes it a great wake-up call for winter nights—or winter mornings, since there is no rule that says you can't have soup for breakfast. Try it sometime and see if it doesn't set you sailing off into the coldest weather.

Pumpkin, I'm reminded by William Woys Weaver's excellent *Heirloom Vegetable Gardening,* is just another name for squash, and you may use hard winter squash and pumpkins interchangeably in this soup. But look for varieties with deep orange-to-red flesh such as Hubbard squash, cheese pumpkin with its distinctive creamy beige rind, or a variety I find in farmers' markets, bright red *rouge vif d'Etampes.* Deep color means deep flavor, and it's also a good indication of beta-carotene and lots of other valuable nutrients.

Instead of chili pepper, add a half teaspoon of harissa if you have it available.

2 tablespoons extra-virgin olive oil

1 medium carrot, coarsely grated or chopped

1 celery stalk, coarsely chopped

1 garlic clove, chopped

1 sweet red pepper, coarsely chopped

1 small fresh red chili pepper, seeded and coarsely chopped, or ½ teaspoon ground or crushed red chili pepper

1½ pounds pumpkin or hard winter squash, peeled and cubed (about 6 cups cubed squash)

1 14.6-ounce can plum tomatoes, chopped, with their juice

2 bay leaves

1 short piece of cinnamon stick

½ teaspoon ground turmeric

sea salt and freshly ground black pepper

1 or 2 tablespoons fresh lemon juice

2 tablespoons finely chopped cilantro

Combine the olive oil, carrot, celery, and garlic in the bottom of a heavy-duty soup pot or saucepan. Set over medium-low heat and cook, stirring occasionally, until the vegetables are soft but not brown, about 10 minutes. Add the chopped peppers, along with the cubed pumpkin, and stir to mix well. As soon as the squash cubes start to sizzle in the bottom of the pan, add the chopped tomatoes, bay leaves, cinnamon, and turmeric, with 2 cups of water. Bring to a simmer and cover the pan. Let simmer gently for about 20 minutes or until the pumpkin is very soft.

When the vegetables are all thoroughly softened, puree the soup, using either a stick blender or a food processor. Return to the rinsed-out pan and adjust the seasoning, adding salt and pepper, along with a tablespoon or two of lemon juice. Just before serving, stir in the cilantro.

Sant'Ambrogio Yellow Pepper Soup

Passato di Peperoni Gialli

FABIO PICCHI MAY BE the best-known chef in Florence, where his Ristorante Cibreo, near the great Sant'Ambrogio market, is a perennial favorite with locals and tourists alike. What characterizes his cuisine is a simplicity and directness that is rare in the world of star chefs these days, and this soup is an excellent example of it. To succeed, however, it requires really good, flavorful sweet peppers from your own or a neighbor's garden, or from a farmers' market. Out-of-season peppers from Dutch or Mexican greenhouses, imported over great distances, simply won't cut it.

There is absolutely no reason why you couldn't make this soup with red peppers but in that case, change the name to *Passato di Peperoni Rossi*. I do not think it would be very good with green peppers.

1 red onion, finely chopped

1 medium carrot, finely chopped

1 celery stalk, including green leaves, finely chopped

¼ cup extra-virgin olive oil

4 sweet yellow peppers, trimmed of seeds and white membranes

1 medium yellow-fleshed potato, peeled

4 cups vegetable broth (page 107), brought to a simmer

1 bay leaf

sea salt and freshly ground black pepper

a pinch of ground red chili pepper or red pepper flakes (optional)

GARNISH:

little cubes of bread toasted in extra-virgin olive oil

grated parmigiano reggiano cheese

Combine the chopped onion, carrot, and celery in a heavy-duty saucepan with the olive oil. Set over medium-low heat and gently sweat the vegetables until they are softened and just beginning to turn color. When their fragrance rises from the pan, you'll know the soffritto is ready.

While the soffritto is cooking, cut the peppers and potato into big chunks. Add them to the soffritto, along with the simmering vegetable broth. Add the bay leaf, salt and pepper to taste, and, if you wish, a pinch of ground red chili or a whole red chili pepper. Return to a simmer, cover the pan, and simmer slowly for 45 minutes to 1 hour. Remove the bay leaf and chili pepper and puree the soup, using a vegetable mill or a stick blender (immersion blender) if you have one. If the puree is too thick, add a little more vegetable broth. Return to the heat briefly to warm up the soup for service, then serve immediately, garnished, if you wish, with olive oil–toasted croutons and grated cheese.

Tuscan Black Cabbage and Pork Soup

Makes 6 to 8 servings

BLACK CABBAGE IS *CAVOLO NERO,* a winter green that is fundamental in the Tuscan kitchen—and in Tuscan vegetable plots where in January you often see the stiff, dark-green-to-almost-black stalks sticking up out of the snowy garden. Like kale and many other members of the Brassica family, *cavolo nero,* they say, improves with a frost, growing sweeter and more tender. And like other Brassicas, too, *cavolo nero* is packed with healthy antioxidants and phyto-nutrients (see "The All-Important Brassicas," page 298).

In North America *cavolo nero* is sometimes called Tuscan kale or lacinato kale. To prepare it, you'll want to remove the tough central ribs. Fortunately, that's easy to do: assuming you're right-handed, hold the root end of the stem in your left hand and wrap your right thumb and index finger around the leaf. Pull sharply to the right and the leafy part will come away, leaving the tough rib to be tossed in the compost.

If you can't find *cavolo nero,* substitute kale, leafy Savoy cabbage, collard greens, or broccoli in this recipe. Collard greens will take a bit longer to cook than the others.

6 cups chicken stock (page 108)

1 pound lean pork, cut in very small cubes

2 or 3 tablespoons extra-virgin olive oil

1 medium white or yellow onion, halved and thinly sliced

1 small dried red chili pepper, crumbled

2 garlic cloves, crushed and chopped

sea salt and freshly ground black pepper

¼ cup minced flat-leaf parsley

[cont. next page]

Bring the stock to a boil, cover the pot, and simmer very gently while you prepare the rest of the ingredients.

In a small skillet over medium heat, sauté the pork cubes in 2 tablespoons of the olive oil until the pork is brown all over. Remove the pork with a slotted spoon and transfer it to the simmering stock.

Turn down the heat to low and sauté the onions in the oil remaining in the skillet. Cook, stirring, until the onions are very soft but not brown. Stir in the crumbled pepper and the garlic and cook for another 3 to 4 minutes, until the garlic has softened, then stir all the contents of the skillet, including the oil, into the simmering stock.

1 pound *cavolo nero,* prepared as described above, slivered

slivered fresh mint leaves or grated parmigiano reggiano for garnish (optional)

Add salt and pepper to the stock, then stir in the parsley and the slivered *cavolo nero.* Cover the pan and cook for about 15 minutes, or until the greens are completely cooked. More mature kale will take longer than fresh, young, new kale.

Serve immediately, garnishing with the fresh mint, if you wish, or with the grated cheese—but not, I think, with both.

Andalucian Gazpacho

Makes 8 servings

GAZPACHO IS ONE of the quintessential Mediterranean soups and, along with paella, what most people call to mind when they think of Spanish cuisine. I learned to make this, not surprisingly, in Andalucia, the hot, dry heartland of Moorish Spain, and it quickly became a family favorite, always part of our weekend picnic baskets. Well chilled, it's deliciously refreshing after a morning at the beach.

3½ pounds ripe, red tomatoes, peeled (page 25) and coarsely chopped (about 6 cups)

1 garlic clove, chopped

½ small red onion, chopped

1 green pepper, chopped

1 long cucumber, peeled and chopped

1 cup extra-virgin olive oil

2 tablespoons sherry vinegar, or more to taste

1 2-inch slice of stale white country-style bread

½ cup cold water

½ teaspoon ground cumin

Put the tomatoes, garlic, onion, pepper, and cucumber in a blender and whirl briefly (in small batches if it's easier) to puree. With the blender lid ajar, pour in the oil and vinegar while you continue to process the vegetables.

Tear the bread into small chunks and soak briefly in the cold water. When the bread is soaked thoroughly, gently squeeze out the excess water and add the soaked bread to the blender along with the cumin and cayenne. Process to incorporate thoroughly.

Taste and adjust the seasoning, adding salt and/or a small quantity of sugar if necessary (sugar brings out the flavor of the tomatoes—½ teaspoon should be adequate). More sherry vinegar also may be added to adjust the flavor. If the thoroughly pureed

a pinch of cayenne pepper

sea salt

sugar

GARNISH

finely diced cucumber, green pepper, onion, and/or hard-boiled egg

soup seems too thick, add ice-cold water until the desired consistency is reached.

The soup should be light and smooth, almost creamy in consistency. If it is still too coarse in texture, you may press it through a sieve. For picnic purposes it is best served thin enough to sip from a mug, but if you're serving it at table, with a soup dish and spoon, a thicker consistency is fine, and you will want to garnish each plate with the traditional gazpacho garnishes—finely diced cucumber, green pepper, onion, and/or hard-boiled egg.

Green Gazpacho

{ Makes 4 to 6 servings

THIS UP-TO-DATE, MODERN, and deeply refreshing version of gazpacho uses avocados, not a traditional Mediterranean fruit but one that has become popular, especially in Spain, in recent years. Many cooks avoid avocado in the mistaken belief that the fruit's high fat content is problematic. But avocados are actually good for you (in moderation, like all good things) since the fat is primarily monounsaturated, just like the fat in olive oil. That fat works to lower "bad" cholesterol while it maintains the "good" HDL cholesterol. Along with all that good fat, they are an important source of many antioxidants. So eat avocados in good conscience—just not every day.

2 slices country-style bread, crusts removed, torn into chunks

3 ripe Hass avocados, peeled and chunked

1 green pepper, cored, seeded, and chopped

½ English cucumber, peeled and chopped

[cont. next page]

Set the chunks of bread in a bowl with water to cover. When most of the water has been absorbed, drain the bread chunks in a colander and press them gently to remove the excess liquid. Set aside.

In a food processor, combine the avocado, green pepper, cucumber, onion, and garlic and process to a smooth consistency. Scrape the avocado mixture into a bowl and set aside.

½ medium yellow onion, chopped

1 or 2 garlic cloves, chopped

½ cup coarsely chopped flat-leaf parsley, leaves only

½ cup coarsely chopped cilantro

fresh juice of 1 whole lemon

½ cup extra-virgin olive oil, preferably Spanish

½ teaspoon ground cumin

a pinch of ground or crushed red chili pepper

1 cup, more or less, of ice water

Now add the bread to the processor, along with the parsley, cilantro, and lemon juice and process till smooth. With the motor running, slowly pour in the olive oil. Add the cumin and chili and continue processing until the mixture is very smooth.

Turn the bread mixture into the bowl with the avocado mixture, folding thoroughly. If the mixture is very thick, stir in ice water until you have the consistency of a thick soup.

Keep the soup chilled until ready to serve.

MEDITERRANEAN BEAN SOUPS

Winter in the Mediterranean is quite mercifully brief, but it can still be harsh, especially in the mountains, where snowfalls always seem to take people by surprise, as if they truly don't belong. Sometimes the snow catches me short too, and I have to walk a mile or so to the bottega in Teverina to get milk or coffee or eggs. *"Ha visto la neve, signora?"* Mrs. Coppini always asks—"Did you see the snow?"—as if the six inches lying on the roads, making them too precarious for driving, might have escaped my attention. And yet it snows every winter three or four times.

These hearty soups of beans, grains, and winter vegetables, cooked for days on the hearth in deep terra-cotta pots, are what keep people going in weather like that, and not just the country folk either. On via Borgognona, just off Rome's ultra-chic Piazza di Spagna, a little Tuscan restaurant called da Nino is, for all its rustic appearance, hugely popular at lunchtime with film people, journalists, and what a friend of mine calls "the in crowd." As you push through Nino's door on one of those blustery February days when the wind whips the rain along the Roman cobblestones in horizontal sheets, you will be greeted by the welcome sight of a big fiasco, the old-fashioned bulb-shaped green-glass jar in which Chianti wines used to be shipped, sitting behind the entry window, filled with white beans simmering away in a bath of water, olive oil, salt, and pepper, with just a branch of sage to flavor them. This is fagiuoli al fiasco, a famous Tuscan country dish, and a more rustic and hospitable flavor on such a wintry day you cannot imagine.

Bean soups are not just Tuscan, of course, but a staple all around the Mediterranean. Before New World beans arrived in Europe sometime after 1492, these soups were made with chickpeas (ceci in Italian, garbanzos in Spanish), lentils, and broad or fava beans. Egyptian foul or ful is another Old World bean, a small dark-skinned fava that was perhaps the very bean that fueled the bellies of the builders of the pyramids—unless that was lentils. These Old World beans still form the basis of some of the region's most loved dishes, but a vast panoply of New World beans are also used.

Vegetarians know that legumes of all kinds should be part of their diet as a healthy, tasty source of protein, but nonvegetarians too will want to boost bean consumption to get valuable folate and fiber, both of which are abundant in legumes. (Folate is a form of vitamin B that is especially good for a healthy heart, while fiber helps to control blood sugar, among other useful functions.) A high consumption of legumes—including chickpeas, lentils, and fava beans—is one reason why the Mediterranean way of eating is especially healthful. As a protein source, beans are just as valuable as meat and with little or no saturated fat, depending on how they're prepared.

Hearty bean soups make filling, main-course dishes that are often even better if they're done ahead. They will thicken, however, if kept overnight or longer, so if you're reheating the soup, be sure to have a kettle of water boiling to add to it as it warms.

Throughout the Mediterranean, these soups are often garnished with a swirl of olive oil at the moment of serving—this is where you'll want to use your finest extra-virgin that you save for special dishes. A sprinkle of minced fresh parsley, basil, cilantro, or other green herb is also great to top off each dish with flavor and color.

Note that 1 cup of dry beans makes about 2½ cups when soaked, or, after cooking, 3 to 3 ½ cups, enough for four main-course servings or six servings as a first course.

Mediterranean Bean Soup

THE BASIC RECIPE

Makes 8 servings

THIS BASIC RECIPE is the soup I cook at home in Tuscany, so it should be called *zuppa di fagioli*. But the principle works, with variations, for many other bean soups. Tuscan cooks use white cannellini beans or cranberry beans (also called *borlotti*), but the soup is just as good with traditional American beans like navy beans, yellow-eyes, and pea beans, or even chickpeas. American big red kidney beans will also do in a pinch, but they are a little crude in flavor for this dish and will give it an unappetizing red color.

1 medium to large onion, coarsely chopped	In a heavy stockpot or soup kettle over medium heat, gently sauté the onion, carrots, and garlic in the oil until the vegetables are soft but not browned, 10 to 15 minutes. Add the drained beans
2 or 3 medium carrots, peeled and coarsely chopped	

1 or 2 garlic cloves, crushed with the flat blade of a knife

2 tablespoons extra-virgin olive oil, plus more to taste for garnish

2 cups dried beans, soaked overnight, drained

8 to 10 cups boiling water

1 tablespoon fresh thyme or 1 teaspoon dried, crumbled

1 or 2 bay leaves, to taste

about ¼ cup chopped flat-leaf parsley, plus more for garnish

sea salt and freshly ground black pepper

to the stockpot along with the boiling water. Add the herbs, except the salt and pepper. (Traditional cooks hold off on the salt until the beans are thoroughly softened; the theory, which I have not been able to prove, is that salt toughens protein and hardens the beans.)

Cook the beans, covered, over low heat for 1½ to 3 hours, adding boiling water from time to time if necessary. Cooking time varies with the age of the beans, and since there is no way to tell whether dried beans are this season's crop, you have to follow your good sense. In any case, if the beans finish cooking before you're ready to serve them, it doesn't matter—they reheat splendidly. When the beans are soft, taste and adjust the seasonings.

Before serving, you may want to remove about 1½ cups of the beans, puree them in a blender or a food mill, and return them to the pot to thicken the soup. If the soup is too thick, on the other hand, it may be thinned by adding hot water or some crushed canned tomatoes with their juices. In any case, be sure to taste the soup and adjust the salt and pepper before serving.

Serve the soup as is, with chopped parsley sprinkled over and a drizzle of the best green olive oil you can buy. Or garnish it with croutons or, to do it in true Mediterranean style, for each serving toast a thick slice of densely textured country-style bread, rub it with a cut clove of garlic, sprinkle it with olive oil and salt, and float it in the middle of the soup plate.

Variation: Add a chopped tomato in season or a dollop of tomato concentrate with the herbs.

Fassolada

Greek White Bean Soup

THIS VERSION OF GREEK BEAN SOUP reverses the usual procedure, sautéing lots of vegetables and adding them halfway through the cooking.

1½ cups large white beans or cannellini, soaked overnight, drained

¼ cup extra-virgin olive oil

3 medium onions, coarsely chopped

2 medium carrots, peeled and sliced

3 celery stalks, coarsely chopped

2 sweet green peppers, diced

3 tablespoons tomato puree

juice of ½ lemon

sea salt and freshly ground black pepper

Drain the beans and place in a heavy soup kettle or stockpot with cool water to cover. Bring to a boil, cover, and simmer for 30 minutes, adding more boiling water as necessary.

Meanwhile, heat the oil in a skillet and gently sauté the onions, carrots, and celery until the vegetables are soft but not browned—about 10 to 15 minutes. Add the peppers and continue cooking for 5 minutes or so, until the peppers are starting to soften.

After the beans have cooked for 30 minutes, pour the vegetables and their oil into the pot with them. Add the tomato puree, stirring to dissolve, and continue simmering for 30 minutes or more, until the beans are very tender. Cooking time will vary with the age of the beans. At the end of the cooking time, stir the lemon juice into the soup. Taste and add salt and pepper if necessary.

Bean and Farro Soup

MANY DIFFERENT KINDS of beans are appropriate for this, but light-colored beans are best—white cannellini or navy beans; streaky red-and-white ones called cranberry beans, Jacob's cattle beans, or borlotti; or heirloom beans such as marfax (marrowfats) and creamy-colored sulphur beans. Darker-colored beans will give the soup an unappetizing color.

Farro is an old-fashioned variety of durum wheat that has become popular recently. *Triticum dicoccum* is the botanical name, officially emmer wheat in English but more often known by its Italian name, farro. It should be easy to find in a specialty shop or online, but if you can't find it, you could substitute kamut, another wheat variety that is often sold in health food stores. Most farro does not need soaking; however, if you are uncertain, test some of the grains beforehand—cook about a quarter of a cup in water for 40 to 50 minutes. If the farro has not softened by that time, it probably will benefit from soaking in water for a few hours or overnight, just like the beans, before cooking.

This soup is often served in Tuscany during the olive harvest—there's no better way to exalt the flavor of new oil than by adding a generous dollop to the soup when you serve it. If you can't get new oil (and in North America few of us can), use the finest and most flavorful oil you can find.

1½ cups beans, soaked overnight and drained

1 medium yellow onion

1 celery stalk, preferably dark green from the outer layer

2 small garlic cloves

1 bay leaf

a pinch of fennel pollen if available, otherwise 2 or 3 fennel seeds

freshly ground black pepper

1 cup farro or kamut, soaked overnight if necessary and drained

1 medium fresh tomato or 2 canned tomatoes, coarsely chopped

sea salt

1 slice country bread for each serving

extra-virgin olive oil for garnish (preferably fresh new oil)

Add the beans to a stockpot with water to cover to a depth of 1 inch. Chop together the onion, celery, and one of the garlic cloves and add to the beans along with the bay leaf, fennel pollen or seeds, and black pepper. Set over medium-low heat and bring to a simmer. Cover the pan and simmer very gently until the beans are tender—this can take anywhere from 40 minutes to an hour or more, depending on the age of the beans. Check from time to time to make sure there is sufficient liquid in the pot—there should always be about 1 inch above the beans. If you must add more water, make sure it's boiling so as not to stop the cooking process.

While the beans are cooking, prepare the farro. Add the drained wheat to a smaller pot and cover with boiling water. Bring to a simmer and cook, covered, until the wheat grains are tender but still have a little bite.

When the beans are done, remove and discard the bay leaf. Use a stick blender to partially blend the beans in their cooking liquid. Or remove and set aside about ⅔ cup of beans and puree the rest in a food processor or vegetable mill; combine the puree with the whole beans and return to the bean pot.

Add the chopped tomato to the beans and cook gently until the tomato melts into the beans—this is really more for color than for taste. Drain the farro, reserving its liquid, and add the wheat grains to the beans. If the soup is too thick, thin it with a little of the farro liquid. Adjust the seasoning, adding more black pepper and salt.

Toast the bread slices. Cut the remaining garlic clove in half and use the half to rub over each slice of toast, then dribble generously with olive oil. Put a slice of toast in the bottom of each soup bowl and spoon the soup over the top. Dribble each serving with more olive oil.

Variation: If you wish, serve the soup with a small handful of grated parmigiano reggiano cheese—and if you have a leftover cheese rind from a piece of parmigiano, toss it into the soup pot with the beans. It gives a very authentic touch—just remember to extract it before you serve the soup.

White Bean, Black Cabbage, and Yellow Squash Soup

Makes 6 servings

MY DAUGHTER THE CHEF insists that beans need not be drained after soaking and that, in fact, if you add bay leaves and garlic to the soaking water, the beans will absorb those flavors as they soak. I have yet to organize a taste test but offer this recipe as a good example of the technique.

Black cabbage is Tuscan *cavolo nero* (page 129), sometimes sold as Tuscan kale or lacinato kale. If you can't find it, use another member of the Brassica family—turnip greens, collard greens, kale, or mustard greens would all be good choices.

Note that if you use vegetable stock, this makes a fine vegetarian meal.

1 cup cannellini or other
white beans

2 bay leaves

2 garlic cloves, crushed with
the flat blade of a knife

4 or 5 cups chicken or
vegetable stock

1 medium yellow onion,
roughly chopped

2 tablespoons extra-virgin
olive oil

1 cup cubed yellow or orange
squash (acorn, butternut, etc.)

1 pound *cavolo nero* or other
greens, prepared as described
on page 129

sea salt and freshly ground
black pepper

¼ cup chopped flat-leaf
parsley

grated parmigiano reggiano
cheese for garnish (optional)

Put the beans in a pan with the bay leaves and the
garlic. Cover with water to a depth of 1 or 2 inches
and leave for several hours or overnight. When
you're ready to cook, add more water if necessary
to cover the beans to a depth of 1 inch. Set the pan
on a low fire and bring to a simmer. Cover and
simmer until the beans are tender, 30 to 50
minutes. Check the beans from time to time and
add *boiling* water if they are drying out. When the
beans are done, remove from the heat. Remove
and discard the bay leaves.

Bring the stock to a simmer, cover, and keep
simmering while you prepare the rest of the
ingredients.

Combine the onion and olive oil in a small skillet
and cook over medium-low heat until the onions
have softened and started to crisp and brown.
Remove them with a slotted spoon and add to the
stock. Add the squash cubes to the skillet and cook,
stirring, until the squash has softened slightly and
started to brown. Add the squash to the soup, along
with any oil left in the pan.

Sliver the leaves of the *cavolo nero* and stir them into
the simmering soup. Let cook for about 15
minutes, until the greens are tender, then stir in the
beans with their cooking liquid. Bring back to a
simmer and taste, adding salt and pepper. Just
before serving, sprinkle the parsley over the soup
and stir it in. Serve the soup, garnishing with
grated cheese and passing more grated cheese at
table.

Egyptian Lentil Soup

{ Makes 6 to 8 servings

T HE FANCY VERSION of this soup is made with a little finely ground lean lamb or beef to enrich the flavor, but a vegetarian version is just as good and more typical of the lentil soup that has nourished Egyptians since the beginning of history. I like to use a mixture of brown and peeled red lentils: the red lentils disintegrate in the soup stock and give it a lovely creaminess. (From Bharti Kirchner, an authority on Indian and Bengali food, I learned that red lentils are called Egyptian lentils, *masur dal* in Hindi—just one more on the list of culinary links between the eastern Mediterranean and the subcontinent.) All brown lentils may also be used, but they will not disintegrate.

1 large onion, coarsely chopped

1 carrot, peeled and coarsely chopped

2 to 3 ounces finely ground lean lamb or beef, to taste (optional)

2 tablespoons extra-virgin olive oil

1 teaspoon ground cumin

1 teaspoon fennel seeds

1½ cups brown lentils, or 1 cup brown lentils and ½ cup red lentils

2 quarts water

1 small dried red chili (optional)

juice of ½ lemon, or more to taste

sea salt and freshly ground black pepper

GARNISH (OPTIONAL)

1 small onion, thinly sliced, the slices warmed and softened, but not cooked, in ¼ cup best-quality extra-virgin olive oil

lemon wedges for serving

In a heavy stockpot or soup kettle, gently sauté the onion, carrot, and ground meat if desired in the olive oil until the vegetables are soft and the meat is very brown—about 15 minutes. Stir in the cumin and fennel and add the lentils and water. Add the chili if desired.

Cook until the lentils are tender, about 30 minutes. Remove the chili. Add the lemon juice and taste for seasoning, adding salt and pepper if desired. Garnish each serving, if you wish, with the onion slices and their oil. Serve with lemon wedges to squeeze over the soup.

Variation: Add a cup of chopped green chard or spinach with the lentils.

Provençal Chickpea Soup

Makes 6 servings

LIKE LENTILS AND FAVA BEANS, chickpeas, called *ceci* in Italian and *garbanzos* in Spanish, are an ancient legume that archeologists find in some of the oldest Mediterranean sites. Even before the invention of agriculture, wild chickpeas seem to have been an important part of the diet of our Mediterranean ancestors, a stable source of protein when wild game was scarce.

There are many, many recipes for chickpea soups and stews all around the Mediterranean. Perhaps the most curious one, from Spain, called *olla gitana* or gypsy stew, includes, in addition to chickpeas, pumpkins, almonds, and pears. But this *soupe aux pois chiches* from Provence is a good deal simpler, in flavor as well as execution. The addition of fennel and orange zest makes it very special.

½ pound dried chickpeas, soaked overnight, drained

2 quarts cold water

sea salt

1 medium onion, sliced

2 leeks, white parts only, rinsed well and sliced

3 tablespoons extra-virgin olive oil, plus a little more for garnish

1 large ripe red tomato, chopped

1 2-inch strip of orange zest, cut into julienne strips

1 teaspoon freshly ground fennel seeds

freshly ground black pepper

6 slices of country-style bread, lightly toasted, for garnish

Drain the chickpeas, place in a heavy soup kettle or stockpot, and add the cold water. Bring to a boil, lower the heat, cover, and simmer until the chickpeas are tender and their skins are loose.

If you wish, remove the chickpeas from their cooking liquid (*don't discard the liquid*) and, when they are cool enough to handle, pull away and discard the skins, a nicety of professional chefs that need not be observed for the family table.

Puree about half the chickpeas with a little of their cooking liquid in a blender or food processor. Return to the soup (that is, the remaining chickpeas and remaining cooking liquid) and stir to blend well. The puree should be creamy but not too thick and studded with whole chickpeas. Taste and add salt if you wish. Cover and keep warm.

In a skillet over medium-low heat, gently sauté the onion and leeks in the oil until soft but not browned—about 10 to 15 minutes. Add the tomato, orange zest, and fennel and cook for 3 to 4 minutes, just long enough to thicken the sauce a little. Then turn it into the soup kettle with the chickpeas and their liquid. Taste and add more salt, if necessary, and lots of black pepper.

Bring the soup back to a gentle simmer and serve over toasted bread with a thread of olive oil drizzled on top.

Chicken and Chickpea Soup from Southern Spain

Cocido Andaluz

Makes 8 to 10 servings

WHEN ANDALUCIAN COOKS make this hearty *cocido,* they start by cooking up a savory broth with a tough but tasty old farmyard bird and the bone from a magnificent salted country ham (jamón serrano). But it's almost impossible to find a bird like that in North America, unless you raise it yourself. Better to make do with a well-flavored stock, preferably one you make at home but otherwise the best you can find in the market.

This is truly a meal in a pot, almost more of a stew than a soup.

8 cups chicken stock (page 108)

1 3½- to 4-pound chicken, or chicken parts, rinsed

½ pound (1 cup) dried chickpeas, soaked overnight, drained

2 or 3 plump garlic cloves, chopped coarsely

3 medium carrots, cut in chunks

2 celery stalks, cut in chunks

2 ripe tomatoes, peeled (page 25) and coarsely chopped

Add the stock and the chicken to a soup kettle along with 2 cups of water, or enough to cover the chicken to a depth of 1 inch. Bring to a simmer over medium heat, then lower the heat, cover the pot, and simmer until the chicken is done, 2½ to 3 hours. If you use chicken parts rather than a whole bird, they will be done in 40 minutes to 1 hour. Add more boiling water from time to time as the stock cooks down. When the chicken is thoroughly cooked, remove it from the stock. Separate the meat from the bones and skin and discard the latter. Set the pieces of chicken aside in a warm place, to be added to the cocido later.

Set the stock over medium-low heat and return to a simmer. Add the drained chickpeas and garlic and

2 leeks, trimmed and sliced about ¼ inch thick

2 medium potatoes, peeled and cut in bite-size chunks

½ cup long-grain rice

1 mild red chili pepper (Anaheim or Spanish ñora) or 1 tablespoon Spanish pimentón dulce (ground mild red pepper)

1 hot red chili pepper (peperoncino or chile arbol) or 1 teaspoon Spanish pimentón picante (ground hot red pepper)

1 cup diced prosciutto or jamón serrano

sea salt

2 hard-boiled eggs, coarsely chopped

a handful of mint, leaves only, chopped

simmer, covered, for about 20 minutes or until the chickpeas have started to soften, then stir in the carrots, celery, tomatoes, leeks, and potatoes. Continue cooking for another 20 to 30 minutes or until the chickpeas are soft, then stir in the rice and the two kinds of pepper, torn into smaller pieces. Adjust the quantities of chili to your taste for more or less *picante* flavors. Continue cooking, covered, for another 10 to 12 minutes or until the rice is done.

Add the diced ham, and a little salt if necessary. Arrange the pieces of chicken in the bottom of a serving dish or in individual serving bowls. Spoon the rest of the cocido over the top and garnish with chopped egg and the chopped mint leaves.

Serve immediately.

Leblebi

Tunisian Chickpea Soup

Makes 6 servings

*L*EBLEBI IS A MAINSTAY of the Tunisian diet, for rich and poor, country folk and city dwellers alike. Similar soups can be found all over North Africa, but what makes leblebi special is the elaborate selection of garnishes. You need not use all of these by any means—a spoonful of capers and a sprinkle of chopped scallions, together with a dollop of olive oil, make a fine soup—although the more garnishes you present, the more the soup becomes worthy of special occasions.

Leblebi can also be made with chicken stock, homemade of course, for an even richer presentation. If you use stock, add a little diced chicken or beef as one of the garnishes.

If you're using commercially prepared harissa (the kind that comes in a tube), add it in small quantities—it is usually much hotter than homemade.

1¼ cups dried chickpeas, soaked overnight, drained

5 cups boiling water, or chicken or vegetable stock

1 teaspoon ground cumin or cumin seeds, or more to taste

1 teaspoon salt, or more to taste

4 fat garlic cloves, coarsely chopped

1 tablespoon harissa (page 279), or to taste

1 medium onion, halved and thinly sliced, slices softened in 1 tablespoon extra-virgin olive oil

6 ½-inch-thick slices of dense country-style bread, preferably day-old

GARNISHES

¼ cup coarsely chopped drained capers

½ cup thinly sliced pickled turnip (page 282)

2 hard-boiled eggs, coarsely chopped, or 1 3½-ounce can best-quality tuna, drained and flaked

a few tablespoons ground cumin

⅓ cup harissa (page 279)

⅓ cup thinly sliced scallion, both white and green parts

a cruet of extra-virgin olive oil

2 lemons, quartered

sea salt and freshly ground black pepper

Drain the chickpeas of their soaking liquid and place them in a 2-quart saucepan or soup kettle. Add the boiling water and place over low heat. Cover and bring the water back to a boil. Cook at a very slow simmer for about 20 minutes or until the chickpeas have started to soften but are not yet ready to eat. Time will vary, depending on the age and size of the chickpeas.

Place the ground cumin in a small bowl and mix with the salt; using the back of a spoon, crush the chopped garlic into the spice mixture to produce a fine, homogenous paste of garlic, salt, and cumin.

Add the garlic-spice paste with the tablespoon of harissa to the simmering soup and stir to mix well. Continue simmering the soup for 5 minutes or so to let the flavors develop, then taste and add more salt, cumin, or harissa if desired.

Continue cooking, covered, another 15 to 20 minutes over very low heat, until the chickpeas are soft. Add the onion slices and their olive oil and cook for 15 minutes longer.

Arrange the garnishes in bowls or saucers on a tray or in a sectioned relish dish, together with the cruet of olive oil, salt, and a pepper mill.

Have ready six individual soup bowls. Remove the crusts from the bread slices and tear a slice into coarse, irregular chunks, each no more than ½ inch thick. Drop the bread chunks from each slice into the bottom of a soup bowl. Ladle about ½ to ¾ cup of the broth over the bread to soften it, then ladle on the chickpeas. Proceed with the rest of the soup bowls and serve immediately, passing the garnishes so that each person can add whatever is desired.

Lentil and Chickpea Soup with Greens

⊱ Makes 6 servings

CHARD IS AN EXCELLENT GREEN to use in this very simple and easy soup, which is a favorite in the Middle East. Chard's fresh sweetness is a nice contrast to the earthy flavors of the legumes. But try it also with spinach or with more pungent collards—you may find that you prefer that combination. If you use collards, strip the green leaves off the tough central stems and discard the stems. Sliver the leaves. (Collard leaves are tougher than either spinach or chard and will require slightly longer cooking.)

½ cup chickpeas, soaked overnight in water to cover, drained

1 garlic clove

1 small dried red chili pepper or 1 teaspoon crushed Aleppo pepper

½ cup lentils (preferably small green or brown lentils)

½ pound chard, coarsely chopped (makes 5 or 6 cups chopped chard)

GARNISHES

3 garlic cloves, coarsely chopped

1 teaspoon sea salt

2 tablespoons freshly squeezed lemon juice

2 tablespoons extra-virgin olive oil

Put the drained chickpeas in a saucepan with water to cover to a depth of 1 inch. Add the garlic clove and chili pepper. Bring to a boil, cover the pan, and simmer the chickpeas for at least 15 minutes or until they begin to soften but are not totally cooked through.

Add the lentils and a cup of boiling water to the chickpeas and simmer, covered, for another 15 minutes or until the chickpeas are almost cooked through. The lentils should be thoroughly done. (It's hard to be precise about cooking times as they depend on the age and size of the legumes.) Now stir in the chard and add 2 or 3 more cups of boiling water. Cook for a final 15 minutes or until the chard is cooked through and the legumes are soft. (Spinach will be cooked in about 7 minutes, while collard greens may take up to 20 minutes.)

While the chard is cooking, crush the chopped garlic cloves in a bowl with the salt. Use the back of a spoon to work the salt and garlic into a paste. Stir in the lemon juice and then the olive oil. When the soup is done and the legumes are tender, stir in the garlic mixture. Taste for salt, then serve the soup immediately.

Catalan Soup of White Beans Garnished with Shrimp

Handsome enough for a dinner party, hearty enough for family supper, this soup from northeastern Spain combines a number of good things that are good for you too—beans, tomatoes, seafood, and of course those ever-present nutritional powerhouses, onions and garlic.

FOR THE BEANS

¼ cup diced jamón serrano or Italian prosciutto

2 tablespoons extra-virgin olive oil

1 medium yellow onion, chopped

4 garlic cloves, chopped

1 cup dried white beans, soaked overnight and drained

sea salt

FOR THE SHRIMP

1 medium yellow onion, chopped

2 or 3 garlic cloves, chopped

¼ cup extra-virgin olive oil

2 pounds ripe, red tomatoes, peeled (page 25), or 1 28-ounce can whole tomatoes, with their liquid, coarsely chopped

1 teaspoon sugar

2 small dried red chilies, crumbled, or to taste

a pinch of saffron threads, crumbled

1 cup dry white wine

To first make the bean soup, in the bottom of a heavy stockpot or soup kettle, combine the diced ham and olive oil and set over medium heat. Cook gently, just until the ham bits start to sizzle, then add the onion and garlic and continue cooking until the vegetables are tender but not browned. Add the drained beans along with about 4 cups of cool water—enough to cover the beans to a depth of 1 inch. Bring to a boil, turn the heat down to simmer, cover the pan, and cook until the beans are tender—30 to 45 minutes, depending on the size and age of the beans. You may need to add water from time to time but it should only be boiling water. When the beans are tender but not falling apart, stir in the salt, remove the pot from the heat, and set aside.

In another saucepan, prepare the sauce for the shrimp. Gently sauté the onion and garlic in the oil until the vegetables are tender but not browned—about 10 to 15 minutes. Add the tomatoes, sugar, and chilies, raise the heat slightly, and continue cooking for 5 to 10 minutes or until the tomato sauce thickens. Stir in the saffron, then add the wine and raise the heat to high. Cook, stirring frequently, until the alcohol has cooked off, about 5 to 7 minutes. Taste the sauce, adding salt and pepper if necessary.

Both the beans and the tomato sauce may be prepared well ahead of time and held until ready to serve—refrigerated if necessary. When reheating

sea salt and freshly ground
black pepper

1½ pounds medium shrimp,
peeled

GARNISHES

¼ cup finely minced flat-leaf
parsley

the zest of a lemon sliced
into fine julienne threads

the beans, you may want to add a little more
boiling water to loosen the bean stock, which gets
quite starchy as it sits.

Reheat the tomato sauce when ready to serve. If
the shrimp are very large, cut them into two or
three pieces. When the tomato sauce is bubbling,
toss in the shrimp and cook very briefly, just until
the shrimp have changed color—not more than 4
minutes.

Serve the hot bean soup in shallow soup plates
with the shrimp in their tomato sauce in the
center of each plate. Garnish with the minced
parsley and a few strands of lemon zest.

Moroccan Harira

Makes 8 servings

*H*ARIRA, A THICK STEW of beans and lentils flavored with a little meat, is
found all over North Africa in one form or another. It's especially popular as a sundown pick-me-up during Ramadan, particularly if the fasting month
falls in winter when hot and peppery harira is most welcome. This is a fine example of the Mediterranean idea of using a small amount of meat to feed a large
amount of people—one pound of beef in an American steakhouse might be expected to feed one person; here it gets stretched with chickpeas, lentils, and tasty
green herbs to make enough for eight.

When I first tasted harira in Marrakesh many years ago, the cook added *smen,*
a very strong-flavored Moroccan preserved butter that tastes like an aged goat's
cheese. If you wish, grate a little aged goat's cheese over each serving to mimic
that flavor.

1 large onion, chopped

8 or 10 small white onions,
peeled but left whole

[cont. next page]

Combine the chopped onion and the whole small
onions in a stockpot with 2 tablespoons of the
olive oil and set over medium heat. Sprinkle with
salt and cook, stirring occasionally, until the

4 tablespoons extra-virgin olive oil

sea salt

1 pound lean boneless beef, diced small

1½ cups chickpeas, soaked overnight, drained

1 tablespoon or more freshly ground black pepper

1 big pinch saffron, crumbled

1 teaspoon powdered ginger

1 3-inch cinnamon stick

2 cups chicken stock

½ cup chopped flat-leaf parsley

½ cup chopped cilantro

2 celery stalks, preferably dark green from outer layer, chopped

1 cup chopped canned tomatoes, with their juice

1 cup lentils, preferably small brown or green lentils, rinsed

2 tablespoons tomato concentrate, tomato extract, or sun-dried tomato paste

1 teaspoon ground cumin

1 teaspoon ground or crushed red chili, or to taste

¼ cup unbleached all-purpose flour

1 teaspoon freshly squeezed lemon juice

lemon wedges for serving

chopped onions are wilted and tender and the whole onions have started to brown a little. Then stir in the diced meat, turn up the heat a little, and cook the meat, stirring, until it has lost its rosy color. Add the drained chickpeas, along with the pepper, saffron, ginger, and cinnamon stick. Add the stock and 3 cups of water and bring slowly to a simmer. Turn the heat down, cover the pot, and cook the soup at a slow simmer until the chickpeas are tender, about 30 to 40 minutes.

While the meat and chickpeas are cooking, chop the parsley, cilantro, and celery together to make a fine mince. Over medium-low heat, gently cook the chopped vegetables with the remaining olive oil in another saucepan or stockpot, stirring occasionally, until the vegetables are soft. Stir in the tomatoes with their juice and continue cooking for about 5 minutes. Add the lentils. By this time, the meat and chickpeas should be done. Extract a cup or two of their liquid and add it to the lentils, along with another 2 cups of boiling water. Bring to a simmer and stir in the tomato concentrate, the cumin, and as much or as little of the chili as you wish. The lentils should simmer for about 20 minutes.

In a small bowl, mix the flour with the lemon juice and a couple of tablespoons of water, stirring to a paste. Add more water gradually, up to ¾ of a cup, stirring to keep lumps from forming, until the flour-and-water paste is the consistency of heavy cream. Stir this mixture into the lentils. Cook very gently, stirring frequently, for 10 minutes. Finally, add the meat, onions, and chickpeas, with any remaining liquid, cover the pot, and cook a final 15 to 20 minutes. The soup should be quite velvety, with the meat, onions, chickpeas, and lentils suspended in it. Taste and adjust the seasoning, adding more salt and pepper if you wish.

Serve the soup immediately, with lemon wedges to squeeze over it.

Turkish Yogurt Soup with Mint

✤ Makes 6 to 8 servings

WISE COOKS ALWAYS HAVE chicken stock on hand, either an excellent, tasty, not overly salted commercial brand on the pantry shelf or, preferably, stock they make at home and freeze. If you make your own stock, add some of the chicken you used to this very easy and delicious Turkish soup. Mixing the yogurt with egg yolk and a little flour helps to stabilize it and keep it from curdling when added to the hot soup. For the creamiest texture, once the yogurt has been added, heat the soup until it is just below the boiling point. If you have white peppercorns, use them instead of the black ones to make a beautiful soup that's the rich color of old ivory.

Turkish cooks use hulled wheat, also called by its Italian name *grano pestato,* for this soup, but you may substitute farro, kamut, or long-grain rice. Whichever of these grains you decide to use must be cooked ahead of time in lightly salted water. Rice will cook in 10 or 15 minutes, but hulled wheat or farro may need to be soaked for several hours before cooking and can take up to 30 minutes to become tender. It would be wise to test-cook a small amount of the grain before you start, just to be sure of cooking times.

6 cups chicken stock, preferably homemade (see page 108, or Note below)

3 cups plain yogurt (low-fat or nonfat if you prefer)

1 egg yolk

1 cup cold water

1½ tablespoons unbleached all-purpose flour

1 cup chopped cooked chicken (use some of the chicken with which you made the stock)

¾ cup cooked hulled wheat, farro, or rice

sea salt and freshly ground pepper

a handful of mint leaves, torn in pieces

Bring the chicken stock to a simmer over medium heat while you prepare the yogurt.

Tip the yogurt into a bowl and beat lightly with a wire whisk.

In a separate small bowl, whisk the egg yolk with a little of the cold water, then whisk in the flour. Mix carefully so there are no lumps, adding water from time to time until you have added all the water. Now beat the egg mixture into the yogurt, again whisking thoroughly.

When the stock is simmering, beat the yogurt mixture into the soup, a little at a time. The yogurt should not come to a boil but it should cook at just below a simmer while the stock thickens to a cream. This will take about 10 minutes but at no time should the soup come to a boil. When the soup is the consistency of light cream, add the cooked chicken and wheat, farro, or rice. Taste and add salt and freshly ground pepper, preferably white pepper. As soon as the chicken and grains are hot, the soup is ready to be served, garnished with the torn mint leaves.

Caution: Do not let the soup come to a rolling boil for fear the egg will curdle and spoil the texture. If you must reheat the soup, be very careful not to overdo it. Whisk the soup fairly constantly as it is reheating.

Variation: Add a chopped fresh green chili pepper (jalapeño or serrano) to the soup with the grains and chicken.

Note: If you are using canned chicken stock, you can boost the flavor very simply by sautéing 4 skinless chicken thighs in a little olive oil until they are brown. Then add the stock called for in the recipe, plus 1 cup more because some of it will evaporate in the cooking. Bring the stock to a simmer and cook for about 30 minutes. Use the meat from the chicken thighs in preparing the soup.

Spanish Meatball Soup

Sopa de Albondigas

⚜ Makes 8 servings

S AFFRON IS THE CHARACTERISTIC SEASONING in Spain, so it's not surprising if it shows up also in meatballs. Use as much or as little as you wish—it has a very distinctive flavor. This plain but tasty soup is often served as a first course at dinner.

1 cup torn pieces of stale bread, crusts removed

¼ cup whole milk

½ cup roughly chopped onions

½ cup chopped flat-leaf parsley

1 garlic clove, smashed

1 pound lean ground meat, either all pork, or a mixture of pork and veal

a pinch of saffron threads, crumbled

1 egg

sea salt and freshly ground black pepper

¼ cup or more fine dry bread crumbs

¼ cup extra-virgin olive oil

8 cups chicken broth (page 108)

1 large leek, trimmed and thinly sliced

Combine the torn bread and the milk in a bowl, mixing to ensure that all the bread is moistened. Set aside for 10 to 15 minutes.

Mince together, or process in a food processor, the onions, parsley, and garlic. Squeeze the bread dry and mix with the vegetables. Add in the meat, saffron, egg, salt, and black pepper and combine well, using your hands to knead the mixture. If it is too wet, add the bread crumbs. (If, on the other hand, it's too dry, add half a teaspoon or more of milk.) Shape the mixture into small balls no bigger than walnuts. You should have 30 to 40 meatballs.

Over medium heat, sauté the meatballs in the olive oil, browning them all over. Bring the chicken broth to a simmer and add the leek slices. As each meatball browns, add it to the simmering broth. When all the meatballs are done, cover the broth and let the meatballs cook at a very low simmer for another 30 minutes. Serve immediately.

Variation: Omit the milk-soaked bread and add to the meat the kind of seasonings used in southern Spain for *pinchitos,* little skewers of meat that are served in tapas bars to have with drinks (see page 101): ½ teaspoon each of ground cumin, hot paprika, ground coriander seeds, turmeric, and ground black pepper. You may need to add more bread crumbs so the mixture will hold together.

BREAKFAST IN THE
MEDITERRANEAN WORLD

Tell me what you eat for breakfast, and I will tell you who you are. Or at least I will tell you what part of the Mediterranean you come from.

In America, breakfast goes two ways. We have either big fat breakfasts (eggs and bacon, toast with butter and jam, home fries on the side) or little skinny ones (cuppa java with skim milk and artificial sweetener). And no matter which we choose, we feel guilty because we know we're not doing it right.

In Mediterranean countries many people don't even consider breakfast a meal. And it's been that way for a long time. In the late Middle Ages, Francesco di Marco Datini, an anxious, fretful, but eminently successful wool merchant from Prato, the industrial town north of Florence, took no breakfast at all. In that, says his biographer Iris Origo, Datini was like most people of his time, in Tuscany and elsewhere. Those who ate breakfast did so only for therapeutic reasons, often to combat the threat of plague. In any case, since coffee and tea were unknown, such a breakfast was but a piece of toasted bread and a glass of wine.

Farm families today have big bowls of half-milk, half-coffee, sweetened with sugar, and perhaps a wedge of stale bread to dip in it, while in cities like Athens, Beirut, Madrid, and Rome the bars and cafés (unlike here, they're often the same thing) are thronged in the early-morning rush hour with workers and students, standing up and hurriedly gulping milky coffee while between sips they nibble on some sort of sweet sticky bun or, in Spain, on crisp *churros,* ropes and twists of deep-fried dough. These bar scenes are a nutritionist's worst nightmare as anxious mothers stuff their children with sugar, fat, and caffeine before putting them happily, smock fronts sprinkled with powdered sugar, on the bus for school.

There are parts of the Mediterranean, though, where breakfast would make even a home economist content: in Morocco, workers stop at street-corner holes-in-the-wall for thick purees of stewed fava beans, mixed with olive oil and redolent of garlic, with glasses of mint tea to wash it down. In Barcelona, along with the obligatory café con leche, breakfasters munch on *pa amb tomaquet* (pahm toh-MAH-kett), glorious small buns of baguette bread, split and lightly toasted, rubbed with garlic and halves of dead-ripe red cherry tomatoes, smashed well into the bread, and topped with olive oil.

My all-time favorite Mediterranean breakfast, however, comes from the Levant. Tewfiq Salah, a large and ebullient Palestinian who served as our occasional driver in Beirut, introduced me to this one morning many years ago at the start of a trip over the mountains to Damascus. Once the introduction was made, I was hooked for life.

The Continental Hotel, where the Beirut drivers had their headquarters, was not far from the university. In the freshness of early morning, when even in summer a breath of cool air off the sea bathes the city, I would walk up the hill to a sidewalk café to join Tewfiq for coffee and bread from a nearby bakery, fresh from the oven, its aromas rich and complex with the fragrance of yeast and roasted wheat. This was usually Arab bread, *khubz arabi,* flat and thick, sometimes lightly sprinkled with za°atar, a delicious mixture of olive oil, wild thyme also called *za'atar,* sesame seeds, and crushed sumac berries with their pleasant, lemony astringency. Sometimes there was also *khubz marqouk,* mountain bread, thin as a flour tortilla and used in a similar way, like a spoon, to scoop up creamy yogurt made from fresh goat's milk. With the yogurt we had olives—fat, aromatic black ones and crisp, bitter green ones—along with young scallions and radishes. And like many Middle Easterners, Tewfiq always began the day with *ful medames* (page 251) made with small, brown Egyptian fava beans.

This kind of breakfast is nutritional perfection—fiber-rich beans and bread, plenty of fresh vegetables, yogurt for its calcium, and an abundance of the good fat, olive oil. And for someone who grew up in New England where, even in boarding school, we had baked beans on Saturday night and warmed-over beans for Sunday breakfast, it doesn't taste all that strange either.

Try it sometime. And if you ever get to Brooklyn, you can eat a Lebanese breakfast in the little Arab restaurants along lower Atlantic Avenue, near Brooklyn Heights. The bread comes from local bakeries, too.

Breads, Pizzas, Flatbreads, and Savory Pies

✧ ✧ ✧

NEAR EPHESUS IN SOUTHERN TURKEY, an old woman makes *saç* bread, thin oniony layers baked on a griddle that looks like an upside-down wok perched over an open fire. In Marrakesh in Morocco, a well-to-do lady rises at dawn to set the dough for the semolina bread she herself makes each day for an extended family that includes half a dozen servants. In the crowded alleys of the medieval souk in Fez, children balance on their heads wooden trays piled with pale, dimpled loaves of dough, on their way to the neighborhood baker. In Egypt, village women bake paper-thin flatbread, as they have for at least 5,000 years, by pressing it against the hot and gritty inside wall of a hand-built mud oven. In Southern Italy and in Greece, when the flames have died in the household oven and the walls are white with heat, housewives thrust in great round grainy loaves made weekly from wheat raised on terraces below the farmhouse and ground at the local mill. And in Naples and Nice and Marseilles, the *pizzaiuoli* work at a feverish pace, flipping flat round disks into domed ovens so hot they could fire pottery, so hot the pizza is done in two minutes flat.

You could spend a lifetime researching, cooking, and writing about all the different breads of the Mediterranean, and in the end you might feel you had only begun. In this part of the world, where the value and power of yeasted grain was probably first encountered and where bread has been such a vital element in the diet since the beginning of history, possibly even earlier, the variety of breads and yeasted products is amazing.

Ceres, in the old religion the goddess of grain and the harvest, retains her power as a symbol of sustenance and life. Bread was one of the holiest offerings solicited for the dead god-kings of Egypt ("thousands of bread and thousands of beer," the ancient formulas intone), just as today it is raised to a sacrament in the Christian Mass. For the same reason, all over the Mediterranean the sacred loaves are baked and blessed each Friday at the beginning of the Jewish Sabbath, and bread, or cake, broken and shared between bride and groom, is the symbol of a new beginning, a new family.

The reason is simple: bread is, for the people of the Mediterranean and their cultural descendants throughout the Western world, the fundamental food. In blessing it and sharing it we recognize, if only tangentially, our connection with each other, with our past as a community, and with the earth that offers us the grain from which we grind the flour to bake our daily bread.

There is a subtler reason at work as well. For in the action of yeast we perceive in a dramatic and immediate form the very beginnings of life itself. Yeast is nothing on its own, a lump of clayey matter or, for most of us today, dry granulated dust that lies inert in the palm of the hand. But mix it with warm water, stir it with ground grain—whether wheat, rye, or barley—knead it and coax it and set it to rest in a hospitable environment, and it begins to stir and grow and come alive. Then pop it into the hot womb of the oven, and it becomes something quite phenomenal, not only symbolic of life but life-giving matter, in and of itself. Food.

Ingredients

Flour

The King Arthur Flour Company in Norwich, Vermont, produces a variety of different flours, including all-purpose flour, bread flour, and artisanal bread flour, all of very high quality. These flours are widely available in stores throughout the Northeast of the United States as well as on the Internet (see www.kingarthurflour.com, an unusually informative and educational web site). Mostly I use King Arthur's unbleached, unbromated all-purpose flour ground from hard red wheat from the western prairies; it is also available as a certified organic flour. The web site lists this flour as between 11.3 and 11.7 percent protein, which is excellent for bread making. Another of King Arthur's flours that gives equally fine results is their "European-Style Artisan Bread Flour," at 11.7 percent protein, made from a mixture of spring and winter wheats to mimic the flours used in traditional European hearth-style breads. Ascorbic acid (vitamin C) is added to enhance yeast growth, but there's also what the company calls "a hint of white whole wheat" in the mixture.

Leavening

In the recipes that follow, I have given instructions for using active dry yeast, the granulated form that comes in little envelopes or is sold loose at health food stores.

But the most traditional and, in my opinion, the best leavening for bread dough is a piece of dough from an earlier baking that has been held back and kept in a cool place for at least 24 hours. You may be more familiar with the name *sourdough* for this process, although when properly maintained the dough should not really be sour at all but rather have the well-developed tang that all fermented foods, from wine to sauerkraut, derive from lactic fermentation. Sourdough is not unique to San Francisco or to Forty-Niners. Since baking began, it has been the most common way to preserve the leaven, in home kitchens as well as commercial bakeries, but since commercial yeasts became widely available, the traditional method has lapsed.

It is so very easy, however, that I urge it on anyone who intends to bake bread at least once every 10 days or so. Well do I remember, from what my children call those hippy-dippy days of yore, bakers who would proudly open a refrigerator to show you a jar of sourdough that they'd kept going for six years or more, a base of nearly solid library paste covered by a thin and yellowish liquid. Like much of what we did in those days, there was something more than a little murky and unseemly about it. There is no reason to go to such lengths, and it may help to get over that if you simply think of each baking as raising a sponge of flour, yeast, and water, then removing a cup of it and setting it aside in a covered glass jar for the next baking.

Some baking instructions will tell you to "feed" your sourdough starter, if you're not able to use it every 10 days or so, with additional flour and water. The irresistible image that springs to mind is of some earnest yuppie on an extended business trip, clutching his jar of sourdough starter so he can feed it regularly while he's away from home. Believe me, this is just too complicated. If you have to go away for a couple of weeks, for heaven's sake, leave behind the sourdough starter or reserved dough or whatever you want to call it. If it isn't any good when you get back, throw it out and start afresh. Life is too short to worry about things like that.

If you want to use the traditional method, start the following recipe. After the first rising, you will have what's called the *sponge*. Before you add the barley, rye, or whole-wheat flour, remove a cup of the sponge, transfer it to a glass container (a mason jar is perfect), cover it, and store it in the refrigerator. (The country bread recipe, having had a cup of starter removed, will make a little less than usual, but that's okay just this once.) The one important thing to remember about starter or reserved dough is that it will work best if it contains nothing but yeast, water, and unbleached all-purpose wheat flour. No eggs, butter, fats, milk, or anything of that ilk should be added to the sponge before the cup of reserved dough has been removed. The starter will keep for ten days. (If you want to keep it longer, you should feed it with equal quantities of unbleached all-purpose flour and tepid water, ½ cup of each. Let the starter come to room temperature, stir in the flour and water, then let it sit at room temperature for an hour or so before returning it to the refrigerator.)

When you want to use starter to make bread, take a cup of reserved dough out of the refrigerator and, using a spatula, scrape it into a bowl. (In cold weather, rinse the bowl with hot water before you add the dough. This will make a warmer, more comfortable environment for the starter.) Simply substitute the cup of starter for the yeast. (I know, this increases the overall quantity of the recipe, but believe me, it will all work out in the end.) Starter works best for true bread recipes rather than quick-rising flatbreads like Arab pita and Neapolitan pizza. But in the very best *pizzerie* of Naples, the traditional leavening to this day is a piece of dough held back from the day before.

You should feel free to experiment with the starter and with other aspects of bread making. Bread is about the most forgiving thing in the entire kitchen repertoire—even when something doesn't turn out the way you wanted or expected, the smells that emanate from baking bread will convince anyone in sniffing range that wonderful things are happening.

Do keep in mind that with any bread or yeast dough, the balance between flour and liquid depends on a number of unpredictable variables, among them most particularly the humidity of the room in which you are working and the age and humidity of the flour. Don't be bound by the quantities in the recipes that follow. If the dough seems very damp and squishy, add more flour; if, on the contrary, it seems dry, add more water. (One easy way to do this is simply to dip your hands in water as you knead—the slight amount of water added to the dough may be sufficient. Or you could spread a thin film of water on the bread board and knead that into the dough.)

If you work with a baking stone, which produces the best texture in breads and pizzas, note that you must put the *cold stone* in the *cold* oven, to avoid cracking the stone. Turn the oven on to the desired temperature and preheat for at least 30 minutes, even though the oven light goes off. The oven will have reached the desired temperature after 5 minutes or so, but it takes a lot longer to heat the stone thoroughly.

Mediterranean Country-Style Bread

✤{ Makes 2 loaves, about 1¼ pounds each

I'VE LEARNED MORE about the art of bread making from Ed Behr, the Vermont-based writer, editor, and general factotum of *The Art of Eating,* a quarterly newsletter, than from anyone in the Mediterranean or elsewhere. Ed seems to have a natural instinct, what my mother would have called "a good hand," for bread. Here's what he taught me:

- Use as little yeast as you can get away with.

- Let the rising be long, cool, and slow.

When you think about it, those are pretty good life principles as well.

This is a very slow-rising bread. Three days may seem excessive, but the bread develops a wonderful flavor and texture, and the bonus is that there's so little to do each day that you almost don't even notice you're making bread. Fifteen years ago I published this recipe in the *New York Times.* The editor of *Food & Wine* magazine called to say it was the best bread she'd ever baked.

2 cups very warm, almost hot, water

1 teaspoon active dry yeast

9 to 11 cups unbleached all-purpose white flour

2 tablespoons sea salt

2½ cups tepid water

2 cups barley, rye, or whole-wheat flour

2 or 3 tablespoons cornmeal or coarse semolina, as needed

Put the very warm water in a large mixing bowl, sprinkle the yeast over it, and stir briefly with a wooden spoon to distribute the yeast through the water. Add 2 cups of the white flour, stir to mix well, cover with plastic wrap, and set aside in a cool place (50 to 70 degrees) to rise overnight. (If you're using starter, mix a cup of starter with warm water and flour, cover, and set aside to rise.)

The next day, if you wish, remove a cup of the starter sponge and store in a glass jar in the refrigerator. Add to the remaining sponge the salt, a cup of the tepid water, and the barley, rye, or whole-wheat flour. Stir or mix thoroughly with your hands. Cover the bowl again, return to a cool place, and let it rise overnight.

On the third day, add the remaining 1½ cups tepid water and about 7 cups white flour. Begin kneading in the bowl, then sprinkle a little flour over a wooden pastry board or wooden countertop and turn the dough out. Knead thoroughly for at least 10 minutes, adding flour as necessary until you have a smooth, elastic dough. Rinse the mixing bowl, dry it, dust it with flour, and put the dough back in. Cover with plastic wrap and set aside at room temperature to rise until it has increased in volume about 2½ times—about 2 to 3 hours.

Turn the dough out on the lightly floured board, punch it down, and knead briefly just to knock any air holes out. Form into two round *(boules)* or long *(baguettes)* loaves and place the loaves on baking sheets (if you're not using a baking stone) or on a wooden peel that has been lightly sprinkled with cornmeal or semolina. Set aside in a warm place (70 degrees or more) to rise rapidly, 30 minutes to an hour, until doubled in size.

If you're using a baking stone, set it in the cold oven and preheat to 500 degrees for at least 30 minutes. If you're using a baking sheet and no stone, simply preheat the oven to 500 degrees. When you're ready to bake, slash the tops of the loaves with a very sharp knife in three or four places. Quickly slide the loaves into the oven, directly onto the hot stone if you're using it, and bake for 15 minutes. Turn the heat down to 350 degrees and bake for 35 minutes longer.

When the bread is done and the crust is golden brown, remove the bread from the oven and let it cool on a rack.

VARIATIONS:

To make Black Olive Bread: When you punch down the dough just before shaping the loaves, add ½ to 1 cup pitted black olives, well drained of any oil or brine, and a tablespoon of finely grated orange zest. Knead these ingredients into the dough before shaping the loaves. You may also find that you must add a little more flour to compensate for the juiciness of the olives.

To make Walnut Bread: When you punch down the dough just before shaping the loaves, add ½ to 1 cup coarsely chopped walnuts to the dough. Knead the dough to distribute the walnuts throughout before shaping the loaves.

To make Barley Bread: Substitute 2 or 3 cups of barley flour for 2 or 3 cups of all-purpose flour in the recipe. In Morocco, where barley bread is a great favorite, it is often baked in 9-inch round bread pans, with a handful of barley grits scattered over the surface of the loaf just before it goes into the oven. Keep in mind that smaller shapes like these will bake more quickly than the hefty loaves described in the recipe.

Fennel and Sesame Bread from Cyprus

Makes 2 loaves; 16 servings

WE USED TO BUY this bread from a bakery on a back street of Kyrenia, the delightful port town on Cyprus's north coast, where we lived for a time in the 1970s. It was called Armenian bread but I later came to realize that it was a Turkish bread, in fact, and the bakery itself was perhaps owned by Turkish Cypriotes. In the heated politics of the day, of which we were blissfully unaware, Armenian was more politically correct than Turkish among the Greek Cypriotes with whom we lived. And now, with unhappy irony, the whole north coast of Cyprus is considered, by the Turks, to be an integral part of Turkey—so, in the interests of world peace, I should probably call this Anatolian bread and let whichever culture is dominant at the moment claim it.

Politics aside, however, it is utterly delicious, fragrant with fennel and thickly coated with sesame seeds like the crisp simit rings that are sold by street vendors all over the Middle East—and yet it really is bread.

As with any bread, the balance between flour and liquid depends on a number of variables, among them the humidity in the air and the age and humidity of the flour.

¾ cup warm water

1 teaspoon active dry yeast

4 cups unbleached all-purpose white flour

1 cup whole-wheat flour

1 teaspoon sea salt

1 tablespoon extra-virgin olive oil plus a little more for the bowl

¼ cup fennel seeds, lightly crushed in a mortar

1 egg white beaten with 2 tablespoons water

⅓ cup or more sesame seeds, as needed

Mix together the warm water (hotter than body temperature but not too hot to hold a finger in it comfortably) with the yeast in a large bowl. When the yeast has dissolved, stir in about 2½ cups all-purpose flour and mix with a spoon. Add the cup of whole-wheat flour and the salt—by now you should be able to mix the sticky flour and liquid together with your hands.

Spread ½ cup or more flour on a bread board and turn the dough out onto the board. Knead well for about 10 minutes, gradually incorporating a tablespoon of olive oil into the bread. Return the kneaded dough to the rinsed-out, lightly oiled bowl, cover with a damp kitchen towel, and set aside to rise for about 2 hours or until the dough has doubled in bulk. The ideal rising temperature is between 60 and 70 degrees, but it won't matter if the temperature is off a little in either direction.

When the dough has doubled, turn it out on the lightly floured board, punch it down, and knead slightly to get rid of any air bubbles. Spread it out and sprinkle the fennel seeds over, then roll up and knead a few more strokes to distribute the fennel seeds evenly throughout.

Cut the dough in half and form each half into a 10- to 12-inch-long sausage. Cover lightly with a damp kitchen towel and set aside for about 30 minutes to rise in the kitchen's warmth. If you're using a baking stone or tiles, set them in the oven and preheat to 425 degrees for at least 30 minutes. Or use a baking sheet with a little cornmeal scattered over it and preheat to 425 degrees.

Just before baking, paint each loaf with the egg-white mixture and pat the sesame seeds thickly all over the top and sides of each loaf. With a very sharp knife or a razor, cut slashes in the top of each loaf. Bake the loaves for about 20 to 25 minutes or until the sesame-flecked crust is russet-gold and the bread feels hollow when you knock the bottom gently.

Southern Italian Semolina Bread

Pane Pugliese

➳ Makes 2 loaves, weighing 2 to 2½ pounds each

S OUTHERN ITALY'S DAILY BREAD is traditionally made with golden semolina, which gives the bread a beautiful creamy yellow crumb that looks as if
eggs had been mixed in the dough. The semolina comes from hard durum wheat
that is grown to this day on the rolling plains of northern Puglia and central
Sicily. In Puglia, the heel of the Italian boot, they say the town of Altamura makes
the best bread in all of Italy. In the rest of the country this crisp-crusted, dense
semolina bread is called *pane pugliese,* bread from Puglia, whether it actually
comes from Puglia or not. But it never tastes as good, they say, as the bread from
Altamura itself.

A good source for semolina is, once again, the King Arthur Flour Company in
Vermont (www.kingarthurflour.com).

FOR THE STARTER OR BIGA

1 cup warm water

½ teaspoon dry yeast

1½ cups unbleached all-purpose flour

FOR THE DOUGH

2 cups warm water

6 to 8 cups semolina, plus a little more for the board

1½ cups room-temperature water

1 tablespoon fine sea salt

extra-virgin olive oil

First make the biga. Put the water in a small bowl, sprinkle the yeast over the top, and leave for 2 to 3 minutes until the yeast dissolves. Gently stir the yeast and water together. Add the all-purpose flour and, using a wooden spoon, stir the flour into the liquid to make a thick slurry. Cover the bowl loosely with plastic wrap or a dampened kitchen towel and set aside in a cool place for several hours or overnight to let the starter develop.

Next day, turn the starter into a larger bowl. Add the warm water and, using your hands, break up the biga in the water. (It will make a sloppy mixture.) Add 2 cups of semolina and work it gradually into the liquid. Cover with a damp cloth or towel and set aside in a cool place (not refrigerated) to rise for 2 to 3 hours until the mass in the bowl has puffed and looks thicker, with bubbles over the surface. This is the first rise.

After the first rise, add the 1½ cups of room-temperature water and 4 to 5 cups of semolina to the mixture, a little at a time—a little flour, then a little water, and so on. Add the salt and mix well, using your hands to knead in the bowl.

Sprinkle a wooden bread board with a cup of semolina and turn the dough out onto it. Work the dough well, kneading to incorporate everything thoroughly. Knead the dough for about 10 minutes, or until it feels silky and smooth, with no hint of stickiness.

Brush a little oil around the inside of the cleaned bowl and add the dough to it, turning to coat it thoroughly. Cover once more with a damp cloth and set aside to rise till doubled, about 2 hours. This is the second rise.

Punch down the dough and form it into two loaves, round or elliptical or long, whatever you prefer. (In Puglia bakers sometimes spread the dough in a rather flat ellipse, then, when it has risen and is ready to bake, flip one half of the ellipse over the other, like a wallet. If you choose to do this, do not slash the loaf as in the directions below.)

Scatter a little cornmeal or semolina over the bread board and set the loaves on the board, covered lightly with a dry cloth.

Set the baking stone in the oven and preheat at 450 degrees for 30 minutes. (The oven light will go off before 30 minutes are up, but continue heating anyway to make sure the stone is heated through.)

Just before setting the loaves in the oven, slash the tops in three or four places with a very sharp knife to let the dough expand. Transfer to the baking stone. Bake for 15 minutes at 450 degrees, then turn the heat down to 350 and continue baking for 45 minutes longer, by the end of which time the loaves should be crisp and golden, with a pleasant hollow knock when they're rapped against the bread board. Remove from the oven and cool on a rack.

Moroccan Semolina Bread

Makes 6 individual breads; 6 servings

SEMOLINA FLOUR, ground from golden durum wheat, is a soft creamy yellow and coarser in texture than regular wheat flour. In North America it's sometimes marketed as pasta flour (it's the flour from which commercial dried pasta is made). In North Africa, semolina flour is used to make couscous, although few home cooks make their own couscous these days, since good ready-made couscous is widely available.

Moroccan cooks also use semolina flour to make the round bread that is served at every meal and is used to sop up the juices of stews, soups, and tagines. The first task of the day for many Moroccan women is to make the family supply of these breads, one per person for each meal. Properly made, this produces crisp-crusted bread with a beautiful yellow crumb. The kneading takes a little longer than with ordinary wheat flour doughs, but kneading, like shelling peas, is a good time for passive meditation—problems get solved while the dough turns to silk. The instructions in my favorite Moroccan cookbook conclude, after detailing the mixing and kneading and molding of the breads: "Send them to be baked at the neighborhood oven."

1 teaspoon active dry yeast

2 cups tepid water

4 cups semolina

1 tablespoon salt

1 cup unbleached all-purpose flour plus about ⅓ cup for the bread board

Rinse a small bowl in hot tap water. Add the yeast to the bowl along with about 3 tablespoons of the tepid water. Set aside while the yeast dissolves.

Put the semolina flour in a large mixing bowl. Make a well in the center and add the yeast mixture and the salt. Pull some of the semolina over the yeast mixture, then pour the rest of the tepid water over the semolina. Set aside for 5 minutes or so to let the semolina absorb the water. Sprinkle the cup of all-purpose flour over the semolina and begin to work the dough, first using a wooden spoon to mix, then, as the mixture becomes raggedy, using your hands. Knead the dough in the bowl with your hands until it is well blended, then turn the dough out onto a lightly floured board and knead for at least 20 minutes, gradually incorporating some of the flour on the board. The mixture will become silky and smooth, though still a little sticky.

After 20 minutes, form the dough into a large ball and set aside. Sprinkle the rest of the ⅓ cup flour on the board. Using a knife or a dough cutter, divide the ball of dough into six pieces. (Don't tear the smaller pieces away with your hands, because you risk tearing the developing gluten structure.) Form each piece into a ball about the size of an orange—each one will weigh approximately ½ pound. As you form each ball, roll it lightly in the flour on the board and set aside. Let the balls rest for about 5 minutes.

Pat each ball into a round flat circle about ¾ inch thick. Set the circles on a wooden peel or bread board and prick each one with a fork in six or seven places. Cover lightly with aluminum foil and set aside to rise for 30 minutes.

If you're using a baking stone, place it in the cold oven and preheat the oven to 450 degrees for 30 minutes. If you're using a baking sheet, simply preheat the oven to 425 degrees.

Place the breads on the stone or baking sheet, close the oven door, and turn the heat down to 400 degrees. Work quickly so that the oven temperature does not have a chance to drop below 400 degrees. Bake the breads for 20 to 25 minutes or until they are golden brown and cooked through.

MEDITERRANEAN-STYLE SANDWICHES

Once you have really good bread, made at least in part with whole-grain flour, you'll want to serve up Med-style sandwiches as an easy lunch or light supper. The region is not short on sandwich ideas, most of them involving lots of good fresh vegetables and plenty of olive oil. Here are a few:

PAN BAGNAT: This renowned and much imitated sandwich comes from the southern coast of Provence, especially around Nice, where it is often served *en plein aire* with a good bottle of Nice's finest vin rosé du Bellet. It is sometimes made with a long baguette, but more often with petits pains, small round buns, not more than about 4 or 5 inches in diameter but with a crispy, not a soft crust. Whether baguette or petit pain, the trick is to split the loaf in half and pull out some of the inner crumb. Then rub the cut surfaces with a cut clove of garlic and dribble with a couple of tablespoons of extra-virgin olive oil. Leave the bread halves to absorb the oil for a bit, then pour off any excess (save it for dressing salad). Cover one-half of the bread with any or all of the following: thinly sliced ripe tomatoes, sliced hard-boiled eggs, anchovy fillets and/or drained flaked tuna, thin slices of cucumber, some pitted black olives, very thin slices of white onion—add as much or as little of any of these ingredients as your fancy dictates. These are considered de rigueur. But you could also add any of the following: sliced gherkin pickles, sweet red peppers slivered, slices of artichoke hearts, either very fresh and raw or pickled, slivered basil leaves, slivered radishes, coarsely chopped flat-leaf parsley. Then sea salt and freshly ground black pepper (judiciously with the salt because you have a number of salty ingredients already), a spritz of red wine vinegar, and top the sandwich with the other half of bread. Weight the sandwich for a good half hour (just put a plate on top with a can of tomatoes or a bottle of wine to weight it) to press it together and let all the good juices commingle. Then slice it in half (or in serviceable lengths if using a baguette) and serve.

PANE CUNZATO ("GARNISHED BREAD"): This Sicilian sandwich reminds me a lot of what's called a muffaletta in New Orleans—in fact, muffaletta is a Sicilian term for a small round soft bun, which is what you should use for this. Cut or tear a round loaf in half and douse the uneven cut surfaces with olive oil. Then add a sprinkling of dried oregano, sea salt, and freshly ground black pepper. Mix together a salad of pitted black and green olives, chopped anchovies, some slivers of roasted red peppers (the kind that come in jars), and, if you wish, some sliced marinated artichoke hearts. But the olives should predominate. Sprinkle with a little lemon juice and add some minced garlic if you wish. Press and weight the sandwich as in the Pan Bagnat above.

TUNISIAN MARKET SANDWICH: Another sandwich made traditionally with a small round individual loaf, no more than 6 or 8 inches across. This one is sold in bakeries in the souq in Tunis's lovely old medina. In this case, you cut off about a fourth of the loaf and pull the crumb out of the remaining, larger piece. Smear garlicky harissa all over the inside, then fill the sandwich with what's called salade tunisienne: sliced boiled potatoes, olives, slices of salt-preserved lemons, capers, tuna, some olive oil, then slices of grilled onions, tomatoes, and peppers. Dip the quarter that you cut off in olive oil or carrot salad, then shove it back into the sandwich to hold all the other ingredients in place.

Pompe à L'huile

Olive Oil Bread from France

Makes one 10-inch loaf; 16 servings

MADELEINE KAMMAN, A GREAT COOK and teacher, introduced me many years ago to this festive bread from Provence. The round golden disk is appropriate for both Christmas and Easter, two feasts of the sun that linger in our modern calendar.

2 cups unbleached all-purpose flour

¼ cup warm milk or water

1¼-ounce envelope active dry yeast

5 tablespoons sugar

3 large eggs

½ teaspoon sea salt

[cont. next page]

Put the flour in a mixing bowl and make a well in the center. Pour the warm milk into the well and sprinkle the yeast on top. Set aside for about 5 minutes while the yeast gradually absorbs some of the liquid. Add a tablespoon of sugar to the yeast and, using a wooden spoon, flick some of the flour from around the sides of the well over the yeasty liquid, covering it completely. Set aside to allow the yeast to develop for at least 30 minutes.

½ cup extra-virgin olive oil plus a little for greasing the bowl and pan

1 tablespoon orange-flower water

2 tablespoons grated orange zest

In a separate bowl, beat 2 of the eggs with the remaining sugar and the salt until the mixture is foamy. Beat in the olive oil, orange-flower water, and grated zest. Pour this mixture into the bowl with the flour and slowly mix in all the flour from around the edges of the bowl. You can use a wooden spoon at first, but once the mixture becomes raggedy, start to use your hands. Eventually you will need to turn the dough out onto a lightly floured board and knead for at least 10 minutes to develop the gluten.

Rinse out the mixing bowl, grease it lightly with a little olive oil, and transfer the well-kneaded dough to the bowl. Cover with a damp cloth and set aside in a warm place to rise. When it is double in bulk—after about 2 hours—turn it out onto the board again, punch it down, and knead very briefly just to knock out any air holes. Return to the greased bowl, cover with the damp cloth, and let rise again until doubled in bulk—about 1½ hours.

Lightly oil a 10-inch round cake pan. Punch the dough down after the second rise, knead again briefly to knock out any air holes, and roll or pat it out in a disk to fit the pan. With a very sharp knife, cut a crisscross or crosshatch pattern about ½ inch deep in the surface of the dough. Cover loosely with a sheet of aluminum foil and set aside to rise until the dough is about 1½ inches high—about 1½ hours.

When you're ready to bake, preheat the oven to 375 degrees. Beat the remaining egg with a teaspoon of cool water and use it to paint the surface of the bread (you will need only about half the egg for this). Cut the crosshatch slashes again. Bake the bread for 20 to 25 minutes. Remove from the oven and cool on a rack before turning the bread out.

Crescia or Ciaccia di Pasqua

Italian Cheese and Pancetta Easter Bread

Makes one 8-inch round loaf; 8 to 10 servings

WITH NUGGETS OF CHEESE and pancetta, this dense bread is made for Easter in central Italy, where the cheese used is pecorino—not hard sour pecorino romano but a slightly aged sheep's milk cheese. Look for pecorino toscano or pecorino sardo.

Pancetta gives a more authentic flavor, but slab bacon might be used instead. If it's very smoky, blanch it briefly in boiling water.

½ cup milk

1 ¼-ounce envelope active dry yeast

½ cup (1 stick) unsalted butter

½ cup fruity extra-virgin olive oil

6 cups cake flour plus more for the board

½ teaspoon sea salt, or more to taste

½ pound sheep's milk cheese (pecorino toscano or pecorino sardo)

1 cup freshly grated parmigiano cheese

2 ounces pancetta, prosciutto, or slab bacon, diced

1 whole egg and 1 egg white

a pinch of saffron threads

sea salt and freshly ground black pepper

Warm the milk to body temperature on the stove. Pour it into a small bowl and sprinkle the yeast over it. Stir with a wooden spoon to dissolve the yeast and set aside for 10 minutes.

Combine the butter and olive oil in a small saucepan and warm on the stove to melt the butter, but don't let it cook.

Add the flour and salt to a large mixing bowl, tossing to distribute the salt evenly. Grate half the sheep's milk cheese on the large holes of a grater and cut the other half of the cheese into small cubes. Add all the cheese, the parmigiano, and the pancetta to the flour and toss with your hands to coat the bits with flour.

Make a well in the center of the flour and pour in the yeast and milk. Beat the whole egg with a fork and add to the yeast along with the saffron threads, crumbling them gently. Add a little salt and pepper. Gradually mix the flour with the liquids, drizzling the olive oil–butter mixture over the flour as you mix. Use a wooden spoon at first and then your hands. Turn the dough out onto a lightly floured board for the final kneading. (Because of the added cheese and ham, the dough will not become smooth and silky like regular bread dough, but it should be soft and well mixed.)

Set the kneaded dough in the mixing bowl, rinsed out, dried, and greased lightly. Cover with a damp kitchen towel and let rise for about 1½ hours.

Butter and flour an 8-inch round springform or cake pan (3 inches deep). Knock the dough down and knead briefly, then press it into the pan, using your knuckles, and set aside, lightly covered, in a warm place to rise again for about 30 minutes.

When the dough has risen, preheat the oven to 400 degrees. Brush lightly beaten egg white over the top of the bread and bake for about 45 minutes or until the top is golden.

PIZZA

Making pizza at home is quick, easy, and fun—or at least it is after you've done it a couple of times. Grown-ups love it almost as much as children do. Even the most recalcitrant young eater usually can be persuaded by pizza—it's a marvelously deceptive way to introduce good-for-you food to rigidly resistant small palates.

So why does pizza evoke squawks of protest from nutritionists? Because they're talking about fast-food pizza as it's served in this country, piled high with saturated fat, sugar, and sodium. The pizza you make at home, on the other hand, is a well-balanced modern Mediterranean meal: a good carbohydrate (the pizza dough) at the center of the plate, dressed with vegetables (tomatoes, onions, fresh peppers) and a little animal protein (anchovies, fresh mozzarella, a few slivers of ham or sausage), the whole bathed in the glow of good monounsaturated fat in the form of extra-virgin olive oil.

On its home ground, pizza is like that, a model of rectitude poised between exuberance and restraint.* On its home ground, too, pizza is almost never made at home. In Italy pizza is the ultimate social food, made in public

*Times are changing, even in Napoli, where I have recently seen, but not tasted, both *pizza al cioccolato,* thickly spread with what looked surprisingly like Nutella, and even more startling, *pizza con patate fritte,* pizza with a topping of french fries.

to be consumed in public, preferably in the company of friends and colleagues. But we live in America, and to the astonishment of Italians, we make pizza at home.

If you find the prospect daunting at first, don't worry. Pizza, like bread in general, is very forgiving, and since it's so fast, a mistake is easily overcome. Everyone who has ever made it, including some of the most gifted chefs in the country, has fallen victim to burned crusts, burned tops, or, the ultimate disaster, jerking the pizza onto the stone only to have the topping slide off, the dough stick to the peel, and a hell of a mess sizzling on the baking stone.

A couple of inexpensive pieces of equipment will help make the process of baking pizza or calzone easier and the results better. A baking stone, a disk or rectangle of composite stone made for use in the oven, or baking tiles (unglazed ceramic tiles from a building supply house) will simulate the effect of the wood-fired masonry ovens traditionally used for pizza and breads throughout the Mediterranean. And a wooden peel, a thin board with a handle and a beveled edge at the far end, makes it easier to slide the prepared dough onto the hot stone.

If you don't want to invest in these, bake your pizza on a cookie sheet or in a shallow pie plate. The crust will be softer, without the pleasing crunch and roasted flavor that comes from the stone, but it will still be a good thing.

Basic Pizza Dough

Makes enough dough for two 8- to 10-inch pizzas;
4 servings as a first course or accompaniment
to a main-course soup or salad

½ teaspoon active dry yeast

1 cup very warm water

2 cups unbleached all-purpose flour

1 cup whole-wheat flour or semolina

1 teaspoon sea salt, dissolved in ½ cup hot water

[cont. next page]

To make the biga, combine the yeast and very warm water in a bowl, stirring gently. When the yeast has dissolved, add about a cup of the all-purpose flour. Stir just until blended. The dough may be lumpy but that doesn't matter. Cover the bowl with plastic wrap or a damp towel and set aside for at least 30 minutes to begin working. Or you may leave the biga in a cool place (not the refrigerator) for several hours or overnight.

½ teaspoon olive oil for the bowl

coarse semolina or cornmeal for the peel, if necessary

When ready to continue, set aside a half-cup of all-purpose flour to use on the bread board. Add the remaining half-cup of flour and the whole-wheat flour or semolina to the biga, stirring to mix. Add half the salt water and stir it in, then as much of the remaining salt water as necessary to make the dough sufficiently soft and ready to knead. You may need as little as ½ cup or as much as a full cup of liquid—much depends on ambient humidity.

Use the reserved half-cup of flour to sprinkle a light dusting on the bread board. Turn the dough out onto the board and knead for 10 minutes, gradually incorporating more flour—but only if it seems necessary. Otherwise, just use enough flour on the board to keep the dough from sticking. Continue kneading until you have a springy, elastic dough that has lost its tackiness.

Rinse and dry the bowl and smear the inside with a little olive oil. Shape the dough into a ball and turn it in the bowl to oil the surface of the dough, then set aside, covered with plastic, to rise for at least an hour in a warm place—the ambient temperature in the kitchen should be sufficient. Or, if it's more convenient, set the bowl in a cooler environment such as an unheated pantry and leave it overnight to develop more complex flavors.

When you're ready to make pizza, set your oven on very high—550 degrees if you can, otherwise, the highest temperature your oven will reach. If you're using a pizza stone, set the cold stone in the cold oven, to avoid cracking the stone, and preheat for at least 30 minutes, even if the oven light goes off, to get the stone as hot as you can before transferring the pizza. If you're using a pizza pan or a sheet pan, you need only heat the oven until it reaches 450 to 550 degrees.

Turn the dough out once more onto the lightly floured board, punch it down, and divide it in two. Keep the half that you're not working with lightly covered with a damp towel.

Knead the dough briefly, then shape it into a ball and stretch it into a rough disk, about 10 to 12 inches in diameter and less than ¼ inch thick, working from the center of the disk outward. You may use a rolling pin to do this, although professional pizzaioli can shape and stretch an immaculate circle with their hands, turning it rapidly and pulling gently on the outer edge of the circle. (My own efforts usually end up with a pretty free-form pizza but it tastes just as good.)

If you're using a wooden peel, sprinkle it quite heavily with semolina or cornmeal and stretch the dough circle over the peel. (If you're using a baking sheet, simply lay the circle of dough on the pan— no need to oil it.) Just before you put the pizza in the oven, add the topping you wish, then dribble a little olive oil over the top.

When the oven is hot, slide the pizza onto the pizza stone with a brisk shake of the peel or simply transfer the pan with the pizza to a rack in the upper part of the oven. Bake for 7 to 10 minutes until the pizza dough is golden and the topping is bubbling. Remove from the oven, slice, and serve immediately. (Some pizza makers like to set the pizza on a rack for a couple of minutes before slicing, in order to let any steam in the dough escape before the dough turns soggy.)

Pizza Napoletana

Traditional Toppings for Neapolitan Pizza

MARGHERITA AND MARINARA are the classic treatments for Neapolitan pizza and have been ever since that unrecorded moment in the 19th century when the New World tomato was firmly and finally wedded to the venerable Neapolitan flatbread called *pizza*. Marinara is a simple sauce, according to the rules established by the True Neapolitan Pizza Association, made of oil, tomatoes, oregano, garlic, and salt. Pizza Margherita is only slightly more complex: oil, tomatoes, grated cheese, mozzarella, basil, and salt. Note the absence of garlic: because this was the favorite of Margherita of Savoy, or so it is said, garlic was left out so that no odor might sully the breath of the queen of Italy.

Pizza can be dressed with chopped or sliced fresh tomatoes, but cooked tomato sauce is more commonly used, even in Naples, where tomatoes at their peak are among the most sensational things I have ever put in my mouth. Leftover sauce freezes well and can be used on pasta or in a soup. Use the recipe for Plain Tomato Sauce (La Pomarola) on page 266.

The quantities for each topping make one 8- to 10-inch pizza. If you wish to make two *pizze alla marinara,* simply double the quantities for the remaining ingredients—but it's more fun to make two different kinds of pizza.

Pizza alla Marinara

Makes one 8- to 10-inch pizza; serving 2 as a starter

THIS IS THE SIMPLEST, purest, and most authentic pizza, the kind you would find in just about any establishment in the Neapolitan heartland. It may startle you by its simplicity but it is really very good. However, although the True Neapolitan Pizza Association might not approve, you could add ¼ cup freshly grated parmigiano cheese to the top of the pizza just before you put it in the oven. In fact, you could add any number of good things—pitted black olives, chopped anchovies, crumbled fresh sausage, crumbled canned tuna. But don't overdo it—with a real Neapolitan pizza you should be able to taste the tomato, the garnish, and the bread itself, as separate flavors that combine to make a miracle.

½ recipe pizza dough (page 171)

semolina or cornmeal for the peel

1 tablespoon extra-virgin olive oil

¾ cup Plain Tomato Sauce (La Pomarola) (page 266)

6 garlic cloves, chopped or thinly sliced

½ teaspoon dried oregano, crumbled

sea salt and freshly ground black pepper

Follow the directions on page 171 for heating the oven and preparing and shaping the pizza dough. Assemble all the ingredients for the pizza before you start to work.

Brush the dough circle with olive oil right out to the edge (you won't use all the oil). Using a wooden spoon or your fingers, spread the tomato sauce over the dough, leaving about a ¼-inch rim around the edge. Distribute the garlic and oregano over the tomato sauce and add salt (if needed) and pepper. Dribble the remaining olive oil over the pizza—be sure to wring the oil out of the brush.

Open the oven door and quickly but smoothly jerk the dough onto the hot stone. Or slide the baking sheet into the oven. Close the door and turn the heat down to 500 degrees. Work quickly so the oven temperature does not have a chance to drop below 500 degrees. Bake for 5 to 6 minutes or until the crust is brown and the top is bubbling.

Pizza Margherita

Makes one 8-to 10-inch pizza; serving 2 as a starter

ONLY SLIGHTLY MORE ELABORATE, this is the pizza said to have been created for the queen of Italy. Note the absence of garlic—to be authentic, leave garlic out of the Plain Tomato Sauce on page 266 (but when nobody's looking, garlic is a good—and healthful—addition).

½ recipe pizza dough (page 171)

[cont. next page]

Follow the directions on page 171 for heating the oven and preparing and shaping the pizza dough.

semolina or cornmeal for the peel

1 tablespoon extra-virgin olive oil

¾ cup Plain Tomato Sauce (La Pomarola) (page 266)

about 3 ounces imported mozzarella di bufala or cow's milk fior di latte, sliced

sea salt and freshly ground black pepper

1 small bunch of fresh basil leaves, rinsed well

¼ cup freshly grated parmigiano cheese

Brush the dough circle with olive oil right out to the edge (you won't use all the oil). Using a wooden spoon or your fingers, spread the tomato sauce over the dough, leaving about a ¼-inch rim around the edge. Distribute the mozzarella slices over the tomato sauce and add salt and pepper. Arrange the basil leaves over the mozzarella, reserving a few for garnish if you wish, then sprinkle with the parmigiano. Dribble the remaining olive oil over the pizza—be sure to wring the oil out of the brush.

Open the oven door and quickly but smoothly jerk the dough onto the hot stone. Or slide the baking sheet into the oven. Close the door and turn the heat down to 500 degrees. Work quickly so the oven temperature does not have a chance to drop below 500 degrees. Bake for 5 to 6 minutes or until the crust is brown and the top is bubbling. Add the reserved basil leaves just before serving.

OTHER TOPPINGS FOR AN 8- TO 10-INCH PIZZA

Remember to keep pizza simple. When you start to pile on layers of cheese, sliced meats, and oil-drenched vegetables, pizza is no longer a healthful alternative. (I just looked up the nutritional breakdown for a Pizza Hut "Double Deep Meat Lover's Pizza," helpfully provided by the Pizza Hut company. One-eighth of a 12-inch pizza, which is considered one serving, has 580 calories, of which 330 are from fat. Bet you can't eat just one!)

Add to this list by using your imagination:

- Add chopped cooked broccoli, cauliflower, or artichokes, mixed with gently sautéed onions and garlic, then top with a thin layer of mozzarella (to keep the vegetables from burning) and a scattering of parmigiano reggiano; dribble extra-virgin olive oil on top.

- Grill red peppers and sliced red onions and distribute over the pizza dough with dabs of fresh goat's cheese; lightly scatter parmigiano reggiano or another hard grating cheese and dribble with extra-virgin olive oil.

- Cook chopped fresh or canned tomatoes with onions, green peppers (maybe a few fresh chilies), and sliced mushrooms, then shave parmigiano reggiano, using a vegetable parer, over the top and dribble with extra-virgin olive oil.

- Spread caramelized onions over the pizza disk, then top with crumbled gorgonzola and broken walnuts, a few dabs of fresh goat's cheese, and a dribble of extra-virgin olive oil.

- Spread the pizza disk with basil pesto, slice fresh ripe tomatoes over the top and real mozzarella on top of the tomatoes, a sprinkle of parmigiano, a dribble of oil, and that's it.

Anna Tasca Lanza's Sicilian Focaccia

Sfincione

Makes 10 to 12 servings

ANNA TASCA LANZA is part of the Tasca d'Almerita wine-making family who have their headquarters at Regaleali, deep in the heart of Sicily on a vast estate where rolling green vineyards produce some of Sicily's most notable wines. Case Vecchie, Anna's own small farm within the estate, is the site of her delightful cooking school, which she now runs with her daughter Fabrizia Lanza. The *sfincione,* a revered tradition, has always been a favorite with students, family, and friends. Don't be put off by the presence of "foreign" cheeses—that's the way they do it at Regaleali.

3 medium onions, thinly sliced

½ cup plus 2 tablespoons extra-virgin olive oil

¼ teaspoon active dry yeast

[cont. next page]

Saute the onions very slowly in ½ cup of olive oil over medium-low heat until golden—this will take about 30 minutes. When done, remove from heat and strain the onions, but keep the oil to use later.

While the onions are cooking, dissolve the yeast in a cup of warm water. Mix the flours and salt

2 cups unbleached all-purpose flour, plus a little more for the board

1 cup semolina

sea salt

1 egg, lightly beaten

6 to 8 anchovy fillets, coarsely chopped

½ pound fresh mozzarella, preferably made from cow's milk, thinly sliced

¼ pound emmental cheese, thinly sliced

¼ pound gouda or edam cheese, thinly sliced

½ cup freshly grated parmigiano reggiano

¼ cup freshly grated caciocavallo or aged pecorino

2 to 3 tablespoons dried oregano, crumbled

½ cup dry unflavored bread crumbs

together in a bowl, make a well in the center, and pour the dissolved yeast into the well. Add the egg and 2 tablespoons of oil. Mix well, working the dough into a ball. Spread a few tablespoons of flour on a bread board and knead the dough for 10 minutes or so, until it is smooth and elastic.

Roll or stretch the dough out into a rectangle to fit a 9 x 12-inch baking sheet, preferably one with raised edges so nothing will spill onto the oven floor. Place the dough in the pan and scatter the anchovy pieces over it. Distribute the sliced cheeses over the anchovies, first the mozzarella, then the emmental and gouda, then spread the strained onions on top. Sprinkle the grated cheeses over the onions, then the oregano, and finally the bread crumbs. Using the palms of your hands, gently press the topping into the dough. Dribble about ¼ cup of the strained oil from the onions over the top. Set aside, covered loosely with plastic wrap or a kitchen towel, in a warm corner of the kitchen and let rise for about 45 minutes.

Preheat the oven to 400 degrees. When the oven is hot, bake the sfincione for 25 minutes, then lower the oven temperature to 325 degrees and continue baking until the cheeses have melted and the top crust is brown, about 20 more minutes. Remove from the oven and let stand for 15 minutes (if you can resist the fragrance) before cutting and serving.

Pissaladière

Provençal Pizza

◈ Makes 4 to 6 servings

THIS IS PROVENÇAL PIZZA, although the name comes not, as you might expect, from pizza but from pissala, a strongly flavored anchovy paste that was once the basis of the pie. Elizabeth David's version, published more than 40 years ago in *French Provincial Cooking,* calls for a rich egg and butter dough and makes something like a savory tart or an eggless quiche. I use olive oil instead of butter but otherwise follow her recipe more or less as she wrote it. It makes, as Mrs. David noted, "a splendid first course at luncheon." In my family it was also considered a superior after-school snack. It's as good at room temperature as it is straight from the oven, something you can't say for most pizzas.

½ teaspoon active dry yeast

¼ cup warm water

1¼ to 1½ cups all-purpose flour

sea salt

1 large egg

4 tablespoons extra-virgin olive oil

1¼ pounds yellow onions, about 2 medium, halved and thinly sliced

1 garlic clove, sliced

2 medium tomatoes, peeled (page 25) and chopped, or 3 canned whole tomatoes, well drained and chopped

2 tablespoons slivered fresh basil leaves or ½ teaspoon dried thyme, crumbled

12 oil-packed anchovy fillets or 3 salt-packed anchovies, prepared as directed on page 40

½ cup pitted black Niçoise or Gaeta olives

freshly ground black pepper

Mix the yeast with the warm water and set aside for about 10 minutes, until it is creamy.

Put a heaped cup of flour in a mixing bowl, add a pinch of salt, and stir to mix. Make a well in the middle of the flour and add the yeast mixture and the egg along with 2 tablespoons of the olive oil. Gradually mix the flour into the liquids and stir to combine well, adding more flour as necessary. Knead with your hands in the bowl, then briefly on a lightly floured board. When the dough is soft and smooth, put it back in the bowl, rinsed out and wiped lightly with a paper towel dipped in a little olive oil. Cover with a damp cloth and set aside to rise in a warm place for 2 hours.

Meanwhile, make the topping. In a heavy skillet over medium-low heat, gently sauté the onion and garlic in the remaining olive oil until the onion is very soft and golden but not brown—about 15 to 20 minutes. Stir in the tomatoes and continue cooking until the tomato liquid has evaporated and the sauce is thick. Add the basil, a little salt, and several grinds of pepper.

Turn the dough out onto the lightly floured board, punch it down, and knead briefly to knock the air holes out. Place the dough in the center of a lightly oiled straight-sided 8-inch pie pan or quiche pan. With your knuckles, press the dough gently but rapidly outward until it is spread over the bottom of the pan and all around the sides. Spread the onion-tomato mixture over the dough. Crisscross the anchovy fillets over the top and fill in the crosses with olives. Place the pie pan on a baking sheet and put it aside to rest and rise while the oven heats.

Preheat the oven to 400 degrees. Place the baking sheet in the middle of the oven and bake for about 20 minutes. Turn the oven down to 350 degrees and bake for another 20 minutes. The crust should be golden and the filling bubbly. Remove from the oven and let sit for 10 minutes or so before serving.

Middle Eastern Pizza

❧ **Makes 16 individual (5- to 6-inch) pizzas**

Fᴿᴏᴍ Bᴇɪʀᴜᴛ ᴛᴏ Dᴀᴍᴀsᴄᴜs to Aleppo to Istanbul, wherever there's a wood-burning bakery oven in an old part of town, the seductive fragrance of these little open-faced pies wafts forth. Called *lahm m'ajin* in Arabic (or *lahm açun* in Turkey), they might be Turkish, or Armenian, or Lebano-Syrian, but they come from that part of the eastern Mediterranean where culinary distinctions are difficult to sort through. In any case, the principle is the same as Neapolitan pizza but the result is very different and decidedly Middle Eastern with flavors of cinnamon, allspice, and cumin, and lamb as the principal ingredient—although you could substitute beef. The tartness in the topping, which is an essential part of the flavor, can come from pomegranate syrup, or from strained yogurt, or from fresh lemon juice—your choice. You could use a normal pizza dough (page 171) for this, but the rich dough described below, with olive oil and yogurt, makes a very tasty alternative.

This makes lovely picnic fare, and it's also a fine lunch with a hefty salad like Greek horiatiki (page 88), Lebanese fattoush (page 87), or Italian panzanella (page 86).

FOR THE DOUGH

3 ½ cups unbleached all-purpose flour plus a little more for the board

1 tablespoon sea salt

½ teaspoon granulated yeast dissolved in ¼ cup warm water

½ cup extra-virgin olive oil

To make the dough, combine the flour and salt in a bowl, tossing to mix well. Make a well in the center and add the dissolved yeast. Flick flour over the yeast mixture to cover completely and set aside for 10 to 15 minutes to start working. (You could leave it longer if it's more convenient, up to 2 hours in a warm kitchen.)

Using a wooden spoon, start to stir the yeast mixture into the flour, gradually adding the oil and

½ cup plain yogurt (nonfat or low-fat is okay)

½ cup warm water

FOR THE TOPPING

2 tablespoons extra-virgin olive oil

½ cup pine nuts

2 medium yellow onions, finely chopped (about 1½ cups)

¾ pound ground lean lamb or beef

1 cup drained, chopped canned whole tomatoes

½ cup finely chopped fresh sweet red pepper

1 cup finely chopped flat-leaf parsley

¼ cup finely chopped cilantro

2 teaspoons ground cumin

1 teaspoon ground allspice, or to taste

2 tablespoons tomato concentrate

1 tablespoon pomegranate syrup or 2 tablespoons strained yogurt or ½ tablespoon fresh lemon juice

½ teaspoon flaked or ground red chili pepper, preferably Aleppo pepper or piment d'Espelette

freshly ground black pepper

strained yogurt for garnish

yogurt. When all the oil and yogurt have been added, the dough will still be quite stiff. At this point, start to work in warm water. You may not need to use all the water. You are aiming for a soft, malleable bread dough. As soon as you can do so, turn the dough out onto a bread board, first sprinkling it with a small amount of flour to keep the dough from sticking. Knead the dough for 5 to 10 minutes, or until it is tender and elastic and has lost its tackiness. You may have to add a little more flour or a little more water during the kneading. Once the dough has reached the right consistency—as soft as your earlobe, or a baby's bottom—set it aside, loosely covered with plastic wrap or a damp kitchen towel, and let it rise for at least an hour.

While the dough is rising, make the topping: combine the olive oil and pine nuts in a skillet and cook over medium heat, stirring constantly, until the pine nuts have started to turn golden but not brown. Remove the pine nuts with a slotted spoon and set aside.

Add the onions to the pan, lower the heat, and cook until very soft and light golden but not browned—about 15 minutes. Combine with all the other ingredients, including the pine nuts, in a bowl and mix well with your hands, adding salt and pepper to taste. Set the meat topping aside.

When you're ready to assemble the pizzas, set the oven on 450 degrees.

Turn the dough out onto a lightly floured board, punch down, and knead briefly to knock out any air bubbles. Divide the dough into quarters and keep the pieces you are not working loosely covered with plastic wrap or a damp towel. Roll a quarter of the dough out on the board until it is very thin—about ⅛ of an inch. Using a cutter or a pan lid for a pattern, cut out circles of dough and set the circles on a baking sheet. You should be able to get four disks of dough, 5 to 6 inches in diameter, from each quarter.

Cover each disk with a thin layer of topping. (If you must bake in batches, only put the topping on just before you put a sheet of pizzas in the oven.) The topping should extend out to the edges, leaving a very thin border exposed. Transfer the baking sheets to the preheated oven and bake for about 10 minutes, or until the pastry is golden but still rather soft. Serve hot from the oven with a dollop of strained yogurt, although they are also very good at room temperature.

Variations:

While Lebanese cooks use pine nuts in their lahm m'ajin, Turkish cooks often substitute walnuts, coarsely chopped.

A Palestinian topping for these little pies, called sfiha in Palestine, is the following, developed from a recipe by Christiane Dabdoub Nasser.

1 tablespoon extra-virgin olive oil

¼ cup pine nuts

2 medium fresh ripe tomatoes, peeled, seeded (page 25), and finely chopped

1 medium onion, minced

3 garlic cloves, minced

1 fresh hot chili pepper (serrano or jalapeño), seeded and minced

¾ pound ground lean beef

sea salt and freshly ground black pepper

½ teaspoon allspice

⅓ cup tahini

2 tablespoons white wine vinegar

Prepare the pine nuts as in the preceding recipe.

If the tomatoes are very juicy, drain them in a sieve or colander and discard the juice. Combine the drained tomatoes and the other minced vegetables in a bowl with the ground beef. Add salt and pepper, the toasted pine nuts, and the allspice and mix well, using your hands.

In a separate small bowl, mix the tahini and the vinegar, stirring to make a smooth paste. Combine the tahini with the meat mixture. Use this as a topping for the pies and bake as described above.

Catalan Pizza

Cocas

Makes 4 servings

Fascinating how theme and variations develop in a great arc around the Mediterranean. The simplicity of a little disk of bread dough, spread with something savory, a mix of onions and garlic cooked in olive oil, eked out with a little salt fish or olives or a crumble of cheese, and toasted in a hot oven obviously has tremendous appeal. In Catalonia, the northeastern part of Mediterranean Spain, pizzas are called *cocas* and exist also in sweet versions. But I prefer the savory kind, as in this one with sweet red peppers playing a starring role—and red peppers, they say, always mark a coca as coming from Majorca, the big island off the Catalan coast. A little cornmeal adds crunch to the dough.

FOR THE DOUGH

1 cup cornmeal

¾ cup boiling water

2 cups unbleached all-purpose flour

1 teaspoon sea salt

1 teaspoon active dry yeast dissolved in ½ cup warm water

2 tablespoons extra-virgin olive oil

FOR THE TOPPING

2 sweet red peppers, finely chopped

2 medium very ripe tomatoes, peeled, seeded (page 25), and chopped

1 medium yellow onion, finely chopped

1 tablespoon minced flat-leaf parsley

[cont. next page]

Add the cornmeal to a small bowl and pour the boiling water over it, stirring to combine well.

Add the flour to a mixing bowl with a good pinch of salt. Make a well in the center of the flour. Pour in the dissolved yeast and a tablespoon of olive oil. Gradually stir the flour into the liquid, using a wooden spoon, then your hands; as you work, add the dampened cornmeal. When the mixture is raggedy, turn it out onto a lightly floured board and knead for about 10 minutes or until it is silky and smooth. Rinse out the mixing bowl, dry it, and rub it lightly with a little oil. Transfer the dough to the bowl, cover with a damp towel or plastic wrap, and set aside to rise for 2 hours or until it has doubled in bulk.

While the dough rises, prepare the vegetables. Mix them all together with the paprika and a little salt.

Preheat the oven to 400 degrees. Turn the dough out onto the lightly floured board. Punch it down and knead lightly to knock out any air holes. Cut the dough into 4 equal parts and form each part into a ball. Roll each ball out to not more than

1 tablespoon sweet paprika

1 tablespoon extra-virgin
olive oil

freshly ground black pepper

¼-inch thickness. Place the dough circles on a lightly oiled baking sheet and turn the edges up very slightly to hold the topping. Drain any excess liquid from the vegetable mixture and spread some of the mixture over each circle. Sprinkle with olive oil and add a little more salt and freshly ground pepper if you wish. Slide the baking sheet into the oven and bake for 5 minutes, then turn the heat down to 300 degrees and bake 20 to 30 minutes longer or until the vegetables are cooked through and the crust is golden.

Variation: Any of the pizza toppings may be used on cocas, which are, after all, but one variation of the basic theme. I recommend the chopped greens with olives, raisins, and pine nuts in the Double-Crusted Pizza from Southern Italy (below).

Double-Crusted Pizza from Southern Italy

Makes 1 double-crust pizza; 6 to 8 servings

1 recipe pizza dough (page 171)

3 pounds mixed greens such as escarole, spinach, chard, broccoli

½ pound yellow onions, halved and sliced

2 garlic cloves, crushed with the flat blade of a knife

¼ cup extra-virgin olive oil

24 black olives, pitted and coarsely chopped

¼ cup golden raisins, plumped in warm water

¼ cup pine nuts

While the pizza dough is rising, prepare the filling. Rinse the greens, trim away the tough stem ends, and slice the tender stems and leaves into 1-inch lengths.

In a saucepan large enough to hold all the greens, gently sauté the onions and garlic in the oil for 4 to 5 minutes, until they are light golden. Stir in the greens and mix well. Clap a lid on the pan and cook for about 5 to 7 minutes or until the greens are wilted. If necessary, add a very little water from time to time to keep the greens from scorching.

When the greens are wilted, add the olives, raisins, pine nuts, and anchovies and stir to combine with the greens. Cook over medium-low heat for just a

6 oil-packed anchovy fillets, coarsely chopped

sea salt and freshly ground black pepper

1 large egg beaten with 1 teaspoon water

few minutes, then taste and add salt and pepper. Set aside until ready to cook.

When the pizza dough is doubled in size, preheat the oven to 375 degrees. Divide the dough into two unequal portions, the larger for the bottom of the pie, the smaller for the top. Lightly grease and flour a 10-inch round straight-sided pie or quiche pan. Roll out the larger piece of dough into a very thin circle large enough to cover the bottom and sides of the pan with a little hanging over the edge. Line the pan with the dough and fill the pie with the vegetable mixture. Roll the second piece of dough into a very thin circle just large enough to fit over the top of the pie. Fold and crimp the edges to hold the crust securely in place. Paint the top with a little of the beaten egg mixture and poke a design or pattern of holes into it to let the steam out. Bake for 40 to 45 minutes or until the pie is golden and crisp. Remove and let sit for 15 minutes before serving.

Spicy Greens and Sweet Cheese in a Greek Savory Pie

Hortopitta or Spanakopitta

Makes 8 servings

ONE OF THE HEALTHIEST parts of the diet of Greek countryfolk, everyone agrees, is the enormous consumption of greens—sweet, bitter, and sour, both wild and cultivated—called generically, *horta*. The range is enormous, so there's almost always something in season, whether lemon balm or purslane, wild fennel or dandelion greens, garden kale or wild chicory. Gathered year-round, greens like these are eaten on their own, tossed into farmhouse cooking pots, or brought to market for city dwellers. The open-air farmers' market in Haniá in western Crete lines both sides of the long street leading down to the port, and most of the vendors stock masses of *horta,* some of it, like beet greens and *rathikia* or wild chicory, identifiable, some of it utterly mysterious.

To mimic the flavor somewhat (but only somewhat) of a Greek hortopitta, combine spinach with any other bitter greens you can find in the market—kale, mustard greens, dandelions, and so forth. The pie may also be made with spinach alone, in which case it's called spanakopitta; it will be somewhat milder in flavor.

The list of ingredients for a Greek savory pie often begins with a pound of butter to be melted and brushed over the delicate, almost transparent leaves of filo pastry. This is delicious but quite indigestible and not, I think, something we want to have set before us more than once or twice a year. In Greek home kitchens, olive oil is more likely to be used, the thick green spicy oil that Greeks adore. The result is both lighter and more digestible and the pastry leaves are crisp, crackly, and very attractive. Incidentally, a plastic spritzer bottle for the olive oil, if you have one, is useful for layering the pastry.

2½ pounds fresh greens, well washed (see headnote for suggestions)

1 medium onion, minced

12 to 18 scallions, both white and green parts, finely sliced

2 tablespoons plus ½ cup extra-virgin olive oil

½ cup finely minced dill

½ cup finely minced flat-leaf parsley

sea salt and freshly ground black pepper

2 large eggs

¾ cup crumbled feta cheese

1 cup Greek mizithra, or ricotta or small-curd cottage cheese

1 tablespoon freshly grated parmigiano reggiano cheese

1 tablespoon plain dry bread crumbs

1 package frozen commercial filo pastry

Make the filling first, placing the greens in a large pot over medium heat. Cover the pot and steam the greens in the water clinging to their leaves for about 15 minutes or until they are very tender. Uncover and stir the greens down periodically.

When the greens are done, drain them in a colander and squeeze them very dry. (If you set the colander over a bowl and save the liquid, you can add it later to a vegetable stock or sauce.) Chop the greens rather coarsely—you should have at least 2 cups of chopped greens—and turn them into a mixing bowl.

Gently sauté the onion and scallions in 2 tablespoons of olive oil over medium-low heat, until the vegetables are very soft but not brown— about 10 to 15 minutes. Add to the greens along with all the other ingredients, one at a time, stirring after each addition. Set the filling aside and prepare the pastry.

Preheat the oven to 375 degrees.

For individual pies, you will need 8 sheets of filo, or one for each pie, plus a couple more for mistakes. Remove the sheets from the package and cover them with a very lightly dampened cloth. Cover the rest of the filo tightly with plastic wrap and return it to its package in the freezer to be used another time.

Add the half cup of olive oil to a spritzer bottle if you have one. Spray a baking sheet lightly with oil, or paint it lightly with a pastry brush. Working quickly, because filo dries out very fast upon exposure to air, remove a sheet of filo and spread it on your work surface, keeping the remaining filo sheets covered with the damp cloth. Open the sheet to its full extent, imagine it divided in half lengthwise, and spray or brush the left half very lightly with oil. Then fold the right half over the left to make a long rectangle, spraying or brushing with oil. Leaving a 1-inch margin around the edge, drop an abundant ¼ cup of filling in the lower right-hand corner of the rectangle. Fold up the lower edge and fold in the right-hand edge of the rectangle, then flip the corner over the filling in a northwesterly direction to make a triangle. Continue flipping the triangle, as if you were folding a flag, until you come to the end of the rectangle. Spray or brush the surface very lightly with oil, trim off any ragged edges with kitchen shears, and set the plump triangle of filo-encased filling on the baking sheet.

When all the filo has been filled, slide the baking sheet into the oven and bake for about 20 mintues or until the tops are golden and crisp.

To make a 10-inch round pie, you will need 12 or more sheets of filo, 6 for the bottom of the pie and another 6 for the top, plus a few extra for mistakes.

Paint or spray lightly the bottom and sides of a 10-inch straight-sided round springform pan with olive oil. Working quickly, remove a sheet of filo, smooth it on the work counter, and brush or spray quickly and lightly with oil. Set the filo in the bottom of the pan, with the excess dough draping up and over the sides. Continue with 5 more sheets of filo, spraying or painting each lightly with oil and stacking them one on top of the other, each sheet crosswise to the one below. Use a light hand with the oil—overdoing it will make the pie greasy.

When all 6 layers are in place, turn the filling into the pie casing, smoothing it out on all sides. Repeat the process of oiling and layering 6 more sheets of filo to make a top for the filling, again setting the sheets crosswise to each other. When the top layers are in place, trim away the excess pastry, leaving about 1½ inches extending beyond the rim of the pan. Spray or brush this extension lightly with water, then roll it in, folding the top and bottom layers together to form a rim around the edge of the pie. Use the remaining oil to spray or brush over the top of the pie. Slide the pie into the preheated oven and bake for about 40 minutes or until the top is golden and crisp.

Variation: To make a Lenten spinach pie, leave out the cheeses and eggs altogether.

Middle Eastern Savory Tarts

Makes 32 little pies

THESE LITTLE TARTS, filled with a stuffing of savory greens, are made all over the Middle East. Housewives pride themselves on a delicate touch with the dough but they are often bakery fare as well, ready for students and workers to pick up for a snack on the run. Palestinian cooks add both lemon juice and sumac, the fragrant sour seasoning made from the crushed red berries of the sumac bush (*Rhus coriaria*—not poison sumac), while in Syria a pungent cheese similar to feta is often mixed in.

Spinach is the easiest green to come by but if you have access to chard or, better yet, to dandelion greens, substitute for half the quantity of spinach below.

I like to make these with the yogurt-and-olive-oil dough for Middle Eastern Pizza (page 180), but you could also use the Basic Pizza Dough on page 171.

Middle Eastern Pizza dough (page 180) or Basic Pizza Dough (page 171)

2 pounds fresh spinach (or 1 pound of spinach and 1 pound of chard or dandelion greens)

¼ cup extra-virgin olive oil, plus a little more to grease baking sheets

1 medium onion, chopped

sea salt if necessary

¼ cup pine nuts or ¼ cup crumbled feta cheese (optional)

freshly squeezed juice of ½ lemon

2 tablespoons sumac

¼ teaspoon allspice

freshly ground black pepper

Whichever dough you decide to use, prepare it ahead of time and set aside to rise.

While the dough is rising, prepare the spinach filling: clean the greens well in several changes of water and discard any tough stems. Chop the greens coarsely. Transfer, with the water clinging to their leaves, to a saucepan and set over medium heat. Cook until the greens are tender (time will vary—spinach cooks quickly, dandelion greens might take quite a bit longer), then drain thoroughly in a colander. If you have a mezzaluna, or a crescent-shaped chopping knife, further chop the greens right in the colander in order to get rid of as much water as possible. As soon as the greens are cool enough to handle, pick up big handfuls and squeeze them gently to get rid of even more water.

While the greens are cooking, combine the olive oil and onion with a big pinch of salt, keeping in mind that, if you plan to use feta in the filling, it may add quite a lot of salt. Mix well, gently crushing the onion bits with the back of a spoon. Set aside until the greens are ready.

Now combine the thoroughly drained greens with all the remaining ingredients, using either pine nuts or feta but not both. Taste the mixture and adjust the salt and pepper.

Use olive oil to grease the baking sheets lightly.

Divide the dough into four smaller portions for greater convenience. While you're working on one portion, keep the others under plastic wrap or a dampened towel so they don't dry out.

Roll a dough portion out on a lightly floured board until it is quite thin. Cut out dough circles about 2½ inches in diameter. You should get eight circles from each portion of dough. At the center of each circle, drop about a tablespoon of the filling. Think of the circle as having three sides and pull up two of them, pinching them together to seal. Then draw up the third side and pinch it to the other two, making a little dough packet roughly shaped like a three-sided pyramid. As each packet is completed, set it on a greased tray. Set the oven at 450 degrees, and let each tray rest for about 30 minutes while the oven is heating.

Transfer the trays to the preheated oven and bake for about 15 to 20 minutes or until the little tarts are golden brown. Remove and serve immediately.

Pasta, Rice, Beans, and Other Grains and Legumes

✤ ✤ ✤

Pasta

I WAS LIVING IN ROME some years ago when an editor at the *International Herald-Tribune* in Paris rang looking for story ideas. Did I ever make pasta at home? he asked. Of course, I said. Well, then, why not write about it for the newspaper? I loved to cook, but I'd never written about it.

Gradually as we talked, I realized with a frisson of anxiety that the editor meant making pasta *from scratch* at home, something no one did in Rome, where there's a *pastificio* making fresh pasta in every piazza as well as shops full of first-rate dried pasta from all the best commercial pasta makers throughout Italy. By then, however, vanity and ambition had won an easy victory over veracity, and I vowed that, if anyone could learn to make pasta, surely I could—and write about it to boot.

So I got out Marcella Hazan's first book, *The Classic Italian Cookbook*, truly a bible for me in those days and still a source of great comfort when the going gets tough, and I read—and weighed and measured and kneaded and rolled and cut and then hung the frangible strips of pasta to dry. Not content with ordinary egg pasta, I made green-colored pasta with spinach as well. We had a very large dining room at the Palazzo Taverna with twelve chairs around the massive table. By the time the children came home from school, all the chairs were draped, backs and seats alike, with ribbons of pasta, and so was the table. Enchantment! "Is it a birthday party?" Nicholas asked.

Fortunately I had a stalwart assistant at the time, Giulia d'Amurri, who kept my fantasies focused and even showed me how to use my thumb to push out orecchiette, or little ears, of pasta—they come, like Giulia's husband, Premio, from Puglia.

For lunch, of course, we had pasta. But how long to cook it fresca-fresca like this, so fresh you could almost eat it out of hand? Giulia knew. She brought an enormous quantity of water to a boil, dumped in a handful of salt and a huge quantity of pasta, gave it a stir with a long wooden ladle, and said: "Basta dire un Ave Maria." It took a little longer than a Hail Mary, but not much.

That was the only time I ever made pasta from scratch by hand, and I see no reason ever to do it again. Imported Italian pasta, like Barilla, De Cecco, and Delverde, to name just a few of the many good imported brands available, is much better than most commercially available "fresh" pasta, which is simply machine-made, machine-extruded pasta that is sold before it is dried. A number of artisanally made dried pastas imported from Italy are available in specialty food shops and in some well-stocked supermarkets. Artisanal production means the pasta has been made the old-fashioned way, extruded through bronze dies and dried slowly at relatively low temperatures, which makes pasta with a slightly rougher surface (to marry better with the sauce) and more of the nutty flavor of wheat. Some of my favorite artisanal pasta brands, available in North America, include Benedetto Cavalieri from Puglia, Rustichella d'Abruzzo, Latini from the Marche, and Setaro from south of Naples.

Making pasta truly by hand is an effort that only the dedicated and gifted can really enjoy as something more than an occasional counter to rainy-day boredom. It is a wonderful product, however, and for those who would like to try, I heartily recommend Marcella Hazan's brilliant first book, now incorporated with her second and published as *Essentials of Classic Italian Cooking* (Knopf, 1992). For the rest of us I offer a bit more than a baker's dozen of quick, easy pasta recipes, ones that require little or no forethought and that prove, if proof be necessary, that pasta—macaroni, spaghetti, vermicelli, tagliolini, whatever—is the original fast food.

Pasta has had something of a bad rap in recent years, after all the low-carb/no-carb fervor and gabble about the Atkins diet. Many good cooks have given up pasta altogether, while others have switched to various types of whole-grain pasta or proprietary products made with a heavy infusion of ground legumes—Barilla in particular makes a product called Pasta PLUS, that my doctor friend David Eisenberg, who is a type 1 diabetic, swears by.

For many reasons I don't agree with this course, except for people like Dr. Eisenberg who have been diagnosed with diabetes. Why? Well, first of all, because millions and millions of Italians eat pasta at least once and often twice a day all year long (annual national consumption is on the order of 60 pounds per person and if each pound of pasta makes five servings, that's a good 300 plates of pasta per person per year). Yet diabetes and obesity are not the problems in Italy that they have become in the United States.

Furthermore, to look at pasta's glycemic load in isolation, without considering how and when pasta is served, gives a very misleading picture. Pasta served with a tomato sauce, made with olive oil, onions, garlic, perhaps some carrot and celery and a few fresh herbs, with a sprinkling of grated cheese over the top gives a very different nutritional picture. And if the pasta portion is a mere 100 grams (about 4 ounces), as is recommended by Italian and other Mediterranean cooks, and is followed by an equally modest *secondo* of meat, fish, or vegetables, it once again shifts the nutritional analysis in a very positive direction.

As far as whole-wheat pasta is concerned, I don't use it simply because, apart from any nutritional boost, it doesn't add anything and in fact detracts from the satisfaction of the pasta experience. No cook that I have ever met in Italy, Greece, or Spain (the latter two countries also major pasta consumers) would consider using whole-wheat pasta. Italian law requires that all commercial pasta be made from hard durum wheat (in the Italian south even homemade pasta traditionally uses durum semolina) and be high in protein, B vitamins such as folate, and minerals.

Cooking Pasta

For American appetites, especially when pasta is the main course offered (that's not a bad idea, either), I count on a pound of pasta for six people. Each pound of pasta, no matter what shape it takes, needs about 5 quarts of very rapidly boiling salted water (a couple of tablespoons of sea salt for this quantity). When the water is boiling furiously, plunge the pasta in and immediately stir with a long wooden spoon. Cover the pan until the water is once again boiling furiously. Then remove the lid and let it cook very briskly, giving it a stir from time to time, until it is done to your pleasure— more or less al dente, which is a very relative term. Of course different shapes and sizes of pasta cook at different rates—only by testing, biting into a strand or a piece, will you know for sure when it is done.

Have a colander ready and a warm bowl in which to put the drained pasta (warm the bowl by adding a couple of ladles of boiling pasta water as it finishes cooking). A moment before the pasta reaches perfection, drain it into the colander and then turn it into the warm bowl (first emptying the bowl of pasta water) to be sauced.

Another method that can be useful for certain recipes is to drain the pasta two or three minutes *before* perfection and then turn it into the sauce on the stove. Let the pasta heat in the sauce that extra two or three minutes: the pasta will absorb the flavor of the sauce, and the whole will be more homogeneous. In either case, unless the recipe specifically states otherwise, dress the pasta as soon as it is done. Never run water over the pasta after it has been drained—that myth about rinsing starch away doesn't hold up. Then serve the pasta immediately.

One other caution: we Americans tend to serve too much sauce for the pasta, almost as if the pasta were there only to eke out the sauce, sort of a Mediterranean-style Hamburger Helper. The reverse, in fact, is true: the sauce is there simply to garnish the pasta. In the recipes that follow, proportions have been calculated Italian style, and it would be a mistake to change them. One of the great cornerstones of the Mediterranean diet is the importance of carbohydrates (pasta, bread, grains, beans) and the role played by savory sauces in lending pleasure and excitement to these essentially rather bland parts of the meal. To reverse that would be to increase the amount of fat, and often the amount of meat, at the expense of those valuable carbohydrates. Besides, it wouldn't taste good.

Pay attention to ingredients. The best-quality canned whole tomatoes are better than fresh tomatoes in many parts of the country and at many times of the year. Garlic should be plump and firm, each individual clove properly swollen to fill its papery husk. Herbs *for the most part* are better fresh than dried—and staples like parsley are always available fresh—although dried oregano, fennel seeds, and bay leaves are exceptions.

Pasta al Pomodoro

Spaghetti or Vermicelli with Tomato Sauce

Makes 6 to 8 servings

PASTA WITH TOMATO SAUCE is what most of us think of when we think of Italian food. And with good reason, as it is ubiquitous.

But there is not just one tomato sauce in Italy. In fact, there are almost as many as there are cooks, with each one insisting on his or her take on this universal condiment as the only authentic and *genuino* way to do it. In the next chapter, on page 266, you'll find my own take on La Pomarola, the Plain Tomato Sauce that Italians make in late summer for the winter store cupboard. The sauce below is slightly different, beginning, as it does, with a soffritto of onion, garlic, carrot, and parsley.

When I think of the injunction to get five-a-day (vegetables) on our tables, I always remember these soffritti, the beginnings of so many Mediterranean soups, sauces, and other dishes. Of course there's not a full serving, according to USDA standards, of onion, garlic, carrot, or parsley in this preparation, but if you're eating that sort of thing on a daily basis, you are getting lots and lots of good vitamins, antioxidants, and all the other benefits of vegetables—plus abundant amounts of flavor.

Tomato sauce can be used with a whole gamut of different pasta shapes, from skinny spaghetti and fat bucatini to short, stubby penne and orecchiette, to flat lasagna and papardelle. And you could simply serve it as it is here, with a glug of extra-virgin olive oil and a handful of freshly grated parmigiano reggiano over the top for a deeply satisfying dish.

Use good-quality whole peeled canned tomatoes for this sauce. In summer, when fresh tomatoes are in season, use ripe red tomatoes that are just about on the verge of falling apart.

1 small onion, chopped	In a heavy saucepan over medium-low heat, gently sauté the onion, garlic, carrot, and parsley in the oil until the vegetables are soft but not brown—about 10 to 15 minutes. Add the tomatoes, raise the heat to medium-high, and cook rapidly, stirring
1 garlic clove, chopped	
1 medium carrot, peeled and chopped	

[cont. next page]

¼ cup minced flat-leaf parsley

¼ cup extra-virgin olive oil

1 28-ounce can whole
tomatoes with their juice,
chopped

¼ cup slivered fresh basil
leaves or ½ teaspoon dried
oregano, crumbled

1½ pounds spaghetti,
vermicelli, tagliatelle, or other
long thin pasta

6 quarts water

sea salt and freshly ground
black pepper

½ cup freshly grated
parmigiano reggiano cheese
(optional)

frequently, until the tomato liquid has evaporated and the tomatoes have reached a thick jammy consistency—about 20 minutes. (If you're using dried herbs, add them with the tomatoes.)

Cook the pasta in boiling salted water according to the directions on page 193.

Taste the sauce and add salt and pepper if necessary. Stir in the fresh basil. When the pasta is done, drain it and immediately turn it into a warmed bowl (use a little of the pasta water to warm the bowl). Top with half the cheese. Turn the pasta in the sauce at the table just before serving. Pass the remaining cheese with the pasta.

Bucatini all'Amatriciana and Penne all'Arrabbiata

THESE TWO PASTAS are favorites in Roman trattorias. *All'amatriciana,* with bits of cured pork called *guanciale* in the sauce, comes from the little town of Amatrice in northern Lazio, the Region of which Rome is the capital. Many of the hosts of the old Roman trattorias and osterias where the common people took their meals also came from Amatrice, and so all'amatriciana became a Roman style of pasta. Penne all'arrabbiata is the same sauce but without the cured pork, and with the addition of enough dried red chilies or chili flakes to justify its name—"enraged pasta." The popularity of these two dishes has benefited considerably from the *nostalgie de la boue* that from time to time afflicts upper-class Romans, intellectuals, film people, and aristocrats, who frequent working-class eating places at times of the night when the working classes are soundly asleep.

Bucatini all'Amatriciana

You could make this with spaghetti or linguine or other types of long skinny pasta, but bucatini are what's used in Rome. Tasty, salty, savory guanciale, made from cured pork cheeks, has become more available in North America in recent years, but if you can't find it, substitute a good lean pancetta. And if that's not available, use slab bacon but blanch it for 3 to 4 minutes in boiling water to rid it of its smoky aroma.

1 large garlic clove, minced

1 medium onion, finely chopped

¼ pound guanciale, if available, or use pancetta or slab bacon, finely diced

3 tablespoons extra-virgin olive oil

1½ pounds tomatoes, preferably plum tomatoes, peeled, seeded (page 25), and chopped, or 1 16-ounce can Italian plum tomatoes with their juice, chopped

sea salt and freshly ground black pepper

1 pound bucatini or other short thick pasta

5 quarts water

freshly grated cheese, preferably pecorino romano

In a saucepan over medium heat, gently sauté the garlic, onion, and guanciale in the oil, stirring occasionally, until the meat renders a little fat and the vegetables just begin to brown—about 15 to 20 minutes. Add the tomatoes and stir to mix. Cook the tomatoes for about 5 minutes, and when they start to give off their juice, lower the heat and simmer, stirring occasionally, until the sauce is dense, about 20 minutes. Add salt and pepper.

Meanwhile, cook the pasta in lightly salted water according to the directions on page 193. Drain it, turn it into a warmed serving bowl, and pour the sauce over it. Serve immediately, passing the grated cheese.

Penne all'Arrabbiata

Makes 6 servings

Control the heat of the dish by using more or less hot red pepper.

¼ cup extra-virgin olive oil

3 large garlic cloves, minced

1½ pounds tomatoes, preferably plum tomatoes, peeled, seeded (page 25), and coarsely chopped, or 1 16-ounce can imported Italian tomatoes with their juice, chopped

1 or 2 dried hot red chilies, broken into pieces, or 1 teaspoon hot red pepper flakes, or to taste

sea salt

1 pound penne or other short thick round pasta

5 quarts water

Heat the oil in a heavy saucepan over medium-high heat and sauté the garlic, stirring constantly, until it is just beginning to turn golden—about 10 minutes. Add the tomatoes and chilies, reduce the heat to medium-low, and continue cooking until the tomatoes are soft and the sauce is dense but not pureed—about 20 minutes. Remove from the heat and taste for seasoning, adding more salt if necessary.

Cook the pasta in lightly salted water as directed on page 193. Drain thoroughly, turn into a warm serving bowl, and pour the sauce over it. Serve immediately.

Spaghetti or Linguine alla Puttanesca

with Tomatoes, Olives, and Capers

Makes 6 to 8 servings

MOST ITALIANS CLAIM this is a famous Roman dish, usually prepared by ladies of the night to revive themselves after their tiring labors. Neapolitan food historian Jeanne Caròli Francesconi contradicts that. In Naples, she says, it was called *alla marinara* until sometime in the late 1940s, when a local celebrity, Eduardo Colucci, playfully rebaptized it *alla puttanesca*. Colucci was known as much for the table he set at his little terrace house on the island of Ischia as he was for the personalities, Italian and foreign, who graced it—and to whom he often served this pasta.

1 medium onion, chopped

2 garlic cloves, chopped

1 medium carrot, peeled and chopped

⅓ cup extra-virgin olive oil

1 whole salted anchovy, prepared as directed on page 40, or 4 oil-packed anchovy fillets

½ cup minced flat-leaf parsley

2 to 3 pounds very ripe fresh tomatoes, seeded (page 25) and chopped, or 1 28-ounce can whole tomatoes with their juice, chopped

½ teaspoon dried oregano, crumbled

2 tablespoons drained capers, preferably large ones

1 cup pitted black olives, preferably Gaeta

sea salt and freshly ground black pepper

1½ pounds linguine, vermicelli, spaghetti, or other long thin pasta

6 quarts water

In a heavy saucepan or skillet over medium-low heat, gently sauté the onion, garlic, and carrot in the oil until the vegetables are wilted but not starting to brown—about 10 to 15 minutes. Chop the anchovy fillets and add them to the vegetables together with half the minced parsley. Cook, stirring and pressing the anchovies with a wooden spoon, until they have melted into the sauce— about 5 minutes.

Now raise the heat slightly to medium or medium-high and add the tomatoes and oregano. Cook rapidly, stirring frequently, until the tomato juice has evaporated and the tomatoes are reduced to a jam—about 20 minutes. Off the heat, stir in the capers and black olives. Taste for seasoning, adding salt and pepper if desired.

While the sauce is cooking, boil the pasta in lightly salted water, following the directions on page 193. Drain the pasta, turn it into a warm bowl, and pour the sauce over. Sprinkle the remaining parsley over the top. Turn the pasta in the sauce at the table immediately before serving.

Variation: Another favorite Neapolitan sauce is made in much the same way but without the onion, carrot, tomatoes, and oregano. It's a quick sauce, to make while the pasta water comes to a boil. Simply sweat the garlic in oil, then add the capers, olives, and parsley. Stir in the chopped anchovies at the last minute and crush them into the sauce. A little finely slivered basil makes a fine garnish.

Pasta alla Checca

Fusilli or Conchiglie with a Raw Tomato Sauce

Makes 6 servings

THIS STYLE OF PASTA can be found all over Italy in the summer, when tomatoes and basil are at their peak. In Rome it's called pasta alla checca. What does *alla checca* mean? No one has ever given me a satisfactory explanation. The sauce should be made in advance, but if you're going to hold it for more than a couple of hours, add the basil only an hour before serving. The raw salsa clings best to curly fusilli or small pasta shells.

Look for the very best, ripest, fullest-flavored tomatoes in local farmers' markets. There's just no point in making this dish unless tomatoes are at their peak. But when they're at their peak, if you're like me, you'll want to make it two or three times a week.

Some cooks sharpen the pasta sauce with a teaspoon of balsamic vinegar, added with the oil.

6 large ripe, red tomatoes

1 garlic clove, minced

2 medium red onions, halved and thinly sliced

1 cup loosely packed basil leaves

sea salt

freshly ground black pepper

½ cup extra-virgin olive oil

1 pound fusilli or conchiglie

5 quarts water

Over a bowl large enough to hold all the ingredients except the pasta, cut the tomatoes into small pieces and mix them and their juices with the garlic and onions. Tear the basil leaves into shreds and add to the bowl. Add a teaspoon of salt, pepper, and oil and toss to mix well. Cover the bowl with plastic wrap and set in the refrigerator until ready to use.

Cook the pasta in boiling salted water according to the directions on page 193. While the pasta cooks, rinse a pasta serving bowl in hot water to warm it. Remove the bowl of sauce from the refrigerator and uncover it. As soon as the pasta is done, drain it and turn it into the warmed bowl. Immediately pour the cold sauce over and mix well. Serve at once.

Mita's Tuscan Sugo

MITA ANTOLINI, MY TUSCAN NEIGHBOR, uses this sauce to dress pasta or gnocchi di patate, little potato dumplings, that she makes for Sunday lunch.

1 medium onion, finely chopped

2 garlic cloves, finely chopped

¼ cup minced flat-leaf parsley

1 celery stalk, finely chopped, leaves and all

1 small carrot, peeled and finely chopped

3 tablespoons extra-virgin olive oil

¼ pound ground very lean beef, veal, or pork

1 chicken liver, cleaned and finely chopped (optional)

⅓ cup dry white wine

1 28-ounce can imported Italian plum tomatoes or 4 or 5 large ripe tomatoes, chopped

sea salt and freshly ground black pepper

1 small bunch of basil, leaves and tender tips, slivered (about ⅓ cup)

1½ pounds tagliatelle or other long flat pasta

6 quarts water

½ cup freshly grated parmigiano reggiano cheese, or more to taste

Sauté the onion, garlic, parsley, celery, and carrot in the olive oil in a skillet over medium heat, stirring frequently, until the vegetables are soft but not brown—about 10 to 15 minutes. Add the ground meat and chopped chicken liver, raise the heat slightly, and cook the meats, stirring constantly, until they have lost all trace of rosiness—about 10 minutes.

Pour in the wine and bring to a boil. Turn down the heat and let the wine cook off until just a few tablespoons are left in the pan—about 5 to 10 minutes. Then turn the can of tomatoes, juice and all, into the pan, raise the heat again, and cook, chopping the tomatoes with a wooden spoon, until the sauce is dense and thick, the tomatoes are reduced almost to a puree, and the juice has cooked down to a few tablespoons—about 20 minutes. Taste for seasoning, adding salt and pepper if desired. Stir in the slivered basil. Set the sauce aside and keep it warm while you prepare the pasta.

Cook the pasta in salted boiling water according to the directions on page 193. Drain the cooked pasta in a colander, turn it into a heated bowl, and immediately dress with the hot sauce. Sprinkle a little of the cheese over the top and pass the remaining cheese at the table.

Pasta with a Seafood Sauce

I HAVE SUGGESTED VERMICELLI or a similar pasta shape for this satisfying dish, but in fact the sauce goes equally well with fusilli or other types of short, twisted pasta. The tomatoes should provide a sweet-tart balance to the seafood but their flavors should not dominate the dish.

2 garlic cloves, thinly sliced

1 sweet red pepper, finely chopped

¼ cup finely chopped yellow onion

2 tablespoons extra-virgin olive oil

¼ cup dry white wine

3 or 4 fresh ripe tomatoes, peeled (page 25) and diced to make 2 cups (or use canned whole tomatoes, well drained and diced)

a pinch of ground or crushed red chili (piment d'Espelette or Aleppo pepper)

sea salt and freshly ground black pepper

½ teaspoon sugar (optional)

½ pound fresh scallops, diced

½ pound fresh shrimp, diced

freshly squeezed lemon juice, to taste

2 or 3 tablespoons slivered basil

1 pound vermicelli, spaghettini, or other long, thin pasta

Combine the garlic, sweet pepper, and onion with the olive oil in a saucepan and set over medium-low heat. Cook, stirring, until the vegetables are soft but not brown. Add the wine and raise the heat slightly. Let the wine simmer vigorously until the alcohol has evaporated and the wine has reduced to a syrupy liquid.

Stir in the tomatoes and continue cooking. If you're using fresh tomatoes, you may want to add a tablespoon or so of water, just until the tomato juices start to flow. Add chili to taste, along with salt and black pepper, and continue cooking until you have a thick sauce. Taste and adjust the seasoning, adding a bit of sugar if you wish.

The tomato sauce may be made well ahead and kept, refrigerated if necessary, until ready to cook the pasta.

When you're ready to cook, bring the sauce to a simmer in a saucepan large enough to hold all the ingredients, including the pasta. In a separate stockpot or pasta pot, bring about 5 quarts of lightly salted water to a rolling boil.

Add the diced scallops and shrimp to the simmering tomato sauce at the same time that you add the pasta to the boiling water. Cook the pasta until it is almost, but not quite, done. Drain it quickly and add to the tomato sauce and seafood mixture. Turn to coat the pasta well with the sauce and let it finish cooking in its own sauce. By the time the pasta has finished cooking, the seafood should also be cooked through. Remove from the heat and add a spritz or two of lemon juice. Transfer the pasta to a heated serving bowl and garnish with the basil. Serve immediately.

Orecchiette alla Barese

Little Ears with Broccoli Rabe

+%{ Makes 6 servings

THE NAME IN ITALIAN gives no hint of it, but *orecchiette alla barese* are always cooked with a sauce made of broccoli rabe or rapini, bitter-sweet greens that are increasingly available in supermarket produce sections. (Like its cousins in the cruciferous vegetable family, broccoli rabe has important health benefits.) If you can't find broccoli rabe, substitute regular broccoli, but the flavor will not be as sharp and interesting.

This quick and easy preparation is a great favorite in the Italian South, especially in the olive oil–producing district around Bari, where the orecchiette are homemade. Orecchiette are a fairly standard variety of dried pasta and available in many supermarkets, but if you can't find them, use farfalle (butterflies), small shells, or fusilli (corkscrews) instead. The preparation is not appropriate for long stringy pasta like spaghetti or linguine.

2 bunches of broccoli rabe or 2 heads of broccoli

sea salt

2 garlic cloves, minced

3 tablespoons extra-virgin olive oil

6 oil-packed anchovy fillets, or to taste

[cont. next page]

Clean and coarsely chop the broccoli rabe. Bring about 1 inch of lightly salted water to a boil in a heavy saucepan. Add the broccoli rabe and cook until it is tender and only a few tablespoons of liquid are left in the bottom of the pan—about 5 to 10 minutes, depending on how finely the vegetable is chopped. Set the pan of broccoli rabe aside, but keep it warm.

In a separate skillet or sauté pan, gently sauté the garlic in the olive oil until it is soft, then melt in

1 teaspoon hot red pepper flakes or 1 small dried red chili, chopped, seeds and all

1 pound orecchiette or other pasta

5 quarts water

freshly ground black pepper

the anchovy fillets by crushing them in the garlicky oil with a fork. Add the red pepper and stir to mix well. Turn the garlic-pepper oil into the broccoli rabe and mix.

Cook the pasta in lightly salted boiling water until done, as directed on page 193. Drain the pasta and immediately combine with the seasoned broccoli rabe. Turn it into a warm serving bowl, add pepper, and serve immediately. (Don't add or pass grated cheese.)

Cauliflower Fusilli

Makes 4 to 6 servings

1 pound (1 small head) cauliflower

sea salt

1 medium yellow onion, chopped

2 tablespoons extra-virgin olive oil

2 tablespoons pine nuts

2 tablespoons golden raisins, plumped in hot water

3 anchovy fillets, chopped

a large pinch of saffron

1 pound fusilli or other type of small, curly pasta

freshly ground black pepper

Grated parmigiano reggiano, caciocavallo, or pecorino cheese (optional)

Break the cauliflower into small florets. In a 6-quart saucepan, bring about 2 inches of water to a rolling boil, add a big pinch of salt, and then the cauliflower. Cook rapidly for about 4 to 5 minutes, or until the cauliflower florets have started to soften but still have firm centers. Remove the cauliflower, using a slotted spoon. *Do not discard the cooking water.*

Combine the chopped onion and oil in a skillet large enough to hold the pasta and cauliflower together. Set over medium-low heat and cook, stirring, until the onion starts to soften and turn golden. Add the pine nuts to the pan and cook, stirring, until they start to turn golden. Drain the raisins and add them to the pan along with the anchovies. Cook for about 5 minutes, stirring occasionally and adding a couple of tablespoonsful of cauliflower water to the pan to keep it from burning. Add the drained cauliflower florets and stir to mix well. Let cook for another 5 minutes, then remove from the heat.

Return the cauliflower liquid to a boil, first adding more water to make about 5 quarts for cooking the pasta. When the water comes to a boil, remove about half a cup and dissolve the saffron in it. Add the pasta to the boiling water and cook until it is done—7 to 10 minutes, depending on your own taste and the shape of the pasta.

When the pasta is done, drain it and add to the cauliflower along with the saffron-infused water. Set over medium heat and let cook, while stirring and tossing, just a few minutes longer, or until the pasta has absorbed much of the liquid in the pan and the ingredients are well combined. Taste and add more salt if necessary and plenty of pepper.

Serve immediately, passing grated parmigiano reggiano if you wish.

Spaghetti con Zucchini, Patate, e Ricotta

Makes 6 servings

THIS IS A MEAGER DISH, one that comes out of the poor peasant culture of Puglia, down in the heel of Italy—meager but rich and delicious in combination, a reflection of how simplicity and poverty and imagination can come together to create something good. As with all simple dishes, the quality of the ingredients is what makes the difference. Use the smallest (no more than 4 inches long) and freshest zucchini you can find and waxy potatoes with good flavor. If you can't find Yellow Finns, red bliss potatoes will do.

At Ristorante Bacco in Barletta, near Bari, they use the local ricotta salata, a hard grating cheese, for this. An aged pecorino, if you can find it, will be good, but don't use pecorino romano, which is too strong for this dish.

sea salt

5 quarts water

[cont. next page]

Have all the ingredients prepared before you start to cook, because the cooking goes very quickly once begun. Fill a serving bowl with very hot water to warm it for the pasta.

3 medium Yellow Finn potatoes, peeled, halved, and sliced ½ inch thick

1 pound spaghetti or spaghettini, broken into pieces about 2 inches long

6 to 8 very small zucchini, thinly sliced

⅓ cup fruity extra-virgin olive oil

lots of freshly ground black pepper

½ cup grated ricotta salata, pecorino, or parmigiano reggiano cheese, or more to taste

In a large pot, bring the lightly salted water to a boil. Add the potato slices and boil for 8 minutes. Add the spaghetti and stir with a long-handled spoon. Cover the pot and bring the water back to a boil. Set the lid ajar and continue boiling for 8 minutes. Add the zucchini slices and boil, uncovered, for 4 minutes or until the potato slices are cooked through and the spaghetti is just tender but not soft and mushy.

Drain, reserving ¼ cup of the cooking liquid. Immediately turn the pasta and vegetables into the warm serving bowl and pour the reserved cooking liquid and olive oil over the pasta. Add salt and pepper and sprinkle 2 or 3 tablespoons of grated cheese over the top. Serve immediately, passing the remaining cheese at the table.

Trenette al Pesto

Makes 6 servings

IN ITALY, PESTO IS FRESHLY MADE at the height of the season when local basil is at its flavor peak. It is a rare treat, one that Italian cooks handle with joy and respect. Italians are discreet with pesto, reckoning that a little of this rich and highly flavored sauce goes a very long way. A big spoonful of pesto may be stirred into a hearty minestrone of summer vegetables (just as it is in the very similar pistou on page 121), and I'm also fond of a small (1 teaspoon, no more) dollop of freshly made pesto to top a grilled or poached fish. In all cases, the accent is on fresh. Otherwise pesto is almost always used only in this classic Genovese dish of slender trenette noodles mixed with a few slices of small new potatoes. The sweetness of the potatoes accents the robust flavor of the sauce, and the contrasting textures of pasta and potatoes add further interest.

Traditionally, as the name implies, pesto is made with mortar and pestle, and many cooks believe that is still the best way to extract the fullest flavor from basil and garlic. It takes time, however, so the following recipe uses a blender or food processor. But someday when you have a little extra time, try making pesto the old-fashioned way, focusing on the materials at hand and the aromas that rise from the mortar. You'll be amazed at where your thoughts might lead.

3 cups packed tender young basil leaves

3 heaped tablespoons pine nuts

1 teaspoon coarse sea salt

½ cup extra-virgin olive oil or more to taste

3 fat garlic cloves, crushed with the flat blade of a knife and very finely chopped

½ cup freshly grated cheese, preferably a mixture of parmigiano reggiano and an aged Tuscan pecorino or pecorino sardo; otherwise, use all parmigiano

sea salt

6 quarts water

3 medium potatoes, peeled and sliced not more than ¼ inch thick

1 pound trenette, linguine, tagliatelle, or other long flat thin pasta

Put the basil, pine nuts, and salt in a food processor or blender and process steadily while you add the oil in a thin but constant stream. The sauce should achieve the consistency of a slightly grainy paste but not a fine puree. Add the garlic and process very briefly, just to mix. When the sauce is the right consistency, transfer it to a bowl and, using a spatula, fold in the grated cheese. (If you're using a mortar, just continue to work in the cheese with the pestle.) If the sauce is too thick, work in more olive oil. Taste and adjust the seasoning.

Pesto can be made ahead and stored in the refrigerator for a few days or in the freezer for a few weeks. If you plan to store it, leave the cheese out. Transfer the pesto to a refrigerator container, pour a thin film of oil over the top, cover, and store. When you're ready to use it, let the pesto thaw if necessary, then stir in the oil on top and the grated cheese.

Bring the lightly salted water to a rolling boil. Drop in the potato slices and boil for 5 minutes, then drop in the pasta. Stir with a wooden spoon, cover the pot, and bring back to a boil. Uncover and boil the pasta and potatoes together for 10 to 12 minutes or until the potatoes are thoroughly cooked and the pasta is done to taste.

While the pasta is cooking, stir a couple of tablespoons of hot pasta water into the pesto. Rinse a pasta bowl with boiling water to warm it.

As soon as the pasta is done, drain it, turn it into the warmed bowl, and pour the pesto over it. Toss gently to mix the pesto and serve immediately, passing more cheese if desired.

Neapolitan Christmas Eve Spaghetti with Walnuts

U Spaghett'anatalina

Makes 4 to 6 servings

PLUMP, FRESH, AND FLAVORFUL, walnuts from the Sorrento peninsula, just south of Naples, are renowned throughout Italy. When the season's crop begins to appear in Neapolitan markets and food shops it's a harbinger of Christmas, when this quick and easy walnut sauce is traditionally served. Remember that walnuts are a terrific source of those all-important omega-3 fatty acids and this is a particularly delicious way to include them on your table.

The Christmas Eve meal in Italy, as in other Mediterranean Catholic countries, is invariably meatless, a relic of what was once the Advent fast that stretched from December 1 to Christmas Eve. The fast is no longer de rigueur for the faithful but most Italians still observe the injunction to go meatless on Christmas Eve.

Use garlic according to your personal taste. This is meant to be a garlicky sauce but it's okay to cut back a little if you wish.

1 cup walnuts, the fresher the better

sea salt

1 pound spaghetti

½ cup extra-virgin olive oil

4 to 6 garlic cloves, minced

4 whole salted anchovies, or 10 oil-packed anchovy fillets, coarsely chopped

½ cup minced flat-leaf parsley

½ cup freshly grated parmigiano reggiano cheese (optional)

Preheat the oven to 400 degrees.

Spread the walnuts out on a cookie sheet and toast in the oven for several minutes, or until the nuts begin to release their fragrance. It's okay if the nuts turn a little golden but don't let them turn deep brown. Remove from the oven and transfer to a kitchen towel spread out on a countertop. Rub the nuts together in the towel to remove and discard as much of the flaky skin as you can. Chop the nuts, or process in spurts in a food processor—you want them to be finely chopped but not pasty. (This can be done ahead, even several days ahead, and the chopped nuts stored in a tightly sealed canister or mason jar.)

When ready to cook, bring 5 quarts of lightly salted water to a rolling boil. Add the spaghetti and cook until almost al dente.

While the pasta water is heating and the spaghetti is cooking, make the sauce: combine the oil and garlic in a large saucepan over low heat and cook gently, stirring occasionally, until the garlic starts to soften. Add the chopped anchovies and continue cooking, using the back of a fork to mash the anchovies into the oil. Stir in the chopped walnuts and cook for about 1 minute.

When the pasta is almost al dente, remove about ½ cup of the pasta water and add it to the sauce. Let it simmer while you drain the pasta, then add the pasta to the walnut sauce, turning to coat the pasta well with the sauce as it finishes its last minute or so of cooking. Taste and add salt if necessary (the anchovies may provide enough salt on their own).

Turn onto a warm platter, sprinkle with parsley and serve immediately, passing grated cheese if you wish.

Variation: Many cooks add ¼ to ½ cup whole-milk ricotta to the sauce toward the end, just before turning the pasta in it. It gives a lovely, unctuous creaminess to the sauce.

Pasta with Pancetta and Beans

Makes 8 to 10 servings

THE BEANS USED IN ITALY are almost always some takeoff on borlotti, those beautiful white beans scrolled with red that are ubiquitous and have many other names. Sometimes they're called scritti or scrignoli, because they look like someone scribbled on them with a red marker pen. You may use other kinds of white or pale beans—Anasazi, Jacob's cattle, navy beans are all good, or try cream-colored cannellini beans. I wouldn't use black beans or red kidney beans in this as the colors of the dish would be completely wrong.

1 cup dried borlotti or other similar beans, soaked overnight

4 tablespoons extra-virgin olive oil, plus more for garnish

1 medium red onion, coarsely chopped

2 plump garlic cloves, thinly sliced

3 to 4 ounces pancetta, diced

1 14-ounce can whole plum tomatoes

sea salt and freshly ground black pepper

1 pound short, stubby pasta such as farfalle or bowties

¼ cup slivered basil leaves

freshly grated parmigiano reggiano

Drain the beans, transfer to a saucepan, and cover with water to a depth of about 1 inch. Set over medium heat and bring to a simmer, then lower the heat, cover the pan, and cook gently until the beans are tender. Time depends on the age of the beans but can vary from 30 minutes to 1 hour. (The beans may be cooked several days ahead and kept refrigerated until ready to use.) When the beans are done, drain them, reserving about 1 cup of bean liquid.

Add 2 tablespoons of the oil to a heavy pan large enough to hold all the ingredients. Set over medium-low heat and add the onion. Cook, stirring, until the onion is soft, then stir in the garlic and pancetta and continue cooking for about 10 minutes, or until the garlic is soft and the pancetta has started to release its fat. (Do not let the onions and garlic brown.)

Add the tomatoes, breaking them up with the side of a spoon. Raise the heat slightly and cook, continuing to break up the tomatoes, until they have reduced to a sauce. Taste and add salt and pepper, then add the beans and reserved bean liquid. Return to a simmer and cook for about 10 minutes, to make a thick sauce.

In a separate saucepan bring about 5 quarts of lightly salted water to a rolling boil. Add the pasta and cook rapidly until the pasta is almost, but not quite, ready to eat. Drain and quickly add the pasta to the bean sauce, tossing to mix well. Sprinkle the pasta with the slivered basil and transfer to a serving bowl. Dribble a thread of olive oil over the top, then serve, with grated cheese to accompany it.

Note: This makes a lot of pasta. If you have leftovers, they are easily converted into a pasta and bean soup by reheating in 3 or 4 cups of chicken or vegetable stock. Be sure to sprinkle the soup with plenty of grated cheese and a dribble of olive oil before serving.

Mushroom Lasagna

Lasagna ai Funghi

Makes 6 servings

IDEALLY THIS DELICIOUS and easy lasagna should be made with wild mushrooms such as porcini (cèpes or boletus) or maitake (hen of the woods), but if they are not available use fresh shiitake mushrooms from the supermarket rather than the little white button mushrooms that have very little mushroom flavor.

If you gather mushrooms yourself (and it's a great family project on a sunny Sunday in the woods), be sure you know what you're doing. Both porcini and maitake are pretty easy to identify, but first-timers should certainly consult a mushroom expert. When in doubt, call your state university's school of agriculture; if they can't help, they should be able to put you in touch with someone who can.

1 ounce dried mushrooms, preferably porcini

½ pound fresh mushrooms, preferably wild (see headnote)

½ cup finely minced yellow onion

1 small garlic clove, finely minced

about ½ cup extra-virgin olive oil

½ cup dry white wine

sea salt and freshly ground black pepper

1 pound lasagna

¼ cup unbleached all-purpose flour

2 cups milk

1½ cups pesto (page 206)

[cont. next page]

Put the dried mushrooms in a bowl and pour over them about 1½ cups of very hot water. Set aside to let them soak for at least 30 minutes, then drain, *reserving the liquid.* Strain the liquid through a fine-mesh sieve to rid it of any bits of soil and set it aside. Rinse the drained mushrooms, then chop coarsely.

Rinse the fresh mushrooms quickly under running water, trimming off any unsightly bits. Slice the mushrooms about ¼ inch thick.

Combine in a medium skillet the dried and fresh mushrooms, the onion, and the garlic, along with 2 tablespoons of the oil and about ⅓ cup of the mushroom-soaking liquid. Set over medium-low heat and cook, stirring occasionally, until the mushrooms have rendered up a lot of their juice and the onion and garlic are softened but not brown. Add the wine, raise the heat to medium, and cook rapidly, stirring, until the juices in the pan have concentrated to a couple of

1 cup whole-milk ricotta

⅔ cup grated pecorino and/or parmigiano reggiano

2 tablespoons unflavored dry bread crumbs

tablespoons. Remove the skillet from the heat and set aside.

Meanwhile, bring a large pot of water to a rolling boil. Add salt and then a few strips of lasagna—this works best if you cook the lasagna in two or more batches, four big lasagna sheets to a batch. Otherwise the sheets may stick together in the pot and are messy to try to separate. Boil the lasagna for about 4 minutes, then, using a slotted spoon, carefully remove the sheets before they are completely cooked and limp. Transfer each sheet to kitchen towels spread out on a countertop, where they will drain.

To make the bechamel, in a small saucepan, heat ¼ cup of the oil and stir in the flour, using a wire whisk to incorporate the flour fully. Cook the mixture, while whisking, for about 3 minutes, until it is very thick, then start to add the milk, about a quarter-cup at a time, and beat with a wire whisk as you do so. Beat the mixture to a thick cream. (This bechamel should be used immediately, otherwise a thick skim will form on the top.)

Set the oven at 375 degrees.

Use about a tablespoon of oil to grease the bottom of a 13 x 9 x 2-inch lasagna or baking dish. Arrange a layer of lasagna strips over the bottom, then cover with about a third of the bechamel. Smear a third of the pesto sauce over that. Spread half the mushroom mixture on top, then top it with dabs of ricotta, using half the ricotta. Sprinkle with about a third of the grated cheese. Make another layer of lasagna, a third of the bechamel, a third of the pesto, and all the remaining mushroom mixture and ricotta. Sprinkle with another third of the grated cheese. Make a final layer of lasagna strips and spread with the remaining bechamel, pesto, and grated cheese. Sprinkle with bread crumbs, then dribble about 2 tablespoons of oil over the top.

Transfer to the preheated oven and bake for about 20 minutes or until the top is bubbling and golden brown. Note, though, that the whole lasagna can be assembled ahead of time and set aside, lightly covered, until you're ready to bake it. It should be served piping hot, with more grated cheese passed at the table.

Variation: Instead of mushrooms, substitute a 9-ounce package of frozen artichoke hearts, each little heart sliced about ¼ inch thick.

Another Variation: Make a tomato-sausage lasagna, using one of the tomato sauces on pages 266–269 instead of the pesto and about ½ pound fresh Italian sausages. Crumble the sausage meat into the oil in the skillet, then when the meat is lightly browned, add the onion, garlic, and mushrooms. Proceed with the recipe as described, substituting tomato sauce for the pesto. (If the sausage meat yields a great deal of fat, remove and discard it before you combine it with the mushrooms.)

Catalan Seafood and Pasta Paella

Fideus a la Marinera

⚜ Makes 6 to 8 servings

ITALY IS THE WORLD CHAMPION of pasta consumption, but the Catalan region of northeast Spain, around the great city of Barcelona, is another part of the Mediterranean where pasta plays an important role in the kitchen. A favorite way to prepare it is in this paella, with lots of savory fish and shellfish to flavor it. The pasta used is called *fideos* in Spanish (*fideus* in Catalan), short, thin noodles similar to spaghettini or angel hair (capelli d'angelo). Broken into shorter lengths, either of these makes a good substitute for the real thing. Like more familiar rice paellas, these glorious pasta paellas are usually served as the main course for a celebration meal.

The cooking process is very different from Italian methods, however. Catalan fideos are almost always cooked right in the pot, along with the other ingredients, rather than cooked separately and then sauced as is done in Italy. Moreover, the pasta is sometimes lightly toasted in olive oil before being stirred into the sauce to finish cooking. Either way, it makes a tasty alternative to Italian-style pasta.

For the fish stock, follow the recipe on page 109, using, if available, the bones from the filleted monkfish and the shells and heads from the shrimp in the recipe. To save on last-minute effort, make stock ahead of time and refrigerate until ready to use. Then bring to a simmer before adding it to the dish. You could also sauté the shrimp and fish and the vegetables several hours ahead, then put everything together just minutes before serving.

This pasta paella is traditionally made in a paella pan but you may use any broad skillet that will fit in your oven.

6 cups fish stock (page 109)

1 pound boneless monkfish

½ pound raw shrimp, preferably with the shells on (the shells to be peeled and added to the fish stock, with the shrimp heads, when it is made)

½ pound fresh squid (calamari)

1 dozen mussels

1 cup dry white wine

3 or 4 garlic cloves, crushed and minced

about ½ cup extra-virgin olive oil

about ½ cup unbleached all-purpose flour

1 leek, trimmed and thinly sliced

2 medium yellow onions, finely chopped

4 ripe red tomatoes, peeled, seeded (page 25), and diced, or 6 canned plum tomatoes, chopped and drained

Bring the stock to a simmer while you prepare the rest of the ingredients. Cut the monkfish fillet into 1-inch cubes and pat dry with paper towels. Peel the shrimp and add the shells to the fish stock, then rinse the shrimp quickly and pat dry with paper towels. Rinse the squid and toss in a colander to dry. Slice into ½-inch rings, then pat dry. Rinse the mussels, discarding any that are gaping, and tug away the beards.

In a saucepan, bring ½ cup of the wine to a boil and add the mussels with about a third of the garlic. Cook rapidly until the mussels have all opened, removing each one as it opens and setting it aside. If, after 8 to 10 minutes, there are mussels that resolutely refuse to open, discard them. Strain the mussel liquid through cheesecloth or a fine-mesh sieve to rid it of any sand or grit, and add the liquid to the stock. Set the mussels aside but keep warm. (Spanish cooks add the whole mussels in their shells to the paella, but you may prefer to discard the shells and just use the mussels themselves.)

Heat 2 or 3 tablespoons of the oil in a large skillet or paella pan over medium heat. Dip the shrimp

2 bay leaves

1 teaspoon Spanish pimentón (paprika or ground red chili), hot or mild

a big pinch of saffron threads, crumbled

sea salt and freshly ground black pepper

12 ounces (¾ of a 1-pound box) fideos noodles, or spaghettini or angel hair pasta, broken into 2-inch lengths

a handful of chopped flat-leaf parsley for garnish

lightly in the flour, shaking to remove any excess, then fry on both sides in the hot oil until golden. Set aside in a warm place and proceed in the same manner with the squid rings, and then the fish cubes.

Lower the heat and add the remaining garlic, leek, and onions to the oil in the pan, adding more oil if necessary. (If you wish to brown the pasta in oil, this is the moment to add it, stirring thoroughly.) Cook, stirring, until the vegetables start to soften. Add the remaining wine and raise the heat slightly. Simmer the wine as you scrape up any brown bits from the bottom of the pan, then stir in the tomatoes, together with the bay leaves, pimentón, and crumbled saffron. Cook for 10 to 15 minutes, or until the tomatoes have dissolved into a dense sauce. Taste and add salt and pepper.

Set the oven at 450 degrees.

If you have not browned the pasta, add it now to the tomato sauce, stir to mix well, then add the fish stock, raising the heat to medium-high. Cook for another 10 minutes, or until the pasta has absorbed a lot of the liquid in the pan. Now arrange the fish cubes, squid rings, shrimp, and mussels over the pasta, nestling the seafood into the pasta and sauce. Cook for another 3 to 4 minutes, just long enough to warm up the seafood, then transfer the pan to the oven and bake for about 5 minutes, or until the top of the dish is lightly toasted. If the dish doesn't get toasty on top, set it under a preheated broiler for 3 to 4 minutes—the pasta should be browned and slightly crisp on the surface.

Remove the dish from the oven and serve immediately, with parsley scattered over the top.

Spanish Cassola with Pasta and Pork

Fideus a la Cassola

🍴 Makes 6 servings

THIS IS A COMPLEX but not difficult dish and the results are splendid. It makes perfect party or celebration fare and the addition of a Catalan *picada,* a pounded nut sauce, gives an extra flavor boost.

If you want to make this a more substantial main course, increase the amount of pork to 1 pound—but don't think of this as a meat-centered dish. The pasta and vegetables should take pride of place.

½ pound lean pork cut into small dice (about ½ inch to a side)

2 tablespoons extra-virgin olive oil

2 medium yellow onions, chopped

1 sweet red pepper, sliced into thin strips

1 bay leaf

4 medium fresh ripe tomatoes, peeled, seeded (page 25), and finely chopped, or use 6 canned plum tomatoes, chopped and drained

1 cup shelled peas, fresh preferred, frozen if necessary

FOR THE PICADA

15 hazelnuts or almonds

1-inch slice country-style bread, crusts removed, fried in 2 tablespoons extra-virgin olive oil

6 or 8 saffron threads, lightly toasted (page 256)

2 garlic cloves, finely minced

Set the oven at 350 degrees.

Sauté the pork dice in olive oil over medium heat until brown, then stir in the onions, red pepper, and bay leaf and cook, stirring, until the pepper strips are soft. Stir in the chopped tomatoes and cook, uncovered, for about 10 minutes or until the tomatoes have dissolved into a sauce. Stir in the peas.

While the tomatoes are cooking, make the picada. Roast the hazelnuts on a tray in the oven until they are golden, being careful not to let them turn dark brown, then chop them coarsely. Fry the bread in 2 tablespoons of olive oil until it is golden on both sides. Toast the saffron, following directions on page 256. Break up the bread and combine in a mortar or food processor with the nuts, saffron, garlic, parsley, and pimentón. Pound or process to a coarse paste, adding another tablespoon of olive oil if it seems necessary.

Bring the stock to a simmer.

Add the noodles to the pork-tomato sauce in the pan and stir to mix well. Add about a cup of the simmering stock to the noodles and as soon as it has been absorbed, add another cup. Keep doing this, just as you would with risotto. After the third

2 tablespoons finely minced flat-leaf parsley

½ teaspoon medium-hot Spanish pimentón (paprika or ground red chili pepper)

1 tablespoon extra-virgin olive oil (optional)

4 cups chicken stock (page 108)

12 ounces (¾ of a 1-pound box) fideus noodles, or angel hair pasta, broken in shorter lengths (about 2 inches long)

½ cup grated parmigiano reggiano or other hard grating cheese

a handful of chopped flat-leaf parsley for garnish

cup of stock has been added, stir in the picada. Continue adding stock until it has all been absorbed. Remove from the heat and let settle for about 5 minutes, then serve with the grated cheese and chopped parsley sprinkled over the top.

Couscous

Couscous is North African pasta, made from durum-wheat semolina and water, the basic carbohydrate, along with bread, on Moroccan, Algerian, and Tunisian tables. Like pasta, it's often served on its own, with a thin but spicy sauce. For special occasions a grander couscous is produced, with a variety of vegetables and meats or fish.

Traditionally cooks made the couscous grains at home, a laborious process. Nowadays, even in North Africa, most couscous is bought ready-made. You can find a good quality at many health food stores; if possible, look for fine-grain couscous from North Africa.

The late President Bourguiba of Tunisia once imagined a north-south line drawn in Libya. East of that line, he said, rice is the staple; west of it is the land of couscous, the Maghreb, the most western—and some would say, the most romantic—region of the Arab world. The cultural differences between the two, he implied, are as sharply defined as the culinary ones.

I give two recipes for couscous, one prepared the traditional way, which involves a certain amount of effort, moistening, steaming, and fluffing the grains—but it's effort that's well worth it for the resulting soft, light texture, with each grain separate and tender. This is really best achieved with a *cous-cousière,* a special two-part pot for preparing couscous, available at kitchen supply stores (or see Resources at the back of the book). The savory stew goes in the bottom half, and the couscous grain goes in the top, so that the steam rising from the stew cooks the grain. You can fabricate a couscousière with a stockpot for the bottom and a colander that will just fit into the top. Line the colander with a double layer of cheesecloth to keep the grains from falling through the holes. (A tight seal between the bottom and top is important to force the steam through the holes of the top and into the couscous. Tunisian recipe books say to dip a strip of muslin in a flour and water paste, but wet strips of newspaper are often used instead.)

The second recipe is a good deal simpler and uses a standard American practice that is quicker and easier and produces acceptable results, even if they don't quite reach the glorious heights of traditional couscous.

As you will see, both these couscous recipes produce a meal in itself rather than a starter, but because they are based on the same sort of staple as pasta, I feel they belong in the pasta chapter. A salad, or a little collection of salads, and some fruit for dessert is all you'll need to add to make a complete meal.

North African Fish Couscous

Couscous de Poisson

❧ **Makes 8 to 10 servings**

FATOUMA MBRAHIM MADE THIS COUSCOUS for me one afternoon in Sidi Bou Said, a compact hilltop village overlooking the sea outside Tunis. She was born in Algeria—her family moved to Tunis after the French war—and she says her couscous, because it uses fruit as well as vegetables, is more Algerian than Tunisian.

In a tiny kitchen equipped with an ancient refrigerator that sat up on table legs, a four-burner stove that ran on bottled gas, a toaster oven, a sink the size of my bathroom sink at home, and a marble countertop that served as cutting board, storage area, and worktable all together, Fatouma turned out a magnificent feast for 26 people, including the couscous with all its accompanying sauces, and a delightful mixture of salads to garnish the main course.

Fatouma's recipe, as you will see, is basically a vegetable couscous with the fish cooked apart in a little of the vegetable sauce. If you wish, you can omit the fish from the meal entirely and serve a vegetarian couscous. The pumpkin featured in many Mediterranean recipes is drier in texture and flavor than our pie pumpkins. A good hard dark orange winter squash (Hubbard, acorn, buttercup, etc.) makes a fine substitute.

½ cup dried chickpeas, soaked overnight

½ teaspoon saffron threads

2 tablespoons harissa (page 279) plus ¼ cup for serving

4 onions, coarsely chopped

2 tablespons plus ½ cup extra-virgin olive oil

4 medium tomatoes, peeled (page 25) and coarsely chopped, or 1 28-ounce can whole tomatoes, drained and chopped

¼ cup canned tomato puree (or use liquid from canned tomatoes)

4 white turnips, peeled and quartered

4 medium russet potatoes, peeled and quartered

4 medium carrots, peeled and cut in chunks

sea salt and freshly ground black pepper

4 cups couscous, preferably fine-grain from North Africa

2 pounds deep-orange squash (acorn, butternut, Hubbard)

2 leeks, cut in chunks

4 medium zucchini, cut in chunks

2 sweet green peppers, quartered

2 quinces (or 2 very firm apples), quartered and cored

1 teaspoon ground cumin

2 pounds fresh fish steaks or fillets: halibut, haddock, snapper, monkfish, or similar fish

1 small green cabbage, cut into wedges

Drain the chickpeas. In a small saucepan, cover the chickpeas with water to a depth of 1 inch. Bring to a boil and cook, covered, for about 20 minutes. Set aside but do not drain.

Crumble the saffron threads into ½ cup warm water and set aside to steep. Mix the 2 tablespoons harissa into ½ cup warm water.

Combine the onions with 2 tablespoons of oil in the bottom of a couscousière and set it over medium–low heat. Cook gently, stirring occasionally, until the onions start to soften, about 15 minutes. Then add the tomatoes, stir, raise the heat to medium, and continue cooking, uncovered, for about 10 minutes or until the fragrance starts to rise. Stir in the diluted harissa and the tomato puree and cook for another 5 minutes.

Add the turnips, potatoes, and carrots to the tomatoes with 4 cups of water, salt, and lots of freshly ground pepper. Bring to a simmer and cook, uncovered, for 15 minutes.

The recipe can be done ahead up to this point. The couscous must be prepared about 1 hour before you start to cook it, and the cooking process itself, while not laborious, will take a good hour and 20 minutes. Give yourself plenty of time, much of which can be spent doing other things while the couscous steams.

About 1 hour before you're ready to cook the couscous, prepare it by tossing the couscous grains in a large, shallow bowl with about a tablespoon of salt to mix well. Then take the remaining ½ cup oil in a measuring cup or jug in your left hand (if you're right-handed) and pour it slowly, a little at a time, over the grains while you stir them with the fingers of your right hand, coating each grain with oil. Add a cup of very hot tap water to the jug and repeat the procedure, mixing the water in a small amount at a time until the couscous has absorbed it. Smooth the top of the couscous and set it aside for about 45 minutes to soften.

Layer the squash, leeks, and zucchini on top of the vegetable stew, then layer the sweet peppers and quince sections on top. Pour the chickpeas with their cooking liquid over the stew. Add the saffron with its soaking liquid, the cumin, and another cup of water.

When the couscous grains are ready, bring the vegetable stew in the bottom of the couscousière to a simmer. Extract about ½ cup of the stew liquid and set it aside for cooking the fish and cabbage sections.

Set the top of the couscousière onto the bottom half, sealing the gap between them with damp strips of newspaper as described on page 218. Rub the palms of your hands lightly with a little olive oil and rub the couscous grains between your palms to get rid of any lumps. Go over it carefully—in a good couscous each grain is separate and soft, which will never happen without this gentle rubbing. Add the couscous to the top of the couscousière, rubbing the grains between your palms as you do so. When all the couscous has been added, gently smooth over the top of the couscous with a wooden spoon and leave, uncovered and without stirring (this is very important), until the steam begins to rise between the grains. This can take up to 30 minutes. Once the steam starts to rise, time the couscous to cook, undisturbed, for 20 minutes.

Meanwhile, in a saucepan that will hold the whole fish or the fish pieces in one layer, cook the fish over medium heat in the reserved liquid from the vegetable stew, adding ½ cup water or more if necessary. Cover the fish and steam until it is done and the flesh flakes easily, about 8 to 10 minutes. Transfer the fish to a platter, reserving the cooking liquid. Cover the fish lightly with a sheet of foil and set it in a barely warm oven while you continue with the couscous.

Put the cabbage sections in a saucepan with the reserved fish liquid, cover, set over medium heat, and cook until done to taste, about 15 minutes. (Slightly underdone cabbage adds a nice texture contrast to the very soft vegetables. The cabbage is cooked apart so that its strong flavor doesn't overcome the more delicate flavors of the stew.) Add the cabbage sections to the fish to keep warm.

When the couscous has steamed for 20 minutes, remove the top of the couscousière and spread the couscous grains out, handling them gently, on a shallow platter or tray. Have ready a cup of very hot tap water with a teaspoon or more to taste of salt dissolved in it. Using a wooden spoon or wooden spatula, repeat the same action as before, pouring the salted water from your left hand, stirring very gently with your right hand, using the wooden spoon until the grains have cooled enough so you can use your fingers. Let the couscous sit for about 10 minutes, resting and absorbing the salted water.

(If you wish, at this point add the juices in which the fish and cabbage cooked back to the vegetable stew.)

Return the couscous grains to the top half of the couscousière and set it once more over the simmering stew, sealing the gap as described above. Again let it steam, uncovered and undisturbed, for 20 minutes.

Mix the ¼ cup of harissa with ¼ cup of hot water to make a sauce to accompany the finished dish.

When the couscous is done, serve it immediately, mounding it on a warm serving platter and garnishing it with all the vegetables, including the cabbage. Dribble a ladleful of the sauce over the couscous and vegetables and over the platter of fish. Serve, passing the rest of the sauce in a bowl along with the harissa garnish.

Simple Couscous with Lamb and Vegetables

Couscous d'Agneau aux Legumes

Makes 6 to 8 servings

THE LAMB AND VEGETABLE STEW for this couscous can be put together very quickly. It does require several hours of cooking, but that doesn't mean the cook has to stand over a hot stove and watch it. Set your burner on the lowest simmer (or make the stew in a Crock-Pot) and you can go off for a bike ride while the stew bubbles away.

Traditional North African cooks go through an elaborate process of steaming and fluffing couscous two or three times (and it really does create an extraordinarily light and fragrant result, as the previous recipe shows), but most of us will be just as happy with the quicker, easier methods used by American restaurant and home cooks alike. Couscous cooked like this is even faster than pasta; a box of couscous should be right next to the linguine and spaghetti on the pantry shelves of anyone who cares about eating well.

2 pounds boned lamb shoulder, cut in stewing chunks

¼ cup extra-virgin olive oil

2 medium yellow onions, halved lengthwise and sliced thin

1 teaspoon mixed ground cloves and cinnamon (see Note)

½ teaspoon powdered ginger

1 teaspoon ground cumin

½ teaspoon ground coriander

a big pinch of saffron threads

sea salt and freshly ground black pepper

Pick over the lamb chunks and remove any thick layers of fat. Heat the oil over medium heat in a heavy casserole large enough to hold all the ingredients. When the oil is hot, add the lamb and cook, stirring and turning the pieces of meat, until they are brown all over. Lower the heat to medium-low and add the onions. Cook, stirring, until the onions have softened.

Stir in the spices, including salt and pepper to taste. Add 4 cups of water and bring to a gentle simmer. Add the soaked and drained chickpeas and the harissa, stirring the harissa into the sauce, then cover the pan and let simmer over very gentle heat for about 1 hour, or until the chickpeas are thoroughly softened and the sauce is thick. (If you must use canned

½ cup chickpeas, soaked overnight, to make 1 cup soaked chickpeas, or use 1 15.5-ounce can chickpeas, well drained

2 tablespoons spicy harissa, or more or less, to taste

2 cups chicken stock or plain water

4 medium carrots, scraped and cut in 2-inch-long pieces

4 small white turnips, peeled and quartered

2 large sweet potatoes, peeled and cut in chunks

¼ small green cabbage, slivered

1 sweet red pepper, trimmed and slivered

½ cup golden raisins

2 cups couscous

GARNISH

a handful of chopped cilantro and flat-leaf parsley, mixed

⅓ cup toasted slivered almonds

chickpeas, hold them in reserve and add with the cabbage, below.)

While the lamb and chickpeas are cooking, bring the stock to a rolling boil. Add the carrots and turnips and cook, covered, until just tender, about 15 minutes. Remove with a slotted spoon and set aside, covered, to keep warm until ready to serve. Add the sweet potato chunks to the stock in the pan and cook briefly, about 10 minutes or just until tender. Remove with a slotted spoon and add to the carrots and turnips. Now drop the cabbage slivers into the water. Cook for 5 minutes, just to wilt the cabbage, then remove and add to the other vegetables.

When the meat and vegetables are ready, prepare the couscous. Bring the stock to a boil again. Taste and if necessary add a pinch of sea salt. Stir in the red pepper slivers and the raisins, which will plump rapidly in the boiling liquid. Let boil for 2 minutes, then add the couscous, stir it in, and immediately remove the pan from the heat, cover it tightly, and set aside for about 5 minutes, during which time the "grains" of couscous will swell and soften.

Spread the couscous on a serving platter, fluffing it with a fork. Spoon the meat and its sauce over the top and arrange the steamed turnips, carrots, and sweet potatoes around the edge, sprinkling the cabbage slivers over the top. Finally, garnish the dish with minced cilantro and parsley and the almonds.

Serve immediately.

Variation: Although the lamb stew is always served with couscous in the Maghreb (North Africa), it is also excellent with rice, cooked in the stock just like the couscous but, of course, for much longer—15 to 20 minutes. And if you want to be totally unorthodox, you could even serve it with steamed new potatoes, rolled in olive oil and a little sea salt.

Note: For the most flavorful cinnamon–clove combination, grind the spices in a coffee grinder just before adding them to the dish. About 12 whole cloves and a 2-inch piece of cinnamon stick should be sufficient to make a teaspoon of mixed spices when ground.

If you like to cook with spices, but don't care for spiced coffee, you may want to keep a coffee grinder specially for spice grinding. Otherwise, to get rid of coffee flavor before grinding spices, wipe out your coffee grinder with a paper towel, then grind a small piece of stale bread in the machine. Repeat the process when you convert back to coffee.

Rice

Second only to wheat in its importance in Mediterranean cooking, rice, in some parts of the region, is considered superior, a grain to be reserved for Sunday dinner and similar special occasions.

Short-grain rice is grown in Italy's Po Valley and Piedmont, in the great wetlands of the Camargue at the mouth of the Rhône in Provence, and in the vast and beautiful Albufera lagoon south of Valencia on the east coast of Spain. In these regions of the western Mediterranean, dishes like risotto and paella have evolved to take advantage of the plump grains that swell as they absorb the liquid and develop a creamy consistency. Risotto should be very creamy but not at all soupy. Paella and similar Spanish preparations aim for something a little drier than risotto but still with the grains enveloped in their aromatic sauce.

Farther east, in Greece, Turkey, and the Levant, long-grain rice, originally from India and Persia, is preferred for pilafs, cooked by first sautéing the rice in cooking fat (butter, oil, sheep's tail fat, or clarified butter) with aromatics and then adding boiling stock or broth. Unlike risotto, the aim with pilaf is a slightly drier, but still moist, rice in which each grain is separate.

Beyond long-grain and short-grain, a number of different types of rice are available in American markets. One of the most attractive is basmati, originally from India, now grown in Texas. Pecan rice and popcorn rice are not (as I thought for years!) rice grains mixed with pecans or popcorn but rather rice with a peculiarly nutty and delicious flavor. Basmati, pecan, and popcorn rice can be used for pilafs, but they are not suitable for risotto or paella.

What about brown rice? It is unquestionably a healthful product, but it is not used in the Mediterranean except by macrobiotics. Brown rice is better for pilaf than for risotto, although you will have to increase cooking times considerably. I have never had any success with brown rice in a risotto or paella—the grains simply don't absorb the liquid properly. Try it, by all means, but be prepared for a dish that is different from what you expected. It will still be full of flavor.

Basic Rice Pilaf

Makes 6 servings

THIS IS THE MOST BASIC rice of all and should be served as an accompaniment to other dishes, whether roasted or grilled meat or fish, vegetables, or beans. The almonds, pine nuts, and raisins are a garnish and may be left out if you wish.

2½ cups chicken stock (page 108)

¼ cup coarsely chopped blanched almonds

¼ cup pine nuts

2 tablespoons extra-virgin olive oil

1 medium onion, finely chopped

1½ cups long-grain rice

1 3-inch cinnamon stick

sea salt and freshly ground pepper

¼ cup golden raisins, plumped in warm water

Heat the stock to a slow simmer while you prepare the rest of the pilaf.

In a saucepan over medium heat, gently sauté the almonds and pine nuts in the olive oil, stirring constantly, until they are brown, about 5 minutes, being careful not to burn them. Remove them with a slotted spoon and set aside.

Add the onion to the oil in the pan and cook, stirring frequently, until the onion starts to soften but not to brown—about 10 minutes. Stir in the rice and continue cooking and stirring until the rice begins to turn a very pale brown—about 5 minutes. Immediately pour in the hot stock, add the cinnamon, and season to taste with salt and lots of pepper. Stir the rice briefly to mix well, then lower the heat and cook, covered, until the liquid has been absorbed, about 15 to 20 minutes. Remove from the heat and, with the pot still covered, set aside for 5 minutes without disturbing. Then remove the lid, discard the cinnamon stick, stir in the reserved nuts and drained raisins, and serve the rice.

Variation: To make a tomato pilaf, omit the almonds, pine nuts, and raisins; chop about a pound of peeled tomatoes, or 2 cups drained canned whole tomatoes, and cook them with the onion and ½ garlic clove, crushed with the flat blade of a knife, before adding the rice. You will need less stock for this pilaf, since the tomatoes will provide quite a bit of juice. Stir in about ¼ cup chopped green herbs (parsley, basil, cilantro) at the end.

For other vegetables, add a pound of leeks, cut into 1-inch slices, or a pound of spinach, torn into pieces, with the onions, and increase the stock to 2½ cups.

Risotto

Plump, short-grain Italian rice, specially grown for risotto and similar techniques, is the only rice to use. Arborio is most widely available in American markets, but you may also find *vialone nano* or even *carnaroli*, the best rice of all but not always available. Note that these are not brand names; rather they're the names of varieties of rice.

Rice for risotto is characterized by a soft, starchy exterior coating that absorbs the cooking liquid a little at a time and swells to the requisite thick, creamy consistency, each grain thoroughly napped with sauce. For this reason risotto rice must never be soaked or rinsed before cooking—that would loosen and dissolve the starchy exterior.

Over the years I've tried making risotto with short-grain brown rice but in the end I have to admit that it just doesn't work. While brown rice can be substituted in long-grain recipes, like rice pilafs, it just makes a gloppy mess with risotti. So use polished risotto rice—it's not the most healthful rice in the world but it won't do you any harm and the rest of the ingredients are darned good for you!

Venetians, who are the best cooks of risotto, say a proper risotto is *all' onda,* that is, like a wave, just rippling with the sauce that is created simply by cooking the rice in an aromatic liquid that may also include a vegetable (or two or three) or seafood. Risotto requires more attention on the part of the cook than pilaf, but the results are well worth it. It is an elegant dish.

Risotto is usually made with quantities of butter, but I find that a mild extra-virgin olive oil is even better.

Asparagus Risotto

≈⅛ Makes 6 to 8 servings

THINK OF THIS RECIPE as a model or basic risotto recipe. You can vary it in many ways, substituting other vegetables, alone or in combination, depending on the season: in spring freshly shelled green peas or fava beans; in summer, peeled and seeded red-ripe tomatoes, zucchini, or sweet peppers roasted and peeled; in autumn, fresh fennel or celery coarsely chopped or chunks of butternut squash; and in winter, artichoke hearts, trimmed and cut in chunks, or small beets, peeled and coarsely grated, for a fantastic pink risotto. You could even try fruit for an interesting challenge. My favorite Roman trattoria specializes in risotto con fragole (strawberries), an absolute knockout.

All risotti follow roughly the same procedure: you sauté very gently some aromatics (onions, garlic, parsley) and the principal flavoring ingredient (asparagus, squash, whatever), then stir in the rice and let it absorb some of the fat (a process called the *tostatura*). Add a little white wine and as soon as the wine has been absorbed, start adding simmering stock or water, in increments of ¼ to ½ cup. As the stock is absorbed, you add more, stirring the while, until the rice is properly al dente, cooked through but still with a little bite at the center. Finally, stir in cheese and/or butter, if you're using it, then cover it firmly and let the rice rest for 10 to 20 minutes before serving it, still hot. The whole process should take no more than 30 minutes, not counting the resting time, and it cannot be speeded up, nor can you successfully partially cook the rice and then reheat it, so plan to make your risotto when the family or guests are ready to come to the table.

6 cups chicken stock (page 108) or vegetable stock (page 107)	Heat the stock to a bare simmer and keep it simmering *very* gently as you prepare the risotto.

[cont. next page]

1½ to 2 pounds fresh asparagus

¼ cup extra-virgin olive oil

1 medium yellow onion, halved and thinly sliced

1 teaspoon sea salt, or more to taste

1 garlic clove, chopped

2 cups rice for risotto (carnaroli, vialone nano, or arborio)

½ cup dry white wine

¾ cup freshly grated parmigiano reggiano cheese

1 tablespoon unsalted butter (optional)

freshly ground pepper, preferably white pepper

Prepare the asparagus, trimming the spears in the usual manner. Break off the heads of the asparagus and set them aside. Break the stalks into two or three pieces.

Add the oil to a heavy kettle or saucepan large enough to hold all the rice when cooked, and set over medium-low heat. Turn the onion, salt, garlic, and the asparagus stalk pieces into the oil, and gently cook, stirring occasionally, until the onion is soft and melting but not brown, and the asparagus is quite limp.

Add the rice to the vegetables and stir to mix well. Cook for several minutes, or until the rice starts to change color and sizzles in the fat. Add the wine, raise the heat slightly, and cook, stirring, until the wine has been absorbed. Now start adding the simmering stock, a half-cup or so at a time and stirring after each addition. As soon as the rice has absorbed the liquid, add more, and continue adding simmering liquid, ladle by ladle, stirring constantly. There should always be liquid visible in the pan—meaning, the rice should never dry out. But do not add all the liquid at once; this will produce boiled rice or pilaf instead of risotto. After 15 minutes, stir in the reserved heads of asparagus.

You may not need to use all the stock, but if it happens that you use up the stock before the rice is ready (unlikely, but it could occur), use boiling water but keep adding liquid. When the rice is done, it will be al dente, with a bit of bite in the center. It should be thick enough to eat with a fork. Each grain should be well coated with the sauce, which will be dense and almost syrupy. The pieces of asparagus stalk will be very soft, while the heads will retain a bit of texture.

Remove the pan from the heat and stir in about ¼ cup of the cheese, the butter, if using, and the pepper. Immediately cover the pan and set it aside for 10 to 15 minutes before serving. When you serve the risotto, pass more cheese at the table.

Risotto con Funghi Porcini

Risotto with Dried Wild Mushrooms

Makes 6 to 8 servings

THIS WONDERFUL DISH is made from the humblest of ingredients, wild mushrooms scavenged in the forest after late-summer rains and dried on racks in the farmyard while the sun is still strong. The best dried mushrooms are funghi porcini, or cèpes, imported from Italy or France, although I have also made *risotto con funghi* with Chinese and Polish dried mushrooms.

Wild porcini can be found in bosky meadows and woodlots all over the northern United States, but they don't have the same intensity of flavor that porcini have in Italy. (On the other hand, our wild chanterelles are streets ahead of Italian chanterelles in flavor.) If you like to go mushrooming and you're confident of what you find, by all means dry your own (see instructions, page 325) to concentrate the flavor.

3 ounces dried porcini

5 cups chicken or vegetable stock (pages 107–108)

1 small yellow onion, minced

2 tablespoons extra-virgin olive oil

2 cups carnaroli, vialone nano, or arborio rice

about ¾ cup freshly grated parmigiano cheese

sea salt and freshly ground black pepper

Prepare the dried mushrooms at least 45 minutes before you're ready to start cooking. Place the mushrooms in a bowl and cover them with hot (not boiling) tap water. Set aside to let the mushrooms absorb the water for at least 30 minutes. Remove the mushroom pieces, *reserving the water in which they soaked.* Put the pieces in a colander or sieve and rinse in running tap water to rid them of any grit. Chop the mushrooms coarsely and set aside.

Now filter the mushroom-soaking liquid through a fine sieve or several layers of cheesecloth to get rid of any grit. Add the mushroom-soaking liquid to the stock for the risotto. When you're ready to start the risotto, bring the stock to a bare simmer and keep it simmering *very* gently while you cook.

In a heavy kettle or saucepan large enough to hold all the rice when cooked, gently sauté the onion in the oil over medium-low heat, stirring continuously until the onion is thoroughly softened but not browned—about 15 minutes. Stir in the rice and turn it for a couple of minutes until it is thoroughly coated with the oniony fat. Now stir in the chopped dried mushrooms and a ladleful (about ½ to ¾ cup—no need to be exact) of simmering stock.

As soon as the rice has absorbed the liquid, add more, and continue adding simmering stock, ladle by ladle, stirring constantly. There should always be liquid visible in the pan. Do not add all the liquid at once; this will produce boiled rice or pilaf instead of risotto. The rice is done when it is al dente, with a bit of a bite in the center. Each grain should be well coated with the sauce, which should be dense and rather syrupy looking. When it is done, the risotto should be thick enough to eat with a fork. (You might not need to use all the liquid.) Total cooking time will be 20 to 30 minutes, depending on how soft you want the rice to be.

Remove from the heat and stir in about ¼ cup of the grated cheese. Set aside for 5 minutes or so to let the flavors settle, then taste for seasoning, adding salt and pepper as desired. Serve immediately, passing more cheese at the table.

Risotto ai Frutti di Mare

Seafood Risotto

Makes 6 to 8 servings

A RATHER FIRM-TEXTURED SEAFOOD is required here. Lobster and shrimp are obvious choices, but you can also use cubed monkfish or any combination of these. Be careful of cooking times in preparing seafood—putting a lot of money into fish only to ruin it by overcooking is one of those things that can seriously depress a cook.

This is a little more complicated than other risotti, but the seafood can be prepared ahead of time with no detriment to the final preparation.

1 pound medium-large (25 count) shrimp, heads removed but shells left on, or 1 live 1½-pound lobster, or ¾ pound cooked lobster meat, or ¾ pound monkfish fillet, cut into small cubes

5 cups fish stock (page 109)

2 to 3 tablespoons extra-virgin olive oil

a pinch of cayenne pepper

2 garlic cloves, minced

1 small yellow onion, minced

1 carrot, peeled and finely chopped

1 celery stalk, finely chopped

2 cups carnaroli, vialone nano, or arborio rice

½ cup dry white wine

¼ cup minced flat-leaf parsley

¼ cup freshly grated parmigiano reggiano cheese (optional)

sea salt and freshly ground black pepper

First prepare the seafood if necessary. Live lobster should be steamed in a very little water until just barely cooked, about 10 minutes, then shelled and the meat cut into bite-size pieces and set aside. Shrimp should be peeled and, if large, cut into smaller pieces and set aside. The shells and other residue can be added to the cooking stock for the risotto, simmered gently for 30 minutes, and strained. (The seafood and the stock can be prepared ahead of time and refrigerated.)

When you're ready to cook, bring the strained stock to a slow simmer and keep it simmering *very* gently while you prepare the risotto.

In a heavy kettle or saucepan large enough to hold all the cooked rice, warm the oil over medium heat and, when it is shimmering, add the seafood. Stir the seafood in the hot oil just until the aroma of the fish begins to rise, about 7 to 10 minutes. The monkfish or shrimp should lose its raw translucence but not be thoroughly cooked. Stir in the cayenne pepper, remove the seafood with a slotted spoon, leaving the aromatic oil behind in the pan, and set aside. (This procedure gives an important flavor boost to the risotto.)

Now lower the heat, stir the garlic, onion, carrot, and celery into the pan, and cook, stirring, until the vegetables are soft but not brown—about 10 to 15 minutes. Stir in the rice and mix until the rice is thoroughly coated with the aromatic oil. Add the wine and cook, stirring, until the rice has absorbed most of it, about 5 minutes.

As soon as the wine is absorbed, start adding the simmering stock. Add a little at a time, ladle by ladle, stirring constantly and not adding more until the previous addition has been mostly absorbed. There should always be liquid visible in the pan.

Do not add all the liquid at once; this will produce boiled rice or pilaf instead of risotto. After the first 20 minutes of cooking, stir in the reserved seafood. The rice is done when it is al dente, with a bit of a bite in the center. Each grain should be well coated with the sauce, which should be dense and rather syrupy looking. When it is done, the risotto should be thick enough to eat with a fork. (You may not need to use all the liquid.) Total cooking time should be about 25 to 30 minutes.

Remove from the heat and stir in the minced parsley and, if desired, the grated cheese. Taste and adjust the seasoning with salt and pepper. Serve immediately.

Panissa

Risotto with Salami and Beans

Makes 6 to 8 servings

THIS IS MY SIMPLIFIED TAKE on a rustic, but rich and sumptuous dish from the rice-growing regions of northern Italy. The original is delicious but heavy. I've cut down on some of the porky ingredients and substituted olive oil for butter. The result, I think, is still delicious but a good deal more digestible. If you serve this as a first course, plan to follow it with a light, simple grill of chicken or fish.

¾ cup borlotti or other speckled beans, soaked overnight

4 cups chicken (page 108) or vegetable stock (page 107)

1 large onion, halved and thinly sliced

1 garlic clove, crushed

2 tablespoons extra-virgin olive oil

Add the drained beans to a saucepan with 2½ cups of water. Bring to a simmer and cook gently, covered, until the beans are tender—about 40 minutes. Add a little more boiling water from time to time if necessary to keep the beans from scorching. When the beans are done, set aside, but do not drain.

Bring the stock to a gentle simmer and keep just below the boiling point while you prepare the risotto.

⅓ to ½ pound salami, skin removed, chopped coarsely

1½ cups Italian short-grain rice, such as arborio, vialone nano, or carnaroli

½ cup well-flavored dry white wine

sea salt and freshly ground black pepper

2 tablespoons freshly grated parmigiano reggiano cheese, or more if you wish

In a large heavy-duty saucepan, combine the onion and garlic with the oil and cook, stirring, over medium-low heat until the onion slices and garlic are softened. Stir in the chopped salami and the rice. Cook, stirring occasionally, for about 5 minutes or until the bits of salami are softened and the rice is well coated with the fat in the pan. Add the white wine, raise the heat slightly, and cook more rapidly, until the rice has absorbed the wine.

Stir in the beans with their cooking liquid and continue cooking until most of the bean liquid has been absorbed. Now cover the contents of the pan with a ladle or two of the not quite simmering broth, stirring to mix well. As the rice absorbs the broth, keep adding more, a ladle or two at a time, stirring as you do so, until the rice is done. The rice should always be just barely swimming in liquid but never awash and never let to dry out.

When the rice is done but still al dente, remove from the heat, taste, and add salt and pepper. Then stir in the 2 tablespoons of cheese, cover the pan and set aside, away from the heat, for 5 minutes or so to combine all the flavors well. Serve the rice, if you wish, with more grated cheese on the side.

Arroz al Horno

Rice Baked in the Oven

+⛊ Makes 6 servings of Arroz al Horno; 16 servings of Cocido only

V ALENCIA IS THE HEARTLAND of Spanish rice growing, and most of it is cultivated in flooded paddy fields around the broad, silvery lagoon of the Albufera, just south of the city of Valencia. On Sundays, Valencians troop out to little beachside and village restaurants to eat rice in one form or another. In an encyclopedic Valencian cookbook I counted two dozen different rice preparations, all of them, justifiably, considered native to the region.

Naturally the best rice cooks come from the great rice-growing regions. Lourdes March, Valencian cook and writer, showed me how to prepare this dish. Spanish cooks like Lourdes use large, round, rather shallow terra-cotta dishes, called *cazuelas* or *cassolas,* for baking *arroz al horno.* A round or rectangular glass ovenproof dish is a good substitute.

Note that the first step produces a rich stock called *cocido.* You can do this well in advance—up to a month, in fact, if you freeze the stock. But if you already have a good, deep-flavored stock on hand in the freezer, use it instead. If you do make the cocido stock from scratch, serve some of the stock as a first course before the rice. Garnish it with toasted garlic croutons and chopped chives or scallion tops.

FOR THE COCIDO

1 6-pound stewing hen, cut in 6 or 8 pieces

½ pound pork ribs or meaty pork bones

2 medium carrots, halved lengthwise

1 large leek, quartered lengthwise and rinsed well

1 white turnip, quartered

3 quarts cold water

1½ teaspoons saffron threads

2 teaspoons sea salt

FOR THE RICE

½ cup dried chickpeas, soaked overnight

4½ cups cocido or well-flavored chicken stock (page 108)

½ cup extra-virgin olive oil

1 large or 2 medium potatoes, peeled and sliced

4 medium ripe tomatoes, 3 cut in half horizontally, 1 peeled and chopped (page 25)

1 small head of garlic

For the cocido: place the hen, pork, carrots, leek, and turnip in a large stockpot. Add the cold water and bring to a simmer over moderate heat. Simmer, covered, for 1 hour, then uncover, skim if necessary, and stir in the saffron and salt. Cover again and simmer for 3 hours. Remove from the heat and let cool for 30 minutes. Strain into a large bowl and let cool completely. Cover and refrigerate overnight. Skim the fat from the surface before using.

(This makes far more cocido than is necessary for Arroz al Horno. What can I say? Freeze what you don't use right away. The stock is delicious on its own or as a base for many soups, stews, and risotti. It can be refrigerated for up to 3 days or frozen for up to 1 month.)

For the rice: drain the chickpeas and put in a saucepan with about 1½ cups of the cocido stock. Set over medium heat and cook, covered, until the chickpeas are soft and most of the liquid has been absorbed, at least 40 minutes. When the chickpeas are done, set them aside with their cooking liquid.

Heat the olive oil in a skillet over medium heat until it starts to shimmer. Then add the potatoes and sauté, turning once or twice, until they're browned—about 10 minutes. Remove from the

1 pound lean boneless pork loin, cut into ½- to 1-inch cubes

sea salt and freshly ground black pepper

1 tablespoon sweet spanish paprika (pimentón)

1½ cups Spanish round-grain rice (arroz bomba) or arborio rice

cooking oil and set aside. Add the tomato halves to the oil, cut side down, and sauté until the cut sides begin to brown (don't turn them over). Remove and set aside. Rub the head of garlic firmly to brush away loose skin, but leave the head itself intact. Add to the oil in the pan and cook, turning frequently, until the outside of the garlic is thoroughly browned—about 10 minutes. Remove and set aside.

Now remove and discard all but 2 tablespoons of the oil in the skillet. Add the pork cubes to the remaining oil and cook, turning frequently, until the pork cubes are thoroughly browned—about 15 minutes. Stir in salt and an abundance of black pepper. Add the chopped tomato and cook for about 2 minutes or until the tomato has softened.

Remove the skillet from the heat and stir in the paprika and rice, mixing well. Set aside.

Before assembling the finished dish, preheat the oven to 400 degrees. Bring the remaining stock or cocido to a simmer on the top of the stove.

Place the reserved garlic in the center of the baking dish. Arrange the pork-rice mixture all around and distribute the chickpeas and their liquid over the top of the rice, pressing them down into the rice a little with the back of a spoon. Nestle the tomato halves in the rice mixture and spread the potato slices over the top.

Pour the simmering stock over the top and bake, uncovered, for 20 to 25 minutes or until the rice is just tender and the stock has been mostly absorbed. Remove the dish from the oven, cover loosely with foil, and let sit for another 5 minutes before serving.

Baked Rice with Vegetables

Tiella di Verdura

A*TIELLA IS A CLASSIC DISH* from Puglia, the long skinny region that takes up the heel of the Italian boot. It's a structured, layered dish of several ingredients, one of which is almost always rice. Like many Mediterranean classics, tiella refers both to the preparation itself and to the dish in which it is cooked, traditionally an earthenware oven dish about 8 to 10 inches in diameter. Of course, if you don't have a Pugliese tiella on hand, you may also make this in a ceramic or glass Pyrex dish, one that's wider than it is tall—a round or oval gratin dish is perfect for the job.

Many recipes for tiella call for arborio rice, the kind that's used in risotto. But Stella Longano, who showed me how to make this one afternoon in a farmhouse outside Monopoli, uses long-grain rice, which she says yields a better result. Have all your ingredients ready and laid out, she counsels, before you start to assemble the dish.

8 ounces (1¼ cups) Carolina long-grain rice

1½ fresh lemons

1½ pounds yellow-fleshed potatoes (Yellow Finns or Yukon Golds)

4 large globe artichokes—about 2 pounds in all (or 1 9-ounce box frozen artichoke hearts)

2 garlic cloves, minced

¾ cup chopped flat-leaf parsley

1 tablespoon dried oregano, crumbled

about ½ cup extra-virgin olive oil

about 1 cup dry, unflavored bread crumbs

Put the rice to soak in water to cover to a depth of 1 inch for 30 minutes, while you prepare the other ingredients.

If you are using fresh artichokes, prepare two bowls of acidulated water, using the juice of half a lemon for each bowl and filling the bowls with cool water. One bowl will be for the sliced potatoes, the other for the artichokes. (If you are using frozen artichoke hearts, simply prepare one bowl for the potatoes.)

Peel the potatoes, slice about ⅛ inch thick, and add the slices to a bowl of acidulated water.

Trim the fresh artichokes of all their hard leaves, rubbing the cut surfaces with the remaining lemon half to keep them from blackening. Slice the artichokes in half lengthwise and, using a grapefruit spoon or a small sharp knife, scrape away the

1½ medium yellow onions, thinly sliced

1 cup canned, drained, chopped tomatoes

¾ cup freshly grated aged pecorino or parmigiano reggiano

sea salt

prickly choke; trim off the sharp points of the internal leaves. Slice the artichokes lengthwise into approximately ¼-inch-thick slices and put them in the other bowl of acidulated water.

If you're using frozen artichoke hearts, simply slice each heart as thinly as you can.

When you're ready to assemble the tiella, set the oven at 375 degrees. Toss together the garlic, parsley, and crumbled oregano and set aside. Smear a little oil around the bottom and sides of a ceramic, glass, or earthenware oven dish about 8 to 10 inches in diameter, or an 11 x 8-inch rectangular dish. Sprinkle 2 tablespoons of bread crumbs over the bottom of the dish and dribble a tablespoon of oil over the bread crumbs.

Drain the potato slices thoroughly and divide roughly into two portions. Layer one portion over the bottom of the dish. (The bottom should be covered with only a slight overlap among the slices.) Distribute about a third of the onion slices over the potatoes and sprinkle with a third of the herb–garlic mixture. Dab about ¼ cup of the chopped tomatoes over the top, then sprinkle with ¼ cup of grated cheese, a pinch of salt, 2 tablespoons of bread crumbs, and a tablespoon of oil.

Drain the rice, squeezing to rid it of as much water as possible, and divide roughly in two portions. Distribute one portion over the top in a thin layer, not covering the potatoes entirely.

Drain the artichoke slices, if necessary, and layer them on top of the rice. Use the remaining rice to top the artichokes. On top of this layer of rice, distribute another ¼ cup of tomatoes, a third of the onion slices, and a third of the herb mixture. Sprinkle as above with ¼ cup of grated cheese, salt, 2 tablespoons of bread crumbs, and a tablespoon of oil.

For the final layer, use the remaining sliced potatoes, dressing them with the remaining ½ cup of tomatoes, plus the remaining onion and the herb mixture. Sprinkle with a little salt, ¼ cup of grated cheese, ½ cup of bread crumbs (to make a thicker layer than the previous ones), and dribble over all about ⅓ cup of oil.

Bring a kettle of water to a boil and add boiling water to the tiella to come about halfway up the container, a depth of about 1½ inches. Transfer to the preheated oven and bake for 1 hour.

Serve hot from the oven or at room temperature.

Paella

Makes 10 servings

THE MOST FAMOUS DISH in the entire repertoire of *la cocina española,* paella is also the most misunderstood and maligned. And that, alas, is true on its home ground as much as abroad.

A true *paella valenciana,* say those who know, can be made *only* with the round, short-grain rice grown in the region from Valencia south and called *arroz bomba* or *Calasparra;* it includes *only* chicken, rabbit, and snails; it is seasoned *only* with saffron and pimentón (paprika); and it should be made *only* over an open fire, preferably of orange wood and vine cuttings. Moreover, it must be made *only* in a wide, round, flat-bottomed pan, itself called a *paella,* a word that comes, so it is said, from the Latin *patella,* for a similar pan. So a paella, it would seem, is a dish cooked in the pan, not necessarily a dish made with rice.

Well, not necessarily. A paella, it turns out, is many things.

"We call all sorts of dishes paella, but real paella is made in the *huerta* [the market gardens], of chicken, rabbit, and garden vegetables—the green things you have in season," says Tinuka Lassala, who comes from Valencia and learned to cook rice from her father. Originally, she explains, paella was cooked *only* by men and *only* for the midday meal. All other rice dishes, those cooked by women and those served in the evening, no matter what their content, were not paella.

I am beginning to get the sense of this, after years of trying to understand. Paella, I think, is a little like barbecue, which once meant an event at which large pieces of meat (whole hogs, whole sides of beef) were cooked outdoors in or over a pit fire by men, usually black, for other men, usually white, to eat. And now it means any kind of grilling over any kind of fire, as long as it takes place outdoors.

Paella, in the same way, once meant a specific dish, also—curiously here in Spain, where men are so protective of their machismo—cooked by men, also cooked outdoors, usually in or close by the fields, *la huerta,* where the vegetables for the paella grow. And just as with barbecue, each cook has his own recipe, often with a secret or two tucked inside, for a paella that is, really, the only true and authentic way to make it "the way our grandfathers did." And, again as with barbecue, the recipes and techniques have been widely dispersed and adopted by all kinds of indifferent and doubtless, truth be told, unskilled cooks, all kinds of equivocal garbage have been thrown into the pot, and the dish has gone forth into the world, minus its reputation and pedigree with but two things intact—the rice and the pan in which to cook it.

The best paella I ever had was in a restaurant on the beach just outside El Grao, the bustling port of Valencia, a restaurant so humble it just escaped shabbiness, a quality that was emphasized by the sand that drifted in on the wind across the dunes outside. The cook was a woman, unusually, but the rest was deeply traditional—there were the open fires of orange wood and vine cuttings on the long kitchen hearth, there were the broad flat pans, there was the rice, the product of the vastly beautiful paddies of the Albufera lagoon south of the city.

Amparo, the cook, red-haired, serene, and stout, made two paellas, one with fish (shrimp, langoustines, squid sliced into rings), one with chicken, rabbit, and snails. She explained the difference between them: for the fish paella, the rice is sautéed in hot oil with the squid and then the liquid is added; for the more traditional one, chicken and rabbit, browned in fat, simmer in a broth to which the rice is added later. "My grandfather made a wonderful paella," she said. "Around here it's the men who make it, y'know."

The following recipe is my adaptation of paella, based on what I've observed over the years from cooks like Amparo, Tinuka, and Lourdes March, another top-notch Valencian rice cook. This paella is not authentic, at least in part because there are so many ingredients, beginning with the rice, that are hard to find in this country. But it is very good. If at all possible, try making it over an open fire (a wood fire, that is, not a charcoal grill), because you can control the heat so much more easily. Failing that, a gas ring (a large gas ring) is second best. If your only heat source is electricity, you'll need to use several burners set at different levels to control the heat.

If you cannot find a paella pan (see Resources), use a large, heavy, flat-bottomed sauté pan or skillet. The skillet must be large enough to hold all the meats and shrimp spread out in one layer, with enough space in between for the rice.

As for ingredients: you must use a round, short-grain rice. Italian arborio rice is an acceptable substitute for Spanish short-grain rice like Calasparra. Rabbit is authentic, but pork can be substituted. The dry beans used in Spain are big white ones called *garrafóns;* use large lima beans instead. The green beans used are flat ones like our romano beans, but any large string beans can be substituted, as long as they are fresh. I also add shrimp to the mixture simply because so many people expect it. If you want to be superauthentic, leave the shrimp out. The recipe calls for 6 cups of chicken stock, but you might need less—the rule is 2 cups of liquid for each cup of rice, but there is a good deal of liquid in the tomatoes and other vegetables.

This large paella is an abundant dish that needs nothing but a crisp green salad to follow.

1 cup large white beans, soaked overnight, drained	Set the beans in a saucepan with 4 cups of water. Bring to a simmer and cook, covered, until the beans are soft but not falling apart, at least 30 to 40 minutes, depending on the age and size of the beans. When the beans are done, set them aside in their cooking liquid.
6 chicken legs and 6 chicken thighs, preferably free-range	
½ cup extra-virgin olive oil, or more if needed	
2 pounds rabbit, cut into small pieces, or country-style pork spareribs, each cut into 3 pieces	In a large, heavy, round flat-bottomed skillet or paella pan, brown the chicken pieces in the olive oil over medium heat, turning frequently to brown on all sides. This will take about 20 minutes. As the chicken browns, remove the pieces and set aside.
1 pound medium-large (25 count) shrimp, unshelled if desired	
3 cups finely chopped white or yellow onion	Add the rabbit or pork to the pan and brown, turning frequently. When the meat is brown on all sides, after about 20 minutes, remove and set aside.
6 to 8 artichokes, prepared as on page 26, quartered, or one 9-ounce package frozen artichoke hearts	Add the shrimp to the pan, raise the heat slightly, and cook quickly, tossing the shrimp. When the shrimp has changed color and become opaque, in 3 to 5 minutes, remove and set aside.

2 cups fresh tomato sauce (page 266), chopped fresh tomatoes, or canned whole tomatoes, drained and chopped

1 teaspoon saffron threads soaked in ¼ cup water

1 pound green beans, cut into 2-inch lengths

2 tablespoons sweet pimentón (paprika)

sea salt

2 rosemary sprigs

6 cups chicken stock (page 108), simmering

4 cups round short-grain rice

Lower the heat to medium-low and, in the oil remaining in the pan, gently sauté the onion until soft and starting to brown, about 15 minutes, adding a little more oil to the pan if necessary.

Meanwhile, bring 2 cups water to a boil in a saucepan and add the drained artichokes. Boil for about 10 to 15 minutes or until the artichokes are just tender. Do not drain.

Add the tomatoes to the onions, raise the heat to medium, and cook, stirring frequently, until the tomatoes thicken and their liquid starts to evaporate—about 20 minutes. Pour in the saffron with its soaking water and stir to mix well. Add the green beans, the artichokes with their cooking water, and the white beans with their cooking water. Stir in the paprika. Cook the vegetables over medium heat, stirring frequently, for about 20 minutes or until the sauce is once again rather thick.

Arrange the pieces of chicken and rabbit or pork around the edges of the pan and sprinkle about 2 teaspoons salt, more or less, over the sauce. Put the rosemary sprigs in the center. Add simmering stock to the pan, a cup at a time, until the liquid comes to the tops of the rivets in a paella pan or about 1 inch from the top of a skillet. Add the rice, sprinkling it around the pieces of meat so that it is completely immersed in the liquid. Don't stir the rice, but use a thin spatula to move it gently down into the liquid. Bring to a boil and cook for about 30 minutes, gradually decreasing the heat as the rice absorbs the liquid. (If you must add more stock to cook the rice thoroughly, it should be simmering.)

When the rice is thoroughly cooked, dry, and tender but not falling apart, add the reserved shrimp, distributing them over the surface. Remove the pan from the heat and let rest for 5 to 10 minutes, then serve immediately.

Quick and Easy Arroz con Pollo (Chicken with Rice)

Makes 4 to 6 servings

THIS FAMILIAR RECIPE, which can be found throughout Latin America but especially in Puerto Rico, Cuba, and other islands in the Spanish Caribbean, is an American take on the true paella valenciana, but it exists in Spain, too, where it's considered a wonderfully tasty and useful dish for when paella itself presents too formidable a challenge. When sweet green peas are in season, a handful is often added to the rice.

1 3- to 4-pound chicken, preferably free-range, cut in 8 pieces

sea salt and freshly ground black pepper

¼ cup extra-virgin olive oil

2½ cups chicken stock (page 108)

2 medium yellow onions, halved and thinly sliced

2 garlic cloves, minced

2 sweet red peppers, chopped coarsely

1 cup peeled (page 25) and chopped ripe tomatoes (or use canned tomatoes)

1 tablespoon sweet Spanish pimentón (paprika)

a big pinch of saffron threads

1 cup Spanish round-grain or arborio rice

2 or 3 tablespoons finely chopped flat-leaf parsley

Rinse and dry the chicken and sprinkle the pieces liberally with salt and pepper.

In a paella pan or large flat skillet, heat the olive oil over medium heat. Add the chicken pieces and brown them thoroughly all over. As they brown, remove and set aside.

In a separate small saucepan, bring the chicken stock to a simmer.

Lower the heat under the skillet to medium-low and add the onions, garlic, and peppers. Cook, stirring, until the vegetables start to soften, then stir in the tomatoes. Cook until the tomatoes start to dissolve into a sauce, then mix in the pimentón and saffron. Stir in 2 cups of the hot chicken stock and the rice. As soon as the stock begins to simmer, add back the chicken pieces. Cover the pan, lower the heat to low, and simmer very slowly until the rice has absorbed all the liquid and the chicken is done—about 20 minutes. If necessary, add the remaining half-cup of stock, all or in part, to the rice as it cooks.

Turn the heat off but leave the covered pan to sit for another 10 minutes before serving. The rice will absorb any remaining liquid. Then remove the lid, scatter parsley over the dish, and serve immediately.

Polenta with Teverina Dried Wild Mushroom Sauce

Makes 6 to 8 servings

POLENTA IS ITALIAN for the American staple cornmeal. There is no need to buy imported Italian polenta since cornmeal is the same thing and what is available in local markets will often be fresher and a good deal cheaper than imported polenta. Most Italian polenta is made from yellow corn, but up in Friuli, in the northeasternmost corner of the country, white corn is often used instead. White or yellow, the important thing is that the meal be stone-ground for the finest flavor. Coarsely ground cornmeal produces a more characteristic polenta than finely ground.

The wild mushrooms prized in Teverina are porcini, harvested every year in late summer and early autumn by countryfolk who scour the hillsides for the elusive treasure. Part of the harvest is eaten fresh or sold in the market in Cortona, but in good years a large part of the yield will be cleaned, sliced, dried in the sun, and stored for wintertime sauces like this one. For more wild mushroom information, see page 324.

Packets of dried porcini, or cèpes as they're called in France, are widely available in well-stocked supermarkets.

1½ ounces dried porcini

1 pound sweet Italian sausage, cut into pieces not more than ½ inch thick

2 tablespoons extra-virgin olive oil

1 medium onion, minced

1 medium carrot, peeled and minced

1 celery stalk, minced

¼ cup minced flat-leaf parsley

1 28-ounce can plum tomatoes with their liquid, coarsely chopped

[cont. next page]

Put the dried porcini in a small bowl, cover with very hot water, and set aside for 30 minutes to soften.

Meanwhile, sauté the sausage in its own fat in a heavy skillet or saucepan over medium-high heat, stirring and turning frequently, until it loses its pink color, about 10 minutes. Drain the sausage slices on a rack spread with paper towels. Drain the fat from the skillet and wipe clean with a paper towel.

When the porcini are soft, drain them in a sieve lined with a double layer of damp cheesecloth set over a small bowl to catch the liquid. Rinse the porcini in running water to rid them of any grit, then chop coarsely. Reserve the chopped porcini and their soaking water.

½ teaspoon chopped fresh thyme or ¼ teaspoon dried, crumbled

3 or 4 rosemary sprigs, to taste, coarsely chopped

sea salt and freshly ground black pepper

1½ cups yellow cornmeal

¾ cup freshly grated parmigiano reggiano cheese

Heat the olive oil in the skillet over medium-low heat and gently sauté the onion, carrot, celery, and parsley until the vegetables are soft but not brown—about 15 minutes. Stir in the tomatoes, thyme, and rosemary. Simmer the sauce gently, uncovered, until it is thickened, about 20 to 25 minutes. Stir in the reserved mushroom liquid, the porcini, and the sausage. Continue cooking, uncovered, for 15 to 20 minutes. The sauce should be very thick. Taste and add salt and pepper if you wish. Set aside, but keep it warm while you make the polenta. Or make a day in advance and store, covered, in the refrigerator until you're ready to cook. Warm the sauce up to simmering before serving.

To make the polenta, bring about 6½ cups of water, lightly salted, to a rolling boil in a heavy medium saucepan. Slowly and steadily pour in the cornmeal, stirring constantly as you pour. When all the cornmeal has been added, reduce the heat to a gentle simmer; cook, uncovered, stirring frequently, until the polenta is thick and creamy, about 20 to 30 minutes.

Pour the polenta into a warm platter—one with a high rim to keep the sauce from spilling over. Make a well or depression in the middle of the polenta and pour the sauce over it. Sprinkle about ¼ cup of the grated cheese over the top and serve immediately, passing the remaining grated cheese at the table.

Bulgur Pilaf

Makes 6 servings

BULGUR OR BURGHUL (it goes by both names) comes from the eastern Mediterranean regions of Turkey, Lebanon, and Syria, and is familiar to Americans who have grown to love tabbouleh, the parsley and bulgur salad that's a staple of Lebanese meze tables and, nowadays, at deli lunch counters (see page 73 for a recipe). In essence, bulgur is wheat that has been steamed, dried, and cracked, an ancient and traditional way of preserving grain through the winter. Do not confuse bulgur with cracked wheat; the steaming and drying process turn it into a very different product, one that does not need any cooking at all, as the tabbouleh recipe shows. However, you can cook bulgur, if you wish, and the result is this delightful pilaf, similar to rice but with the nutty flavor of the wheat itself to balance the tomato and onion.

3 cups chicken or vegetable stock (pages 107–108)

1 medium onion, chopped

2 tablespoons extra-virgin olive oil

1¼ cups medium-grain bulgur

1 large ripe tomato, coarsely chopped, or 3 canned tomatoes, drained and coarsely chopped

sea salt and freshly ground black pepper

¼ cup minced flat-leaf parsley

Bring the stock to a gentle simmer over medium-low heat.

In another heavy saucepan over medium-low heat, gently sauté the onion in the oil until it is soft but not brown—about 10 to 15 minutes. Add the bulgur and stir to coat well with the oil. Stir in the tomatoes, raise the heat to medium, and cook briefly, 4 to 5 minutes, to soften the tomato. Add the simmering stock and a little salt if desired. Cover and cook over medium heat for 5 minutes, then lower the heat and simmer for 10 to 15 minutes or until the bulgur is tender and little steam holes form on the surface. Remove from the heat and set aside, covered, for 10 minutes. Uncover the pot, taste the bulgur, and add more salt if desired and plenty of pepper. Just before serving, stir in the parsley and fluff the grains.

Variation: For a delicious change of pace, try this recipe with farro. Available in specialty food stores, farro is the pearled or husked grains of emmer wheat, a hard-grain durum wheat that may be an ancestor of modern hybrid wheats. It will need about 15 to 20 minutes longer cooking than bulgur.

Beans and Pulses

Dried beans and pulses—lentils, kidney beans, lima beans, chickpeas (or garbanzos), broad beans (or fava beans), and so on—come in such variety, and the varieties change so often from place to place, that they deserve an encyclopedia of their own. Lentils, chickpeas, and fava beans are Old World beans, with a history that goes back almost to the very beginnings of Mediterranean agriculture. Esau's biblical mess of pottage was probably a well-cooked stew of lentils made savory with garlic and leeks and quite possibly with a little olive oil on top.

New World beans, which also go back to the beginnings of agriculture, only on *this* side of the globe, include the whole panoply that botanists call kidney beans or *Phaseolus* (the name of the genus) and were unknown in the Mediterranean until sometime after 1492. Unlike the potato and the tomato, which were slow to gain acceptance, New World beans were quickly adopted all over Europe, presumably because they could be cooked and eaten in ways that were already very familiar. And they quickly became very important in the everyday fare of people, especially in the Mediterranean, with its almost vegetarian diet. Long before our ancestors understood protein and its critical role in human development, they knew that beans, properly prepared, can give the same sense of nourishment and ample satisfaction that meat does and that beans cooked with a small amount of meat—a little chopped bacon or ham, a wing of preserved goose, or a few sausages—are even more satisfying, extending that small amount of meat to serve many more people than the meat might do on its own.

The world of beans is vast. I look for new varieties every time I travel and bring them home both to eat and to plant. In the market in San Sebastian in the Atlantic north of Spain, I found black beans that were as shiny as agates (and very precious too, I could tell by the price), while in Roman markets there are tiny lentils like delicate green and brown shells, almost too pretty to eat. In this country too there are dozens of varieties, many quite regional—I think of Sivvy beans in the Carolina Lowcountry, Jacob's cattle beans and yellow eyes in Maine, and Anasazi beans in New Mexico and Arizona.

Everywhere in the Mediterranean, simple, humble bean dishes are served as main courses, first courses, or part of an hors d'oeuvre. Chickpeas or garbanzos in Provence, pale cannellini beans or speckled borlotti in Tuscany, small green flageolets or haricots secs, dark lentils, white or brown favas, dried beans or fresh—whatever the local beans of choice, they are handled in a similar fashion from Beirut to Barcelona and back again. The beans are soaked overnight (unless they are fresh), the soaking water is discarded, fresh water is added to the pot, often with aromatics (but no salt), and the beans are cooked until very tender. Then they are drained and mixed with good olive oil, a little vinegar or lemon juice, and more flavorings—garlic, onion, chopped green herbs, spices like cumin or red pepper flakes. Served at room temperature, they make a substantial addition to meze tables, and they can also be gussied up with seafood and made to star as a main course at dinner. Fashionable Florentine restaurants serve white Tuscan beans topped by a healthy dollop of best beluga caviar—garlic and sapphires in the mud, perhaps, but it works.

Beans are truly nutritional powerhouses. They're low in calories and fat, so you can feel comfortable about adding a good dollop of olive oil or a handful of diced ham or pancetta to the cooking pot. And at the same time, they're an excellent source of protein, with plenty of B vitamins, especially elusive folic acid; lots of fiber, chiefly the so-called "sticky fiber" that sweeps up cholesterol and keeps our insides clean and tidy; and a surprisingly high quotient of antioxidants, at least one of which is suspected of offering protection against overexposure to ultraviolet radiation. (I'm not about to suggest a big bowl of bean soup before you go off to the beach this summer. . . but that time might come.)

I could go on and on, listing the virtues of beans, but one other advantage stands out: beans are cheap, cheaper than any other protein resource, and for that reason alone they should be an integral part of the family menu. Beans can be stodgy, it's true, but cooked the way they are in the Mediterranean, with garlic and lemon, olive oil and aromatics, they become truly seductive.

Dried beans store well and should always be in your pantry cupboard, but beware of beans that have been kept too long—the older they are, the longer it will take to cook them. Buy beans from a store with a quick turnaround or, better yet, directly from a farmer who can tell you exactly when they were harvested. Despite my predilection for fresh food freshly prepared, I keep a few emergency cans of high-quality cooked beans, especially chickpeas and white cannellini, in the pantry. I look for canned beans that are organically raised and preserved with nothing but water and salt. Rinsed quickly under running water and added to a soup, dressed with a little oil and lemon and tossed with chips of onion, or combined with pasta, those cans of beans have often meant the difference between success and failure in providing for unexpected guests.

The great problem with beans, of course, is flatulence, which can produce both snickers and a goodly amount of discomfort for those who are sensitive to the digestive gases produced by beans. The problem can be dealt with, if not eliminated entirely, by discarding the water in which the beans have soaked. (I think it was Elizabeth David who told how French country women save the bean water to use in the laundry for getting rid of stubborn stains. I've never tried it, though I think of it every time I pour the soaking water down the drain.)

Tuscan Beans with Olive Oil and Aromatics

Makes 6 to 8 servings

LIKE BREAD, beans are a wonderful foil for great olive oil, which may be why the Tuscans, who produce some of the world's finest oils, are also among the world's champion bean eaters. Use a fine, estate-bottled, green, fragrant olive oil (it need not be Tuscan) with these.

The following is a model recipe and can be adapted to many different kinds of beans, including non-Mediterranean beans like Mexican black beans or Asian adzukis. Remember that cooking time can vary greatly with the size and age of the beans.

1½ cups dried white beans, such as cannellini, soaked overnight and drained

any or all of the following aromatics: 1 small onion, quartered; 1 garlic clove, lightly crushed; 4 or 5 fresh sage leaves; 2 bay leaves; 12 black peppercorns; 1 small dried hot red chili

¼ cup best-quality extra-virgin olive oil

sea salt and freshly ground black or white pepper

1 tablespoon minced flat-leaf parsley

Set the beans in a saucepan and add 3½ cups water and any or all of the aromatics. Do not add salt. Bring the water to a boil, turn the heat down, cover the beans, and simmer gently for 30 minutes to 1½ hours, adding *boiling* water from time to time if necessary to keep the beans from scorching. Be attentive: if the water gets low, the beans will scorch very quickly. Cooking time depends on the size and age of the beans, which is hard to assess. At the end of 30 minutes, start testing the beans to judge how tender they are and continue testing periodically until the beans are done. They should be very tender but not falling apart.

Remove the beans from the heat and drain them, *reserving the cooking liquid.* Discard the aromatics used in cooking the beans. At this point, if you wish, remove about ½ to ¾ cup cooked beans and crush them gently, using a fork, in about ½ cup of the reserved cooking liquid. Then stir in the crushed beans with the whole cooked beans. Add more cooking liquid if you wish to reach the desired consistency. Or leave all the beans whole and add ½ cup or more of the reserved cooking liquid.

While the beans are still hot, add olive oil and stir to coat the beans well. Dress them with one of the following combinations or devise your own:

- 1 garlic clove, minced, and 6 scallions, both white and green parts, sliced on the diagonal

- a little chopped raw onion and finely slivered fresh green chilies

- the juice of ½ lemon along with ½ teaspoon ground cumin and chopped fresh hot red chilies or a pinch of hot red pepper flakes

- finely minced fresh green herbs—basil, dill, fennel tops, chervil, sage, lovage, borage, or others

After dressing the beans, taste and add salt and freshly ground black or white pepper if desired.

Plain beans, dressed with oil and lemon juice or vinegar, can also be served as a first-course or antipasto salad, garnished with a little handful of pitted black olives, coarsely chopped if large; or a small can of best-quality tuna, flaked over the top along with a little handful of capers; or 3 or 4 medium shrimp per serving, peeled, quickly sautéed in olive oil, and tossed with salt, pepper, and a green herb; or—if you're feeling extravagant—a big spoonful (as much as you can afford) of best-quality caviar or salmon roe.

Whatever the flavors or garnishes, however, the beans should be sprinkled with minced parsley before serving. Serve hot or at room temperature.

Greek Baked Beans

THIS IS MY ADAPTATION of a recipe favorite from Diane Kochilas, whom I first met in New York years ago when she was a young journalist writing about food. Later she went back to her father's native country, where she married, started a family, and quickly became one of the most prominent Greek food writers. A fierce defender of Greek traditions, Diane also teaches Greek cooking at her home on the Aegean island of Ikaria.

If you can't find true Greek *gigantes* ("giant" beans), available in most Greek neighborhood markets, use any large white beans for this recipe. Baking beans in the oven's gentle heat, instead of stewing them on top of the stove, gives a finer finish—the beans seem both softer and more compact, and the skins don't separate the way they do sometimes when beans are boiled fiercely.

This recipe makes a *lot* of beans. Any leftovers can be frozen to use later in a soup or stew, or you could mash them and reheat in a little olive oil, just like Mexican refried beans, and serve them with steamed bitter greens as a super-healthy vegetarian meal.

1 pound Greek gigantes (giant) beans, soaked overnight and drained

⅓ cup extra-virgin olive oil

2 medium red onions, finely chopped

2 cups raw ripe plum tomatoes, peeled and chopped, or use canned plum tomatoes, drained and chopped

3 tablespoons honey

2 tablespoons tomato concentrate, or tomato extract, or sun-dried tomato paste

2 bay leaves

Put the beans in a large saucepan with water to cover to a depth of about 1 inch. Bring to a boil, then lower the heat to simmer, cover the pan, and simmer very gently for 40 to 50 minutes, or until the beans are starting to soften but not yet ready to eat. Periodically, skim off any foam that rises to the top. When the beans are ready, remove from the heat but do not drain.

Set the oven at 325 degrees.

Using 3 tablespoons of the oil, cook the onions in a skillet over medium-low heat, stirring frequently, until the onions are very soft and starting to brown.

Using a slotted spoon, transfer the hot beans from the saucepan to an oven dish, preferably a bean pot—a terra-cotta or ceramic dish that is taller than it is wide (lacking such a pot, you could also use an

¼ cup fresh herbs, minced (dill is preferred by Greeks, but you could also use un-Greek basil, or a tablespoon of mint and a tablespoon of thyme)

¼ cup red wine vinegar

sea salt and freshly ground pepper

ordinary casserole or soufflé dish, but a bean pot is preferable). Stir in the remaining olive oil, the onions, and the chopped or crushed tomatoes. Dissolve the honey and tomato concentrate in about 1 cup of the hot bean water and add to the beans, mixing carefully and tucking the bay leaves in with the beans. There should be just enough liquid in the pot to barely cover the beans—add a little more if necessary, but make sure it is boiling hot. Cover the pot securely with aluminum foil (and the pot lid if available), transfer to the preheated oven, and bake for about 1½ hours. Check the beans from time to time and add a little more boiling bean liquid or plain water if necessary.

Remove the bean pot from the oven. The beans should be meltingly tender at this point. Stir in the fresh herbs and the vinegar, along with salt and pepper. Return the bean pot, uncovered, to the oven and let the beans bake for another 15 minutes to absorb all the flavors.

Egyptian Beans with Olive Oil and Lemon
Ful Medames

Makes 6 servings

THESE ARE THE BEANS that Lebanese and Egyptians eat for a hearty breakfast with yogurt and bread. *Ful medames* are a delicious staple all over the Middle East, not just for breakfast but throughout the day. My son Nicholas quotes a saying he picked up on his travels: ful, he says, are the rich man's breakfast, the shopkeeper's lunch, the poor man's supper. The aroma of these beans on the stove can send displaced Middle Easterners into paroxysms of desire.

The beans used are very fragrant, small brown favas, called Egyptian fava beans or *ful* (FOOL). They are available in Middle Eastern shops (see Resources at the back of the book for suppliers).

2 cups dried Egyptian ful or other beans, such as chickpeas, cannellini beans, or Great Northern beans, soaked overnight and drained

2 garlic cloves, peeled

1 teaspoon sea salt

½ cup fresh lemon juice

¼ cup extra-virgin olive oil

½ cup finely chopped flat-leaf parsley

6 or 8 scallions

1 lemon, cut into wedges

Place the drained beans in a saucepan, and cover with fresh water. Set over medium heat and bring to a boil. When the beans are boiling, turn the heat down to a steady simmer, cover the pan, and cook, just simmering, until the beans are thoroughly tender. Count on 1 hour, more or less, depending on the freshness of the beans. Add a little boiling water from time to time to make up for the water that is absorbed by the beans—the beans should always be covered with water. When the beans are done, remove from the heat and drain, *reserving the cooking liquid*.

Crush the garlic with the flat blade of a knife and chop it slightly. Put the chopped garlic in a bowl with the salt and, using the back of a spoon, mash the garlic to a paste with the salt. Add the lemon juice and mix well.

Remove about 1 cup beans and mash them with about ½ cup of bean liquid to a coarse, runny texture with a fork. Mix with the garlic, then, using a slotted spoon, add the unmashed beans and stir to combine it all well. If the mixture is too dry, add a little more of the bean-cooking liquid. Stir in the olive oil and pour onto a deep serving platter. Garnish the platter with parsley, scallions, and lemon wedges and serve, hot or at room temperature, with Arab flatbread (pita) to use as scoops.

Turkish Beans with Potatoes, Celery Root, and Carrots

Makes 6 to 8 servings

2 cups dried large white beans, soaked overnight

2 bay leaves

Drain the beans and put in a large heavy saucepan with the bay leaves and fresh water to cover to a depth of 1 inch. Bring to a boil, turn the heat

1 medium onion, coarsely chopped

2 garlic cloves, crushed with the flat blade of a knife

¼ cup extra-virgin olive oil plus more for serving if desired

1 large potato, peeled and cut into chunks

1 medium celeriac (celery root), peeled and cut into chunks

2 medium carrots, peeled and cut into chunks

sea salt and freshly ground black pepper

¼ cup finely minced flat-leaf parsley

down, and simmer, covered, for 30 minutes. Check the water from time to time and add more boiling water if necessary. The beans should always be covered with water.

While the beans are cooking, gently sauté the onion and garlic in the oil in a large heavy saucepan until they are soft but not brown—about 10 to 15 minutes. Add the potato, celery root, and carrots and stir to coat well with the oil. Cook over medium heat for about 10 minutes or until the vegetables start to soften. The vegetables should not brown.

When the beans have cooked for 30 minutes, add the vegetables with more boiling water if necessary to cover. Add ½ teaspoon salt and continue cooking until the beans are very tender—another 30 minutes or longer, depending on the size and age of the beans.

When the beans are very tender, remove from the heat and taste, adding more salt if necessary and lots of pepper. Just before serving, stir in the parsley. Add more olive oil at the table if desired.

Tunisian Chickpeas with Spicy Vegetables

Makes 6 to 8 servings

TUNISIANS SOMETIMES SERVE a combination of different beans in this peppery sauce, though chickpeas on their own are fine, too. Don't be limited by the vegetable selection listed—add, subtract, or substitute at will, keeping in mind cooking times and balance of flavors.

1 cup dried chickpeas, soaked overnight

2 medium onions, coarsely chopped

[cont. next page]

Drain the chickpeas and set aside. In a large heavy saucepan over medium-low heat, sauté the onion in the oil until it is soft and just beginning to brown—about 10 minutes. Stir the tomato puree

1/3 cup extra-virgin olive oil

2 tablespoons tomato puree

1 tablespoon harissa (page 279) or 1 dried red New Mexico or Anaheim chili

1 cup cold water

1 cup very hot water

3 medium carrots, peeled, cut in half lengthwise, and sliced about 1 inch thick

2 small white turnips, peeled and cut into rough chunks

sea salt

1 pound Swiss chard, preferably green, but red will do

4 red or green sweet peppers

about 1 cup yellow winter squash in chunks: butternut, acorn, Hubbard, or any other firm-textured squash

freshly ground black pepper

1/4 cup minced flat-leaf parsley

minced cilantro and lemon wedges for garnish

and harissa into the cold water, add to the onions, and bring to a slow simmer.

If you're using a dried red chili instead of the harissa, rinse any dust off the outside, break the chili into pieces, discarding the stem (for less heat, discard the seeds and inner white membranes), and soak in the hot water for about 30 minutes. Add the chili pieces and soaking water to the onions with the tomato puree.

Have a teakettle of boiling water ready. Stir the onion-chili mixture and simmer for 5 minutes to develop the flavors. Then stir in the drained chickpeas and add boiling water to cover to a depth of 1 inch. Reduce the heat and simmer the beans, covered, for about 40 minutes, stirring from time to time and adding a very little boiling water if necessary.

Add the carrots and turnips to the stew along with water to cover, adding a teaspoon of salt if you wish. Continue cooking, covered, for 10 minutes.

While the carrots and turnips are cooking, trim the chard of any coarse or fibrous stem ends, then slice across the leaves to make thin chiffonades. Slice the sweet peppers lengthwise into strips no more than 1 inch wide. Add the chard, pepper strips, and squash chunks to the beans along with more water if necessary. Cook for 10 to 15 minutes, by which time all the vegetables should be soft and the beans should be very tender. If there's too much soupy liquid in the pan, raise the heat and cook, uncovered, to reduce the pan juices.

Taste and adjust the seasoning, adding more salt if desired and a lot of black pepper. If the bean stew isn't hot enough, stir in a little more harissa or ground red chili (not commercial chili powder). Stir in the parsley and serve, garnished with minced cilantro and lemon wedges if you wish.

Slow-Cooked Chickpeas with Orange Zest and Lemon Juice

Revithia me Portokali

Makes 6 servings

THIS WONDERFULLY FRAGRANT DISH originated with Aglaia Kremezi, Greek food writer and cooking teacher. Chickpeas are innately healthful but what is even more appealing here is the delicious combination of flavors that sing of the Mediterranean. If you use vegetable stock, this makes a great addition to the vegetarian repertoire.

⅓ cup extra-virgin olive oil plus more to garnish

3 medium yellow onions, halved and thinly sliced (2 cups)

3 garlic cloves

½ green or red sweet pepper, thinly sliced

1 cup coarsely chopped celery, including green leaves

1 pound (2½ cups) dried chickpeas, soaked overnight and drained

a big pinch of ground or crushed red chili (Aleppo pepper or piment d'Espelette)

1½ cups chicken or vegetable stock, preferably homemade (pages 107–108)

1 3-inch segment orange zest

2 bay leaves

½ cup dry white wine

½ cup chopped flat-leaf parsley

2 tablespoons Dijon mustard

¼ cup fresh lemon juice, or to taste

sea salt and freshly ground black pepper

Set the oven at 250 degrees.

In a flameproof casserole over medium heat, heat the oil and sauté the onions and garlic for 4 minutes, or until soft. Stir in the sliced sweet pepper and celery, chickpeas, and ground chili, then add the stock or water, the orange zest, and the bay leaves. Bring to a simmer, and cover the dish with a double layer of aluminum foil and then the lid.

Transfer the casserole to the oven and cook for 3 hours or until the chickpeas are very tender. Add the wine, parsley, mustard, and lemon juice, stirring to mix very well. Cover the casserole tightly once again and return it to the oven to continue cooking for another hour, by which time the chickpeas should be tender all the way through. Taste and adjust the seasoning, adding salt and black pepper. Dribble with a little more olive oil and serve hot, or warm, or at room temperature.

Catalan Chickpeas with Tomatoes and Toasted Almonds

Makes 6 to 8 servings

Excuse me for adding yet another chickpea recipe but I do love these legumes. They have *such* a satisfyingly meaty flavor and texture! I was not surprised to read that Richard Ford, eminent British traveler in early 19th century Spain, wrote that "chickpeas are the potatoes of the land." Indeed, the Spanish seem to have more good ideas for chickpeas than almost anyone else in the Mediterranean. This is one of their best.

To toast almonds, simply spread them on a cookie sheet and set in a preheated 350-degree oven for 10 to 15 minutes, stirring occasionally, or until the almonds are nicely golden all over.

1½ cups chickpeas, soaked overnight

1 onion, finely chopped

¼ cup extra-virgin olive oil

2 very ripe tomatoes, peeled (page 25) and finely chopped

a big pinch of saffron threads, toasted

3 garlic cloves, coarsely chopped

⅓ cup toasted, chopped almonds

½ cup chopped flat-leaf parsley

sea salt and freshly ground black pepper

2 hard-boiled eggs for garnish (optional)

Drain the chickpeas and transfer to a saucepan with enough boiling water to cover to a depth of about 1 inch. Bring to a simmer and cook the chickpeas, partially covered, until they are tender, 30 minutes to 1 hour, depending on the age of the chickpeas. Add a little boiling water from time to time as necessary.

While the chickpeas are cooking, combine the onion and olive oil in a skillet and set over medium-low heat. Sauté the onion, stirring, until it is soft, then stir in the tomatoes and cook for about 20 minutes longer, cooking away all the liquid from the tomatoes so that they sizzle with the onions in the pan. Tip this mixture into the chickpeas and stir well.

To toast the saffron, fold it into a piece of clean white typing paper. Set the paper envelope in a pan over medium-low heat. Keep turning the paper until it starts to turn brown. Remove immediately and unwrap the saffron, which will have become crisp and darker.

Combine the toasted saffron, garlic, almonds, parsley, and a pinch of salt. Pound the mixture in a mortar or process it in a food processor until it's a coarse paste, thinning it with a little of the liquid from the chickpeas. Stir the paste into the chickpeas, tasting for salt and pepper.

Serve the chickpeas, if you wish, garnished with the eggs, peeled, chopped, and sprinkled over the top of the dish.

ABOUT LENTILS

The finest lentils are the smallest—little brown *lenticchie* from Umbria in Italy or slate-colored *lentilles du Puy* from central France—but they are very hard to find in this country and very expensive if you do find them. Ordinary grayish brown lentils will have to do instead, but don't use Indian lentils in Mediterranean recipes unless instructed specifically to do so. In Indian cuisine, lentils are meant to disintegrate somewhat and form a delicious, thick sauce for rice and other staples. In Mediterranean cuisine, the opposite end is desired: lentils are intended, for the most part, to remain intact, especially when served as an accompaniment or a salad.

Lentils are often cooked with some sort of preserved pork or bacon, and delicious they are. In Italy, good luck in the new year comes from eating as many lentils as possible for Capo d'Anno, the first of the year. New Year's lentils are served with cotechino, a large pork sausage delicately flavored with nutmeg that is poached and sliced and accompanied by a piquant salsa verde.

Pellegrino Artusi's Lentils with Aromatics

◆◆◁ Makes 6 servings

P ELLEGRINO ARTUSI CAME FROM EMILIA but lived in Florence in the late 19th century. It was there, shortly after Italy became a unified country again for the first time since the fall of the Roman Empire, that he compiled what is widely accepted as the first truly national Italian cookbook, *La Scienza in cucina e l'Arte di mangiar bene* (*Science in the Kitchen and the Art of Eating Well*). It is a remarkable collection of delicious recipes and genial commentary, and is still in use in Italian kitchens to this day. Artusi recommends these lentils to go with cotechino or zampone, two savory poached sausages. It's a favorite combination to eat on New Year's Day, each lentil consumed foretelling additional riches to be accumulated in the year ahead. But if you don't have a cotechino, Artusi's lentils will also make an excellent accompaniment to roast pork or roast lamb.

½ pound brown or green lentils

2 small onions, peeled

1½ garlic cloves, peeled

1 bay leaf

sea salt and freshly ground black pepper

1 small carrot, peeled and finely chopped

2 tablespoons minced flat-leaf parsley

½ celery stalk, finely chopped

2 tablespoons extra-virgin olive oil

½ cup chicken stock (page 108)

Pick the lentils over carefully to get rid of any small stones or pieces of grit. Rinse them under running water. Place in a saucepan over medium heat with about 3 cups of water. Add one of the onions, a garlic clove, the bay leaf, and salt and pepper and bring to a boil. When the water is boiling, turn it down, cover the lentils, and simmer for 20 to 30 minutes—or until the lentils are thoroughly cooked and tender. (Time varies even more than with other legumes, depending on the age of the lentils.)

While the lentils are cooking, prepare the rest of the vegetables. Finely chop together the remaining onion and the ½ garlic clove. Combine in a heavy saucepan with the carrot, parsley, and celery and sauté gently in the olive oil until the vegetables are soft but not brown—about 15 minutes. Stir in the stock or, if you're planning to serve with a cotechino or zampone sausage, the same quantity of degreased liquid in which the sausage was cooked. Simmer gently. When the lentils are tender, drain them and stir into the vegetable mixture. Simmer for 5 minutes to concentrate the flavors. Serve the lentils with the sliced sausage or with slices of roast pork (see recipe for àrista, page 432).

Cumin-Scented Lentils and Rice

Mujaddarah

⚜ **Makes 2 servings as a main dish; 4 to 6 as a side**

A FAVORITE CLASSIC LENTIL DISH from Lebanon, Syria, and Palestine.

1 cup small green or brown lentils

2 bay leaves

¾ cup long-grain rice, rinsed briefly under running water

sea salt and freshly ground black pepper

1½ teaspoons ground cumin

1 medium yellow onion, halved and very thinly sliced

¼ cup extra-virgin olive oil

Rinse the lentils in a colander under running water. Bring a cup of water to a rolling boil and add the rinsed lentils, along with the bay leaves. When the water returns to a simmer, lower the heat, cover the pan, and simmer the lentils for about 15 to 20 minutes or until the lentils are just tender and all the water has been absorbed.

In a separate pan, bring another cup of water to a rolling boil. When the lentils have cooked for 15 to 20 minutes and their water has been absorbed, add the rinsed rice to the lentils along with the cup of boiling water, the salt, pepper, and cumin. Bring to a simmer once more, cover, and cook until all the liquid has been absorbed and both the lentils and the rice are thoroughly tender but have not become mushy. Watch the pot as you cook and, if the pot becomes too dry before the lentils are done, add a little more boiling water as necessary.

While the lentils and rice are cooking, sauté the onion slices in the olive oil over low heat until they are golden brown. Keep the heat low and stir from time to time, more often as the onions start to brown. This can take as much as 20 to 30 minutes, but be patient—if the onions cook too quickly they will burn and turn acrid.

When the lentils are ready to serve, mound them in a serving dish and garnish the top with the golden onions and the oil in which they cooked. Serve immediately.

Dressings, Sauces, Condiments, and Preserves

✧ ✧ ✧

Salad Dressings

I N THE MEDITERRANEAN KITCHEN salads are dressed simply, with a rich and flavorful olive oil, the very best extra-virgin oil the cook can afford, often the product of the family's own groves of stately olive trees. To this good oil will be added a little (often a very little to American taste) vinegar or lemon juice, salt, and pepper. This is the quickest and easiest dressing in the world to prepare, and when you have the best oil you can find and the quality of your other ingredients matches it, there is no need for a cupboard full of bottled dressings.

Mediterranean cooks are puzzled by the American rage to change the flavor of good oil by steeping intense aromatics in it. Add the aromatics to the dressing, not the oil, and use it right away. Additions of chili or garlic, rosemary or basil will disguise the character of an indifferent oil, such as canola or corn oil, but steeping chili peppers or garlic in the best extra-virgin olive oil only masks its lush, fresh, and elegant flavor.

Whether vinegar or lemon juice, acid should be added with a judicious hand. American salad dressing is both overly sweetened and overly acid by Mediterranean standards. This would be simply a matter of taste were it not for the wine issue—an acid dressing makes salad inappropriate to serve with wine, and there's always wine to finish at the end of the meal and perhaps a bit of cheese to go with the salad. Ergo . . . a good oil-to-acid proportion is about three to one; four to one is better if you expect to have wine with the salad. A few drops of balsamic vinegar are not inappropriate in a dressing for a very simple green salad, but balsamic vinegar should not be treated as an expensive cure-all for salad dressing woes—rather, it's a precious ingredient to be treated with respect and understanding.

Lemon and Garlic Dressing for Salads or Vegetables

Makes ¼ cup; enough for 4 to 6 servings of salad

THIS DRESSING IS COMMON throughout the eastern Mediterranean for plain green salads, for composed salads, and as an all-purpose dressing for steamed fresh vegetables (artichokes, asparagus, green beans) or crudités—raw or parboiled fresh seasonal vegetables served as a first course. It's delicious poured over hot steamed new potatoes, sprinkled with a little chopped tarragon or chives.

½ garlic clove, crushed with the flat blade of a knife

1 teaspoon fine sea salt

1 tablespoon fresh lemon juice

3 tablespoons fruity extra-virgin olive oil

freshly ground black pepper

Chop the garlic coarsely and put it in the bottom of a clean, dry salad bowl with the salt. Using the back of a spoon, crush the salt and garlic together to make a smooth, homogeneous paste. Add the lemon juice and stir to dissolve the salt, then add the olive oil. Mix all together well in the bottom of the bowl. Pile on the salad, but don't mix it until you're ready to serve. When you serve it, toss the salad in the dressing and add some pepper.

Vinaigrette

French Salad Dressing with Mustard and Vinegar

Makes ½ cup; enough for 8 servings of salad

G O EASY ON THE MUSTARD—this isn't *sauce à la moutarde*. For plain green salads or for sliced fresh tomatoes at the height of the season, these are the proportions to use, the mustard counterpointing the sauce as garlic does in the preceding recipe. For steamed artichokes or leeks, increase the quantity of mustard to 1 teaspoon. On the other hand, a very thick and mustardy vinaigrette, with perhaps a tablespoon of mustard, makes a pungent sauce for grilled squid and octopus.

½ teaspoon Dijon mustard

2 tablespoons aged red wine vinegar or sherry vinegar

½ cup fruity extra-virgin olive oil

½ teaspoon sea salt, or more to taste

freshly ground black pepper

In a salad bowl or a small bowl, mix the mustard with the vinegar until it is thoroughly dissolved. Add the oil and salt and beat vigorously with a fork or wire whisk to blend. Taste the dressing and adjust the seasoning, adding more salt if necessary—but mustard is often very salty. Just before pouring it over the salad, grind in black pepper to taste.

Variation: Substitute 3 tablespoons bitter (Seville) orange juice for the vinegar and use on a plain green salad or bean salad garnished with a handful of roasted walnuts.

An Anchovy Sauce for Bitter Greens

Makes a scant ½ cup; enough for about 6 servings of salad

T HIS DRESSING IS MADE expressly for puntarelle, or chicory shoots, a delight of the early-spring table in Rome. They're sold already cleaned, a tedious task, in the Campo dei Fiori market. I haven't seen puntarelle in other parts of Italy, and the few times I've found them in New York greenmarkets, they have been disappointing. But the pungent sauce can be used for other greens as well, especially bitter greens like endive and chicory. It's even good with plain romaine lettuce.

2 garlic cloves, crushed with the flat blade of a knife

4 to 6 oil-packed anchovy fillets, to taste, or 2 whole salt-packed anchovies, prepared as directed on page 40

1 tablespoon red wine vinegar or sherry vinegar, or more to taste

¼ cup extra-virgin olive oil

freshly ground black pepper

Pound the garlic cloves in a mortar with the coarsely chopped anchovy fillets. When the paste is very smooth, stir in the wine vinegar. Slowly beat in the olive oil, using a fork to mix well. Taste and adjust the seasoning, adding pepper if desired. (There should be sufficient salt from the anchovies.)

Tomato Sauces

Tomato sauces of various kinds from silky smooth to chunky rustic, and with various ingredients from onions and garlic to chopped ham, anchovies, and minced meat, and flavored moreover in a variety of hues—garlic, rosemary, basil, fennel, cumin, cilantro, chili, parsley, cinnamon, clove, and on and on—tomato sauces in their infinite variety are so ubiquitous throughout the Mediterranean that they could be considered truly a defining element in the cuisine. And yet, and yet . . . they are "only" 500 years old, less actually, which is a very, very short time in terms of the Mediterranean kitchen. It can come as a surprise to discover that tomatoes were introduced from the New World well after 1492 and were not widely adopted until a good 350 years after that date. In fact, there are places in the Mediterranean where tomatoes were not part of the kitchen culture until well into the twentieth century. I've always been amused by a statement in Norman Lewis's lovely book *Voices of the Old Sea,* an account of life in a Catalan fishing village in the 1940s, in which the decadence of modern life is attributed, at least in part, to "the widespread consumption of tomatoes—recently introduced into local agriculture—which reduced fertility and lowered the birthrate." And that was less than a hundred years ago.

Myself, I wouldn't push that point too far. Tomatoes were also long known as love apples and suspected of contributing mightily to amorous inclinations, quite possibly because of their bright red color, indicating the flush of passion. In any case, whether passionate or decadent, tomatoes presented new opportunities for that tart-sweet flavor combination that has always been a Mediterranean favorite. I describe a few different sauces from different regions below. See also the Italian tomato sauce for pasta on page 195. All these recipes are simple and easy, but you should feel free to experiment, altering flavors or adding to them as your own palate dictates. I've said it many times but it's worth repeating once more: nothing in the Mediterranean kitchen is set in stone. The goal of a good Mediterranean cook is to exalt the flavors of good ingredients through straightforward techniques—and there's no better illustration of that than these simple but ubiquitous sauces.

In the past, I've given fairly detailed instructions for canning tomato sauces like these but lately I've come to see that freezing presents a much easier alternative, one that probably has a carbon footprint equivalent to canning. If you're interested in canning tomatoes (or bottling, a more exact term), I suggest you look at one of my earlier books, *The Essential Mediterranean* or *Cucina del Sole*. Or simply go online to the U.S. Department of Agriculture, which provides detailed instructions for canning just about anything.

In recent decades, we Americans seem to have totally lost sight of the fact that tomatoes are a highly seasonal vegetable (I know, I know, tomatoes are really a fruit), to be appreciated only in the fullness of time. When tomatoes are at the height of their season (which here in the northeastern United States where I live much of the year means September), and only then, they are succulent, sweet, and packed with flavor. And that's the point at which they are both cheap enough and of sufficiently high quality to justify the effort of preserving, whether by canning or freezing.

And they do justify it.

Because come January, a freezer or pantry full of tomato sauces, preserved at their peak of ripeness, just ready to be defrosted or un-jarred, then turned into pasta sauces, pizza toppings, soups and stews, what-have-you—that represents a treasure to be envied and emulated.

Plain Tomato Sauce

La Pomarola

THIS IS THE SIMPLEST of all tomato sauces—any simpler and it would be just crushed cooked tomatoes (which is not a bad idea). Make this with fresh tomatoes at the height of the late-summer season when they are full of flavor. Made in quantity, when tomatoes at the farmers' market or farmstand are abundant and cheap, the sauce freezes very well. I used to emulate my Tuscan country neighbors and put up jars and jars of tomato sauce for the winter, but lately I've been convinced that it's a whole lot easier to freeze the sauce in one-cup to one-quart containers so I have it available throughout the rest of the year. Pound for pound, between the two methods I suspect the carbon footprint is pretty equal.

When fresh ripe tomatoes are no longer in season, and you don't have your own sauce, whether frozen or canned, on hand, you can make this with canned tomatoes—Muir Glen makes a very good organic product, and there are also imported canned tomatoes from Italy, although the best of these are wildly expensive and cheaper brands are not very reliable.

This is the basic sauce to use for Neapolitan pizza classics.

2 or 3 garlic cloves, sliced (optional)

2 tablespoons extra-virgin olive oil

4 pounds fresh tomatoes, cut into chunks, or 1 28-ounce can whole tomatoes, with their juice, chopped

1 teaspoon sea salt (omit if using canned tomatoes)

½ teaspoon sugar (optional)

In a heavy saucepan over medium-low heat, cook the garlic in the olive oil until it starts to soften, about 5 minutes. Do not let the garlic brown as it will make the sauce acrid—if the garlic browns, toss it out and start all over again with fresh oil and fresh garlic.

Add the tomatoes, salt and sugar if you wish, raise the heat slightly and cook rapidly, stirring frequently, while the tomatoes give off their juice and cook down to a thick mass—15 to 20 minutes. Canned tomatoes will take a little less time as they are already cooked. Watch the mixture carefully toward the end to make sure it doesn't scorch.

Put the sauce through the medium disk of a food mill. (Don't use the food processor or blender because it will grind up the tomato seeds and make the sauce bitter. The food mill will hold back most of the seeds and skin, letting just the pulp go through.)

If the sauce seems too thin, return it to medium-low heat and continue cooking, stirring constantly and watching very carefully, until it has reached the right thick saucy consistency.

Variation: Use this sauce as a model or basic tomato sauce and play around with it wherever your imagination leads, making variations as you see fit. A marinara sauce, for instance, is very similar except it has additional garlic (up to 4 cloves) and herbs, perhaps a pinch of ground or crushed red chili pepper and a couple of teaspoons of dried oregano. Depending on how you're planning to use the sauce, you might crush a few chopped anchovies with the garlic, or add some crumbled sausage or a little ground beef or pork to make a more robust sauce. Stir in slivers of zucchini and sweet red peppers along with the tomatoes to give the sauce a summery flavor. Or, when the sauce has finished cooking, flake into it a small can of oil-packed tuna, along with chopped black olives and capers, to make something close to a puttanesca sauce (or see the recipe on page 198).

See also the recipe for Tomato Sauce for Pasta on page 195.

Greek Domata Saltsa

Makes about 5 cups

WITH ITS SPICY EASTERN FLAVORS, this sauce is excellent with any grilled, baked, or roasted fish. Use it in any Greek preparation that calls for tomato sauce—moussaka for instance, or Greek makaroni or rice pilaf.

4 pounds ripe red tomatoes, preferably plum tomatoes, peeled (page 25), or 1 28-ounce can plum tomatoes with their juice

¼ cup extra-virgin olive oil

¼ cup grated yellow onion

1 tablespoon sugar

1 2-inch stick of cinnamon

2 bay leaves

1 cup red wine

sea salt and freshly ground black pepper

Chop the raw tomatoes or put them through the coarse holes of a vegetable mill. Add the tomatoes and oil to a heavy saucepan and set over medium heat. Stir in the onion, sugar, cinnamon, and bay leaves and bring to a simmer. Cook, uncovered, at a steady, low simmer for 15 minutes, then add the wine, salt, and plenty of black pepper. Continue cooking, stirring occasionally, for another 45 minutes, at which point the sauce should be dense but not at all dry. Remove and discard the bay leaves and cinnamon stick.

The sauce will be quite chunky. To give it a finer texture, put it through the vegetable mill once again.

Provençal Sauce de Tomates

Makes about 3 cups

SIMONE BECK, Julia Child's partner in *Mastering the Art of French Cooking,* used to make this sauce in late summer when the tomatoes of Provence were at their finest. It can be used in any southern French recipe that calls for tomato sauce, such as an eggplant gratin made by layering fried eggplant slices with the sauce in a baking dish, then topping with a mixture of bread crumbs, minced parsley, and grated cheese, and baking in a hot oven until the surface bubbles and browns.

3 pounds ripe red tomatoes, preferably plum tomatoes

2 tablespoons extra-virgin olive oil

about ¾ cup minced yellow onion (1 medium onion)

3 or 4 large garlic cloves, crushed and chopped

fresh thyme sprigs

Wash and quarter the tomatoes and add to a heavy saucepan with a tablespoon of the oil. Cook, uncovered, for about 15 minutes or until they have softened and rendered up a lot of their juice. Transfer the tomatoes and their juice to a food mill and put them through the coarse disk. Return the pureed tomatoes to the rinsed-out saucepan.

In a small skillet, gently cook the onion in the remaining tablespoon of olive oil until it is soft and

½ teaspoon dried Greek or Sicilian oregano

½ teaspoon crushed fennel pollen or fennel seeds

1 2-inch piece of dried orange peel

1 bay leaf

sea salt and freshly ground black pepper

1 or 2 tablespoons sugar

lightly golden but not brown. Stir the onion into the tomato puree along with the garlic cloves, thyme, oregano, fennel, orange peel, and bay leaf. Mix well and simmer gently, uncovered, over medium-low heat, for about 20 to 30 minutes, or until the sauce is thick. Taste and season with salt and pepper, along with sugar if it seems necessary.

When the sauce is thick, remove the orange peel and bay leaf. If you wish, put the sauce through a food mill again before using it.

Coulis de Tomates

Makes 5 to 6 cups

CALL THIS FRENCH KETCHUP, if you will. It should cook down until it is as thick as American ketchup; it's just as useful to have on hand in the pantry or freezer. Freeze this in half-cup containers, as you will rarely use it in large quantities. Use the coulis to boost the flavor of soups, sauces, and savory baked dishes.

10 pounds ripe, red, peak-of-the-season tomatoes

2 pounds yellow onions, coarsely chopped

5 tablespoons extra-virgin olive oil

2 entire heads of garlic

sea salt and freshly ground black pepper

3 or 4 thyme branches

3 bay leaves

4 rosemary branches

1 tablespoon dried oregano

1 cup coarsely chopped or torn basil, leaves only

Wash the tomatoes and check them over carefully, cutting away any bruises or spoiled areas. Cut the tomatoes in chunks and put them in a wide, deep saucepan. Set over low heat and slowly bring to a simmer. There should be plenty of juice from the tomatoes, but if necessary add a very little water to keep the tomatoes from scorching. Cook, stirring occasionally, until the tomatoes have completely fallen apart into a sauce. Put the sauce through a food mill, to get rid of seeds and skins. Return the sauce to the pan and set over medium-low heat.

Meanwhile, further chop the onions, or process them briefly in a food processor. Add the onions to a skillet with the olive oil and cook, stirring frequently, over medium-low heat until the onions are softened and reduced. While the onions are cooking, separate and peel the garlic cloves and toss the garlic in with the onions. Add salt and pepper to taste and stir the onion–garlic mixture into the tomatoes.

Add the thyme, bay leaves, rosemary, and oregano, and continue cooking slowly, uncovered, for about 1 hour longer. Stir in the basil and taste, adjusting the seasoning.

Puree the coulis, using either the food mill or the processor. It should be at least as thick as heavy cream and very tasty. Transfer to small containers and freeze until ready to use.

Sauce Verte

French Green Sauce for Fish

Makes about 1 cup; enough for 6 to 8 servings

THIS SAUCE IS OFTEN SERVED as an accompaniment to a plain poached salmon (page 351) or other large whole fish. It's delightful on plain steamed vegetables—perhaps a selection of green broccoli, white cauliflower, and small orange carrots. If you serve it with vegetables, cut down the number of anchovy fillets—or leave them out entirely if you don't care for the flavor. For the finest texture, use a mortar and pestle; for speed, use the food processor as directed for salsa verde (following recipe).

1 quart water

a small bunch of fresh watercress, leaves and tender stems only, about 2 loosely packed cups

10 fresh spinach leaves, stems discarded, about 2 loosely packed cups

Bring the water to a rolling boil and drop in the watercress and spinach. Boil for 60 to 90 seconds or until the leaves are soft. Drain well in a colander. Finely chop the greens on a cutting board.

Tear the bread into chunks—you should have about 1 cup—and put in a small bowl. Cover with water and let the bread absorb the water for about a minute, then drain and squeeze as dry as you can. Set aside.

1 1-inch-thick slice of stale country-style bread, crusts removed

1 tablespoon drained capers, or more to taste

4 oil-packed anchovy fillets, chopped, or 1 salt-packed anchovy, prepared as directed on page 40 and chopped (optional)

2 tablespoons minced shallot

1 tablespoon minced fresh tarragon leaves

¼ cup minced flat-leaf parsley

⅓ to ½ cup fruity extra-virgin olive oil to taste

2 tablespoons white wine vinegar or sherry vinegar or lemon juice, or to taste

sea salt and freshly ground black pepper

In a mortar, pound the capers and anchovies, if desired, to a paste. Add the shallot, tarragon, and parsley and pound to mix well, then add the blanched chopped greens and continue pounding. Pound in the soaked bread and, when the mixture is smooth and homogeneous in texture, start to add the olive oil, as if for a mayonnaise, a little at a time and turning constantly with a small wooden spoon. Once about half the oil has been incorporated you can add the rest in a thin, steady stream, stirring continually. Add oil until the sauce is the desired consistency. Stir in a tablespoon of the vinegar or lemon juice. Taste the sauce for seasoning, adding salt, pepper, and more vinegar or lemon juice as desired.

Salsa Verde

Italian Green Sauce for Fish or Meat

Makes about 2 cups; enough for 12 servings

A N ITALIAN EDITION OF SAUCE VERTE, salsa verde goes with bollito misto, a northern Italian extravaganza of simmered veal, chicken, sausage, tongue, and more; but it's even better with plain poached, steam-poached, grilled, or oven-baked fish. Make it in a processor, following these directions; or, for a finer texture, make it with a mortar and pestle, as directed in the preceding sauce verte recipe. In essence, this is another version of pesto.

6 ounces shelled walnuts, about 1½ cups

½ cup coarsely chopped flat-leaf parsley

[cont. next page]

First toast the walnuts. Set the oven at 350 degrees. Spread the walnuts in a single layer on a sheet pan. When the oven is hot, transfer the pan to the oven and toast the walnuts for 5 to 10 minutes, being careful not to burn the nuts. Remove from

1 tablespoon coarsely chopped basil

2 garlic cloves, coarsely chopped

2 small cornichons

yolk of 1 hard-boiled egg

½ cup extra-virgin olive oil

1 tablespoon red wine vinegar or sherry vinegar or fresh lemon juice

sea salt and freshly ground black pepper

the oven and toss the walnuts in a clean dry kitchen towel, rubbing the nuts to release as much of their bitter tannic skins as you can. (The skins won't disappear entirely, and you don't want them to do so because a little of that bitter tannin is good in the sauce.)

Transfer the nuts to a food processor.

Add the parsley, basil, garlic, and cornichons. Turn the machine on and add the egg yolk. Continue processing, adding the olive oil in a slow stream, until the sauce is very smooth. Add the vinegar and process to mix well. Taste for seasoning, adding salt, pepper, and more vinegar if necessary.

Turkish Walnut Sauce for Fish or Vegetables

Tarator

+✥{ Makes 2 to 3 cups

IN LEBANON AND SYRIA, tarator is usually made with tahini (sesame paste), while in Bulgaria it may be a simple blend of cucumbers and yogurt, but in Turkey tarator almost always denotes a sauce based on walnuts.

Walnuts are always on nutritional short lists of powerhouse foods, primarily for their antioxidants and their high quotient of omega-3 fatty acids. It's hard to dislike walnuts although some people object to the tannic flavor of their skins. You can get rid of that by roasting the shelled nuts in a 350-degree oven for a few minutes, or by dropping them in boiling water for 30 to 45 seconds, then rubbing the nuts with a kitchen towel to get rid of a lot of the skins.

The bread crumbs should be fresh, untoasted crumbs from a slightly stale country loaf. The easiest way to make these is to remove the crusts and tear the inner crumb into chunks, then process in the food processor to a fairly uniform fine consistency.

Tarator is often served with steam-poached or fried seafood, especially with fried mussels or squid rings, but it's also good with steamed vegetables, such as green beans or small new potatoes. It should be made a couple of hours before you intend to serve it, to let the flavors develop fully.

1 cup freshly processed bread crumbs

2 to 3 teaspoons finely chopped garlic (2 cloves)

½ teaspoon sea salt

2 cups walnuts, skinned if desired

¼ to ½ cup extra-virgin olive oil

1 tablespoon white wine vinegar

1 teaspoon pomegranate syrup, or more to taste (optional)

Traditionally, this sauce was made by pounding the ingredients in a mortar, but it is much easier with a food processor. Add the bread crumbs to the processor bowl, along with the garlic and salt, and process briefly, in spurts, then add the walnuts and continue processing until you have a coarse, rather chunky paste. With the motor running, blend in about ½ cup of room-temperature water, processing to a thick cream. Continue blending in about ¼ cup of the oil and the vinegar. Taste the sauce from time to time as you blend in the oil and vinegar—it should have a pleasant tartness but not be sharp with vinegar. Adjust the seasoning as you blend. Finally, blend in the pomegranate syrup if available.

Variation: In some parts of the Balkans, Turkish tarator is turned into a soup: omit the bread thickening and simply process the walnuts, garlic, and salt with the olive oil. Blend in the vinegar and then stir in about 4 cups yogurt and ½ cup cold water. Serve cold or at room temperature.

Skordalia

Greek Garlic Sauce for Fish or Vegetables

Makes 1 cup; 8 to 10 servings

SKORDALIA CAN BE MADE with either firm-textured country bread or a baked potato or, as in this recipe, both. If you use potato, however, you *must* make the sauce with a mortar and pestle, because a blender or food processor will do strange and unpleasant things to the texture of potatoes.

This sauce often accompanies salt cod for the Friday meal in Greece, but it's also traditional to serve it with little boiled beets—the beets will color the sauce pink where it touches them. In Macedonia, according to Greek cooking authority Diane Kochilas, the bread might be replaced with a cup of finely chopped walnuts.

1 large russet potato, about ½ pound

1 inch-thick slice of firm country bread, crusts trimmed

3 large garlic cloves, chopped

sea salt

½ cup extra-virgin olive oil

¼ cup strained yogurt (page 278)

juice of ½ lemon, or more to taste

Preheat the oven to 500 degrees and bake the potato for at least an hour or until it is very soft. Discard the potato skin and mash the flesh with a fork. You should have about ⅔ cup.

Tear the bread into chunks, place in a bowl, and cover with cool water. Leave for just a minute or so, for the bread to absorb the water, then drain and squeeze the bread as dry as you can.

With a mortar and pestle, pound the garlic with about a teaspoon of salt until it is very smooth. Add the bread and continue pounding until the mixture is creamy, then pound in the potato flesh. Add the olive oil as if for a mayonnaise, a little at a time and stirring constantly. When about half the oil has been added, stir in the strained yogurt (an unorthodox touch to lighten the sauce). When all the oil has been added, you should have a thick, homogeneous, rather creamy mass. Stir in the lemon juice. Taste the sauce and adjust the seasoning, adding more salt, pepper, and lemon juice if desired.

Variation: Some cooks stir in ¼ to ⅓ cup of salted capers, refreshed in water, drained, and coarsely chopped, added with the yogurt.

Aïoli

Garlic Mayonnaise

 Makes 1¼ cups; 6 to 8 servings

Aïoli, sometimes called the "butter of Provence" because it is so integral to the cuisine, is simply a mayonnaise incorporating quantities of fresh garlic—usually two cloves per person in Provence. That is a lot, and you might wish to use less (I do—three or four cloves for this recipe), but since the whole point of aïoli is garlic, by all means don't stint. The quality of the garlic is most important—it should be fresh and plump with swollen cloves. Reject any shriveled cloves or any in which the core is developing a green sprout.

Traditionally aïoli is made with egg yolks and garlic pounded in a mortar. A lighter sauce can be made in the blender with a whole egg and an egg white, but the blender does odd things to the taste of garlic, so I prefer to make the lighter mayonnaise in the blender, then fold in the garlic paste separately by hand. I always use organic eggs, but if you're not sure of your egg source and worried about salmonella, don't try this recipe.

1 whole egg

1 egg white

sea salt

1 to 1½ cups fruity extra-virgin olive oil as needed

juice of ½ lemon, or more to taste

4 to 8 garlic cloves, coarsely chopped

Make the mayonnaise by whirling the egg and egg white in a blender with a little pinch of salt. Remove the center knob from the blender lid and, with the blender churning, start to pour in the olive oil, a very thin thread at first, until the mixture starts to thicken. Stop the blender and pour in a few tablespoons of lemon juice, then start the blender again and continue adding oil, a little more thickly as the mixture emulsifies and mounts. When all the oil has been added, turn the blender off and set aside.

Combine the garlic in a small bowl or a mortar with a teaspoon of salt and pound the garlic or crush it with the back of a spoon until you have a thick and homogeneous paste. Now use a spatula to scrape the mayonnaise into the garlic paste and turn gently to incorporate everything. Taste and add more salt and lemon juice if desired.

If the mayonnaise breaks down and separates while you're blending it, remove it all from the blender and start over again with a fresh egg. Whirl the egg until it is light and add, bit by bit, the broken-down mayonnaise and more oil and lemon juice. It should be easy to reconstitute the mayonnaise. Then proceed as directed.

Sauce Rouille

Makes about ¾ cup of sauce; enough for 6 servings

THIS SIMPLE, COLORFUL SAUCE adds body and interest to Provençal fish stews and soups. A spoonful is dropped in the center of each bowl of soup for serving, and the rest is passed at the table, heaped in a small china bowl. It is also a fine garnish for any plain grilled or poached fish. To French tastes it's a fiery sauce; to Mexicans and many Americans it's on the mild side. Like the romesco sauce that follows, it can be made more or less hot by adjusting the amount of chilies.

2 sweet red peppers

2 fresh New Mexico (Anaheim) chilies or dried chilies soaked in hot water for 20 to 30 minutes

2 garlic cloves, crushed and chopped

sea salt

3 tablespoons dry unseasoned bread crumbs

⅓ cup extra-virgin olive oil

cayenne pepper or Tabasco sauce, if desired

Roast and peel the fresh peppers and chilies, following the directions on page 26.

If you're using dried chilies, remove them from the soaking water, discard the seeds and membranes, and scrape the red pulp away from the skins with a spoon. Discard the skins.

In a mortar, crush the garlic to a paste with a little salt. Add the peppers and chilies with the roasting juices and pound with the pestle to a homogeneous mass. Stir in the bread crumbs, then the olive oil. Taste and add a little cayenne if desired to make a hotter sauce.

Note that the sauce may be made in a food processor but be careful not to overprocess. It should have texture and not be totally smooth.

Variation: In Provence the sauce is sometimes made like a mayonnaise or an aïoli, an egg yolk stirred with olive oil to a compact mass, then the pounded red peppers and garlic stirred in. This is rich. Another alternative uses a whole egg and an egg white, as in the aïoli on page 275.

Salsa Romesco

Makes about 1¼ cups; 8 to 10 servings

A CATALAN SAUCE for fish and seafood, this is characteristic of a number of Spanish sauces in which almonds, bread, and garlic are fried and then pounded in a mortar or whirled in a blender. The process gives a pleasantly rough texture and a complex and rather nutty flavor. This is a variation of the sauce with grilled shrimp on page 393. Almonds, bread, and garlic fried in olive oil sounds Arab to me—did this come to Spain with the Moors?

Try salsa romesco with grilled or steam-poached fish or stir a healthy dollop into a bowl of fish stew. Spaniards often refer to this sauce as *muy piquante,* very hot, but I don't think most Americans, accustomed to Mexican and Southeast Asian food, will find it so. If you want to make it hotter, add more chilies.

2 dried New Mexico (Anaheim) chilies

1 small dried hot red chili, or more to taste

½ cup extra-virgin olive oil

6 whole garlic cloves

½ cup blanched almonds

1 2-inch-thick slice of stale country-style bread, crusts removed

1 medium very ripe tomato

1 tablespoon sherry vinegar, or more to taste

sea salt (optional)

Break up the dried chilies, discarding some or all of the seeds (which is where the heat is concentrated). In a small skillet over medium-low heat, fry the chilies in ¼ cup of the olive oil until the color starts to change, about 3 to 5 minutes. Transfer the chilies with a slotted spoon to a blender or food processor. In the oil remaining in the pan, fry the whole garlic cloves, stirring frequently, until golden brown, about 5 to 7 minutes. Remove them and add to the chilies. Add the almonds to the pan and fry (adding a little more olive oil if necessary), stirring, until golden brown, about 5 minutes. Add to the chilies. Finally, add 2 tablespoons oil to the pan and fry the bread on both sides until golden, about 5 to 7 minutes. Add to the chilies, breaking the bread into smaller pieces, together with any oil remaining in the pan.

Process or blend the fried ingredients in brief spurts, stirring down occasionally, to get a coarse bread-crumb texture.

Slice the tomato in half; squeeze out and discard the seeds. Chop the tomato coarsely and add to the blender with the vinegar. Process to a coarse paste.

Now, with the blender running, add the remaining oil in a thin stream until it is thoroughly blended in and you have a thick, mayonnaise-like mass but with texture from the bread and almonds. Remove and scrape into a bowl. Taste and adjust the seasoning, adding salt if you wish or a little more vinegar.

Labneh

Lebanese Strained Yogurt

❦ Makes 1½ to 2 cups, depending on how long you let it drip; 32 servings

THOUGH OFTEN CALLED *yogurt cheese,* this isn't, of course, cheese at all since no rennet or other coagulant is used. It's simply thickened yogurt in which the whey has been drained away.

Labneh is a marvelous substitute for fresh cheeses, however. In Lebanon it's

---

PERSILLADE AND GREMOLATA

Two Pick-Me-Ups for Tired Food

A Provençal persillade or an Italian gremolata is not really a recipe so much as a technique. Here's how it works: suppose a piece of fish is cooked a little too simply, or a sauce, no matter how carefully directions were followed, comes out tasting a little faded, lacking in verve and interest. Then a French or Italian cook will turn to a persillade or a gremolata to perk up the dish, adding it at the very end, either stirring it into the sauce or sprinkling it over the top of meat or fish—or braised beans or vegetables.

To make a persillade, simply mince together a little handful of flat-leaf parsley and a couple of garlic cloves, more or less to taste. For a gremolata, add the finely chopped or grated zest of half a lemon. Gremolata is traditionally served over the top of Milanese osso buco, but it adds vigor and sparkle to other dishes as well.

---

used as a spread for warm pieces of Arab bread (pita), especially at breakfast, and it's always among the dishes on the table for a meze. Beat the labneh with a little sugar or honey and vanilla and substitute it for whipped cream, crème fraîche, or clotted cream; serve it with fresh fruits or with any of the fruit desserts or sweet cakes in the dessert chapter, pages 444–464.

For a different taste, make labneh with low-fat or nonfat yogurt, add a mixture of chopped green herbs (basil, tarragon, sorrel, lovage) and a little finely minced garlic to make a low-fat substitute for those high-fat French garlic cheeses. Just don't try to substitute labneh or yogurt for cream in cooking—it breaks down when heated to the boiling point.

Experiment with different brands of yogurt until you find one that pleases you. Small producers often make the best. Just be sure it's a pure yogurt made with acidophilus and other living cultures and with no added pectin, gelatin, or other thickeners.

Use a colander lined with a triple layer of cheesecloth. Pour a quart of pure yogurt into the cheesecloth and set the colander in the sink or in a bowl to catch the whey. Set a plate or a piece of plastic wrap or aluminum foil lightly over the top to keep the dust off and leave for up to 24 hours. The yogurt just gets thicker as it keeps on dripping. When it's the thickness you desire, scrape it into a refrigerator container, cover it, and refrigerate it. It will keep for 10 days or more. Any whey that drifts to the top can be poured off before using.

An especially useful device is a plastic draining cone made for straining yogurt (see Resources). I set the cone over a tall, straight-sided measuring jug—the mouth of the jug is just wide enough for the cone to sit down in the jug without falling through.

Harissa

North African Hot Sauce

Makes ½ to ¾ cup; about 8 servings as a garnish

T HIS HOT PEPPER SAUCE adds piquancy to all manner of North African stews and couscous and is often eaten on its own, smeared on a piece of bread. Commercial harissa is available in tubes, but this version, similar to what's sold in the great Central Market in Tunis, is far superior. As with any hot sauce, you can vary the heat by balancing medium-hot and very hot chilies. Some cooks add a very little cumin to the blend. The chilies used in Tunisia are different from the ones I have suggested. The goal is to achieve a complex and pleasing balance of piquant flavors.

Harissa will keep for a long time in the refrigerator if it is spooned into a clean glass jar and the top is covered with olive oil. Use a spoonful any time you want to spark up a sauce or a soup—it's especially good with any kind of bean or legume soups, and it's essential with North African couscous.

12 medium-hot dried chilies (New Mexico or Anaheim)

2 hot dried chilies (pasilla or ancho)

1 very hot dried chili (arbol)

2 tablespoons coriander seeds

1 tablespoon cumin seeds

1 teaspoon caraway seeds

sea salt

4 or 5 garlic cloves, coarsely chopped

about ¼ cup extra-virgin olive oil

Rinse the chilies quickly in running water, then break off the tops and shake out the loose seeds. Set the chilies in a bowl and cover with very hot water. Set a plate over the chilies to weight them down and keep them under water. Set aside for 20 to 30 minutes to soften.

Meanwhile, roast the coriander, cumin, and caraway seeds in a dry skillet over medium heat until the aromas of the spices start to rise. Transfer to a mortar with a pinch of salt and pound to a grainy powder. Add the chopped garlic and pound to a paste.

Drain the chilies and discard most of the seeds and membranes. Using a spoon, scrape the softened pulp into the mortar. Pound with a pestle to a coarse paste. Pound in about ¼ cup oil, a tablespoon at a time. Taste and add salt if desired. The sauce should be very thick but easy to spread. If you're not going to use it right away, put it in a jar, smoothing the top with the bowl of a spoon, and pour a little more oil over the top to seal it. It will keep, refrigerated, for 2 to 3 weeks.

Moroccan Preserved Lemons

SALT-PRESERVED OR PICKLED LEMONS have a strange and delectable flavor that utterly mystifies those who taste them for the first time in a fish or meat stew. These are used for Moroccan Chicken with Preserved Lemons and Olives (page 412) and Tunisian Fish with Preserved Lemons and Olives (page 373), but once you've tried them in those dishes, you'll find other uses for them as well. I was introduced to these years ago through Paula Wolfert's masterpiece *Couscous and Other Good Food from Morocco,* and they've been an important part of my pantry ever since. I sometimes even add a little slice of preserved lemon to a Bloody Mary for Sunday lunch.

Use a 3½- to 4-pint glass canning jar or any similar lidded jar (it need not be self-sealing since it is the salt that preserves the lemons).

24 to 36 fresh whole lemons, preferably organic

1 or 2 cups pickling, kosher, or sea salt

If you can't find certified organic lemons, scrub the lemons well with a brush under running water.

Fill a clean preserving jar with boiling water, first standing it on a layer of newspapers or kitchen towels. Leave it for 10 minutes or so, then turn the water out. If for any reason you are interrupted in your work and can't immediately start to fill the jar with lemons, repeat this process. The jar should be sterilized with boiling water immediately before you fill it.

Hold a lemon upright and slice down carefully from the bud end to the stem end, stopping about ½ inch from the stem end. Give the lemon a quarter turn and slice again. The lemon will be quartered, but the quarters will be firmly attached at the stem end. Open the lemon slightly and pack the insides with salt, then press the lemon down in the bottom of the jar. Do this with all the lemons, pressing them very firmly so that they yield up a considerable quantity of juice. Fill the jar up to the top, with an inch to spare. Add ⅓ cup of salt.

If insufficient juice has been released to completely cover all the lemons, squeeze enough fresh lemon juice to cover them right up to the top. Add another 2 tablespoons pickling salt to the top of the jar and screw the lid on tight.

Now set the jar of lemons aside to pickle for at least 3 weeks—although preserved lemons will last a good deal longer, several months at least. Every couple of days, invert the jar and leave it standing on its head for a couple of days, then right it again. This will redistribute the salty juice over all the lemons.

Lebanese Pickled Turnips

Makes 12 servings

PINK PICKLED TURNIPS are great favorites in Lebanon and Syria, where they often play a significant role on the meze table, their delicate rosy color as significant a contrast to the pale cream of hummus and baba ghanouj as their sharp fermented flavor is to the sweet earthiness of eggplant and chickpeas. Use small white turnips, the ones that have a light violet blush around the tops—the big yellow-fleshed, purple-skinned ones just won't do the trick. You will also need a 3½- to 4-pint mason or other type of preserving jar or two smaller ones. The jars need not be self-sealing.

2 pounds white turnips

1 medium beet, peeled and sliced

3 garlic cloves, peeled (optional)

pickling, kosher, or sea salt

1¼ cups white wine vinegar

2½ cups water

Make sure the preserving jar is scrupulously clean. Immediately before using it, fill it with freshly boiling water and let the water sit for 10 minutes before turning it out.

Peel the turnips. Quarter or halve them if large and fill the preserving jar with turnips, layering slices of beet in among them from time to time. If you wish, add the garlic cloves as well. For quart jars, add 1 tablespoon salt; for half-gallon jars, add 2 tablespoons. Mix the vinegar and water and pour the liquid over the turnips in the jar so that they are completely covered. Close the jar tightly and set aside in a cool (but not refrigerated) place. Invert the jar every few days to redistribute the salt. The pickles will be ready to eat in a week to 10 days but can be kept, refrigerated, for up to 1 month.

Vegetable Dishes

✧ ✧ ✧

AT MORE VEGETABLES," government diet specialists thunder, and the American Cancer Society chimes in: "Five a day! Five a day!"

Everywhere the message is unmistakable—we Americans have to get more fresh vegetables into our diets, and the way to do that is not by doubling an order of french fries and ketchup to go with a lunchtime burger. Most people who give even a little thought to the relationship between food and health need no persuading that fresh fruits and vegetables, full of vitamins and fiber along with important antioxidants, polyphenols, and other trace elements that are even now not well understood, are the very foundation of a healthy diet. They know too that we should all be consuming more vegetables, including beans and grains, and a good deal less meat and meat products.

This is not a new or revolutionary idea. No less a patriot than Thomas Jefferson, writing to a friend in 1819, said: "I have lived temperately, eating little animal food, and that not as an aliment, so much as a condiment for the vegetables which constitute my principal diet." Yet today, less than one-third of American adults and, somewhat more shockingly, only 20 percent of American children consume the recommended five servings a day.

Yet, if the message is unmistakable, the method is less than clear. Five a day of *what* exactly? And how am I supposed to do it? Say I have cereal and yogurt at breakfast (because I need the fiber and the calcium) and a half sandwich and a cup of soup at lunch (because I work in a midtown office and that's the most acceptable lunch available). Then I come home tired but willing to put a little effort into the evening meal both because cooking is a good way to come down off a high-tension workday and because I care about the quality of what I put into my body and the bodies of those I nurture and cherish. What should I cook for dinner?

Adding vegetables to the diet doesn't necessarily mean staring at a plate of naked broccoli at suppertime. As Mediterranean cooks know well, vegetables can be slipped into an overall menu plan in dozens of different ways, ways moreover that don't just add bald quotients of nutrients to the diet but add appetizing flavor and color, verve and excitement to the plate. Think of a piece of grilled meat or fish on a plain white dinner plate. It was prepared in the proper manner, brushed with olive oil, sprinkled with fresh herbs, cooked until just done, and there it sits—interesting, but . . . as Gertrude Stein said of the city of Oakland, "There's no there there."

But add to that grilled meat or fish what Italians call the *contorno* (the word comes from the decorative arts and means "cornice" or "border"). Make the *contorno* broccoli, just for the sake of the argument. Only make it steamed lightly until very tender, so that the deep green color shines, then chopped coarsely and turned in a little *salsina* of warm olive oil with some minced garlic and broken fragments of red chili pepper. A few drops of lemon juice, a few grains of salt, and the *contorno* becomes what it was intended to be—delicious on its own and even more delicious as a border around that plainly grilled piece of meat or fish (see recipe, page 355). It decorates, enhances, and adds to the value, both visual and gustatory, of the plate.

Precede that with a cup of lemony Tomato-Rice Soup (page 122) that you may have made a few weeks back and kept frozen in single-serving quantities, or a quickly made carrot or beet salad (pages 81–83); follow it with an apple, an orange, or a bowl of fresh seasonal berries, and you've almost fulfilled your five-a-day commitment. All that remains is to add fruit to your breakfast yogurt and make sure your lunchtime soup is a hearty, beany mixture, and you're there. Anything else you add is, as it were, icing on the cake—the fruit-and-veg cake, that is.

Vegetables are the heart and soul of Mediterranean cooking; grains and beans may be the backbone of the diet, but vegetables are what bring delight to these frankly rather stodgy staples. And not just as an accompaniment to what sits in the center of the plate, for vegetables are often served in their own right. An artichoke, at the height of its late-winter season, is seen as a special thing, something deserving of treatment on its own. As such it may be served as a first course with nothing more to garnish it than a little vinaigrette or green sauce into which the tender ends of the leaves are dipped before scraping them, in that sexy, intimate way of artichokes, between the teeth. Fresh peas in June, the tiny tender *piselli romaneschi* that are raised in little market gardens around Rome, issue forth from the kitchen almost as a stew, mixed with bits of cured-pork *guanciale* and impregnated with olive oil, a first course so tender and juicy it must be eaten with a spoon. Or leeks in winter, fat and alabaster-white, plainly steamed and cooled to room temperature, are served, with stunning simplicity, all by themselves with a mustardy vinaigrette that points up the sweet earthiness, the ancient nature of this fundamental vegetable.

Whatever the vegetable (and I could go on and on listing vegetables that are served on their own in this manner), the treatment makes it a star, to be appreciated for precisely what it is and nothing more. But it does something more than that, something a little more spiritual and philosophical. For in the Mediterranean it is a clear if unstated principle that you don't eat artichokes in August or fresh peas in February or leeks in June or fresh fava beans in October. Acknowledging there is a season for each of these things forces us to recognize and salute their rarity and worth. It ties us ever more deeply to the agriculture that sustains us all, that is the foundation of our life on the planet, and it gives us (or at least it gives me) a sense of humble gratitude for all that went into creating this perfection, the skill of the farmer and the cook, the richness of the earth, the rain and sun and wind that urged the plant to fruition.

In shifting from a meat-based diet to a largely plant-based diet, keep in mind that you will need to increase the quantity of vegetables in each individual serving. Because they lack fat, vegetables are less filling than meat; moreover, vegetables prepared in a Mediterranean style are so delicious that people just naturally seem to want more of them. I find, for instance, that it takes ½ pound of a vegetable like broccoli to make one serving as an accompaniment to a main-course meat or fish. If I am serving broccoli on its own or with other vegetables, I might increase that to ¾ pound, depending on whether it's for lunch or dinner and how many courses come before or after.

One question comes up more often with vegetables than with any other food: should I buy organic? My answer to that is a resounding, but qualified yes, but with certain restrictions. Yes, because the term organic properly means that the soil in which the vegetables have grown is as healthy as it can be, and the healthiest vegetables can only come from healthy soil. It used to be said that there was no difference in nutritional values between organic and, shall we say, in-organic (or conventional) cultivation. But the jury is no longer out on that question and it is unmistakably clear now that, all things being equal, organically raised vegetables (and fruits and other things you might want to put in your mouth) are better for you overall, not just better for you because they don't have pesticides and chemical fertilizers added to their nutritional profiles but because they are actively and positively more full of goodness. Michael Pollan, in his recent book *In Defense of Food,* gives some USDA statistics on the decline of nutritional values in basic foodstuffs since the widespread adoption of chemical fertilizers in the 1950s: vitamin C down 28 percent, riboflavin (aka vitamin B_2) down 38 percent, calcium down 16 percent, and so on. And, although the present book is concerned with the environment only in a peripheral way, organic cultivation of our food also means healthier, greener, more pleasurable surroundings for us all, farmers and neighbors, city and country alike.

That said, however, there are many farmers and food producers who have chosen, for various reasons from the political to the economic, not to apply for organic certification—yet whose growing methods are as sustainable, if not more so, than many of the large, industrial organic producers. By scouting around farmers' markets and farm stands, by asking smart (and not smart-ass) questions, you will find out who they are and you will want to buy and eat their products. For myself, I would far rather eat an apple harvested from a neighboring Maine farm where the farmer practices Integrated Pest Management, spraying her trees rarely and only in response to a threatened infestation—I would far rather have that apple than one raised halfway around the world by strictly organic methods and shipped by air to my local supermarket's warehouse in New Jersey before it is further trucked to Maine. In other words, organic is fine but locally grown is also important, and, most important of all: *neither course should be taken as an exclusive, rigid commitment.* All those writers and bloggers who are suddenly telling us how they managed for a year (an entire year!) to eat nothing that had been grown more than 100 miles from their own back doorsteps—excuse me, but I'm really not ready yet to give up olive oil, wine, and citrus fruits, none of which can be produced successfully within a thousand miles from my Maine back doorstep.

So, yes, buy organic, but more important, buy fresh, raw, unprocessed food, as much of it as possible grown on farms not too far from your kitchen. How far is not too far? That's up to you to decide. The best test may be the one devised by that preeminent farmer Eliot Coleman: the most important thing to know is the first name of the person from whom you buy your vegetables. Farmers' markets, farm stands, community-supported agriculture (CSA— where you give the farmer money in the spring and she gives you vegetables throughout the growing season), and other ways of connecting solidly with local agriculture are really critical. It's not always possible for people who live in inner cities to do this, and it often appears to be more expensive than buying conventional products, but it's worth it in the end. Our governments, at the city, state, and federal level, should be doing a whole lot more to support healthy diets—and our public health system's commissioners should demand it. I don't believe it's too late yet to reestablish the vital connections that were broken throughout the last century.

Plainly cooked vegetables are made more interesting by adding some sort of very simple sauce. See Chapter Five for some appropriate sauce recipes. The following are suggestions for combinations.

Vegetables to Serve with a Light, Mustardy Vinaigrette

Steamed or poached artichokes, asparagus, beets, broccoli, green beans, leeks, steamed greens (spinach, chicory, broccoli rabe).

Mix up the vinaigrette (page 263), adding finely chopped or minced green herbs if appropriate, and simply toss the finished vegetables in it while still warm. For best flavor, serve the vegetables hot or at room temperature but not chilled.

Vegetables to Serve with Extra-Virgin Olive Oil and Freshly Grated Cheese

Steamed or poached asparagus, broccoli, cauliflower, cabbage, green beans, zucchini.

When the vegetables are tender, drain them and return to the pan. Add about a tablespoon of very fruity olive oil and a tablespoon of freshly grated parmigiano, feta, manchego, or other cheese for each pound of vegetables. Toss the vegetables over low heat just long enough to warm the oil and soften the cheese. With the oil and cheese you can also add sea salt, freshly ground black pepper, and minced fresh herbs if you wish.

Grilled Vegetables

Eggplant, tomatoes, zucchini, onions, peppers.

Slice them thickly (leave peppers whole or in halves), paint with olive oil, and grill over charcoal or wood embers until tender. Serve sprinkled with a few drops of lemon juice.

Pureed Vegetables

Beets, carrots, celeriac, potatoes, turnips, cut into chunks.

Steam until very tender, then put through a vegetable mill (much better than a food processor) and beat in a little yogurt and/or fruity olive oil, salt, pepper, and herbs.

Quick Grated-Vegetable Sautés

Turnips, beets, cabbage, carrots, celery root.

Grate on the large holes of a grater and sauté in 1 or 2 tablespoons of extra-virgin olive oil, adding sea salt, pepper, and perhaps a little pinch of sugar or a thread of tomato sauce, if desired.

Vegetables à la Grecque

Artichokes (hearts only), mushrooms, fennel, small baby onions, carrots, very fresh zucchini.

Poach in 3 parts water to 1 part extra-virgin olive oil along with the juice of ½ lemon, 1 teaspoon whole peppercorns, 1 teaspoon whole coriander seeds, a little thyme and parsley, and a bay leaf. Cook, uncovered, until the water boils away and the vegetables are very tender; serve with their aromatic juices poured over them.

VEGETABLES AND ANTIOXIDANTS

Scientific chatter about the traditional Mediterranean diet inevitably comes around to antioxidants, which are said to be one of the most significant aspects of the diet in terms of supporting good health. Population studies have consistently shown that people who eat substantial amounts of fruits and vegetables, good sources of antioxidants, have a lower risk of cancer, heart disease, and some neurological diseases. But what are antioxidants exactly, why are they so valuable, and how can we get more of them?

The answer to the last question is quick and easy: eat more vegetables and fruits, in greater varieties, at least five servings a day, better yet nine, ten, or more, choosing from green leafy vegetables, cabbage-family vegetables, onions and garlic, and bright-colored squashes, melons, tomatoes, and citrus.

The answers to the other two questions are a little more complicated, probably more so than you really want to know, so I'll try to be as brief and straightforward as I can.

Our bodies produce nasty molecules known as free radicals, all day every day, as the result of both natural processes, like breathing and aging, and unnatural ones, like exposure to tobacco smoke, environmental pollutants of all kinds, and even simple sunlight which, as we know, can be both health giving and harmful. Through a complex chemical process, these free radicals swimming through our metabolism initiate oxidation, and oxidation leads to cell damage that, research is beginning to show, may be linked to cancers, heart disease, and even diabetes. And the damage begins with those wretched free radicals, many of which are unavoidable.

Enter the antioxidants, which interfere with the oxidation process, by neutralizing the free radicals responsible for it. But that's not all they do—some antioxidants actually help to repair cell damage while others may improve immune function and possibly lower the risk of infection.

Phytochemicals, vitamins, and other nutrients available from plant sources, i.e., from fruits and vegetables, and from products such as olive oil and wine that are derived from fruits and vegetables, are all antioxidants. They include familiar vitamins like C, E, and beta-carotene, but also less well-known phytonutrients such as allyl sulfides, from the onion family, isoflavones from the soy and cabbage families, and flavonoids from many different fruits and vegetables. Vegetables also provide nutrients such as copper, zinc, and iron that are not antioxidants as such but are used by the body to ensure specific biological reactions that bring about antioxidant effects.

But we don't actually eat indole-3-carbinols or genistein or resveratrols or allyl sulfides; we eat broccoli and cabbage, garlic and onions, tomatoes, carrots, parsley, and celery. And we drink red wine. All of which are excellent sources of these inestimably valuable antioxidants. Don't reach for the supplement bottle just yet. The best strategy for good health is to eat antioxidants in their natural state, with a diet abundant in fruits and vegetables. Fortunately, the Mediterranean diet is exactly that, and in fact, nutritional researchers have proposed that a major reason for the effectiveness of the diet is not one or two or many antioxidants, but rather the presence of so many of them all together, even some as yet undiscovered, acting as an ensemble, strengthening each other, just as a chorus of many different voices is stronger, and often more pleasing, than a single voice alone.

And when you go to market for your antioxidants, keep in mind that, according to researchers from the University of California at Davis reporting in the *Journal of Agricultural and Food Chemistry*, organically raised tomatoes have much higher levels of flavonoids than conventionally grown tomatoes—and the case is similar for other organically raised vegetables and fruits. So eat your antioxidants—and for best results, make them organically grown at that.

All vegetables are good for you, but some are higher in antioxidants than others. If you're concerned about getting enough healthy fruits and vegetables, think about eating as many different varieties as possible. Be sure to include some or all of the following at least four or five times a week, depending on the season: citrus fruits, melons, red grapes; tomatoes (both raw and cooked); onions, leeks, and garlic, all members of the great Allium family; leafy greens, both raw and cooked; cabbage-family vegetables (including many Asian vegetables—bok choy, Chinese broccoli—that respond well to Mediterranean treatments); nuts, especially walnuts and almonds; and deep-colored fruits—blackberries, pomegranates, and blueberries (not exactly Mediterranean but awfully good nonetheless). Some other foods are good sources of antioxidants as well, including especially red wine, tea (an important beverage in many parts of the Mediterranean), and of course that eternal friend of the Mediterranean diet, extra-virgin olive oil.

Artichokes

Braised Artichokes and Potatoes

Makes 6 to 8 servings

DOWN BY THE TIBER in the old Roman ghetto, a few restaurants still specialize in Roman Jewish food. Probably the most famous dish is deep-fried *carciofi alla giudea,* whole artichokes plunged into a vat of olive oil and fried until they look like bronzed chrysanthemum souvenirs of a long-ago football game. Because they're made with chokeless Roman artichokes, you don't have to worry about any nasty spines when you eat them. The flesh of the artichoke is roasted and sweet. An unforgettable treat!

Well, you can't really do this without spineless artichokes, something we don't seem to have in this country (although an enterprising grower could develop a good market). This recipe is a takeoff on the idea, with potatoes added.

8 small, firm artichokes

8 small potatoes, peeled

1 medium onion, halved and finely sliced

2 garlic cloves, coarsely chopped

sea salt and freshly ground black pepper

[cont. next page]

Prepare the artichokes as described on page 26, quartering them and removing the chokes. Drain them and put them with the potatoes in a saucepan large enough to hold all the ingredients. Sprinkle the onion and garlic around the other vegetables; add a little salt and pepper and the thyme and bay leaves. Pour the olive oil over the vegetables and set the pan over medium heat.

¼ teaspoon dried thyme, crumbled

2 small bay leaves

⅓ cup extra-virgin olive oil

juice of ½ lemon

lemon wedges for serving

When the oil starts to sizzle, add the lemon juice and enough boiling water to come about halfway up the artichokes. Cover the pan tightly and cook for 30 minutes. Then remove the lid, raise the heat, and cook until all the water has evaporated and the artichokes and potatoes are sizzling in the oil, about 10 to 15 minutes longer.

Remove from the heat and serve immediately, with lemon wedges for squeezing over the vegetables.

Artichoke Parmigiana

Parmigiana di Carciofi

Makes 6 to 8 servings

W E ALL KNOW EGGPLANT PARMIGIANA but this is how a parmigiana is put together in wintertime, when no eggplants are available. Layered, baked dishes like this are so characteristic of the Italian South that they are truly symbolic of the cuisine. Note that parmigiana has nothing at all to do with the northern city of Parma nor with the glorious parmigiano reggiano cheese of that region. In fact, though you may use parmigiano in this dish, it's much more typically done with a well-aged pecorino cheese from the South.

Use a good-quality fresh mozzarella here, the kind that's sold in its brine, and not the rubbery tough stuff that's sold as mozzarella in many supermarkets, which bears no resemblance to the real thing.

½ cup unbleached all-purpose flour

sea salt

about 1¼ cups extra-virgin olive oil

6 or 8 large artichokes

1 lemon, cut in half

½ pound fresh mozzarella, thinly sliced

Make a batter for the artichokes: put the flour in a bowl with a pinch of salt and, using a fork, gradually beat in about ¼ cup of water. Beat in 2 tablespoons of the oil, then add more water until the batter is the consistency of heavy cream. (Some cooks beat in a tablespoon or two of dry white wine along with the oil to give the batter more flavor.) Set the batter aside to rest while you prepare the artichokes.

⅓ cup freshly grated aged pecorino or parmigiano cheese

1½ cups plain tomato sauce (page 266)

freshly ground black pepper

Trim the stems of the artichokes, cut away the pointed tops of the leaves, and break off the outside leaves until you reach the tender insides. Constantly rub the cut surfaces with a lemon half to keep them from darkening. Slice each artichoke in half lengthwise and, using a serrated grapefruit spoon, scoop out the prickly choke. Cut the cleaned artichokes in vertical slices about ¼ inch thick. Squeeze the remaining lemon half into a bowl of cool water and toss the slices in the acidulated water.

Put about 1 inch of oil in the bottom of a skillet over medium-high heat. When the oil has reached frying temperature (about 360 degrees), working rapidly, dip the artichoke slices in the batter and fry until crisp and golden. Remove the slices as they finish cooking and drain on paper towels.

The recipe may be prepared ahead up to this point. When ready to continue, heat the oven to 425 degrees.

Lightly oil the bottom and sides of a rectangular terra-cotta or glass oven dish. Arrange half the fried artichoke slices over the bottom of the dish, covering with thin slices of mozzarella and a sprinkling of half the grated cheese. Dot with half the tomato sauce, adding salt and pepper. Arrange the remaining ingredients in a second layer, finishing with tomato sauce and grated cheese.

Transfer to the preheated oven and bake for 30 minutes.

May be served hot but is best slightly warmer than room temperature.

Asparagus

This is one of the many vegetables that have suffered from overexposure. We now have asparagus in markets year-round, much of it grown in Mexico and of indifferent quality. My asparagus memories go back to my Maine childhood, when it was the first green vegetable, if you don't count dandelions, of the spring. Like many Maine professional men, my father, although a lawyer with a busy practice, was a first-rate gardener. He was particularly proud of his asparagus patch and would go out to the garden in season to gather enough fresh asparagus for our favorite breakfast, poached asparagus on toast. That early Maine asparagus had a flavor (still has) that nothing from Mexico can beat. I still believe that asparagus should be eaten only when it's in season locally. If in Mexico that means year-round, in Maine, as in the Mediterranean, it still means springtime.

Castelvetro's Grilled Asparagus

Makes 6 to 8 servings

IN THE EARLY 17TH CENTURY, Giacomo Castelvetro fled to England from Venice and the hounds of the Inquisition. A man of great culture and humanity, he became concerned that the English diet was poor in fresh vegetables. So, as one of the earliest advocates of the virtues of the Mediterranean diet, he set himself the task of introducing a more healthful table to his English friends. The result was *A Brief Account of the Fruits, Herbs & Vegetables of Italy*, dedicated in 1614 to that great gardener and patron of the arts, Lucy, Countess of Bedford.

This is a remarkable book, a treasure chest of honest, sage, and lucid advice about cultivating and cooking a range of fruits and vegetables so amazing that our modern produce markets look humble by comparison. What makes the book exceptional is Castelvetro's sensibility in the kitchen as much as in the garden. The book rings as true today as it must have done nearly 400 years ago. The Italian original has been translated by Gillian Riley and published as *The Fruit, Herbs & Vegetables of Italy* (Viking, 1989).

This recipe is based on the gentle 17th-century gourmet's directions for grilling asparagus.

3 pounds plump seasonal asparagus

¼ cup extra-virgin olive oil

Preheat the oven broiler or prepare a charcoal fire for grilling. Rinse the asparagus and trim it of any tough ends. The stalks should be roughly equal in length. Place the asparagus in a shallow bowl and

sea salt and freshly ground black pepper

3 tablespoons fresh bitter (Seville) orange juice or 2 tablespoons sweet orange juice and 1 tablespoon lemon juice

add the olive oil. Roll the asparagus around to coat it well with the oil.

Sprinkle another plate with salt and lots of freshly ground black pepper, stirring with a fork to mix the grains well. Roll each spear of asparagus in the salt and pepper mixture to coat it, not too thickly. Lay the spears on a grid and broil or grill carefully, about 6 to 8 inches from the heat. The asparagus should cook through and be lightly and pleasantly browned on the outside in about 10 minutes.

Heap the asparagus in a clean shallow bowl and pour the citrus juice over, stirring gently to mix well. Serve immediately or set aside at room temperature, stirring occasionally, to absorb the flavors.

Andalucian Asparagus

✦ Makes 4 to 6 servings

CLARA MARIA DE AMEZUA is Spain's foremost cooking teacher and a tireless promoter of Spanish ways in the kitchen. This is her method for cooking asparagus in a manner that's typical of Spain's vast southern region of Andalucia.

2 pounds young asparagus

¼ cup extra-virgin olive oil, or more if needed

4 garlic cloves, peeled

12 blanched almonds

1 2-inch slice of crusty country-style bread, crusts removed, cut into cubes

1 tablespoon very-good-quality sherry vinegar

sea salt

Preheat the oven to 400 degrees. Trim the asparagus, rinse, and set aside.

Heat half the olive oil in a saucepan over medium heat. Add the garlic, almonds, and bread and sauté, stirring constantly, until all the ingredients are nicely browned—about 5 to 7 minutes. Do not let them burn. Transfer the almonds, garlic, and bread cubes with a slotted spoon to a food processor or blender. Add the vinegar and about ½ teaspoon salt and process briefly until the mixture is a coarse meal.

In the oil remaining in the pan, sauté the asparagus over medium-low heat until the stalks change color and start to become tender—about 5 to 7 minutes. (You may need to add another tablespoon or two of oil.) Remove the asparagus and place in an ovenproof gratin dish. Bring a cup of water to a boil and pour it over the asparagus. Then sprinkle the almond-bread mixture over the top. Bake for 15 minutes or until the asparagus is thoroughly cooked and most of the liquid has boiled away. Serve immediately.

Beets

If beets are young and tender, their tops can be cooked and served with them. Cook the tops and roots separately so that any sand clinging to the roots will not get mixed into the tops. Cut the tops to within an inch of the roots, rinse them carefully, chop into 1-inch pieces, and steam them in about 1 inch of boiling water. In a separate pan, boil the rinsed beets. Drain, slip the skins off, and cut them into slices or chunks, depending on their size. Mix them in with the beet tops and serve with a vinaigrette (page 263) or with olive oil and lemon juice.

Larger beets are delicious baked in the oven. The flavor is quite different and, naturally enough, drier than boiled beets. Just like baked potatoes, they can go in a 375-degree oven all on their own, though they will take longer than potatoes—about 1 hour. Once cooked, they may be dressed like boiled beets, with olive oil and either vinegar or lemon juice and a mighty sprinkling of fresh chopped herbs.

In Greece, small young beets, boiled in abundant salted water until they are tender, are drained, the skins slipped off, and served with skordalia (page 273). Or try the recipe for beet salad from Tunisia on page 81.

Beets with Yogurt and Tahini

Makes 4 to 6 servings

WHILE THIS IS A GREAT ADDITION to a meze or buffet table, it's also a lovely dish to accompany a simple piece of fried or grilled fish.

1 pound cooked beets, peeled (3 medium beets)

½ cup strained yogurt (see page 278)

sea salt

3 or 4 garlic cloves, crushed and minced

½ cup fresh lemon juice

¼ cup sesame paste (tahini)

Cut the beets in chunks in a serving bowl.

In a separate small bowl, mix together the strained yogurt, salt, garlic, lemon juice, and tahini. Pour over the beets and mix gently.

Serve at room temperature.

Broccoli and Broccoli Rabe

Italian cooks are in a class by themselves when it comes to broccoli and its stronger-flavored relative broccoli rabe—or broccoletti di rape or rapini, two other names by which this amazing vegetable is also known in American markets. Broccoli rabe's Chinese cousin, called variously *choy sum* or Chinese (white) flowering cabbage, is equally good in these recipes.

Steamed Broccoli or Broccoli Rabe with Garlic and Chili Pepper

Makes 6 to 8 servings

3 pounds fresh broccoli or broccoli rabe

2 garlic cloves, thinly sliced

½ cup extra-virgin olive oil

1 dried red chili pepper, or more to taste

½ teaspoon sea salt, or more to taste

A head of broccoli can be cooked as a single unit, but it's easier to trim away the thick lower stems and cut the head into individual florets with a couple of inches of stem attached. Rinse in a colander and set aside.

Broccoli rabe should be rinsed carefully and any yellow leaves and coarse stems cut away and discarded. For convenience in cooking, cut the flowering stems and leaves into 2-inch-long pieces.

For broccoli: bring about an inch of lightly salted water to a rolling boil and add the broccoli. Cook, partially covered, until the broccoli is starting to soften but not quite tender—about 5 minutes, depending on the thickness of the broccoli stems.

THE ALL-IMPORTANT BRASSICAS

Broccoli and broccoli rabe, cauliflower, Brussels sprouts, cabbage and kale, turnip greens and mustard greens, and their many sisters and cousins are all members of a family botanists call the *brassicas*—*B. oleracea* for broccoli, *B. rapa* for turnips and mustard greens. (You will also sometimes see the family referred to as cruciferous vegetables because of the cross-marking at the tip of the emerging flower bud that is characteristic of all family members.)

Brassicas are worth mentioning because they all, without exception, have a huge nutritional impact, full of beta-carotene and vitamins C and K; of minerals like calcium, phosphorus, and potassium; and of riboflavin and folacin. While the balance of these elements may change from one variety to another, they are all important. Moreover, they're excellent sources of dietary fiber. And most important of all, but little recognized until very recently, like all green vegetables, these leafy brassicas are excellent sources for the alpha-linolenic acid that is the parent of vital omega-3s.

So critical are these vegetables that at least one of them should appear on your table every day.

Fortunately this is not difficult. Throughout history people have recognized the importance of these vegetables, and one or more of them are characteristic of just about every food culture in the earth's temperate zones (they are difficult to grow in the tropics). This means that the family has become wide-ranging, with an enormous variety of textures, shapes, and flavors—though always with that underlying peppery sharpness, especially in their raw state, that marks all brassicas. Don't assume that only brassicas typical of Mediterranean kitchens and gardens are suitable to use in Mediterranean-style cooking. Asian cuisines also have an interesting range of brassicas (bok choy, gai choy or Chinese mustard, gai lon or Chinese broccoli, and many more). They are increasingly available in American produce markets, and I often use them in these Mediterranean recipes.

While the broccoli is cooking, in a skillet large enough to hold all the broccoli, gently sauté the garlic in the oil over medium-low heat. Add the chili, broken into smaller pieces or sliced. (For less heat, discard the pepper seeds and membranes.) Cook the garlic and pepper together, stirring, until the garlic is soft but not brown.

As soon as the broccoli is ready, drain it and turn it immediately into the hot garlic and chili oil. Cover the skillet and shake it to distribute the oil. Cook over medium heat for 10 to 12 minutes or until the broccoli is tender. Serve immediately, using any pan juices as a sauce.

For broccoli rabe: follow the directions above but you will not add water to the pan because broccoli rabe will cook in the moisture clinging to its leaves after rinsing. Sauté the garlic and chili in the oil and add the uncooked broccoli rabe directly into the skillet. Cook for about 12 to 15 minutes or until the broccoli rabe is tender.

Sautéed Greens with Garlic and Oil

Makes 6 servings

A RECIPE SIMILAR to the preceding is a great way to treat all manner of greens available in farmers' markets and supermarket produce sections, especially in wintertime when hot-weather vegetables like tomatoes and peppers are less interesting. I'm thinking of various kinds of kale, including newly fashionable Tuscan or lacinato kale, as well as turnip greens, collards, mustard greens, and the like. Spinach and chard are also valuable cool-weather greens—and all of these, of course, besides being tasty seasonal additions to the table, have terrific nutritional impact. Beyond antioxidants, these vegetables are all great sources of omega-3 fatty acids, which are so valuable in combating the chronic diseases associated with Westernized diets.

Any of these greens may be prepared in the following manner. Remove tough stems if necessary, chop the greens if you wish, rinse carefully (very carefully in the case of spinach, which tends to be sandy, especially if it comes from a local farm), and boil in the water clinging to the leaves, adding a little more water if the greens start to stick, until the greens are tender. The time will vary, from 10 minutes or less for fresh young spinach to as much as 30 minutes for more robust collards. Once the greens are tender, drain and chop. Then continue with this very simple procedure.

3 pounds fresh greens, cooked as described above

3 garlic cloves, chopped

¼ to ⅓ cup extra-virgin olive oil

1 dried chili pepper

sea salt

1 or 2 tablespoons aged wine vinegar or fresh lemon juice

In a saucepan large enough to hold all the greens, sauté the garlic very gently in the oil over medium-low or low heat until the garlic is very soft but not taking color. Add the dried chili pepper, broken in bits (for less heat, discard the seeds and white membrane before adding to the pan), and stir it in. Add the chopped greens and stir and turn them in the aromatic oil until they have completely absorbed it. As soon as the greens start to sizzle in the heat of the pan, remove from the heat, stir in salt and vinegar or lemon juice to taste, and serve immediately, on their own or poured over lightly toasted slices of country-style bread that have been rubbed lightly with a cut clove of garlic and dribbled with a small amount of olive oil.

Variation: Lebanese cooks serve greens like this with chopped onions added to the greens and a tasty onion garnish made by sautéing a good pound of very thinly sliced onions in extra-virgin olive oil until they are golden brown and crisp, then draining them well and sprinkling them over the top of the greens when they're served.

Cabbage and Kale

Cabbage is a vegetable that is so easily ruined by overcooking that it's a wonder anyone bothers to eat it anymore. And in fact, not many people do. It's one of those vegetables people seem to get more often in restaurants than anywhere else, and there too it's served with an indifference that borders on contempt. The obligatory creamy coleslaw in a sticky sweet and sour sauce is not cabbage at its finest. Nor is the smell of overcooked cabbage—the cabbage in a big pot of water that sat on the back of the stove and simmered all day, lending its unforgettable aroma to tenement staircases.

Poor cabbage! Fortunately, smart young chefs are beginning to take a look at the maligned vegetable and devise ways to make it more acceptable. It isn't hard, especially when you combine cabbage with olive oil, garlic, and aromatic herbs. Cabbage should be cooked either briefly in a large quantity of water or—if you must cook it a long time, as in recipes for braised cabbage—in a small quantity of oil and/or stock.

Sizzling Cabbage with Garlic

Makes 8 servings; ¼ cabbage per serving

USE SMALL, FIRM ROUND CABBAGES or crinkly-leaved Savoy cabbages. Peel away the outer layer of leaves and rinse before using.

2 small cabbages

sea salt

1 garlic clove, minced

½ cup extra-virgin olive oil

freshly ground black pepper

Preheat the oven to 400 degrees. Quarter the cabbages and remove part of the central stem, but leave enough to hold the leaves together.

Bring lightly salted water to a rolling boil. Boil the cabbage quarters rapidly for 5 to 7 minutes, until the cabbage starts to soften but does not get limp.

Combine the garlic and oil in a shallow bowl like a soup plate. Drain the cabbages and immediately dip each quarter in the olive oil, turning it to coat each side. Then set the quarters in an oval gratin dish and sprinkle with salt and pepper. Pour any remaining oil over the cabbages in the dish, cover the dish with aluminum foil, and slide the dish into the oven for about 5 minutes or just long enough to set the oil really sizzling. Remove the foil and let the cabbages sizzle a little longer—no more than 5 minutes—then serve immediately in the sizzling pan with slices of crusty country-style bread for sopping up the juices.

Sweet and Sour Cabbage

IF YOU THINK of sweet and sour combinations as something characteristic of Asian cuisines, think again: some of the most ancient recipes we know from the Mediterranean world (and that means going back at least to Classical Greece) set great store by the flavor blend of tart and sweet. And since cabbage is one of the oldest vegetables in the Mediterranean repertoire, it seems appropriate to give it this treatment, which actually comes from Italy by way of Elizabeth David. David used sugar in her recipe but honey is better and more authentic. Pancetta is what's called for in Italy; if you use bacon instead you will have a nice smoky flavor that goes well with cabbage.

1 green medium cabbage, weighing approximately 2 pounds

2 tablespoons extra-virgin olive oil

2 tablespoons minced pancetta or bacon

1 small onion, finely chopped

2 large ripe tomatoes, peeled, seeded (page 25), and chopped

1 tablespoon tomato concentrate, tomato extract, or sun-dried tomato paste dissolved in 2 tablespoons hot water

sea salt and freshly ground black pepper

1 tablespoon red wine vinegar

1 tablespoon honey

Cut the cabbage into thin strips, discarding the hard center stalks. Set aside.

In a saucepan large enough to hold all the cabbage, combine the oil and pancetta and set over medium heat. When the pancetta fat starts to run and sizzle, add the onion and cook, stirring, until the onion is soft but not brown. Add the tomatoes and the dissolved tomato paste and let cook until the tomatoes melt and dissolve into a thick sauce. Then stir in the cabbage, along with salt and pepper and the vinegar. Let cook for about 15 minutes, stirring occasionally, until the cabbage is thoroughly wilted. Be careful that the cabbage doesn't burn— if necessary, add a spoonful or two of boiling water. When the cabbage is wilted, stir in the honey and let cook for another 5 to 7 minutes, until you have a thick and flavorful sauce that naps the cabbage.

Braised Cavolo Nero with Chestnuts

PEELING CHESTNUTS IS TEDIOUS but worth it for the fine rich flavor and the textural contrast they add to any cabbage dish. When we're in Italy for Thanksgiving, this robustly flavored dish is a favorite on our table, made with *cavolo nero,* a type of very dark green kale that stands in the garden all winter, getting sweeter with each frost. It's an important source of vitamins when there's nothing else fresh to eat, and it's a magnificent source of all the powerful antioxidants the cabbage family comes armed with. Cavolo nero is increasingly available—often sold as Tuscan kale or lacinato kale.

24 fresh chestnuts

1 medium onion, diced

2 tablespoons extra-virgin olive oil

2 ounces slab bacon, diced (optional)

1 cup chicken stock (page 108)

2½ pounds cavolo nero (lacinato kale), or use ordinary kale

sea salt and freshly ground black pepper

Preheat the oven to 350 degrees. Prepare the chestnuts. With a sharp paring knife, carefully cut a cross on the rounded side of the chestnut, cutting right through the tough peel and into the flesh. When all the chestnuts are done, spread them out on a cookie sheet and roast for about 15 minutes or until the chestnuts have burst open along the cuts. Remove from the oven and peel the chestnuts, pulling away both the outer shell and the furry inner skin that clings to the nut. Stubborn chestnuts should be returned to the oven for further toasting.

In a pan large enough to hold all the chestnuts, cook the onion in the olive oil until it is soft but not brown—about 10 minutes. Add the bacon if desired and continue cooking until the bacon starts to render its fat—about 5 minutes. Turn the peeled chestnuts into the pan, raise the heat to medium, and stir the chestnuts to coat them with fat. When the fat starts to sizzle, pour in the stock, cover the pan, lower the heat to medium-low, and cook for 20 to 35 minutes, until the chestnuts are tender but still firm.

Meanwhile, clean the cavolo nero and cut away the hard stems. Hold a bunch of the leaves together in your hand and sliver the leaves every ½ inch or so. When all the cavolo nero is prepared, rinse it carefully in a colander under running water. Transfer to a large saucepan and cook it in the water clinging to the leaves, watching carefully and adding a very little boiling water if necessary to keep it from sticking. Cook for about 20 minutes or until the cavolo nero is very tender.

When the kale and chestnuts are done, combine them with their juices. Set over medium–high heat and cook rapidly, stirring frequently, to reduce the juices and concentrate them. Taste and add salt and pepper if desired. A few drops of lemon juice can also be added.

Variation: If you don't want to bother with the chestnuts, cook the cavolo nero with the pancetta and onions. Add a cup of cooked white beans as a garnish.

Carrots

Finely chopped carrot and celery, along with onion and garlic and some-times a little minced parsley, form the *battuto* or *soffritto,* which, like the French mirepoix, forms the basis of so many soups, stews, and sauces in the Mediterranean kitchen. I mention this because, in our urge to get more fresh vegetables into the diet, we might ignore this very good and efficient source. A medium carrot, minced and cooked in a sauce that will eventually serve six or eight people, may not seem like much in the way of a vegetable, but looked at as one part of a multifaceted and vitamin–rich combination, it takes on more importance.

See also the recipes for carrot salads, pages 82–83.

Carrots in Agrodolce

Italian Sweet and Sour Carrots

Makes 6 servings

Finishing vegetables in a sweet-and-sour sauce is an old Italian technique that I learned years ago from Elizabeth David's *Italian Food*. Mrs. David suggested the method for zucchini, but I find it works very well with fresh sweet carrots. This is also a good way to treat baby onions.

3 pounds firm, tender carrots, peeled and sliced no more than ½ inch thick

sea salt

1 tablespoon minced shallot or onion

¼ cup extra-virgin olive oil

freshly ground black pepper

3 tablespoons red wine vinegar

1 tablespoon sugar

2 tablespoons minced flat-leaf parsley

Drop the carrots into a pan of rapidly boiling lightly salted water. Cook for about 5 minutes or long enough to tenderize the carrots slightly but not cook them through. Drain the carrots.

Cook the shallot or onion in the olive oil over medium-low heat until just softened—about 5 to 10 minutes. Add the drained carrots and stir to coat the slices well with the oil. Grind some black pepper over, add a few tablespoons of hot water, cover the pan, and cook gently for about 5 minutes. Uncover the pan and pour in the vinegar. When the vinegar is boiling, add the sugar and stir the carrots in the liquid while it cooks down to a small amount of syrup that coats the carrots nicely. When the carrots are cooked, turn them out in a warm serving bowl, sprinkle with the parsley, and serve immediately.

Oven-Braised Carrots

Makes 6 to 8 servings

2 medium onions, halved and sliced

¼ cup extra-virgin olive oil

[cont. next page]

Preheat the oven to 375 degrees. In an ovenproof casserole, gently stew the onions in the olive oil over medium-low heat until they are soft but not browned—about 10 to 15 minutes.

3 pounds young, tender carrots, peeled

1 cup chicken or vegetable stock (page 108 or 107)

sea salt and freshly ground black pepper

⅓ cup freshly grated parmigiano reggiano cheese

Cut the carrots in half lengthwise, then into sections about 2 inches long. Add the carrots to the casserole and stir to mix well. Pour in the stock with salt to taste and a good quantity of black pepper. When the stock comes to a boil, cover the casserole with a lid or heavy aluminum foil and bake for about 40 minutes or until the carrots are very soft.

Remove the casserole from the oven, stir the carrots, and sprinkle the cheese over the top. Return to the oven, uncovered, and cook until the stock has reduced to a few tablespoons of bubbling syrup and the cheese is melted. Serve immediately.

Carrots in a Chermoula Sauce

✺ Makes 6 to 8 servings

A MOROCCAN MIXTURE of aromatics suspended in oil, chermoula is used as a sauce for vegetables or a marinade for fish. Feel free to change the quantities or to add and subtract—each cook in Morocco has his or her own balance, which, it is always claimed, is the only authentic and genuine chermoula. Only cumin and sweet paprika seem to be constants, although cilantro is almost always present. If you don't care for the flavor of cilantro, use parsley instead. This is the version Sakina el-Alaoui, a fine Marrakesh cook, uses for carrots and zucchini. I've also used it successfully with autumn squashes, split in half and roasted in a 375-degree oven until tender, then dressed with the chermoula.

2 pounds carrots, peeled and cut into 2-inch chunks

FOR THE CHERMOULA

1 garlic clove, crushed with the flat blade of a knife

2 tablespoons minced cilantro

2 tablespoons minced flat-leaf parsley

If the carrots are very thick, cut each chunk in half lengthwise. Put the carrots into a saucepan and just barely cover with boiling water. Cook, partially covered, until they are soft and tender—about 15 minutes.

Meanwhile, chop the garlic and mix with the cilantro, parsley, salt, paprika, and cumin. Beat in the oil and lemon juice. Taste and adjust the

½ teaspoon sea salt

1 teaspoon sweet paprika, preferably Spanish pimentón dulce

¼ teaspoon ground cumin

3 tablespoons extra-virgin olive oil

juice of 1 lemon

seasoning, adding more salt or lemon juice if you wish.

As soon as the carrots are done, drain them and while they are still hot pour the chermoula sauce over. Stir gently to cover the carrot pieces with the sauce. Set aside to marinate for at least 30 minutes before serving. Serve at room temperature.

Cauliflower

Cauliflower with a Veil of Grated Cheese

Makes 6 to 8 servings

1 tablespoon extra-virgin olive oil

about 3 pounds firm white cauliflower

2 cups chicken or vegetable stock (page 108 or 107)

½ cup coarsely grated aged cheese, such as aged pecorino or manchego, asiago, or parmigiano reggiano

sea salt and freshly ground black pepper

Preheat the oven to 400 degrees. Lightly oil a gratin dish large enough to hold all the cauliflower.

Break the cauliflower into small florets of uniform size. Bring the stock to a boil in a pan large enough to hold the cauliflower. Add the cauliflower, cover, and steam for about 8 to 10 minutes or until the cauliflower is just tender. Using kitchen tongs, remove the cauliflower, reserving the cooking liquid, and place in the gratin dish. Dribble the remaining olive oil over the cauliflower and set the dish aside but keep warm while you finish the sauce.

Rapidly boil down the stock remaining in the pan until you have just a few tablespoonfuls of syrupy sauce. This should take 7 to 10 minutes.

Spoon the sauce over the cauliflower, then distribute the cheese over the top. Add salt and pepper. Transfer the dish to the preheated oven just long enough for the cheese to melt and brown very lightly. Remove from the oven and serve immediately.

Gratin of Cauliflower with Tomato Sauce

3 tablespoons extra-virgin olive oil

1 garlic clove, chopped

1 medium yellow onion, chopped (about 1 cup chopped onion)

3 or 4 anchovy fillets, chopped

2 cups canned plum tomatoes, with their juice

sea salt

ground or crumbled dried red chili pepper, to taste

¼ cup finely chopped or slivered basil or flat-leaf parsley

2 pounds cauliflower, trimmed and broken into florets

3 tablespoons dry bread crumbs

½ cup coarsely grated parmigiano reggiano cheese

¼ cup finely chopped blanched almonds

To make the tomato sauce, combine a tablespoon of oil with the garlic and onion in a skillet over medium heat. Cook, stirring, until the vegetables have softened, then stir in the chopped anchovies and continue cooking, mashing the anchovies into the oil with a fork. Add the tomatoes with their juice and raise the heat to medium. Cook the tomato sauce rapidly, breaking up the tomatoes with a cooking fork or a big spoon. Simmer for about 20 minutes or until the sauce is thick, then add salt and a big pinch of chili. When the sauce is thick, remove from the heat and stir in the basil or parsley. Set the sauce aside.

Set the oven at 425 degrees.

Bring a few inches of lightly salted water to a rolling boil and add the cauliflower. Cover and cook for 5 to 7 minutes or until the cauliflower is just tender all the way through. Drain the cauliflower and set aside.

Rub a tablespoon of oil over the bottom and sides of an oval gratin or other oven dish. Sprinkle a tablespoon of bread crumbs over the bottom and sides of the dish. Arrange the cauliflower in the dish and spoon the tomato sauce over it. Combine the grated cheese, almonds, and remaining bread crumbs and sprinkle over the top. Dribble the remaining tablespoon of oil on top and transfer the dish to the preheated oven to bake for about 15 minutes or until the top is brown and the sauce is bubbling.

Serve immediately, piping hot, or let cool to room temperature.

Chard with Onions and Black Olives

Makes 6 servings

THE SWEETNESS OF CHARD is a nice foil with pungent black olives, but this dish is also good with escarole, dandelion greens, or spinach, depending on the season.

3 pounds of greens, cleaned, rinsed, steamed, and chopped

1 bunch scallions, trimmed and sliced on the diagonal

3 tablespoons extra-virgin olive oil

⅓ cup pitted chopped black olives

freshly ground black pepper

2 tablespoons aged red wine vinegar

Prepare the greens as described in the headnote on page 299.

Combine the sliced scallions and the olive oil in a skillet large enough to hold all the greens. Set over medium heat and cook, stirring, until the scallions have started to soften. Stir in the black olives, then add the chopped greens, mixing well to distribute the olives throughout.

When the greens begin to sizzle in the oil in the pan, add plenty of black pepper and the vinegar. Stir once more, then let the vinegar come to a simmer. As the vinegar starts to cook away, remove the greens from the heat and serve immediately.

GARLIC

I know of no recipe in all the Mediterranean for garlic on its own, with the exception of Spanish garlic soup (page 125). But the importance of garlic in cuisines all over the region is undeniable. Whether a mere whisper, a half a clove crushed and mixed with lots of other ingredients, or a prominent flavoring in itself (as in the lamb recipe on page 425), garlic is, as the old saw has it, as good as ten mothers in terms of what it does for us and for our food. It acts as an antibiotic and an antiviral, it's a powerful antiseptic, it boosts immune activity, it lowers cholesterol, it keeps the blood thin, it helps lower blood pressure, it's good for the cardiovascular system—and, understandably, it's particularly effective at keeping vampires away. The antioxidant allicin is one of garlic's important properties but curiously allicin is only released when garlic is crushed or finely chopped. For that reason, when it's appropriate, it's a good idea to add raw garlic to your food. When you add garlic to a soup or sauce at the start of cooking, for the most efficient use, plan to stir a little chopped raw garlic into the dish at the very end, too.

Eggplant

One of the most endearing traits of the Turks is their candid pride in their own cuisine. Every Turkish cookbook begins with two pronouncements: (1) that Turkish is one of the world's three great cooking styles, the other two being French and Chinese; and (2) that there are at least 200 recipes for preparing eggplants in traditional Turkish cookery. One might dispute the primacy of the "great" cuisines, but one would not dispute the prominence of eggplant in Turkey and in every country from the Balkans around through North Africa where the influence of Turkish culture and the Turkish kitchen has been felt. Eggplants have a uniquely voluptuous flavor and texture—which is probably why the Turks, a sensuous people, love them so much.

Eggplants, or aubergines to give them their English name (which is closer to the names used in the Mediterranean), actually came into the Mediterranean with the Arabs, but the vegetable achieved apotheosis with the introduction of New World tomatoes, so much so that there is scarcely a recipe for eggplant that doesn't include tomatoes in some form, even if it's just a tablespoon of tomato paste diluted with water and added to a sauce.

We used to think that eggplant was a nutritionally neutral vegetable, that is, not bad for you but not particularly good for you either except as a platform for tomatoes, sweet peppers, garlic, and onions. In recent years, though, researchers have found that eggplant, like most traditional vegetables, does indeed have nutritional benefits in the form of some powerful antioxidants, including one in particular called chlorogenic acid. Eggplant is almost invariably used in combination with other ingredients and that may well be the source of its benefits, since modern researchers are beginning to explore the possibility that, in many of these traditional dishes, the sum is indeed greater than its parts—in other words, that eggplant and tomatoes, just for instance, may have a greater nutritional impact together than either vegetable has on its own.

The greatest problem with eggplant is its ability to soak up oil or any other kind of cooking fat. For traditional cooks this was hardly a problem, particularly when the fat was something as delicious as fresh green olive oil or perhaps the salt-preserved tail fat from a fat-tailed sheep.

For contemporary cooks the problem of fat absorption is said to be solved by salting the cut eggplants, whether in slices or chunks, and setting them aside to let the bitter juices drain away. I don't find our modern eggplants to be particularly bitter, but I am persuaded that salting them reduces their ability to absorb oil to any significant degree. I salt eggplant slices or chunks when I fry them, but otherwise not. In Spain, I learned recently, cooks soak eggplant slices in milk for several hours for a similar effect.

When it's appropriate, you can control the amount of oil by slicing the eggplants rather thickly, painting the slices on both sides with a small amount of oil, and grilling or broiling them. This is one of the best vegetables for grilling over charcoal or wood embers. The creamy flesh absorbs a delightful smokiness from the fire. Small eggplants can be cut in half, the cut sides scored and dribbled with olive oil, before grilling; larger eggplants should be sliced—lengthwise if you wish. For other eggplant recipes, see ratatouille (page 66) and roasted eggplant salad (page 56).

The number of eggplant types available in American produce markets seems to increase each season. Best for Mediterranean preparations are the familiar dark violet to black pear-shaped ones, sometimes called *Italian*. Look for eggplants that are not more than 6 to 8 inches long and have a good heft to them. Lighter eggplants have been stored too long and lost moisture.

Karni Yarık

Turkish Eggplant Stuffed with Meat and Rice

Makes 8 servings

OF THE WHOLE REPERTOIRE of Turkish ways with eggplant, this is one of the most popular and a good illustration of how a small amount of meat can be used as a flavoring, rather than a primary ingredient, to add richness to main-course vegetable presentations. Serve *karni yarık* as a main course with cacık (page 59) on the side and a copious salad such as fattoush (page 87).

Dried mint, rather than fresh, is used here for its sweet intensity.

1¼ cups finely chopped yellow onion

about ¼ cup extra-virgin olive oil, or more if needed

[cont. next page]

Prepare the stuffing: in a skillet over medium-low heat, gently cook the onion in 2 tablespoons of the olive oil. After about 5 minutes, when the onion starts to soften, add the green peppers. Cook for 10 to 15 minutes or until the vegetables are soft but not browned. Remove the vegetables from the skillet, along with the cooking oil, and set aside.

1 cup finely chopped sweet
green pepper, preferably
cubanelle or Italian long
peppers

½ pound lean ground lamb

1¼ cups chopped fresh or
well-drained canned Italian
plum tomatoes

1 tablespoon dried mint

1 tablespoon ground cumin

½ teaspoon hot red pepper
flakes

sea salt and freshly ground
black pepper

1 cup cooked long-grain rice
(about ½ cup raw)

¼ cup minced flat-leaf parsley

8 small eggplants (one per
serving) or 4 larger ones,
halved

1 very ripe tomato, thinly
sliced

⅓ cup freshly grated
parmigiano reggiano cheese

Add the lamb to the skillet and sauté quickly,
raising the heat and stirring constantly until the
lamb is thoroughly browned—about 5 to 7
minutes. (If the lamb is especially lean, you
might need to add a teaspoon or more of olive
oil.) Scrape the lamb with its fat into a sieve to
drain. Discard the fat and return the lamb to the
skillet along with the onion-pepper mixture.
Add the chopped tomatoes and seasonings and
mix well. Cook, stirring occasionally, over
medium-low heat until the tomatoes have
released all their liquid and the sauce has thickened
but not dried out—about 15 minutes. Taste and
adjust the seasonings.

Remove the skillet from the heat and stir in the
rice and parsley, mixing well. Set aside until you're
ready to use it. (The stuffing can be prepared a day
or more ahead of time and refrigerated, but bring
it back to room temperature before proceeding
with the recipe.)

Preheat the oven to 350 degrees. Rinse the
eggplants. Leave them whole, but prick them with
a fork in half a dozen places. (If you use larger
eggplants, cut them in half lengthwise, score the
cut surfaces in a crisscross pattern no more than ½
inch deep, and then paint them with a very little
olive oil.) Place the eggplants on a lightly oiled
baking sheet (cut side up if you're using halves) and
bake for 30 to 40 minutes or until the flesh is soft.
Set aside until cool enough to handle.

Using a table knife and spoon, gently cut a slit
down one side of the whole eggplants so that
you can open them up and push the flesh to
either side—but don't cut them into two separate
halves. Pile up several heaped tablespoonfuls of
stuffing in the center of each eggplant. (If you're
using halved eggplants, break up the cooked flesh
with the tines of a table fork to make room for the
stuffing.) Be careful not to cut through the
eggplant skin.

Set the stuffed eggplants in a lightly oiled rectangular roasting pan. Raise the oven temperature to 450 degrees. Place one or two tomato slices on top of each eggplant and dribble a teaspoon of olive oil over each. Sprinkle a little grated cheese on top of the tomato slices. Bring a teakettle of water to a boil and pour water into the roasting pan to a depth of about ½ inch. Bake for 15 to 20 minutes or until the tops are nicely browned.

Set the eggplants aside until you're ready to serve. They should be served warm or at room temperature but not cold.

Eggplant Stuffed with Ricotta and Herbs

THIS IS A RARE RECIPE for eggplant, one that doesn't include tomatoes. It goes back to pre-tomato Italy and was inspired by the great gourmet Castelvetro's instructions for preparing eggplant.

3 or 4 small eggplants (½ eggplant per serving)

sea salt

1 medium onion, chopped

2 garlic cloves, minced

⅓ cup extra-virgin olive oil

⅓ cup long-grain rice, parboiled for about 8 minutes to soften the grains

¼ cup minced flat-leaf parsley

¼ cup minced green herbs such as borage, lovage, basil, summer savory, thyme, oregano, or a combination

¾ cup ricotta cheese

[cont. next page]

Cut each eggplant in half lengthwise and, using a small paring knife or a grapefruit spoon, carefully hollow out the halves, leaving a shell not more than ½ inch thick. Sprinkle a little salt over the eggplant shells and turn them upside down to drain in a colander or on a cake rack while you proceed with the recipe. Coarsely chop the eggplant flesh.

In a sauté pan over medium-low heat, gently sauté the chopped eggplant with the onion and garlic in 2 tablespoons of the olive oil until the vegetables are thoroughly softened but not brown—about 15 minutes. Remove the pan from the heat and stir in the rice, herbs, and ricotta. Add Tabasco if you wish. Mix well, taste, and add salt and pepper if desired.

Preheat the oven to 350 degrees. Rinse the eggplant shells to rid them of excess salt and pat

dash of Tabasco sauce or cayenne pepper (optional)

freshly ground black pepper

½ cup toasted unseasoned bread crumbs

¼ cup freshly grated parmigiano cheese

the insides dry with paper towels. Lightly oil a baking dish. Mound the stuffing loosely in each shell and set the shells in the baking dish. Sprinkle the tops with the bread crumbs and cheese and drizzle the remaining oil over them.

Add about ½ inch of boiling water to the baking pan and bake for 30 to 40 minutes or until the tops are golden brown. Remove from the oven and let cool slightly before serving.

Eggplant in a Sauce of Peppers and Tomatoes

Makes 4 to 6 servings

B ECAUSE THIS DISH is customarily served at room temperature, it can be made well ahead. Don't, however, serve it chilled from the refrigerator— room temperature is when it's at its best.

about 1 pound eggplant (2 small or 1 large)

sea salt

2 large sweet peppers, preferably green and red

¼ cup extra-virgin olive oil

1 medium yellow onion, chopped

1 garlic clove, chopped

3 large very ripe tomatoes, peeled, seeded (page 25), and chopped

½ cup slivered basil

1 tablespoon salt-cured capers, rinsed and chopped

freshly ground black pepper

Cut the eggplant, unpeeled, into 1-inch cubes. Set them in a colander, sprinkle liberally with salt, and put a plate over them with a weight (a can of tomatoes is fine) on top. Set the colander in the sink or over a bowl to drain for about 1 hour, then rinse the salt off and dry the cubes thoroughly with paper towels, pressing to extract most of the moisture.

Core the peppers, discarding the seeds and white membranes, and chop into big pieces.

In a large skillet over medium heat, sauté the eggplant cubes in the olive oil until they are brown. (The cubes must be very dry to brown.) As the cubes brown, remove them from the oil and set aside. When all the eggplant has browned, lower the heat to medium-low or low and add the peppers, onion, and garlic to the pan. Cook gently until the peppers and onion are soft. Do not let the onion or garlic brown.

Return the eggplant to the skillet, along with the chopped tomatoes, stirring to mix everything together well. Cook for about 20 to 30 minutes or until the tomatoes are reduced to a thick sauce that naps the eggplant and peppers. Stir in the slivered basil and capers. Add black pepper and, if necessary, salt.

You may serve this immediately but it's customary to serve it at room temperature.

Onsa's Eggplant Tajine

Tagine d'Aubergines

Makes 8 servings as a main course; 10 to 12 servings as a starter

ONSA MAHJOUB IS MARRIED to the family that makes what is arguably Tunisia's finest olive oil. Once when I was visiting the Mahjoubs, collecting recipes from Onsa's seven sisters-in-law, she promptly invited me to taste *her* specialty—a tagine of layered eggplant, pumpkin, and chicken. It was delicious and it has one great virtue beyond that: it can be made ahead and served at room temperature; in fact, it's better at room temperature than it is steaming hot.

2 pounds eggplant (2 medium eggplants)

sea salt

2 pounds pumpkin or dark-yellow squash such as Hubbard or butternut

1½ cups plus 2 tablespoons extra-virgin olive oil

12 ounces (¾ pound) skinless, boneless chicken, in bite-size pieces

[cont. next page]

Slice the eggplant on the diagonal, about ¼ to ½ inch thick. Arrange the slices in a colander, sprinkling each layer liberally with salt. Set a plate on top of the eggplant and weight it (a can of tomatoes works fine for this). Set the colander in the sink for about 1 hour to drain any bitter juices from the eggplant.

Peel the pumpkin or squash and cut in slices about ¼ to ½ inch thick. Set aside.

Mix the chicken in a saucepan with a tablespoon of olive oil and the chopped scallions. Add water

7 or 8 plump scallions (1 bunch), chopped to make ¾ cup

¼ cup capers, well drained

2 or 3 long green Italian peppers

½ cup grated gruyère cheese

6 eggs

just barely to cover, bring to a boil, lower the heat to a simmer, and cook until the chicken is tender, about 10 minutes. Drain and add the chicken and scallions to a food processor with another tablespoon of oil, the capers, and a pinch of salt. Process to make a coarse paste—you'll have about 1½ cups when done.

Bring 1½ cups of olive oil to frying temperature (360 degrees) in a deep skillet or frying pan and add the pumpkin slices, a few at a time. Fry on both sides until the pumpkin turns a deeper shade of golden orange, then remove and drain on a rack or in a colander.

Rinse the eggplant slices carefully under running water to get rid of excess salt, then pat them very dry with paper towels. When the pumpkin is done, fry the eggplant slices in the same oil, turning once, until golden brown on both sides. Remove to a rack or colander to drain well.

Lower the heat slightly and add the whole, rinsed peppers to the pan. Cook, turning frequently, until the transparent outer skin of the peppers has started to lift off and the peppers themselves are softened. Remove and set aside, preferably in a paper bag, to soften.

(The recipe may be done well ahead to this point and the final dish assembled about an hour before you're ready to serve it.)

When you're ready to do the final baking, preheat the oven to 375 degrees. Line the bottom of an oval gratin dish with half the drained eggplant slices. Arrange half the pureed chicken over the eggplant and sprinkle with about ¼ cup of the grated cheese. Arrange the pumpkin slices over this. Beat one of the eggs with a fork in a small bowl and drizzle over the pumpkin. Then add the rest of the chicken, the remaining cheese, and the remaining eggplant slices.

Cut the peppers in quarters lengthwise, discarding the stem and core and any white veins from the insides. Lift away the transparent skin where it's easy to do that (you don't need to be too finicky about this). Slice the pepper quarters lengthwise about ¼ inch thick and use the slices to make a lattice over the eggplant.

Now beat the remaining eggs together well and pour over the top of the dish, tilting the dish to get egg all around it. Transfer to the preheated oven and bake for 40 minutes or until the tagine is set and firm, lightly browned on top, but not tough and rubbery.

Remove and let sit for 20 minutes or so before serving.

Favas or Broad Beans and Peas

Fava beans, or broad beans, to give them their proper English name, are not well known in this country. All the more curious since they were a familiar staple of colonial kitchen gardens. Nowadays, they're more likely to be known by their Italian name, *fave* or favas, and to be available only in Greek or Italian neighborhood produce shops. Why this should be so is a culinary mystery. The fact is that they are delicious, with a delicately earthy flavor that becomes exaggerated and even unpleasant as they mature.

Most American cookbooks, if they mention broad beans at all, suggest not only shelling them from the thick green pods (lined with a soft fuzz in which the beans lie like green babes in a nursery) but also peeling away the outer skin from each bean. To which I say, if you have to go through all that, favas ain't worth eating.

Broad beans should be eaten as they are in the Mediterranean, when they are young and tender and the pods are limber rather than stiff and tough. Shell them if you wish, although the most slender beans can be eaten pods and all, just topped and tailed and cut into lengths like string beans. Or you can mix the two together, shelled beans and beans in the pod, as Middle Eastern cooks do. It is hard to find fava beans of this quality here, but they are very easy to grow and don't take up a lot of space in the home garden, where they happily tolerate cold weather. (In Mediterranean gardens the seeds are planted at Christmas, about 3 inches underground, and the plants spring up in early March, so there are usually plenty of broad beans for a late Easter.)

Peas, on the other hand, may be one of the few vegetables that are really popular with Americans, although we tend to consume far more of them frozen than we ever do fresh. But can anything in the whole vegetable kingdom actually compare with sweet June peas lightly simmered when they're still dewy fresh from the garden? Well, yes, as any gardener knows, the one thing that beats that is standing in the garden row itself, just about twilight, and eating peas, pod by pod, out of hand—that is truly Edenic fare.

The market gardens that surround Rome and supply much of the produce for the city are famous for the quality of both fava beans and tiny sweet *piselli romaneschi,* which arrive next in spring's progression. A *scorpacciata,* which my dictionary translates as "blowout," is how Romans celebrate the delicious evanescence of this season—they eat their fill and then eat some more, because their time is so brief.

Don't even think of trying the recipe below unless you raise your own vegetables or otherwise have access to the very finest quality of fresh, young produce.

Fava (Broad) Beans or Peas Roman Style

✴ Makes 6 servings

L IKE MANY ROMAN PREPARATIONS, these are traditionally made with *strutto,* a very fine and tasty lard, and *guanciale,* the cured cheeks of pork, a mixture of fat and lean. That is still the best way (and remember that lard is lower in cholesterol than butter), but since good lard and cured pork cheeks are all but impossible to find in this country, I have adapted the recipe.

¼ cup finely diced onion

⅓ cup extra-virgin olive oil

2 or 3 slices of pancetta or prosciutto, diced

3 to 4 pounds tender young fava (broad) beans or peas, shelled or, if the favas are tender, cut up like string beans

In a saucepan large enough to hold all the beans, gently cook the onion in the olive oil until it is very soft but not brown—about 10 to 15 minutes. Add the prosciutto and stir until the fat starts to run, about 5 to 7 minutes. Add the beans and stir to coat them well. Pour in the stock and add the salt, pepper, parsley, and thyme.

1 cup chicken stock
(page 108) or water

sea salt and freshly ground
black pepper

1 tablespoon minced flat-leaf
parsley

½ teaspoon minced fresh
thyme or ¼ teaspoon dried,
crumbled

Raise the heat to a fast boil. Cook quickly, without covering, so that the beans retain their bright color and all their flavor. By the time the cooking is done and the beans are tender, there should be just a few spoonfuls of rather syrupy liquid in the bottom of the pan, good for sopping up with wedges of country bread. Remove from the heat and serve immediately.

Koukia me Anginares

Broad Beans with Artichokes

Makes 6 servings

THIS GREEK DISH, which is substantial enough to be a main course (perhaps with some bread and a good sheep's milk cheese to go along with it), requires not only top-quality fava beans but also fresh small young artichokes, preferably the lovely violet ones, two to a serving. These are almost impossible to find in this country, so use larger artichokes, counting on one to a person.

12 small artichokes or 6 large
ones

1½ pounds fresh young fava
beans

1 medium onion, coarsely
chopped

2 tablespoons minced dill

1 teaspoon minced mint
leaves

½ cup extra-virgin olive oil

juice of 1 lemon

sea salt and freshly ground
black pepper

Prepare the artichokes as described on page 26. Large artichokes should be quartered and the chokes removed.

Shell the fava beans. The youngest and slenderest can be kept in the pods but should be topped and tailed, like green beans, and cut into approximately 1½-inch lengths. Put the beans, onion, and herbs in a pan large enough to hold all the vegetables. Add the olive oil and set the pan over medium-low heat. Cook, stirring frequently, for 10 to 15 minutes or until the onions have softened but not browned. Then push the drained artichokes into the bean mixture and add the lemon juice, a little salt and pepper, and water just to come to the tops of the vegetables. Cover tightly and cook, just simmering, for about 20 minutes or until the artichokes are tender enough to be pierced by the point of a knife. Remove from the heat and let stand for 20 to 30 minutes before serving.

Fennel

For inexplicable reasons, fennel (the blanched white bulb, that is, not the seeds) is often called *anise* in American produce markets. If you don't know what to look for, ask the produce manager for anise—that's fennel, and you won't find it called anything else in cookbooks.

Italians believe raw fennel cleanses the palate and often serve it as an end-of-the-meal salad, thickly sliced and dressed with a little olive oil and lemon juice or wine vinegar. It is also occasionally served braised with a sprinkling of grated parmigiano reggiano or aged pecorino cheese; follow the directions for Cauliflower with a Veil of Grated Cheese (page 307). Greek cooks marinate thick fennel slices with olive oil, salt, and pepper, then grill the slices over charcoal or wood embers.

Provençal Marinated Fennel

Makes 6 to 8 servings

FENNEL IS SO DELICIOUS RAW that we often forget how good it can be when cooked. This treatment from Provence makes something very similar to the preparation called "*à la grecque*" (page 289).

6 firm fennel bulbs

6 tablespoons extra-virgin olive oil

sea salt and freshly ground black pepper

1 small celery stalk, thinly sliced

1 thin leek, thinly sliced

2 garlic cloves, crushed with the flat blade of a knife

Trim the fennel bulbs, slicing off some of the root end and removing the tough outer leaves. Then slice lengthwise into ¼- to ½-inch slices.

In a skillet or saucepan large enough to hold all the fennel, combine the olive oil with salt and pepper, the sliced celery and leek, crushed garlic, thyme, and bay leaves. Set over medium heat and as soon as the vegetables start to sizzle, add the pine nuts. Cook briefly, just until the pine nuts start to brown, then put in all of the fennel slices, spooning

1 tablespoon thyme leaves

2 bay leaves

1 tablespoon pine nuts

1 cup dry white wine

1 tablespoon sultana raisins or dried currants

1 tablespoon minced flat-leaf parsley

the other ingredients over them. Add the wine and raise the heat slightly to bring the wine to a boil, then lower the heat to simmer, cover the pan (with aluminum foil if you don't have a lid), and let the fennel cook for 15 minutes or until it is just tender.

Remove the cover and stir in the raisins and parsley. Continue cooking, uncovered, until the liquid has reduced to a syrup.

The fennel may be served hot from the pan, but it is really much better at room temperature with some of its cooking liquid spooned over.

Green Beans

What kind of green beans? Well there are the flat, broad ones called romano beans and little haricots verts, as narrow as shoelaces, and deep violet beans that turn green when cooked, and sturdy crisp round pole beans, like Blue Lake and Kentucky Wonder, cherished by American gardeners. Fresh green beans, like sweet corn and dead-ripe juicy tomatoes, are one of summer's great pleasures, not to be confused with the flaccid long-distance things that decorate supermarket produce sections out of season. Test the beans before you buy: if they break in two with a satisfying snap, they are ready to eat.

Green beans, steamed whole if they're small, broken into 2-inch pieces if they're larger, are an elegant hot first course, dressed with a light vinaigrette or just with plain olive oil, lemon juice, and salt and pepper. Cook a large quantity, at least ¾ pound per serving, and heap them in a big china bowl. They're so good they're addictive, like potato chips, and there are almost never enough.

Cooking times in the next two recipes may come as a surprise since we've heard for years about not *over*cooking vegetables. Yet Mediterranean cooks often stew green beans, and other vegetables too, for a long time, especially in combinations like these. The result is a remarkably good-tasting exchange of flavors.

Green Beans with Olive Oil and Tomatoes

GREEN BEANS STEWED until meltingly tender in a thick and aromatic sauce of fresh tomatoes are ubiquitous throughout the Mediterranean. When fresh green beans are at their peak in local markets, consider increasing the quantities and making this a main course, perhaps with salad, a wedge of cheese, and some good bread. It's a way of honoring the goodness of things as simple and ordinary as beans.

3 pounds green beans, topped and tailed, cut into 2-inch lengths if desired

1 cup finely chopped onion

1 garlic clove, finely chopped

¼ cup extra-virgin olive oil

2 cups chopped fresh tomatoes or chopped drained canned whole tomatoes

1 teaspoon sugar

1 teaspoon sea salt, or more to taste

1 tablespoon fresh lemon juice

In a saucepan large enough to hold the beans, cook the onion and garlic in the oil over low heat until the onion is thoroughly golden and starting to brown—about 10 to 15 minutes. Rinse the beans and, with the water that clings to them, turn them into the onions. Stir to mix everything together well, cover, and lower the heat to medium-low. Cook for about 5 minutes, just to meld the flavors.

Uncover the pan and add the tomatoes, sugar, and salt. Cover again and cook for about 20 minutes or until the beans are thoroughly softened and the tomatoes have dissolved into a sauce that naps the beans. Add a little boiling water from time to time if the sauce starts to stick. Stir in the lemon juice. Taste and adjust the seasoning, adding more salt if necessary.

Variation: Middle Eastern cooks add pinches of ground cumin and allspice to the tomato sauce that flavors the beans.

Fassolakia Yiahni

Ragout of Fresh Green Beans

Makes 6 servings

DIANE KOCHILAS was one of the first food writers to introduce Americans to the great and delicious variety of regional Greek food. This recipe is adapted from her first book, *The Food and Wine of Greece*. Diane tops the dish with crumbled feta cheese to make a main-course offering.

¼ cup extra-virgin olive oil

2 medium onions, halved and very thinly sliced

1 garlic clove, chopped

3 pounds fresh green beans, topped and tailed

4 medium potatoes, peeled and cut into chunks

4 or 5 fresh, ripe tomatoes, peeled (page 25) and coarsely chopped, or 1 28-ounce can whole tomatoes, drained and chopped

1 small dried hot red chili (optional)

sea salt and freshly ground black pepper

In a pan large enough to hold all the vegetables, warm the olive oil over medium-low heat. Add the onions and garlic and cook, stirring occasionally, until the onions are meltingly soft—about 10 to 15 minutes. Add the beans and potatoes and stir with a wooden spoon for a few minutes, until the vegetables are coated with oil and beginning to soften.

Add the tomatoes and chili and season with salt and pepper. Add a few tablespoons of water and cover the pot tightly. Simmer for about 1 hour, adding a little boiling water from time to time if necessary. The vegetables are done when they are very soft and the tomatoes are reduced to a thick sauce that naps the vegetables. The dish can be served hot but is more traditionally served at room temperature.

Leeks

Leeks are an essential ingredient in most broths and stocks, but they are also quite wonderful on their own, milder than onions but with a similar rich flavor. Gardeners blanch leeks, usually by hoeing soil up around the growing stems to retain their creamy whiteness. This leaves sandy traces between the leaves, so they need careful cleaning. To clean leeks, insert a knife tip about 1½ inches from the base and slide it back toward the green tips to slice the leek in half, leaving it attached at the base. Cut away the tough green leaves, but leave a little green for a more attractive presentation. Rinse very well in running water to get rid of the sand.

Oven-Braised Leeks

8 fat leeks, rinsed well

2 cups chicken or vegetable stock (page 108 or 107)

⅓ cup extra-virgin olive oil

juice of 1 lemon

1 celery stalk, cut into 1-inch pieces

¼ teaspoon dried oregano, crumbled

1 bay leaf

1 teaspoon black peppercorns

1½ teaspoons coriander seeds

sea salt and freshly ground black pepper

Preheat the oven to 375 degrees. Arrange the leeks in a single layer in a shallow ovenproof pan or gratin dish.

In a medium saucepan, combine all the remaining ingredients except salt and pepper. Bring to a boil and simmer for about 10 minutes, then pour over the leeks. Add a little salt and ground pepper to taste.

Cover the pan tightly with aluminum foil and bake for 15 to 20 minutes or until the leeks are just soft. Remove the foil and continue baking for 5 to 10 minutes or until the juice in the pan is reduced to a syrupy liquid and the leeks are starting to brown. Set aside and cool to room temperature before serving. Serve with crusty country-style bread for sopping up the juices.

Mushrooms

Mushrooms used in Mediterranean cooking are almost always wild, and the variety is staggering. Among the favorites most frequently seen in market stalls are fat porcini or cèpes (*Boletus edulis*), lovely apricot-colored chanterelles, and trompettes de la mort (a sort of black chanterelle that, despite the name—trumpets of death—is thoroughly safe to eat). There are also the dangerous but delicious ovoli or *Amanita caesarea*—dangerous because they are closely related to the deadly *Amanita phalloides,* or death cap, especially in the infant, egglike stage that gives them the name *ovoli*. Italians make a delicious salad from fresh ovoli, thinly shaved and combined with julienne strips of celery and shards of parmigiano cheese, all dressed with good oil and lemon juice and sometimes with a few shavings of white truffle over the top.

Mushrooms like these grow in deciduous woods and fields throughout the United States, but I cannot in good conscience recommend that you gather your own unless you know what you are about. If you are ignorant but curious, get in touch with a local mycological society—your local extension agent or state university school of agriculture should be able to help you.

Porcini or cèpes are the easiest mushrooms to recognize and are abundant in many parts of this country. If you find a lot, you might want to dry them for a source of intense flavor to add to stews, soups, and sauces. Here's how you do it:

Collect firm, healthy specimens, without any trace of bugs or slugs. Brush away any earth or leaves clinging to them, but *do not wash them*. Slice them about ½ inch thick and arrange the slices on a screen. Place the screens in the sun on a dry day and just leave them. You'll have to turn them occasionally and bring them in at night when the dew starts to collect. If they don't dry sufficiently in one day, set them out again in the morning. Alternatively, you can set them in a very slow oven, or use a commercial dehydrator. When the slices are thoroughly dry and powdery, they can be stored in a tin canister—but don't put them in plastic bags, or they'll mildew and turn soft.

Fresh wild mushrooms are increasingly available in the produce sections of well-stocked supermarkets. Shiitake, portobello, and cremini mushrooms, although cultivated, often have good flavor. But if you can't find wild or flavorful cultivated mushrooms, cook dried porcini with fresh commercial button mushrooms, as in the following recipe, to give the supermarket variety a taste of the wild.

Gratin of Mushrooms and Potatoes

Makes 4 to 6 servings

D RIED MUSHROOMS should be soaked before being used in very hot, but not boiling, water, then drained (don't discard the water!) and thoroughly rinsed to remove all traces of grit. The soaking liquid should be strained through a fine-mesh sieve and added to the cooking juices for flavor; or it can be frozen and added to soups and sauces. The flavor of dried wild mushrooms can vary enormously from one packet to the next. Keep that in mind in following this recipe and don't hesitate to alter the amount suggested if you find the flavor stronger or milder than you expected.

¾ ounce dried porcini, or
more to taste

[cont. next page]

Soak the mushrooms, following the directions above. When they're softened, strain the liquid into a bowl through a sieve lined with a double layer of

½ pound fresh commercial mushrooms

¼ cup extra-virgin olive oil

1 pound baking potatoes, peeled and thinly sliced

sea salt and freshly ground black pepper

2 medium tomatoes, thinly sliced, or 4 canned whole tomatoes, drained and coarsely chopped

¼ cup grated parmigiano reggiano cheese

¾ cup grated fresh mozzarella cheese

cheesecloth. Rinse the mushrooms carefully, squeeze dry, and chop coarsely.

Wipe the commercial mushrooms with a damp paper towel to remove any grit. Slice them about ¼ inch thick and sauté in 2 tablespoons of the olive oil in a heavy skillet over medium-high heat. Cook for about 5 minutes, stirring frequently. The mushrooms should be just starting to soften.

Preheat the oven to 400 degrees. Brush an oval gratin dish with a tablespoon of the remaining olive oil. Arrange the potatoes in a layer in the dish and pour in the mushroom-soaking liquid with a little salt and pepper. Scatter the fresh and dried mushrooms over the potatoes. Arrange the tomatoes in a layer over the mushrooms. Sprinkle with a little more salt, if desired, and more pepper. Drizzle the remaining tablespoon of olive oil over the top. Bake until the potatoes are just tender, 20 to 25 minutes.

Remove the dish from the oven. Combine the grated cheeses and sprinkle on top of the tomatoes. Return the dish to the oven and bake until the cheese is melted and forms a golden crust, about 10 minutes. Remove from the oven and let stand for about 15 minutes before serving.

Fricassee of Wild Mushrooms

Makes 4 to 6 servings

IF YOU DO FIND a good source of wild cèpes or porcini mushrooms, try this Tuscan way of preparing them.

about 4 pounds fresh wild mushrooms

Clean the mushrooms very well, brushing with a soft brush to remove earth or forest detritus and cutting away any spoiled or wormy bits. Do not

1 medium yellow onion,
chopped fine

⅓ cup extra-virgin olive oil

sea salt and freshly ground
black pepper

2 eggs

2 tablespoons fresh lemon
juice

4 to 6 thin slices country-
style bread, lightly toasted

clean with running water as porcini especially will become soggy; if necessary, use a damp towel to clean them. Cut the cleaned mushrooms in chunks.

In a skillet over medium-low heat gently sauté the onion in the oil until it is soft but not brown. Add the mushrooms and stir to mix. Raise the heat to medium and cook the mushrooms, stirring frequently. They will first absorb most of the oil, then, as they cook down, release it again. When they do so, add salt and pepper.

Beat together in a small bowl the eggs and lemon juice. Remove the mushrooms from the heat and immediately add the egg mixture, mixing fast so that the eggs form a thick cream rather than scrambled eggs. Have ready the toasted bread slices on individual plates and pour the mushroom cream over the bread. Serve immediately.

Okra

Okra Middle Eastern Style

Makes 4 to 6 servings

EXCEPT IN SOME PARTS of the South, okra is not well known in the United States. That may be because the okra on offer in supermarket produce sections is all too often old and tough. And that's a pity because it's a delicious vegetable when you can buy it fresh from the farmer who grew it. If you don't happen to have an okra farmer in the neighborhood, widely available frozen okra is an acceptable alternative.

Okra, in the same family as hollyhocks, has a slightly sticky quality that some people find disagreeable while others think it's part of okra's charm. In any case, that stickiness, which is contained within the pod, leaks out if the stem end is cut off the pod. Just trim the conical stem with a paring knife without slicing through the surface of the pod.

2 pounds fresh okra

3 tablespoons extra-virgin olive oil

1 medium yellow onion, chopped

3 ripe fresh tomatoes, peeled (page 25) and chopped, or use canned tomatoes

2 garlic cloves, thinly sliced

2 to 3 tablespoons finely minced cilantro

fresh lemon juice

sea salt and freshly ground black pepper

Trim the stem end of each okra pod as described in the headnote. Rinse the okra pods and toss them in a kitchen towel to dry them.

Add the oil to a skillet and set over medium heat. When the oil is hot, toss in the okra pods and sauté, stirring and rolling the pods about until they turn bright green and soften slightly. Remove with a slotted spoon and set aside.

Add the chopped onion to the same oil and lower the heat to medium-low. Cook the onion gently until it is softened but do not let it brown. As soon as the onion is soft, stir in the tomatoes and garlic and cook, stirring occasionally, until the tomatoes have thickened to a sauce. Now return the okra to the pan, along with about a cup of boiling water (the water should just come to the tops of the vegetables). Raise the heat and cook rapidly until most of the liquid has evaporated and the okra pods are tender. Stir in the cilantro and lemon juice, along with salt and pepper, then serve immediately.

Variation: In Beirut, Najwa Rawda, a fine Lebanese home cook, showed me a more substantial version of this dish when she browned in olive oil about a pound of very lean veal, cut in half-inch cubes, then added the meat to the okra along with the tomatoes.

Onions

Walnut-Stuffed Roasted Onions

Makes 6 servings

ONCE UPON A TIME, onions like these were roasted in the fireplace embers until their skins were blackened. Nowadays, we roast them in the kitchen oven instead and the walnut stuffing gives them extra appeal.

5 tablespoons extra-virgin olive oil

6 large yellow onions, unpeeled

½ cup diced pancetta or prosciutto

1 cup chopped walnuts

1 cup chicken stock (page 108)

sea salt and freshly ground black pepper

½ teaspoon thyme leaves

Set the oven at 375 degrees.

Rub 2 tablespoons of the olive oil all over the outsides of the unpeeled onions. Set them directly on the oven rack and roast for 40 minutes or until the onions are tender all the way through.

Remove the onions from the oven (do not turn off the oven). As soon as the onions are cool enough to handle, slice off the tops so that you can get at the insides. Using a serrated spoon, pull out the insides, leaving two or three layers intact on the outside. Chop the insides coarsely.

Heat another 2 tablespoons of oil in a skillet and add the pancetta dice. Cook, stirring, until the pancetta starts to yield up its fat and the little dice begin to turn brown. Stir in the walnuts and chopped onion, then add half the chicken stock, along with salt, pepper, and thyme. Let cook on medium heat for about 10 minutes or until the stock reduces slightly and naps the other ingredients.

Arrange the empty onions in a very lightly oiled baking dish and fill them with the walnut-pancetta stuffing. Add the remaining stock to the dish. Dribble a little of the remaining olive oil over the tops of the onions and add the rest to the baking dish. Transfer to the oven and bake another 20 minutes or until the onion tops are lightly browned. Remove from the oven and serve immediately.

Red Peppers with Garlic, Sausage, and Olives

Makes 4 to 6 servings

ANOTHER EXAMPLE of typical, traditional Mediterranean dishes, in which a very small amount of meat goes a very long way. You could serve this as a first course before one of the hearty bean-based soups on pages 134–138. If you use hot Italian sausages in this dish, you might want to omit the chili pepper.

3 or 4 fresh Italian-style sausages, hot or sweet as you prefer

3 tablespoons extra-virgin olive oil

2 pounds sweet peppers, preferably red ones

1 fresh chili pepper (optional)

1 medium yellow onion, halved and thinly sliced

4 garlic cloves, chopped

½ cup dry sherry

½ cup pitted black olives

1 3-inch strip of orange zest, finely slivered

⅓ cup slivered basil leaves

sea salt

Open the sausages and discard the skins. Coarsely crumble the sausage meat, then combine it with a tablespoon of the olive oil in a skillet over medium heat. Cook, stirring, until the meat is thoroughly browned, then remove with a slotted spoon, discarding the fat, and set aside.

Roast and peel the sweet peppers and the chili, as directed on page 26. Slice the sweet peppers lengthwise about ½ inch thick, the chili pepper in slivers, and set aside.

Add the rest of the oil to the skillet in which you browned the sausage and stir in the onion and garlic. Cook over medium-low heat until the onions are soft and melting, but not brown. Stir in the sherry and let it bubble up and cook, then add the pepper strips, olives, and slivered orange zest. Cook very briefly, just to combine the flavors, then stir in the sausage meat. If there's a lot of liquid in the pan, raise the heat slightly and cook down to a few syrupy tablespoons. Just before serving, stir in the slivered basil and salt if necessary.

Patatas à la Riojana

Potatoes Simmered in a Spicy Stew

A NA ESPINOSA COMES from a little pueblo near the cathedral city of Burgos in Old Castile, the heartland of Spain. These potatoes are her grandmother's recipe, but a similar sort of potato stew is served almost daily throughout the region. Sometimes, she says, it's the main dish of a meal, especially if enriched with sausages or meaty pork spareribs cooked along with the potatoes. This version has just a small amount of sausage for flavoring. Vegetarians can omit the sausage.

The chilies used in Spain have just enough heat to make you sit up and take notice. The best ones to use here are dried New Mexico (Anaheim) chilies. Removing seeds and inner membranes before soaking will also cut down on the heat of the chilies.

½ cup chopped onion

¼ cup extra-virgin olive oil

3 pounds potatoes, peeled and thickly sliced

about 6 ounces Spanish-style paprika-flavored chorizo or garlicky kielbasa, cut into ¼-inch-thick slices

1 sweet green pepper, thickly sliced

¼ cup coarsely chopped flat-leaf parsley

2 tablespoons sweet paprika, preferably Spanish pimentón dulce

[cont. next page]

In a deep kettle that will hold all the ingredients, sauté the onion in the oil over medium-high heat until it starts to soften but is not browned—about 10 minutes. Add the potatoes and continue cooking, stirring to mix well. Add the sausage, again stirring, and when the potatoes are just beginning to brown along their edges—about 10 minutes—add a cup of water. Cook for about 5 minutes. The potatoes will absorb much of the water during this time.

Add a second cup of water when the first has been pretty well absorbed, together with the green pepper, parsley, and sweet paprika.

Remove the chilies from the soaking liquid and discard the seeds and membranes. With a spoon

3 dried red New Mexico (Anaheim) chilies, soaked in water

¼ teaspoon hot paprika

sea salt

edge, scrape away the inner red pulp. Discard the skins and add the pulp to the potatoes, stirring to mix well. Cook for 8 to 10 minutes, until the potatoes are tender. Add the hot paprika and stir carefully to mix without breaking up the potatoes. Taste and add salt if desired. The potatoes should be fork-tender with just a little rich red sauce to spoon over their tops. Serve immediately.

Gratin or Tian of Potatoes

Makes 6 to 8 servings

THIS TRADITIONAL PROVENÇAL PREPARATION is proof that a good gratin need not be swimming in butter, cream, and cheese like the delectable ones from the Dauphiné. Potatoes are much more frequently used in the Mediterranean than we might expect.

¾ cup chicken stock (page 108)

3 pounds waxy potatoes, such as red bliss, peeled and thinly sliced

2 garlic cloves, minced

⅓ cup fruity extra-virgin olive oil

sea salt and freshly ground black pepper

2 bay leaves

Preheat the oven to 375 degrees. Bring the stock to a simmer in a small saucepan.

Toss the potatoes and garlic in a bowl with the olive oil until the potatoes are well coated. Arrange the slices in an oval gratin dish. Add salt and pepper to taste and tuck the bay leaves in with the potatoes. Pour the simmering stock over them. Cover the gratin dish with aluminum foil and bake for 40 minutes, by which time the potatoes should have absorbed most of the stock. Uncover the pan and continue baking for 10 minutes to brown the tops of the potatoes. Serve immediately.

Variation: Other vegetables, cut the same size as the potatoes, can be added to the gratin—turnips and celery root are obvious choices, but non-root vegetables would be good, too, such as thinly sliced winter squash or pumpkin.

Garlic-Roasted Potatoes with Black Olives

Makes 6 servings

2 pounds potatoes, unpeeled, cut into chunks, or whole small new potatoes

4 garlic cloves, chopped

3 rosemary sprigs

1 small hot dried red chili, crumbled

sea salt and freshly ground black pepper

¼ cup extra-virgin olive oil

24 large black olives, pitted and coarsely chopped

2 tablespoons minced flat-leaf parsley

Preheat the oven to 425 degrees. In a bowl, toss the potatoes with the garlic, rosemary, chili pepper, salt and pepper, and olive oil. Spread the potatoes about an inch or more thick in a small roasting pan or a gratin dish—thick enough so that you can't see the bottom of the pan through the potatoes. Roast, stirring occasionally with a wooden spoon, for about 25 minutes or until they are golden brown.

Remove from the oven and stir in the olives. Taste and add more pepper and salt if desired—the olives may be sufficiently salty. Sprinkle with parsley and serve.

Spinach

Remember how fast Popeye's muscles bulked up as he emptied the spinach can when danger threatened? He knew what he was doing, and so did your mother when she popped a spoonful of spinach on your plate. Loaded with iron, folate, and a whole host of antioxidants, spinach is a natural nutritional defense against everything from cardiovascular disease to osteoporosis. Better yet, it's delicious—much nicer in these recipes than anything Popeye was chugging out of that can!

Spinach is said to have originated in the East, possibly in Persia, and was brought into the Mediterranean by the Arabs when they swept across North Africa and into Spain, southern France, and Sicily. Certainly the many preparations of spinach with pine nuts and dark or golden raisins suggest an Arab origin.

Note that when spinach is not available, Mediterranean cooks don't hesitate to substitute fresh green chard.

Garbanzos kon Spinaka

Sephardic Spinach with Chickpeas from Greece

THIS RECIPE IS ADAPTED from a favorite and most unusual book, *Cookbook of the Jews of Greece,* by Nicholas Stavroulakis, founder of the Jewish Museum of Athens and a profound scholar of Mediterranean culture. Greek Jews came from two directions, the Sephardic from Spain, from which country they were expelled in 1492, and the Romaniote Jews from Palestine, who emigrated much earlier. Stavroulakis points out that there were Jews in Thessalonica at the time Saint Paul visited them in his evangelizing efforts, and they must have been there long before.

As with many Jewish recipes, nothing marks this as specifically Jewish— spinach is cooked with chickpeas all over the Mediterranean. But it was given to Stavroulakis by a Greek Jew from Larissa. And its name is Ladino, the language of Sephardic Jews, a dialect of old Spanish mixed with words of Turkish and Greek origin. It's tempting to see this as a recipe the Sephardim brought with them from Arab Spain to Greece.

This is delicious served over steamed rice and makes a first-rate vegetarian main course.

1 large onion, thinly sliced

2 tablespoons extra-virgin olive oil

1½ cups chickpeas, soaked overnight, or use the quick-soak method (page 25)

1 pound fresh spinach

½ cup minced dill

juice of 2 lemons

sea salt and freshly ground black pepper

Gently sauté the onion slices in the olive oil over medium-low heat until the onions are soft but not browned—about 10 to 15 minutes. Drain the chickpeas and add them to the onions, turning them to coat with the oil. Cover with water— about 1 cup will do—and simmer gently until the chickpeas are tender, about 40 minutes, adding a little *boiling* water from time to time if necessary.

Meanwhile, clean the spinach thoroughly, rinsing it in several changes of water and cutting away the thick stems. When the chickpeas are tender, add the spinach with the water clinging to its leaves and the dill and continue cooking very slowly until the spinach is tender—about 10 minutes. At the end of the cooking time, stir in the lemon juice and adjust the seasoning, adding salt if necessary and pepper.

Ligurian Spinach with Golden Raisins and Pine Nuts

Makes 4 to 6 servings

THIS WAY OF PREPARING spinach comes from Liguria, a region on the northwest coast of Italy but part of a culinary culture that extends in an arc from the Cinque Terre up and around Provence and down to the Catalan coast south of Barcelona. You'll find similar preparations all through that region.

2 pounds fresh spinach

¼ cup golden raisins

¼ cup pine nuts

3 tablespoons extra-virgin olive oil

½ medium onion, minced

½ garlic clove, minced with the onion

sea salt and freshly ground black pepper

a pinch of freshly grated nutmeg (optional)

Rinse the spinach carefully in two or three changes of water. Place the spinach in a large pot over medium heat, cover, and cook, stirring occasionally, in the water clinging to the leaves for about 10 minutes—don't overcook the spinach. Drain thoroughly and chop coarsely. You should have about 3 cups spinach. (The spinach can be cooked and chopped well ahead of time and then refrigerated until you're ready to use it.)

Cover the raisins with very hot water and set aside to refresh and plump.

In a saucepan over medium-low heat, gently sauté the pine nuts in the olive oil until golden, about 7 to 10 minutes, being careful not to burn them. Remove them from the oil and set aside. Add the onion and garlic to the oil and cook, stirring frequently, until soft but not brown—about 10 minutes. Stir in the chopped spinach and mix to combine thoroughly. Just before serving, drain the raisins and stir them into the spinach along with the toasted pine nuts. Add salt, pepper, and a little nutmeg if desired. Serve immediately.

Spinach with an Andalucian Sauce

✦ Makes 4 servings on its own; 6 servings to accompany meat or fish

S INCE IT WAS Arab gardeners who introduced spinach to Andalucia—and then to the rest of Spain and Europe—it seems only appropriate to include a recipe for an Andalucian treatment of this perfect vegetable. This one comes by way of my old friend Elisabeth Luard, who lived in the south of Spain for many years and continues to explore the country's foodways. It's typical of the region around Jaen, still to this day the largest producer of extra-virgin olive oil in the world.

For the chilies, use Spanish ñoras if you can find them. Otherwise, dried Anaheim or New Mexico chilies will be fine. Don't confuse Spanish pimentón with pimentón de la Vera. The latter is smoked paprika, and while it is delicious in many things, it's not for this dish.

2 dried red chili peppers, preferably anchos or Spanish ñoras

2 pounds fresh spinach, carefully rinsed

6 tablespoons extra-virgin olive oil

2 garlic cloves, roughly chopped

1 1-inch-thick slice stale country-style bread, cubed (about 1 to 1¼ cups cubed bread)

1 tablespoon mild Spanish paprika (pimentón)

sea salt

fresh lemon juice (optional)

Set the chilies in a bowl of warm water and leave to soak and soften for about 2 hours. Then take a spoon and carefully scrape away the soft inside flesh of the peppers, discarding the seeds and skins. Add the flesh to a food processor.

Cook the rinsed spinach in the water clinging to its leaves for about 5 minutes or until the spinach is very soft. Drain thoroughly in a colander and set aside.

Heat ¼ cup of the oil in a skillet large enough to hold all the ingredients, including the spinach. Add the garlic and sauté gently until it starts to take color. Use a slotted spoon to remove the garlic and transfer to the processor. Add the bread cubes to the oil in the pan and sauté until golden on all sides. Add to the processor, along with the paprika, a couple of teaspoons of water, and the remaining olive oil, then process, pulsing, to make a paste.

Return the drained spinach to the skillet with the oil left in it. Set over medium heat and when the spinach starts to sizzle, stir in the paste, mixing thoroughly. Add a little salt, turn down the heat, cover the pan, and let cook for about 10 minutes, just until the flavors come together. A quick squeeze of lemon juice (optional) at the end adds a nice touch to the dish.

Serve immediately—Elisabeth recommends serving the spinach with fried or toasted bread rubbed with garlic.

Variation: In Jaen, the spinach sometimes serves as a bed for fried eggs—one or two for each serving.

Squash

Except for zucchini, we don't think of squash as a Mediterranean vegetable. Yet pumpkins and winter squash also have a role to play, most often in combination with other vegetables, as in couscous (page 217). Moroccan chermoula makes a fine sauce for barely steamed chunks of autumn squash.

Sautéed Squash with a Chermoula Sauce

Makes 6 to 8 servings

about 1½ pounds autumn squash such as turban, acorn, butternut, or kabocha

¼ to ½ cup extra-virgin olive oil

ingredients for chermoula sauce (page 306)

Cut the squash in half and remove the seeds and fibers from the center. Peel the squash and cut into 2-inch chunks. Heat the oil in a skillet over medium heat and sauté the squash pieces until lightly brown on all sides. Remove and set aside but keep warm.

Mix together the chermoula sauce, following the directions on page 306. While the squash is still warm, pour the chermoula over it, stirring gently to mix well without breaking up the squash. Set aside to marinate for at least 30 minutes before serving. Serve at room temperature.

What would the Mediterranean table be without tomatoes? Well, it would be an ancient Mediterranean table, since this amazing New World fruit arrived in the Mediterranean only after 1492 and did not become widely used until long after that. Giacomo Castelvetro's great compendium, written in 1614, doesn't even mention tomatoes, and although they appeared as botanical curiosities in early herbals, the first European recipes that we know of are in Antonio Latini's cookbook published in Naples in 1692. Still, tomatoes did not become widespread until the later 19th century.

Today they flourish: in early summer there are pinkish-green salad tomatoes, plump and tasty and intended to be eaten raw and somewhat under-ripe; later there are dead-ripe tomatoes, packed with juice, and plum-shaped tomatoes full of flesh to be turned into sauces; and later still, in the dead of winter, you can glimpse the welcome sight of little winter tomatoes, small globes as bright red as a Christmas ornament, the whole plant inverted and hanging by its roots from a market stall.

Provençal Stuffed Tomatoes

Makes 6 servings

6 large very ripe but firm tomatoes

½ teaspoon sea salt

1 large garlic clove, crushed with the flat blade of a knife

1 oil-packed anchovy fillet or 1 salted anchovy, prepared as directed on page 40

3 tablespoons finely chopped flat-leaf parsley

3 to 4 tablespoons toasted unseasoned bread crumbs, to taste

Cut each tomato in half horizontally and gently squeeze out the seeds inside. Set the tomato halves, cut side up, on a lightly oiled baking sheet. Preheat the oven to 425 degrees.

Mix the salt and garlic in a mortar and pound with the pestle until you have a paste. Then pound in the anchovy and the parsley. When the parsley has been thoroughly incorporated, add a tablespoon of the toasted bread crumbs and mix well. Add a tablespoon of the olive oil and stir to make a thick paste.

Using a narrow spatula, smear some of the garlic paste on each tomato half. Mix the remaining bread crumbs with the basil leaves and sprinkle

3 tablespoons extra-virgin olive oil

1 tablespoon chopped basil leaves

over each tomato half. Then drizzle the remaining oil over the halves.

Bake the tomatoes on the baking sheet for about 20 minutes or until they are thoroughly softened and starting to brown on top. Remove and serve hot, or set aside and serve at room temperature later.

HOTHOUSE TOMATOES MADE TO TASTE LIKE SOMETHING ELSE

This is not so much a recipe as a trick, to be used when you can't get good fresh tomatoes and still feel they must be a part of your table. What the trick does is concentrate the small amount of flavor in these tomatoes and intensify it. It comes from my daughter Sara, who, after a childhood spent happily munching her way around the Mediterranean, grew up, to the surprise of no one but her parents, to become a restaurant chef.

Preheat the oven to 200 degrees. Rinse as many tomatoes as you need, cut out their cores (where the stems are), sprinkle in a few grains of salt and pepper and a few drops of extra-virgin olive oil, and set them in a well-oiled roasting pan. Place the pan in the oven and, after about an hour at this slow heat, sprinkle a little more salt and drizzle a little more oil over each tomato. The skins of the tomatoes will have cracked and the tomatoes themselves settled in the pan a little as their juice has evaporated. After another hour of roasting, sprinkle a little finely minced garlic over the cracked tomatoes, along with a few grains of sugar. Continue roasting for up to 3 hours, from time to time adding a little more oil, salt, and sugar—but the sugar in very small quantities because you don't want the tomatoes to dissolve into jam.

Serve these as an accompaniment to grilled meat or fish, or mix them with other vegetables to add sparkle. Or chop them coarsely and mix with pasta for a delicious first course.

Gratin of Purple-Topped Turnips

Makes 6 servings

2 tablespoons extra-virgin olive oil, plus a little to oil the dish

2½ pounds purple-topped turnips, scrubbed and sliced not more than ¾ inch thick

sea salt

¼ cup finely chopped shallot

½ garlic clove, finely chopped

1 cup chicken stock (page 108)

¼ cup minced flat-leaf parsley

2 tablespoons finely grated parmigiano reggiano cheese

freshly ground black pepper

Preheat the oven to 400 degrees. Lightly oil an oval gratin dish. Prepare the turnips while you bring a large pan of lightly salted water to a rolling boil. Drop the turnip slices in and cook for about 5 to 7 minutes, until they're just tender. Drain and arrange the slices in the gratin dish.

Meanwhile, cook the shallot and garlic in the olive oil in a saucepan over medium-low heat, stirring occasionally, until the vegetables are tender but not brown—about 10 minutes. Add the stock and parsley and, when the stock is boiling, pour it over the turnip slices in the gratin dish. Sprinkle with the cheese and a little pepper. Cover with aluminum foil and bake for 20 to 30 minutes or until the turnip slices are very tender. Remove the foil, baste the slices with a little of the pan juices, and bake for 5 minutes more, just to glaze the top of the turnips. Serve immediately.

Zucchini and Zucchini Blossoms

Young, firm zucchini, not more than 6 inches long, can be steamed whole in lightly salted water for just a few minutes until tender, then cut into chunks and turned while still hot in the chermoula described on page 306. Sliced zucchini are very good sautéed in olive oil, or use them in the recipe for *agrodolce* (page 305); zucchini need not be parboiled, as the carrots are, before being cooked in the sauce.

Kolokythia Yakhni

Greek Zucchini Stew

THIS METHOD can be adapted for many other vegetables, such as green beans, broad beans, or even little new potatoes. Or a combination of two or three vegetables might be used.

2 medium onions, sliced

⅓ cup extra-virgin olive oil

1 pound tomatoes, chopped, or 1 14- to 16-ounce can whole tomatoes, drained and chopped

1 teaspoon sugar

½ cup water

sea salt and freshly ground black pepper

2 pounds small zucchini, cut in half lengthwise unless very small

1 teaspoon minced mint leaves

1 teaspoon minced dill

In a saucepan over medium-low heat, gently stew the onions in the olive oil until soft but not brown—about 10 minutes. Add the tomatoes and sugar and cook for another 10 minutes. Then pour in the water, add salt and pepper, and stir well. When the tomato sauce has come back to a boil, add the zucchini with the mint and dill. Cook gently until the zucchini is very tender, about 15 minutes. Let stand for 20 minutes before serving.

Fiore di Zucchini Fritti

Fried Zucchini Blossoms

Makes 6 servings, counting 4 blossoms for each person
You may need more than 4 blossoms per person—
in fact, you may end up frying until all the zucchini plants
in the garden have been stripped of their flowers

FOR THOSE WHO HAVE ACCESS to the flowers of zucchini, this is a wonderful way to use them. One is always told to use only the male flowers of the zucchini, but I must confess I can't tell the difference. Don't worry about using female flowers (the ones that produce the zucchini fruit)—I have never met a gardener who complained about an underabundance of zucchini.

These are as addictive as potato chips—and probably about as healthful, too. Be prepared to spend your time at the stove frying up zucchini blossoms while your loved ones gather around and consume them as fast as they emerge.

24 just-picked zucchini
blossoms

1 cup olive oil and 1 cup
canola oil

1 cup cool water

1 cup unbleached all-purpose
flour

sea salt and freshly ground
black pepper

coarse sea salt for serving

Rinse the blossoms lightly in running water and set aside in a colander to drain. Put the oils in a deep frying pan and heat up gradually over medium heat.

Put the water in a bowl and sift over it about ½ cup of the flour, beating with a fork as you sift it in. Continue adding flour, beating as you do so, until the batter is the consistency of light cream. Add salt and black pepper.

Test the oil temperature by dropping a little cube of plain bread in it. When it's hot enough, the bread cube will sizzle and quickly turn golden brown. Dip a zucchini blossom in the batter, coating it completely. Briefly hold it over the bowl to let excess batter drain off, then drop it in the hot fat. Let it sizzle on one side until golden brown, then turn with a long-handled kitchen fork and cook briefly on the other side. Remove with the fork or a slotted spoon and set on a rack over paper towels to drain.

You can do about six of these at a time without reducing the temperature of the oil too much. Don't try to crowd the pan. When all the zucchini blossoms have been fried, if they have not already been eaten, pile them up in a bowl, sprinkle with a little coarse salt, and serve.

Mixed Vegetable Dishes

Turkish-Style Oven-Braised Winter Vegetables

Makes 8 servings

THERE IS SOMETHING COMFORTING about the mixed vegetable dishes of the eastern Mediterranean. Greek and Turkish cooks are particularly gifted at roasting, braising, and stewing vegetables for hours in a little savory extra-virgin olive oil and whatever aromatics the cook has to hand. These are substantial dishes that can easily be the focus of a meal, especially with a good crusty country loaf and a chunk of feta or other firm cheese.

Don't be limited by the vegetable suggestions here—if others are available, use them. Fennel, artichoke or celery hearts, and beets are all good suggestions, though beets should be added with caution to avoid turning the whole thing pink.

1 cup dried small white beans, soaked overnight

about ½ cup extra-virgin olive oil

1 medium celery root, peeled and cut into 1-inch cubes

½ pound Jerusalem artichokes, peeled and cut into 1-inch cubes

3 large carrots, peeled and cut into 1-inch cubes

[cont. next page]

Preheat the oven to 450 degrees. Drain the soaked beans and place in a saucepan with water to cover to a depth of 1 inch and 2 tablespoons of the olive oil. Cook gently until the beans are tender—time depends on the age and size of the beans. When done, set aside in their cooking liquid.

Place all the vegetables except the scallion greens in a large roasting pan with the remaining olive oil, the lemon juice, and salt and pepper. Fill the pan

3 small white turnips, peeled
and cut into 1-inch cubes

2 medium potatoes, peeled if
desired and cut into 1-inch
cubes

15 scallions, green tops sliced
diagonally and white parts
left whole

4 large garlic cloves, crushed
with the flat blade of a knife

juice of ½ lemon, or more to
taste

sea salt and freshly ground
black pepper

lemon wedges for serving

halfway with boiling water and place, uncovered,
in the preheated oven for 30 minutes or until
the vegetables are thoroughly cooked and
starting to brown on top. Remove and sprinkle
the chopped scallion greens over the
vegetables. Cover the roasting pan lightly
with foil and set aside until the beans are
ready.

When the beans are tender, add them with
their cooking liquid to the roasted vegetables,
distributing them evenly. The dish can be
reheated, covered with foil, in the oven
before serving, but it is usually served at
room temperature. Serve with lemon
wedges.

Roots, Shoots, and Squash

Roasted Winter Vegetables

Makes 8 servings or more, depending on what else is served

PEEL THE ROOT VEGETABLES and cut them in chunks about 1 to 1½ inches
to a side. You can do this ahead of time and store the cut vegetables in a
plastic bag in the refrigerator for a few days until you're ready to cook. Then all
you have to do is toss the vegetables with oil and herbs and put in a preheated
oven. If you pre-cut celery root, sprinkle a little lemon juice over the cut surfaces
to keep it from darkening.

Store and cook the beets separately from the others; otherwise the beets may
bleed their color onto paler vegetables.

If you don't have all of the vegetables listed, don't worry, just add more of
what you do have. You may also make substitutions—other winter root vegetables like potatoes or delicious parsnips, which seem to be utterly unknown in the
Mediterranean, can take the place of some of the vegetables on this list. When I

couldn't find white turnips, I once substituted daikon radishes, again unheard of in the Mediterranean but they gave a nice oriental turnipy touch to the combination.

1 pound beets (about 3 medium beets), peeled and cut in chunks

about ½ cup extra-virgin olive oil

juice of ½ lemon

sea salt and freshly ground black pepper

about 2 tablespoons of fresh herbs, finely minced (parsley, sage, rosemary, thyme, winter savory, chives or scallion tops)

1 teaspoon medium-strength ground or crushed red chili

2 medium onions

1 pound carrots, cut in inch-thick slices (3 medium carrots)

1 pound celery root, peeled and cut in chunks

1 pound small white turnips, peeled and cut in chunks

1 medium sweet potato, peeled and cut in chunks

1½ pounds hard winter squash, peeled and cut in chunks

2 leeks, cut in chunks

8 garlic cloves, cut in half

Set the oven at 450 degrees.

Toss the beets in a bowl with about 2 tablespoons of olive oil and a teaspoon of fresh lemon juice. Sprinkle with salt and pepper. Combine the minced herbs with the chili and sprinkle a pinch of the mixture over the beets, then transfer to a baking dish. Since the beets will take 20 to 30 minutes longer to cook than the other vegetables, place them in the oven now and cook for a total of 1 hour and 15 to 20 minutes or until the beets are tender.

While the beets are cooking, prepare the rest of the vegetables. Peel the onions and slice off their tops but leave them attached at the stem end, merely trimming away any bits of root. Quarter each onion and add to a big bowl, along with the chunks of carrot, celery root, turnip, and sweet potato.

Rub about a tablespoon of olive oil over the bottom of an oven dish large enough to hold all the vegetables in one or two layers.

Add the remaining oil to the bowl of vegetables, along with the remaining lemon juice, mixed herbs and chili, and salt and pepper to taste. Mix, using your hands, so that all the vegetable chunks are impregnated with the herby oil. Arrange the vegetables in the oven dish and transfer to the preheated oven. Bake for 20 minutes, then remove the dish and add the squash chunks. Stir the vegetables to mix them well and return to the oven. At the same time, give the beets a stir.

After another 20 minutes, remove the oven dish again. This time add the leeks and garlic, stir, and return to the oven, first giving the beets another stir. The vegetables should be done after another 15 minutes of cooking. Test by piercing a carrot chunk with a sharp pointed knife. It should slide right in without resistance.

Remove the vegetables from the oven. Test the beets at this time—they may need a few more minutes baking. Arrange the vegetables on a platter, garnishing them, if you wish, with more freshly chopped herbs and another spritz of lemon juice. Pile the beets on top just before you send them to the table.

Mediterranean Summer Stew of Vegetables

꙰{ Makes 6 to 8 servings

THIS IS A DISH for people like me, who are weary of the so-called crisp-tender vegetables served in fashionable restaurants. Don't be limited by the vegetable suggestions in the recipe. Your local farmers' market may provide a different and equally enticing selection—perhaps fresh young fava beans, so tender you can eat them pod and all, or later in the season shell beans, okra, and any of the variety of summer squashes. When young spring onions are available, the kind with the outer skin still fresh enough to eat, I like to use them, with their green tops, instead of yellow or white onions.

A heavy terra-cotta braising dish, wider than it is tall, is traditional for these vegetable preparations, though it should be used with a gas burner and a Flame-Tamer. Send the vegetables to the table in the handsome dish in which they are cooked.

¼ cup extra-virgin olive oil

2 medium fresh spring onions or yellow or white onions (not scallions), thinly sliced

3 garlic cloves, crushed with the flat blade of a knife

2 medium potatoes, peeled and cut into chunks, or 12 small new potatoes

Warm the olive oil over medium-low heat in a pan large enough to hold all the vegetables. Add the onions and garlic and stew very gently, stirring occasionally, until the onions are meltingly soft—about 10 to 15 minutes.

When the onions are soft, arrange the potatoes over them, then add the beans and peppers. Distribute the thyme over the beans. Add the

1 pound or more green beans, topped and tailed and broken in half if very long

3 small sweet peppers, both green and red, cut into strips

3 or 4 thyme or oregano sprigs, to taste

3 long narrow zucchini, cut into 1-inch chunks

3 large firm but ripe tomatoes, cut into chunks

sea salt and freshly ground black pepper

1 tablespoon minced flat-leaf parsley

zucchini chunks and then the tomatoes. Sprinkle a little salt, if desired, and pepper on top, cover tightly (use a double layer of heavy-duty aluminum foil to cover a terra-cotta pot), and stew over low heat for about 45 minutes or until the vegetables are thoroughly cooked. Check the liquid occasionally—there should be plenty, but if necessary add up to ¼ cup boiling water.

When the vegetables are soft and meltingly tender, remove the dish from the heat and set aside, still covered, until ready to serve. If necessary, they can be warmed up a little just before serving, but they are best a bit warmer than room temperature. Sprinkle with the parsley just before serving.

Fish and Seafood

✧ ✧ ✧

S PURRED BY QUESTIONS about the healthfulness of high-fat animal products, Americans are eating more fish than ever before. Still, the high point for annual fish consumption recently was just over 16 pounds per person, compared to 84 pounds of chicken and 67 pounds of beef. Moreover, what the increase reflects is that people who have always eaten fish are simply eating more, while those who didn't eat fish still don't.★

Pity them! Not only is fish good for you—low in fat and cholesterol for those who are concerned about heart disease (and who isn't?) and full of high-quality proteins, vitamins, and valuable trace minerals like selenium, copper, and zinc that are hard to get from other sources—it's also just plain good. And fish is quick and easy to prepare. As Mediterranean cooks know well, fish and seafood generally benefit from the simplest preparations— poaching, steaming, roasting, or grilling, whether whole fish, boneless fillets, or steaks. The sauce for the fish is most often prepared apart, whether a plain and delicious mix of good olive oil, lemon juice, and a sprinkling of fresh herbs or a slightly more complex combination like Lebanese samki harra (page 369), made with chopped garlic and cilantro and flavored with hot chilies and cumin.

★When the first edition of this book was published in 1994, the consumption statistics for fish and beef, at 14.8 and 63 pounds respectively, were not hugely different from today. Both fish and beef have increased slightly. What has changed enormously is U.S. consumption of chicken, which has nearly doubled, from 46 pounds in 1994 to 84.3 pounds in 2005. Over-all, it seems that in that period Americans have greatly increased their consumption of all animal-derived protein. We'd be much better off converting at least half of that to vegetables.

The supply of fresh seafood in American fish markets and supermarket fish counters has improved enormously in recent years, especially with the development of farm-raised fish like catfish, tilapia, and salmon. Don't be put off by fish labeled "fresh-frozen." That may seem an anomaly, but if the fish is handled correctly and flash-frozen at sea or on shore soon after it is caught, fresh-frozen can be even better than many so-called fresh varieties, which may have been carried at sea, iced down in the hold of the fishing vessel, for as long as 10 days before reaching port. (Be sure to ask if the fish has been frozen, especially if you're not planning to use it right away. If it has been thawed at the fish market, which often happens, you will not want to refreeze it without cooking it first.)

It may come as a surprise to learn that a good deal more than half of all the seafood consumed worldwide comes from fish farms. Shrimp, salmon, sea bass, Arctic char, sea bream, turbot, mussels, oysters and clams, and fresh water species such as tilapia and catfish are among the species you may find at your supermarket or neighborhood fishmonger. Much has been written about the merits and especially the relative safety of eating farmed fish. Whether wild or farmed, however, it's important to understand that, with the exception of some sport fish caught in contaminated inland waters, most seafood is safe to eat under most conditions, fully as safe as other sources of protein in our diets, including beef, pork, chicken, eggs, and butter. And seafood of all kinds is an important contribution to a healthy diet. Drs. Eric Rimm and Dariush Mozaffarian from the Harvard School of Public Health surveyed two decades of scientific studies on the subject of seafood safety and contamination. "The benefits of eating fish," they argued incontestably in the *Journal of the American Medical Association,* "greatly outweigh the risks."

A report published a few years back in the journal *Science* reached the alarming conclusion that toxin levels in farmed salmon were far in excess of those in wild salmon and pose a definite health risk. But Dr. Mozaffarian pointed out that levels of PCBs (polychlorinated biphenols) and dioxins in fish are low, "similar to other commonly consumed foods such as beef, chicken, pork, eggs, and butter. . . . [T]he possible health risks of these low levels . . . are only a small fraction of the much better established health benefits of the Omega-3 fatty acids. [F]or farmed salmon, the cardiovascular benefits are greater than the cancer risks by a factor of at least 300:1. With the exception of some locally caught sport fish from contaminated inland waters, the levels of PCBs and dioxins in fish should not influence decisions about fish intake."

The authors blame the media for "greatly exaggerating the unsubstantiated claim of a health risk from fish." Rather, they concluded, a far greater health risk comes from *not* eating fish.

Despite the claims of environmentalists (and I consider myself a dyed-in-the-wool environmentalist on all issues but this one), farmed salmon is just as safe as wild salmon, it has a similar content of omega-3 fatty acids and, if raised in an environmentally sustainable manner, as much farmed salmon is, it is an optimal source of seafood.

A word about shellfish and cholesterol: despite the bad rap they used to get, most mollusks and crustaceans are low in cholesterol. (Errors in measurement by food scientists led to the mistake.) Clams, mussels, and scallops have fewer than 35 milligrams of cholesterol in 100 grams (about 3½ ounces) of raw fish (the yolks of large eggs have 225 milligrams each); lobster has 95 milligrams, shrimp (America's favorite seafood after canned tuna) 150, and squid 230. But even with squid's relatively high count, many nutritionists recommend it except for people on rigidly low-cholesterol diets. The reason? Squid, like most other seafood, is very low in fat. Only 13 of the 92 calories in a 3½-ounce serving of squid come from fat, and the small amount of fat is made up partly of omega-3 fatty acids, which may be valuable in combating heart disease.

Although some of the health benefits attributed to fish may simply be the result of eating less meat (every time you eat a portion of fish, you eat one less of meat), there is considerable evidence that fish is more healthful in and of itself. One major reason, scientists believe, is the presence of polyunsaturated omega-3 fatty acids, which interfere with the formation of blood clots and help to prevent the buildup of plaque in blood vessels. Blood clots and plaque are initial steps in the progression of atherosclerosis, which, if uncorrected, can lead to heart disease.

Omega-3 fatty acids in fish may also act against inflammatory and immune reactions, which characterize diseases like arthritis and psoriasis; and there is growing evidence of their positive role in the prevention of certain cancers, as well as improving blood sugar control in type 2 diabetes. DHA, one of the omega-3 fatty acids found in fish, is crucial for brain development. (Didn't your mother tell you that fish was brain food? And of course, as in so many other things, she was right!)

The fish richest in omega-3 fatty acids are those denizens of deep, cold waters that carry fat in their muscles, especially Atlantic salmon, mackerel, herring, bluefish, albacore, and bluefin tuna. Swordfish is also a good source of omega-3 fatty acids. White-fleshed fish like cod, haddock, halibut, and snapper, because they don't carry fat in their muscle tissue, are not great sources of omega-3 fats, but they should not be avoided for that reason. On the contrary: as very-low-fat sources of protein, they should be a significant part of the diet.

Much traditional advice to the buyer of seafood is old-fashioned—look for rosy gills, we are told, or clear eyes or shiny skin. Professional chefs in fancy restaurants may have that luxury, but the rest of us seldom get to look at gills, eyes, or skin these days because fish usually comes to us already cut into fillets or steaks, rarely as whole fish. I rely on my nose to tell me when fish is fresh and when it is not. It's pretty infallible. If you do make a mistake, don't be afraid to take the offending beast right back to the person you bought it from and ask for a refund. You may not get it, but you will have made your point.

Many of the species traditionally used in the Mediterranean are rarely available here—or there, for that matter—but fortunately fish recipes and preparations are highly adaptable. In the recipes that follow I have suggested a number of different varieties where it is appropriate. I often substitute haddock, cod, halibut, or snapper, even farm-raised catfish or salmon, in Mediterranean recipes, and they work just fine. Salmon, especially, although not a traditional Mediterranean fish, is appearing in Mediterranean markets at a rapidly increasing rate, primarily because of the marketing skill of Norwegian aquaculturists. Monkfish, widely available in American fish markets, is always an appropriate choice for Mediterranean preparations, and bluefish and mackerel, if they are small, can be substituted for sardines—though if you have access to fresh sardines, snap them up and rush them home as quickly as you can. To my mind, there's no better fish in the world than a sparkling-fresh sardine, wrapped in a grape leaf blanket with its little head poking out and grilled over charcoal embers.

For more delicious seafood recipes, see also pages 110–119 in the chapter on soups for Mediterranean seafood soups.

Poached Whole Fish

The Basic Recipe

Makes 16 to 20 servings

POACHING, OR VERY GENTLY BOILING, fish in water to cover is traditionally reserved for whole fish, usually a rather large fish, such as a whole salmon or sea bass. It makes an elegant presentation for a dinner party or wedding feast.

The technique requires not only a large fish but a large kettle in which to cook it. A fish-poaching kettle is a long, oval, deep pan. Old-fashioned French poaching pans come with a rack inside, very convenient for lifting the whole fish out once it is cooked. If your fish kettle lacks a rack, use a double layer of cheesecloth instead. Set in the middle of the cheesecloth, the fish can be lowered into the simmering liquid and retrieved when it has finished cooking.

For the Fish: Place the fish in the kettle and cover it with cool water. Then remove the fish and measure the quantity of water. This will tell you how much liquid you need to cover the fish. If the stock and wine available do not measure up, don't worry—just add water to bring the liquid up to the right level.

Place the liquid and herbs in the fish kettle and bring to a very slow simmer—the liquid should be just shuddering. Put the fish on the rack or the double layer of cheesecloth and gently lower it into the liquid. Cover and let it continue cooking at a shuddering simmer. The so-called Canadian rule dictates that fish should cook for 10 minutes for each inch of thickness, measured at the thickest part of the fish, but this often leads to overcooking. For a whole fish, I use the Canadian rule minus 10 minutes—thus a 4-inch-thick salmon cooks for 30 minutes and no more. Fish this large continues to cook from interior heat once it is removed from the pan.

Grasping the rack or the cheesecloth (use rubber gloves and old kitchen towels to protect your hands from the heat), lift the fish out of the pan and set it on a platter to cool slightly.

To serve the fish immediately, place it on a warm platter and remove the top layer of skin between the head and the tail (the part that will be eaten) while the fish is still warm. Spoon a few tablespoons of fish stock over the flesh to keep it from drying out.

Pour over it about half of the following mixture, beaten together with a fork before it is poured.

FOR A 6-POUND WHOLE SALMON OR SEA BASS

4 to 6 cups fish stock (page 109) or water and wine simmered for 20 minutes with a few bay leaves, a sliced onion, and a few parsley sprigs

1 or 2 cups good-quality dry white wine as needed

a little handful of whatever green herbs you will use for garnish—parsley, basil, dill, tarragon, thyme

¼ garlic clove, mashed to a paste with ½ teaspoon sea salt

½ cup best-quality extra-virgin olive oil

3 tablespoons fresh lemon juice

sea salt and freshly ground white pepper

1 tablespoon finely minced flat-leaf parsley, basil, dill, tarragon, thyme, or other herbs

Garnish the platter with sprigs of the herb used in the sauce. Pass the remaining sauce for guests to serve themselves.

A homemade mayonnaise, incorporating some of the minced fresh herbs, or an aïoli (page 274) can also be served with the room-temperature fish.

Steam-Poached Fish Fillets or Steaks

THE BASIC RECIPE

Makes 6 to 8 servings

THE TECHNIQUE called *steam-poaching* (or *poach-steaming*) is similar to poaching but requires less liquid. Fillets or steaks can be poached in an ordinary large skillet or saucepan—preferably one with a lid that fits securely on top, though a large sheet of heavy aluminum foil, in a pinch, makes a perfectly good lid. This is a good, quick, easy preparation for people who want to eat a very-low-fat diet or just a single light dish to recover from a feast. In addition to the fish listed here, salmon is a good choice; though somewhat higher in fat than the others, it is an excellent source of beneficial omega-3 fatty acids.

2 pounds boneless fish fillets or steaks: haddock, cod, snapper, monkfish, bass, sole, or similar fish

1 cup fish stock (page 109), fish stock and dry white wine, or half wine and half water plus 1 bay leaf, ¼ teaspoon dried thyme, crumbled, a few parsley sprigs, and a pinch of sea salt, if desired

[cont. next page]

To determine the cooking time, measure the fish fillets or steaks at the thickest part (an *approximate* measure will do). Place the liquid in a shallow skillet large enough to hold all the fish in one layer. Slowly bring the liquid to a bare simmer. Lower the fish pieces into the simmering liquid and immediately clap a lid on the pan. Or cover the pan with aluminum foil, pressing it down around the edges. Cook at a very slow simmer for about 7 minutes for each inch of thickness. The fish is done when it is opaque all the way through (check steaks next to the bone to be sure they are done). Using a spatula, remove the fish pieces and place on a warm platter.

olive-oil-and-lemon sauce
from preceding recipe,
mayonnaise, aïoli (page 274),
or sauce rouille (page 276)

Raise the heat to high and boil the liquid down to about one-third the original quantity. Stir in the olive-oil-and-lemon sauce and pour half of it over the warm fish pieces. Serve immediately, passing the rest of the sauce for guests to help themselves. (If you're using mayonnaise or aïoli, set aside half of it in a little china bowl to be passed at table. Off the heat, carefully mix the reduced poaching liquid, a spoonful at a time, into the remaining mayonnaise or aïoli, then spoon the mixture over the pieces of fish and garnish the platter with a sprinkling of minced fresh herbs.)

Baked or Roasted Fish

The Basic Recipe

✳ Makes 6 to 8 servings

Fish suitable for baking include whole fish; chunks or center cuts, with the bone, of large fish such as haddock, sea bass, salmon, or similar fish; and fish steaks cut 1½ to 2 inches thick. For whole fish or center-cut chunks you'll need about ½ pound per person; for boneless steaks or thick fillets, at least ¼ pound per serving.

¼ cup extra-virgin olive oil

at least 3 pounds whole fish
or center-cut fish chunks, or
½ to 2 pounds boneless
steaks or thick fillets

¼ cup dry white wine or
fresh lemon juice

1 garlic clove, minced

sea salt and freshly ground
black pepper

1 tablespoon fresh or dried
herbs: fresh parsley, rosemary,
dill, or cilantro, fresh or dried
thyme or oregano

Preheat the oven to 425 degrees. Rub a small amount of olive oil over the bottom of a roasting pan large enough to hold all the fish in one layer. Rub the fish or steaks with a little more oil and place in the pan. Combine the remaining olive oil with the wine, garlic, salt, pepper, herbs, and hot pepper. Pour the mixture over the fish, making sure all the pieces are well coated.

Roast the fish for 15 to 20 minutes—steaks will take less time than whole fish or chunks. Baste the fish frequently with the pan juices. Remove the fish from the oven and test for doneness—the flesh should be opaque all the way through to the bone.

½ teaspoon hot red pepper flakes (optional)

lemon wedges and best-quality extra-virgin olive oil for serving

If the fish is not done, return it to the oven for another 5 to 10 minutes.

When the fish is cooked, transfer it to a warm serving platter or warm plates and spoon the juices over the top. Serve immediately with lemon wedges and a little pitcher of best-quality extra-virgin olive oil.

Grilled Fish

THE BASIC RECIPE

Makes 6 to 8 servings

FISH STEAKS, cut 1½ to 2 inches thick—halibut, swordfish, and tuna are all good choices—are really best for grilling. Fillets are usually too delicate, and large whole fish are tricky—too often the outside is charred before the inside is cooked. If you're lucky enough, however, to find *small* whole fish, such as sardines, imported red mullet, small mackerel, or bluefish, they will be exquisite cooked over charcoal or the embers of a wood fire for a real Mediterranean-style treat.

Count on ¼ pound boneless fish steaks per serving, a little more with the bone in, and add a little extra for enthusiastic appetites.

1 teaspoon finely minced garlic, about 3 cloves

½ cup extra-virgin olive oil

¼ cup fresh lemon juice, orange juice, or dry white wine

1 tablespoon balsamic vinegar or sherry vinegar

a pinch of cayenne pepper or hot red pepper flakes (optional)

[cont. next page]

Combine all the ingredients except fish and lemon wedges and mix well. Using a pastry brush, paint the fish steaks liberally on both sides and set them aside, lightly covered with a piece of aluminum foil, to marinate for at least 30 minutes.

Build up a fire, using good hardwoods if you're cooking in a fireplace or the best hardwood charcoal (not fake-wood briquettes) if you're using a grill. Let the fire burn brightly and die down until you have a nice bed of hot coals or embers. Large pieces of fish can be set directly on the grill,

½ teaspoon ground cumin, or 1 teaspoon or more chopped fresh herbs such as rosemary, dill, parsley, thyme, cilantro, basil, or mint, or ½ teaspoon dried thyme or oregano, crumbled

freshly ground black pepper

2 pounds fish steaks

lemon wedges for garnish

but to prevent smaller ones from falling through and burning up, you may want to use a special grid made for fish.

When you're ready to cook, brush a little plain olive oil on the cooking surface and set it 4 to 6 inches from the source of heat. Arrange the fish steaks so that they have equal access to the heat source. Cook for about 4 to 5 minutes on each side, turning once. Test for doneness—fish should be opaque all the way through—by inserting the tip of a sharp knife near the bone or in the center of a boneless piece of fish. Remove immediately to a hot platter.

The remaining marinade should be heated just to the boiling point and either poured over the cooked fish or passed at the table along with lemon wedges.

Saucing Plainly Cooked Fish

Check the chapter on sauces, pages 261 to 283, for other ideas about dressing plainly cooked fish. Many of the small dishes in Chapter One are also appropriate. Try any of the following: Turkish cacik (page 59), tapénade (page 52), mechouia (page 63), eggplant salad (page 56), or mhammara (page 58).

ABOUT TUNA AND SWORDFISH

Tuna and swordfish are springtime treats in Rome, served with tiny sweet peas, *piselli romaneschi*, from the market gardens of the Roman *campagna*. For me this particular combination was always associated with the season's first opportunity to dine al fresco at Passetto, a lovely restaurant just outside Piazza Navona. The cook used thin tuna or swordfish steaks, just ½ inch thick, quickly sautéing them on both sides in a mixture of butter and fragrant oil, and served them with a *contorno* (accompaniment) of delicate peas cooked until they became a creamy not-quite puree of intense flavor and sweetness.

The finest tuna of all is bluefin but I must urge you not to consume it—not to order it in a restaurant nor to buy it if you see it on sale, which would be rare indeed. Largely because of an insatiable Japanese demand for bluefin tuna for the finest sushi and sashimi, populations of this noblest of all fish are seriously depleted throughout the world ("critically endangered," according to the Blue Oceans Institute, an environmental organization that focuses on the sea). But there are many other, equally delicious members of the tuna family, such as yellowfin and albacore, that are suitable for Mediterranean dishes.

In buying tuna and swordfish, look for moist fish with good clear color and no off tints or aromas. Yellow flesh in swordfish means it's old, as does a dark brown color in tuna. Usually both fish exhibit distinctive dry edges or gaping layers of flesh when they've been kept around too long. But as with other fish, your nose will tell you—tuna, especially, gets a strong ammonia odor when it's over the hill. Both tuna and swordfish are better fresh than frozen—or "previously frozen," in the current marketing parlance.

Fresh tuna and swordfish are usually available as steaks. Very thick ones—up to 4 inches—are best cooked with the oven-roasting technique described on page 354. For other purposes I prefer steaks that are not more than 2 inches thick. Although the flavor of tuna and swordfish is very different—tuna is usually more assertive, more unmistakably fish yet with a meaty quality that is very appealing—they can be used interchangeably in the following recipes.

Pressures on Atlantic swordfish stocks have eased somewhat in recent years; still, I look in seafood markets for swordfish that has been caught by harpooning or trolling. With these two fishing methods, bycatch is not the problem that it is with long-lining the big fish.

Braised Tuna or Swordfish in White Wine

A Pan-Mediterranean Recipe

Makes 4 servings

1 medium onion, thinly sliced

1 crushed garlic clove, chopped

[cont. next page]

In a heavy sauté pan large enough to hold the tuna and vegetables comfortably, gently sauté the onion, garlic, and pepper strips in the oil over medium-low heat until the vegetables are soft—about 10 to 15 minutes.

1 sweet red pepper, cut into julienne strips

1 tablespoon extra-virgin olive oil, or more if needed

1 fresh tuna or swordfish steak, approximately 1½ inches thick, weighing 1 to 1¼ pounds

sea salt

1 cup dry white wine

½ cup pitted black olives, preferably Kalamata, coarsely chopped

1 tablespoon drained capers, coarsely chopped

1 tablespoon finely shredded lemon zest

Pat the fish steak dry with paper towels. Push the vegetables to the edge of the pan and turn the heat up to medium-high. Quickly sear the fish on both sides, adding more oil if necessary. The vegetables shouldn't brown, however—remove them with a slotted spoon if they start to brown and put them back when you've finished the fish. When the fish is nicely seared on both sides, sprinkle it with a little salt. Add the wine to the pan and let it come to a boil. Then turn the heat down to low, cover the pan, and braise the fish and vegetables in the wine for 8 to 12 minutes, depending on how well done you'd like the fish.

Add the olives, capers, and lemon zest and stir to mix well with the vegetables. Continue cooking just until the olives are heated through—about 3 to 5 minutes. Then transfer the fish to a heated platter and distribute the vegetables over and around it. Turn the heat to high and rapidly boil down any juices remaining in the pan until reduced to 2 or 3 tablespoons of syrupy glaze. Add to the fish and serve immediately.

Provençal Braised Tuna or Swordfish

⇥ Makes 6 to 8 servings

THIS IS AN ADAPTATION of a method mentioned in René Jouveau's lovely *Cuisine Provençale de Tradition Populaire*. Note that the only fat comes from the olives and the fish itself, the amount depending on the type of fish used.

2 large onions, roughly chopped

2 large ripe tomatoes, roughly chopped, or canned whole tomatoes, drained and chopped

Preheat the oven to 375 degrees. Strew half the chopped onion in a heavy kettle or casserole, preferably one with a tight-fitting lid. Cover the onion with half the chopped tomatoes and top them with a layer of half the sliced lemons. Sprinkle with salt, pepper, and about a third of the

1 large lemon, very thinly sliced

sea salt and freshly ground black pepper

2 tablespoons coarsely chopped rosemary needles

2 pounds tuna or swordfish steak, 1½ to 2 inches thick, skinned if necessary

⅓ cup chopped black olives, preferably oil-cured

2 bay leaves

3 or 4 thyme sprigs

1 cup dry white wine

rosemary. Set the fish on top—it can be in several pieces, but they should fit together to make a compact layer. Add a little more salt and pepper and half the remaining rosemary. Spread the remaining lemons over the fish, followed by the remaining tomatoes and remaining onions. Top the final onion layer with a little more salt and pepper and the remaining rosemary and strew the black olives over all. Tuck the bay leaves and sprigs of thyme into the pot and pour the white wine over all.

Seal the kettle with heavy-duty aluminum foil, then add the lid. Bake for 1½ hours.

Salade Niçoise Royale

Makes 8 servings

TRADITIONAL SALADE NIÇOISE was always served as an hors d'oeuvre or first course, and purists refused to admit tuna, or even potatoes, to the composition of this Provençal favorite. Gradually, however, over the years, canned tuna—but always the very best oil-packed white tuna—began to creep in more and more. And then someone had the brilliant idea of using a piece of fresh tuna, grilled like a steak over live coals, and voilà, salade Niçoise had become a main-course dish. You will still find traditionalists who turn up their noses at this modern version, but it makes a wonderful summertime treat and splendid fare for a special celebration, especially since so much of the dish can be prepared in advance. For an elegant presentation, roast the peppers over the grill until the skins are black and blistered, following the directions on page 26. Slice the peeled peppers into long thin fingers and use as described.

1 pound fresh green beans, the smaller the better, trimmed

1 pound small waxy potatoes such as red bliss, Yellow Finn, or Russian fingerling

[cont. next page]

The green beans, potatoes, and eggs can be prepared well ahead of time—in the morning, say, for an evening meal. Simply rinse the beans and place in an inch of rapidly boiling salted water. Cook until the beans are tender—about 7 to 10 minutes—or to taste. Remove from the heat, drain, and immediately

9 tablespoons extra-virgin olive oil

3 tablespoons red wine vinegar

sea salt and freshly ground black pepper

3 or 4 hard-boiled eggs (optional)

1 head of romaine lettuce, green leafy tops only

1 pound fresh ripe red tomatoes

1 large red onion, very thinly sliced

1 sweet green pepper, very thinly sliced

1 sweet red pepper, very thinly sliced

½ cup black Niçoise or Gaeta olives, pitted

8 oil-packed anchovy fillets (optional)

½ to ¾ cup tightly packed basil leaves

2 pounds fresh tuna steak, about 2 inches thick

1 garlic clove, finely chopped

1 teaspoon sea salt

2 tablespoons finely minced fresh chives or scallion greens

1 tablespoon drained capers, rinsed and chopped

refresh in cold running water to preserve the color. Set aside as soon as the temperature has reduced and cover lightly with a piece of foil.

Scrub the potatoes and cook them in rapidly boiling salted water to cover until they are done, about 20 to 30 minutes, depending on the size and variety; be careful not to overcook. When done, remove from the heat, drain immediately, and run a little cold water over them to halt the cooking process. Peel them if you wish. Small potatoes can be served whole, but larger ones can be sliced rather thickly—not less than ¼ inch thick. Potatoes should be dressed immediately while still warm. Mix together 3 tablespoons of the olive oil and 1 tablespoon of the wine vinegar, adding salt and pepper to taste; pour over the potatoes and toss gently. The potatoes will absorb most of the dressing. Set aside until ready to assemble the salad.

If you're planning to use live coals to cook the fish, prepare the fire about an hour before you plan to serve so as to have plenty of time for a good bed of coals to build up. (If you're using an electric or gas grill or broiling the fish in the oven, just preheat for about 5 to 10 minutes.)

While the fire is readying itself, arrange the elements of the salad on a large oval platter, leaving room in the center of the plate for the fish. Arrange the lettuce as a bed for the other ingredients. Slice the tomatoes and sprinkle with salt. Pile the tomatoes at one end of the platter, pile the potatoes at the other end, and arrange the beans along both sides. Scatter the onion and pepper rings over the vegetables and arrange the black olives and anchovies on top. Slice the eggs and add the slices. Finally, strew fresh basil leaves over everything.

Set the grill or broiling pan about 5 or 6 inches away from the heat. Paint the grill or pan with a little of the olive oil—the oil will smoke a little when it's hot enough. Place the tuna steak on the

grill or in the broiling pan and cook for about 8
minutes on each side, turning once. Like red meat,
high-quality tuna is best if it's not thoroughly
cooked—a little pink or even red in the middle is
tasty. Remove the fish from the grill when it's done
and drop it in the center of the salad platter.

While the tuna is cooking, prepare the dressing:
Crush the garlic and salt together in a small bowl,
using the back of a spoon, until it is a paste. Then,
using a fork, beat in the remaining oil and vinegar
along with the chives, capers, and salt and pepper.

As soon as the tuna is in place, pour the dressing
over the vegetables and serve immediately.

Sicilian Swordfish in Foil Packets

Makes 2 servings

THIS IS A FINE RECIPE for entertaining because there's no last-minute mess
to contend with. You can prepare the packets ahead of time and pop them
in the oven for 15 minutes before serving. Use any good-quality imported green
olives—the small, firm, rather bitter green ones are fine—but in the absence of
good-quality green olives, imported black olives will do. Though usually made
with swordfish, the recipe works just as well with yellowfin or albacore tuna, or
with fresh halibut or salmon steaks.

Note that the recipe is for only two servings, but it can be expanded indefinitely.

1 swordfish, tuna, or other
fish steak, about 1½ inches
thick, weighing about ½ to ¾
pound

a little flour for dusting the
fish

2 tablespoons extra-virgin
olive oil

1 small onion, chopped fine

[cont. next page]

Dust each side of the fish steak lightly with flour,
shaking off the excess. Heat 1 tablespoon oil in a
sauté pan over medium-high heat and sauté the
fish quickly in it just until it is golden on each side.
(It will continue cooking later.) Remove the fish
and set aside.

Lower the heat and in the oil remaining in the pan
gently sauté the onion and garlic until they are
soft, about 10 to 15 minutes, adding the second

1 small garlic clove, chopped fine

1 tablespoon golden raisins, plumped in hot water, drained

1 tablespoon pine nuts

1 celery stalk, chopped fine

1 tablespoon salt-packed capers, rinsed and drained

6 large green olives, pitted and coarsely chopped

2 canned plum tomatoes, chopped

sea salt and freshly ground black pepper

2 bay leaves

1 tablespoon fine dry bread crumbs

tablespoon of olive oil if necessary. Then add the raisins, pine nuts, celery, capers, and olives and cook for 2 to 3 minutes. Add the tomatoes, raise the heat slightly, and cook over medium heat for another 2 to 3 minutes, until the sauce is thick.

Place the fish on a large square of aluminum foil or parchment paper. Pile the sauce on top, add salt, pepper, and a few bread crumbs, and fold up the ends of the foil to form a loose but tightly sealed packet. The fish can be prepared well ahead of time and refrigerated, but allow time to bring it back to room temperature before cooking.

When you're ready to cook, preheat the oven to 425 degrees. Put the room-temperature packet on a cookie sheet or in a shallow baking pan and roast for 15 minutes. Remove. Divide the steak into 2 serving pieces and serve with the sauce spooned over them.

Variation: You can also prepare this in a single baking dish or gratin dish, piling the sauce on top of the fish pieces and baking in a hot oven for 15 to 20 minutes, until the fish is thoroughly cooked and the sauce is bubbly on top.

North African Spiced Marinated Fish

Chermoula

Makes 6 servings

THIS DELICIOUSLY FRAGRANT MARINADE will lend flavor interest to just about any kind of fish or seafood, especially bland, farm-raised catfish and tilapia. But it's even better with salmon, either steaks or fillets, and wonderful with big, meaty chunks of swordfish or halibut. In fact, I can't think of any seafood that won't benefit from a bath in this Moroccan mix.

half a large bunch fresh cilantro

half a large bunch flat-leaf parsley

8 garlic cloves, crushed with the flat blade of a knife

1 teaspoon sea salt, or more to taste

1 tablespoon freshly ground cumin, or more to taste

1 tablespoon ground or crushed dried red chili pepper (piment d'Espelette or Aleppo pepper is best), or more to taste

1 tablespoon ground mild red paprika, or more to taste

½ cup extra-virgin olive oil

¼ cup freshly squeezed lemon juice

6 to 8 small salmon steaks, each weighing about 5 ounces

Chop together the cilantro and parsley to make 1 cup of very finely minced fresh herbs.

Crush the garlic with the salt to make a smooth paste (you can do this in a mortar, or simply, using the back of a spoon, crush the garlic and salt together in a small bowl). Combine the garlic, minced herbs, cumin, chili, paprika, olive oil, and lemon juice in a small saucepan or skillet. Set over medium heat and warm just until the mixture is very hot but do not let it boil. (You should be able to hold your finger in it to a count of ten.) Taste the mix and adjust the seasoning, adding more of the salt, peppers, oil, or lemon juice if it needs it.

Set the fish steaks in an oven dish large enough to hold them all in one layer. Pour the warm marinade over the fish and cover with plastic wrap. Set aside for an hour or so, refrigerating if necessary. (The fish can marinate for several hours or even overnight if refrigerated.)

When you're ready to cook, set the oven at 450 degrees.

Uncover the fish and transfer the dish, with the marinade, to the preheated oven. Every 5 minutes or so, baste the fish with some of the marinade. Bake for about 20 minutes or until the fish is done and flakes easily when tested with a fork.

Serve immediately, spooning a little of the marinade over each serving.

Braised Salmon or Halibut Steaks

✤ Makes 8 servings

2 pounds salmon, halibut, swordfish, or other fish steaks, about 1 inch thick

[cont. next page]

Lightly dredge the fish steaks in a little flour, shaking them to remove excess. In a pan over medium-high heat, fry the steaks in 2 tablespoons

a little flour for dredging the fish

3 tablespoons extra-virgin olive oil

3 medium yellow onions, thinly sliced

1 garlic clove, minced

1 or 2 bay leaves

1 teaspoon sea salt, or more to taste

½ teaspoon sweet paprika

juice of ½ lemon

of the oil just long enough to brown them, 2 to 3 minutes on each side. They will not be cooked through. Transfer the steaks to an oven dish that will hold them in one layer. Preheat the oven to 375 degrees.

Add the onions, garlic, bay leaves, and salt to the pan in which the fish cooked, together with the remaining tablespoon of olive oil. Stir to mix with the oil and cook, covered, over medium-low heat, stirring occasionally, until the onions are very soft and golden brown—about 10 to 15 minutes. At the end of the cooking time, remove the bay leaves and stir in the paprika and lemon juice. Mix well and return to the heat just long enough to warm up the lemon juice.

Distribute the onion mixture over the top of the fish steaks, covering them as much as possible. Bake for 20 to 25 minutes or until the top is golden brown and the steaks are thoroughly cooked.

Salt-Baked Whole Fish

Makes 6 to 8 servings

I'M NOT SURE where this recipe originated—I first had it in the south of Spain, later in the south of Italy—but it has become widely, wildly, and deservedly popular in recent years for its simplicity of execution and its fresh, direct, and uncomplicated flavor. That flavor, of course, depends entirely on the quality of the fish itself. You must have a whole fish for this—head, tail, bones, everything but the innards. Only the best will do. A whole snapper would be my choice here, though the preparation would also be fine with a whole salmon, or any other large whole fish; thin, flat fish like sole and small halibut will not be successful. Just be sure you have an oven dish, and an oven, that are large enough for the fish.

This is a spectacular presentation for a dinner party.

1 whole fresh snapper or salmon (head and tail included), weighing at least 4 pounds (cleaned weight)

4 pounds coarse sea salt

2 egg whites

lemon wedges for serving

very fine extra-virgin olive oil for serving

Set the oven at 425 degrees.

Rinse the fish carefully, inside and out. Pat dry with paper towels. Measure the thickness of the fish at its thickest part.

Pour the sea salt into a large bowl, add the egg whites, and mix vigorously until all the grains of salt are coated with egg white. Spread about a third of the salt over the bottom of a large rectangular or oval oven dish big enough to hold the whole fish. The bottom layer should be at least 1 inch thick. Set the fish on top, then cover it completely with the rest of the salt. It is important to encase the fish completely in salt, so that no part of it is visible. The topmost part of the fish should be covered at least 1 inch thick.

Transfer the oven dish to the preheated oven, turn the heat down to 400 degrees, and bake a 2-inch-thick fish for 20 minutes, a 3-inch-thick fish for 30 minutes.

Remove the fish from the oven. The salt will have formed a hard crust over the fish. It's fun to present the fish like this at the table, then dramatically crack the crust with the handle of a knife or with a small hammer. As you remove the crust, you will be pulling away the fish skin and, of course, any scales. The flesh will be pleasantly salty and very moist.

Serve with wedges of lemon and a cruet of the finest extra-virgin olive oil you can find for dressing the fish.

Baked Fish with Capers and Olives

→⟨ Makes 6 to 8 servings

Many kinds of fish are appropriate for this treatment, including tuna and swordfish. Or try thick salmon, sea bass, haddock, cod, snapper, or grouper fillets or halibut steaks or thick slices of monkfish. This dish could as easily be Greek as Italian—if you want to make it more so, add a teaspoon of dried oregano with the bread crumbs.

4 teaspoons extra-virgin olive oil

2 pounds boneless fish

1 cup very ripe tomatoes, peeled and seeded (page 25), or 1 cup drained imported canned tomatoes

½ teaspoon sugar

1 teaspoon fresh lemon juice

1 tablespoon drained capers, rinsed

¼ cup chopped pitted green olives, preferably large imported Italian olives

sea salt and freshly ground black pepper

½ cup unseasoned dry bread crumbs

Preheat the oven to 400 degrees. Use a teaspoon of oil to coat the inside of a baking dish large enough to hold all the fish in one layer. Place the fish in it.

Chop the tomatoes and mix with the sugar and lemon juice in a small bowl. Add the capers and olives and mix again. Taste for seasoning and add salt and pepper as desired. Pile the tomato sauce on top of the fish pieces. Distribute the bread crumbs over the top and drizzle on the remaining oil. Place in the oven and bake for 35 to 40 minutes or until the fish is thoroughly cooked, the sauce very bubbly and browned.

Roasted Fish with a Citrus Sauce

→⟨ Makes 4 servings

The best citrus to use for this remarkably flavorful dish is bitter or Seville oranges (sometimes sold in Cuban markets as "sour oranges"). As the name suggests, these are a good deal less sugary than our most common juice and navel oranges—they're actually the oranges traditionally used for the finest English orange marmalade and are called Seville oranges because they grow along the cobblestoned streets in the old Barrio Santa Cruz of Sevilla in southern Spain, a glorious spectacle in early spring when the sweet fragrance of orange blossoms perfumes the air. You may find these oranges in Hispanic and Latino markets in January and February, but if they're unavailable, use a combination of oranges and lemons, as described in the recipe.

Whatever citrus you use, make sure it's certified organic; otherwise, you should scrub the fruit well with warm water and soap to get rid of any surface pollutants or wax.

Swordfish is often used for this dish in the Mediterranean, but halibut, cod, and hake are all good, as is just about any meaty, white-fleshed fish. Adjust the cooking times to reflect the thickness of the fish you use and if the sauce is still too liquid when the fish is done, simply remove the fish to a warm platter and boil down the sauce to concentrate the juices.

2 small Seville oranges; or use 1 blood or juice orange and 1 lemon

1¼ pounds fresh swordfish, about 1¼ inches thick

a little unbleached all-purpose flour for dusting the fish

2 tablespoons extra-virgin olive oil, plus a little more if necessary

2 garlic cloves, finely minced

1 medium yellow onion, finely minced

¼ to ⅓ cup finely minced flat-leaf parsley

1 teaspoon ground cumin

a pinch of ground or flaked red pepper (optional)

sea salt and freshly ground black pepper

a pinch of sugar (optional)

Set the oven at 400 degrees.

Grate the zest of the oranges and squeeze them for their juice.

Cut the fish into 4 to 6 serving pieces, and pat dry with paper towels. Dust the pieces lightly with flour on both sides, shaking off the excess.

In a skillet over medium heat, heat the olive oil. Add the fish pieces to the hot oil and cook quickly, just browning the pieces on each side, about 1½ to 2 minutes to a side. Remove and set the fish pieces in one layer in an oven dish in which they will just fit.

Lower the heat to medium-low and add the garlic, onion, and parsley to the skillet (you may need to add a little more oil if the fish has absorbed most of it). Cook gently, stirring, until the vegetables are quite soft but do not let them brown. Stir in the cumin, along with the red pepper, if using, and the salt and pepper, then add the orange zest and juice. Raise the heat slightly and cook, stirring, until the liquid comes to a boil. Let it boil for about 30 seconds, then remove from the heat and taste. If the sauce is too sour, stir in a big pinch of sugar and return to the heat briefly, just to dissolve the sugar in the sauce. Pour the sauce, with its vegetables, over the fish and set the dish in the hot oven.

Bake the fish for about 20 minutes, then remove. If the liquid in the pan is very juicy, transfer the fish to a warm serving platter, then boil down the sauce slightly to thicken (remove it to a saucepan if your oven dish is not flameproof) before pouring it back over the fish on the platter.

Serve immediately.

Lebanese Ways with Fish

We lived in Beirut in the early 1970s, right before Lebanon lurched into a 15-year war of unparalleled brutality. Most of the people I knew in Beirut have long since fled, gone to the earth's far corners. Most of them still harbor a heart-stabbing desire for the city that once was—sparkling, vivacious, beautiful, and temperamental, perched on its peninsula over the dazzling sea and backed by the stormy, snowcapped range of Mount Lebanon.

Not the least of Beirut's charms was the city's incredibly evolved cuisine that drew from a cross-cultural mix of all the people who had stopped there or passed through—Arabs and Persians, Egyptians, Turks and Armenians, Greeks, French, Italians, and of course the Lebanese themselves, fierce defenders of a heritage that went back to the ancient Phoenicians. The people of the coastal cities, Tyre and Sidon, Beirut and Byblos, had been seafarers and traders since the days of old Phoenicia, and seafood thus was a rich part of their diet, whether prepared in the French manner on the terrace of the glamorous seaside St.-Georges Hotel or in a more rustic fashion in the little outdoor restaurants that surrounded the Crusader port of Byblos, one of the oldest cities in the world. The following recipes are among treasured mementos of that time.

Samki Harra

Lebanese Fish in a Cilantro-Chili Sauce

U SE THE HOT CHILI JUDICIOUSLY in this recipe. Mediterranean food is not intended to be as piquant as, say, Mexican. The goal is a sense of heat but not overwhelming hotness.

1 cup chopped walnuts

2 pounds boneless firm-textured white fish fillets such as cod, scrod, haddock, or snapper

a little flour for dusting the fish

4 to 5 tablespoons extra-virgin olive oil as needed

2 cups finely chopped onion

4 garlic cloves, coarsely chopped

1 cup chopped cilantro

3 cups fish stock (page 109)

1 teaspoon hot red pepper flakes, or to taste

½ teaspoon ground cumin

¼ cup fresh lemon juice, or more to taste

sea salt and freshly ground black pepper

Pound the walnuts, using a mortar and pestle, almost to a paste. Or process them in a food processor. Set aside.

Dust the fish pieces lightly with flour. Heat 2 tablespoons of the olive oil in a skillet over medium to high heat and, when the oil is almost smoking, sauté the fish, a few pieces at a time, for 2 to 3 minutes on each side. Don't worry about thoroughly cooking the fish since it will continue to cook in the sauce. As each piece is done, remove and set aside. (You may need to add a little more oil from time to time.)

When all the fish has been sautéed, discard any remaining oil and wipe the pan out with paper towels. Add 2 tablespoons fresh oil and over medium-low heat gently cook the onion and garlic until thoroughly softened and starting to brown—about 15 to 20 minutes. Add the cilantro and stir to incorporate thoroughly. Then add the stock, reserved walnut paste, hot pepper, and cumin. Cook the sauce over gentle heat for about 15 minutes, stirring occasionally, to develop the flavors. Then add the reserved fish pieces and continue cooking for 8 to 10 minutes or until the fish flakes apart easily.

Transfer the fish pieces to a warm platter. Add the lemon juice to the sauce, mixing thoroughly. Taste and adjust the seasoning, adding more lemon juice, salt, black pepper, or red pepper if desired. Pour the sauce over the fish.

Serve immediately, accompanied by plain boiled rice or rice pilaf (page 225).

Kousbariya

Lebanese Fish Baked in a Tomato-Cilantro Sauce

Makes 8 servings

2 pounds firm-textured white fish fillets such as cod, scrod, haddock, or snapper

a little flour for dusting the fish

¼ cup extra-virgin olive oil

1 medium onion, halved and thinly sliced

1 garlic clove, chopped

3 very ripe tomatoes, seeded and chopped, or 4 canned whole tomatoes, drained and chopped

1 tablespoon ground cumin

1 cup minced cilantro

sea salt and freshly ground pepper

Cut the fish into serving-size pieces about 1 inch thick. Lightly dust the fish pieces with flour. Heat 2 tablespoons of the olive oil in a heavy sauté pan over medium to high heat and, when it is almost smoking, add the pieces of fish. Sauté the fish, a few pieces at a time, for 2 to 3 minutes to a side. (The fish will continue cooking later.) Remove each piece as it is cooked and set aside.

When all the fish is done, discard the frying fat and wipe the pan out with paper towels. Add the remaining 2 tablespoons of oil to the pan and over medium-low heat gently sauté the onion and garlic until soft but not brown—about 10 to 15 minutes. Add the tomatoes and cook, stirring occasionally, until the tomatoes have given off their juices and started to thicken—about 10 minutes more. Stir in the cumin and cilantro. Taste for seasoning and add salt and pepper if necessary.

Preheat the oven to 350 degrees. Arrange the fish pieces in a shallow baking or gratin dish and cover them with the sauce. Bake for about 20 minutes or until the fish is thoroughly cooked and the sauce is bubbling. Serve immediately.

Samak Tajen

Lebanese Baked Fish with Tahini

NOT TO BE CONFUSED with a Moroccan or Algerian tagine, this luscious fish is called, in Lebanese Arabic, tajen or tajin, with the accent on the first syllable. The richness of the sweet onions and sesame-paste tahini contrasts beautifully with a fairly lean fish such as haddock or halibut. But a rich sauce like this simply won't work with a fatty fish like salmon, tuna, or bluefish.

A fish tajen is usually served at room temperature but if you prefer it hot from the oven—by all means, serve it that way.

1 to 1½ pounds boneless haddock or halibut fillets, cut in 4 to 6 pieces

sea salt and freshly ground black pepper

1 teaspoon ground cumin

¾ cup fresh lemon juice

1 pound yellow onions

¼ cup extra-virgin olive oil

¼ cup pine nuts

½ cup tahini (sesame paste)

2 garlic cloves, crushed and minced

2 tablespoons finely minced flat-leaf parsley

Pat the fish fillets dry with paper towels and set them in a shallow baking dish. Combine the salt, pepper, and cumin with half the lemon juice and sprinkle this over the fish, turning the fish to coat with the marinade. Cover with plastic wrap and set aside to marinate for several hours, refrigerated if necessary.

When you're ready to cook, let the fish come up to room temperature. Set the oven at 350 degrees.

Cut the onions in half lengthwise, then slice thinly lengthwise to make what Lebanese call onion "wings."

Heat the olive oil in a skillet over medium heat and add the pine nuts. Cook, gently stirring and keeping an eye on them, until the nuts are golden. Remove with a slotted spoon and set aside.

Add the onion wings to the oil in the skillet, turn the heat down to medium-low, and cook, stirring occasionally, until the onions are very soft and starting to brown.

Combine the tahini with about ½ cup of water, adding the water a little at a time and stirring it in before adding more. The tahini will get quite thick.

After all the water has been added, start stirring in the remaining lemon juice, again, a little at a time. When all the lemon juice has been added, stir in the garlic and a pinch of salt.

Add the pine nuts and onions to the tahini sauce and stir to mix well. Pour this sauce over the fish in the baking dish and transfer to the preheated oven. Bake the fish for 40 minutes or until the sauce is very thick and slightly brown. Just before serving, sprinkle the fish with minced parsley.

Serve with more lemon wedges, if you wish, although the sauce should be quite lemony enough.

Roast Fish with Fennel, Potatoes, and Carrots

⚜ Makes 6 servings

THE BEST FISH for this is what the French call a *darne de saumon,* a center cut of salmon, but any kind of thick salmon fillets will work well. Other thick cuts of fish such as halibut or swordfish, snapper or monkfish, will do very nicely, too.

In many markets, fennel (or "Florentine fennel") is known as anise.

If you wish, you could prepare and roast the vegetables a couple of hours ahead of time. Then reheat them and add the fish just minutes before serving.

1 pound fingerling or new potatoes, peeled and quartered or thickly sliced

6 medium carrots, peeled and cut in chunks

sea salt

2 large (or 4 small) bulbs of fennel, including green tops

Set the oven at 400 degrees.

Bring a pot of lightly salted water to a rolling boil. Add the potatoes and carrots and boil vigorously for about 5 minutes, just to soften them slightly. Drain thoroughly and transfer to a bowl.

Cut the green tops off the fennel and set aside. Cut the bulbs into halves if they're small, into quarters or

1½ cups small grape tomatoes (optional), cut in half

4 garlic cloves, coarsely chopped

1 lemon, preferably organic

¼ to ⅓ cup extra-virgin olive oil plus 2 tablespoons

freshly ground black pepper

6 pieces of boneless fish fillet, cut about 1 inch thick and each weighing 4 to 5 ounces

¼ cup chopped fresh green herbs: thyme, basil, parsley, rosemary, or a mixture

eighths if they're large. Add to the vegetables in the bowl, along with the tomatoes, if using, and garlic.

Grate the lemon zest and add to the green fennel tops. Squeeze the juice of half the lemon over the vegetables. Slice the other half very, very thin and add to the vegetables. Add the ¼ cup (or more) of olive oil and toss to coat all the vegetables with oil and lemon juice. Spread the vegetables in an oven dish and roast for 30 to 40 minutes or until all the vegetables are tender and can be pierced easily with the point of a knife.

Meanwhile, use the remaining olive oil to rub over the fish. Sprinkle with a little salt and pepper and set aside.

Combine the fennel tops and lemon zest with the chopped herbs and sprinkle most of this on top of the fish, reserving a small amount for a garnish at the end.

When the vegetables are cooked, lay the fish fillets on top of the vegetable layer and return to the oven. Bake for 10 to 15 minutes or until the fish is done all the way through.

Serve immediately, sprinkling the reserved lemon-herb mixture over the top.

Tunisian Fish with Preserved Lemons and Olives

Makes 6 servings

AT THE ELEGANT RESTAURANT Dar El Jeld at the top of the old medina in Tunis, they make this traditional fish preparation from the southern quadrant of the Mediterranean with fillets of sea bass, or loup de mer. Farmed sea bass are widely available in American markets, but other fish are also suitable:

monkfish, haddock, cod, snapper, or any other firm-textured white fish with rather plump fillets (not sole or flounder). Madame Jait, one of the restaurant's proprietors, told me the dish is "not Tunisienne but Tunisoise," meaning from Tunis the city, with its cuisine of the Mediterranean littoral, not Tunisia the country, which draws more deeply from Africa and the desert for inspiration. At Dar El Jeld they do not add harissa or hot pepper to the sauce, as they would farther south, just a little cumin stirred in at the end—"because to add it sooner," says Madame Jait, "would make the sauce bitter."

1½ pounds fish fillets

sea salt and freshly ground pepper

about ½ teaspoon saffron threads

½ garlic clove, minced

1 medium onion, minced

2 tablespoons extra-virgin olive oil

1 medium green sweet pepper, cut into long strips

1 medium very ripe tomato, finely chopped, or 1 tablespoon tomato puree diluted with 1 cup hot water

1 tablespoon harissa (page 279) or ½ teaspoon ground medium-hot dried red chili (not chili powder) (optional)

¼ cup drained capers, rinsed and coarsely chopped

1 preserved lemon (page 281), rinsed and cut into small pieces

½ cup pitted olives, preferably mixed green and black

2 tablespoons white wine vinegar

½ teaspoon ground cumin

Rinse the fish fillets in running water and pat dry with paper towels. Sprinkle on both sides with salt, pepper, and the crumbled saffron. Set the fillets aside on a rack until you're ready to cook them.

In a skillet over medium-low heat, gently cook the garlic and onion in the oil until the onion is soft but not brown—about 10 to 15 minutes. Add the green pepper strips and cook just until wilted, then add the tomato and, if you wish, the harissa. Continue cooking over low heat until the sauce is reduced and thickened—about 5 to 10 minutes.

Add the fish pieces to the sauce and cook for about 7 to 10 minutes or until done. Transfer the fish pieces to a heated platter. Stir the capers, preserved lemon, and olives into the fish sauce along with the vinegar. Simmer for 5 minutes, adding the cumin at the very end. Taste and adjust the seasoning, adding salt if necessary.

Pour the sauce over the fish on the platter, arranging the lemons and olives around the edge. Serve immediately, accompanied by rice pilaf (page 225) or plain steamed potatoes to sop up the sauce. At Dar El Jeld the plate is garnished with cherry tomatoes and little onions about the same size, both cooked in the fragrant sauce of the fish.

Herb-Crusted Fish Fillets in a Marinara Sauce

THIS IS ANOTHER MODEL RECIPE that can be varied in several directions— by adding cumin, a spoonful of harissa, and a little chopped salt-preserved lemon to the tomato sauce to give a more North African flavor, for instance, or chopped capers and black or green olives to give a Provençal touch to the dish. It's an excellent sauce with almost any kind of meaty fish—halibut, monkfish, or salmon—but it's also first-rate with scallops. Best of all, the tomato sauce can be made ahead, then warmed to simmering before it is served with the quickly sautéed fish.

1½ to 2 cups **Plain Tomato Sauce** (page 266)

a pinch of ground or flaked red chili pepper, such as piment d'Espelette or Aleppo pepper

a pinch of sugar (optional)

fresh lemon juice, to taste

1 pound fish cut in 4 serving-size pieces

½ cup unbleached all-purpose flour

1 egg

½ cup dry unflavored bread crumbs

2 tablespoons finely chopped flat-leaf parsley

2 tablespoons finely chopped basil

2 tablespoons finely chopped chives

Follow the recipe for Plain Tomato Sauce, adding ground or flaked chili, sugar, and lemon juice. Cook till the sauce is thick and almost jammy. Set aside. If you're planning to use it right away, keep it warm, otherwise refrigerate it but bring it back to simmering before adding to the fish.

Pat the fish pieces dry with paper towels. Set up three soup plates in a row, one with the flour, one with the egg, lightly beaten with a fork, and one with the bread crumbs. Combine the chopped herbs with the bread crumbs and toss to mix well.

Dip each piece of fish first in the flour, dredging it lightly, then in the egg, and finally in the herb and bread crumb mixture.

Add 2 or 3 tablespoons of oil to a flat-bottomed skillet and set over medium heat. When the oil is hot, drop the fish pieces in and quickly brown them on each side, turning once. They should be done, brown and crisp on each side, in just 2 to 3 minutes. Remove the fish pieces to a warm serving platter and top with the thick tomato sauce. Serve immediately.

Variation: The sauce is also very good with fresh shrimp, although they will not need breading. Instead, sauté the shrimp quickly in the oil and stir the chopped herbs into the tomato sauce right before serving.

Gratin of Fish and Spinach

Makes 6 servings

THIS DISH IS TRADITIONALLY MADE with salt cod, but I find it difficult to persuade Americans, outside of some more adventurous restaurant chefs, that there is virtue in that old-fashioned treat. Make this with any firm-textured white fish, such as haddock or snapper; salmon fillets are also a good choice, setting up a nice contrast between the pink fish and the deep green spinach.

2 pounds fresh spinach, rinsed well

1 medium onion, chopped

1 garlic clove, chopped

2 tablespoons extra-virgin olive oil

1 tablespoon Dijon mustard

sea salt and freshly ground black pepper

1½ pounds fish fillets, the thicker the better

juice of ½ lemon, or more to taste

¾ cup fine dry unseasoned bread crumbs

Cook the spinach in a large kettle over medium heat, using only the water clinging to its leaves, for about 10 to 15 minutes. When spinach is tender, remove from the heat, drain, and chop rather coarsely.

In a small saucepan or skillet over medium-low heat, gently sauté the onion and garlic in 1 tablespoon of the oil until the onion is softened but not browned—about 10 to 15 minutes. Stir in the mustard and combine this mixture with the chopped spinach, stirring to mix it all together. Taste and add salt and pepper if desired. (The recipe can be prepared ahead up to this point.)

When you're ready to cook, preheat the oven to 450 degrees. Lightly oil the bottom and sides of an oval gratin dish large enough to hold the fish in one layer. Spread half the spinach mixture in the bottom of the dish, then set the fish pieces on top. Sprinkle with salt, pepper, and the lemon juice. Then top with the remaining spinach. Strew the bread crumbs over the top and drizzle the remaining tablespoon of oil over the crumbs.

Bake for about 20 to 30 minutes, depending on the thickness of the fillets, or until the fish is thoroughly cooked and the spinach is bubbling. Serve immediately.

Halibut with a Spanish Almond Sauce

Pescado en Pepitoria

Makes 6 servings

M OST RECIPES FOR THIS SPANISH CLASSIC "en pepitoria" involve chicken, but the saffron-fragrant almond-rich sauce is even better with fish steaks. Halibut and swordfish are both good choices. You could make the pepitoria sauce ahead of time for an easier last-minute preparation.

Traditional Spanish cooks make pepitoria using a mortar and pestle, and it's true that it makes the best textured sauce. But it's a pretty laborious preparation for Americans, who will feel more comfortable, no doubt, using a food processor, although it's a good idea to crush the saffron and cinnamon in a mortar. If you don't have a mortar, add the saffron and ground cinnamon directly to the sauce mixture in the food processor and dribble in the vinegar or lemon juice.

¼ cup extra-virgin olive oil

4 garlic cloves, slivered

½ cup blanched slivered almonds

about 1 cup cubes of rustic country bread, crusts removed

a big pinch of saffron threads

1 1-inch piece of cinnamon bark, broken into bits, or ½ teaspoon ground cinnamon

[cont. next page]

Warm the oil over medium-low heat and add the garlic slivers. Cook until the garlic is soft but do not let it brown. Remove with a slotted spoon and set aside in a saucer.

Raise the heat slightly and add the almond slivers to the oil. Cook, stirring, until the almonds are toasted golden brown. Be careful not to let the almonds burn. Remove with a slotted spoon and set aside in another saucer.

Now add the bread cubes to the same oil and sauté, stirring and turning, until each cube is dark

sea salt and freshly ground
black pepper

1 tablespoon aged sherry
vinegar or freshly squeezed
lemon juice

½ cup chopped flat-leaf
parsley

1 cup finely chopped yellow
onion

1 cup finely chopped leek,
white and pale green parts
only

½ cup instant flour (Wondra)

1½ pounds boneless halibut
steaks, about 1 inch thick

½ cup fish stock (page 109)
or dry white wine if fish
stock is unavailable

½ cup dry sherry

golden on all sides. Remove and add to the
almonds.

Combine the saffron and broken cinnamon bark
with a teaspoon of salt in a mortar and crush to a
powder. Sift through a sieve to make sure you don't
have any large pieces of cinnamon left. Scrape into
a small bowl and add the vinegar or lemon juice
and several turns of black pepper.

Combine the sautéed garlic slivers with the parsley
in a food processor and process in brief spurts until
you have a puree. Add the almonds and bread and
again, using brief spurts, process until the sauce is a
grainy texture. Be careful not to overprocess—the
texture should be crisp and crunchy, not bready.
Add the saffron mixture and process very briefly,
just long enough to mix.

(The sauce may be made ahead to this point but if
you are not going to cook the fish right away,
obviously you won't need to turn on the oven.)

When you're ready to start cooking, turn the oven
on to 400 degrees.

You should have plenty of oil in the skillet, but if
not add a few tablespoons more and set over
medium-low heat. Add the onion and leek to the
pan and cook very gently, stirring frequently, until
they are very soft, then remove, using a slotted
spoon, and set aside.

While the onions and leeks are cooking, sprinkle
the fish steaks on both sides with salt, pepper, and
instant flour. As soon as the vegetables have been
removed from the skillet, raise the heat and add the
fish steaks. Brown them quickly on both sides, then
transfer the fish to an oven dish. Spoon the
reserved onion mixture over the top of the fish,
cover the dish with foil, and set in the preheated
oven to bake for 20 minutes.

Add the fish stock (or white wine) and sherry to
the skillet in which the fish was sautéed. Set over

medium heat and boil down, scraping up the brown bits in the pan and concentrating the wine. When the liquid is reduced to half a cup, stir in the almond-saffron pepitoria sauce.

Remove the fish from the oven after 20 minutes. Take the foil cover off the oven dish and spoon the pepitoria sauce all over the fish, mixing it lightly with the pan juices. Return the dish, uncovered, to the oven for an additional 10 minutes.

Remove and let set briefly—10 minutes or so— before serving.

Sardines in a Fennel-Spiked Tomato Sauce

Makes 4 to 6 servings

S ARDINES ARE NOT ALWAYS EASY to find in American fish markets, but when I find them, I snap them up. Fish lovers know that sardines are among the most delicious fish of all, rich and meaty in flavor and easy to eat because the central spine lifts out easily, leaving two small fillets for the happy diner. Of course, it goes without saying but I'll say it anyway, like all so-called "oily fish"— truly an unfortunate name—they are exceedingly rich in omega-3 fatty acids and tremendously good for you. If you can't find sardines, try this with young fresh mackerel or small bluefish, sometimes called (inaccurately, it turns out) blue snapper.

With oily fish, freshness is of even more critical importance, so let your nose be the judge before you buy.

1 onion, halved and sliced very thin

2 or 3 tablespoons of extra-virgin olive oil, plus a little more for oiling the oven dish

[cont. next page]

Set the oven at 425 degrees.

In a saucepan over medium-low heat, gently sauté the onion slices in a couple of tablespoons of oil until they are soft but not beginning to brown. Add the chopped tomatoes, raise the heat to medium, and cook the tomatoes, stirring from time to time, for about 10 minutes or until most

1 pound ripe tomatoes, peeled, seeded (page 25), and chopped, or use a 14-ounce can imported plum tomatoes, lightly drained and chopped

1 tablespoon fennel seeds, cracked in a mortar or with a rolling pin

1 tablespoon finely grated orange zest

sea salt and freshly ground black pepper

1½ pounds impeccably fresh sardines, tinker mackerel, or bluefish

2 tablespoons unseasoned bread crumbs

⅓ cup dry white wine

of the juice has evaporated and the tomatoes have reduced to a thick jam. Stir in about half the cracked fennel seeds and the orange zest and add salt and pepper.

If your fishmonger has not dressed the fish, open each fish up by slitting along the belly. Remove the entrails, then bone the fish by removing the central spine and the bones attached to it. Either butterfly the fish (that is, let each fish lie open like a book) or, with larger fish, separate each one into fillets. Rinse briefly under running water.

Use a little more oil to spread on the bottom of a rectangular or oval oven dish that is large enough to hold all the fish in one layer. Spread all but about half a cup of the tomato sauce all over the bottom. Arrange the fish on top of the tomato sauce. Sprinkle with bread crumbs and the remaining cracked fennel, then with the wine. Dot with the remaining tomato sauce and transfer to the preheated oven for about 20 minutes. When the fish is done, serve it immediately.

Oven-Roasted Fish with Vegetables

❧ Makes 8 servings

S URROUNDED AS IT IS by three seas—the Atlantic, the Mediterranean, and the Mar Cantábrico arm of the Atlantic—Spain is famous for the quality of seafood in markets, restaurants, and homes. All the more curious, then, that the Spanish are champion meat eaters and have been ever since the entire nation received a papal dispensation from Friday fish to lend strength for the crusade against Islam. Today we know the Christian forces would have been even stronger, and possibly brainier, had they eaten seafood. (True, they won in the end—but it took them 700 years, all told, to do so.) Despite their predilection for meat, modern Spanish home cooks favor oven-roasting fish for its quick, easy preparation and lack of fuss.

Besugo, or sea bream, is the fish of choice in Spain, but any large fish with firm-textured white flesh will do. Red snapper is ideal. The fish should be cooked whole for the best flavor.

1 whole 4-pound red snapper, cleaned and scaled

sea salt

1 lemon, thinly sliced

⅓ cup extra-virgin olive oil

2 medium onions, halved and thinly sliced

2 pounds small new potatoes, peeled and sliced ¼ inch thick

2 large peppers, preferably 1 red and 1 green, sliced ¼ inch thick

1 medium tomato, sliced ¼ inch thick

a pinch of saffron threads, crumbled and dissolved in ¾ cup dry white wine

2 tablespoons dry unseasoned bread crumbs

Rinse the fish inside and out and pat dry. With a sharp knife, make three deep vertical slashes, almost to the bone, on each side of the fish. Sprinkle a little salt over each lemon slice and press a slice into each of the slashes. Tuck the remaining lemon slices into the belly cavity.

In a large skillet, heat 2 tablespoons of the oil over medium-low heat. Add the onions and sauté gently, stirring occasionally, until they are soft but not brown, about 10 to 12 minutes. Using a slotted spoon, remove the onions from the oil and spread them in a roasting pan large enough to hold the fish.

Preheat the oven to 400 degrees. Add another tablespoon of oil to the pan and over medium-high heat fry the potato slices, turning occasionally, until they are golden brown, about 15 minutes. Using the slotted spoon, remove the potatoes from the oil and distribute over the onions in the baking dish. Now add the pepper strips to the pan and cook, stirring occasionally, until softened, about 5 minutes.

Set the fish on the bed of potatoes and onions and distribute the pepper strips and tomato slices over it.

In a small bowl, whisk the remaining oil with the saffron-infused wine until blended. Pour over the fish and sprinkle the bread crumbs, with a little salt if you wish, on top.

Bake for 35 to 40 minutes or until the fish is firm and cooked through. Remove from the oven, cover lightly with aluminum foil, and set aside for 10 minutes or so before serving.

Baked Fish Fillets in a Herb Marinade

QUICK AND EASY, this simple technique should be in every cook's reper-toire because it can be expanded or contracted to serve any number, and adapted to almost any kind of fish. Plus, you can vary the seasonings any way you want, using, for instance, more or less garlic, or other types of herbs—basil, thyme, cilantro, oregano, but just one at a time, please. If you want to make an herb topping that's more Provençal and less North African, for instance, substi-tute chopped black olives and sun-dried tomatoes for the salt-preserved lemon and the harissa.

I've used halibut here, but just about any other kind of firm-textured fish could be used—monkfish, cod or Pacific cod, mahimahi, salmon, haddock, and so forth.

3 tablespoons finely minced flat-leaf parsley

1 bay leaf

1 garlic clove

1 small yellow onion

half a salt-preserved lemon if available (page 281)

½ teaspoon harissa or chili pepper paste, if available (page 279)

2 tablespoons extra-virgin olive oil

1½ pounds halibut fillets at least ½ inch thick

2 tablespoons dry white wine, or a little more if necessary

¼ cup salted capers, rinsed, drained, and chopped coarsely

freshly ground black pepper

Chop together the minced parsley, bay leaf, garlic, onion, and salt-preserved lemon, if you have one, until very fine—almost a paste. Mix with the harissa and a tablespoon of the oil. Pat the fish fillets dry with paper towels, then spread the paste over the top of the fish. Set in a deep dish and sprinkle with the wine. Cover and set aside in a cool place, or refrigerate, for at least 1 hour and up to 12 hours.

When you're ready to cook the fish, turn the oven on to 400 degrees. Smear the remaining tablespoon of oil over the bottom of an oven dish large enough to hold the fish in one layer. Set the fish in the dish and pour any of the marinade juices over the top. Sprinkle the fish with the chopped capers and black pepper.

Transfer to the preheated oven and bake for 15 to 20 minutes or just until the fish is cooked through and the top coating is sizzling. Serve immediately, preferably in the dish in which the fish baked, garnishing the fillets, if you wish, with some freshly minced herbs and lemon wedges.

Pan-Fried Haddock with Little Green Lentils and a Bright Green Sauce

T HE COMBINATION OF FISH and legumes is an old one and surprisingly delicious. In this case the lentils, their flavors accented with little dice of pancetta and a hint of chili, provide a creamy contrast to the crisp textures of the fried fish.

This is a recipe that is adaptable to many different kinds of seafood—I have made it successfully with diver-caught scallops, and with medium shrimp, both quickly sautéed in olive oil like the haddock in the recipe. It would also be quite splendid with cubes of swordfish, large enough that two or three cubes make a serving.

The lentils may be made well ahead and kept warm until ready to serve. If they start to stick together, add just a little more boiling water to them and give them a stir over medium heat before adding to the fish.

¾ cup extra-virgin olive oil

3 tablespoons diced pancetta or prosciutto

1 small yellow onion, finely chopped

1 medium carrot, finely chopped

1 celery stalk, finely chopped

1 small leek, finely sliced

2 cups small lentils (lentilles du Puy or Castelluccio lentils from Umbria)

1 small branch of rosemary

1 small dried red chili pepper

2 bay leaves

6 cups simmering water, or vegetable or chicken stock (pages 107–108)

[cont. next page]

Combine 2 tablespoons of the oil with the pancetta in a saucepan large enough to hold all the other ingredients. Cook over medium heat until the fat in the pancetta starts to run, then stir in the chopped vegetables and the sliced leek. Continue cooking for about 10 minutes, stirring the vegetables in the fat and lowering the heat if necessary—the vegetables should just melt but not turn brown.

Meanwhile, rinse the lentils quickly under running water and when the vegetables in the pan have softened, stir in the lentils, along with the rosemary, chili pepper, and bay leaves. Mix well, then add about 4 cups of the simmering water or stock, keeping the rest of the water or stock warm in case you need it later. The lentils should be covered to a depth of 1 inch.

Return to a simmer and lower the heat so that the lentils cook at a steady simmer. Cover the pan and

½ cup minced flat-leaf parsley

2 cups basil, leaves only, rinsed and dried

2 pounds fresh haddock or other white-meat fish fillets (see headnote for suggestions)

¼ cup unbleached all-purpose flour

sea salt and freshly ground black pepper

cook until the lentils are tender—about 30 minutes, although the time will depend on the age of the lentils. Add a little more simmering water or stock from time to time if necessary.

While the lentils are cooking, prepare the green sauce. Combine the parsley and basil leaves, which must be completely dry, with a half cup of olive oil in a food processor and process in brief spurts until you have a brilliant green basil-flavored oil. Restaurant chefs then strain the oil but home cooks will leave it as is and take pleasure in the irregular texture. Set aside.

Cut the fish into serving sizes. Pat dry with paper towels. Combine salt and pepper with the flour and dip each piece of fish briefly in the flour, shaking off the excess. Add 2 or 3 tablespoons of oil to a skillet and set over medium-high heat. When the oil is very hot and shimmering on the surface, add the fish and sauté quickly until brown on each side—2 to 3 minutes to a side should be plenty. (You may have to do this in batches, in which case, keep the cooked fish warm while you finish cooking the rest.)

Arrange the lentils on a serving platter (or on individual plates if you wish), with the fish on top and some of the green sauce spooned over each piece of fish. Pass the rest of the parsley-basil sauce at the table.

Serve immediately.

A Seafood Extravaganza
with Oranges and Ouzo

Makes 10 servings

S ERVE THIS DELECTABLE COMBINATION of fresh ocean flavors with a plain rice pilaf cooked in fish stock, if you have it, with a pinch of cinnamon.

When buying squid or scallops, be sure to request those that have not been treated with sodium tripolyphosphate (STP), said to be a benign treatment to maintain freshness and quality. It's hard to tell with scallops but squid that has been treated is a pure, bleached, dead-looking white. Either squid or scallops treated with STP will leach out a good deal of nasty-looking liquid when sautéed—and the fish never, in fact, browns properly but rather sits in the pan, stewing in its juices.

Scrupulous fishmongers sell untreated scallops as "dry" scallops, meaning they are natural, without STP.

Ouzo is the universal Greek aperitif, anise-flavored and slightly sweet, like French Pernod. It should be available in well-stocked liquor stores but Pernod may be substituted.

2 pounds firm-textured, white-meat fish, such as halibut, mahimahi, or monkfish

1 pound medium shrimp, preferably with the shells on (optional)

½ pound calamari (squid) or scallops (optional)

¼ cup extra-virgin olive oil

1 large red onion, cut in half and sliced very thin

1 garlic clove, finely chopped

1 large fennel bulb

[cont. next page]

Rinse all the seafood and pat dry with paper towels. Cut the fish into serving portions, but leave the shrimp and scallops, if you're using them, whole. If you're using calamari, separate the tentacles from the hoods and slice the hoods in rings. Cut the tentacles in half.

Combine the olive oil, sliced onion, and garlic in a heavy saucepan or large skillet and set over medium-low heat. Cook, stirring occasionally, until the onions are soft but do not let them brown.

While the onions are cooking, slice the fennel bulb in half lengthwise, then slice very thin crosswise. Chop the fennel greens and set aside. Add the sliced fennel to the onions, cover the pan, and continue cooking until the fennel is soft.

1 large ripe red tomato, or 2 medium, peeled, seeded (page 25), and chopped to make 1 cup (or use canned whole tomatoes, well drained)

½ cup freshly squeezed orange juice

finely grated zest of 1 orange, preferably organically raised

⅓ cup Greek ouzo

¾ cup pitted green olives, preferably Greek

sea salt and freshly ground black pepper

Once the fennel has softened, stir in the tomato, orange juice, grated zest, and ouzo and raise the heat to medium. Cook rapidly, uncovered, until the liquid in the pan has reduced and become thicker, about 10 minutes. Add the fish and calamari and/or scallops to the pan, spooning the sauce over the seafood. Let the sauce simmer for about 7 minutes, then gently stir in the shrimp and let cook an additional 4 to 5 minutes or until the shrimp and all the rest of the seafood are cooked through. Finally, stir in the olives and the chopped fennel greens, then taste the sauce, adding salt and plenty of black pepper.

Serve immediately.

ABOUT SHRIMP

Shrimp is far and away America's favorite seafood, replacing canned tuna in recent years. That's partly because of availability—a lot of the shrimp available in our markets is farmed, and a lot is frozen, meaning it's much easier to get shrimp to market in good condition than it once was. I prefer truly fresh shrimp overall, but it's not always easy to find, and frozen shrimp offers a good alternative. This is one seafood that takes particularly well to freezing, so much so that even what looks like fresh shrimp in your markets may have been previously frozen—but your supplier should be able to tell you, and if she can't, she should not be your supplier. Previously frozen shrimp, which is then thawed for sale in a supermarket seafood section, rarely has the fine flavor and firm texture of either frozen or fresh shrimp, but last choice on anyone's shopping list should go to shelled and deveined shrimp, whether fresh or frozen, as they will have lost a good deal of flavor.

It's easy to tell when shrimp is good, or perhaps I should say it's easy to tell when it's bad—when it has a decidedly un-fresh aroma. As with other seafood, your nose will tell you immediately what's going on.

One way to perk up frozen shrimp is to brine it before cooking it. Mix a quarter cup of salt and a quarter cup of sugar with a cup of boiling water and stir to dissolve. Then add 2 cups of ice water to chill it down quickly. Add the shrimp to this and refrigerate for several hours or overnight.

Most Mediterranean connoisseurs prefer shrimp cooked in their shells, believing, correctly, that the shells add a great deal of flavor. But most Americans don't like to deal with shrimp shells on their plates. Use your own judgment in the shrimp recipes that follow, but keep in mind that when grilling shrimp, the shell helps protect the tender meat from the intense heat of the grill.

Deveining the shrimp is not usually necessary unless the veins are especially large.

North African Shrimp Tagine

Makes 4 to 6 servings

TAGINE REFERS BOTH to the cooking vessel and to the dish that's cooked in it. This one, with its fragrant combinations of cilantro and cumin, salted lemons and olives, inevitably calls up the seductive aromas and flavors of Moroccan kitchens.

A Moroccan tagine is an earthenware cooking pot, round and rather shallow with a high conical dome that comes to a peak on top. You don't need an authentic tagine from the Marrakesh souq to make this recipe, but if you want to try it with a real tagine, you can find one on the web site tagines.com. Any earthenware cooking vessel with a tightly fitting lid will work, however, and even an ordinary heavy-duty saucepan, one that will hold a couple of quarts, will do.

If fresh ripe tomatoes are not in season, use canned plum tomatoes but keep the juice to add to the tagine if necessary.

The tagine may be served on its own, if you wish, but couscous or rice will help soak up the delicious juices.

½ cup finely minced flat-leaf parsley

[cont. next page]

Combine the parsley, cilantro, ginger, pimentón, saffron, olive oil, and lemon juice in a bowl. Pick over the shrimp and rinse briefly under running

¼ cup finely minced cilantro

1 tablespoon finely minced fresh ginger

1 tablespoon medium-hot Spanish pimentón (paprika) or other ground red chili pepper, such as piment d'Espelette or Aleppo pepper

a big pinch of saffron

⅓ cup extra-virgin olive oil

freshly squeezed juice of 1 lemon

1½ pounds medium shrimp, peeled, tails left on

8 fresh ripe plum tomatoes, peeled (page 25) and chopped, or use 8 drained canned tomatoes, chopped, juice reserved

2 fat garlic cloves, minced

1 teaspoon ground cumin

sea salt and freshly ground black pepper

3 medium carrots, peeled and sliced diagonally

1 large or 2 medium sweet red onions, halved and sliced longitudinally

4 medium red potatoes, partially peeled, sliced

1 sweet red or yellow pepper, very thinly sliced

1 medium-hot green chili pepper, very thinly sliced

1 whole salt-preserved lemon (page 281), thinly sliced

½ cup green or black olives, pitted

water. Add the shrimp to the bowl, stirring to mix well. Set aside to marinate for no longer than 30 minutes. The shrimp may become mushy if marinated for too long.

Meanwhile, combine the chopped tomatoes with the garlic and cumin in a saucepan and bring to a simmer. Cook, uncovered, over medium heat for 20 to 30 minutes or until the tomato sauce is thick, adding juice from the can or a little water from time to time to keep the sauce from scorching. When the sauce is thick, add a little salt and plenty of black pepper.

Spread about ¾ cup of the tomato sauce in the bottom of a tagine or other cooking pot, then layer the carrots over the sauce. Sprinkle the onion slices over the carrots, then layer the potato slices on top. Finally distribute the pepper slices over the potatoes and spoon the remaining tomato sauce on top. Cover the pot, set it over medium-low heat, and cook the vegetables until they are tender, 20 to 30 minutes. From time to time, if necessary, add a little water, or juice from the canned tomatoes, to the pan to keep it from scorching.

When the vegetables are tender, layer the marinated shrimp on top of the tagine. Add the slivers of salted lemon and the olives, then pour anything left of the marinade over the top. Cover the tagine once again and cook until the shrimp is done—about 10 minutes.

Check the sauce and if it is very thin and soupy, remove the cooked shrimp and set aside in a warm place. Raise the heat under the tagine and cook rapidly until the sauce thickens, then return the shrimp and serve in the tagine, sprinkling a little freshly chopped cilantro over the top if you wish.

Skewered Shrimp with Garlic, Lemon, and Olive Oil

Makes 8 servings

THIS IS ONE OF THOSE recipes whose simplicity belies its dramatic effect on the taste buds. The shrimp can be cooked under a gas or electric grill but achieve their most noble flavor when grilled over charcoal or wood embers. Use the largest shrimp you can find for this dish, although the marinade is also good with smaller specimens. The shrimp are delicious served with a *contorno,* or accompaniment, of white cannellini beans. This is one recipe where you'll want to leave the shells on and peel the shrimp at the table.

4 pounds fresh shrimp, preferably very large, with their shells on

½ cup extra-virgin olive oil

1 teaspoon sea salt

freshly ground black pepper

3 or 4 garlic cloves, to taste, finely minced

3 tablespoons fresh lemon juice

½ bay leaf for each shrimp

¼ cup minced fresh green herbs such as parsley, basil, or tarragon

lemon wedges for garnish

Spread the shrimp out in a shallow glass or ceramic baking dish. Combine the oil, salt, pepper, garlic, and lemon juice, beating to mix well. Pour over the shrimp and set aside to marinate for at least 30 minutes, turning the shrimp occasionally in the marinade. (Refrigerate the shrimp if you're holding them longer than 30 minutes.)

Build up a charcoal or wood fire in plenty of time to have a good bed of hot coals when you're ready to cook. Or preheat an oven broiler and adjust the rack.

Thread the shrimp on skewers, alternating with halves of bay leaf. Lightly oil a grill and set the skewers on the grill over the fire, about 4 inches from the source of heat. Grill for about 3 minutes on each side. As soon as the shrimp are done, transfer to a heated platter. Sprinkle with the herbs and serve immediately with the lemon wedges.

Variation: Scallops, threaded horizontally, are equally good marinated and grilled on skewers. Or alternate scallops and shrimp for a handsome presentation.

Tomato and Pepper Gratin of Shrimp and Scallops

THIS TASTY COMBINATION was inspired by a recipe from a Basque chef friend, Teresa Barrenechea, who does something similar with plump sea scallops. Scallops, like the Basques themselves, are from the Atlantic coasts of Spain and France, not the Mediterranean, but this is clearly a Mediterranean-derived recipe. I mix shrimp and scallops together but you could also make this with some cubes of firm-textured fish, such as swordfish or monkfish.

If you buy scallops, be sure they have not been treated with STP (sodium tripolyphosphate). The ones you want will be marketed as "dry scallops." STP is an allegedly safe additive that keeps scallops and other seafood white and plump. It leaches out when the seafood is cooked and makes a nasty contribution to any sauce, plus you will be unable to brown the seafood properly.

Instead of pimentón, you could use piment d'Espelette, Aleppo pepper, or any other kind of ground red chili pepper that is not wickedly hot. Do not use Spanish pimentón de la Vera, as its smoky flavor is unpleasant in this dish.

The seafood may be fried ahead of time and kept warm, and the topping may also be made ahead, leaving just a quick pass under a preheated broiler before presenting the gratin at the table—and the look of the dish is almost as gratifying as the taste.

6 tablespoons extra-virgin olive oil

1 cup finely chopped yellow onion

1 garlic clove, finely chopped

1 sweet red pepper, slivered

4 canned plum tomatoes, drained and chopped

1 teaspoon mild Spanish pimentón (paprika)

sea salt and freshly ground black pepper

Combine 2 tablespoons of the oil with the onion and garlic and set over medium heat. As the vegetables start to sizzle and soften, lower the heat and add the pepper slivers. Stir to mix well and let cook until the pepper slivers are soft, then stir in the tomatoes, pimentón, and salt and pepper to taste. Let cook about 4 to 5 minutes longer. If the vegetables start to stick to the pan, add a small amount of water or white wine to loosen them. When the vegetables are done, set aside. This step may be done well ahead.

When you're ready to prepare the seafood, rinse it

1 pound sea scallops

1 pound medium shrimp, peeled

¼ to ½ cup instant flour (Wondra)

½ cup dry white wine

2 tablespoons chopped flat-leaf parsley

1 tablespoon fine dry bread crumbs

under running water if necessary, then dry thoroughly with paper towels. Set a skillet over medium heat and add 2 tablespoons of the oil. Spread the instant flour in a soup plate and dip each scallop in, shaking off any excess. Add the scallops to the hot oil and fry briefly, browning on each side, about 1½ to 2 minutes to a side. Set the browned scallops aside but keep warm.

Follow the same procedure with the shrimp, adding another tablespoon of oil if necessary.

While you're cooking the scallops and shrimp, preheat the broiler.

When the shrimp are done, add the white wine to the skillet and cook, stirring up all the brown bits and reducing the wine slightly to burn off the alcohol. Stir the tomato-pepper topping into the wine and mix well, then remove from the heat.

In an oval gratin dish, arrange the shrimp and scallops in a single layer. Top with the tomato-pepper mixture. Sprinkle with parsley and bread crumbs, then top with a thin thread of the remaining oil (you don't have to use all of it if you don't wish to).

Set in the preheated broiler and broil for about 5 to 7 minutes or until the top is lightly browned and sizzling.

Remove and serve immediately.

Catalan Shrimp in a
Sweet Red Pepper Sauce

THIS RECIPE and the next are often made with Mediterranean rock lobster (the kind that have no claws), but they are just as good, possibly even better, with shrimp. This dish is delicious with a rice or bulgur pilaf (pages 225, 244); or try it with steamed wheat berries.

2 sweet red peppers or good-quality jarred Spanish red peppers (pimientos de piquillo)

2 pounds medium-large (25 count) shrimp

3 tablespoons extra-virgin olive oil

½ medium onion, minced

¼ cup minced flat-leaf parsley

4 medium very ripe tomatoes, peeled, seeded (page 25), and chopped, or 1½ cups chopped well-drained canned tomatoes

½ cup dry white wine

1 tablespoon cognac

½ teaspoon saffron threads

½ teaspoon cayenne pepper

Roast and peel the red peppers, following the directions on page 26. Cut the prepared peppers into strips and set aside.

Peel the shrimp and devein if necessary. Heat 2 tablespoons of the oil in a sauté pan over medium heat and sauté the shrimp, stirring frequently, for a couple of minutes on each side. Remove the shrimp from the oil and set aside.

Lower the heat to medium-low, add the remaining tablespoon of oil to the pan, and gently sauté the onion and parsley until the onion is soft but not browned—about 10 to 15 minutes. Add the peppers and tomatoes and cook until most of the tomato juice has boiled away and the sauce is thick and jammy—about 20 minutes.

Add the wine and cognac and raise the heat to boil away the alcohol, then stir the reserved shrimp back in together with the saffron and cayenne. Stir to combine well and cook for an additional 2 or 3 minutes, until the shrimp are thoroughly warmed and the flavors have melded. Serve immediately.

Grilled Shrimp with Almonds

Makes 6 servings

THIS IS ONE TIME when the shrimp should be served with their shells on—messy, yes, but utterly delicious.

2 tomatoes, peeled, seeded (page 25), and chopped

½ cup blanched almonds

6 tablespoons extra-virgin olive oil

2 garlic cloves, peeled

1 teaspoon minced flat-leaf parsley

½ teaspoon freshly ground black pepper

1 teaspoon hot red pepper flakes

juice of ½ lemon

2 tablespoons sherry vinegar

2 pounds medium-large (25 count) shrimp

Prepare a charcoal fire or preheat a gas or electric grill. Set the chopped tomatoes to drain in a fine-mesh colander or sieve.

In a small sauté pan over medium-low heat, toast the almonds in a tablespoon of the oil, stirring frequently, until the almonds are golden brown—about 5 to 7 minutes—being careful not to burn them. Transfer the almonds to a mortar, food processor, or blender. In the oil remaining in the pan, gently sauté the garlic cloves, stirring frequently, until they are golden—about 15 minutes. Add the garlic to the almonds along with the parsley, black pepper, and hot pepper. Pound in the mortar or process or blend, gradually adding in the drained tomatoes to make a thick sauce. (If you're using a food processor or blender, be careful not to overprocess; the mixture should be a little granular from the almonds.)

Transfer the sauce to a bowl and beat in the lemon juice and vinegar. Reserve 2 tablespoons of the remaining oil and beat the rest into the sauce. Set the sauce aside.

Toss the shrimp with the reserved 2 tablespoons oil. Cook the shrimp on the hot grill, about a minute to a side, until the shells are papery and the flesh is thoroughly cooked. Pile the shrimp on a platter and serve the sauce in a separate bowl (less messy); or pour the sauce over the hot shrimp and serve (very messy but delicious).

Midye Pilaki

Turkish Potato and Mussel Stew

Makes 6 to 8 servings

S ERVE THIS IN SOUP plates with lots of crusty country bread, toasted if you wish, to sop up the delicious juices.

6 dozen mussels, about 6 pounds

2 medium onions, halved and thinly sliced

6 garlic cloves, peeled

¼ cup extra-virgin olive oil

2 large ripe tomatoes, peeled, seeded (page 25), and diced, or 4 canned whole tomatoes, drained and diced

2 large potatoes, peeled, halved, and sliced about ¼ inch thick

2 medium carrots, peeled and cut into chunks

sea salt and freshly ground black pepper

⅓ cup finely chopped flat-leaf parsley

Pick over the mussels, discarding any that are gaping. Clean them under running water, removing any beards that cling to the shells. In a heavy wide shallow pan, bring about 2 inches of water to a boil. Add the mussels, cover the pan, and steam until all the mussels have opened, stirring occasionally to make sure all the mussels are cooked—about 7 to 10 minutes. Remove the mussels from the pan (do not discard the water). Discard any that have not opened. Remove the mussels from the shells and discard the shells. Put the mussels aside in a dish, covered with a spoonful of their cooking liquid to keep them from drying out.

Strain the mussel liquid through a double layer of cheesecloth or a fine-mesh sieve. You should have about 2 cups of cooking liquid. Set aside.

In the rinsed and dried pan, gently sauté the onions and garlic in the olive oil until the vegetables are soft but not browned—about 10 to 15 minutes. Add the tomatoes and cook for just a few minutes to release their juices. Add the potatoes and carrots together with the mussel liquid, cover the pan, and cook the vegetables over medium-low heat until the potatoes and carrots are tender and have absorbed most of the liquid— about 20 to 30 minutes. Stir the mussels back in and continue cooking very gently, just long enough to heat the mussels thoroughly. Taste the sauce and add salt and pepper—additional salt might not be necessary if the mussels are salty. Off the heat, stir in the parsley. Serve immediately.

Peppery Steamed Mussels

Pepata di Cozze

A PEPPERY STEW of mussels, this is as far from Normandy's moules mari-nière as the Mediterranean is from the North Atlantic. These are often served as a first course but they're equally satisfying as a main course, especially if served over slices of toasted country-style bread that has been rubbed with a little garlic and dribbled with olive oil.

This recipe comes from Puglia, the long, thin heel of Italy's boot, where mussels and oysters have been cultivated in brackish lagoons along the coast since Roman times. These are Mediterranean black mussels, *Mytilus galloprovincialis,* which are a little different from our more common Atlantic blue mussels, *M. edulis.* The Mediterranean critters have a softer, more delicate flavor and a creamier texture. But farmed Atlantic mussels, widely available from fishmongers and at good supermarket seafood counters, are fine for this recipe.

Farmed mussels, fortunately, do not need the intense cleaning that wild mussels require, but they must have their beards, that hairy black stuff, removed. Give the beard a sharp tug or cut it with a paring knife and pull it away. Do not do this until you are ready to cook the mussels, however, as they die shortly after the beard is removed. And a dead mussel is a mussel that should be discarded.

Female mussels have a rich, reddish-orange flesh, while males are paler and cream colored.

1 celery stalk, preferably one of the dark green outer stalks, with leaves

1 garlic clove

a handful of flat-leaf parsley

1 red sweet pepper, cut into julienne strips

zest of 1 organic lemon, cut into julienne strips

[cont. next page]

Chop together the celery, garlic, and parsley to make a coarse mixture. Transfer, along with the strips of red pepper and lemon, to a saucepan large enough to hold all the mussels in a layer no more than two mussels deep. Add the oil, stirring to mix, and set over medium-low heat. Cook gently, stirring occasionally, until the vegetables are soft but do not let them brown. Add the anchovy bits and continue cooking, mashing the anchovy pieces into the oil with a fork.

¼ cup extra-virgin olive oil

2 or 3 anchovy fillets, coarsely chopped

½ cup dry white wine

1 teaspoon freshly squeezed lemon juice, or more to taste

1 tablespoon very coarsely ground black pepper, or more to taste

4 pounds mussels

Add the wine and lemon juice to the pan and as soon as it starts to simmer, stir in the black pepper. Now add the mussels, raising the heat to high, and cook, stirring and tossing, until the mussels are fully open. (If after 10 minutes there are still unopened mussels, discard them.)

Using tongs, remove the mussels from the pan to a deep heated serving bowl. Boil the pan juices down, if necessary, to about ½ cup, pour over the mussels in the bowl, and serve immediately.

Poultry and Meat

✧ ✧ ✧

W HEN I WROTE the first edition of this book, back in 1993, American eating habits were changing—possibly, it seemed, for the better. Beef consumption had fallen by 26 percent in the immediately previous decades, while chicken, seen as a healthier alternative, had risen by a whopping 75 percent. But this optimistic picture was not to last. Looking back from today's perspective, we can see that our overall meat consumption has climbed steadily, despite the occasional glitch up or down, throughout the second half of the last century and into the first decade of this one. In 1950, Americans consumed 144 pounds of meat per person—that is, meat purchased at the retail level, as cuts ready for cooking, or in restaurants and other types of food service. In 2007, the projected figure is 222 pounds per person per year—an increase of more than 50 percent.

Although beef consumption reached its peak back in 1975, with an astounding 85 pounds per person annually (that's a quarter pound of beef a day, every day of the year, for every man, woman, and child in the United States), it is still today, at 66 pounds, 50 percent greater than it was in 1950. And chicken—that healthier alternative, once the symbol of the working-class family's Sunday lunch—could you possibly guess how much more chicken we consume now than we did in 1950?

Four hundred percent, that's how much more. Hardly, in such quantities, a healthier alternative.

Although there are many other factors to consider in the mess of our American diet (a more sedentary population, increased consumption of fast food, and a hugely increased intake of high-fructose corn syrup in the form of sweetened drinks), it seems clear that one cause of our national epidemic of obesity has to be found in this enormous quantity of meat.

These dietary changes are invading the countries of the Mediterranean as well, and elsewhere throughout the developed world, and they are having similarly unhappy effects on the health of populations. If the traditional Mediterranean diet included meat only rarely, often in very small quantities, today in Greece, Spain, Italy, France, and urban centers of the eastern Mediterranean, most people expect to have meat on the menu several times a week if not more often, and in quantities much greater than their parents or grandparents consumed.

Scientists, nutritionists, dietitians, even some government health specialists advise us that our lives would be healthier, happier, and more productive if we would just cut down on the amount of meat we eat. The customary restaurant serving of a pound-per-person slab of well-marbled beefsteak, its edges curling with crisply browned fat, its cholesterol-rich juices forming a savory puddle for a butter-drenched baked potato topped with a dollop of sour cream, is assuredly nutritional madness.

But you just can't get around the fact that most of us who are not vegetarians really *like* to eat meat. There are complex physiological, psychological, and cultural reasons behind this, not the least of them being that meat adds depth, richness, and complexity of flavor to dishes that vegetables, no matter how fresh and delicious, can't supply. Moreover, quantities of meat on the table have always served as a cultural marker for high status, which is one good reason why government agencies like the federal Department of Agriculture promote the image of an American table groaning under the weight of all that meat.

I am not a vegetarian. But years of living and working in Mediterranean countries have taught me that meat does not need to be, in fact still in many places seldom is, at the center of the plate. The trick in traditional Mediterranean kitchens is to use meat in small quantities, more as a flavoring ingredient than as the focus of a dish. The best example of this is a pasta sauce in which ½ to ¾ pound of meat makes enough sauce, with tomatoes and other vegetables, for six to eight servings. The sauce is savory with herbs, spices, dried wild mushrooms, and other aromatics, but the richness comes from the meat flavor.

Sauces are not the only example of this principle. Many traditional meat dishes are made with almost more vegetables than meat and are intended to be served, like a sauce, with a carbohydrate, whether pasta, rice, potatoes, or polenta. Even at festive meals, Mediterranean cooks precede the meat with a vegetable-sauced pasta or light soup and follow it with fruit, plain or cooked, depending on the season. Although meat is at the center of the plate in such meals, it is only one plate in the succession of the menu, and the rest of the plates are all determinedly nonmeat.

Please note that in the following recipes I have counted on a serving size, in general, of 3 to 4 ounces of whatever meat is served—not counting bones. All recent health and nutrition research concurs that there is no need for healthy, normal humans, whether children or adults, to consume more than that amount daily, and a growing body of evidence suggests that excess consumption can cause cumulative health problems that go well beyond weight and cholesterol counts.

If this looks like a small amount of meat on your plate (and it will, I am certain), you should add more grains, legumes or beans, and vegetables to extend it. Most of the following preparations, for instance, go well with rice, baked or steamed potatoes, steamed bulgur pilaf, cornmeal polenta, steamed barley, or some of the small pasta shapes (small shells, orzo, elbows, etc., but not spaghetti or linguine) that are intended for this purpose.

Precede the meat dish with a light vegetable or bean soup, a salad of raw or cooked vegetables, or a plate of a single vegetable that is the star of the current season. (In early summer, for instance, try a plate of plain little green string beans. Fresh from a market garden, lightly steamed and dressed with oil, lemon, and a little garlic, they are ever so much more desirable than asparagus imported out of season from Mexico.) Follow the meat with a green salad and a small piece of cheese, or fresh fruit, or a simple, easy-to-make sweet, and you have a very substantial meal.

As much as possible I use meat from animals that have been raised humanely, in unconfined spaces with plenty of room to range. I also look for meat from animals that have been fed nonmedicated feed and have been given drugs only when necessary to fight off disease. The two conditions go hand in hand, for animals raised in confinement, whether chickens in battery cages or pigs and veal calves in cramped stalls, are exposed to innumerable sources of infection and need to be medicated to stay alive long enough to be slaughtered. When I take an antibiotic or, heaven forfend, a hormone, I want a dosage prescribed by my medical advisers for my specific condition and not an obscure quantity prescribed by some distant animal-feed manufacturer and dosed to the animal willy-nilly by the factory farm manager.

I also wish to give voice to a respect for life that has been the source of ethical questions since the beginning of human self-consciousness. Since we take life to sustain our own lives, it seems to me unquestionable that we owe an indulgence to the life we take, at least that that life be lived in dignity and lost with a sense of respect on the part of those who take it.

For me, the finest food begins with the finest ingredients. All else being equal, the meat of animals raised humanely, whether chickens, hogs, or so-called "wild" venison, is better in flavor and texture and contributes more to the dish than that from commercial factory farms.

FASTING AND FEASTING IN THE MEDITERRANEAN

At the beginning of the last century l'Isle-sur-la-Sorgue, a substantial country town in the Vaucluse region of Provence, had only two butcher shops. Not surprising perhaps in a rural area where many people probably got their meat from farmyard animals like chickens and rabbits. What is surprising, though, René Jouveau, chronicler of Provençal food lore, tells us, is that the two butcher shops were open *only* twice a year, at Christmas and Easter.

Like other people of the Mediterranean at that time, the people of l'Isle-sur-la-Sorgue, it seems, scarcely ate meat at all, especially beef. Lamb was for Easter, turkey for Christmas, and for the rest, on Sundays if they were fortunate they might have a roasted chicken, rabbit, pigeon, or duck. And if they were not fortunate, Sunday might see little more than an extra dollop of olive oil and an extra cut of cheese to go with the daily beans and bread.

This was the pattern in country districts throughout the Mediterranean until sometime well after World War II, long periods of meager diet punctuated by brief and welcome bouts of feasting. It was the pattern in Greece in the 1950s when butcher shops were closed during Lent and other fasts, and it was the pattern in Crete and southern Italy when the Seven Countries Study (see Appendix I) was initiated in the early 1960s.

The cycle of fasting and feasting was reinforced by religious proscriptions, especially among Christians. In the Orthodox tradition, observant laypeople fasted during the following periods: Wednesdays and Fridays throughout the year except during Easter and Pentecost weeks and for 10 days after Christmas; the 48 days leading up to Easter; the 40 days before Christmas; the 15 days culminating in the Feast of the Assumption on August 15; and, in honor of the Apostles, from the end of Pentecost Week to June 29, the Feast of Saints Peter and Paul. Fasting, for Greeks, Syrians, Bulgarians, and other members of the Orthodox community, means no meat, eggs, or dairy products all the time and no oil, wine, or fish during particularly acute periods. (During Lent, for instance, oil and wine are permitted on Saturdays and Sundays, and fish is allowed on the two feast days that fall in Lent, Annunciation, on March 25, and Palm Sunday.) Fully a third of the year, then, is given over to a very meager diet during which meat and dairy are completely excluded—and that's not counting Wednesdays and Fridays—although how many people in the Orthodox church still observe these stringent rules is not clear.

The Catholic tradition is more lenient. Long ago, a papal dispensation released Spaniards from the weekly obligation to abstain from meat so as to conserve their strength to battle the Infidel. In other parts of the Catholic community today, Lent is observed only by the pious and penitent, Fridays have ceased to be meatless, and other fasting periods seem to have been largely forgotten.

This is a pity, not just for religious reasons (perhaps for that as well), but because the obligation to abstain from meat and dairy products for long periods throughout the year was clearly beneficial to physical well-being as much as to spiritual health. I mention this particularly because it seems like a good practice, especially for people who have no interest in becoming totally vegetarian, to observe days or periods of abstention from meat and dairy products.

The total fast of Yom Kippur is also now but one day a year, but among pious Jews traditionally there were weekly abstentions on Mondays and Thursdays, the days when the Torah was read. Moslems fast in a rather different manner. Throughout Ramadan, the month-long period that commemorates the revelation of the Koran, Moslems abstain from food and drink (and tobacco and sexual intercourse as well) from daybreak until sunset, when traditionally the fast is broken with a few dates or a small cake like knaife or katayef, honey-drenched sweets with fresh cheese or chopped nuts. Men go to the mosque to pray; women prepare or supervise the preparation of an evening meal that must be nourishing enough to provide for the next 24 hours.

Throughout the Mediterranean, every long period of fasting was broken by a feast, and none more glorious in the Christian world than Easter. To me this is the quintessential Mediterranean feast, summing up in its emotional surge and its iconography the fundamental Mediterranean belief in a god (or goddess) who dies and returns to life and in some mystical way redeems humanity from the terror and mystery of our own dying. It is a powerful myth, deeply embedded in the history of the region.

In the Orthodox church, the long fast of Lent culminates in an even more rigorous Passion Week fast, when every scrap of fat is banned from the diet. Greeks break the fast on Easter Eve, after midnight Mass. When the Orthodox priest delivers the poignant and stirring pronouncement "Christ is risen!" it is the signal for a round of feasting that begins almost immediately with *magheritsa,* a rich thick broth of organ meats, butter, oil, and eggs, an eruption of goodness and flavors that burst or explode in the mouth after the long, lean weeks of Lent. *Magheritsa* is traditionally made with all of the innards, including the lungs, tripe, and carefully rinsed intestines, of the lamb that was slaughtered for the Easter feast. And the feasting continues the next day, with the same lamb roasted or stewed and shared abundantly among family and friends, along with buttery sweet cakes, often made in Easter symbols like the lamb and the dove.

This profusion of meat, butter, sugar, and eggs is typical of Easter celebrations throughout the Mediterranean. It is a way of eating that is not, of course, to everyone's taste and certainly not particularly healthful if it were to become an everyday affair. But it's worth remembering that a rich and meat-laden diet is *not* the stuff of everyday consumption. It's a feast, and a feast by its very nature is a very special occasion.

ABOUT CHICKEN

Like most Italian farmers, my Tuscan neighbors raise their own chickens and rabbits. The chickens run free in the farmyard, their diet supplemented only by cracked corn raised on the farm; the rabbits are in hutches, fed from herbaceous grasses gathered in huge bunches from the fields each day. The meat of these animals is incomparable, full of savor and juice and texture.

Our modern, commercially raised chickens are the tomatoes of the animal world—overbred, overmedicated, mass produced, tasteless, and with a mushy texture that adds nothing to soups or stews.

Seek out sources of good, naturally raised, preferably free-range birds, which, fortunately, are becoming more available—and less expensive as they do so. If you can't find free-running birds, insist on birds that have been fed pure, nonmedicated feed. They don't need that garbage in their diet, and neither do you.

Salt-Marinated Roast Chicken with Lemon, Garlic, and Herbs

Makes 4 to 6 servings

THE SIMPLEST AND MOST DELICIOUS Mediterranean meal imaginable centers around a plain, humble, but nonetheless beautiful roast chicken. There are so many ways to serve it—

- on its own with an uncomplicated green salad;

- garnished with a whole selection of root vegetables—potatoes, carrots, little turnips, perhaps some celery root if you can find it—cut in chunks and braised in the pan drippings while the bird roasts;

- alternatively, garnished with summery vegetables, such as eggplant, tomatoes, zucchini, peppers, all cut in chunks and added to the pan to roast along with the chicken;

- with a savory rice pilaf, or—and this is a great eastern Mediterranean favorite—bulgur wheat toasted with onions and pine nuts and steamed in a light stock made from the innards of the bird.

So often with roast chicken (or any other bird, for that matter), by the time the thighs are cooked through, the breast meat is overdone, dry and unappetizing. Salting the bird liberally inside and out, as described below, and refrigerating, lightly covered, overnight or longer (up to three days) helps to solve that problem. I don't know the science behind it, but the technique works to balance out the moistness in a very satisfying way.

The best, most flavorful chicken, I'm convinced, comes from free-range birds that have been left in relative liberty to move around a chicken yard. I buy chickens like these in my local farmers' market and in health food stores and co-ops. Not only is the flavor more developed but, it seems to me, the texture of the birds is more interesting, not tough but with a pleasant chewiness that is a long way from the mushy texture of industrially produced birds.

If you don't have time to marinate the chicken in salt, not to worry. It's almost as good without the salt marinade—but in that case, sprinkle the bird inside and out with about a teaspoon of sea salt.

3½- to 4-pound roasting chicken, preferably free-range

3 teaspoons sea salt

2 plump garlic cloves

1 fresh lemon, preferably organic

2 or 3 tablespoons extra-virgin olive oil

freshly ground black pepper

HERBS (OPTIONAL)

4 rosemary sprigs

4 flat-leaf parsley sprigs

1 tablespoon minced thyme or ½ tablespoon dried oregano, crumbled

½ cup dry white wine for the sauce or gravy

Rinse the chicken thoroughly inside and out in cool running water, then dry it well, inside and out, with paper towels. Rub the chicken all over, inside and out, with salt, using the full 3 teaspoons. Wrap the chicken loosely in plastic wrap and set in the refrigerator overnight or for two to three days.

When ready to cook, set the oven at 450 degrees.

Remove the chicken from the refrigerator, unwrap it, and pat it dry all over with paper towels, rubbing off any excess salt. (The chicken will have absorbed some of the salt flavor during the marinating.) Set the chicken on a rack in a roasting pan.

Crush the garlic cloves with the flat blade of a knife, discarding the skins. Toss the garlic into the cavity of the bird. Grate the zest of the lemon and set aside. Cut the lemon in half and cut one of the halves into four pieces, reserving the other half. Toss the smaller pieces into the cavity, squeezing gently to release a little juice.

Pour a tablespoon of oil in the palm of your hand and rub the upper part of the chicken all over with the oil. Grind a liberal quantity of pepper over the surface of the bird.

If you wish to add the herbs, strip the leaves (needles) from the rosemary and chop, along with the parsley and lemon zest. Add either fresh thyme or dried oregano (not both) and mix well. Use this mixture to slip between the skin and flesh of the chicken breasts, gently forcing the skin and flesh apart without tearing the skin. (If this is difficult, rub half the mixture over the surface and scatter the rest inside the cavity.)

Transfer the pan to the preheated oven and let the chicken roast, breast up, for 15 to 20 minutes, until it is turning golden. If the breast starts to blacken and blister, reduce the heat to 375 degrees. Roast for another 10 minutes, then turn the bird so the back is uppermost. Dribble another tablespoon of olive oil over the back and grind lots of black pepper on top. Roast for 30 minutes, then turn the bird once more. Squeeze the juice of the reserved lemon half over the breast and return to the oven for a final 20 minutes. The bird will have roasted for an hour and 15 to 20 minutes and should be well done. (If you prefer it slightly less cooked, roast the final turn for just 10 minutes.)

The chicken is done when a meat thermometer inserted in the inner thigh reads 180 degrees (don't let the thermometer touch the bone, as it will give a faulty reading), or when the juices run clear yellow when you pierce the thigh with a fork. Remove from the oven and set the bird aside for 15 minutes or so before serving.

If you wish to make a sauce for the chicken, remove and discard as much of the fat from the pan as you can. Add wine to the pan and over medium-high heat bring the wine to a boil, scraping up all the brown bits with a wooden spoon. When the wine has reduced by half and made a rather syrupy glaze, turn all the juices into a sieve set over a bowl. Press the solid bits to extract as much flavor as possible.

If there's still a lot of fat in the sauce, set it in the refrigerator—or better yet, the freezer—for 15 to 20 minutes to let the fat rise and start to solidify. That will make it easier to remove and discard it, but be sure to reheat the sauce before serving it with the carved chicken. There should be just enough thick, rich sauce for a tablespoon or two with each serving.

Roast Chicken with a Middle Eastern Stuffing

Makes 6 servings

A MIDDLE EASTERN STUFFING, with its saffron, cinnamon, and cumin flavors, lends a hint of the exotic to a plain roasted chicken. Cook the rice or wheat berries in water ahead of time until not quite done—still with a little resistance to the bite. They will finish cooking as part of the stuffing.

4½- to 5-pound chicken

2 minced garlic cloves

sea salt

5 tablespoons extra-virgin olive oil

2 tablespoons lemon juice

1 big pinch saffron

about ¼ pound lean ground beef

1 cup finely minced onion (1 medium yellow onion)

¼ cup toasted pine nuts

¼ cup toasted slivered almonds

freshly ground black pepper

1½ cups cooked rice, peeled wheat berries, or farro (½ cup dry grains will yield approximately 1½ cups cooked)

2 tablespoons currants or sultanas, soaked in hot water and drained

½ teaspoon ground cinnamon

½ teaspoon ground cumin

3 tablespoons chicken stock, made from the giblets (see recipe)

Remove the giblets from the chicken and set aside. Rinse the bird inside and out and pat dry with paper towels.

In a small bowl, using the back of a spoon, crush the garlic cloves and a big pinch of salt to a coarse paste. Stir in 2 tablespoons of the oil and the lemon juice. Use this to rub all over the chicken, inside and out. Cover lightly and set aside, refrigerated if necessary, to marinate for several hours or overnight.

Put the saffron in a small bowl or measuring cup with about ¼ cup of warm water and set aside to steep while the chicken marinates.

Rinse the giblets—liver, heart, neck, and stomach if included—and cover with water in a small saucepan. Add a little salt and pepper and set over medium-low heat. When the water comes to a boil, cover the pan, lower the heat to a simmer, and simmer for about 45 minutes, adding a little boiling water from time to time if necessary. This will provide plenty of stock for the stuffing and for basting the bird. When the stock is done, remove the giblets and mince them. You should have about ½ cup, but don't worry if there's less—you can make up the difference later with the ground beef. When you're ready to start cooking, measure the amount of chopped giblets that you have and add enough ground beef to make 1 cup in all.

Combine the minced onion with a tablespoon of oil and set over medium-low heat. Cook, stirring, until the onions start to soften, then stir in the pine nuts and almonds. Add the meats and continue cooking, breaking up the ground meat with the side of a spoon, until the beef has lost its red color and the mixture is crumbly. Transfer to a bowl, with any juices left in the pan. Add all the remaining ingredients (black pepper, cooked grains, currants, cinnamon, cumin, and chicken stock). Add the remaining 2 tablespoons of oil and the saffron in its soaking water, and mix well.

Set the oven at 450 degrees.

Set the chicken on a rack in a roasting pan and fill the cavity with the stuffing you have prepared. (If you have extra stuffing, put the leftovers in a small oven dish, dribble olive oil over the top, and roast for about 20 minutes or until the grains are thoroughly cooked and a nice crust forms on the top.) Tie the legs together over the gap to keep the filling from spilling out. Spoon any leftover garlic-oil marinade over the bird and transfer to the preheated oven. Roast for 30 minutes, basting the bird midway with the pan juices or a little of the reserved giblet stock. When the skin is starting to turn deep golden, lower the heat to 350 degrees and continue roasting, still basting frequently.

After another hour of roasting, start to test the chicken for doneness. There are several ways to tell when it's done: the leg joint moves easily in its socket; when breast and thigh meat are pierced with a small knife, the juices run clear yellow; a meat thermometer, inserted in a thigh but not touching the bone, will read 180 degrees.

When the chicken is done, remove from the oven and set aside for at least 15 minutes before carving and serving, with the stuffing and a little of the pan juices spooned over.

Pollo al Chilindron

Spanish Chicken with Sweet Peppers

Makes 8 servings

I<small>N THIS</small> S<small>PANISH</small> <small>WAY</small> of cooking chicken, tomatoes are sometimes added and cooked down with the peppers. I prefer the purity of the sweet pepper flavor. If you can't find any slightly hot peppers (such as Anaheim or New Mexico peppers), add a little ground or crushed red chili, such as Aleppo pepper or piment d'Espelette, to the pepper mixture. (But don't use chili powder, which is a mixture of chili pepper, cumin, and other seasonings for making chili con carne.)

The chicken parts should be small—legs separated from thighs, breast halves cut in half again. If you use boneless chicken, the quantity needed for the recipe will be less—2 to 3 pounds should be plenty for 8 servings. Serve with steamed rice, spooning some of the sauce on top.

4 pounds chicken parts
(8 pieces)

sea salt and freshly ground black pepper

6 tablespoons extra-virgin olive oil

8 flavorful red and green peppers, preferably both sweet and slightly hot

2 medium onions, halved and thinly sliced

2 garlic cloves, sliced

1 teaspoon chopped fresh thyme or ½ teaspoon dried, crumbled

12 fat green Italian or Greek olives, pitted and coarsely chopped

½ cup amontillado sherry

½ cup water or chicken stock (page 108)

Cut away any excess fat or skin from the chicken pieces. Sprinkle the pieces with salt if you wish and liberally with pepper. In a large skillet over medium heat, fry the chicken pieces in ¼ cup of oil until they are golden brown on all sides, 5 to 7 minutes to a side.

Meanwhile, slice the peppers lengthwise about ½ inch thick.

When the chicken is done, remove it from the skillet and set aside to drain. Discard the cooking fat and wipe out the pan. Preheat the oven to 375 degrees.

Add the remaining 2 tablespoons of oil to the pan and gently sauté the onions and garlic over medium-low heat, stirring frequently, until the vegetables are very soft but not beginning to brown—about 10 to 15 minutes. Add the thyme and the pepper strips and continue cooking and stirring until the peppers are soft and limp, about 15 minutes. Mix in the olives.

2 tablespoons fresh orange juice, *not* canned or frozen concentrate

Put the chicken in an ovenproof casserole or dish. Pile the pepper and onion mixture over the chicken pieces to cover them thoroughly. Add the sherry, stock, and orange juice to the skillet, raise the heat to medium-high, and boil, scraping up any brown bits left in the bottom of the pan. Pour the liquid over the peppers.

Bake the chicken for about 30 minutes or until the meat is thoroughly cooked and the sauce is sizzling.

Niçoise Chicken with Tomatoes and Black Olives

Makes 6 to 8 servings

THIS IS A CLASSIC DISH from the Comte de Nice, that bit of the Riviera that seems so much like Italy. Italians may consider it heresy, but in Nice this is often served with wide pasta noodles on the side.

6 tablespoons extra-virgin olive oil

3 medium onions, coarsely chopped

2 garlic cloves, chopped

1 tablespoon minced fresh thyme or 1 teaspoon dried, crumbled

a small handful of finely chopped flat-leaf parsley

3 to 4 pounds chicken breasts and legs, cut into 6 or 8 pieces

sea salt and freshly ground black pepper

[cont. next page]

In a large skillet, heat 3 tablespoons of the olive oil, add the onions and garlic, and sauté over medium-low heat until the onions are very soft and starting to brown, about 10 to 15 minutes. Add the thyme and parsley and cook a few minutes longer, stirring to mix well. Set aside.

Cut away any excess fat or skin from the chicken pieces. Rub the chicken pieces all over with salt and pepper. In a separate pan, sauté the chicken pieces in the remaining oil until they are well browned on all sides—about 5 to 7 minutes to a side. Add the tomatoes and wine, stirring to scrape up the brown bits from the bottom of the pan. Turn the heat up to medium-high and cook, uncovered, stirring occasionally, until the liquid has reduced and the tomato sauce is thickened—about

6 very ripe tomatoes, peeled
(page 25) and chopped, or 1
28-ounce can whole
tomatoes, well drained and
chopped

½ cup dry white wine or
vermouth

½ cup small black Niçoise
olives

juice of ½ lemon

20 to 25 minutes. Test the chicken for doneness—
there should be no trace of pink.

Stir in the reserved onion-herb mixture, the olives,
and the lemon juice. Return to a boil and cook for
5 minutes, stirring frequently—or just long
enough to reduce the juices once more. Serve
with rice, polenta, or bulgur pilaf (pages 225, 243,
244)—or with wide pasta noodles.

Baked Chicken Breasts with a Pomegranate Glaze

Makes 4 servings

I'M NOT A BIG FAN of skinless boneless chicken breasts, which became a fad years ago at the height of the somewhat misguided anti-fat campaigns. To my mind, there's no point in eating chicken unless you can taste it and those denatured breasts are dry and tasteless. On a healthy chicken, the skin contributes a great deal to the flavor. But this is one dish that you *could* make with skinless boned breasts, if you insist, since the pomegranate glaze contributes mightily to its taste. And if the chicken breasts come from a plump bird that has grazed in some freedom and developed flavor, it will be all to the good.

Pomegranates, those cheerful round red fruits often seen in wintertime fruit bowls, have quickly gained a reputation as superfruits, so thoroughly packed are they with antioxidants, especially deep red anthocyanins. Bottled pomegranate juice concentrate is widely available but make sure it is unsweetened. One brand to look for is Woodstock Farms Organic Pomegranate Juice Concentrate. Also available in Middle Eastern stores is pomegranate syrup, sometimes called pomegranate molasses. An excellent brand is Mymouné from Lebanon. If the syrup is available, just use half a cup and don't bother boiling it down—obviously it's already a syrup. Simply mix with the flavorings and bring to a simmer.

4 boneless chicken breasts, weighing a total of about 1½ pounds

1½ teaspoons ground cumin

sea salt and freshly ground black pepper

2 garlic cloves, minced

2 tablespoons extra-virgin olive oil

2 cups unsweetened pomegranate juice concentrate

1 tablespoon sugar

1 tablespoon Dijon-style mustard

1 fresh pomegranate, if available

Rinse the chicken breasts and dry well with paper towels.

Mix 1 teaspoon of the cumin with salt and pepper, the garlic, the olive oil, and 2 tablespoons of the pomegranate juice. Rub this all over the chicken pieces and set aside for an hour or more to marinate.

Combine the remaining pomegranate juice concentrate with the remaining ½ teaspoon of cumin, the sugar, and the mustard in a small saucepan. Set over medium-high heat and cook rapidly, stirring occasionally, for about 10 minutes or until the sauce thickens into a syrup and reduces to about ¾ cup.

When you're ready to cook, turn the oven on to 400 degrees. Set the chicken pieces on a rack in a baking dish. Add any excess marinade into the saucepan with the pomegranate glaze. Reheat the glaze to simmering and paint the chicken breasts thoroughly with it. (You don't need to use it all, as you will be doing this again two or three times before the chicken is done.)

Transfer the dish to the hot oven and bake for about 10 minutes, then remove the chicken and turn the oven down to 350 degrees. Brush the chicken again with the glaze and return it to the oven. After another 10 minutes, brush the chicken again with glaze and return to the oven for a final 5 minutes. (If at any time the glaze is burning on the bottom of the baking dish, add a very small amount of boiling water to the dish.)

While the chicken is baking, prepare the fresh pomegranate: using the curved bottom of a soup spoon, thump the pomegranate vigorously all over the surface. Don't worry about hitting it too hard. Then cut the pomegranate in half over a bowl to catch the juice. Most of the seeds should have been dislodged by your thumping and will fall out into the bowl. Use a teaspoon to extract the rest.

Discard any of the bitter white membrane mixed in with the jewel-like pomegranate seeds.

When the chicken is done, transfer to a heated serving platter or individual plates. If there's a lot of glaze left in the baking dish, boil it down to a thick syrup. Slice the chicken diagonally, pour the thickened glaze over the slices, and garnish them with the pomegranate seeds.

Moroccan Chicken with Preserved Lemons and Olives

Makes 8 servings

SAKINA EL-ALAOUI IS A FINE Moroccan home cook who takes great pride in the quality of food on her table. She prepares her chickens, which are very small (a half chicken makes one serving) in the traditional manner, rinsing them thoroughly, inside and out, in cold water, then rubbing them all over, inside and out, with salt and cut lemon quarters. She removes all visible traces of fat and any fibrous elements from the birds and rubs the salt and lemon juice between the skin and the flesh on the chicken breasts. Once the birds have been thoroughly cleaned, she freezes each one individually for use later on.

Moroccan cooks use *olives rouges,* lovely red and violet half-ripened olives (Sakina's are preserved at home in a paste of salt and the juice of bitter oranges), but any good-quality salt- or brine-cured olives can be substituted. Preserved lemons add an unusual and enticing flavor, but they must be made a good three weeks in advance. If you wish, use fresh lemons—the flavor will not be the same, but it's still a good dish.

about 5 to 6 pounds chicken, preferably small chickens weighing no more than 2 or 2½ pounds, including livers and giblets

1 lemon, cut into quarters

Remove all traces of fat and any fibers from the chickens. Rinse thoroughly, inside and out, in cool running water. Rub them all over, inside and out, with lemon quarters, being sure to rub between the skin and the flesh of the breasts. Rub salt all

a handful of fine sea salt

½ cup minced cilantro

½ cup minced flat-leaf parsley

2 tablespoons minced garlic

1 tablespoon ground ginger

freshly ground black pepper

¼ teaspoon saffron threads

2 whole preserved lemons
(page 281)

¼ cup water

½ cup extra-virgin olive oil

4 medium onions, halved and
very thinly sliced

1 tablespoon sweet paprika

1 tablespoon unsalted butter
(optional)

1 cup best-quality black or
violet olives

over the chickens. Set aside in a cool place to drain for at least 30 minutes or refrigerate the chickens, covered, overnight. Trim any greenish spots off the livers and pull away and discard the giblet linings.

When you're ready to cook, rinse the chickens again in cool running water and pat them dry with paper towels. Set aside.

In a heavy pot or kettle large enough to hold all the chickens, mix the cilantro, parsley, garlic, ginger, and pepper. Crumble the saffron into the herbs. Cut one of the preserved lemons into small pieces and add to the mixture along with the water.

Mix the seasoning together well, then put the chickens in the pot and use your hands to rub them all over, inside and out, with the seasoning sauce. Add the giblets to the middle of the pot, pour the olive oil over, and set the kettle over very low heat. As the chicken begins to sizzle in the sauce, add the onions and shake the pan to distribute them evenly around the birds. Cover the pan and cook very slowly until the chickens are thoroughly cooked and the onions have almost disintegrated into the sauce. After 30 minutes of cooking, add the livers to the pot, together with the paprika, shaking the kettle to distribute the paprika in the sauce. Total cooking time will be 1½ to 2 hours.

When the chickens are thoroughly cooked, remove them from the sauce. Cut whole chickens into halves or quarters and arrange them on a warm platter. Take the gizzards and hearts out of the sauce, cut them into small bits, and stir them back in. Using a fork, coarsely crush the livers in the sauce. The sauce should be quite thick; if it seems too thin, let it boil down, stirring frequently, until it is the right consistency. Add the butter if desired and the olives. Swirl the pan to distribute the olives and emulsify the sauce. Pour the sauce over the chickens on the platter and garnish with strips of peel from the second preserved lemon. (If you're not using preserved lemons, garnish the chickens with a little grated fresh lemon zest.)

Lebanese Garlic-Marinated Chicken on the Grill

Makes 6 to 8 servings

THIS IS ANOTHER GOOD RECIPE for skinless, boneless chicken breasts since the olive oil compensates for the dryness of the meat, but if you prefer, by all means, leave the skin on. For the finest flavor and texture, use chicken breasts from naturally raised free-range birds. For extra garlic flavor, serve it with Lebanese toum bi zeit (garlic sauce) from the recipe that follows. Precede it with a chilled gazpacho (page 130) and serve the chicken with fresh pita bread or slices of a crusty country loaf and a massive green salad for a memorable summer Sunday lunch.

2 pounds boneless chicken breasts, skin removed if you wish

4 garlic cloves, crushed with the flat blade of a knife

1 teaspoon sea salt

½ cup fresh lemon juice

¾ cup extra-virgin olive oil

1 teaspoon sweet paprika

freshly ground black pepper

Chicken breasts are usually sold split in half. Cut each breast half in half again and put them in a bowl.

Chop the garlic coarsely and in a small bowl crush it with the salt, using the back of a spoon, until you have a smooth paste. Stir in the lemon juice, oil, paprika, and pepper. Beat well with a fork and pour the marinade over the chicken pieces. Mix well, using your hands, and turn the pieces to coat them liberally with the marinade. Cover and refrigerate for 4 or 5 hours or overnight.

When you're ready to cook, prepare the grill, leaving plenty of time for it to heat up if you're using charcoal or wood. When the fire is hot enough, place the chicken pieces on the grill and set the grill a good 8 inches from the source of the heat. Use the marinade remaining in the bowl to baste the chicken frequently as it cooks. Grill for 10 minutes or longer on each side, turning each piece once. Test for doneness and serve hot or at room temperature.

Anissa's Garlic Sauce

Toum bi Zeit

Makes ¾ to 1 cup

I HAD STRUGGLED FOR YEARS to get this sauce right—clear white, creamy, and pungent. But it was only when my Lebanese friend and food writer Anissa Helou offered the suggestion of strained yogurt instead of the customary dampened bread or mashed potato that the whole thing began to come together for me. This is delicious but—obviously—for garlic lovers only. It is best made with a mortar and pestle, as a food processor brings out an acrid flavor.

6 plump fresh garlic cloves, crushed with the flat blade of a knife

1 teaspoon sea salt

⅓ to ½ cup extra-virgin olive oil

3 to 4 tablespoons strained yogurt (page 278)

Chop the garlic cloves coarsely, then combine them with the salt in a small bowl or a mortar. Using the pestle or, in the case of a small bowl, the back of a spoon, crush the garlic and salt together until you have a smooth paste. The garlic should be thoroughly crushed, almost to a cream.

Slowly beat in the olive oil, stirring constantly, as if you were making a mayonnaise. Add at least ⅓ cup of oil but if you can do so without the sauce breaking, add as much as ½ cup. At the end, gently stir in the yogurt, incorporating it fully into the sauce.

Brick Chicken or Guinea Hen

Pollo o Faraona al Mattone or al Diavolo

Tuscans call this celebrated method of grilling pigeons or very young chickens *pollo al mattone* because the bird is traditionally flattened with a brick or *pollo al diavolo* because the peppery seasoning is as hot as the dickens. Tuscan chickens don't weigh much more than a couple of pounds each, so half a chicken, flattened with a weight, is ideal for each serving.

Chickens in our markets tend to be much larger—4 pounds is considered a small chicken. If you use a chicken that size, have it cut in four pieces (two breast halves, two legs plus thighs) and don't bother trying to flatten them. Simply marinate and grill them, and call them *pollo al diavolo*.

Alternatively, if you can find guinea hen (*faraona* in Italian), they are perfect for the brick treatment, but it requires a certain amount of fiddling in the kitchen so it's not for everyone. If you have heavy cooking tiles or bricks made for use with food (not construction bricks), you can heat them in the oven. But an easier way is to use two heavy black iron skillets, one slightly smaller than the other so that it will fit inside. Heat both of the skillets for 20 to 30 minutes in a 500-degree oven just before you're ready to start cooking. Turn on a stovetop burner to high and put the larger skillet on the burner. (You must have your blower or fan on high as well.) Immediately, add the chicken pieces—they should just fit in the larger skillet—then set the smaller skillet on top to weight the pieces. The bottoms of the chicken pieces cook from the heat of the burner, obviously, but the tops of the chicken partially cook also with the heat and weight of the skillet. Then, once the chicken is turned to do the other side, the skillet should go back on top.

1½ cups extra-virgin olive oil

1 teaspoon sea salt

1 tablespoon freshly ground black pepper

1 tablespoon hot red pepper flakes, or to taste

1 tablespoon chopped rosemary leaves

Mix the olive oil with the salt, black pepper, red pepper, rosemary, parsley, and thyme and set aside, covered, for several hours or overnight.

Prepare the chicken by cutting away excess yellow fat from the insides of the birds. Flatten small chicken halves, if available, by laying them skin side up on a board (a flattened chicken will cook more

1 tablespoon finely chopped flat-leaf parsley

1 tablespoon fresh thyme or 1 teaspoon dried, crumbled

4 to 5 pounds chicken, cut into 8 or 10 pieces

juice of 1 lemon

lemon wedges for garnish

evenly on the grill). Cut away the wing tips and pound each chicken half smartly with the flat side of a meat cleaver or a Chinese cleaver—this should crack the breastbone. Larger chickens, cut in pieces, do not need this treatment.

Place the chickens in a dish or on a platter large enough to hold them all in one layer. Cover them with the flavored olive oil. Leave to marinate in the oil, turning occasionally, for at least 1 hour. Or refrigerate, covered, for several hours or overnight.

Prepare the grill, leaving plenty of time for it to heat up if you're using charcoal or wood. When the fire is hot enough, place the chicken pieces skin side down on the grill and set the grill a good 8 inches from the source of the heat. Add the lemon juice to the oil remaining in the platter and use the lemon-oil mixture to baste the chickens frequently as they cook. Grill for 15 minutes on each side, turning each piece once.

Or cook chicken on top of the stove, following directions in the headnote. Test for doneness: the juices should run clear yellow when chicken is thoroughly cooked.

Serve the chicken piled on a platter and garnished with lemon wedges. Accompany with ratatouille or with fresh salad greens, dressed simply with oil and lemon juice.

Braised Duck with Wild Fennel

Anatra alla Finocchietta

Makes 4 servings

WILD FENNEL POLLEN, called finocchietta, is a favorite aromatic that Tuscan country cooks use with a certain abandon. I'm not sure that it is actually the pollen—it's gathered from ubiquitous wild fennel plants at the time when the blossoms have faded somewhat but before the seeds start to form, so it seems like a mixture of dried blossoms and the pollen that still feeds them. It goes almost automatically with pork dishes, and is a special ingredient of the Tuscan salami called finocchiona, as well as the stuffing for that great roast pig, porchetta, that you find in Tuscan and Umbrian country markets. But it's used with other dishes too, as in this recipe where it flavors duck breasts.

You can find finocchietta or wild fennel pollen from a number of sources (see page 465). You could also substitute fennel seeds, first crushing them in a mortar or a spice grinder; the flavor will be somewhat different but still delicious. Most butcher shops will have frozen boneless duck breasts, usually sold in 1½ pound packages, which should be enough for four people. Occasionally you will find fresh duck breasts on offer—when you do, snatch them up and rush them home to your kitchen for this treat.

In restaurant kitchens, two breast halves are tied together around the finocchietta filling, as if they were a small, compact porchetta, but for home cooking, you could simply braise each breast half on its own. If you wish to tie the breasts together, you'll need kitchen string.

2 boneless duck breast halves

freshly ground black pepper

sea salt

2 or 3 garlic cloves, crushed and minced

a big pinch of very finely minced rosemary

1 tablespoon wild fennel pollen (or fennel seeds, see headnote)

2 tablespoons extra-virgin olive oil

½ cup dry sherry or Tuscan vin santo

Set the duck breasts, skin side up, on a countertop or work board. Using a sharp paring knife, cut a few small slits in the duck skin, scoring it to release the fat as the bird cooks. Sprinkle quite generously with pepper.

In a small bowl, using the back of a spoon, crush together about a teaspoon of salt with the minced garlic to make a paste. Add the rosemary, wild fennel pollen (or crushed fennel seeds), and the oil. Rub this paste all over the duck breasts, but concentrate most of it on the fleshy insides of the breasts. Tie the two breasts together, skin side out, to make a compact little roast, and set that aside to marinate for about 30 minutes.

Turn the oven on to 400 degrees.

Set a black iron skillet or other heavy skillet (one that can go in the oven) over medium-high heat and preheat it for a minute or two until it is very hot. Add the duck "roast" and brown it on all sides, turning it regularly, until it is nice and brown all over. (If it gives off a lot of fat, remove much of it and set aside—it's great for sautéing potatoes.) When the duck is brown, transfer it to the preheated oven and roast, turning it once or twice, for about 25 minutes. (For rare duck, 20 minutes will be plenty of time.)

Remove the duck from the oven, transfer it to a heated platter, and pour off the pan juices. Let the fat rise to the top and spoon it off (again, reserving to fry potatoes). Add the sherry or vin santo to the skillet and set over medium heat, bringing the wine to a boil and scraping up any browned bits. Reduce to a couple of tablespoons and return the degreased pan juices to the pan.

Slice the duck and pour the pan juices over the slices for serving.

Alternatively, if you want to make individual breast halves, rub each one with the paste, set aside to marinate as described above, then brown in the skillet. The oven roasting, however, will be much shorter—about 15 minutes for rare, 20 minutes for more well done.

Variation: Several times I've mentioned potatoes deliciously sautéed in duck fat. You could also steam potatoes until they are just tender, slice or chunk them, then finish them off in the oven with the duck, rolling them about in the rendered fat, first adding salt and another big pinch of chopped fresh rosemary.

ABOUT RABBIT

Growing up in Maine, I never ate rabbit, nor did I know anyone who did. The first rabbit I ever knowingly consumed was in the home of a French friend in Paris, a woman who took great pride and pleasure in the fine, traditional table she set for her family after she came home from the office every day. The meal she prepared was *lapin à la moutarde,* a very typical and familiar French presentation with a wonderfully savory mustard sauce.

Rabbit is a farmyard animal throughout the Mediterranean, as familiar on the table as chicken or duck. My Tuscan neighbors raise rabbits in hutches along with their chickens and geese, and they often serve rabbit, fragrant with olive oil and rosemary, that has been braised in the outdoor bread oven after the bread has come out, as part of a Sunday feast. I have grown to love this meat for its delicious flavor, its supple texture, and its adaptability to many styles and sauces. Moreover, it's very low in fat—lower even than skinless white-meat chicken. As for the Thumper factor, well—we eat lamb and veal without any problems, so what's the big deal about rabbit?

If you're unfamiliar with rabbit, try these recipes, braising it in white wine with onions and plump green olives or in vermouth and stock with dried wild mushrooms. Rabbit also lends itself well to many traditional chicken stews—coq au vin, for instance, can as easily be made with tender pieces of rabbit. Or try *pollo al chilindron* (page 408) or the Niçoise-style braised chicken (page 409).

It's hard to find good fresh rabbit in this country, although persistence may pay off in a farmer who is willing to provide you with what you're looking for. Otherwise, you will have to make do with frozen rabbit. Thaw frozen rabbit slowly in your refrigerator so as not to toughen the delicate meat. If you can't find rabbit at all, you can use chicken in these recipes instead.

Braised Rabbit Garnished
with Green Olives and Onions

◆❀ Makes 8 servings

W ITH ITS PEPPERY SAUCE, this dish is delightful with a lentil puree. Prepare the lentils as in the recipe on page 258 and, when they're very soft, whirl them with their juices in a food processor or put them through the medium disk of a food mill.

Instant flour may seem like an anomaly in a traditional Mediterranean dish, but it's a trick restaurant chefs use to achieve a smooth sauce, and it works.

2 2- to 2½-pound rabbits, cut into about 6 pieces each

1 cup dry white wine, or more if necessary

6 tablespoons extra-virgin olive oil

½ garlic clove, crushed lightly

2 tablespoons minced flat-leaf parsley

1 teaspoon dried thyme, crumbled

2 bay leaves

½ teaspoon sea salt, or to taste

24 small pearl or pickling onions, peeled

1 tablespoon instant flour (Wondra)

24 plump green olives, pitted

1 teaspoon freshly cracked black pepper

Rinse the rabbit pieces under cool running water and set them in a large mixing bowl. Pour the white wine, 4 tablespoons of the oil, garlic, parsley, thyme, bay leaves, and salt over them and stir to coat the pieces with the marinade. Cover and set aside for several hours or refrigerate overnight.

In a heavy casserole or saucepan large enough to hold all the rabbit, sauté the onions in the remaining 2 tablespoons of oil over medium heat, stirring frequently, until they are golden brown— about 10 to 15 minutes. Remove the onions with a slotted spoon and set aside.

Remove the rabbit pieces from the marinade, reserving the marinade. Pat the pieces dry with paper towels and brown them in the oil remaining in the pan, turning frequently—about 10 minutes. When all the rabbit pieces are well colored, sprinkle the flour over them. Cook for about 5 minutes, stirring constantly with a wooden spoon, to distribute and brown the flour. Return the browned onions to the pan and pour in the marinade, adding a little wine or stock or water if necessary to bring the liquid just to the top of the meat and onions. Bring to a boil, scraping up any bits that adhere to the pan. When the liquid is boiling, turn the heat down to a simmer, cover the pan, and simmer gently for about 1 hour or until the meat is falling off the bone.

Remove the meat and onions from the pan and arrange them on a heated serving platter, the meat in the center, the onions around the edge. Strain the sauce through a sieve to remove all the aromatics and let the strained sauce sit for a few minutes so that the fat rises to the surface. Skim away the fat and return the sauce to a clean small saucepan. Simmer the sauce over medium-low heat for about 5 minutes to reduce it and thicken it slightly. Add the olives for the last few moments, just long enough to heat them, then remove them with a slotted spoon and distribute them over the onions. Taste the sauce for seasoning, adding a little more salt if necessary. Stir in the cracked black pepper and pour the sauce over the meat in the platter. Serve immediately.

Angelo Pellegrini's Braised Rabbit with Wild Mushrooms

Makes 8 servings

ANGELO PELLEGRINI WAS an accomplished cook and gardener, a wine-maker of distinction (partly helped by the fact that his wine grapes came from the vineyards of his good friend Robert Mondavi), and a fine writer. "I am convinced," he once wrote, "that no one, much less one in moderate circumstances, can satisfy a cultivated palate every day of the year without a garden and a cellar of his own." He made this rabbit dish for me in the kitchen of his Seattle home one sunny summer morning shortly before he died. I will never forget it.

¾ ounce dried porcini

1 small celery stalk, leaves included

Put the mushrooms in a bowl and cover them with very hot water. Set aside to soak. Chop together the celery, parsley, herbs, and chili and set aside.

4 flat-leaf parsley sprigs

2 or 3 tarragon sprigs

3 or 4 thyme sprigs

4 sage leaves

2 wild mint sprigs, if available

1 small dried red chili, seeds and membranes removed

2 2- to 2½-pound rabbits, cut into about 6 pieces each

½ cup unbleached all-purpose or instant flour (Wondra)

sea salt and freshly ground black pepper

¼ cup extra-virgin olive oil

2 ounces Italian pancetta or blanched bacon, minced almost to a pulp

kidneys and livers from the rabbits or 2 chicken livers, chopped

1 tablespoon tomato puree

¼ cup dry vermouth

½ cup chicken stock (page 108)

½ teaspoon arrowroot

Put the rabbit pieces in a paper bag with the flour, salt, and pepper. Shake the bag vigorously to coat the meat. Over medium-high heat in a heavy stewing pan large enough to hold all the meat, sauté the rabbit pieces in the olive oil, turning frequently. As the pieces brown—in about 15 to 20 minutes—remove them and set aside.

When all of the rabbit pieces are browned, add the pancetta to the pan and stir over medium-high heat. When the pancetta starts to brown, add the rabbit livers and kidneys or the chicken livers. Stir well and lower the heat slightly. Add the herb mixture and continue cooking for about 5 minutes, stirring occasionally and taking care not to burn the vegetables. Return the rabbit pieces to the pan with their juices.

Remove the mushrooms from their soaking liquid. *Do not discard the liquid.* Rinse the mushrooms rapidly under running water, chop them coarsely, and add them to the pan with the rabbit. Strain the mushroom liquid directly into the pan through a sieve lined with a paper towel. Add the tomato puree, vermouth, and stock, stir, and bring to a slow simmer. When the liquid starts to bubble, sprinkle the arrowroot over and stir to mix well. Cover the pan and leave the rabbit to cook over low to medium-low heat for 1 hour.

Dr. Pellegrini liked to serve this rabbit with polenta (page 243).

Moroccan Tagine of Beef or Lamb with Sweet Turnips and Apricots

🌿 **Makes 10 to 12 servings**

S AKINA EL-ALAOUI MADE this deservedly famous Moroccan tagine for me one bright September morning in her sunny kitchen in Marrakesh. Sakina used quinces from the trees in her back garden, but they are not easy to find in this country so I have substituted dried apricots and little purple-topped turnips.

A tagine is both the preparation and the dish in which it is cooked—a round earthenware dish with a conical top. You can find all sorts of tagines for sale at www.tagines.com, but you could also use a good solid heavy-duty stew pot, such as Le Creuset makes, with a close-fitting lid. The beauty of a tagine, apart from the wonderful exchange of flavors that takes place, is the fact that just about everything for the meal gets cooked together in one pot, making a lot less work for the cook.

This is a tagine for a large party. It will easily serve 10 people and needs nothing more than a green salad and a simple dessert or fruit to follow. In Morocco it's often served with semolina bread (page 164).

3 pounds boneless lean beef or lamb, cut into small chunks

¼ cup extra-virgin olive oil

1 teaspoon freshly ground black pepper

1 teaspoon ground ginger or 1-inch-length fresh ginger, peeled and cut in half lengthwise

a big pinch of saffron threads, crumbled

sea salt

4 large red onions, halved and thinly sliced

3 garlic cloves, thinly sliced

3 medium tomatoes, chopped, or 1 14- to 16-ounce can whole tomatoes, drained and chopped

Brown the meat in the oil over high heat in a tagine, a heavy saucepan, or a flameproof casserole, stirring occasionally so that the meat browns all over, about 15 to 20 minutes. Add the aromatics and salt and stir to mix well. When the aroma of the spices begins to rise, stir in the onions, garlic, and tomatoes, lower the heat, and cook, stirring frequently, just until the onions begin to soften, about 15 minutes. Add enough water to the pan just to cover the contents, cover the pan with a tight-fitting lid, and cook over medium-low heat until the meat is done—about 1½ hours. Check the water level from time to time, adding boiling water as necessary. The contents of the pan should always be just barely covered with liquid.

After the meat has cooked for 1½ hours, drain the apricots and add them to the pan, along with the

1 cup dried apricots, soaked in water to cover until soft

10 to 12 small purple-topped white turnips, peeled and quartered

1 3-inch piece of cinnamon

8 small zucchini

¼ cup minced flat-leaf parsley

⅓ cup minced cilantro

turnips and cinnamon stick. Let cook for 15 minutes, while you prepare the zucchini.

Cut the zucchini in half lengthwise, then in half again horizontally, to make 32 pieces of zucchini. Add to the stew along with the parsley and cilantro. Stir to mix very well and cook for about 10 minutes longer or until the zucchini is tender but not falling apart.

Serve the tagine on a large deep platter. Using a slotted spoon, transfer the meat from the stew to the center of the platter. Set the apricots and turnips around the edge of the meat and the zucchini chunks around the outer edge of the platter.

If the meat sauce is thin, bring it to a rapid boil and cook over high heat to reduce it and thicken it. Pour the thickened sauce over the meat and serve immediately. Any syrup remaining from the apricots may also be poured over the dish before serving.

Stifado of Lamb

✤ Makes 6 to 8 servings

STIFADO IS A GREEK WAY of braising or stewing in red wine and red wine vinegar. Lamb stifado is a typical dish in tavernas all over Greece; on the island of Cyprus we ate stifados of octopus and tiny onions flavored memorably with cinnamon, cloves, and allspice. Many cooks like to marinate the meat beforehand in the wine and vinegar, but with lamb, the marinating is not necessary.

This dish is especially delicious with rice or tiny orzo pasta, cooked separately in a little of the stifado liquid.

3 pounds small white onions, peeled

[cont. next page]

In a heavy casserole over medium-low heat, gently sauté the onions and garlic in the oil until the onions are just starting to turn brown—about 10

4 garlic cloves, crushed with
the flat blade of a knife

¼ cup extra-virgin olive oil

2 pounds boneless lean lamb,
cut into small stewing pieces

1 14- to 16-ounce can
whole tomatoes, drained and
coarsely crushed

2 tablespoons tomato puree
diluted with ½ cup water

2 bay leaves

1 3-inch cinnamon stick

4 allspice berries

4 whole cloves

1½ teaspoons ground cumin

1 cup dry red wine

½ cup red wine vinegar

sea salt and freshly ground
black pepper

to 15 minutes. Push the onions and garlic out to the edges of the pan and add the meat to the center. (Or remove the onions and garlic and set aside, if it is more comfortable, returning them to the pan after the meat has browned.) Turn the heat up to medium and quickly brown the meat all over—about 15 to 20 minutes.

When the meat is thoroughly browned, stir in the tomatoes, tomato puree, bay leaves, cinnamon, allspice, cloves, and cumin. Add the red wine and vinegar and enough water to barely cover the meat and vegetables, along with a very little salt and pepper if desired. Cover the pan tightly and simmer very slowly for at least 2 hours. It can cook for as long as 4 hours and, like most wine and onion preparations, is even better reheated the day after it's made. If you're going to serve it immediately after cooking, however, let it stand away from the heat for about 30 minutes before serving.

Souvlakia or Kebab

Skewered Lamb with Grilled Vegetables

⚜ Makes 8 to 10 servings

IN THE EARLY 1970S, when the terrible ethnic war that would soon wrack the nation was still just a small cloud on a very distant horizon, Lebanon was perfect picnic country. There were cobble beaches on the one hand, forests and mountain meadows strewn with blossoms on the other, and a full panoply of ruined Roman temples and Crusader castles where you could set up camp with a ravishing view of snowy mountain peaks, the shimmering sea, olive groves and orchards, hilltop villages, and, off in the distance, another Roman or Crusader ruin.

Lamb on skewers was a favorite picnic food, easy to prepare, easy to transport, easy to set up and cook on the spot. In the photographs in food magazines, the ingredients are craftily arranged on skewers, a cube of lamb, a cherry tomato, a piece of green pepper, a chunk of onion, and so on. The arrangement looks pretty, but it makes better sense, since all these ingredients cook at different rates, to skewer the lamb and roast the vegetables apart.

For picnics, whether in Roman ruins or American backyards, I like to serve this with cacık (page 59) and rounds of pita bread. Tuck the grilled meat and vegetables into the bread and drizzle a little garlicky cacık over for a Middle Eastern sandwich. The gazpacho on page 130, served in chilled mugs, goes well with this, too.

The meat should be plenty for 10 people. Select the quantity of vegetables according to taste and what looks good in the market. The vegetables listed here are the traditional ones. Eggplant and zucchini, cut into thick slices, painted with olive oil, and grilled on both sides, are not bad with this either, and in America grilled fresh sweet corn, still wrapped in its outer husks, goes splendidly with the rest. For a Mediterranean touch, try good extra-virgin olive oil with salt and pepper on your corn instead of butter—the combination is alluring.

3 pounds boneless lean lamb, preferably leg, cut into 1½-inch cubes

¼ cup extra-virgin olive oil

2 tablespoons fresh lemon juice

¼ cup minced flat-leaf parsley

3 garlic cloves, finely minced

½ teaspoon hot red pepper flakes

freshly ground black pepper

2 bay leaves, crumbled

red onions, unpeeled, cut into quarters

sweet red and green peppers, cut in half lengthwise and cored

hot red and green chilies, cut in half lengthwise and cored

[cont. next page]

Mix the lamb with the oil, lemon juice, parsley, garlic, red pepper flakes, black pepper, and bay leaves. Stir with your hands to distribute the aromatics thoroughly. Cover and place in the refrigerator for several hours or overnight. Stir the meat occasionally. (If this is for an away-from-home picnic, prepare the vegetables at the same time and store each type in its own plastic bag in the refrigerator. If you're cooking at home, there's no need to prepare the vegetables until just before you're ready to cook.)

Prepare the grill when you're ready to cook, leaving plenty of time for it to heat up if you're using charcoal or wood. Set the cooking grid about 5 to 6 inches from the fire. Thread the meat cubes on skewers and prepare the vegetables if you didn't do it the day before. You will want to grill the meat in the center of the grill and the vegetables along the side, where the fire is a little less intense. But the vegetables take longer than the meat, so start with them. Just be sure to leave enough room in the middle for the meat.

small ripe but firm tomatoes, cut in half, or whole cherry tomatoes

sea salt

lemon wedges to squeeze over the grilled meat and vegetables

Brush the onion quarters all over with the marinade remaining in the bowl. Set the onion quarters skin side down on the outer edge of the grill. Now do the same with the peppers and chilies and then the tomatoes. In each case the vegetable will cook only on its skin side, but the heat of the grill will penetrate, and the blistering skin of onions, peppers, and tomatoes gives a wonderfully seductive aroma to the whole. Cherry tomatoes especially will cook much more quickly than anything else. Watch them carefully—if they split open, they may drop through to the fire. As soon as all the vegetables are in place, put the meat skewers in the center. They should take about 7 to 8 minutes—3½ to 4 minutes on each side, brushing them frequently with the remaining marinade. They are done when they are crisp on the outside and still pink within. Leave them on a little longer if you don't like rare meat, but don't overcook.

If you time this carefully, everything will come out right at the same time. But don't worry. Most people don't time it that carefully, and the point of a picnic is to have a good time.

Sprinkle salt to taste over the meat and vegetables and serve with lemons to squeeze over.

One last thought: wrap pita breads in foil packages—no more than 4 breads to a package—and set them at the edge of the grill while it's warming up. Remove them when you put the vegetables on, but don't open them. The foil will retain enough heat to keep them warm until you're ready to open them and slip the meat and vegetables inside.

A Rich Beef Stew from Provence

Provençal Daube de Boeuf

> *...An exquisite scent of olives and oil and juice rose from the*
> *great brown dish ... with its shiny walls and its confusion of savoury*
> *brown and yellow meats and its bay leaves and its wine. ...*
> —Virginia Woolf, *To the Lighthouse*

Makes 8 servings

THOUGH IT HAS LITTLE to do with the Mediterranean, one of my all-time favorite novels is *To the Lighthouse* and especially the scene where Mrs. Ramsay, with exquisite grace, serves a daube de boeuf to her guests assembled around the candlelit table, a recipe, Virginia Woolf tells us, handed down from her French grandmother. I like to think that Mrs. Ramsay's daube was a lot like this. To be authentic, use a good robust red wine from Provence, a Gigondas, for instance, or a Côtes du Rhône.

2½ pounds boneless lean beef, cut into 10 chunks

FOR THE MARINADE

½ cup extra-virgin olive oil

1 medium carrot, peeled and sliced

1 medium onion, sliced

1 celery stalk, sliced

¾ cup robust, dry red wine

¼ cup red wine vinegar

¼ cup brandy

2 tablespoons coarsely chopped flat-leaf parsley

1 4-inch strip of orange zest

2 garlic cloves, coarsely chopped

¾ teaspoon fresh thyme leaves or ¼ teaspoon dried, crumbled

[cont. next page]

Put the meat in a deep china or glass bowl and pour all the marinade ingredients over it. Turn the meat with your hands to distribute the aromatics evenly throughout. Cover the bowl and refrigerate overnight or for 4 to 5 hours.

The next day, preheat the oven to 300 degrees. Remove the pieces of meat, reserving the marinade. Dry the meat well with paper towels and sprinkle a little instant flour over it to help the browning. In a large heavy casserole, brown the meat in 2 tablespoons of olive oil over medium-high heat. (You may have to do this in batches, removing pieces as they brown.)

When all the meat is brown, return it to the pan and pour the marinade over it. There should be just enough liquid to come to the top of the meat. Add a little more wine if necessary. Set the pan over medium-low heat and, while it is warming up, prepare the carrots, shallots, and olives and add them to the pan with the tomatoes.

3 bay leaves, broken in two

freshly ground black pepper

FOR THE STEW

a little instant flour (Wondra)
for sprinkling on the meat

2 tablespoons extra-virgin
olive oil

8 medium carrots, peeled and
cut into chunks

18 fat shallots or 18 very
small pearl onions, peeled

24 pitted olives, preferably a
mixture of black and green

1 14- to 16-ounce can whole
tomatoes, drained and
chopped

sea salt and freshly ground
black pepper (optional)

When the sauce is simmering, cover the pan tightly and bake for at least 3 hours. It is actually better prepared a day ahead of time, in which case you can refrigerate the daube once it is cooked, first letting it cool down to room temperature. Before you heat it up the next day, remove the fat, which will have congealed on the surface. Taste the daube and adjust the seasoning, adding salt and pepper if you wish.

These daubes are often served with wide pasta noodles, like tagliatelle, though Mrs. Ramsay probably served hers with potatoes.

Veal Stew with Wild Mushrooms

Makes 4 to 6 servings

WHEN WE LIVED in Spain, we would go out in early December looking for a Christmas tree in the forests of the Gredos Mountains north and west of Madrid, where Spanish friends had a *finca,* a large farm. After a long day tramping through the pine groves we were treated to a late *merienda* in the cottage of the bailiff who managed the place. In the fireplace embers, his wife cooked a plain tortilla of potatoes and onions (page 91) to go with the rough wine of the farm and followed it with chestnuts so fresh they could be eaten out of hand like apples. One year, when we were ready to leave, the bailiff's wife handed me a piece of newspaper wrapped around a cache of chanterelles she had gathered that morning. They were dewy fresh, apricot-colored, and their aroma had some of the sweet fruitiness of apricots, too. They were perfect in the veal stew I was planning for supper.

Chanterelles are one of two kinds of wild mushrooms I feel comfortable about gathering, the other being porcini or boletus. (I would feel comfortable about morels, too, but I never seem to find them.) They are unmistakable—though if you're unfamiliar with them, check carefully with a mushroom guidebook or preferably an experienced mushroomer before you try. If you come across them, by all means, use them in this very simple dish. Morels and porcini are also excellent choices, but if you can't find fresh wild mushrooms, use a mixture of commercially available fresh shiitake and white button mushrooms. Add a handful of dried porcini, soaked in warm water as in the directions for Angelo Pellegrini's Braised Rabbit with Wild Mushrooms (page 422).

This is especially good with a well-seasoned, freshly steamed polenta; or make the polenta ahead, slice it thickly when it is cool and firm, and sauté the slices on each side in a few tablespoons of good extra-virgin olive oil.

If you can't find good-quality, humanely raised veal, by all means substitute beef or lamb.

2 pounds fresh wild mushrooms

2 medium onions, finely chopped

½ garlic clove, minced

¼ cup minced flat-leaf parsley

3 tablespoons extra-virgin olive oil

1½ pounds boneless veal shoulder, cut into small stewing pieces

1 cup dry but fragrant white wine

1 teaspoon minced fresh thyme or ½ teaspoon dried, crumbled

sea salt and freshly ground black pepper

a few drops of fresh lemon juice, optional

Wild mushrooms must be cleaned carefully before they are cooked, but they should never be washed. Trim the tough stem ends and any soft spots. (In Tuscany they say that if you throw the trimmings out the kitchen door, you'll get mushrooms next year in the spot where they landed.) Brush away any leaves or twigs that cling to the mushrooms, working gently with a soft brush or a sponge dipped in water and squeezed very dry. Chanterelles should be kept whole; large porcini should be sliced thickly, smaller ones cut into halves or quarters; morels can be kept whole unless they're large, in which case cut them in half. Set the prepared mushrooms aside.

In a heavy skillet large enough to hold all the ingredients, sauté the onions, garlic, and parsley in the oil over gentle heat, stirring constantly, until the onions are just soft—about 10 to 15 minutes. Push the vegetables out to the sides of the skillet, raise the heat to medium, and brown the veal pieces in the oil. (The vegetables can be removed for this process and returned to the pan after the meat is browned if that's more convenient.)

When the meat is brown, stir in the mushrooms and cook rapidly, stirring frequently. The mushrooms will absorb oil at first, then give off a good deal of liquid. When the liquid is bubbling—after about 15 to 20 minutes—add the wine and a little water or stock if necessary to bring the liquid just to the top of the meat. Add the thyme and salt and pepper to taste. Cook, uncovered, at a steady simmer for about 20 minutes. Then raise the heat to high and cook for 5 minutes. The liquid should reduce to about ⅓ cup of syrupy glaze. If the liquid reduces too much, add a little more wine or water during the cooking process. Remove from the heat, taste, and adjust the seasonings, adding a few drops of fresh lemon juice if you wish. Serve immediately.

Àrista di Maiale

Florentine Roast Loin of Pork

Makes 10 to 12 servings

THERE IS A STORY that's always told about àrista. It sounds apocryphal, but no less an authority than Pellegrino Artusi, the great 19th-century cook, gastronome, and recipe compiler, says the dish was served at a church council meeting in Florence in 1430, in Artusi's words, "to smooth out some differences between the Roman and Greek Churches." When the Greek bishops were served this famous Florentine roast, they were heard to murmur "Àrista! Àrista!," which in Greek means "This is really terrific!" And àrista it has been ever since.

Àrista di maiale, pork loin roasted in rosemary and garlic, is served all over Tuscany, in farmhouse kitchens, at bourgeois tables, in trattorie and tavole calde. The best is roasted on a rotating spit, a *girarrosto,* before the fire, but it is also put into the bread oven after the bread comes out. It is good hot straight from the oven and even better cold the day after. Sliced very thinly and put between two slices of country bread, it makes a terrific sandwich, and it often appears on an antipasto tray along with sliced sausages and prosciutto.

Ask the butcher to bone out a loin roast of pork but leave the undercut attached. This will give you two pieces of unequal size, attached at the bottom. When opened out flat, it will look like a book that is open about two-thirds of the way through. You will also need butcher's twine to tie the roast once you have stuffed it.

Hot from the oven, this is delicious with roasted potatoes. Or, if you wish, add peeled potatoes, carrots, and onions to the roasting pan for the final hour of cooking, turning the vegetables in the pan juices and basting them from time to time. Cold the next day, àrista makes a fine accompaniment to Lentil and Green Olive Salad (page 79).

4 pounds boneless pork loin in one piece

7 or 8 rosemary sprigs

4 garlic cloves, chopped

1½ teaspoons sea salt

freshly ground black pepper

2 tablespoons extra-virgin olive oil

½ cup dry white wine

Preheat the oven to 375 degrees. Open the pork loin out on a worktable or cutting board. Strip the needles from 4 rosemary sprigs and combine them with the garlic. Chop the two together to make a coarse mixture. In a small bowl, combine the garlic and rosemary with a teaspoon of salt and a good quantity of black pepper. Add a tablespoon of the olive oil and mix well. Rub the inside of the pork with this mixture. Roll the two sides of the pork together and tie them with butcher's twine every 2 inches or so along the whole length of the roast. As you tie, work the remaining rosemary sprigs in under the twine so that the rosemary is evenly dispersed on the outside of the pork.

When the pork is tied up, rub the outside with the remaining salt and olive oil. Set it on a rack in a roasting pan and roast for 1 hour, basting with the wine and the pan juices every 20 minutes or so. Then reduce the heat to 325 degrees and continue roasting and basting; a 4-pound boneless loin should be done in about 1½ hours. If you prefer your pork very well done, leave it in the oven for 2 hours in all. As soon as it is done, remove from the oven and set aside for 10 minutes before slicing. Degrease the pan juices and serve them with the pork.

Afelia

Cypriote Braised Pork with Wine, Cinnamon, and Coriander

Makes 6 to 8 servings

Note that coriander seeds rather than the fresh herb (cilantro) are used in this dish. Crush the seeds with a mortar and pestle or grind them coarsely in an electric coffee grinder. Cypriote red wines are quite heavy, so a richly flavored California Cabernet Sauvignon would be fine for the sauce—and to drink with it. Oven-roasted potatoes in olive oil or rice makes a nice accompaniment.

2 pounds boneless lean pork, cut into 1- to 2-inch pieces

2 cups dry red wine

2 tablespoons crushed coriander seeds

1 3-inch cinnamon stick, broken in two

½ cup extra-virgin olive oil

24 small white onions, peeled

2 bay leaves

sea salt and freshly ground black pepper

Place the pork pieces in a bowl with the wine, coriander, and cinnamon. Stir to mix well, cover, and refrigerate for 8 hours or overnight.

When you're ready to cook, remove the pork from the marinade, reserving the marinade. Dry the meat with paper towels and brown it in the oil over medium-high heat in a pot large enough to hold the pork and onions. Turn the pork to brown it well on all sides. This will take about 20 minutes. As the pork browns, transfer the pieces to a plate and reserve.

When all the pork is brown, add the onions and stir them in the oil just until they start to take on a little color—about 10 to 15 minutes. Return the pork pieces to the pan together with the reserved marinade. Add the bay leaves, a little salt if desired, and several grinds of pepper. Cover tightly, turn the heat to low, and cook slowly but steadily for at least 2 hours or until the pork pieces are fork-tender and the sauce is thick and almost syrupy. If the pork pieces are done but the sauce is still watery, remove the pork and the onions and boil the sauce down to the desired consistency. Serve the pork with its sauce.

Braised Pork with Sweet and Hot Peppers

Makes 4 to 6 servings

1 medium onion, chopped

2 garlic cloves, chopped

2 tablespoons extra-virgin olive oil

¾ pound lean boneless pork loin or tenderloin, cut into ½-inch slices

½ teaspoon sea salt, or more to taste

freshly ground black pepper

1 rosemary sprig

¼ cup dry red wine

¼ cup water

1 tablespoon balsamic vinegar

6 red and green peppers, both hot and sweet, sliced into long strips

In a large skillet over medium heat, gently sauté the onion and garlic in the oil until the vegetables are soft and beginning to brown—about 15 minutes. Push the vegetables to the sides of the pan and add the pork pieces. Sauté the pork, turning to brown it on both sides—about 10 to 15 minutes. Sprinkle salt and pepper over the pork and add the rosemary needles, stripped away from the sprig. Add the wine, water, and vinegar and stir to mix everything together. Arrange the pepper slices over the top. Cover the pan and steam together gently, over medium-low heat, until the peppers are softened, about 20 to 25 minutes. Serve with rice or bulgur pilaf (pages 225, 244).

ALMOST VEGETARIAN

The next recipes are good examples of almost-vegetarian cuisine, preparations in which a small amount of meat acts as a flavoring or base for a dish that is made up primarily of vegetables. If you're trying to cut down on the quantity of meat you eat but don't want to become a vegetarian, these are for you. Dishes like these have the added advantage that they can be made well in advance and, in fact, seem to benefit from a day of rest between cooking and serving. Bring them slowly back to serving temperature. Accompany with a rice or bulgur pilaf (pages 225, 244) and a green salad.

Gratin de Haricots au Porc

A Simple Cassoulet

THE CLASSIC VERSION of cassoulet is a production that nowadays is largely left to restaurant kitchens. It involves copious quantities of meat, both fresh and preserved, garlic sausages, and goose preserved in its own fat. All that aromatic fat gives the dish extraordinary succulence and a voluptuous texture, but it is not something modern palates will want to contemplate more than once or twice a year—or a lifetime.

This is a much simpler version and yet very good, another example of how a small amount of meat can be used to complement and flavor other elements of the meal, in this case beans.

The recipe might look complicated at first, but it is really very straightforward. Partially cook the beans, then roast the pork, then combine them for a final exchange of flavors in the oven. For ease of preparation, you can cook the beans and pork a day ahead and refrigerate them until ready to finish, an hour or two before you want to serve the gratin.

1 pound small white beans, soaked overnight, drained

2 medium onions, 1 cut in half, 1 halved and thinly sliced

¼ cup coarsely chopped flat-leaf parsley

2 garlic cloves, crushed with the flat blade of a knife

1 bay leaf

2 medium carrots, peeled and chopped

freshly ground black pepper

3 tablespoons extra-virgin olive oil

1¼ pounds lean pork in one piece for roasting

Combine the beans in a saucepan with the halved onion, parsley, garlic, bay leaf, carrots, pepper, and 2 tablespoons of olive oil. Add boiling water to come to about an inch above the beans and set on medium-low heat. As soon as the water simmers, cover the pan, lower the heat, and simmer for about 40 minutes or until the beans are just tender but not falling apart. Check the water level from time to time, adding a little *boiling* water when necessary to keep the beans covered.

Meanwhile, preheat the oven to 350 degrees. Use the point of a knife to make little ½-inch-deep incisions all over the pork and insert a garlic slice in each slit. Rub the pork with the remaining olive oil and about a teaspoon of salt. Grind some pepper over the pork and rub it in with your hands. Strew the onion slices and the thyme over

2 garlic cloves, thinly sliced

sea salt

1 teaspoon chopped fresh thyme or ½ teaspoon dried, crumbled

½ cup dry white wine

1 cup fine dry unseasoned bread crumbs

the bottom of a small roasting pan and set the pork on top of the onions. Pour half the wine over it and roast the pork for about 40 minutes, basting every 10 minutes with the pan juices. Remove the pork from the oven and turn the heat down to about 275 degrees.

Drain the beans, reserving the cooking liquid. Discard the onion halves and bay leaf. Spread half the beans in the bottom of a wide bean pot or casserole. Cut the pork into small pieces (don't worry if it's pink in the middle) and distribute the pieces over the beans, along with the onion slices from the roasting pan. Add the rest of the beans on top of the pork.

Pour the wine into the roasting pan and set it over high heat until the wine bubbles. Stir to bring up all the brown bits adhering to the pan, and when the alcohol has cooked off, add the liquid to the beans. Pour in about a cup of the reserved bean cooking liquid or more if necessary to come just to the top of the beans. Sprinkle half the bread crumbs over the top and set the casserole in the oven. After 30 minutes, gently stir the bread crumbs into the top layer of beans and add half the remaining bread crumbs. Repeat this after another 30 minutes or so. This will help to form a crust or gratin on top of the beans. The total cooking time will probably be about 1½ hours. Check the liquid level from time to time and add more cooking liquid or boiling water if necessary. If a crust has not formed by the end of the cooking time, drizzle a tablespoon of olive oil over the top, raise the heat to 400 degrees, and cook for another 10 minutes, until the top is golden.

Variation: This dish also works very well with lamb, in which case you might wish to add a good deal more garlic.

Lamb Baked with Potatoes, Eggplant, Tomatoes, and Zucchini

Makes 8 servings

1 pound boneless lean lamb shoulder, cut into pieces no more than ½ inch to a side

3 to 4 tablespoons extra-virgin olive oil as needed

1 large onion, coarsely chopped

2 garlic cloves, crushed with the flat blade of a knife

2 large potatoes, peeled and cut into cubes

4 large very ripe tomatoes, cut into chunks, or 1 28-ounce can whole tomatoes, with liquid, coarsely chopped

2 medium zucchini, cut into ½-inch-thick slices

1 large eggplant, cut into 1-inch cubes

½ teaspoon ground cinnamon

2 tablespoons minced flat-leaf parsley

2 bay leaves

1 tablespoon sweet paprika

1 teaspoon dried thyme or oregano, crumbled

sea salt and freshly ground black pepper

½ cup dry red wine

Preheat the oven to 325 degrees. In a heavy saucepan or skillet, brown the meat in 2 tablespoons of the olive oil over high heat, turning frequently so that the meat browns uniformly. When all the meat is brown—after about 20 minutes—remove it from the pan with a slotted spoon and distribute it over the bottom of an ovenproof casserole or large soufflé dish.

Add the onion and garlic to the oil remaining in the pan, lower the heat to medium-low, and cook, stirring frequently, until the onion has softened— about 10 to 15 minutes. Remove the onion and garlic and distribute over the meat. Add another tablespoon of oil to the pan, raise the heat to medium, and sauté the potato cubes, stirring, until they start to brown along the edges—about 10 minutes. Remove the potatoes and distribute over the onions.

Add the tomatoes, zucchini, and eggplant to the pan and cook, stirring to bring up any bits that have adhered to the pan. Stir in the spices and herbs, a little salt and pepper, and the wine. Cook over medium heat for about 10 minutes to reduce the tomatoes to a thick sauce. Pour the sauce over the vegetables in the oven dish. Cover the casserole with aluminum foil and set in the oven. Bake for 1 hour, uncovering for the last 15 minutes of baking. The vegetables and meat should be very tender. Serve immediately.

Lamb or Veal with Artichokes

＊ Makes 8 servings

BALQISS WAS THE SEVENTH DAUGHTER of a seventh daughter, a magical woman in Arab folklore. She kept house for us in Beirut and tended the baby while I delved into the basement library of the American University. Walking home from a six- or seven-hour library stretch, dazed, thoroughly grubby, and longing for food and a bath, preferably in that order, I would catch the deliciously compelling aromas of her cooking from far down Rue de Californie. This was one of her favorite recipes, one that often greeted me when I arrived home.

3 tablespoons extra-virgin olive oil

1 pound boneless lean lamb or veal, cut into small cubes

6 fat scallions, both white and green parts, coarsely chopped

2 medium yellow onions, coarsely chopped

2 large garlic cloves, chopped

10 artichokes, prepared as directed on page 26 and quartered

2 teaspoons unbleached all-purpose flour

⅓ cup fresh lemon juice

¼ cup minced flat-leaf parsley

¼ cup minced cilantro

sea salt and freshly ground black pepper

Heat the oil in a saucepan large enough to hold all the ingredients. Over medium heat, cook the meat cubes, turning frequently, until the meat is thoroughly browned—about 20 minutes. Lower the heat to medium-low and add the scallions, onions, and garlic. Sauté until the onions are soft but not brown, about 10 to 15 minutes, then add just enough water to come to the top of the meat, cover the pan, and cook gently for about 20 minutes.

Drain the artichoke quarters and add to the pan with the meat, stirring to mix well. Blend the flour with a little water to get rid of any lumps, then add more water to make ½ cup and stir the mixture into the stew. Add the lemon juice and more boiling water to bring the level up to the top of the artichokes and meat. Cover the pan and cook for 20 minutes longer or until the artichoke quarters are tender. Remove the lid and simmer for another 10 to 15 minutes to reduce and thicken the sauce. Add the parsley and cilantro, taste, and adjust the seasoning, adding salt, pepper, and lemon juice as desired. Serve the artichoke stew over a mound of rice or bulgur pilaf (pages 225, 244).

Variations: Other vegetables could be used instead of artichokes for this basic Lebanese way to combine a vegetable with a small amount of meat.

POULTRY AND MEAT ✦ 439

I have had this stew, called yakhnet, with green beans and with okra—you would need 1 to 1½ pounds of either. A little chopped tomato, not more than ¾ cup, gets added with the vegetable, and cinnamon and allspice are favored spices to use with these.

Turkish Meat and Winter Vegetable Stew

Lamb with Celery Root, Carrots, Potatoes, and Leeks

Makes 8 servings

G NARLED AND DUSTY-CREAM-COLORED celery root, or celeriac, is often available in produce markets in the winter. It should feel firm when you press it and hefty in the hand—lightweight ones are probably dried out and spongy inside. The flavor is decidedly celery and pleasantly pungent when raw. Cooking it softens and sweetens the flavor.

If you can't find celery root, use thoroughly un-Mediterranean parsnips instead—the flavor will be different, but the texture will be similar.

1 pound boneless lean lamb or beef, cut into small cubes

2 tablespoons extra-virgin olive oil

2 medium onions, coarsely chopped

sea salt

1 tablespoon unbleached all-purpose flour

½ cup chicken stock (page 108) or water

5 medium waxy potatoes, peeled and cut into large cubes

2 medium celery roots, peeled and cut into large cubes

In a heavy saucepan or casserole over medium-high heat, brown the meat in a tablespoon of the oil, turning frequently to brown evenly on all sides. When the meat is brown, in about 20 minutes, turn the heat to medium-low and add the onions with another tablespoon of oil. Cook the onions gently, stirring frequently, until they are soft but not brown—about 10 to 15 minutes. Add a little salt and the flour and stir until the flour has been completely blended into the meat and onions. Pour in the stock, bring to a simmer, cover the pan, and cook for 20 to 25 minutes, stirring occasionally.

Uncover the pan and add the vegetables, stirring to mix them well with the meat sauce. Add a little more water or stock just to come to the top of the

4 medium carrots, peeled and cut into 2-inch lengths

3 fat leeks, trimmed, rinsed, and cut into 2-inch lengths

2 garlic cloves, crushed with the flat blade of a knife

1 teaspoon dried thyme, crumbled

freshly ground black pepper

1 tablespoon fresh lemon juice

vegetables. Add the garlic, thyme, and black pepper, cover the pan again, and cook the vegetables until they are tender but not falling apart—about 20 minutes. At the last moment, stir in the lemon juice. Taste and adjust the seasoning, adding more salt, pepper, or lemon juice if desired. Sprinkle with the parsley and serve.

LIVING AND EATING IN THE MEDITERRANEAN

Like most people in the late Middle Ages, Francesco di Marco Datini, the Prato merchant whose life was so brilliantly detailed by Iris Origo in *The Merchant of Prato*, took only two meals a day. In Italy these were *desinare*, or dinner, at *terce*—that is, the middle of the morning—and *cena*, or supper, at sundown. In summer, when the sun set late, a *merenda* or snack might fill the gap between. But two meals were recommended—for the sake of body as well as soul. Origo quotes a certain Paolo da Certaldo: "Order your day so that you do not eat more than twice, dinner in the morn and supper at night, and do not drink save at meals, and you will be much more healthy. . . . Cook once a day in the morning and keep part for the night; and eat little at supper, and you will keep well."

Certaldo's advice is followed throughout much of the Mediterranean today. Most people eat a very light, almost insignificant breakfast, a copious lunch sometime well after midday, followed by a rest if not a siesta, and a light, late supper, often made up of leftovers from lunch with perhaps a little plate of soup or fresh salad to enliven the meal. In between these meals there are small snacks—merende, meriendas, or casse-croûtes—often in the form of a tiny triangle of a sandwich or a little square of pizza, but always freshly made, never packaged or mass produced. (A bar that doesn't provide freshly made snacks like this doesn't survive for long.)

Is this a healthier way to live than America's on-the-run eating style, which, more often than not, features a very light lunch and a heavier meal in the evening? On the evidence, it would seem so, though it's almost impossible to structure a scientific test. Dietitians tell us that calories consumed at midday are metabolized more quickly than those consumed in the evening. And experience confirms that late, heavy meals lead to restless nights and dyspepsia in the morning.

Certainly the Mediterranean way is more civilized, even though times are changing and offices and shops are increasingly pressured to stay open through the day. Still, even in busy Mediterranean capitals, all who are able to do so, no matter what their social class or professional status, stop what they're doing at one o'clock in the afternoon and go home or to a restaurant for lunch with family and friends. This is not a mere pause in the day's occupation, but a full-scale halt, a shifting of the gears, for what is a social highlight and one of the most enjoyable moments of the day.

Whole families take part in mealtimes. It's not that they're all out in the kitchen chopping onions (usually there's a grandmother or an aunt or a sister temporarily out of work who takes charge of the cooking), but rather that they all have something to contribute, from the youngest on up. Mediterranean people have a limitless interest in food. You sense this when you sit down at a family table—everyone comments, usually favorably (usually with good reason), talking about how the sauce is flavored or the sweetness of the cheese, about what it was like the last time they had it, or how it's different at Aunt Elena's house, or remembering the time they all went mushrooming in the hills above Nice.

The merchant from Prato, though something of a Puritan, was also enormously interested in the quality of his victuals. When Francesco was working in Florence, his wife, Margherita, kept him supplied with the products of their country estate in Prato, sending down to Florence eggs, cheese, fresh produce, and the chickens, capons, and partridges that he especially loved. Francesco and Margherita paid strict attention to what was on their table, an attitude that holds true for many Mediterranean people to this day, rich and poor alike.

Even deep in the heart of a modern city, a guest at a noble table (noble by money or noble by blood but *magari*, as Italians say, noble all the same) will not be surprised to find that the food—the roasted chickens, the grilled meats, the fresh salads, the oil in the cruet, and the wine in the crystal glasses—all comes from the family's own estates, much of it produced under the direct and astute surveillance of the head of the family. And in that it will be no different from, if more abundant than, the same food served in a farmhouse kitchen.

Mary McCarthy once pointed out that in England and America rich and poor eat very differently, while in Italy and France rich and poor eat alike except that the rich eat more. That may not be as true as it once was, but in Mediterranean countries food is still a major link that ties together all social and economic classes in a network of common interests and values and pleasures.

Foreigners often remark that Italians spend their time at table talking about what they're eating right now, what they had at the last meal, and what they're going to have at the next. There's a certain sweet truth in that, and not just for Italians. When the gods of good eating are listening in heaven, they hear at mealtime the same welcome chorus all over the Mediterranean. *"Sahteen!"* they hear. *"Buon appetito! Bon appétit!"*

And we lack even the words to make a translation.

A Few Sweets

✧ ✧ ✧

I
T IS SIX O'CLOCK in the afternoon, late spring in Tuscany, and warm
enough to go about without a jacket even in the narrow, deeply shaded
streets of Cortona. Along the stone-paved via Nazionale, which ambles
through the heart of the old Etruscan hill town, corrugated steel shutters
bang up, one after the other, as shops reopen after the long siesta. It is the
hour of the *passeggiata,* not just in Cortona but all over the Mediterranean,
in bustling cities and quiet towns, even in country villages. The streets fill
gradually, but by seven o'clock they are thronged with strollers of all ages,
young, old, babies in prams, elderly ladies arm in arm, students clutching
book bags, little children darting between the legs of their parents, people
coming and going, stopping to chat, moving in and out of cafés and bars,
sharing coffee, a glass of wine or something stronger, and above all, sweets.

This is the time of day when Mediterranean people pause in whatever
they're doing for a little social intercourse over something sweet. It might be
as simple as an ice cream or sherbet, as elaborate as the syrup-and-nut confections of Greece and Lebanon, a little wedge of fruit-and-rum-laced cake
in southern Italy, butter-filled cookies in Barcelona, a dollop of rice pudding in Turkey, or a crust of sweet pastry with jam on top in Tuscany.

At holiday time the sweets grow more elaborate—special sweet breads
and cakes associated with Christmas and Easter, marzipan candies for All
Souls' Day, fried delights for Hanukkah, Carnival, or the end of Ramadan,
rich tortes for the Feast of the Epiphany when the Three Kings arrive at the
manger bearing gifts. One characteristic that all these confections share,
along with those consumed during the late-afternoon *passeggiata* or *paseo,* is
that they are almost never made at home. Elaborate sweets are made in the

pastry shop, the pasticceria, zacharoplasteion, or pâtisserie, which is often a very different place from the bakery, just as daily bread is a very different thing from such sweet delights. Only rarely are sweets made at home, and then they are usually of the very simplest sort.

The kind of sweet desserts we Americans consume at the end of a meal—cakes, cookies, fudgy chocolate confections—are regarded with bewilderment in Mediterranean countries, where more often than not a meal ends with fruit, plain and simple, raw or cooked, or on special occasions perhaps a glass of sweet wine and a cookie to dip in it. It is a much saner way to conclude a repast. If the meal has been abundant—and the abundance may mean nothing more than good bread and cheese and a hearty vegetable soup—nothing more is required.

I've selected the sweet cakes, cookies, and puddings in this chapter with that in mind. The fruit desserts and suggestions are self-explanatory. The rest, although made in home kitchens, are either special holiday sweets or intended to be served, for instance, to guests who drop in on Sunday afternoon.

If you feel you must serve a sweet at the end of the meal, keep the quantities very small—Paula Wolfert pointed out to me that the sweets served in Turkish homes with little cups of strong black Turkish coffee are no bigger than the coffee cups themselves.

SERVING FRESH FRUIT

As with other produce, I like as much as possible to put only organically produced, pesticide-free fruits on my table. That's not always easy to do, however, and during apple season in New England, for instance, I'd rather have apples from regional farms, raised under principles of integrated pest management (using pesticides selectively and only when necessary, rather than systematically throughout the growing season) than organically raised strawberries from Chile.

Still, you can't buy everything locally. There's no way we'll ever get local citrus fruits in New England or even very good figs. Buying locally is a good principle, but it's not the whole story.

A dramatic and appetizing presentation might focus on just one variety of fruit, piling it up in extravagant abundance in a handsome bowl—translucent yellow Bartlett pears, for instance, or Macoun apples, dark, velvety plums too juicy to eat except over a plate, New Jersey peaches when they're so tender a thumb can dent the flesh, Door County cherries, red and glowing like currants, or the first tangerines and mandarin oranges of the season, enhanced with some of their dark green leaves. In decorator's terms, an opulence of fruit piled up in a bowl like this "makes a statement." But it's also an invitation to a certain delicious kind of greed—and we all need more fresh fruit in our lives, so a little greed is in order.

Another fine way to serve fruit is in a fresh fruit salad, perhaps calling it *macédoine* or *macedonia* to give it new dimension. Cut a selection of fruit into uniform pieces, peeling those varieties that seem to warrant it, mix them together in a glass bowl, and add a very little sugar and a few tablespoons of liqueur or wine or citrus juice.

Don't overdo the varieties, however—three or four different fruits, carefully selected to balance one another's flavors, present a better display than eight or nine. Too many fruits in the macédoine leads inevitably to the supposition that the cook simply cleaned out the refrigerator fruit drawer before dinner.

Don't overdo the addition of other flavorings, either—it's a mistake to think that, if 2 tablespoons of Grand Marnier are good, 4 tablespoons will be that much better. Restraint is the key. The point is simply to enhance the flavors, which is why fortified sweet wines and herbal liqueurs are used. Lemon juice, orange juice, or the juice of bitter or Seville oranges can be just as sharp and interesting with fresh fruit.

Other suggestions for serving fresh fruit:

- peaches, peeled and sliced and dressed with a very little aromatic red wine (not more than a tablespoonful per serving) and a sprinkling of sugar

- fresh little seasonal strawberries, rinsed briefly and served with a little balsamic vinegar (artisanally made aceto balsamic tradizionale if you can afford it) and a saucer of powdered sugar to dip them in

- berries of any sort—raspberries, blackberries, blueberries, huckleberries, cloudberries—with the juice of blood oranges or Meyer lemons

- oranges, the skin and white pith peeled away, thinly sliced and dressed with a little sweet white moscato wine (try this with a few grains of freshly cracked black pepper for a startling contrast)

- melons with wedges of lemon or lime to squeeze over them (more traditional at the start of the meal but also good for dessert)

- if you can find them, fresh figs, so ripe they fall apart in your hands, are too extravagantly delicious to need garnishing with any other flavor; eat them out of hand, preferably sitting in the sun under the fig tree

Nicholas's Favorite Braised Pears in Red Wine

My son Nicholas was six years old when he discovered these pears in a restaurant on the via Crispi in Rome. He was just coming off a two-year diet of peanut butter and jelly sandwiches (on whole-wheat bread, of course), and I thought he would slide off his chair with pleasure at the soft buttery winy taste of them. Thirty years later, he still asks for via Crispi pears when he comes home.

The pears should be firm. Overripe pears will cook too quickly and disintegrate. They can be cooked on top of the stove but are best baked in the oven at a low temperature. I use a copper pan that is small enough that all the pears can stand upright and tall enough so that their stems aren't crushed when the pan is covered.

6 very firm yellow or green pears with their stems attached

½ lemon

1 3- to 4-inch cinnamon stick, broken in two

2 cups strong red wine—a California Cabernet Sauvignon or a Côtes du Rhône

½ cup water

½ cup sugar

Preheat the oven to 275 degrees. Peel the pears with a vegetable parer, leaving the stems intact. Place them upright in a deep ovenproof dish. Pare the zest away from the lemon half and add it to the pears. Cut away and discard the white pith and thinly slice the lemon half. Add the slices along with the cinnamon to the pears.

Bring the wine, water, and ¼ cup of the sugar to a boil. Pour the boiling wine over the pears, cover them with a lid or a piece of heavy-duty aluminum foil, and bake for 1½ hours or until the pears are very soft.

Remove the pan from the oven. If the liquid is not syrupy, remove the pears from the pan and set them aside, standing upright on a small platter, to cool to room temperature. (Do not refrigerate; they'll get too cold.) Boil the liquid down, adding more of the sugar if necessary, until it is a thick syrup. Discard the cinnamon, lemon slices, and zest. Spoon the syrup over the pears, a little at a time. Serve at room temperature.

A Compote of Turkish Dried Fruits and Nuts

Makes 8 servings

ONE OF TURKEY'S leading exports is high-quality dried fruits, especially apricots and figs, and the country is also the world's leading producer of hazelnuts, so this winter dessert is particularly apt. You can use all figs or all apricots, but the two together, alternating in the dish, are particularly attractive.

These are traditionally served with a clotted cream called *kaymak,* but they are also good with strained yogurt (page 278) that has been sweetened to taste with sugar or honey and flavored with ¼ teaspoon vanilla extract if desired.

To toast the nuts, spread them on a baking sheet in a 350-degree oven for about 15 minutes or until they are a light golden brown. Be careful not to over-roast them.

about 1½ pounds mixed dried figs and apricots

½ cup finely chopped toasted hazelnuts

½ cup finely chopped toasted walnuts or almonds

½ cup sugar

1 cup water

Put the dried fruits in a large mixing bowl and pour boiling water over them to cover. Set aside to soften for about 15 minutes. Butter the bottom of a shallow round straight-sided ovenproof dish just large enough to hold all the fruit. Preheat the oven to 350 degrees.

Combine the nuts in a food processor with ¼ cup of the sugar. Process very briefly in spurts to grind the nuts coarsely—they should not become a paste.

When the dried fruits are softened, drain them and alternate them in the prepared dish.

Mix the remaining sugar with the water, bring to a boil, and cook for 5 minutes. Pour the syrup over the fruits in the dish, cover with foil, and bake for about 20 minutes. Remove the foil, sprinkle the sugar and nut mixture over the fruits, and return the dish to the oven for 15 minutes.

Turkish Apricots Stuffed with Sweet, Thick Yogurt

Makes 6 servings

I N TURKEY THESE LUSCIOUS APRICOTS are stuffed with *kaymak,* a sweet, rich but rather bland cream made traditionally, like Italian mozzarella, from the milk of water buffalos. There's nothing remotely like that here, but yogurt, drained overnight to make labneh (strained yogurt) and mixed with sugar, can be used instead. The taste is quite different but still delicious. Use nonfat yogurt if you wish. Turkish cooks would not add the wine, but I think it lends a little complexity to the flavors.

¾ pound dried apricots, preferably imported from Turkey

¼ cup sugar, plus more to taste for the labneh

2 tablespoons sweet dessert wine such as Moscato or Sauternes

½ cup thick strained yogurt made from 1 pint yogurt (page 278)

2 tablespoons finely chopped pistachio nuts, or more if desired

Put the apricots in a pan with water to cover to a depth of 1 inch. Bring to a boil and simmer, uncovered, until the apricots are plump—10 to 15 minutes.

Drain the apricots, reserving the cooking water. Measure out ¾ cup of the cooking water and return it to the pan with the ¼ cup sugar. (Discard the rest of the cooking water.) Cook, stirring, until the sugar has dissolved, then add the wine. Return the apricots to the pan and continue cooking for about 20 minutes or until they are very soft. Remove the apricots and set aside to cool. Do not discard the cooking syrup.

While the apricots are cooking, blend the labneh with sugar to taste until it is smooth. Start with 2 tablespoons of sugar and add more if desired.

When the apricots are cool enough to handle, open each one and spoon in a rounded tablespoon or more of the yogurt, pressing the apricot halves around it to hold it in place. (The apricots should not be closed up over the yogurt, however. They should look like an old-fashioned whoopie pie, with the yogurt oozing out.)

Arrange the apricots on a serving dish and spoon some of the reserved syrup over each one. Garnish with pistachios.

Zaleti

Venetian Cornmeal Cookies

Y OU CAN FIND *zaleti* year-round in the territory around Venice, but they are traditional for Carnival and the pre-Lenten frenzy. Like many sweets and savories from that time of the year, they hark back to ancient magic related to worship of the sun, and they remind us of that in their shape and color— round and bright yellow with cornmeal and egg yolks. Some cooks add grated lemon zest instead of vanilla, and some add chopped candied fruit instead of the currants and pine nuts. (The currants here are dried black Zante grapes, not red currants. If you can't find them, use raisins instead.) In fact there may be as many different recipes as there are cooks, and each has its own claim to authenticity.

½ cup dried currants or raisins, either black or golden

¼ cup grappa, vodka, or rum

¾ cup yellow cornmeal

¾ cup unbleached all-purpose flour

a pinch of sea salt

1 teaspoon baking powder

½ cup (1 stick) unsalted butter plus butter to grease the cookie sheet

3 large egg yolks

½ cup sugar

⅓ cup pine nuts

Preheat the oven to 375 degrees. Put the currants in a little bowl with the liquor and set aside to macerate for 20 to 30 minutes.

Combine the cornmeal, flour, salt, and baking powder and sift to mix well. Set aside.

Use a little butter to grease a cookie sheet. Heat the stick of butter in a small pan over low heat until it is just barely melted but not separated and foaming.

Beat the egg yolks until thick and lemon colored. Slowly beat in the sugar and then the melted butter. When all the butter has been incorporated, add the sifted dry ingredients and mix well with a wooden spoon.

Drain the currants and add to the batter together with the pine nuts. Stir to distribute throughout the batter. Set aside to rest for about 15 minutes, then drop by spoonfuls on the greased cookie sheet. Bake for 10 minutes, until the cookies are browning around the edge. Remove to a wire rack to cool.

Kourabiedes

Greek Butter-Almond Cookies

> **Makes 3 to 4 dozen cookies**

I FIRST MET THESE in their Greek incarnation, although they are deservedly popular throughout the eastern Mediterranean. In Lebanon and Syria they're called ghraybeh, and made often without almonds, or with hazlenuts instead. Rich with butter and sugar, they are especially treasured at Christmastime, when Greek cooks stick a whole clove into each cookie, a symbol of the gifts of the magi. I don't do that—I don't like biting down on a whole clove, and these are so good you can quickly forget, in your enthusiasm, to remove the clove beforehand.

To toast the almonds, spread them on a baking sheet in a 350-degree oven for about 15 minutes or until they are a light golden brown. Be careful not to over-roast them.

2 cups blanched almonds, toasted

2 tablespoons granulated sugar

2 cups (4 sticks) unsalted butter

1 large egg yolk, lightly beaten

¼ cup good cognac

1 teaspoon pure vanilla extract

2½ cups cake flour

½ teaspoon baking powder

a pinch of sea salt

1 cup confectioners' sugar

Preheat the oven to 350 degrees. Divide the almonds into two batches. Process one batch in the food processor with the granulated sugar until it is finely ground but not a paste, being careful not to overprocess. Finely chop the second batch of almonds on a cutting board with a sharp knife. They should be smaller than rice grains but not as fine as coarse cornmeal.

In a large mixing bowl, beat the butter until it is very light, pale colored, and fluffy. Using a spatula, stir in the egg yolk, cognac, and vanilla and beat briefly just to combine with the butter.

Combine the flour, baking powder, salt, and ½ cup of the confectioners' sugar. Sift this over the butter, about a quarter of it at a time, folding in after each addition. Add all the almonds and stir or knead with your hands to mix together very well. The dough should be soft but not sticky, and you should be able to roll a small ball of it easily between your palms. If it's too sticky, refrigerate for 20 minutes to chill.

Shape and bake the cookies in batches. Roll a rounded tablespoon of the dough, gently and quickly, between your palms to make a ball and set the balls on an ungreased cookie sheet, leaving about ½ inch between them. Bake for about 10 to 12 minutes or until the cookies are pale golden. They should not be brown.

Transfer the cookies to a wire rack set over a sheet of aluminum foil. Let them cool for 10 to 15 minutes, then sift the remaining confectioners' sugar over them. (The sugar that falls between the cookies onto the aluminum foil can be reused in the next sifting.) The cookies keep very well in a tin for several weeks.

Ricotta Cake

Ciambella di Ricotta

Makes one 9- to 10-inch cake; 8 to 10 servings

RICOTTA COMES FROM the valuable leftovers, or rather the second stage, of cheese making. If you go into a traditional, old-fashioned cheese dairy late in the morning after the cheeses have been set, you can see how it's done. The protein-rich whey that has drained from the cheese itself is reheated (re-cooked = ri-cotta), sometimes with a little fresh milk added, until the proteins blossom, small puffs that look like cotton buds rising to the top of the liquid. Collected in a strainer the fresh ricotta is sometimes served up, warm and smoky from the fire, perhaps with a dribble of local honey, a rare and wonderful treat.

In this simple Italian cake, ricotta takes the place of more usual butter. If you can find sheep's or goat's milk ricotta, possibly from a farmer who makes cheese, it's even better, but most of us will make do with cow's milk ricotta from the supermarket. I would not advise using skim-milk ricotta, as it is too dry to make a good cake. The ricotta should be drained in a fine-mesh sieve or a double layer of cheesecloth overnight.

butter and flour for the cake pan

15 ounces well-drained ricotta (goat's or sheep's milk, if available, otherwise whole cow's milk)

2 cups unbleached all-purpose flour

1 teaspoon baking powder

½ teaspoon baking soda

½ teaspoon sea salt

3 eggs

1 cup sugar

grated zest of 1 lemon, preferably organic

1 tablespoon pure vanilla extract

1 tablespoon dark rum

¼ cup whole milk if necessary

confectioners' sugar (optional)

Set the oven at 350 degrees. Butter and flour a 9- or 10-inch cake pan.

Puree the ricotta through the fine disk of a food mill.

Combine the flour, baking powder, baking soda, and salt and toss with a fork to mix well.

Beat the eggs in a bowl until they are light and foamy. Gradually beat in the sugar, then the lemon zest, the vanilla, and the rum. Beat in the ricotta and then, using a rubber spatula, fold in about a third of the flour mixture. Continue folding in flour until everything has been combined. The batter should be quite thick but still pourable. If it seems too heavy, fold in the whole milk, using as little as necessary to give the batter a good consistency.

Turn the mix into the prepared cake pan and transfer to the preheated oven. Bake for 50 minutes, checking from time to time to be sure the cake is baking evenly. When the cake is firm in the middle, golden on top, and pulls away from the sides of the pan, remove from the oven and let cool on a rack. Then turn it out and, if you wish, sprinkle the cool surface with confectioners' sugar.

Torta di Polenta Gialla

Cornmeal Cake

Makes one 9-inch cake; 8 servings

THIS IS A LOVELY, LIGHT citrusy cake, based on one that's made through-out Italy's Po Valley region. It will keep for a week or more, but it's so delicious it will doubtless disappear long before then. Serve it, if you wish, with a little sherbet on the side or with lightly sweetened berries.

butter and flour for the cake pan

1 vanilla bean

1 cup sugar

¾ cup (1½ sticks) unsalted butter

3 large eggs, separated

½ cup very finely ground blanched almonds

3 tablespoons fresh orange juice

½ cup yellow cornmeal

½ cup unbleached all-purpose flour

1 teaspoon baking powder

a pinch of sea salt

2 tablespoons potato starch or arrowroot

¼ cup confectioners' sugar (optional)

Preheat the oven to 325 degrees. Lightly butter and flour a 9-inch round cake pan.

Chop the vanilla bean as finely as you can and put it in a blender with the sugar. Blend until the vanilla is thoroughly pulverized. (If you don't have a vanilla bean, you can simply stir in ½ teaspoon pure vanilla extract with the orange juice later.) In a medium mixing bowl, cream the butter until light and fluffy. Using a sifter to hold back any pieces of vanilla that didn't disintegrate, slowly sift the vanilla sugar into the butter, a little at a time, beating continuously. Add the egg yolks, one at a time, beating after each addition. Stir in the almonds and orange juice. Add the cornmeal and stir to mix very well. Set aside.

Mix together the flour, baking powder, salt, and potato starch. Place in a sifter and set aside.

In a separate bowl using clean beaters, beat the egg whites to stiff peaks. Stir about a quarter of the egg whites into the batter, then sift about a third of the flour mixture over it. Fold the flour into the batter with a spatula. Continue adding egg whites and flour two more times, folding after each addition, ending with the remaining egg whites.

Pour the batter into the prepared pan and bake for 20 to 30 minutes or until the cake is golden brown and springs back to the touch.

Set aside on a rack to cool. Remove from the pan
and sift a little confectioners' sugar over the top
before serving if you wish.

Tunisian Orange–Olive Oil Cake

Gâteau à l'Orange

Makes one 9-inch cake; 8 servings

THIS DELICIOUS ORANGE–OLIVE OIL cake is a favorite recipe from the
Mahjoub family, makers of very fine extra-virgin olive oil and other traditional products in northern Tunisia. The Mahjoubs make it with a blood orange
called maltaise de Tunisie, which gives the cake a beautiful red blush color, but
when I can't get blood oranges, I make it with small thin-skinned Florida juice
oranges. (Thick-skinned navel oranges won't work.) It's important to use organically raised oranges, since the whole fruit, skin and all, is called for; otherwise,
scrub the oranges very carefully with warm soapy water.

butter and flour for the
cake pan

2 cups unbleached all-
purpose flour

1 teaspoon baking powder

½ teaspoon baking soda

2 small, organically raised
oranges, preferably blood
oranges (about ¾ pound)

⅓ cup extra-virgin olive oil

4 large eggs

1½ cups sugar

1 teaspoon pure vanilla
extract

confectioners' sugar
(optional)

Preheat the oven to 375 degrees. Butter and flour a
9-inch springform cake pan.

Sift together the flour, baking powder, and baking
soda.

Slice off the tops and bottoms of each orange
where the skin is very thick and discard. Cut
the oranges into chunks, skin and all, discarding
the seeds, which will make the batter bitter.
Transfer the orange chunks to a food processor
and pulse to a chunky puree. Add the olive oil,
pouring it through the feed tube while the
processor is running, and mix to a lovely pink
cream.

In a separate large bowl, beat the eggs until very
thick and lemon colored, gradually beating in the
sugar. Beat in the vanilla.

Fold about a third of the flour mixture into the eggs, then about a third of the orange mixture, continuing to add and fold in the dry and liquid mixtures until everything is thoroughly combined.

Pour the batter into the prepared cake pan and bake for 20 minutes, then lower the temperature to 325 degrees and bake 30 minutes longer or until the cake is golden on top and a toothpick inserted in the center comes out clean.

Remove and let cool. Then invert on a cake rack and dust lightly, if you wish, with confectioners' sugar.

Greek Olive Oil and Citrus Cake

Makes one 9-inch cake; about 8 to 10 servings

VERY DIFFERENT from the previous recipe, this is another take on the combination of citrus and olive oil.

butter and flour for the cake pan

1 orange

1 lemon

3 cups cake flour

1 teaspoon baking soda

1 tablespoon ground cinnamon

2⅓ cups dried currants

1 cup light-flavored extra-virgin olive oil

1½ cups sugar

1 tablespoon brandy

Butter and flour a 9-inch round cake pan and set aside. Grate the zest of the orange and lemon and mix together. Squeeze the orange and lemon juice and mix with the zest.

Sift the flour with the baking soda and cinnamon. Add the currants, stirring to distribute them evenly throughout the flour.

In a medium bowl, beat the oil, adding the sugar a little at a time. When all the sugar has been added, fold in about a third of the flour mixture. Add about a quarter of the juice and zest and fold in. Continue alternating flour and juice, folding after each addition, until it has all been mixed. Finally, add the brandy and mix well. Pour the batter into the prepared pan and bake for 1 hour. Remove from the oven and cool on a rack before removing from the pan.

Walnut Cake with Mastic

THIS IS A WONDERFUL CAKE for afternoon tea—deliciously crunchy with walnuts and delicately sweet, with the fragrance of mastic. Serve it with seasonal berries, perhaps with a dollop of plain thickened yogurt on top of each slice. Like many Greek recipes, this one came to me from Greek food authority Diane Kochilas.

Mastic (*masticha* in Greek, giving the *ch* that rough, back-of-the-throat sound) is the resin of a peculiar bush (*Pistachio lentiscus*) that only grows on the Greek island of Chios. It can be chewed like gum but it also hardens into crystals that look like rock candy and this is what you will need for this recipe. Mastic is exported from Chios and used as a flavoring for breads and sweets all over the eastern Mediterranean. The flavor is soft, pleasant, flowery, yet with a refreshing hint of licorice, too. You should be able to find mastic in Greek and Near Eastern specialty grocers or from web sites such as www.greekproducts.com.

If you simply can't find mastic, make this with unflavored extra-virgin olive oil. It will still be a delicious cake.

½ cup mastic-flavored extra-virgin olive oil (see recipe steps)

butter and flour for a 10-inch springform pan

1 cup walnut meats

1 cup unbleached all-purpose flour

½ teaspoon baking soda

½ teaspoon baking powder

a pinch of sea salt

6 medium eggs, separated

1 cup sugar

¾ cup plain nonfat yogurt

To make mastic-flavored olive oil, crush a small lump of mastic, about ½ teaspoon, and stir it into 1 cup of extra-virgin olive oil in a small saucepan. Set the pan over medium-low heat and warm, stirring, until the mastic has completely dissolved. Do not let the oil come to a boil. As soon as the mastic crystals are dissolved, remove from the heat and set aside. Let cool. Store in a covered glass jar in a dark cupboard.

Preheat the oven to 300 degrees. Butter and flour a springform pan. Spread the walnuts on a sheet pan and set in the preheated oven for 15 to 20 minutes or until they are lightly toasted. Let cool, then chop fine—or grind to a fine texture in a food processor but do not process them into a paste. The walnuts should still be a bit grainy.

Combine the flour, baking soda, baking powder, and salt and toss with a fork to mix well.

Beat the egg yolks, gradually beating in ½ cup of the sugar. Beat until the yolks are thick and pale. Beat in the olive oil and the yogurt. Add the flour mixture to the egg yolks and fold the flour in.

With clean beaters, beat the egg whites to soft peaks, then sprinkle the remaining ½ cup of sugar over them and beat to stiff peaks. Fold the beaten whites gently into the yolk mixture, then turn the batter into the prepared pan.

Transfer to the preheated oven and bake for 60 to 70 minutes or until the top is golden, the center is firm, and the cake pulls away a little from the sides of the pan.

Remove and transfer to a cake rack. When the cake is cool, remove it from the pan.

Karydopita Nistisimi

Lenten Walnut Cake

Makes 8 servings

A T A REMARKABLE CONFERENCE on the foods and wines of Greece that was held many years ago in Thessaloníki, organized by Oldways Preservation & Exchange Trust, the highlight was a banquet, if that's not an oxymoron, of Greek Lenten foods called "The Joys of Fasting." The traditional Orthodox Lenten fast is rigorous—not only no meat, but no animal products of any kind, including eggs and butter. Yet the foods offered at this festive fast table were rich with the flavors of fresh vegetables and perfumed with herbs and good olive oil. *Karydopita,* topped with poached apricots in a sauce flavored with orange-flower water, was the fitting conclusion.

The recipe was devised by Aglaia Kremesi and Vali Manouilidi for the conference. This version is adapted somewhat from their recipe.

FOR THE SYRUP

½ cup sugar

½ cup honey

1 cup water

1 tablespoon orange-flower water or fresh lemon juice

FOR THE CAKE

a little olive oil for greasing the pan

1 teaspoon baking soda

¼ cup brandy

½ cup sifted unbleached all-purpose flour

½ cup sugar

1 teaspoon baking powder

½ teaspoon ground cinnamon

¼ teaspoon ground cloves

½ cup extra-virgin olive oil

½ cup fresh orange juice

2 cups walnut halves, finely chopped, about 1½ cups

¾ cup dry unseasoned bread crumbs

1 tablespoon grated orange zest

FOR THE TOPPING

½ cup apricot jam

2 tablespoons water

Make the syrup: boil the sugar and honey with the water for 15 to 20 minutes, until it is reduced to about ¾ cup. Off the heat, mix in the orange-flower water or lemon juice. Set aside to cool, then refrigerate.

Preheat the oven to 375 degrees. Using a paper towel dipped in olive oil, grease a 9-inch round springform pan.

Add the baking soda to the brandy. In a large mixing bowl, combine the flour with the sugar, baking powder, cinnamon, and cloves, tossing to mix well. Make a well in the center. Pour in the oil, orange juice, and brandy and gradually mix together, stirring with a wooden spoon. Mix in the nuts, bread crumbs, and orange zest and pour the batter into the prepared pan. Bake for 40 to 60 minutes or until the cake is firm in the center and pulling away from the sides of the pan.

When the cake is done and while it is still hot, pour the cold syrup over it and set aside in the cake pan to cool. Over very low heat, melt the jam with 2 tablespoons of water, stirring constantly. When the cake is cool, remove the springform and brush the apricot topping over the cake.

Crostata di Marmellata

Italian Jam Tart

Makes 8 to 10 servings

THIS ITALIAN FARMHOUSE TART is made very simply with *pasta frolla* and either very-good-quality jam or fresh fruit cooked with sugar to make a jam. Cherries, peaches, apricots, apples, plums in their seasons can go into the *crostata*.

This recipe uses nothing but very-good-quality jam. If you wish, make your own, using about a pound of soft fruits such as cherries, raspberries, or blackberries and cooking them down with about ½ cup of sugar to make about 1½ cups of jam.

1 cup unbleached all-purpose flour

¼ cup cake flour or pastry flour

¼ cup sugar

a pinch of sea salt

6 tablespoons (¾ stick) unsalted butter at room temperature

1 large egg, lightly beaten

grated zest of ½ lemon, preferably organic

butter for the pan

1½ cups good-quality jam, preferably homemade

1 large egg for the glaze

1 teaspoon water

Make the *pasta frolla* at least an hour ahead of time. Mix together the flours, sugar, and salt, tossing with a fork. Add the butter, cut into pieces, and, working rapidly, rub it into the flour mixture. Make a well in the center. Add the egg and lemon zest and use a fork to mix well. Form the dough into a soft ball, wrap it in plastic or foil, and refrigerate for at least 1 hour.

When ready to make the crostata, remove the dough from the refrigerator. Preheat the oven to 350 degrees. Butter a 9-inch straight-sided tart pan, preferably one with a removable bottom.

Roll out approximately two-thirds of the *pasta frolla* very quickly into a 10-inch circle. This is easiest to do between sheets of wax paper. Line the tart pan. Or, if it is easier, press the pastry dough into the tart pan and up the sides. The dough should be about ⅛ inch thick. Spread the jam over the tart.

Between sheets of wax paper, roll out the remaining pastry dough, cut it into strips, and make a lattice on top of the tart.

Beat the egg with the water and brush a little of the wash over the lattice. Slide the tart into the oven and bake for about 20 minutes or until the crust is golden. Cool and serve at room temperature.

Clafoutis

A CLASSIC FRENCH COUNTRY DESSERT, clafoutis is as simple as a batter cake with fruit—which, in fact, is what it is. The recipe is adapted from a clafoutis served for dessert years ago (and probably still served to this day) at Domaine Tempier, the great Bandol wine estate where Lulu Peyraud, now in her late eighties, continues to preside. In early summer the clafoutis was made with cherries but it could be adapted to many seasonal fruits—peaches, plums, berries, even apples or pears in the autumn. Whatever you choose, you will need about a pound of fruit, and of course the fruit should be pitted and/or peeled where necessary. Because berries are very juicy, you should double the amount of flour when using them.

2 to 3 tablespoons very cold unsalted butter

1 pound of cherries or small greengage plums, halved and pitted, or 4 or 5 small pears or apples, peeled and cored

¼ cup coarsely chopped or slivered blanched almonds

3 eggs

⅔ cup sugar

½ teaspoon sea salt

½ cup unbleached all-purpose flour

1¼ cups whole milk

Set the oven to 375 degrees.

Use about a tablespoon of the butter to butter generously a baking dish just large enough to hold all the fruit in one thick layer. Set the fruit in the buttered dish, cut sides down, and scatter with the almonds.

Beat the eggs to a froth in a mixing bowl, then beat in about ½ cup of the sugar. Add a pinch of salt, then fold in the flour and finally the milk. Pour the batter over the fruit in the baking dish.

Sprinkle the remaining sugar over the batter, then dot with the remaining butter.

Transfer to the preheated oven and bake for 45 minutes to 1 hour or until the top is golden with the fruit just poking through.

Remove from the oven and set aside for 30 minutes or so before serving.

Torrijas

Spanish Sweet French Toast with Citrus Syrup

Makes 6 servings

A UNIVERSAL SPANISH FAVORITE, *torrijas* are similar to *pain perdu* or sweet-ened French toast. In Jerez, Rosario Vazquez sprinkles a little cinnamon sugar over her *torrijas,* while in Madrid, Ana Espinosa serves this simple dessert with an appealing orange sauce. Other cooks might dip *torrijas* in warm honey or sugar syrup. The garnish changes from region to region, but the *torrijas* are the same.

1¼ cups fresh orange juice, from 4 oranges

1 tablespoon fresh lemon juice

⅓ cup plus 1 tablespoon Spanish brandy

⅓ cup plus 1 tablespoon orange liqueur such as Grand Marnier

⅓ cup plus 1 tablespoon port

zest of ½ orange, cut into julienne strips

5 tablespoons sugar

1 quart whole milk

zest of ½ lemon

1 3½-inch cinnamon stick

6 or 8 ¾-inch-thick slices of crusty plain white bread

¼ cup extra-virgin olive oil

3 large eggs, well beaten

Mix the juices, liquors, orange zest, and sugar together in a small saucepan and bring to a boil over medium-low heat. Simmer for about 25 minutes or until the liquid is reduced to about 1¾ cups of syrup. Set aside, but keep warm. (Or prepare the syrup ahead and heat it up when you're ready to make the torrijas.)

In another saucepan, combine the milk with the lemon zest and cinnamon and bring just to a simmer over low heat. Steep over very low heat (not even simmering) for about 20 minutes.

Place the bread slices in a rectangular dish in which all the slices will fit without overlapping. (If you don't have a large enough dish, prepare the torrijas in 2 or 3 batches.) Remove and discard the lemon zest and cinnamon stick. Pour the milk over the bread and leave for a few minutes.

When you're ready to cook, heat the skillet over medium heat. Add 2 tablespoons of the olive oil. Carefully dip a slice of soaked bread in the beaten egg, turning it to coat both sides. Cook, turning once, until nicely browned and firm, exactly as you would for French toast. Repeat with the remaining oil and bread.

Arrange the *torrijas* on a platter, drizzle a little of the orange syrup over each slice, and pass the remaining syrup in a pitcher.

Sütlaç

Turkish Rice Pudding

Makes 5 cups; about 8 servings

S OFT, SWEET, AND DELICATELY PERFUMED, this is one of the most soothing desserts imaginable. In Istanbul you buy your *sütlaç* ready-made at the pudding shop, but it's very easy to prepare at home.

1 quart whole milk

zest of 1 lemon

1 3-inch cinnamon stick

½ cup short-grain rice (rice for risotto is fine)

a pinch of sea salt

2 cups water

1 tablespoon rice flour

1 tablespoon cornstarch

¾ cup sugar

GARNISHES (OPTIONAL)

ground cinnamon, rose water, and/or finely chopped pistachios

In a saucepan, heat the milk almost to boiling, add the lemon zest and cinnamon, and steep the milk for about 30 minutes. Keep it just below boiling temperature.

In a covered pan over medium-low heat, simmer the rice with a pinch of salt in 1½ cups of the water until it is very soft and all the water has been absorbed—about 30 minutes. If the water is absorbed before the rice is soft, add a little more *boiling* water to the pan. When the rice is soft, remove the lemon zest and cinnamon stick from the milk and pour the milk into the pan with the rice. Bring to a simmer and cook for 30 minutes.

Put the rice flour and cornstarch in a small bowl and slowly mix in about ½ cup water to make a smooth paste. Add this slowly to the simmering milk and rice, stirring constantly. Cook for 10 minutes, stirring constantly. Finally, add the sugar and continue cooking for 10 to 15 minutes or until the mixture is thickened.

The hot pudding may be served in a bowl or in eight individual pudding dishes. If you wish, add 2 tablespoons of rose water to the pudding while it is still hot and before you spoon it into the bowls. Or, once it is in the serving dishes, sprinkle a little cinnamon on top. Add a little spoonful of chopped pistachios and serve lukewarm or at room temperature.

❧{ RESOURCES }❧

WHERE TO FIND IT

The Internet has truly brought the Mediterranean home to North Americans. Products, implements, pots and pans, tools, and foodstuffs that once required a trip to a far-off ethnic neighborhood—or even to the Mediterranean itself—are now at our fingertips, requiring nothing more than a valid credit card and a double-click of the computer mouse. The following are some of my favorite sources but when in doubt—Google will find it for you.

For specialized kitchen tools and equipment (paella pans, baking stones, couscoussières, yogurt strainers, etc., etc.):

The Baker's Catalogue (kingarthurflour.com) for special baking equipment, pans, and tools

The Bridge Company (bridgekitchenware.com), New York City's premier supplier of kitchenwares of all kinds

La Tienda, Williamsburg, Virginia (tienda.com), for Spanish cooking equipment, earthenware cassolas, also table and glassware from Spain

Sur la Table stores nationally (SurLaTable.com)

Tagines.com for Moroccan earthenware and other tagines

Williams-Sonoma stores nationally (williams-sonoma.com)

For all sorts of food products, from extra-virgin olive oils to salts to cheeses to pasta products to grains and beans—you name it:

I've noted, where relevant, a site's home base—a personal visit is always the best way to see the gamut of products. And where a site is specialized in a particular cuisine I've also taken note. Otherwise, these are good general suppliers of a great variety of high-quality Mediterranean ingredients.

The Baker's Catalogue (kingarthurflour.com) for a wide variety of flours and many other baking ingredients

Chefshop.com (notably, a great variety of ground and crushed red chilies)

Dayna's Market (daynasmarket.com), for Middle Eastern foods

Formaggio Kitchen, Cambridge, Massachusetts (formaggiokitchen.com)

Kalustyan's Spices and Sweets, New York City (kalustyans.com), for mostly Middle Eastern (also South Asian) ingredients

La Tienda, Williamsburg, Virginia (tienda.com), for Spanish foods, including jamón serrano and, new to the market, jamón de bellota

The Mozzarella Company, Dallas, Texas (mozzco.com), for cow's milk mozzarella *(fior di latte),* goat's milk ricotta and feta, and other specialty cheeses made on-site

Murray's Cheese Shop, Greenwich Village, New York City (murrayscheese.com), for fine imported and specialty cheeses

The Olive Oil Source (oliveoilsource.com) for extra-virgin olive oils from all over the world

Rockridge Market Hall, Oakland, California (markethallfoods.com)

Theoliveoilsecret.com is not a site for purchasing olive oil but is full of good information that should be in every potential olive oil purchaser's pocket.

Titan Foods, Astoria, Queens (titanfood.com), for Greek foods, located in the capital of Greek America

Todaro Brothers, New York City (todarobros.com), for Italian ingredients

Vivande Porta Via, San Francisco (vivande.com), for a small but choice selection of Italian ingredients

Zingerman's Deli, Ann Arbor, Michigan (zingermans.com)

The Mediterranean Diet and Health

by ANTONIA TRICHOPOULOU, *MD, Professor of Nutrition and Biochemistry, Athens School of Public Health, and Director, World Health Organization Collaborating Center for Nutrition Education in Europe; and* DIMITRIOS TRICHOPOULOS, *MD, Vincent L. Gregory Professor of Cancer Prevention and Epidemiology, Harvard School of Public Health*

How do we know that people in a particular area of the world have a healthier diet than our Western diet? Epidemiology, the study of disease patterns, provides the answer.

The frequency of most diseases varies substantially around the world. For diseases of infectious or occupational origin the importance of the environment, whether physical, chemical, or biological, is clear. But for many other common chronic diseases, including those of the circulatory system and cancer, the role played by the environment has not always been obvious. Studies of migrants have shown that whatever the disease pattern in their country of origin, they tend to acquire, sooner or later, the disease pattern of their host country, even when they remain relatively isolated within ethnic communities. For instance, the frequency of cancer of the large intestine is much lower in Japan than in the United States but rises to American levels within 20 years among Japanese immigrants to this country. We can conclude, then, that outside factors, collectively termed *environment*, whether imposed by others or created by individuals themselves through personal choices about food, behavior, or lifestyle, are critical determinants of disease. This is not to imply that heredity is not important; it is, but genes are usually evenly distributed among nonisolated population groups and thus influence who *within* a population will develop disease. And most genes exercise their effects through interactions, whether simple or complex, with the environment.

Among the many environmental factors, qualitative or quantitative deviations from the ideal diet represent, as a group, the most important factor in the genesis of the most common killer diseases, including coronary heart disease and several forms of cancer. This should not be surprising. Only factors that vary widely among countries and population groups can account for the remarkable variability of disease patterns around the world, and few aspects of human conditions or behavior vary as much as diet. Of course, the human diet is unusually complex, involving hundreds of chemical components, and from the evolutionary point of view it is frequently challenging, since humans are the only animals who process and cook their food.

Nobody knows for sure what the ideal diet *is,* but there are good reasons to believe that the Mediterranean diet may come closer to it than any other realistic diet. What exactly is the Mediterranean diet? What evidence do we have that adopting this diet can benefit our health?

The *Mediterranean diet* is a loose term, and some doubt remains as to what precise dietary patterns apply. However, there are common elements in the diets of most Mediterranean people, and to the extent that they share lower rates of diet-related diseases, this looseness of definition represents an advantage: several variations on the Mediterranean diet may be equally beneficial. As a rule, the Mediterranean diet is low in saturated fat with added fat mostly in the form of olive oil; high in complex carbohydrates from grains and legumes; and high in fiber, mostly from vegetables and fruits. Total fat may be high—around 40 percent of total energy intake in Greece, as mentioned in the chapter Making the Change—or moderate (around 30 percent of total energy intake, as in Italy). In all instances, however, the ratio of monounsaturated to saturated fats is high (usually two to one or more). This is because olive oil, which contains 60 percent or more of monounsaturated oleic acid, is the principal fat in the Mediterranean region. The large quantities of fresh vegetables and of cereals and the abundance of olive oil guarantee high intakes of beta-carotene, vitamin C, tocopherols (vitamin E), various important minerals, and several possibly beneficial nonnutrient substances such as polyphenols and anthocyanins.

Since Homeric times, the diet of the Mediterranean has been based on wheat, olives and olive oil, legumes, green vegetables, seasonal fruits, and wine. Other components of the diet include onions and garlic, cheese and yogurt (mainly from goat's milk), and, to a certain extent, fish, fowl, and eggs. Because of limited availability, red meat has been used infrequently and, as a rule, in small quantities. Few adults in the Mediterranean region will find it difficult to recognize this pattern as the essence of their traditional diet. In comparison to the average American, the average Italian consumes 3 times as much pasta, bread, and fresh fruit; almost twice as much tomatoes and fish; 6 times more wine; and 100 times more olive oil—but 30 percent less meat from any source, 20 percent less milk, and 20 percent fewer eggs.

Any overview of the actual foods and dishes consumed in the Mediterranean region must emphasize the large quantities of whole-grain bread that accompany every meal. Pasta (not just in Italy but also in Greece and in North Africa in the form of couscous) is regularly used, frequently in addition to bread, as an added component in several soups, as a supplement to various dishes, or as a separate dish. Abundant complex carbohydrates, as well as plant proteins, are contributed by whole grains and cereals and also by legumes. In Greece bean soup, prepared with large quantities of olive oil, is considered the national food, credited with the survival of Greeks in their poverty-stricken country through the millennia.

The Mediterranean diet is frequently, and rightly, associated in the minds of many Americans with that lively salad made from fresh vegetables, olive oil, and feta cheese, known in this country as *Greek salad*. Usually prepared with tomatoes, cucumbers, onions, and olives, the original Greek salad is different from its American variant; in the Greek version, vegetables are fresher and tastier, olive oil is much more abundant, and the serving is much larger. A Greek fresh vegetable salad can also be made from just greens, herbs, olive oil, and lemon juice; again, feta cheese, made from goat's or sheep's milk, is frequently added. It is worth noting that cheese is consumed in large quantities along the northern Mediterranean shore—in fact, Greeks and French lead the world in per capita cheese consumption.

In Greece, vegetables are usually cooked, especially in olive oil, and vegetable combinations include eggplant, zucchini, beans or okra, and almost always tomatoes, onions, and herbs. Vegetables also dominate many meat dishes, and, in the absence of meat, feta cheese is regularly added to most vegetable stews.

As might be expected, fish has been an important food for Mediterranean people since antiquity. Meat, however, has not been consumed in large quantities in the region until recently, mainly because it's been expensive and in short supply. The changing pattern has been implicated in the increasing incidence of diverticular disease and perhaps cancer of the large bowel.

Wine consumption is high in the European Mediterranean countries, but widespread abuse of hard liquor is not. For millennia wine has been consumed in moderation, almost always during meals and as a rule in the company of friends—the ancient Greek word *symposium* means "drinking in company," but with a connotation of intellectual interchange. The philosophy that shaped the Mediterranean attitude toward wine consumption is best expressed in a passage from Plato's *Symposium* that many modern epidemiologists would approve: "I prepare but three kraters for prudent men; the one is for health, the one they drink first; the second is for love and pleasure; the third for sleep. The fourth is not ours, but belongs to licentiousness."

By the late 1950s the hypothesis linking diet in general to coronary heart disease was gaining widespread support, although reliable data linking dietary habits of individuals to their risk of developing coronary heart disease were lacking. The existing evidence was indirect: diet, in particular the composition of dietary fat, had been shown to be a critical determinant of serum cholesterol, with saturated fat increasing and polyunsaturated fat reducing serum levels; serum total cholesterol had been established as a major risk factor for coronary heart disease. At that time no distinction was made between low- and high-density lipoproteins (LDL and HDL or "bad" and "good" cholesterol).

In an effort to evaluate the hypothesis of a relationship between diet and coronary heart disease and to explore several other aspects of the etiology of this disease, Ancel Keys, MD, and his colleagues set out to undertake what turned out to be one of the most celebrated studies in modern epidemiology, the Seven Countries Study. The study involved 12,763 men aged 40 to 59 years. The men were enrolled between 1958 and 1964 in 16 study groups or cohorts: 2 in Greece, 3 in Italy, 2 in Croatia and 3 in Serbia (both then part of Yugoslavia), 2 in Japan, 2 in Finland, 1 in the Netherlands, and 1 in the United States. The men were interviewed and examined so that information was available for virtually all characteristics that later were identified as major risk factors for coronary heart disease, including blood pressure, serum cholesterol, tobacco use, physical activity, dietary habits, and several others. After a follow-up period that lasted for at least 10 years, the study generated several important results; findings continue to be reported by investigators active in some of the original study centers. Among the most important findings were that the Mediterranean groups had lower mortality rates from *all causes together* than the northern European and American groups; that the difference in mortality and incidence was particularly striking with respect to coronary heart disease; that the mean percentages of calories from saturated and polyunsaturated fats in the diets of the groups could account to a considerable extent for the differences in mean levels of serum cholesterol among them; and that the mean percentage of calories from saturated fats could account to a considerable extent for the differences in the incidence of coronary heart disease among the groups (an effect that could have been mediated through the detrimental effect of saturated fats on serum cholesterol).

Results subsequently reported from other investigations provided direct support for many of the findings of the Seven Countries Study and indirect support for others. Data assembled by the World Health Organization have confirmed the low rates of coronary heart disease in Mediterranean countries not only in the late 1950s but even now, when the traditional diet is not so closely followed. In 1990 the annual mortality from this disease per 100,000 persons of a "standard" age was 243 among men and 132 among women in the United States, whereas it was, respectively, 139 and 64 in Italy, 106 and 47 in Spain, 137 and 59 in Greece, and 91 and 40 in France. Mediterranean countries are also characterized by lower rates, as compared to those in the United States and northern Europe, of several non-smoking-related cancers, including those of the large bowel, breast, prostate, and ovary. The consequences of these disease patterns create surprising contrasts. According to the most recent (1992) World Health Organization data, men at the peak of their lives (45 years) have longer life expectancy in Greece than in any other European or North American country, even though Greek men are notorious for their high tobacco consumption, they rarely exercise in a systematic way, and they are served by a rather modest health-care system.

For logistical reasons the dietary data in the Seven Countries Study were analyzed only as group averages and not for each individual subject in the study. Although this is not an optimal analysis, there can be no doubt that many of the differences in disease occurrence between Mediterranean groups on the one hand and northern European and North American groups on the other were due to differences in dietary patterns. For age-adjusted data, only major differences in other important disease-causing factors or conditions could explain the observed large differences in disease incidence. Such factors are genes, widespread epidemics, tobacco smoking, and low socioeconomic class. But none of these factors is likely to have played a major role: migrant studies have eliminated a genes-based explanation; no major infectious epidemic was selectively affecting northern Europe and North America; and poverty and tobacco smoking have been, if anything, more common in Mediterranean countries.

The Seven Countries Study confirmed that a diet low in saturated fat, like the Mediterranean diet in virtually all its variations, can reduce total serum cholesterol and risk of coronary heart disease. In the process, however, the Mediterranean diet came to be perceived as just another low-saturated-fat diet. Scientists from the

Mediterranean countries have tried to argue that there is much more to the Mediterranean diet than its low intake of saturated fats, but the majority of the educated public was too preoccupied with the polyunsaturated-to-saturated-fatty-acid ratio and the "reduce total fat" commandment to pay much attention. It was only in 1991 that a major editorial in the influential *New England Journal of Medicine,* by the distinguished scientists Frank Sacks and Walter Willett, revived interest in the Mediterranean diet. These authors pointed out that high levels of serum HDL cholesterol are probably as important for the prevention of coronary heart disease as low levels of serum LDL (and total) cholesterol. They argued further that a diet low in saturated fat but high in monounsaturated fat, which would reduce LDL cholesterol and increase HDL cholesterol, appears to be at least as good as a diet low in saturated fats and high in carbohydrates. Although both monounsaturated fat and carbohydrates are effective in reducing LDL, carbohydrates do not increase HDL cholesterol as much as monounsaturated fats do. Furthermore there is experimental evidence and limited human data justifying some concern about the long-term safety of a diet high in polyunsaturated fats, the diet that has been promoted by the American Heart Association, whereas the safety of a high-monounsaturated-fat diet has been demonstrated through the centuries in the people of the Mediterranean region. Willett and his colleagues and other authors also have provided evidence that partially hydrogenated vegetable fats, the basis of margarine and vegetable shortening, far from being safer than saturated animal fats, may actually increase the risk of coronary heart disease. So, it appears that among the realistic alternatives open to people accustomed to the Western diet, the Mediterranean diet stands out as apparently healthier.

Although most scientists believe that diet can in fact play a role in coronary heart disease by contributing to high cholesterol levels and subsequent atherosclerosis, an increasingly influential minority theorizes that diet may also interfere with the blood-clotting events that trigger acute coronary episodes (mainly myocardial infarction and sudden cardiac death). According to this hypothesis, long-chain polyunsaturated fatty acids, of what is chemically described as omega-3 type, have beneficial effects, including a reduction in blood-clotting tendency and blood viscosity and an increase in the breaking up of blood clots. These fatty acids are provided mainly by fish, but also by several plants, and there is indeed evidence that eating fish may reduce the risk of coronary heart disease. Although fish is not a defining characteristic of the Mediterranean diet, it is obviously an important part of it—certainly more important than red meat in the time-honored traditional diet of the Mediterranean.

There has been a tendency to associate the health effects of the Mediterranean diet with its fat composition, but perhaps equally important is the fact that almost all variants of this diet are high in complex carbohydrates (bread, pasta, legumes) and rich in fresh vegetables and fruits. Complex carbohydrates and fiber, derived from vegetables, fruits, cereals, or legumes, seem to play a major beneficial role in protecting against constipation, diverticular disease, and perhaps colorectal cancer and coronary heart disease. But the protective role of fresh vegetables and fruits is likely to extend to a much wider range of diseases. They have been consistently reported to be protective against, or at least inversely associated with, several common types of cancer, including those of the esophagus, stomach, large bowel, liver, pancreas, lung, bladder, cervix, and even ovarian and breast cancers. Whether the effects of vegetables and fruits are due to their high content of antioxidant vitamins like beta-carotene, vitamin C, and vitamin E, other vitamins like folate, certain minerals and trace elements, or other compounds is not clearly established. Antioxidants are strong candidates as protagonists in the disease-preventing capacity of vegetables and fruits. They are believed to prevent or neutralize the effects of oxidative processes that may be involved in the development of cancer, atherosclerosis, other chronic diseases, or aging itself. In most instances the protective effect seems to be more strongly associated with vegetables and fruits themselves than with any particular constituent nutrient or nonnutrient. Nevertheless, certain vitamins appear to protect against certain diseases in high doses that can be taken only in the form of supplements. This may be particularly true with respect to vitamin E and coronary heart disease. This field of research is rapidly developing, and it is not conclusively established that very high doses of vitamins are required. In any case it would be prudent to assume that whether vitamin supplements are taken or not, fresh vegetables and fruits should be plentiful in the diet, and the Mediterranean diet is as plentiful as any.

There are several other dimensions to the Mediterranean diet, and very few of them are linked to adverse health effects. Total fat intake, including intake of monounsaturated fat, is considered a risk factor for cancers of the large bowel and perhaps those of the prostate and the pancreas. However, the incidence of these cancers is generally lower in the Mediterranean region than in northern Europe or North America. It appears that red meat (and possibly animal protein and fat) is a more important determinant of cancer of the large bowel than monounsaturated fat, although other explanations may also apply. Consumption of red meat has been low in the traditional Mediterranean diet, although recent data suggest rapidly increasing trends. Salt intake is probably unnecessarily high in several Mediterranean countries, and this may contribute to the modestly high incidence of stroke and stomach cancer in some of these countries. Total energy intake is rather high in the European Mediterranean countries, but in the absence of excess prevalence of obesity in the region, this is actually an advantage—it implies higher energy expenditure and therefore higher levels of physical activity. Physical exercise is an important protective factor for coronary heart disease and possibly cancers of the large bowel and the prostate. Finally, the relatively low intake of milk is partly compensated by the high cheese consumption that covers, in most instances, the requirements for osteoporosis-preventing calcium.

The deleterious effects of excessive alcohol intake, both long-term and short-term, are well documented. By contrast, light to moderate drinking has been shown consistently to be associated with reduced risk of coronary heart disease by about 25 percent. Since coronary heart disease is the principal cause of death among both men and women in the developed countries, it is not surprising that light to moderate drinking has been associated with longevity and has been singled out as a likely explanation for the very low coronary mortality of the French, the so-called French paradox. Light to moderate drinking should be interpreted as two to three glasses per day for men or one to two glasses per day for women; a lower level is indicated for women because of their presumed higher sensitivity, as well as concerns that alcohol may slightly increase the risk for breast cancer.

It has been shown in several studies that alcohol increases the levels of "good" HDL cholesterol and, at least in theory, all alcoholic drinks should impart similar degrees of protection against coronary heart disease. This would be true even in lay quantitative terms, since the servings of most alcoholic beverages, including spirits, wine, and beer, contain approximately equal amounts of alcohol. Most epidemiologic studies have supported this hypothesis, but some authors have argued that wine, and in particular red wine, may be more beneficial, possibly because the latter contains compounds with antioxidant properties. Probably more important than the chemical differences between wine and other alcoholic beverages is the way wine is drunk, particularly in the Mediterranean countries—almost always during meals and in the company of family or friends, under conditions that favor moderation and discourage acute intoxication. Mature people and societies can find the balance that maximizes the beneficial health effects of wine and minimizes its adverse effects, but the balance can be a precarious one.

It is not clear whether the identified health-promoting aspects of the Mediterranean diet can fully explain the otherwise unexplained good health of Mediterranean people. Some scientists have proposed that the freshness of plant foods, various interactions among components of diet, or the pattern of eating and drinking may have elusive and difficult-to-identify synergistic effects. Others have argued that the relaxing psychosocial environment in most Mediterranean countries, the preservation of the extended family structure, the stress-releasing afternoon siesta habit, and even the mild climatic conditions may complement the beneficial effects of diet. Nevertheless few, if any, deny the central role of diet in the constellation of favorable conditions surrounding the Mediterranean people.

The Mediterranean diet and lifestyle are not the product of unusual insight or wisdom. They were shaped by climatic conditions and environmental constraints, and in many instances they represent adaptive responses to poverty and hardship. Furthermore, many of their important health-promoting components are not unique to the Mediterranean region but can be found in other areas of the world and other population groups. Still, several variations of the Mediterranean diet can be considered realistic models of a prudent diet that fits our current understanding of healthy nutrition. Indeed, it is the convergence of recent results from methodologically superior nutritional investigations with the dramatic ecological evidence represented by the Mediterranean natural experiment that has created the present momentum toward the Mediterranean diet. It would appear logical for non-Mediterraneans to adopt critical elements of this diet in their food habits and for Mediterraneans to reverse the trends that tend to draw them away from their health-promoting nutritional traditions.

Both authors of this report were born and raised in Greece, but both have traveled and lived in several parts of the world. In the process, we have come to realize that individuals as well as ethnic groups can learn a lot from the experience and the cultural tradition of others. It seems to us that a healthy diet may represent one of the most important contributions of the Mediterranean people to others around the world. It is tasteful, lively, and highly variable—and it can be an integral and important component of a health-promoting lifestyle.

APPENDIX II

Pyramid Schemes

The Mediterranean Diet Pyramid evolved from a conference held in Cambridge, Massachusetts, early in 1993, called "Traditional Diets of the Mediterranean." Jointly organized by Oldways Preservation & Exchange Trust, a Boston-based non-profit organization (of which I was then a founding director) with an interest in food issues, and the Harvard School of Public Health, the conference brought together a distinguished group of scientists, public health officials, scholars, and experts on diet and health from around the globe to consider the traditional Mediterranean diet and the health benefits that might derive from it.

There was a considerable and cohesive body of research to examine, and in the years since, the consensus has grown that the traditional diets of the Mediterranean, as described by Dr. Antonia Trichopoulou and Dr. Dimitrios Trichopoulos in Appendix I, "The Mediterranean Diet and Health," represented a way of eating that is most likely a major factor in the generally excellent health profiles of the people who follow it. As the Trichopouloses explain, this sense of the traditional diet is based primarily on research that began with the highly commended Seven Countries Study in the late 1950s and early 1960s. (It is not to say that this traditional diet has been followed by all Mediterranean peoples at all times in their long history, but rather that there are certain common threads, particularly the overall reliance on fresh vegetables, legumes, seafood, wheat as the basic carbohydrate, and, above all, olive oil as the principal fat. But obviously, at many times and in many places, people ate very different things, some equally good for you and some not so great.)

At the time of the first Mediterranean Diet conference—there have been at least three since then—it was thought useful to offer a pyramid of dietary recommendations to counter the U.S. Department of Agriculture's own pyramid representing USDA's Dietary Guidelines for Americans. In its latest incarnation, the USDA pyramid has been revised slightly but still includes the startling recommendation that two to three servings daily of 2 to 3 ounces from the group labeled "meat, poultry, fish, dry beans, eggs & nuts" could be considered healthful. It doesn't take a mathematician to work out that 3 ounces three times a day could well mean 9 ounces of red meat daily, hardly wise counsel for optimum health. (You can see a copy of this pyramid at nal.usda.gov/fnic/Fpyr/pmap.htm.)

The Mediterranean Diet Pyramid, which was copyrighted by Oldways Preservation & Exchange Trust, is shown in its current version, with thanks to Oldways for permission to publish it, on page 477. It does not rely on serving sizes but stresses instead the relationships among various food groups with suggestions as to how frequently they should be consumed. Most radically, the very tiptop of the pyramid, a place for food to be consumed *monthly* rather than daily or weekly, is reserved for what looks unmistakeably like a sizable beef steak (maybe even a 9-ounce steak), while the place of extra-virgin olive oil in a healthful diet is graphically illustrated by including it with cheese and yogurt, fruits, vegetables, beans and legumes, and carbohydrates, all recommended for consumption every day. Oldways has gone on to develop diet pyramids for Asians, Latin Americans, and vegetarians, but its focus has remained the Mediterranean and the nonprofit organization now offers a "Med Mark program," for food and drink products that fulfill what the organization believes to be the parameters of a traditional Mediterranean diet. On its web site (oldwayspt.org) Oldways describes this as a way both to move people toward more healthful diets and to boost appropriate companies' bottom lines.

The Harvard School of Public Health, the other partner in that 1993 conference, not to be outdone by Oldways or USDA, now has its own pyramid, called the Healthy Eating Pyramid, which includes the advice that a plant-based diet is healthiest of all, and advises against the consumption of red meat, refined grains, potatoes, sugary drinks, and salty snacks—all aspects of the traditional American diet, the web site says, that are "really unhealthy." HSPH further takes USDA to task for promoting recommendations that "have often been based on out-of-date science and influenced by people with business interests in their messages."

If readers detect a note of skepticism in my tone, it's because I am not especially impressed with any of these pyramid schemes. While initially attractive graphics, they are not really useful or in the long run at all meaningful. I find it hard to accept that the American public is so subliterate that the message about dietary change can only come from a colorful illustration. This is not to say that any of these organizations are mistaken or misguided in their advice—although USDA's recommendation to eat plenty of meat and not much olive oil is a little off track—rather that the method they've chosen to get their message out simply, to my mind, misses the mark.

The Traditional Healthy Mediterranean Diet Pyramid

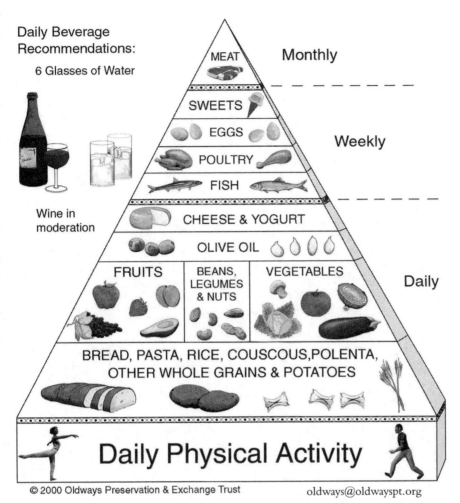

Daily Beverage Recommendations:

6 Glasses of Water

Wine in moderation

MEAT — Monthly

SWEETS

EGGS — Weekly

POULTRY

FISH

CHEESE & YOGURT

OLIVE OIL

FRUITS BEANS, LEGUMES & NUTS VEGETABLES — Daily

BREAD, PASTA, RICE, COUSCOUS, POLENTA, OTHER WHOLE GRAINS & POTATOES

Daily Physical Activity

oldways@oldwayspt.org

For more information, please contact Oldways Preservation & Exchange Trust at 266 Beacon Street, Boston, MA 02116, Telephone: 617-421-5500, Fax: 617-421-5511, web site: www.oldwayspt.org.

BIBLIOGRAPHY

Scientific and Technical Publications Relating to Health Aspects of the Mediterranean Diet

Greco, Luigi. "Mediterranean Diet in Italy: Historical and Socioeconomic Perspective." *Nutrition, Metabolism and Cardiovascular Diseases* 1 (1991): 144–47.

Kafatos, Anthony, et al. "Coronary-Heart-Disease Risk-Factor Status of the Cretan Urban Population in the 1980s." *American Journal of Clinical Nutrition* 54 (1991): 591–98.

Keys, Ancel, et al. "The Diet and 15-Year Death Rate in the Seven Countries Study." *American Journal of Epidemiology* 124, no. 6 (1986): 903–15.

Kromhout, Daan, et al. "Food Consumption Patterns in the 1960s in Seven Countries." *American Journal of Clinical Nutrition* 49 (1989): 889–94.

Mozaffarian, Dariush, and Eric B. Rimm, "Fish Intake, Contaminants, and Human Health." *Journal of the American Medical Association* 296 (2006): 1885–99.

Renaud, S., and M. de Lorgeril. "Wine, Alcohol, Platelets, and the French Paradox for Coronary Heart Disease." *The Lancet* 339 (June 20, 1992): 1523–26.

Sacks, Frank M., and Hannia Campos. "Polyunsaturated Fatty Acids, Inflammation, and Cardiovascular Disease: Time to Widen Our View of the Mechanisms." *Journal of Clinical Endocrinology & Metabolism* 91, no. 2 (2006).

Scarmeas, Nikolaos, Yaakov Stern, Ming-Xin Tang, Richard Mayeux, and Jose Luchsinger. "Mediterranean Diet and Risk of Alzheimer's Disease." *Annals of Neurology,* at http://www3.interscience.wiley.com/journal (April 18, 2006).

Schleifer, David. "Fear of Frying." http://www.nplusonemag.com (May 21, 2007).

Serra-Majem, Lluís, and Elisabet Helsing, eds. "Changing Patterns of Fat Intake in Mediterranean Countries." *European Journal of Clinical Nutrition* 47, Suppl. no. 1 (September 1993). (The entire issue of the journal consists of papers, by the editors and other research scientists, delivered at a seminar on the subject held in Barcelona in 1992.)

Trichopoulou, Antonia, Tina Costacou, Christina Bamia, and Dimitrios Trichopoulos. "Adherence to a Mediterranean Diet and Survival in a Greek Population." *New England Journal of Medicine* 348, no. 26 (June 26, 2003): 2599–2608.

Willett, Walter C., M.D., et al. "Relation of Meat, Fat, and Fiber Intake to the Risk of Colon Cancer in a Prospective Study Among Women." *New England Journal of Medicine* (December 13, 1990): 1664–72.

Willett, Walter C., M.D., and Frank M. Sacks, M.D., "More on Chewing the Fat: The Good Fat and the Good Cholesterol." Editorial. *New England Journal of Medicine* (December 12, 1991): 1740–42.

Young, Lisa R., and Marion Nestle. "Expanding Portion Sizes in the U.S. Marketplace: Implications for Nutrition Counseling." *Journal of the American Dietetic Association* 103, no. 2 (February 2003).

Cookbooks and Books About Food

Algar, Ayla. *Classical Turkish Cooking.* New York: HarperCollins, 1991.

Andrews, Colman. *Catalan Cuisine.* New York: Atheneum, 1988.

Artusi, Pellegrino. *La Scienza in cucina e l'Arte di mangiar bene.* Firenze: Giunti Marzocco, 1984.

Barron, Rosemary. *Flavors of Greece.* New York: Morrow, 1991.

Castelvetro, Giacomo. *The Fruit, Herbs & Vegetables of Italy.* Gillian Riley, trans. New York: Viking, 1989.

David, Elizabeth. *French Provincial Cooking.* New York: Harper & Row, 1962.

Davidson, Alan. *Mediterranean Seafood,* rev. ed. Baton Rouge: Louisiana State University Press, 1981.

El Glaoui, Mina. *Ma Cuisine marocaine.* Paris: Jean-Pierre Taillendier/ Sochepress, 1987.

Field, Carol. *The Italian Baker.* New York: Harper & Row, 1985.

Francesconi, Jeanne Caròli. *La Cucina napoletana.* Roma: Newton Compton Editore, 1965.

Gray, Patience. *Honey from a Weed.* New York: Harper & Row, 1986.

Halici, Nevin. *Nevin Halici's Turkish Cookbook.* London: Dorling Kindersley, 1989.

Hamady, Mary Laird. *Lebanese Mountain Cookery.* Boston: Godine, 1987.

Hazan, Marcella. *The Classic Italian Cook Book.* New York: Knopf, 1976; revised and reprinted in *Essentials of Classic Italian Cooking.* New York: Knopf, 1992.

Helou, Anissa. *Lebanese Cuisine.* New York: St. Martin's Press, 1998.

———. *Mediterranean Street Food.* New York: Morrow, 2006.

Jenkins, Nancy Harmon. *Cucina del Sole.* New York: Morrow, 2007.

———. *The Essential Mediterranean.* New York: HarperCollins, 2005.

———. *Flavors of Puglia.* New York: Broadway, 1997; Congedo Editore, 2006.

———. *Flavors of Tuscany.* New York: Broadway, 1998.

Jouveau, René. *Cuisine provençale de tradition populaire.* Berne: Éditions du Message, n.d.

Keys, Ancel, and Margaret Keys. *Eat Well & Stay Well.* Garden City, NY: Doubleday, 1959.

Khayat, Marie Karam, and Margaret Clark Keatinge. *Food from the Arab World.* Beirut: Eastern Art, 1978.

Kochilas, Diane. *The Food and Wine of Greece.* New York: St. Martin's Press, 1990.

———. *The Glorious Foods of Greece.* New York: Morrow, 2001.

Kouki, Mohamed. *Cuisine et patisserie tunisiennes.* Tunis-Carthage: Las Charguia, 1991.

Kremezi, Aglaia. *The Foods of Greece.* New York: Stewart, Tabori & Chang, 1993.

————. *The Foods of the Greek Islands.* New York: Houghton
Mifflin, 2000.

Luard, Elisabeth. *The Food of Spain & Portugal.* North Vancouver, BC:
Whitecap, 2004.

March, Lourdes. *El Libro de la paella y de los arroces.* Madrid: Alianza, 1985.

Médecin, Jacques. *Cuisine Niçoise.* London: Penguin, 1983.

Middione, Carlo. *The Food of Southern Italy.* New York: Morrow, 1987.

Nestle, Marion. *What to Eat.* New York: North Point Press, 2006.

Olney, Richard. *Simple French Food.* New York: Atheneum, 1983.

Pollan, Michael. *In Defense of Food: An Eater's Manifesto.* New York: Penguin
Press, 2008.

Richardson, Paul. *A Late Dinner: Discovering the Food of Spain.* New York:
Scribner, 2007.

Roden, Claudia. *A Book of Middle Eastern Food.* New York: Vintage, 1974.

Rosenblum, Mort. *Olives: The Life and Lore of a Noble Fruit.* New York: North
Point Press, 1996.

Simeti, Mary Taylor. *Pomp and Sustenance: Twenty-Five Centuries of Sicilian Food.*
New York: Holt, 1991.

Stavroulakis, Nicholas. *Cookbook of the Jews of Greece.* Athens: Lycabettus
Press, 1986.

Tamzali, Haydee. *La Cuisine en Afrique du Nord.* Hamamet: Michael
Tomkinson, 1990.

Uvezian, Sonia. *Recipes and Remembrances from an Eastern Mediterranean Kitchen.*
Beirut: Siamanto Press, 2004.

Weaver, William Woys. *Heirloom Vegetable Gardening.* New York: Holt, 1997.

Wolfert, Paula. *The Cooking of the Eastern Mediterranean.* New York: Morrow, 1994.

————. *Couscous and Other Good Food from Morocco.* New York: Harper &
Row, 1974.

Wright, Clifford A. *A Mediterranean Feast.* New York: Morrow, 1999.

Books About the Mediterranean

Attenborough, David. *The First Eden: The Mediterranean World and Man.* Boston:
Little, Brown, 1987.

Bradford, Ernle. *Mediterranean: Portrait of a Sea.* London: Hodder & Stoughton, 1971.

Braudel, Fernand. *The Mediterranean and the Mediterranean World in the Age of
Philip II.* New York: Harper & Row, 1972.

————. *The Structures of Everyday Life* (Vol. I of *Civilization & Capitalism*). New
York: Harper & Row, 1981.

Fitzgerald, Robert, trans. *The Odyssey of Homer.* New York: Vintage Classics, 1990.

Fox, Robert. *The Inner Sea: The Mediterranean and Its People.* New York:
Knopf, 1993.

Norwich, John Julius. *The Kingdom in the Sun.* London: Longman, 1970.

Origo, Iris. *The Merchant from Prato.* New York: Knopf, 1951; reprinted, Boston:
David Godine, 1986.

Simeti, Mary Taylor. *On Persephone's Island: A Sicilian Journal.* New York:
Knopf, 1986.

METRIC CONVERSION CHART

Liquid Measures

U.S. Measures	Fluid Ounces
1 teaspoon	⅙
2 teaspoons	¼
1 tablespoon	½
2 tablespoons	1
¼ cup	2
⅓ cup	2⅔
½ cup	4
⅔ cup	5
¾ cup	6
1 cup/½ pint	8
1¼ cups	10
1½ cups	12
2 cups/1 pint	16
2½ cups	20
3 cups/1½ pints	24
3½ cups	27
3¾ cups	30
4 cups/2 pints	32
4½ cups	36
5 cups	40
6 cups/3 pints	48
7 cups	56
8 cups	64
9 cups	72
10 cups/5 pints	80

Solid Measures

U.S.	Metric Equivalent	U.S.	Metric Equivalent	U.S.	Metric Equivalent
1 oz.	25 g.	7 oz.	200 g.	1¾ lb.	800 g.
1½ oz.	40 g.	8 oz./½ lb.	225 g.	2 lb.	900 g.
2 oz.	50 g.	9 oz.	250 g.	2¼ lb.	1000/1 kg.
3 oz.	60 g.	10 oz.	275 g.	3 lb.	1 kg. 350 g.
3½ oz.	100 g.	12 oz./¾ lb.	350 g.	4 lb.	1 kg. 800 g.
4 oz./¼ lb.	110 g.	16 oz./1 lb.	450 g.	4½ lb.	2 kg.
5 oz.	150 g.	1¼ lb.	575 g.	5 lb.	2 kg. 250 g.
6 oz.	175 g.	1½ lb.	675 g.	6 lb.	2 kg. 750 g.

Oven Temperature Equivalents

Fahrenheit	Celsius	Gas Mark	Heat of Oven
225°	110°	¼	Very cool
250°	120°	½	Very cool
275°	140°	1	Cool
300°	150°	2	Cool
325°	160°	3	Moderate
350°	180°	4	Moderate
375°	190°	5	Moderately hot
400°	200°	6	Moderately hot
424°	220°	7	Hot
450°	230°	8	Hot
475°	240°	9	Very hot

INGREDIENTS AND COOKING TERMS

U.S.	British
All-purpose flour	Plain flour
Arugula	Rocket
Baking pan	Baking tin
Baking soda	Bicarbonate of soda
Beets	Beetroot
Broil, broiled	Grill
Celery root	Celeriac
Cheesecloth	Muslin
Cilantro	Fresh coriander
Cookies	Biscuits
Corn	Sweet corn
Eggplant	Aubergine
Fava beans	Broad beans
Flame Tamer	Heat diffuser
Heavy cream	Double cream
Light cream	Single cream
Pie plate	Flan dish
Plastic wrap	Cling film
Powdered sugar	Icing sugar
Romaine	Cos lettuce
Skillet	Frying pan
Tart dough	Shortcrust pastry
Tart pan	Flan tin
Tart shell	Pastry case
Vanilla bean	Vanilla pod
Walnut meats	Walnut kernels
Zucchini	Courgettes